DIANA K. IVY • SHAWN T. WAHL

Texas A&M University-Corpus Christi   Missouri State University

third edition

Kendall Hunt
publishing company

NONVERBAL COMMUNICATION
FOR A LIFETIME

Book Team
Chairman and Chief Executive Officer   Mark C. Falb
President and Chief Operating Officer   Chad M. Chandlee
Vice President, Higher Education   David L. Tart
Director of Publishing Partnerships   Paul B. Carty
Senior Developmental Coordinator   Angela Willenbring
Vice President, Operations   Timothy J. Beitzel
Permissions Editor   Tammy Hunt
Cover Designer   Faith Walker

Cover image © Shutterstock, Inc.

www.kendallhunt.com
Send all inquiries to:
4050 Westmark Drive
Dubuque, IA 52004-1840

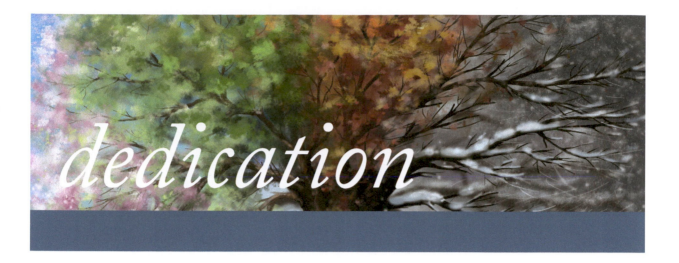

dedication

For all of us who remain students of nonverbal communication . . .

contents

contents

brief contents

CHAPTER FIVE
Physical Appearance: The Body as Nonverbal Communication   141

CHAPTER SIX
Kinesics: Body Movement, Gestures, and Posture   183

contents

contents

preface

We are excited to share the third edition of this textbook with you. As instructors, typically our question when planning a course is, What do we want students to know and learn? Students often wonder what they're supposed to know and learn from a course as well. Anyone who's ever taught a course in nonverbal communication knows how challenging it is and likely supports this claim: The topic of nonverbal communication is supported by a vast, multidisciplinary research base, making it fascinating yet complex to teach and study. Instructors have to make difficult choices about content because there's simply too much material to work through with students over the course of one term.

Many authors who approach this subject for a textbook feel overwhelmed by the amount of material at their disposal. Questions arise about what to present and what to leave out, how to organize such a wealth of information, and how to translate it into accessible language for students. Part of the challenge is that the material is so provocative! Students "take to" the material and generally find it fascinating and applicable to their daily lives, so their enthusiasm for the material represents another kind of challenge (the good kind).

One response we've made to this challenge has been to develop **an organizing feature** in the form of a **model** (described below) which we believe will help instructors guide students through the territory. In this text, we provide 12 tightly focused chapters in which material drawn from the research bases of communication, psychology, education, and other disciplines, as well as popular literature, is explored with relevance to our model. This book doesn't attempt to cover the entire nonverbal world, because its authors live in the real world—a world confined by 16-week semesters (or, for some of us, 12-week quarters). We've made difficult choices regarding the content, based on our years of experience teaching courses in nonverbal communication and experimenting with texts written by colleagues across the country. What we've ended up with is what we believe represents the best work in the field, including classic and contemporary research from a variety of methods, as well as popular literature and online contributions. Our goal is to expose students to both the breadth and depth of information regarding nonverbal communication, without overwhelming them.

Nonverbal communication is one of the most grounded, practical, and useful topics within the discipline of communication that a college student will explore. We make every attempt in this book to translate material into meaningful applications for students. But the beauty of studying nonverbal communication is that its practicality is based on decades-long, intense, oftentimes persnickety research. Nonverbal communication research is difficult to accomplish, especially if one wishes to do it well, meaning in a way that advances our understanding of human behavior. We strive in this book to provide a **balance of theory and application**, but everyone who writes a textbook says that; everyone has that as a goal. How successful we are is up to our readers, but we believe that the best approach to the instruction of nonverbal communication, as well as the textbooks that serve as tools for conveying that instruction, is to offer students practical ways to use information that is based on sound research and theory.

OUR ORGANIZING DEVICE: THE REFLEXIVE CYCLE OF NONVERBAL COMMUNICATION DEVELOPMENT

We've found that developing an organizing structure or device lends coherence to a textbook. In addition, such a structure helps students make connections between the material and their lives. In Chapter 2 of *Nonverbal Communication for a Lifetime*, we introduce the **Reflexive Cycle of Nonverbal Communication Development, a model in five phases** that can continue to be put into use over the course of one's lifetime. The model was developed from discussions between us, as authors, about how people come to learn nonverbal behavior, how and why they make changes in their behavior as they grow and mature, how they perceive others' nonverbal cues and interpret them so as to make sense of what's happening around them, how they use their own nonverbal communication to have an impact on others, and then how those behaviors are altered or reinforced as a result of this ongoing process.

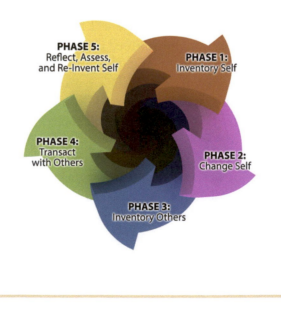

Two aspects of **reflexivity** drew us to this principle as a guiding feature for the model in this book: First, reflexivity means to refer back to the subject of a sentence, and you'll no doubt notice that we put a good deal of emphasis in this text on the individual, albeit within a social context. A common lay understanding of the study of nonverbal communication is that it involves "reading other people's body language." We spend some time in this book explaining how there is no "language of the body," but many people believe that studying nonverbal communication is merely learning to read other people's cues and interpret them more accurately. To us, this is only part of the picture. To become a skilled, astute perceiver of the nonverbal realm, we must first enhance our awareness of our own nonverbal communication before we can attempt to fully understand others' nonverbal cues. Our intent to stress this aspect led to the reflexive approach and the development of a cycle model to illustrate it.

A second feature of reflexivity is that actions are accomplished automatically rather than purposefully. Having our nonverbal abilities become automatically effective in every situation is a goal to work toward or an ideal to approach, with the realization that we can never reach perfection. A cycle, as opposed to a hierarchical, building-block structure or a linear series of lines or arrows, indicates a repetitive, process goal—**a goal about "becoming," not "arriving."** Improving our nonverbal sending and receiving abilities is a constant process throughout our lifetimes. Studying this topic, experiencing diverse people and situations, and working to enhance our abilities to send nonverbal signals as well as to receive and interpret them from others more accurately, so that we work toward such abilities becoming more automatic or reflexive, are practical steps toward the goal of improving our communication over our lifetime.

The Reflexive Cycle includes the following **five phases**:

PHASE 1: INVENTORY SELF. This first phase reflects the continuous process of becoming more aware of our own nonverbal communication. We have little hope of improving our communication abilities if we're unaware of the current skills we possess, as well as areas we need to work on. So the first challenge the Reflexive Cycle poses is to inventory our own nonverbal behavior—to work toward becoming more aware of how we communicate without or in conjunction with words.

PHASE 2: CHANGE SELF. The second step in the Reflexive Cycle is to make any **changes** to our nonverbal communication that we deem necessary, based on the inventory we completed in Phase 1. This phase involves coming to a decision about those things that are working well, meaning those behaviors we don't want to change or that don't need alteration, as well as those areas that need some work. Students need to understand that, just as many of our nonverbal behaviors have taken time to develop and have become ingrained, it takes time to "un-learn" or alter default or commonly used behaviors.

PHASE 3: INVENTORY OTHERS. A course or a book on nonverbal communication tends to make us better "people watchers." Phase 3 of the Reflexive Cycle challenges students to **inventory others' nonverbal behavior** closely, to pay attention to a wider range of cues at a more microscopic level than they're used to doing. The text provides labels for the behaviors students observe, as well as research findings to help them better understand how nonverbal communication functions in social settings.

PHASE 4: TRANSACT WITH OTHERS. In Phase 4 we interact with others and mutually affect one another's nonverbal behavior. We prefer to call this process *transaction*, because it implies a shared creation of meaning that occurs in a simultaneous, ongoing manner. We don't exist in a vacuum, but in a social context in which the behavior of others affects the behavior of ourselves. Phase 4 is about communicating with people, verbally and nonverbally, while still maintaining an awareness of nonverbal cues—our own and those other people exude.

PHASE 5: REFLECT, ASSESS, AND RE-INVENTORY SELF. We come full circle in the Reflexive Cycle when we move through Phase 5, which calls upon us to **reflect and assess** the process we've undertaken. An important goal is to be purposeful or mindful in this entire undertaking, this process of understanding nonverbal complexities and applying that understanding to behavior, so that we can reflect on what we've learned, assess triumphs as well as mistakes, and continue to further develop our nonverbal skills.

The cycle is ongoing; we never stop evolving in our understanding and use of nonverbal communication. If we continuously work through the **Reflexive Cycle**, we believe we'll be more able to enact nonverbal skills appropriate to varying situations, such that these skills become "second nature." The full model of the Reflexive Cycle is presented in Chapter 2, but small versions of the cycle appear at various points throughout chapters, with one or more phases of the cycle highlighted. The highlighting of certain phases means that content corresponding to one or more phases is being discussed in the paragraph or paragraphs adjacent to the icon. We offer the icon reminder simply as a device to reinforce for students the connection between textbook information and different phases in the cycle.

OVERVIEW OF THE BOOK ■ ■ ■

Consistent with the first two editions, the book is organized into three parts. In **Part One**, Chapter 1 provides context for the study of nonverbal communication within the larger realm of human communication. It also contains the **fundamentals**, in terms of reasons for studying the topic, how nonverbal contrasts with verbal communication, and the basic nature of nonverbal communication. Chapter 2 introduces the Reflexive Cycle of Nonverbal Communication Development and overviews codes of nonverbal behavior that are explored in the second part of the book.

   Part Two contains seven chapters devoted to the primary **codes** of study within the realm of nonverbal communication: environment; space (proxemics) and territoriality; physical appearance; body movement, gestures, and posture (kinesics); facial and eye expression; touch (haptics); and vocal expression (vocalics). Each chapter covers key information and research related to the code, as well as applications of the information to situations relevant to students' lives.

   The final three chapters (**Part Three**) constitute our **applications** section, in which material on nonverbal codes or categories of cues are related to three contexts for communication. Chapter 10 is a cutting-edge treatment of nonverbal communication as affected by technology. Probably nothing has impacted the study and enactment of nonverbal cues more than technology, specifically the pervasive use of mobile phones and the increasing impact of online communication and social media in our culture. Chapter 10 explores communicative aspects that traditionally have been viewed as verbal messages for their nonverbal properties. Chapter 11 examines critical nonverbal cues in two relevant settings for students: professional and educational environments. Finally, Chapter 12 delves into more personal waters, focusing on nonverbal cues relevant to biological sex and psychosocial gender, identity, sexuality, and intimate relationships.

PEDAGOGICAL FEATURES

We provide **ten pedagogical features** in this book. Each chapter contains two opening features to help instructors deliver course content and to enhance student learning.

Chapter Outlines detail the organization of each chapter, while *Chapter Objectives* help students prioritize information so that they can learn more efficiently.

Case Study—a brief provocative example to gain attention from readers as they delve into new topics and preview the nature of the discussion that lies ahead. In most chapters, cases represent actual events that either students journaled as a course requirement in our nonverbal communication courses or that emerged through class discussion.

The *Out of the Classroom, Onto the Page* box provides excerpts of discussions that emerged from our teaching of nonverbal communication at our respective universities. These boxes contain snippets of classroom exchanges, followed by questions or challenges to readers to consider how the examples apply to their own lives.

Remember boxes go beyond simple listings of key terms to provide brief definitions for students' review. These boxes appear intermittently within each chapter as a reminder to students of important concepts they will want to retain.

Chapters contain *What Would You Do?* boxed features that provide a challenge or dilemma involving nonverbal communication, then pose a question to students as to how they would handle the situation. This feature is designed to help students apply textbook material to real-life experiences.

Because nonverbal communication research is prolific and fascinating, we highlight one study in the *Spotlight on Research* feature within each chapter. The research chosen for each spotlight box is selected for its cutting-edge qualities, relevance to students' lives, or impact on the field of nonverbal communication.

To close each chapter, we provide a *Summary* section that highlights key information (but doesn't reveal so much that the summary is all a student needs to read!). Next we include *Discussion Starters* that instructors may use as a means of generating class discussions about chapter content, as actual assignments, or as thought provokers for students to consider on their own time. Finally, complete *References* to the research base cited within the text appear at the end of each chapter. Students may find these references useful as they prepare assignments and/or conduct their own research projects. Instructors may use the references to gather additional material for their own research or to supplement instruction.

INSTRUCTIONAL SUPPLEMENTS ■ ■ ■ ▬▬▬▬▬▬▬▬▬▬

An online Instructor's Manual is provided through Kendall Hunt Publishers, upon adoption of the text. The IM contains chapter outlines that can serve as class notes for instructors or students, keyword listings, and suggested class activities, as well as PowerPoint slides containing outlines and graphics for each chapter that can stimulate class discussion. In addition, an online Test Bank is available for instructors' use. Test items in multiple choice, true/false, and essay formats appear for all chapters.

ACKNOWLEDGMENTS ■ ■ ■ ▬▬▬▬▬▬▬▬▬▬

This project has certainly been a team effort; thus there are many people to acknowledge and thank. The authors wish to thank the people we've been privileged to work with at Kendall Hunt Publishing, including Senior Developmental Coordinator Angela Willenbring and Director of Publishing Partnerships Paul Carty, who offered great assistance, encouragement, and suggestions.

Thanks also go to Ivy's colleagues in the Department of Communication and Media at Texas A&M University-Corpus Christi, particularly Department Chair David Gurney, College of Liberal Arts Dean Mark Hartlaub, and President Kelly Quintanilla, for their unwavering support and tolerance of endless book-writing stories. Thanks are also extended to Shawn's colleagues in the College of Arts and Letters and School of Communication Studies at Missouri State University. Both authors are especially grateful to research assistants Joshua Cavazos, Mandee Spendler, Ashley Billig, and Dominic Pecoraro. We also thank Instructor's Manual preparer Garrett Ruzicka for his contributions to this work.

No project for the benefit of college students can succeed without the help of college students. We have thousands to thank from our current universities, as well as the universities at which we've worked over the years, for being sources of inspiration for the creation of this book. Students of nonverbal communication deserve our thanks for providing the motivation to write this text and the fuel for a good deal of its content.

Finally, we thank our families, friends, and colleagues for their listening ears, thought-provoking questions, lively discussions, and persistent belief in this book and its authors. Ivy owes a great deal of gratitude to her late parents, Herschel and Carol Ivy, who sacrificed and supported so she could receive an excellent education. Ivy also thanks sister Karen Black, nephew Brian Black, niece Sumitra Black, and grand-nieces Mackenzie and Sidney Black for their constant and generous praise over the years for her scholarly achievements. Special thanks go to Steve and Sue Beebe for being role models, both in life and as textbook authors. Shawn thanks his mother, Evelyn Wahl, who was always there to listen and provide support during the writing process; his brothers, Larkin Wahl and Shannon Wahl, for their confidence and support; and his pugs, Jake (RIP) and Bentley (B-Pug) for providing love and balance.

Diana K. Ivy, *Corpus Christi, Texas*
Shawn T. Wahl, *Springfield, Missouri*

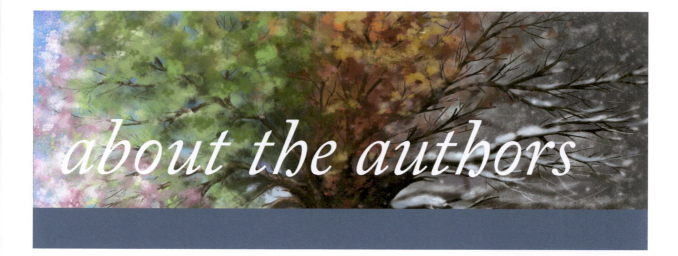

about the authors

Diana K. Ivy, Ph.D., Professor of Communication at Texas A&M University-Corpus Christi, has been teaching communication at the college level for 37 years, including such undergraduate and graduate courses as nonverbal, interpersonal, relational, gender, and instructional communication. She has co-authored two other textbooks, *Communication: Principles for a Lifetime (7th edition)* and *GenderSpeak: Communicating in a Gendered World (6th edition)*, and has published articles in *Communication Education, Southern Communication Journal,* and *Women & Language.* She was Speaker of the Faculty Senate and Director of the Women's Center at her university, has held multiple offices in the National Communication Association, hosted a call-in radio show, "Call Me Ivy," and completed post-doctoral coursework at Oxford University, studying C. S. Lewis and communication.

Shawn T. Wahl, Ph.D., is Dean of the College of Arts and Letters and Professor of Communication at Missouri State University (MSU). He also was Department Head of Communication at MSU. Prior to MSU, he served as Department Head of Communication and Mass Media at Angelo State University and as the founding Director of Graduate Studies in Communication at Texas A&M University-Corpus Christi. Shawn has co-authored six other textbooks, including *The Communication Age: Connecting and Engaging (3rd edition), Business and Professional Communication: Keys for Workplace Excellence (4th edition), Public Speaking: Essentials for Excellence (7th edition), Public Relations: Strategies for Professional Success, Persuasion in Your Life (2nd edition),* and *Intercultural Communication in Your Life (2nd edition).* He has

xxi

published articles in a variety of national communication journals, including *Communication Education, Communication Studies, Communication Research Reports, Communication Teacher, Basic Communication Course Annual,* and *Journal of Family Communication.* He is an active member of the National Communication Association, served as the 2016 president of the Central States Communication Association, and completed the Management Development Program at Harvard. In addition, Shawn has worked across the globe as a corporate trainer, communication consultant, and leadership coach in a variety of industries.

part one

Chapter 1: Foundations of Nonverbal Communication

Chapter 2: Nonverbal Communication Development: A Reflexive Approach

chapter one

FOUNDATIONS OF NONVERBAL COMMUNICATION

chapter outline

After studying this chapter, you should be able to
1. contrast communication with human communication,
2. explain how encoding and decoding function in the communication process,
3. define verbal and nonverbal communication,
4. provide five reasons for studying nonverbal communication,
5. describe the six means by which nonverbal communication functions with verbal communication,
6. offer four ways that verbal communication contrasts with nonverbal communication, and
7. discuss four elements that reveal the nature of nonverbal communication.

"I hate my cubicle at work; I just need more space."

"When we talk, could you look at me instead of your phone?"

"That guy just looks shifty—something about his face makes me wonder if he's telling the truth."

"When I get nervous, I can't seem to control my hands; they just flap around. My knees shake, too, and I wonder if people can see that."

"You have the craziest colors in your house, but somehow it all works."

What do these excerpts of conversation all have in common? They all refer to a fascinating form of human communication that occurs without words—nonverbal communication. Think about it for a moment: How do you convey sarcasm? If your coworker came into your office, plopped down a bunch of files, and said, "No weekend for you; we have a new project," how would you say "Great, thanks" in a way that would convey the sense of sarcasm you feel? You'd probably draw out or elongate the words, emphasize the word *great*, and roll your eyes toward the heavens to signify that you're anything but happy about the extra work. You'd use all these behaviors to accompany your words, to provide context for how the words are to be interpreted. Your vocal inflection (sometimes called "tone"), pacing, and emphasis, accompanied by eye behavior, would give your coworker the true meaning of your message. You'd use nonverbal communication to help get your verbal meaning across accurately. Nonverbal communication is something we use every day as we relate to other people and make our way in the world.

Before we define terms related to nonverbal communication, let's first explore what exactly *communication* is. Communication has been defined in many ways—in fact, one research team counted more than 126 published definitions (Dance & Larson, 1972). Here's the definition we prefer: **Communication** is "the process of acting on information" (Beebe, Beebe, & Ivy, 2019,

p. 5). A person says or does something, causing others to say or do something in response. From this definition, we can see that communication isn't unique to human beings. If you call out to your dog using its name, your dog will likely perk up, look at you, start wagging its tail, and come over to you. The dog responds to your verbal and nonverbal actions, so communication has occurred.

Human communication can be defined as "the process of making sense out of the world and sharing that sense with others by creating meaning through the use of verbal and nonverbal messages" (Beebe et al., 2019, p. 5). As human beings, we're driven to make sense out of the world; communication helps us do that. But, unless you're a hermit and completely cut off from the rest of civilization, that's not enough. We're also driven to share our sense of the world with others and receive their responses so we can repeat the process and be even better equipped to make sense out of our world, share that sense again with others, and so forth. When we share our sense of the world with others, we **encode** our messages (put our thoughts, emotions, and ideas into words or actions) with verbal and nonverbal cues to help others understand what we mean. When receivers respond to or **decode** our messages (interpret our thoughts, emotions, and ideas), we find out if an exchange of meaning has successfully occurred. In one sense, this exchange of message and response is a co-creation of meaning, in that both parties play a role in experiencing a meaningful exchange. While the person initiating the exchange can't control how the listener interprets the message, the goal is for the listener to understand the meaning of the message as the sender intended it.

So what are verbal communication and nonverbal communication, and how do they function in this exchange we've just described? **Verbal communication** is the words we choose to use and, on some occasions, the nonwords we use (such as "uh-huh" and other vocalizations that aren't really words but are interpreted as words). Very simply put, **nonverbal communication** includes all those ways we communicate without words. A fancier definition is this: "Nonverbal communication is communication other than written or spoken language that creates meaning for someone" (Beebe et al., 2019, p. 70).

To make it more complicated, one important exception to this definition, pertaining to people who are deaf, warrants mention. When hearing people watch deaf people sign to each other, the signs they use look like nonverbal gestures, but to deaf people they are actually language—either individual words or phrases—that have direct meanings for receivers of such signs (Fox, 2008; Grossman & Kegl, 2007; Kaneko & Mesch, 2013). Sign language is verbal communication in exchanges with people who are deaf.

What kinds of behaviors are included in what we term *nonverbal communication*? Our

Sign language is verbal communication in exchanges with people who are deaf.

walk, stance, posture, and footsteps are a form of nonverbal communication. What we wear and how we look, move, and gesture, as well as the facial and eye expressions we make, are all included in this fascinating topic we're studying. At what distance do you prefer to stand when talking to people? Your use of space is a form of nonverbal expression, as is the environment you create for yourself and protect, and the environments you enter into. When you call a close friend on the phone, how does he or she know it's you? The sound of your voice—not the words you use—has nonverbal elements related to pitch, rate, volume, and so forth, that become recognizable to others. When a friend needs a hug, your touch sends a powerful nonverbal message.

BASIC TERMINOLOGY IN THE STUDY OF NONVERBAL COMMUNICATION	
Communication:	Process of acting on information
Human Communication:	Process of making sense out of the world and sharing that sense with others by creating meaning
Encode:	Send verbal and nonverbal cues to help people understand what we mean
Decode:	Receive and interpret verbal and nonverbal cues to understand what people mean
Verbal Communication:	Words you choose to use
Nonverbal Communication:	Communication other than written or spoken language that creates meaning for someone

Remember!
1.1

WHY STUDY NONVERBAL COMMUNICATION?

Some students take a nonverbal communication course, like the one you're taking, and assume that they've somehow become completely aware of their own behavior, as well as perfect or near-perfect interpreters of others' behavior. It's unwise and inappropriate to assume that we can become omniscient about how we behave nonverbally or develop into infallible judges of others' nonverbal cues, because human beings are unique, complicated, and ever-changing creatures.

Four goals are important for our study:
- to deepen our understanding of nonverbal communication,
- to heighten our awareness of how we come across to others,
- to sharpen our powers of observation, and
- to develop greater skill in interpreting meanings behind our own and others' nonverbal actions.

Try to remain keenly aware of the idiosyncratic, complex nature of nonverbal communication. We all hope to "catch more clues," but we should avoid making the mistake of believing that studying nonverbal communication will magically allow us to read people's deepest meaning, and that our interpretations will always be correct. Below we provide five reasons for focusing on nonverbal communication.

Nonverbal Messages Communicate Feelings and Attitudes

If you were really happy and excited about something, how would other people know? Would they know from the words you say, or from the fact that you're shouting and talking a mile a minute? When you're mad, are your appearance and actions different than when you're upbeat? Of course they are, unless you have an extremely well-developed poker face. Videos or pictures of you in different moods can be quite revealing, because your face, body, and voice communicate volumes about what's going on inside you.

Nonverbal communication is a primary tool for humans to convey our attitudes and feelings, as well as to understand others' emotional states (Argyle, 1988; Charles & Campos, 2011; Künecke, Wilhelm, & Sommer, 2017; Planalp, 2008; Yoo & Noyes, 2016). As one expert in nonverbal communication research, Albert Mehrabian (1972, 1981), concluded, the most important source of emotional information is the face, which can communicate as much as 55% of the meaning of a message. Vocal cues such as pitch, volume, and intensity communicate another 38% of the emotional meaning. Thus, about 93% of how we feel is communicated nonverbally; as little as 7% of our emotion is communicated through the words we choose to use. Just realizing those percentages and what they mean is powerful. If we struggle to understand the emotional states of other people (particularly people who are really close or especially important to us), we should pay more attention to nonverbal than verbal cues.

Nonverbal Messages Are More Believable Than Verbal Ones

You're in the reception area, waiting for a job interview, and you *really* want this job. You're wearing an outfit that no doubt makes you uncomfortable but gives you the requisite "power look," and you're probably sweating a bit, no matter the temperature in the room. You fidget and shift positions in your chair, check for the hundredth time to make sure your résumé is firmly planted in your portfolio, and repeatedly glance up at the clock on the wall.

We should pay more attention to nonverbal cues to understand the emotional states of other people.

© Thaninee Chuensomchit/Shutterstock.com

The receptionist notices your behavior, and, in an effort to make small talk and ease the situation, he or she says, "There's no reason to be nervous." You reply, "Oh, I'm not nervous at all. I'm really looking forward to this opportunity." Try as you might to look and sound convincing, do you think the receptionist will believe you?

If the receptionist is a savvy nonverbal communicator, she or he will ignore your verbal protestations, pay attention to your nonverbal cues, and determine, correctly so, that you're nervous about the interview. This example illustrates how nonverbal cues carry the truer weight of a given message than does verbal communication—a version of the old adage, "Actions speak louder than words." Nonverbal communication is both intentional and unintentional, whereas verbal communication is always intentional. What we mean by this is that we *choose* language, even if that choice is accomplished in a split second in our brain. But we may not always choose our nonverbal actions; some actions are innate—they just happen, often leaving us wishing that they didn't happen. For example, most people who blush really wish they didn't, but there's little they can do about it once it starts.

Let's face it: Some things are simply out of our control, and many nonverbal behaviors are no exception. But certain forms of nonverbal behavior *are* within our control (such as frowning when we open a disappointing gift, before we realize the need to mask the look of disappointment). Nonverbal communication is important to study because, when verbal and nonverbal information contradict, as they often do, the wisest thing to do is to attend to and believe the nonverbal. We shouldn't be distracted by what a person says in such a situation, because the truer message usually lies in the nonverbal behavior.

Nonverbal Messages Are Critical to Successful Relationships

Ray Birdwhistell is another name you need to know, because, like Mehrabian, he produced fascinating research on nonverbal communication in the early years of its study. In *Kinesics and Context* (1970), Birdwhistell contended that as much as 65% of the way human beings convey meaning in our messages is through nonverbal channels. This means that only about 35% of how we get our message across is accomplished through our use of language. A good illustration of how this operates is when we find ourselves attempting to communicate with someone who doesn't speak our language. Nonverbal cues become very important in these situations. We're likely to slow down the pronunciation of our words and use more volume—even though saying words more loudly and slowly won't make us any more intelligible if the person doesn't speak our language! We're also likely to exaggerate head nods and arm and hand gestures, which we hope will translate into some form of meaning for the listener. In these situations, the 65% figure is likely to go much higher as we rely heavily on nonverbal cues to get our message across.

In situations in which communicators share the same language, nonverbal cues still play a major role in making impressions on others, which underlies the formation of relationships. In fact, research suggests that we make judgments about other people very quickly, based on nonverbal information (Naumann, Vazire, Rentfrow, & Gosling, 2009; Petrician, Todorov, & Grady, 2014; Re

Kelly's had a really rough, long day; she's finally driving home from classes at the university. All she wants to do is take a hot bath and hit the sheets, but the driver in the car in front of her seems to be really taking his time. He's going about 10 miles *under* the speed limit; Kelly can't get around him because of another car in the lane next to her, so she's frustrated. When she finally reaches a break in the traffic, she angrily wheels out of her lane to pass the slow car in front of her. As she pulls even with the car, she yells at the driver and gives him "the finger." Just as her middle finger hits the air, she realizes that the driver of the car is one of her professors. He looks over, recognizes her, and glares. If you were in this situation, *what would you do?*

Would you slow down, pull even with your professor's car, and make some kind of nonverbal "I'm sorry" signal or laugh like it was all a big joke? Would you speed away to remove yourself from an embarrassing situation? The next time you saw the professor in class, would you say something? Or would you remain silent, hoping that he didn't recognize you in the car? Would you try to meet with the professor during office hours to try to explain your behavior, or would that be drawing undue attention to an already awkward situation?

& Rule, 2016; Rule & Ambady, 2009; Ryan, 2016). We may decide whether a date is going to be pleasant or dull during the first 30 seconds of meeting our date, before he or she has had time to utter more than "hello."

Nonverbal cues are important not only in the early stages of relationships but also as we maintain, deepen, and sometimes terminate those relationships. The more intimate the relationship, the more we work to understand our partner's nonverbal cues. Long-term couples often spend less time verbalizing their feelings and emotions to each other than they did when they were first dating; each learns to

Since we often make judgments about people very quickly, our nonverbal cues take on greater importance when meeting and interacting with others.

© Mila Supinskaya/Shutterstock.com

interpret the other's subtle nonverbal cues. If a spouse or partner is silent during dinner, the other spouse or partner may deduce that the day was a tough one and decide to give the person some extra space. In fact, all of us are more likely to use nonverbal cues to convey negative messages than to announce our explicit dislike of something or someone (Burgoon, Stern, & Dillman, 1995; Yoo & Noyes, 2016). We also use nonverbal cues to signal changes in the level of satisfaction with a relationship. When we're in conflict with a partner or simply want to slow things down, we may start using a less enthusiastic tone of voice, make less eye contact, smile less, and engage in less physical contact with our partner; when we want to accelerate the level of a relationship, we will likely do the opposite (Guerrero, Andersen, & Afifi, 2017; Guerrero & Floyd, 2006).

Nonverbal Messages Are Superior to Verbal Messages in Some Situations

People tend to be awkward at funerals or when speaking to people who are grieving—have you noticed this? We hope you don't have much experience at funerals (unless it's your profession) or in contexts involving a good deal of grieving, but, sadly, we all encounter and experience grief in our lives. In those moments, what do you do or say to someone who's grieving? What do you prefer someone say to you if you're grieving? Prolific author C. S. Lewis (best known for his *Chronicles of Narnia* books), in *A Grief Observed* (1961), written after the death of his beloved wife, said this:

> An odd byproduct of my loss is that I'm aware of being an embarrassment to everyone I meet. At work, at the club, in the street, I see people, as they approach me, trying to make up their minds whether they'll "say something about it" or not. I hate it if they do, and if they don't. I like best the well brought-up young men, almost boys, who walk up to me as if I were a dentist, turn very red, get it over, and then edge away to the bar as quickly as they decently can. Perhaps the bereaved ought to be isolated in special settlements like lepers. (pp. 10–11)

In situations where words just can't be found, aren't necessary, or don't help you offer a true expression of how you feel, nonverbal communication is superior (if enacted appropriately, of course).

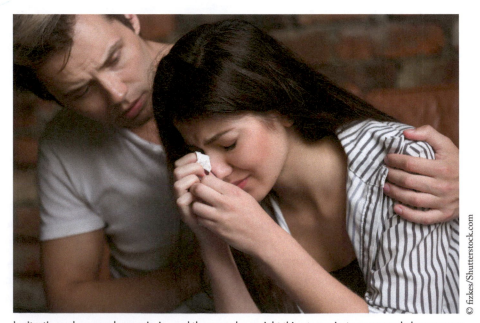

© fizkes/Shutterstock.com

In situations where people are grieving and there may be no right thing to say, just your nonverbal presence or a sensitive, appropriate touch may be the best way to communicate your support.

When words fail, such as in times of great sadness and grief, nonverbal actions may prove to be the best route if you want to show support by simply being there, offering an appropriate touch or facial expression, or avoiding staring at people who are obviously grieving, causing them to feel more publicly exposed and vulnerable.

Nonverbal Messages Serve Various Functions

Nonverbal cues can work independently or in tandem with verbal language to convey meaning. First, nonverbal cues can *substitute* for verbal messages. For example, you go to a crowded concession stand at a ballgame; the server won't be able to hear you over the roar of the crowd, so instead of shouting your order for two bags of popcorn, you put up two fingers in the air and point to the popcorn machine to signal what you want.

We often use nonverbal actions in connection with words to *complement* our communication or to clarify or extend the meaning of our words. This complementary function allows us to convey more information, leading to a more accurate interpretation by receivers of our communication (McNeill, 2000; Rowbotham, Holler, Lloyd, & Wearden, 2011). At the concession stand, if you shout your order while holding up two fingers and pointing to the popcorn machine, the gestures complement the verbal message to make you more understandable to the server. Complementary cues also help color our expressed emotions and attitudes. For example, a long, heavy sigh may reveal how tired or bored you are. The length of a hug while you tell someone you've missed him or her can convey the depth of the emotion you're feeling.

Do you think she can tell how bored he is with this conversation?

On occasion, our nonverbal cues *contradict* rather than complement our verbal cues. The classic example is a person who has a frowny expression on her or his face, whose arms are crossed defensively, who won't make eye contact and keeps a distance from you, but who, if asked if he or she is mad, will reply, "No, I'm not mad." This person's body is shouting, "I'm mad," but the verbal message is just the opposite. (As we said earlier, when the verbal and the nonverbal contradict, the wiser approach is to believe the nonverbal.)

Nonverbal behaviors may also serve a *repeating* function. Say you're back at that same concession stand, ordering two more bags of popcorn. (You *really* like popcorn.) You may shout your order the first time, but upon seeing that the server can't hear you, you put up two fingers and point to the popcorn machine. In this example, you use verbal communication first, followed by a nonverbal signal that repeats the message, thus clarifying the communication that's exchanged.

Communicating Nonverbally with Patients with Dementia

Let's face the harsh reality: None of us is getting any younger. While you may feel like you have a huge amount of life stretching out before you (and you're likely right about that), all human beings age. As we age, our communicative and physical abilities change. And as conditions like Alzheimer's disease and dementia remain challenges worldwide, research is focusing on the importance of nonverbal cues when relating to people suffering from conditions that rob them of their ability to form speech.

The international research team of Maggie Ellis and Arlene Astell (2017) developed an Adaptive Interaction approach that is helping medical professionals, caregivers, family members, and friends find a way to communicate with people who can no longer form words. Rather than being shunted off in a corner or kept in bed in isolation, patients whose ability to verbally communicate is compromised can be reached by caregivers who are trained in intensive use of nonverbal cues, both in terms of sending cues to patients and, more importantly,

reading patients' nonverbal cues. The research involved direct observation of patients' behavior, the coding of patients' repetitive and consistent nonverbal responses to questions and other prompts, and comparisons across patients. Findings led to the training of medical personnel and other caregivers to improve their ability to read and interpret such nonverbal cues as sounds, movements (e.g., head nods, head shakes), eye gaze, and facial expressions.

Regarding their research results, Ellis and Astell (2017) concluded the following: "Findings suggest that Adaptive Interaction provides a mechanism for people living with dementia who have no functional verbal language production to demonstrate a desire and ability to communicate. The study highlights that interaction partners need to be responsive and adaptive to the needs of nonverbal people with dementia" (p. 18).

Care to know more about this study? If so, check out Ellis, M., & Astell, A. (2017). Communicating with people living with dementia who are nonverbal: The creation of Adaptive Interaction. *PLoS ONE, 12* (8): e0180395.

One of the more fascinating functions of nonverbal communication is its ability to *regulate* conversation. Most conversations occur in a series of turns at talk by the interactants, but just how do we signal that we want a turn? Such nonverbal cues as leaning forward, making or breaking eye contact, raising our eyebrows, breathing in sharply, uttering the first few sounds in a word as we try to interrupt or signal that we want to talk, murmuring "uh-huhs" and "um-hms" in response to someone else's communication, raising a hand in a more formal or professional setting—all these behaviors serve to regulate the flow of conversation (Ekman, 1965).

Finally, nonverbal behaviors often *accent* or provide emphasis for a verbal message. At the loud concession stand, it may take you a while to get the attention of a server, so you may find yourself shouting your order and waving two fingers in the air to get attention and service. Good public speakers learn how to accent their remarks with nonverbal cues that reinforce and add intensity to certain messages in the minds of listeners (Beebe & Beebe, 2017).

Public speakers develop their nonverbal skills, like the use of complementary and accenting gestures, to help get their points across and impress audiences.

© Matej Kastelic/Shutterstock.com

WHY STUDY NONVERBAL COMMUNICATION?

Remember! 1.2

- Nonverbal communication is a primary means of communicating feelings and attitudes.
- Nonverbal messages are usually more believable than verbal messages.
- Nonverbal communication is critical in the initiation, development, and sometimes termination of relationships.
- Nonverbal messages are superior to verbal messages in some situations.
- Nonverbal messages can substitute for, complement, contradict, repeat, regulate, and accent verbal messages.

CONTRASTING VERBAL AND NONVERBAL COMMUNICATION

Verbal and nonverbal communication can be distinguished by several factors. First, verbal communication is *discontinuous*, whereas nonverbal communication is *continuous*. While some people may talk a blue streak, making you think that their verbal communication is continuous, talk actually occurs in a stop-start fashion. However, nonverbal communication occurs continuously; it precedes verbal communication, accompanies it, and continues even after conversations are over. Take your basic greeting: You see someone coming your way on the sidewalk and recognize the person as someone you know. As you near, you make eye contact and raise a hand in a friendly waving gesture. Coming within hearing range of each other, you each say a quick "hello," sustain the eye contact, turn toward each other, pass each other, and then walk away. Nonverbal communication is present throughout this whole exchange, but the verbal exchange was only two words.

A second contrast is this: Verbal communication employs the use of a *language*, with grammar, rules, and syntax (patterns of construction). In school, we studied the proper use of language and rules to follow that make for the clear, appropriate construction of verbal messages. Nonverbal communication is messier than that. Although people have conducted studies to determine a sort of nonverbal grammar and syntax and to categorize its use into discrete, recognizable, and consistent patterns, such efforts have failed to receive wide support (Birdwhistell, 1970; Dittmann, 1977). Nonverbal communication is simply too complex, too culture- and context-specific, and too idiosyncratic to form into some kind of language.

One of the more interesting efforts to make nonverbal communication into a form of language was contributed by Julius Fast, who wrote the popular book *Body Language* in 1970. Fast contended that certain body gestures, movements, and facial expressions had directly translatable meanings—in all situations, for all people, across time. If you were savvy and observant enough, you could quickly and easily interpret the meanings of certain nonverbal behaviors. For example, Fast's book instructed that if a woman was sitting near a man with her legs crossed and she pumped her foot up and down, that meant she was attracted to the man. This seems overly simplistic and somewhat ridiculous for our current day and time, but Fast's body language approach caught on within popular culture in the 1970s. His book is still in print today, and people still talk about reading someone's "body language."

So let's get something straight right here and now: **There is no "language of the body."** As we've said, nonverbal communication is too complex, personal, cultural, and contextual to be easily translated into some sort of language. What if you were standing outside a classroom, waiting to go in for a class, and you had your arms crossed over your chest? What might be the range of interpretations of such a stance? Some observers might think you were angry and hostile; others might deem you aloof and withdrawn, as though your arms were protecting your body or shielding you from interaction with (or invasion by) other people. Some might think nothing of it, believing you were just comfortable standing that way. Still others might think you were just physically cold; we often cross our arms when we're cold or get the shivers. For our female readers, yet another explanation might be that your bra strap just broke and you're trying to hold things up and together (if you know what we mean). In just this one simple example of a single behavior, we generated five possible interpretations. So believing that every time we see a nonverbal signal it automatically translates into some direct meaning is just folly.

A third distinction between verbal and nonverbal communication is that language has to be *learned*, while nonverbal behavior is both *learned* and *innate*. Babies babble as they learn to use their voices, but it's a deliberative process to learn a language. A good deal of nonverbal behavior is innate or genetically hardwired, as evidenced in studies of children who are sensory deprived, meaning they don't have use of one or more senses. In one line of research, children both blind and deaf responded to stimuli with facial expressions similar to those of sighted and hearing children. These sensory-deprived children produced patterns of movement, as well as facial expressions, related to such emotions as sadness, happiness, anger, disgust, surprise, and fear, similarly to their sighted and hearing counterparts in the studies (Eibl-Eibesfeldt, 1973, 1975; Galati, Miceli, & Sini, 2001; Galati, Scherer, & Ricci-Bitti, 1997; Galati, Sini, Schmidt, & Tinti, 2003). Further evidence favoring the nature part of the nature–nurture debate comes from studies of twins who were separated at birth and raised in different environments, yet for whom many nonverbal behaviors, such as walk, posture, gestures, and vocal attributes such as pitch and tone, were strikingly similar (Bouchard, 1984, 1987; Farber, 1981; Segal, 1999).

However, notice that we say that nonverbal communication is both learned *and* innate, because a good deal of how we communicate nonverbally is learned behavior. Certain gestures, touches, facial expressions, and vocalizations are learned through our culture and upbringing. For example, adults in the 1970s will likely never forget that the

What are some possible interpretations of this crossed-arms position? Might this woman be angry, closed off, or simply cold in this room? Even simple nonverbal cues are open to multiple interpretations.

index and middle finger, when extended upward together, signal "V for Victory," mainly because that gesture is so readily associated with former President Richard Nixon. If you're a University of Texas fan, you learn the "hook 'em horns" hand gesture very quickly, but if you're an OU Sooner or an Aggie, you learn equally as quickly to turn that "hook 'em" gesture upside down. A couple of decades ago, most people wouldn't dismiss someone else's communication with the expression, "Whatever." Prevalent use of this response in the 21st century has taught us to add a vocally higher pitch on the "what" part and a lower pitch on the "ever" part so that the appropriate sarcasm or tone of dismissal is conveyed.

A final distinction between verbal and nonverbal communication is that verbal communication is believed to be processed primarily in the *left hemisphere* of the brain, in which logical, abstract, and analytical thinking reside—thinking that is particularly helpful for the learning and use of language. Nonverbal communication is processed primarily in the *right brain hemisphere*, which tends to be the area in which artistic or creative abilities reside and emotional or affective information is processed (Buck & Van Lear, 2002; Hopkins, 2007). These right-brain abilities are particularly well suited to the production and interpretation of nonverbal cues (Andersen, Garrison, & Andersen, 1979; Bowers, Bauer, & Heilman, 1993). However, we should mention that researchers continue to call into question the view that brain hemispheres work separately and contain separate strengths; brain functioning may be more complex than the right-left distinction would suggest (Jung-Beeman et al., 2004; Newman, 2003; Sukel, 2012).

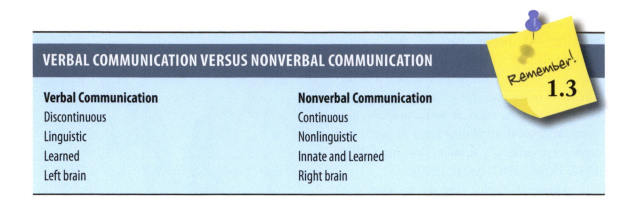

THE NATURE OF NONVERBAL COMMUNICATION ▪ ▪ ▪ ▪

Many times we've wished we had a dictionary of nonverbal behavior so we could simply turn to a page, look up a certain behavior, and find a description of exactly what that behavior means. Such a reference book works well for verbal communication, but no such book exists to help decode nonverbal cues. Below we provide four challenges inherent in the interpretation of nonverbal communication.

Nonverbal Communication Is Culture-Bound

It's imperative to take cultural factors into account when deciding which culturally appropriate cues to exhibit and when attempting to interpret the nonverbal cues of members of other cultural groups (Axtell, 1998; Hess, Blaison, & Kafetsios, 2016; Matsumoto & Hwang, 2013; Matsumoto & Juang, 2016; Vennekens-Kelly, 2012). Intercultural communication scholars Samovar, Porter, McDaniel, and Sexton Roy (2014) warn that one culture's friendly or polite action may be another culture's obscene gesture. For example, making the "okay" sign in the United States typically signals agreement or that everything is alright, but in parts of Europe it could communicate to someone that you think she or he is a big fat loser, a zero (Crislip, 2018). In Brazil, the "okay" sign is interpreted as an extremely crude gesture (that corresponds to a body part most people don't talk about). Scholars, cultural enthusiasts, and travel writers continually provide tips to help travelers avoid common gaffes in foreign countries, such as Americans extending too intimate or too much touch when meeting new people (Bartlett, 2015; Cortez, 2017; Nummenmaa, Glerean, Hari, & Hietanen, 2014).

Is there such a thing as a culturally universal nonverbal cue? Cross-cultural research suggests commonalities, if not universalities, in the expression of human emotions (Jack, Garrod, Yu, Caldara, & Schyns, 2012). When humans from almost every culture are happy, they tend to smile; when they're unhappy, they tend to frown; and when meeting or greeting others, they tend to raise or flash their eyebrows (Argyle, 1988). Expressions of pride are also fairly universally recognizable emotional cues (Tracy & Robins, 2008). In many cultures, young children wave to signal that they want their parents, raise their arms to be picked up, and suck their thumbs to comfort themselves (Collett, 1984; Eibl-Eibesfeldt, 1972; Ekman & Friesen, 1971; Hall, 1959, 1966; Shuter, 1976). This research shows some commonalities underlying the way humans communicate emotion, yet each culture develops unique methods as well (Hess, Blaison, & Kafetsios, 2016; Matsumoto, Olide, Schug, Willingham, & Callan, 2009; Matsumoto & Yoo, 2005; Szarota, 2010; Yang, 2010).

This means "okay" in the United States, but it might be seen as an offensive gesture in another country.

Nonverbal Communication Is Rule Governed

When we say that nonverbal communication is rule governed, we don't mean the typical connotation for the term *rule* that involves lots of dos and don'ts. What we mean is that expectations or assumptions about appropriate nonverbal behavior, which most people learn through their culture, are always operating. We may be aware of some of our own rules about nonverbal behavior, but we're unaware of many of these rules *until they're violated*.

Watch young children who are in the process of learning culturally rooted rules of behavior. You may be standing in line at the grocery store and feel something brush past your legs; you look down and realize that a young child has made a beeline for the candy display. She or he didn't care what was in the way (your body); the point was to make the straightest, fastest approach to that candy as possible before being detected by a parent. Imagine the absurdity of an adult doing the same thing—bumping into you in an effort to retrieve some highly desirable candy. In each culture around the world, children go through a process of learning rules about appropriate touch and distance from other people, among other lessons.

Here's another example that resonates with people these days: Have you been annoyed lately when you paid your hard-earned money to enjoy a night out at the movie theater, only to be treated to someone answering his or her cell phone *and carrying on a whole conversation* during the movie? Or how about those people who talk at full volume to their companions in the theater, as if they were at home in their living room watching TV? Until this happens to you, you may be unaware that you have a rule about appropriate behavior in a movie theater. Rules may be broad and sweeping, such as a rule about greeting strangers with a handshake instead of another more personal touch, or they may be micro-rules, such as the movie theater rule that applies primarily to only one context and can vary from person to person.

Nonverbal communication scholar Judee Burgoon and various colleagues developed a model for how nonverbal communication functions, termed the **expectancy violations model** (Afifi & Burgoon, 2000; Burgoon, 1978, 1983, 1993, 1995, 2016; Burgoon & Dunbar, 2006). We explore this model in more depth in Chapter 4 on proxemics and territoriality, because that was the original focus of the research, but here's a synopsis: The model suggests that we develop expectations for appropriate nonverbal behaviors in ourselves and others, based on our cultural backgrounds, personal experiences, and knowledge of those with whom we interact. When those expectations (or rules) are violated, we experience heightened arousal (we become activated or more engaged in what's happening), and the nature of our interpersonal relationship with the other person becomes a critical factor as we attempt to interpret and respond to the situation.

Our tendency in a rules violation situation is to attempt to adapt to or correct the violation by nonverbal means before resorting to verbal communication. We're more likely to back away from a "close talker" than to say to her or him, "Please back up; you're violating my personal space." We all violate nonverbal rules from time to time; it's at those moments when we become acutely aware that rules or expectations of appropriateness have a powerful influence on nonverbal communication (Bevan, 2003; Bevan, Ang, & Feams, 2014; Cohen, 2010; Ramirez & Wang, 2008).

© Historical/Contributor/Getty Images

President Lyndon B. Johnson was a notorious "close talker." But since he was also regarded as a highly rewarding communicator, according to expectancy violations model, people refrained from trying to correct the president's behavior.

Nonverbal Communication Is Ambiguous

People within a culture who speak the same language attach similar meanings to most words. But the meaning of a nonverbal cue is known only to the person displaying it; the cue may not be intended to have any meaning at all. So another aspect of nonverbal communication that makes it complex, albeit fascinating to study, is that it's ambiguous. We can take a course in nonverbal communication, study the research, and hone our people-observing skills, and still be wrong by a mile when we interpret someone's nonverbal communication.

OUT OF THE CLASSROOM
onto the page

No matter your view on the "FWBR" (friends with benefits relationship), you will probably agree that they are more prevalent now than in years past, or at least people seem more open about them than they used to be. Some students find such relationships morally bankrupt. Others think FWBRs are no big deal, and attach no judgment to those who engage in them. Still others avoid FWBRs because, either in their own experience or the experience of a friend, one or the other person in the friendship develops romantic feelings and ends up getting hurt. What could have been just a friendship (no "benefits") may also end because of hurt feelings.

But here's a sliver of a recent discussion in one of our nonverbal communication classes; the topic was expectancy violations theory. Jordan asked classmates and the professor for their take on something that had happened to him; he wanted to know if the behavior "was cool" or not. He described a situation where his partner in an FWBR got drunk at a party and started openly flirting with him, in front of everyone. She touched him inappropriately and announced (quite loudly) that she had "intimate knowledge" of Jordan's body. Jordan found her behavior very embarrassing and he shortly thereafter ended the FWBR; their friendship never recovered. Jordan's classmates had varying opinions about the situation, with most saying that his friend's behavior "wasn't cool" and was absolutely a violation of expectations, verbally and nonverbally. However, some felt that Jordan's ending the FWBR as well as the friendship was overly harsh, given that the friend was intoxicated.

It seems like partners in an FWBR have a lot of rules about appropriate and inappropriate nonverbal and verbal communication, especially communication that betrays the secrecy of the arrangement. The problem is, many FWBR couples don't openly discuss the rules and boundaries of the connection, which can lead to embarrassment and the end of any sort of relationship.

For instance, some people struggle to express their feelings nonverbally. Their voices may go monotone, or they may project frozen facial expressions, like a "poker face." They may use sarcasm or tease us, but their deadpan expressions make us think their negative comments are sincere. Or what about in those situations where someone attempts to deceive you? If you know the person well and know that he or she tends to look you in the eye most of the time, when she or he avoids eye contact with you, does it necessarily mean deception is occurring, or might there be some other explanation? Often it's challenging to draw meaningful conclusions about other people's behavior, even if we're very familiar with them.

One strategy that helps us interpret in these dilemmas is called **perception checking**. It's wise to observe in detail the nonverbal cues in a given situation, make our own interpretation of those cues, and then do one of two things (or both): (1) run our interpretation by another observer, to get a second opinion or more input before we draw a conclusion (**indirect perception checking**), or (2) use a more straightforward approach, in which we ask the people we're observing how they feel or what's going on (**direct perception checking**). Remember earlier in this chapter, when we warned about not assuming that our interpretation of nonverbal cues is necessarily the right one? Perception checking can improve the chances of our interpretation being more accurate, but it's not a *guarantee* of accuracy.

Nonverbal Communication Is Multichanneled

We know our students are the ultimate multitaskers. Yes, we realize that you can take notes on a professor's lecture, check Facebook on your laptop, respond to texts on your cell phone, and leap over tall buildings in a single bound—you're superhuman! Just like multitasking, nonverbal cues register in our senses from a variety of sources simultaneously. But you can pay close attention to only one source of stimuli at time, even if you switch or vary your attention very quickly.

Let's take a deception situation again as an example: You wonder if the person you're dating is lying to you about where she or he was the night before, when you were supposed to spend time together (you got stood up). You look for nonverbal clues of deception, such as little eye contact; eyes shifting back and forth, rather than focusing; hands touching the face, particularly the forehead or eyebrows; taking longer than usual to respond to your questions; providing lengthier-than-normal explanations; and expending nervous energy through the hands and feet. While we can process only one nonverbal signal at a time, just as we can focus on only one task at a time, we're aware of the cluster or sum total of someone's behavior. One gesture or vocal cue, in isolation, won't tell the whole story, so we gauge the *package* of behavior to determine the truthfulness of the person's communication. It boils down to this suggestion: When trying to interpret the meaning of a single nonverbal behavior, look for clusters of corroborating nonverbal cues, in conjunction with verbal behavior, to get the most complete picture you can.

chapter one

THE NATURE OF NONVERBAL COMMUNICATION

Nonverbal communication is . . .

Culture-bound:	Nonverbal behaviors are generated, taught, and understood within the context of the culture in which they occur.
Rule governed:	Expectations or assumptions about appropriate nonverbal behavior, which most people learn through their culture, are always operating.
Ambiguous:	Nonverbal behavior is difficult to interpret accurately because the meanings for different actions vary from person to person.
Multichanneled:	Nonverbal cues register in our senses from a variety of sources simultaneously, but we can attend to only one nonverbal cue at a time.

SUMMARY ■ ■ ■

In this chapter, we provided fundamental information pertinent to the study of nonverbal communication. We defined *communication* and *human communication*, including the process of encoding and decoding, and then defined *verbal* and *nonverbal communication*. Recall this definition: Nonverbal communication is communication other than written or spoken language that creates meaning for someone.

Next we provided four reasons for studying nonverbal communication. We described nonverbal communication as a primary means of conveying feelings and attitudes. We examined the believability of nonverbal messages compared with verbal messages, and the role nonverbal communication plays in the initiation, development, and sometimes termination of relationships. We contended that, in certain situations, nonverbal communication is preferable to or more appropriate than verbal communication. Finally, we explored how nonverbal messages can substitute for, complement, contradict, repeat, regulate, and accent verbal messages.

While nonverbal and verbal cues often work together, some differences exist in the two modes of communication. First, verbal is discontinuous, whereas nonverbal is continuous, meaning that nonverbal messages are sent nonstop, whether or not someone is talking. Second, verbal communication involves the use of a language, with its own grammar and patterns; nonverbal is nonlinguistic, meaning that it is too individually and culturally based to be viewed as a language. Third, verbal communication is learned, but nonverbal communication is both learned and innate. Finally, while researchers continue to debate and investigate this issue, the prevailing view is still that verbal communication is processed primarily in the left hemisphere of the brain, while nonverbal communication is processed primarily in the right hemisphere.

In our final section of this chapter, we discussed the culturally bound nature of nonverbal communication, meaning that nonverbal behaviors are generated, taught, and understood within the context of the culture in which they occur. Nonverbal is also rule governed; expectations or assumptions about appropriate nonverbal behavior are always operating, which most people learn through their culture. Nonverbal behavior is ambiguous, in that it is difficult to interpret nonverbal cues accurately because the meanings for different actions vary from person to person. And, finally, nonverbal communication is multichanneled: Nonverbal cues register in our senses from a variety of sources simultaneously, but we can attend to only one nonverbal cue at a time.

We trust that your reading of this introductory chapter has provided an understanding of some of the basic terminology and the nature of our topic under study. In the second chapter of this opening section of the book, we explore in more depth some of the generally recognized categories of nonverbal behavior, and then provide a model of how human beings can endeavor to expand our awareness of nonverbal cues, in ourselves and other people, and use that awareness to improve our nonverbal communication skills so as to enhance our personal and professional lives.

DISCUSSION STARTERS ▪ ▪ ▪

1. If we didn't have nonverbal cues, how would human beings communicate their feelings and attitudes to one another? How would we know where we stand in a relationship without our partner's use of nonverbal cues to communicate emotions?

2. When verbal and nonverbal cues contradict, we've advised you to believe the nonverbal because these behaviors often carry the truer weight of a message. But can you think of a situation in which we should pay more attention to verbal than nonverbal cues? When are our words more important than our actions?

3. Discuss the pros and cons of the "body language" approach to studying nonverbal communication.

4. What are some common nonverbal mistakes or violations that nonnatives frequently make when they travel in the United States? That Americans make when they travel abroad? How do these mistakes reveal the culture-bound nature of nonverbal communication?

5. What rules or expectations do you have about appropriate nonverbal communication? For example, how close do you let most people stand while speaking to you? Does it depend on who it is? Do you think your rules should just be unspoken and understood by most people in your social circle, or will you have occasion to explain your rules or expectations about nonverbal cues to someone? How are you likely to handle it if/when your rules or expectations are violated?

REFERENCES ■ ■ ■

Afifi, W. A., & Burgoon, J. K. (2000). The impact of violations on uncertainty and the consequences for attractiveness. *Human Communication Research, 26,* 203–233.

Andersen, P. A., Garrison, J. D., & Andersen, J. F. (1979). Implications of a neurological approach for the study of nonverbal communication. *Human Communication Research, 16,* 74–89.

Argyle, M. (1988). *Bodily communication* (2nd ed.). London: Methuen.

Axtell, R. E. (1998). *Gestures: Do's and taboos of body language around the world.* New York: John Wiley.

Bartlett, E. (2015). A body map of the places it is inappropriate to touch someone in social situations. Retrieved from https://www.indy100.com/article/a-body-map-of-the-places-it-is-inappropriate-to-touch-someone-in-social-situations--ZJBADUpSOe

Beebe, S. A., & Beebe, S. J. (2017). *Public speaking: An audience-centered approach* (10th ed.). Boston: Pearson.

Beebe, S. A., Beebe, S. J., & Ivy, D. K. (2019). *Communication: Principles for a lifetime* (7th ed.). Boston: Pearson.

Bevan, J. L. (2003). Expectancy violation theory and sexual resistance to close, cross-sex relationships. *Communication Monographs, 70,* 68–82.

Bevan, J. L., Ang, P-C., & Feams, J. B. (2014). Being unfriended on Facebook: An application of expectancy violation theory. *Computers in Human Behavior, 33,* 171–178.

Birdwhistell, R. L. (1970). *Kinesics and context.* Philadelphia: University of Pennsylvania Press.

Bouchard, T. J., Jr. (1984). Twins reared apart and together: What they tell us about human diversity. In S. W. Fox (Ed.), *Individuality and determinism* (pp. 147–184). New York: Plenum.

Bouchard, T. J., Jr. (1987). Diversity, development, and determinism: A report on identical twins reared apart. In M. Amelang (Ed.), *Proceedings of the meetings of the German Psychological Association—1986.* Heidelberg, Germany: German Psychological Association.

Bowers, D., Bauer, R. M., & Heilman, K. M. (1993). The nonverbal affect lexicon: Theoretical perspectives from neuropsychological studies of affect perception. *Neuropsychology, 7,* 433–444.

Buck, R., & Van Lear, A. (2002). Verbal and nonverbal communication: Distinguishing symbolic, spontaneous, and pseudo-spontaneous nonverbal behavior. *Journal of Communication, 52,* 522–541.

Burgoon, J. K. (1978). A communication model of personal space violations: Explication and an initial test. *Human Communication Research, 4,* 129–142.

Burgoon, J. K. (1983). Nonverbal violations of expectations. In J. M. Weimann & R. P. Harrison (Eds.), *Nonverbal interaction* (pp. 77–111). Beverly Hills, CA: Sage.

Burgoon, J. K. (1993). Interpersonal expectations, expectancy violations, and emotional communication. *Journal of Language and Social Psychology, 12,* 30–48.

Burgoon, J. K. (1995). Cross-cultural and intercultural applications of expectancy violations. In R. L. Wiseman (Ed.), *Intercultural communication theory* (Vol. 19, pp. 194–214). Thousand Oaks, CA: Sage.

Burgoon, J. K. (2016). Expectancy violations theory. In C. R. Berger & M. E. Roloff (Eds.), *The international encyclopedia of interpersonal communication.* New York: John Wiley & Sons. doi:10.1002/9781118540190

Burgoon, J. K., & Dunbar, N. E. (2006). Nonverbal expressions of dominance and power in human relationships. In V. Manusov & M. L. Patterson (Eds.), *The SAGE handbook of nonverbal communication* (pp. 279–297). Thousand Oaks, CA: Sage.

Burgoon, J. K., Stern, L. A., & Dillman, L. (1995). *Interpersonal adaptation: Dyadic interaction patterns.* Cambridge, UK: Cambridge University Press.

Charles, S. T., & Campos, B. (2011). Age-related changes in emotion recognition: How, why, and how much of a problem? *Journal of Nonverbal Behavior, 35,* 287–295.

Cohen, E. L. (2010). Expectancy violations in relationships with friends and media figures. *Communication Research Reports, 27,* 97–111.

Collett, P. (1984). History and study of expressive action. In K. Gergen & M. Gergen (Eds.), *Historical social psychology* (pp. 371–396). Hillsdale, NJ: Erlbaum.

Cortez, J. (2017, May 15). Don't make these cultural mistakes when you travel abroad. Retrieved from https://www.tripsavvy.com/cultural-mistakes-to-avoid-abroad-3259977

Crislip, K. (2018, April 20). Hand gestures in the world with more than one meaning. Retrieved from https://www.tripsavvy.com/hand-gestures-with-more-than-one-meaning-3149620

Dance, F. E. X., & Larson, C. (1972). *Speech communication: Concepts and behavior.* New York: Holt, Rinehart, & Winston.

Dittmann, A. T. (1977). The role of body movement in communication. In A. W. Siegman & S. Feldstein (Eds.), *Nonverbal behavior and communication.* Potomac, MD: Erlbaum.

Eibl-Eibesfeldt, I. (1972). Similarities and differences between cultures in expressive movements. In R. A. Hinde (Ed.), *Nonverbal communication.* Cambridge, UK: Royal Society and Cambridge University Press.

Eibl-Eibesfeldt, I. (1973). The expressive behavior of the deaf-and-blind born. In M. von Cranach & I. Vine (Eds.), *Social communication and movement* (pp. 163–194). London: Academic Press.

Eibl-Eibesfeldt, I. (1975). *Ethology: The biology of behavior* (2nd ed.). New York: Holt, Rinehart, & Winston.

Ekman, P. (1965). Communication through nonverbal behavior: A source of information about an interpersonal relationship. In S. S. Tomkins & C. E. Izard (Eds.), *Affect, cognition, and personality* (pp. 390–442). New York: Springer.

Ekman, P., & Friesen, W. V. (1971). Constants across cultures in the face and emotion. *Journal of Personality and Social Psychology, 17,* 124–129.

Ellis, M., & Astell, A. (2017). Communicating with people living with dementia who are nonverbal: The creation of Adaptive Interaction. *PLoS ONE, 12* (8): e0180395. https://doi.org/10.1371/journal.pone.0180395

Farber, S. L. (1981). *Identical twins reared apart: A reanalysis.* New York: Basic Books.

Fast, J. (1970). *Body language.* New York: M. Evans.

Fox, M. (2008). *Talking hands: What sign language reveals about the mind* (Reprint ed.). New York: Simon & Schuster.

Galati, D., Miceli, R., & Sini, B. (2001). Judging and coding facial expressions of emotions in congenitally blind children. *International Journal of Behavioral Development, 25,* 268–278.

Galati, D., Scherer, K. R., & Ricci-Bitti, P. E. (1997). Voluntary facial expression of emotion: Comparing congenitally blind with normally sighted encoders. *Journal of Personality and Social Psychology, 73,* 1363–1379.

Galati, D., Sini, B., Schmidt, S., & Tinti, C. (2003). Spontaneous facial expressions in congenitally blind and sighted children aged 8–11. *Journal of Visual Impairment and Blindness, 97,* 418–428.

Grossman, R. B., & Kegl, J. (2007). Moving faces: Categorization of dynamic facial expressions in American Sign Language by deaf and hearing participants. *Journal of Nonverbal Behavior, 31,* 23–38.

Guerrero, L. K., Andersen, P. A., & Afifi, W. A. (2017). *Close encounters: Communication in relationships* (5th ed.). Thousand Oaks, CA: Sage.

Guerrero, L. K., & Floyd, K. (2006). *Nonverbal communication in close relationships.* Mahwah, NJ: Erlbaum.

Hall, E. T. (1959). *The silent language.* Garden City, NJ: Doubleday.

Hall, E. T. (1966). *The hidden dimension.* New York: Doubleday.

Hess, U., Blaison, C., & Kafetsios, K. (2016). Judging facial emotion expressions in context: The influence of culture and self-construal orientation. *Journal of Nonverbal Behavior, 40,* 55–64.

Hopkins, W. D. (Ed.). (2007). *The evolution of hemispheric specialization in primates.* New York: Academic.

Jack, R. E., Garrod, O. G. B., Yu, H., Caldara, R., & Schyns, P. G. (2012). Facial expressions of emotion are not culturally universal. *Proceedings of the National Academy of Sciences of the USA, 109,* 7241–7244.

Jung-Beeman, M., Bowden, E. M., Haberman, J., Frymiare, J. L., Arambel-Liu, S., Greenblatt, R., et al. (2004). Neural activity when people solve verbal problems with insight. *PLoS Biology, 2,* e97. doi:10.1371/journal.pbio.0020097

Kaneko, M., & Mesch, J. (2013). Eye gaze in creative sign language. *Sign Language Studies, 13,* 372–400.

Künecke, J., Wilhelm, O., & Sommer, W. (2017). Emotion recognition in nonverbal face-to-face communication. *Journal of Nonverbal Behavior, 41,* 221–238.

Lewis, C. S. (1961). *A grief observed.* New York: HarperCollins.

Matsumoto, D., & Hwang, H. (2013). Cultural similarities and differences in emblematic gestures. *Journal of Nonverbal Behavior, 37,* 1–27.

Matsumoto, D., & Juang, L. (2016). *Culture and psychology* (6th ed.). Boston: Cengage.

Matsumoto, D., Olide, A., Schug, J., Willingham, B., & Callan, M. (2009). Cross-cultural judgments of spontaneous facial expressions of emotion. *Journal of Nonverbal Behavior, 33,* 213–238.

Matsumoto, D., & Yoo, S. H. (2005). Culture and applied nonverbal communication. In R. E. Riggio & R. S. Feldman (Eds.), *Applications of nonverbal communication* (pp. 255–277). Mahwah, NJ: Erlbaum.

McNeill, D. (Ed.). (2000). *Language and gesture.* New York: Cambridge University Press.

Mehrabian, A. (1972). *Nonverbal communication.* Chicago: Atherton.

Mehrabian, A. (1981). *Silent messages* (2nd ed.). Belmont, CA: Wadsworth.

Naumann, L. P., Vazire, S., Rentfrow, P. J., & Gosling, S. D. (2009). Personality judgments based on physical appearance. *Personality and Social Psychology Bulletin, 35,* 1661–1671.

Newman, J. D. (2003). Vocal communication and the triune brain. *Physiology & Behavior, 79,* 495–502.

Nummenmaa, L., Glerean, E., Hari, R., & Hietanen, J. K. (2014). Bodily maps of emotions. *Proceedings of the National Academy of Sciences, 111,* 646–651.

Petrician, R., Todorov, A., & Grady, C. (2014). Personality at face value: Facial appearance predicts self and other personality judgments among strangers and spouses. *Journal of Nonverbal Behavior, 38,* 259–277.

Planalp, S. (2008). Varieties of emotional cues in everyday life. In L. K. Guerrero & M. L. Hecht (Eds.), *The nonverbal communication reader: Classic and contemporary readings* (pp. 397–401). Long Grove, IL: Waveland.

Ramirez, A., Jr., & Wang, A. (2008). When online meets offline: An expectancy violations theory perspective on modality switching. *Journal of Communication, 58,* 20–39.

Re, D., & Rule, N. O. (2016). Making a (false) impression: The role of business experience in first impressions of CEO leadership ability. *Journal of Nonverbal Behavior, 40,* 235–245.

Rowbotham, S., Holler, J., Lloyd, D., & Wearden, A. (2011). How do we communicate about pain? A systematic analysis of the semantic contribution of co-speech gestures in pain-focused conversation. *Journal of Nonverbal Behavior, 36,* 1–21.

Rule, N. O., & Ambady, N. (2009). She's got the look: Inferences from female chief executive officers' faces predict their success. *Sex Roles, 61*, 644–652.

Ryan, R. (2016). *60 seconds and you're hired* (Rev. ed.). New York: Penguin.

Samovar, L. A., Porter, R. E., McDaniel, E. R., & Sexton Roy, C. (2014). Approaches to intercultural communication. In L. A. Samovar, R. E. Porter, E. R. McDaniel, & C. Sexton Roy (Eds.), *Intercultural communication: A reader* (14th ed., pp. 1–3). Boston: Cengage Learning.

Segal, N. L. (1999). *Entwined lives: Twins and what they tell us about human behavior.* New York: Dutton.

Shuter, R. (1976). Proxemics and tactility in Latin America. *Journal of Communication, 26*, 46–55.

Sukel, K. (2012, August 12). Can we quit it with the "right brain, left brain" stuff already?! *Big Think.* Retrieved from http://bigthink.com/world-in-mind/can-we-quit-it-with-the-right-brain-left-brain-stuff-already

Szarota, P. (2010). The mystery of the European smile: A comparison based on individual photographs provided by Internet users. *Journal of Nonverbal Behavior, 34*, 249–256.

Tracy, J. L., & Robins, R. W. (2008). The nonverbal expression of pride: Evidence for cross-cultural recognition. *Journal of Personality & Social Psychology, 94*, 516–530.

Vennekens-Kelly, E. (2012). *Subtle differences, big faux pas: Test your cultural competence.* Scottsdale, AZ: Summertime.

Yang, P. (2010). Nonverbal gender differences: Examining gestures of university-educated Mandarin Chinese Speakers. *Text & Talk, 30*, 333–357.

Yoo, S. H., & Noyes, S. E. (2016). Recognition of facial expressions of negative emotions in romantic relationships. *Journal of Nonverbal Behavior, 40*, 1–12.

chapter two

NONVERBAL COMMUNICATION DEVELOPMENT: A REFLEXIVE APPROACH

chapter outline

chapter objectives

Attraction affects how we communicate, both verbally and nonverbally. How do your nonverbal cues change when you are in the presence of someone you're attracted to? Do you process that attractive person's nonverbal cues differently because of the attraction you feel?

Danielle has an intriguing dilemma: She's really attracted to a guy in one of her classes but is unsure what to do—if anything—about her attraction. And this is no ordinary guy. Wu is an international student, working on a degree in computer science. He comes from a country where the customs and language are quite different from those found in the United States, although Wu speaks very good English. Danielle's attraction is *major*, such that she's finding it hard to concentrate on what her professor and classmates discuss each day—that is, until Wu jumps into the class discussion. Then she hangs onto every word.

She hasn't told anyone about her attraction, but she wonders: Does Wu even realize I'm in his class? Has he noticed me? Do I act differently because of this attraction I feel? Can other people tell I'm attracted to him? What do I do if Wu doesn't make a move? Do I make the first move? What *is* the first move?

If Danielle decides she doesn't want to pursue the object of her attraction and doesn't want Wu to know she's attracted to him, she will work to suppress any sign that she likes him so that he and other people won't detect what she feels. But if she wants Wu to know she's attracted, she will behave in ways that let her interest be known. What exactly *are* those ways? What are appropriate behaviors in American culture for a young woman to let a young man (from another cultural background, no less) know she's interested, without seeming too aggressive or, worse, promiscuous?

Attraction to another person is a feeling most of us have experienced, so Danielle's challenge with Wu is an example we'll use in this chapter to help us explore how nonverbal communication operates in human behavior. Using Danielle's situation, we'll work from a model we've developed that enhances our understanding of how people come to know themselves better as communicators, how they change and improve their communicative abilities, how they affect others' communication, and how they, in turn, are affected by the process of affecting others.

THE REFLEXIVE CYCLE OF NONVERBAL COMMUNICATION DEVELOPMENT

Nonverbal communication is a fascinating and complex area of study; you probably know that by now, since you're taking a course in this subject. But you may be wondering: How can I get a handle on this topic? How can I make sense out of all this information and make it useful for me so I get something practical out of it, something that can enhance my relationships and improve my life? Those are the perfect questions to ask.

We believe they're perfect questions because—as self-serving as this sounds—we asked them, too, as we began envisioning this book. Our challenge was, first, to sift through the vast amounts of information available on the topic of nonverbal communication and to piece it together so it formed a coherent structure that would make sense to professors and students. Second, we wanted to find a way to deliver that information so its reception had the potential to deepen people's understanding and improve their lives. In a nutshell, those are the goals of this book.

To accomplish those goals, we developed the model you see in Figure 2.1, the Reflexive Cycle of Nonverbal Communication Development. We encourage you to embrace this model and make it work for you as you continue to deepen your understanding of how nonverbal communication functions and to improve your nonverbal skills as a communicator. In the next few pages, we first examine what it means to be "reflexive," since this property is at the core of the model and key to your understanding and application of it. Then we explore each phase of the cycle, using Danielle and Wu's example to help us better understand how the model functions.

FIGURE **2.1**
Reflexive Cycle of Nonverbal Communication Development

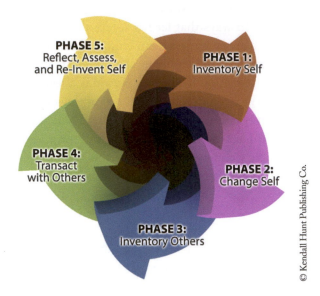

What Does "Reflexive" Mean?

Been to the doctor for a physical lately? If so, your doctor likely banged on your kneecap with one of those rubber mallets to see if you had healthy reflexes. According to the online *Oxford Dictionary*, a reflex is "an action that is performed without conscious thought as a response to a stimulus." Some nonverbal behaviors are reflexive in that they are automatic responses to stimuli. These behaviors are both innate and learned, but they occur with little or no intentional decision making or forethought. Think about biting into a lemon that's just been cut in half; does that thought make you cringe? You likely experienced some sort of facial response (such as crinkling the bridge of your nose) at the thought of biting into that lemon, so your nonverbal response was **reflexive**—accomplished automatically rather than purposefully.

Wouldn't it be great if we could learn to produce nonverbal signals and respond to other people with cues that are appropriate for every circumstance we experience in life? It would be interesting if we could enact those behaviors so seamlessly that they became automatic. For certain, that's an ideal beyond any of our grasps. But if we view it as a goal to work toward, an ideal to approach—realizing that we can never reach perfection—then it becomes an intriguing prospect.

What we describe is a *process* goal, a goal about "becoming," not "arriving." That's why the model is a *cycle*, not a straight line or arrow going upward, indicating that the reflexive process repeats. It's a constant process throughout our lifetimes, as we encounter diverse people, varied situations, and new information (Dashtipour, 2012; Elliott & du Gay, 2009; Giddens, 1991). Improving our nonverbal effectiveness through study, exposure to people and situations, and conscientious intent to enhance our nonverbal abilities so that we work toward such abilities becoming more automatic or reflexive—that's a practical, encouraging goal that can motivate us over our lifetimes.

A dictionary explanation for the term *reflexive* is "referring back to the subject" as in, "I, myself, have always wanted to travel to Australia." In this statement, the word *myself* refers back to the subject of the sentence, *I*. Communication scholars have described **reflexivity** as "a form of self-critical yet compassionate self-examination," explaining that "through reflexivity, we come to moments of self-discovery" (Medved & Turner, 2011, p. 109). Others have explained it as "bending back, by going more deeply into the self in order to understand others" (Jorgenson, 2011, p. 115). In *Concepts of the Self*, Anthony Elliott (2013) contends that reflexivity is a "self-defining process that depends upon monitoring of, and reflection upon, psychological and social information about possible trajectories of life" (p. 45). Note that in the reflexive model, the cycle focuses on the individual. As we explain each phase of the cycle, you'll see why the self, within a social context, receives so much attention in our exploration of nonverbal communication.

Phase 1: Inventory Self

Remember Danielle, the student who had the hots for her classmate Wu? One of the first things Danielle was concerned about was this: Does Wu (or anyone else) know I'm attracted to him? This question reflects the first phase of the Reflexive Cycle—the continuous process of becoming more aware of your own nonverbal communication (see Figure 2.2). We have little hope of improving our communication abilities if we're unaware of the current skills we possess, as well as areas we need to work on. But this becomes a particularly challenging task in the nonverbal realm because we're unaware of a good deal of our nonverbal communication.

Two of the most prolific scholars in the field of nonverbal communication, whose work we referenced in Chapter 1 and will reference many times throughout this book, are Paul Ekman

FIGURE 2.2
Reflexive Cycle of Nonverbal Communication Development, Phase 1

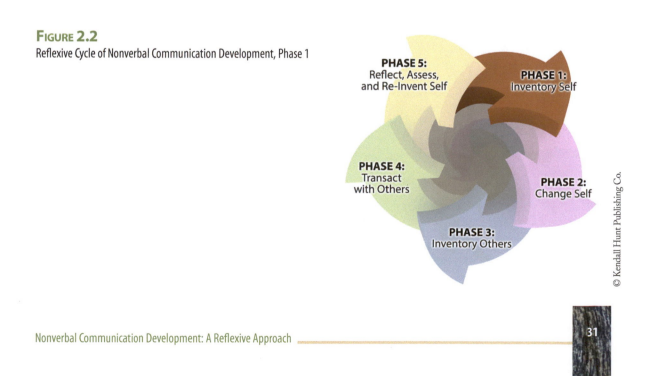

and Wallace Friesen. Ekman and Friesen (1968) explored the nature of nonverbal communication, characterizing it as behaviors often enacted unconsciously, meaning with little intent. They contended that most people were unaware of the nonverbal cues they produced; people's lack of awareness made them unable to make conscious decisions to alter their nonverbal behavior. If we don't realize what we're doing, how can we assess it and possibly change it? The first challenge the Reflexive Cycle poses is to inventory our own nonverbal behavior—to attempt first, on our own, to become more aware of how we communicate without as well as in conjunction with words.

Our best advice to Danielle, who's attracted to her classmate Wu, is to take an honest inventory of her nonverbal behavior, at least as much as she can figure out on her own. During her next class with Wu, she should make mental notes (or even written ones) about how she's feeling and how she believes she's coming across to others during the class session. She should track such things as feelings of warmth in her skin (maybe even blushing), because her skin temperature might rise due to her feelings of attraction. How about eye contact? Does she look at Wu in class? How close or far away does she sit from where Wu sits? Research and our own experience have shown that students are predictable and habitual in their choice and maintenance of seating in a classroom where there is no assigned seating arrangement (Burgess & Kaya, 2007; Douglas & Gifford, 2001;

People improve as communicators by first becoming more aware of how they nonverbally communicate with others (phase 1 in the Reflexive Cycle).

Fassinger, 2000; Hill & Epps, 2010; Koen & Durrheim, 2010). Does Danielle stay in her original seat in class, or does she change her seating position in regard to Wu's chosen seat? Such nonverbal indicators speak volumes about how Danielle feels about Wu, her fears about her attraction (and what to do, if anything, about it), and how others will react to her if they learn of her attraction. If Danielle really wants to better understand herself as a nonverbal communicator, her first challenge is an honest, reflexive self-examination (inventory).

How does this apply to you? If a friend were to impersonate you, what would that look and sound like? Is there something particularly striking or memorable about your walk, voice, or facial expressions? Inventory, first, those nonverbal elements that other people have made you aware of throughout your life. For a real eye-opener, record yourself and watch the playback; note your posture, your walk, how you tend to sit (e.g., slouched, straight, legs crossed at the knees or ankles). Record yourself in conversation with someone, and note how you use such behaviors as gestures, facial and eye expressions, touch, and tone of voice. Granted, this isn't a natural expression of nonverbal behaviors, because the recording is a prescribed event, one where the purpose is known, but it will give you some insights and a greater awareness of how you use nonverbal cues to express who you are and communicate with others.

A second aspect of this inventory involves asking others for feedback about your nonverbal behavior. You can make significant changes by conducting your own inventory, but others' feedback is useful. For example, some people believe that whatever emotion they feel shows up in their facial expressions, as if they're an "open book." But when they ask others about this behavior, they may get different perceptions. Some people may agree that their faces portray their emotions, but others may perceive more discretion or more of a "poker face." Such feedback is good information for those of us working on our nonverbal skills. The goal in this phase is to move nonverbal cues more into the realm of the known rather than the unknown, the aware rather than the unaware, so that we operate more consciously as communicators.

As you progress through this course and this text, heightened awareness of your own nonverbal behavior will come to you. But here's our warning: Be brave. Learning this much about yourself can be daunting, because bad will be mixed in with the good. No one's perfect; you'll no doubt have to confront some behaviors that have developed over time and that you may not completely understand, much less like and want to continue doing. You may realize that some of your nonverbal behaviors look and sound like those of your parents. (This may be horrifying or pleasant, depending on your feelings about your parents!) It does take real courage to face yourself honestly, take stock of who you are and how you communicate, be open to and seek others' feedback, and challenge yourself to make meaningful changes. But realize that awareness is the beginning phase of truly understanding the power of nonverbal communication in our relationships and interactions with others.

OUT OF THE CLASSROOM
onto the page

A student in one of your authors' undergraduate nonverbal communication classes described to the class her recent experience with the "inventory self" phase of the Reflexive Cycle (even though she didn't know to call it that at the time). She had some trouble at her part-time job, where she'd recently not been selected for a promotion to a job with more responsibility and oversight of other workers. She interviewed for the position and thought she had a good chance at getting it, given that she'd worked there for a few years and had gotten positive reviews from supervisors. When she didn't get the job, she mustered up some courage and asked the manager who interviewed her for some feedback on how she could have done better in the interview. The manager's response was vague—something about her lacking assertiveness that was necessary when supervising others. The feedback left her with more questions than answers.

Still irritated by the situation, she decided to participate in a job interview training program offered by her campus's career services office. She was videotaped doing a mock interview with one of the career services staff members, then she forced herself to watch and listen to the recording. (Sometimes recorded feedback of oneself is hard to handle!) She noticed that while her face, eyes, and body positions exuded confidence, her voice did not. She had a vocal behavior that nonverbal communication scholarship terms "upspeak." Upspeak is when every statement ends with an upward pitch change, as though all sentences were turned into questions. The result is that a person using upspeak sounds unsure, as though every statement needs affirmation from others in conversation. Our student realized that her use of pitch made her sound unconfident and a bit "ditzy," as she put it. She set her sights on moving this vocal behavior from the unaware category into her awareness; she began consciously working to sound more certain and to avoid the pitch shift at the end of her statements. At the point at which the student shared this story with the class, she was in the process of changing this behavior that had once been out of her realm of awareness. She was hopeful that altering this one small nonverbal cue would affect how others perceived her.

Phase 2: Change Self

The second step in the Reflexive Cycle (see Figure 2.3) is to change our nonverbal communication, based on the inventory we completed in Phase 1. When we say *change*, we also mean to come to a decision about things that work well, behaviors we don't want to change or that don't need alteration. Danielle may discover, once she thinks about her behavior in the class with Wu, that how she's behaving toward Wu suits her at this point in time; no changes are needed or comfortable at present. Or she may realize that she's either being too obvious or too subtle about her attraction to Wu. Maybe she'll ask trusted classmates if her attraction to Wu is noticeable, only to learn that no one has noticed. If Danielle's goal is to get Wu's attention, to get him to become interested in her, and, ultimately, to see if a relationship with Wu is possible, then she most likely will have some changes to make in her verbal and nonverbal communication.

Let's take two simpler, more personal examples: Are you someone who tends to use a lot of hand gestures in conversation? Do people tell you, "You couldn't talk if your hands were tied together"? Maybe you have a bad habit of interrupting other people, perhaps out of exuberance or because it's hard to control your energy when you have something you want to say. By studying nonverbal communication or possibly through common, everyday interaction, you may decide you want to change your behavior. You inventoried yourself, including putting the feedback from others to good use, and are now working to change something in your nonverbal repertoire. The outcome is that you consciously work to restrict your hand movement when you talk to people, or dedicate yourself to being a better listener rather than letting your energy overtake you and lead to an interruption. Just as many of our nonverbal behaviors have taken time to form—many may have taken a lifetime to develop and become ingrained—it will take time to "unlearn" or alter routine or commonly used behaviors. But with conscious effort, over time your new approach will become habit or more automatic (reflexive).

FIGURE 2.3

Reflexive Cycle of Nonverbal Communication Development, Phase 2

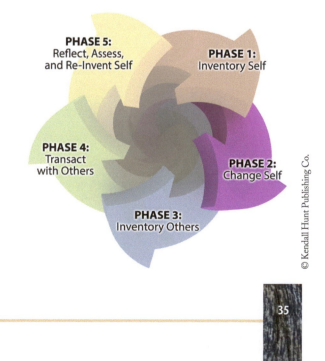

PHASE 5: Reflect, Assess, and Re-Invent Self

PHASE 1: Inventory Self

PHASE 4: Transact with Others

PHASE 2: Change Self

PHASE 3: Inventory Others

© Kendall Hunt Publishing Co.

Phase 3: Inventory Others

Are you a people watcher? Taking a course in nonverbal communication and reading this book will make you more of a people watcher—at a more microscopic level—than you probably deemed possible. In fact, students in our nonverbal communication classes tell us that the course "makes them weird," in that they process way more information about people than they did before studying this topic.

Phase 3 (see Figure 2.4) challenges you to inventory others' nonverbal behavior closely, to pay attention to a wider range of cues at a more microscopic level than you're used to doing—no matter how fascinated you are, generally, by people. You'll likely accomplish this phase *covertly* and *overtly*.

Covert observation means noting nonverbal cues subtly and without detection. To pull this off, you'll first want to sharpen your powers of unobtrusive observation. This means that you get out of your own head whenever you have the chance, that you "divorce to self from the situation," meaning your attention to yourself and your needs are subverted so you can more carefully clue in to others. Then you appropriately observe the nonverbal behaviors of other people without drawing attention to yourself. Note that we said "appropriately"; too much people watching can get weird, as in stalking someone.

What Phase 3 challenges you to do is to observe everyday, commonplace behavior—not to create some circumstance in which unordinary behavior might emerge. For example, since staring is considered rude in U.S. culture, you won't want to take up staring at people as a means of observing their nonverbal behavior. Crowded social spaces are excellent venues for covert observation, but you want to seek every opportunity you can find, put on your people-watching hat, and take in the scene around you, noting behaviors you find effective and those you do not. And you don't necessarily

FIGURE 2.4
Reflexive Cycle of Nonverbal Communication Development, Phase 3

have to inventory others' behaviors from a distance; you can be actively engaged in a conversation with several people and still clue in to the nonverbal cues flying back and forth. You're a participant in the conversation, but you're also inventorying the fascinating array of behaviors as they occur.

In a more **overt** manner, you may also find occasion to ask people directly about their own nonverbal behavior or the nonverbal cues of others. This strategy is termed **perception checking**, discussed also in Chapter 1, and it's a useful tool that you're no doubt already using to some extent.

Phase 3 of the Reflexive Cycle challenges you to observe people's nonverbal communication on a level you might not have done before (without making yourself a nuisance).

Referring to our earlier example, Danielle has perceived some things about Wu, but she wants to bounce her views off of other people to get more information and a better understanding of the situation. She may ask some classmates very casually, "Hey, what do you think of that Wu guy in our class?" Or she may be more direct, explaining to friends or classmates that she's attracted to Wu and then soliciting their opinions of or perceptions about him. This is an ongoing process of becoming more socially competent through inventorying—in as much detail as possible—others' ways of expressing themselves nonverbally. The saying goes that "imitation is the sincerest form of flattery," so you may find that others behave in ways you want to emulate, that you want to adopt others' nonverbal skills into your repertoire as a communicator.

Phase 4: Transact With Others

You've inventoried yourself in an effort to become more aware of nonverbal cues you give off to others. You've decided what aspects of your nonverbal repertoire you like and want to retain, as well as those things you want to begin to change. You've sharpened your powers of observation in terms of others' nonverbal communication. Now, in Phase 4 (see Figure 2.5), we interact with others and mutually affect one another's nonverbal behavior. We prefer to call this process **transaction**, because it implies a shared creation of meaning that occurs in a simultaneous, ongoing manner (Beebe, Beebe, & Ivy, 2019). As compared to verbal communication in which, generally, messages are produced one at a time as interactants take turns at talk, in the nonverbal realm messages are exchanged continuously and the sheer act of exchange shapes the interaction.

Phase 4 is about communicating with other people, verbally and nonverbally, while still maintaining an awareness of nonverbal cues—yours and theirs. We recognize that this is a challenge,

PHASE 5:
Reflect, Assess, and Re-Invent Self

PHASE 1:
Inventory Self

PHASE 4:
Transact with Others

PHASE 2:
Change Self

PHASE 3:
Inventory Others

© Kendall Hunt Publishing Co.

because we often become concerned or preoccupied with ourselves in social situations, sometimes just wondering how other people perceive us, whether they like us, whether we sound intelligent or silly, and so forth. But that's what this process is all about—becoming increasingly aware, on a daily basis, of the critical role nonverbal behavior plays in the process of communicating with others. The more you clue in to how you're nonverbally communicating, how others are nonverbally communicating, and how, in turn, all that nonverbal communication affects ongoing interaction, the more successful and savvy a communicator you'll become.

Back to Danielle and Wu: Danielle inventoried her own nonverbal behavior regarding her attraction to Wu, then she started working on some subtle changes she believed would make her a more effective communicator. Next, she inventoried Wu's nonverbal behavior—overtly and covertly—to try to assess any interest he might have in her and how he interacts with people in general. Now she believes she is ready to attempt some kind of exchange with Wu. As a subtle beginning, Danielle might try to make more eye contact with Wu, in hopes that he'll notice her. She might speak up more in class, following up any comments Wu makes, trying to

©Kolett/ Shutterstock.com

In Phase 4 of the Reflexive Cycle, people communicate and affect each other. This is a common occurrence, but students of nonverbal communication will pay special attention to the nonverbal cues of others, as well as themselves, during conversation.

draw his attention. In such a nonverbal-only transaction, Danielle's behavior is affected by what she hopes to make happen with Wu; whether Wu will notice and respond, such that a transaction occurs, is anyone's guess. Wu might not be as attuned to nonverbal signals as Danielle is, so she may decide that more direct contact is necessary, like catching Wu after class and introducing herself, in the hopes of sharing a good first conversation.

Phase 5: Reflect, Assess, and Re-Inventory Self

We come full circle in the Reflexive Cycle when we move through Phase 5 (see Figure 2.6), which asks you to reflect on and assess the process you've just undertaken. Try to be purposeful or mindful in this entire undertaking, this process of understanding nonverbal complexities and applying that understanding to behavior, so you can reflect on what you've learned, assess triumphs as well as mistakes, and continue to further develop your nonverbal skills. Remember that the cycle is ongoing; we never stop evolving in our understanding and use of nonverbal communication.

Perhaps Danielle's reflection and assessment might go something like this: Danielle first inventoried her own nonverbal behavior toward Wu once she realized she was attracted to him and wanted to do something about it. She observed Wu in class and talked to some trusted classmates, seeking their perceptions of him. She saw him interact with friends in the student center on campus and took in information about his friends (none of them looked like deviants); she also didn't see him with anyone who looked like a girlfriend or boyfriend, so that gave her courage. Next she decided that her first move toward Wu (who seemed unaware of her interest in him) would be to catch him in the hallway and talk to him about something discussed in class. She introduced

FIGURE 2.6
Reflexive Cycle of Nonverbal Communication Development, Phase 5

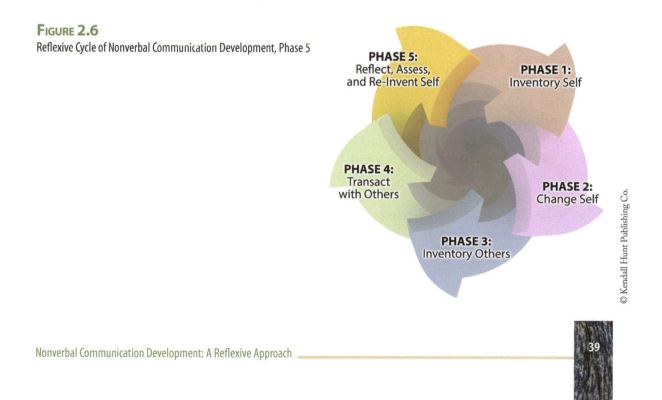

herself, resurrected one of Wu's comments from class, and asked him to tell her more as they walked across campus. She carefully inventoried Wu's nonverbal behavior, as well as his words, looking for any signs that he might be interested in her or attracted to her, too. Detecting Wu's positive response to her, Danielle next chose to extend an offer to Wu to study together for an upcoming exam in the class they had together. Wu accepted, and the relationship was off and running. We're happy to say that they're now married and living happily ever after with three kids and a dog. (So what if our example sounds like a fairy tale? We wanted a happy ending.)

If Danielle is a person who wants to learn and grow from her experiences, she will now enact Phase 5 by overviewing this whole process with Wu and her attention to nonverbal cues—her own as well as Wu's. She'll reflect on the nonverbal signals, look for any missteps or missed opportunities, assess whether she did the right thing or if she could have done some things differently, and then continue the process by re-inventorying her nonverbal behavior. If the process works optimally, Danielle will have expanded her nonverbal repertoire of behavior and will be better equipped to cope with and respond to other new situations and people.

The process of gaining skill in sending and receiving nonverbal communication is ongoing, as the Reflexive Cycle indicates.

Remember that the Reflexive Cycle is a continuous process of moving nonverbal communication out of the "unaware" and into the "aware." One framework, attributed to Abraham Maslow, helps explain what we mean. The framework contends that people function at one of four levels:

1. **Unconscious incompetence:** We're unaware of our own incompetence. We don't know what we don't know.
2. **Conscious incompetence:** At this level, we become aware or conscious that we're not competent; we know what we don't know.
3. **Conscious competence:** We're aware that we know or can do something, but it hasn't yet become an integrated skill or habit.
4. **Unconscious competence:** At this level, skills become second nature. We know something or can do something but don't have to concentrate to be able to act on that knowledge or draw on that skill (Beebe et al., 2019).

If you continuously work through the Reflexive Cycle, you'll draw closer to the fourth level described above, unconscious competence. You'll be more able to enact nonverbal skills appropriate to varying situations, such that these skills become "second nature." The Reflexive Cycle is a constant process of discovery, but, as we've described it, it's not for the faint of heart. It takes work and a real commitment to improving your ability to nonverbally communicate.

WHAT WOULD *YOU* DO

Mike's coworker reeks. It's a combination of less-than-desirable hygiene, a remnant pot-smoking smell, and a weak attempt at a cover-up with cheap cologne. Unfortunately, Mike's cubicle is right next to "Pig Pen's" and their supervisor rarely drops by, so management isn't aware of the problem. Sure, the guy gets his work done, but at the expense of his coworkers who have to put up with the various odors. The guy seems not to know how badly he smells; as the TV commercial says, "he's gone nose blind."

If you were in this situation, *what would you do*? If you really liked the job and didn't want to quit, how would you cope with the situation? Would you attempt to increase your coworker's awareness of nonverbal cues by gently explaining to him that you find his cologne offensive (too powerful a nonverbal cue), or make up a story like an allergy to his cologne? (Maybe you don't want his cologne usage to stop, because not wearing it might be worse.) Would you rat on him to your supervisor? Would you simply ask for a transfer to another cubicle or another area within the organization, thereby decreasing your proximity to him?

Making Effective Use of the Reflexive Cycle

Now that you have a greater understanding of each phase in the Reflexive Cycle, let's talk about how to use this model as you work through material in this book. A smaller version or icon of the Reflexive Cycle will appear at various points throughout the chapters, with one or more phases of the cycle highlighted. The appearance of the icon should signal to you, "Aha, the Reflexive Cycle is in play here." The highlighting of certain phases means that content corresponding to one or more phases is being discussed in the paragraph or paragraphs adjacent to the icon. We offer the icon reminder simply as a device to reinforce for you the connection between textbook information and different phases in the cycle. For example, in the chapter on proxemics (use of space), we ask you to inventory your rules or expectations about space, including such things as how much space you prefer around you in daily interaction, who is allowed to "invade" your space without it being perceived as a violation, and how you react if

someone gets too close to you in conversation. To the side of the paragraphs on this material, you'll see the Reflexive Cycle icon, with the first phase (Inventory Self) highlighted, because the text corresponding to the icon focuses on becoming more aware of your own space issues. Pay attention to the presence of these icons as you read, because they'll reinforce for you the practical applications we encourage you to make with the information you're learning.

CODES OF NONVERBAL COMMUNICATION

Since human nonverbal behavior is so diverse and vast, the need arises for classifications. The primary categories or **codes** of nonverbal information researchers have studied, and which we'll explore in subsequent chapters in this text, include the following: environment; space and territory; physical appearance; body movement, gestures, and posture; facial expression; eye expression; touch; and vocal expression. Although we concentrate on these codes as they're exhibited in mainstream Western culture, recognize that they're enacted differently in other cultures (Samovar, Porter, & McDaniel, & Sexton Roy, 2014).

REMEMBER

Remember!
2.1

Reflexivity	Actions accomplished automatically rather than purposefully; referring back to the self
Covert observation	Appropriately observing nonverbal behaviors of other people without drawing much or any attention to ourselves
Overt observation	Asking people directly about their own nonverbal behavior or the nonverbal behavior of others
Perception checking	Asking direct or third-person parties for their perceptions, which we can compare with our own
Transaction	Shared creation of meaning that occurs in a simultaneous, ongoing manner
Unconscious incompetence	Being unaware of our own incompetence
Conscious incompetence	Becoming aware or conscious of our own incompetence
Conscious competence	Realizing we know something or can do something, but it hasn't yet become an integrated skill or habit
Unconscious competence	Knowing we can do something but not having to concentrate to be able to act on the knowledge or draw on the skill

Environment

Picture your car as you last left it. (For those of you who don't currently have a car, picture a car—inside and out—that you can imagine yourself owning.) If you gave one of your professors your keys and he or she got in your car and started the engine, what would happen? Would the car choke to life, as though it hadn't had an oil change in a decade, or would it hum? Would your car reveal what all you'd eaten in the past week? Is half your wardrobe in that car? Would your back seat be condemned by the health department? How long ago did that "new car smell" wear off, and what replaced it? Would some form of music (maybe containing X-rated language) come blaring through the speakers? What impressions of you would your professor get, just by sitting in your car? Whether or not you've ever thought of it as such, your car is a form of **environment** that reveals a good deal, nonverbally, about you.

As one scholar put it, "People cannot be understood outside of their environmental context" (Peterson, 1992, p. 154). The environment is important to the study of nonverbal communication in two ways: (1) The choices we make about the environment in which we live and operate reveal a good deal about who we are, and (2) our nonverbal behavior is altered by various environments in which we communicate.

First, the physical environments in which we function can be seen as extensions of our personalities (Biemiller, 2008; Billig, 2006; Gifford, 2014; Scannell & Gifford, 2017). We may not be able to manipulate all the elements of our environment, but to whatever extent we're allowed, we'll put our "signature" on our physical environs, such as our homes, rooms, and offices, to make them unique and personal (Gosling, Ko, Mannarelli, & Morris, 2002; Wells & Thelen, 2002). The environments we create for ourselves often speak volumes about those relationships we deem most important, as well as our own importance (Altman, Brown, Staples, & Werner, 1992; Lohmann, Arriaga, & Goodfriend, 2003). Who has the higher status in an office building—the person in the corner office with wall-to-wall windows, high atop a skyscraper, or the person on a lower floor in a cubicle amidst other cubicles in high traffic? Many environmental cues signal status in American culture and in the work world (Vilnai-Yavetz, Rafaeli, & Schneider-Yaacov, 2005).

Second, our behavior, perceptions, and even our physical and mental fitness may be altered because of the physical environments in which we find ourselves (Andrade, Lima, Devlin, & Hernandez,

If your job demanded you work in a space like this, how might you make your cubicle more personal, more an extension of your personality? How would this work environment affect your verbal and nonverbal communication with coworkers?

© Kolett/Shutterstock.com

2016; Paul, Mandal, Ramachandran, & Panwar, 2010; Rashid & Zimring, 2008; Syndicus, Weise, & van Treeck, 2018). Such things as lighting, air quality, temperature, noise, and smells at our workplaces affect our mental and physical health (Hadavi, 2017; Kozusznik, Peiro, Soriano, & Escudero, 2018).

Space and Territory

You arrive to class a bit early; you put your stuff down at your usual seat, then head to the vending machine in the hall to grab a snack to help you get through the many hours left in your day. When you come back to your classroom, someone is not only sitting in the seat where you left your stuff, but that person has also moved your stuff one seat away from where you left it. How would you react? Would you feel uncomfortable or violated because a classmate invaded "your" space and touched your stuff? Or would you roll with the punches, assuming that two classmates simply wanted to sit together? For decades research has explored the fascinating subject of **proxemics**, or how people (and animals) create and use space and distance, as well as how they behave to protect and defend that space (Hall, 1959, 1966; Kabo, 2017; Li & Li, 2007; Sluzki, 2016; Szpak, Nicholls, Thomas, Laham, & Loetsher, 2016).

Every culture has well-established ways of regulating spatial relations. Normally, we don't think much about the rules or norms we follow regarding space, until those rules are violated. Violations can be alarming, possibly even threatening. How physically close we are willing to get to others relates to how well we know them, to considerations of power and status, and to our cultural backgrounds (Beaulieu, 2004; Hellmann & Jucks, 2017; Matsumoto, 2006).

The study of how people use space and objects to communicate occupancy or ownership of space is termed **territoriality** (Brown & Robinson, 2011; Costa, 2012; Erlandson, 2012; Lyman & Scott, 1999). You assumed ownership of your seat in the classroom when you put your stuff there, and you likely felt that you had the right to that seat because you got there first and "staked out your territory." You may have reacted negatively because your sense of personal space was invaded, but also because your classmate broke a cultural rule governing territoriality. Or you may not have reacted negatively because your rules about space and territory allow for a wide berth of behavior.

We communicate our ownership of space with **territorial markers**—objects and actions that signify an area has been claimed (Goffman, 1971). Did you put a sign up on your bedroom door when you were a kid, saying something like "Jason's Room: Keep out on pain of death"? The most common form of territorial marker is a lock. We lock our doors and windows, cars, offices, briefcases, TVs (using V-chips), and computers, and password protect all kinds of accounts and information to keep out intruders. We can be territorial about our identities, people we're in relationships with, and our time.

Physical Appearance

What do we tend to notice about people when we first see them? Most of us would answer the face, including the eyes, but others might answer the person's walk, stance, or general body motion.

Generally, before we hear someone's voice or register other nonverbal elements about the person, we've taken in nonverbal cues related to their **physical appearance**, or physical attributes of the face and body. Thus, appearance is a very important topic to study, since it's generally the first nonverbal cue people perceive. (Obviously, we're talking about face-to-face encounters, not situations where you meet people online.)

People from many diverse cultures place a premium on appearance, including such physical factors as body weight, skin color and texture, hairstyle, and adornments such as clothing and jewelry. Similar to other cultures, Americans place significant emphasis on looks, as we discuss in depth in Chapter 5. For example, Americans tend to vote for taller-than-average and better-looking political candidates, especially for the office of president, because we associate good looks and height with higher status (Hart, Ottati, & Krumdick, 2011; Schubert, Curran, & Strungaru, 2011; Tenner, 2004). Americans put such pressure on ourselves and others to be physically attractive that our self-esteem may decline when we realize we can't match up with some perceived ideal (Darlow & Lobel, 2010; Hill, Ogletree, & McCrary, 2016; Wrench & Knapp, 2008).

Clothing is another significant nonverbal cue. While clothing functions primarily to maintain decency, as well as to keep our bodies protected and warm, it also communicates our culture (Aliakbari & Abdollahi, 2013; Droogsma, 2007; Morris, 1985). Unique T-shirts, baseball caps, baggy pants, as well as other aspects of appearance, termed **artifacts** (e.g., jewelry, tattoos, piercings, makeup, cologne, eyeglasses), are displays of culture. While we don't believe that "clothes make the man," clothing and artifacts do affect how we are perceived by others (Dunden & Francis, 2016; Pham, 2011; Zestcott, Bean, & Stone, 2017).

A famous couple can shape perceptions of "ideal beauty."

Body Movement, Gestures, and Posture

What happens if people try to communicate when they don't share a common language? Most people end up looking extremely foolish by using exaggerated gestures or slowly, deliberately, and loudly mouthing words the listener can't understand. In such situations, we try to compensate for our lack of verbal understanding with nonverbal remedies. Even people who speak the same language often use gestures to make a point.

Kinesics is a general term for the study of human movement, gestures, and posture (Birdwhistell, 1960). Technically, movements of the face and eyes are contained within this category, but because our faces and eyes can produce such a wealth of information, we discuss them as separate codes.

Our kinesics provide valuable information to others. We develop a certain pattern of walk, stance, and posture, which becomes recognizable by others who come to know us. Body movements are affected by our moods and emotions, our physical health and conditioning, and also by technological innovations (Kim, Cheon, Youm, Son, & Kim, 2018). College students tend to walk differently (less efficiently) nowadays because most are looking at their cell phones instead of where they're going or people they're walking with (Lamberg & Muratori, 2012). Some people carry themselves in ways that convey pride and confidence, while others look as though the weight of the world were on their shoulders. Judgments about our competence, confidence, and personality can come from the observation of basic kinesic cues (Gurney, Howlett, Pine, Tracey, and Moggridge, 2017). Some people "talk with their hands," meaning they use a lot of gestures to complement what they're saying, while others prefer using fewer gestures, perhaps viewing them as distracting (Armstrong & Wagner, 2003). The body in motion is a fascinating, complex subset of nonverbal behavior that we study in more depth in Chapter 6.

Some people like to "talk with their hands" to make a point.

Facial Expression

This may sound sort of "duh," but our faces reveal our emotions—more than our body movements, tone of voice, and so forth (Buck, 2016; Ekman & Friesen, 1975). You cook a dish for the first time and serve it to your romantic partner or friend. You interview for a job you really want, and nervously watch the interviewer for some clue as to how she or he will respond to your résumé. In both situations, you scan the other person's face, eagerly awaiting some reaction. When trying to infer what another person feels by focusing on his or her **facial expression**, it helps if we know the person well, can see her or his whole face, have plenty of time to observe, and understand the situation that prompted the reaction (Fischer & LaFrance, 2015; Halberstadt, Dennis, & Hess, 2011; Hurley & Frank, 2011; Künecke, Wilhelm, & Somer, 2017; Wang, Huifang, Yexin, & Fan, 2016).

As adults, we come to realize that there are times when it's inappropriate and unwise to reveal our emotions fully, such as crying in front of superiors when we've been passed over for promotion or becoming visibly angry when we receive a grade that's lower than we expected. Masking emotions by controlling our facial expressions is a skill most of us learn at some point early in our lives (Cole, 1986; Gadea, Aliño, Espert, & Salvador, 2015). But at other times, having a "poker face"

can endanger our relationships. Consider aloof, distant parents who can't separate themselves from their work to enjoy the company of their own children, or romantic partners who can't tell how their partners feel about them because emotional displays have been squelched. The best approach is a balance of control and spontaneity. We want to stay real and human, to be able to reveal to others what we feel, but at times doing so can be inappropriate or damaging.

Eye Contact

You've probably heard that old English proverb, "The eyes are the windows to the soul." Can people see into your soul by looking into your eyes? Are you comfortable making eye contact with most people, or only with people you know well? **Eye contact** is extremely important in U.S. culture, as well as in many other cultures around the world (Quintanilla & Wahl, 2016). Americans often judge others—especially their trustworthiness, sincerity, and confidence—on the basis of whether they make or avoid eye contact (Lawson, 2015; Tang & Schmeichel, 2015). But there are limits to how much eye contact is considered appropriate; too little may be a sign of deception or a lack of confidence, whereas too much (staring) can be invasive or perceived as rude (Garland-Thomson, 2009; Mann et al., 2012; Vrij, Mann, Leal, & Fisher, 2010). As an interesting exercise, inventory your own eye behavior, thinking about when you're apt to look at someone and when you're likely to avert your gaze.

Eye contact plays a significant role in the judgment of a person's credibility in casual, everyday conversation, but it's particularly critical in a public presentation setting (Beebe, 1974; Beebe & Beebe, 2017; Napieraliski, Brooks, & Droney, 1995). A classic example illustrating the importance of eye contact and judgments of credibility comes from the first televised presidential debate, in which John F. Kennedy appeared comfortable and confident as he made eye contact with television cameras. It seemed as though he was looking at the American people rather than a TV camera. Richard Nixon, on the other hand, at times moved his gaze nervously from side to side and gener-

ally made less eye contact with the camera and the viewing audience, creating the perception that he was shifty, untrustworthy, and lacking confidence (Tiemens, 1978).

Touch

Touch, or body contact, is the most powerful form of nonverbal communication; it's also the most misunderstood and has the potential for severely negative consequences if not enacted appropriately. Typically, touch is a nonverbal expression of affection

© Matej Kastelic/Shutterstock.com

Do you feel anxious on a plane because of the possibility of unavoidable touch, due to the crowded conditions?

or intimacy, but what happens when we touch others accidentally or unintentionally? Think about a crowded airplane; if you're in that unlucky middle seat in a row, you might touch elbows, arms, hips, or legs with strangers on either side of you. The longer the flight, the more you may get used to this kind of unavoidable touch, or the more anxious it may make you, such that you can't wait to get off that plane.

Studies on touch (or **haptics**, as it's called in research) have shown that human contact is vital to our personal development, well-being, and physical and psychological health, as well as relationship development (Floyd, 2016a, 2016b; Hesse & Mikkelson, 2017). Many factors affect the amount of touch we need, initiate, tolerate, and receive. Physical contact evidenced in our families is the biggest influence, because those early experiences shape our views of appropriate and inappropriate touch and our comfort levels in extending touch to others, as well as receiving others' touches. Cultural background has a significant effect as well (Jung & Fouts, 2011; Mansson et al., 2016). Some cultures are high-contact and touching is quite commonplace, such as in some European and Middle Eastern cultures where men kiss each other on the cheeks in greeting. Other cultures are low-contact, such as some Asian cultures where displays of affection are rare and considered inappropriate (Andersen, 2011; Matsumoto & Hwang, 2013).

Vocal Expression

As we mentioned regarding the face, the voice is a significant vehicle for communicating our thoughts and emotions (Karpf, 2006). **Paralanguage** or **vocalics** includes such aspects as the pitch, rate, and volume at which we speak; it also pertains to having a nasal, raspy, or breathy voice. Ever had a parent or teacher rebuke you for your "tone of voice"? Tone is accomplished through the flexible mechanism of the voice.

Imagine that your spouse, romantic partner, or best friend purchased and modeled a new outfit, asking you what you thought. If you really hated the person's new outfit, would you say enthusiastically, "That looks GREAT!"—which could either be a little white lie designed to prevent hurt feelings or an expression of sarcasm? Or would you say, "That looks nice," in a halfhearted way? The ability to convey these different reactions is accomplished primarily by the human voice.

Beyond revealing our thoughts, emotions, and the nature of our relationships with others, our voices also convey how self-confident, knowledgeable, and attractive we are, and influence how we are perceived by others (Frank, Maroulis, & Griffin, 2013; Hodges-Simeon, Gaulin, & Puts, 2010; Imhof, 2010). If you were to listen to a presentation given by someone who mumbled, spoke very slowly and softly, continually mispronounced words, and used "uh" and "um" in every pause, you'd likely view that speaker as less credible and persuasive than one who spoke clearly, rapidly, fluently, and with appropriate volume (Beebe & Beebe, 2017; Hughes, Wood, & Foulkes, 2016; Christenfeld, 1995; Goberman, Hughes, & Haydock, 2011).

CODES (CATEGORIES) OF NONVERBAL COMMUNICATION

Environment	How people create and behave in spaces
Space (proxemics)	How people create and use proximity and distance; includes behavior to protect and defend space
Territorial markers	Cues that indicate ownership and occupancy of space
Physical appearance	Physical attributes of the face and body; typically the first nonverbal cue people perceive in face-to-face situations
Body movement, gestures, and posture (kinesics)	People's use of movements of the body to convey information, emotions, and attitudes
Eye contact	Conveys trustworthiness, sincerity, honesty, interest, and respect
Facial expression	Reveals thoughts and expresses emotions
Touch (haptics)	Study of human bodily contact; communicates the nature of the relationship between people
Vocal expression (vocalics, paralanguage)	Communicates emotion and clarifies the meaning of messages through such elements as pitch, rate, and volume

NONVERBAL SENDING AND RECEIVING ABILITY ■ ■ ■ ▬▬▬

Our goal in writing this book is to help students become more aware of nonverbal communication—nonverbal messages we send to other people, as well as the nonverbal cues others communicate. This ongoing process involves sharpening both sending and receiving powers. But for a moment, let's consider people beyond ourselves, because we have a prime example within our culture of people whose sending and receiving skills must be at their absolute best—our safety depends on it.

Unless you've been living under a rock, you know that national security is a prime concern for us all. We live in an increasingly dangerous world, and all too frequently we hear of some threat to our national security somewhere. In response to those threats, a group of ordinary citizens are trained to do extraordinary jobs every day, because they work for the U.S. Transportation Security Administration (TSA). First, think about air marshals, who undergo rigorous training just to be able to blend in with ordinary passengers on a plane but must also be able to assess and respond to dangerous situations instantly. Marshals' nonverbal communication skills must be finely honed so they convey "normal" nonverbal cues and don't call attention to themselves when they fly right along with the rest of us. Plus, they must be excellent processors of others' nonverbal information so they can anticipate a potential threat.

Next, think about the people who staff the security checkpoints at airports. Yes, many of us sigh when we think about how long it often takes to get through airport security before we can be on our way, but none of us can deny the importance of these security professionals' efforts to protect our safety. The TSA employees checking us through security must fine-tune their powers of observation, because they play critical roles in air travel safety.

A TSA training program called SPOT (short for Screening of Passengers by Observation Techniques) was initiated in 2010

The traveling public's safety depends on the ability of TSA employees to detect and accurately interpret people's nonverbal cues.

and is still in use today. The program involves behavioral observation and analysis techniques so that agents can spot travelers who exhibit signs of deception (Burns, 2010; Winter & Currier, 2015). The training program helps agents put aside passengers' physical characteristics so they can focus on an array of nonverbal cues (red flags) that could indicate deceit or undue anxiety, plus indications that someone is concealing illegal items or substances in clothing or possessions. While the program has come under fire in recent years for how some TSA agents react to disabled persons and minority group travelers, the track record of the TSA in combating air travel terrorism is exemplary (Israel, 2017; Martin, 2017).

Now, back to us good old ordinary citizens: How do we become better senders of nonverbal communication, as well as better interpreters of all the nonverbal cues we receive from others?

Nonverbal Sending (Encoding) Ability

We've talked at length in this chapter and in Chapter 1 about awareness—developing more awareness of the nonverbal communication we convey to other people. Thus, the first step of the Reflexive Cycle is a self-inventory. But some nonverbal signals we give off are beyond our control, such as physical features that communicate unintended messages to observers. Maybe someone's eyes are set closely together, giving us the sense that the person is shifty or not to be trusted. A person with large eyes may be seen as naive, and a heavy-lidded person may be thought of as sleepy or "out of it." People often make judgments about character, intellect, ability, and personality from flimsy nonverbal elements. Since we can't alter these kinds of cues sent without our control to other people, let's focus on the nonverbal cues we send that we *can* control or work to improve.

In his review of the topic of nonverbal skill acquisition, scholar Ronald Riggio (2006) discusses nonverbal sending abilities, also called nonverbal encoding skill or nonverbal expressiveness: "The ability to convey nonverbal messages to others, particularly the sending of emotional messages, is a critical skill for social success, and a fundamental component of the larger construct of communication competence" (p. 87). Research has focused more attention on nonverbal receiving ability than on sending ability, but some efforts are noteworthy in that they help us better understand how people can improve their ability to send nonverbal cues.

Prolific scholar Ross Buck and colleagues developed a technique, modified but still used in research today, in which subjects are video-recorded while viewing and talking about emotion-evoking images (Buck, 1978, 2005; Buck, Miller, & Caul, 1974; Buck, Savin, Miller, & Caul, 1972). Viewers of the recordings attempt to correctly identify the emotion being portrayed by each subject, primarily through the subject's facial and vocal expressions. Another approach is to record subjects who are asked to pose their facial expression in such a way as to convey a particular emotion; they may also be asked to read a sentence or phrase, with the intent of conveying facially and vocally a particular emotion. Viewers of the recordings attempt to correctly identify the emotion being portrayed. The people encoding the nonverbal cues can then receive feedback about how well they expressed various emotions nonverbally, to help them improve their encoding skills. One ingenious aspect of these techniques is that they can test both encoding and decoding abilities.

Studies on encoding ability have found that women tend to be more nonverbally expressive than men, especially when it comes to communicating positive emotions such as surprise and happiness (Burgoon & Bacue, 2003; Fischer & LaFrance, 2015; Hall, 2006; Ivy, 2017; Woodzicka, 2008). Women tend to smile more than men, but women are expected to smile more and have more general facial animation than men, in many cultures (Ellis, 2006; Panjwani, Chaplin, Sinha, & Mayes, 2016; Smith, LaFrance, Knol, Tellinghuisen, & Moes, 2015). Conversely, men tend to be better encoders of the emotions of anger and sadness, as well as better able to suppress or control their emotional display, compared with women (Bauer & Murray, 2018; Guerrero, Jones, & Boburka, 2006; Hess, Adams, Grammer, & Kleck, 2009).

One of the best ways to enhance your nonverbal sending ability is simply to engage in the process of daily living but to place more emphasis on the role of nonverbal communication in social interaction. Many people think of communicating as merely talking, but you—as a student of nonverbal communication—realize that verbal messages are only a small part of the communicative encounter. Nonverbal cues will tell you volumes more than verbal, so focusing on nonverbal broadens your horizons. Experience in different social situations and with different people, especially people from varying cultural backgrounds, is great training if you want to improve in this area. The key is to make a concerted effort to *learn something* from every encounter.

As the phrase goes, "watch and learn." Observing role models you think are nonverbally savvy is another excellent way to enhance encoding skills. For example, imagine you've heard a public speaker you thought was excellent. You liked the way the speaker made consistent eye contact with audience members but wasn't distracted by anyone; the way she or he wasn't tied to notes but seemed to have the speech "down"; the confident use of gestures to add emphasis to the remarks; and the even, flowing voice that kept the audience at constant attention. Can you try to emulate these winning behaviors the next time you make a presentation? Realize that, as infants, we imitated people's facial movements, especially movements of the mouth; as early as 9 months of age, we mimicked our mother's facial expressions (Field, 1982; Field, Woodson, Greenberg, & Cohen, 1982; Termine & Izard, 1988). As we grew and learned, we continued to model the nonverbal behaviors of those around us—most importantly, those of our parents and siblings (Ekman & Friesen, 1967; Schofield, Parke, Castaneda, & Coltrane, 2008). But that process shouldn't stop just because now we're adults and making our independent way in the world.

In addition to experience and role modeling, we need to remain open to other people's feedback about our nonverbal communication. If you exhibited an annoying nonverbal behavior, would you choose to remain oblivious to it, possibly missing out on some social opportunities or potential relationships simply because no one dared bring it to your attention, or would you rather face the truth about yourself? Which option generates more personal growth?

Nonverbal Receiving (Decoding) Ability

Nonverbal researchers have been prolific on the subject of nonverbal receiving or decoding ability for several decades. Various diagnostic tools and tests have been developed, but we choose here to focus on two of the most prevalent, used in past and present research.

In the 1970s, psychologist Robert Rosenthal and colleagues developed the Profile of Nonverbal Sensitivity (PONS), still used in research today (Rosenthal, Hall, DiMatteo, Rogers, & Archer, 1979). The PONS test contains 45 minutes of audio and video segments. In each 2-second segment, a woman enacts a scene and portrays different emotions and attitudes. For example, in one scene, the woman displays happiness related to seeing a baby; in another scene, she criticizes someone for being late, displaying negative emotions of exasperation and irritation. Eleven scenes are depicted; some reveal just the face, some just the body, some the face and body combined, some have no audio, some have audio but with the actual speech content (words) masked, and so forth. When taking the PONS, segments are presented and subjects decode what's happening and which emotion is portrayed in each segment. Subjects' responses are scored for accuracy by type of segment, either single channel or multichannel. In a nutshell, the PONS test measures a person's ability to recognize people's emotional or attitudinal states within certain situations (Hall, 2005; Janusik, 2018). A shortened version of the test—the MiniPONS—has since been developed and tested, with excellent results; this more convenient version is currently being used in nonverbal research (Banziger, Scherer, Hall, & Rosenthal, 2011).

Research using the PONS test shows that, across various cultures and nationalities, girls and women tend to score higher than boys and men, particularly when it comes to decoding facial expressions. This female advantage extends from grade school through adulthood (Gulabovska & Leeson, 2014; Hall, 1984; Hall, Andrzejewski, & Yopchick, 2009; McClure, 2000; Rosenthal et al., 1979; Rosip & Hall, 2004). The sex difference has been documented by other nonverbal decoding tests as well, with U.S. and non-U.S. subjects alike (Baron-Cohen, Wheelwright, Hill, Raste, & Plumb, 2001; Hall, Murphy, & Schmid Mast, 2006; Horgan, Schmid Mast, Hall, & Carter, 2004). While the sex difference is a general trend, other research focusing on specific emotions and non-verbal cues has found that females are less accurate decoders of angry expressions in males (Rotter & Rotter, 1988; Wagner, MacDonald, & Manstead, 1986), as well as nonverbal cues of deception in general (Zuckerman, DePaulo, & Rosenthal, 1981).

Another measure of decoding ability, the Diagnostic Analysis of Nonverbal Accuracy (DANVA), was developed and tested by researchers (Nowicki & Carton, 1997; Nowicki & Duke, 1994; Nowicki, Glanville, & Demertzis, 1998; Nowicki & Mitchell, 1998). The DANVA appears in multiple versions, some of which contain images of Caucasian and African American adults making facial expressions to convey four primary emotions (happiness, sadness, fear, and anger), Caucasian adults expressing the same four emotions vocally, and Caucasian children expressing these emotions facially. People depicted in the DANVA speak the same basic sentence but try to convey nonverbally a particular emotion, and subjects are scored by how accurately they identify the different emotions. One advantage of the DANVA is that both posed and spontaneous expressions of emotions are communicated, whereas the PONS test contains only posed depictions of emotion, which some scholars believe to be one of its limitations (Riggio, 2006).

Researchers using such measures as the PONS test or the DANVA have detected a trend according to age, in that nonverbal decoding skills generally increase from childhood into adulthood but plateau as people hit their 20s and 30s (Charles & Campos, 2011; Nowicki & Duke, 1994, 2001; Pitterman & Nowicki, 2004). Studies have resulted in lower scores on the PONS test for older adults when compared with younger adults, suggesting that age-related changes in memory and attention may affect decoding ability (Krendl & Ambady, 2010; Lieberman, Rigo, & Campain, 1988).

Beyond research techniques, time and patience enhance our receiving ability. You've already learned a good deal about nonverbal communication from reading this chapter, studying this topic in class, and living as many years as you have. But enhancing interpretive skills requires, first, an awareness of the importance of nonverbal elements in the communication process. A second requirement is the willingness and emotional maturity to make our own behavior secondary to that of someone else. In other words, if we're so wrapped up in ourselves that we can think about and deal only with how *we're* feeling, what *we're* thinking, and what *we* want at a given moment, we can't possibly hope to take in others' nonverbal cues, interpret them accurately, and respond appropriately.

Nonverbal Learning Disabilities

Throughout this book, we stress the importance of enhancing your ability to encode and decode nonverbal communication effectively, but what if your brain simply didn't allow you to do this? For a small percentage of the population, processing nonverbal information is nearly impossible; Nonverbal Learning Disabilities (NLD) are the culprit. This set of disabilities stems from a neurological dysfunction that affects the right hemisphere of the brain, where nonverbal functioning generally occurs (Murphy, 2016). Only relatively recently have psychologists, educators, and medical experts begun to focus on disabilities that affect people's (especially children's) ability to send and receive nonverbal messages. Some characteristics of NLD include the following:

- Lack of ability to comprehend nonverbal communication, especially facial expressions of emotion
- Deficits in tactile (touch) perception
- Greater risk of developing psychopathology and social problems
- Significant deficiencies in social judgment and social interaction
- Problems in math, reading comprehension, and handwriting
- Problems with organization, problem solving, and higher reasoning
- Strong verbal and auditory attention and memory skills
- Lack of image, poor visual recall

- Faulty spatial perception and spatial relations
- Lack of coordination
- Severe balance problems
- Difficulties with fine motor skills
- Frequent tantrums, difficulty being soothed by others, feeling easily overwhelmed
- Fear of new places and changes in routines
- Increased susceptibility to depression and anxiety with age (Agaliotis & Kalyva, 2006; Cornoldi, Mammarella, Goldenring Fine, & Siegel, 2016; Galway & Metsala, 2011)

Children and adolescents with NLD may continue to have difficulty into adulthood; they may actually fare worse over time than those who have only verbal learning disabilities (Bloom & Heath, 2010; Martin, 2013). Many people have both verbal and nonverbal learning disabilities. Part of what complicates NLD is that people with the condition find it a challenge to integrate new information into their lives, so they're relatively inflexible when confronted with new and different circumstances. In addition, they often struggle to apply what they learn from one situation to another. Because children and adolescents with NLD are frequently verbally adept, even precocious, other factors are presumed to be the problem, such as laziness or boredom; thus, NLD is often diagnosed late in a child's or adolescent's development (Bloom & Heath, 2010).

A parenting website ran a feature on NLD in 2007 so that parents of children and adolescents with the disability could better understand it. This article explains:

One of the most salient consequences of having NLD is the impairment in social functioning. Few of us realize how much of our social interactions are based on our understanding of the nonverbal cues of communication. Eye contact, hand gestures, tone of voice, body language, and posture are some of the many signals to which we attend when we speak with someone else. Children who miss the nonverbal cues of communication often feel uncomfortable with their peers and may gravitate toward adults, who admire their broad knowledge, or to younger children, who will gladly take direction from them. (Spier, 2007)

Various treatments have been developed to cope with the disability, such as occupational therapy, social skills training, academic support in weak subjects, and cognitive behavioral therapy or coaching to help with coping skills. Research continues to search for a better understanding of the causes of NLD, as well as for more effective treatments for the condition.

If you'd like to read more about Nonverbal Learning Disabilities, here are a few sources we recommend:

Cesare Cornoldi, Irene C. Mammarella, Jodene Goldenring Fine, and Linda S. Siegel's *Nonverbal Learning Disabilities* (2016).
Maggie Mamen's *Understanding Nonverbal Learning Disabilities: A Common-Sense Guide for Parents and Professionals* (2014).
Marilyn Martin's *Helping Children with Nonverbal Learning Disabilities to Flourish: A Guide for Parents and Professionals* (2013).
Michael Brian Murphy's *NLD from the Inside Out: Talking to Parents, Teachers, and Teens about Growing up with Nonverbal Learning Disabilities* (2016).

Remember to take into account the cultural backgrounds of those with whom you communicate, as we discussed in Chapter 1. Avoid automatically attaching your own cultural frame of reference when you decipher nonverbal cues. As we've stated, the context within which nonverbal cues are communicated plays an important role. Be aware of your surroundings and other situational factors when interpreting the meaning of nonverbal actions. Here's another important point: Be prepared to fail. We all struggle to make sense out of others' actions; no one has this skill down pat. We have to use our interpretive failures to learn lessons we can apply to the next encounter.

Enhancing Your Nonverbal Skills: Mehrabian's Framework

You see one of your friends talking to someone outside a classroom at your college. You can't quite make out who she's talking to, but you sure can tell she likes the person. She's leaning toward the person, gesturing more than is typical for her, and seems to be smiling and making lots of eye contact. As you get closer to your friend, you can hear her voice—she's laughing a lot and her voice pitch seems higher than normal. What's going on here?

Albert Mehrabian (1972, 1981), a scholar whose work we cite often in this book, believed that you could observe people interacting and make relatively accurate judgments as to how much they like one another (if at all), how interested each person is in the conversation, and whether one person is more dominant or in control of the conversation than the others. His research generated three primary dimensions: immediacy (liking or pleasure), arousal (activation or interest), and dominance (power or status).

Why do we like some people and dislike others? Sometimes we can't put a finger on the precise reason. Mehrabian contends that **immediacy**—nonverbal behavior that communicates liking and engenders feelings of pleasure—is a probable explanation. The principle underlying immediacy is simple: We like and respond positively to people who tend to display immediacy cues, and we avoid or respond negatively to those who don't. Immediacy cues include the following:

- *Proximity:* Close, forward lean
- *Body orientation:* Face-to-face or side-by-side position
- *Eye contact:* Eye gaze and mutual eye gaze
- *Facial expression:* Smiling and other pleasant facial expressions
- *Gestures:* Head nods, movement
- *Posture:* Open and relaxed, arms oriented toward others
- *Touch:* Culture- and context-appropriate touch
- *Voice:* Higher pitch, upward pitch (Argyle, 1988)

Back to your college friend talking to someone outside a classroom: Her nonverbal immediacy cues of body posture, proximity to the other person, pleasant facial expressions, and vocalics like laughing and an animated tone all clue you that your friend likes the person she's talking with (Guerrero & Floyd, 2006).

The second component in Mehrabian's framework is **arousal**, but we don't mean sexual arousal; the term in this case simply means activation or interest. Arousal prepares the body for action, with such physiological indications as increased heart rate, blood pressure, and brain temperature. The face, voice, and movement are primary nonverbal indicators of arousal. Your college friend can show interest (arousal) in the person she's talking with by maintaining a close conversational distance, giving consistent eye contact, possibly extending a slight touch to the person, using a more direct body orientation, and smiling (Farley, 2014; Lakens & Stel, 2011; Wilt, Funkhouser, & Revelle, 2011). (Some of the cues that indicate immediacy or liking also indicate arousal or interest.) Use caution, however; arousal cues can indicate interest in the *topic* of conversation, not necessarily the people conversing.

The third dimension of Mehrabian's framework communicates the balance of power in an interaction or relationship. **Dominance** cues communicate status, position, and importance. Back to your friend's conversation outside the classroom, the more dominant or controlling person in the interaction may exhibit a more relaxed body posture; less direct body orientation to the more submissive person; a downward head tilt; and less smiling, head nodding, and facial animation (Bailey & Kelly, 2015; Civile & Obhi, 2016; Dunbar & Abra, 2010; Gonzaga, Keltner, & Ward, 2008; Hullman, Goodnight, & Mougeotte, 2012; Langner & Keltner, 2008).

Using Mehrabian's list of nonverbal immediacy behaviors, do you think the people in this photo like each other? Are they a "couple" or is it more casual than that?

When you attempt to interpret someone's nonverbal communication, realize that a good deal of room for error exists. People are complex, and they don't always send clear signals. But the more you learn about nonverbal communication and the more you become aware of your own communication and the communication of others, the greater your chances of accurately perceiving and interpreting someone's nonverbal message.

MEHRABIAN'S FRAMEWORK

Remember!
2.3

Immediacy	Nonverbal cues that communicate liking and engender feelings of pleasure
Arousal	Nonverbal cues that communicate stimulation or activation
Dominance	Nonverbal cues that communicate status, position, and importance

SUMMARY ■ ■ ■

In this chapter, we introduced the Reflexive Cycle of Nonverbal Communication Development, which serves as a structuring device and a learning reinforcement for the rest of the text. This model enhances our understanding of how people come to know themselves better as communicators, how they change and improve their communicative abilities, how they affect others' communication, and then how they are, in turn, affected by the process of affecting others.

We first examined what it means to be reflexive, since this property is at the core of the model. We explored reflex action, meaning those behaviors that are accomplished automatically rather than purposefully, as well as the sense of reflexivity as referring back to the self. The Reflexive Cycle emphasizes the individual within a social context. Then we outlined each phase of the cycle, beginning with Phase 1: Inventory Self, which involves taking stock of our own nonverbal behavior to become more aware of how we communicate without or in conjunction with words. A second aspect of this inventory activity involves asking others for feedback about our nonverbal behavior. We have little hope of expanding or refining our nonverbal abilities if we lack awareness of how we nonverbally communicate to others.

Phase 2 of the Reflexive Cycle is to change our nonverbal communication, based on the inventory we completed in Phase 1. In this phase, we consider our strengths and weaknesses, in terms of our own nonverbal communication, and work to alter those behaviors we believe need changing or work to add nonverbal cues to our repertoire. Phase 3 challenges us to inventory others' nonverbal behavior closely, meaning that we pay attention to a wider range of cues at a more microscopic level than we're used to doing. We discussed covert observation, in which we carefully clue in to the nonverbal behaviors of other people without drawing much or any attention to ourselves. We also discussed overt observation—specifically, a strategy termed *perception checking*, in which we ask people directly about their perceptions of their own nonverbal behavior or the nonverbal behavior of others.

In Phase 4, we interact with others and mutually affect one another's nonverbal behavior, a process we termed *transaction* because it implies a shared creation of meaning that occurs in a simultaneous, ongoing manner. Through communicative transactions, we grow, learn, evolve, and are shaped by other people, and they by us. Finally, Phase 5 involves reflection and assessment of the entire cycle, our process for understanding nonverbal complexities and applying that understanding to behavior. Remember that the reflexive process repeats; it's a constant cycle throughout our lifetimes as we encounter diverse people and varied situations.

In the last half of the chapter, we introduced primary nonverbal communication codes or categories of nonverbal behavior that research has explored. These eight areas include environment; space and territory; physical appearance; body movement, gestures, and posture; facial expression; eye contact; touch; and vocal expression. Research findings for each code were presented to illustrate what we'll be exploring in more depth in subsequent chapters.

We next considered research techniques that have been developed to assess people's nonverbal encoding and decoding abilities. Finally, we explored more commonplace ways to enhance our skills as nonverbal communicators so that we can continue to improve our social competence. Mehrabian's framework helps us accurately interpret nonverbal cues along three dimensions: immediacy, arousal, and dominance. Nonverbal cues related to these dimensions reveal a great deal about communicators.

DISCUSSION STARTERS ■ ■ ■

1. What does the concept of reflexivity mean, and how can it be applied to the study of nonverbal communication?

2. Why is the reflexive model structured as a cycle, instead of as a straight line or some other configuration? What are the implications of such a structure for the enhancement of nonverbal communication abilities?

3. Work through a personal example—either something you encountered in the past or are presently experiencing—to help you make sense of the Reflexive Cycle of Nonverbal Communication Development. Does it help you analyze the situation? What changes do you need to make?

4. What are the eight codes or categories of nonverbal communication? Provide examples of nonverbal behaviors that correspond to the different codes.

5. How can we enhance our encoding and decoding skills as communicators? Why is it important to become more sensitive expressers, as well as interpreters, of nonverbal cues?

REFERENCES

Abkar, M., Kamal, M. M. S., Mariapan, M., Maulan, S., & Sheybanic, M. (2010). The role of urban green spaces in mood change. *Australian Journal of Basic and Applied Sciences, 4,* 5352–5361.

Agaliotis, I., & Kalyva, E. (2006). Nonverbal social interaction skills of children with learning disabilities. *Research in Developmental Disabilities, 29,* 1–10.

Aliakbari, M., & Abdollah, K. (2013). Does it matter what we wear? A sociolinguistic study of clothing and human values. *International Journal of Linguistics, 5,* 34–45.

Altman, I., Brown, B. B., Staples, B., & Werner, C. M. (1992). A transactional approach to close relationships: Courtship, weddings, and placemaking. In B. Walsh, K. Craik, & R. Price (Eds.), *Person-environment psychology: Contemporary models and perspectives* (pp. 193–241). Hillsdale, NJ: Erlbaum.

Andersen, P. A. (2011). Tactile traditions: Cultural differences and similarities in haptic communication. In M. Hertenstein & S. Weiss (Eds.), *The handbook of touch: Neuroscience, behavioral, and health perspectives* (pp. 351–371). New York: Springer.

Andrade, C. C., Lima, M. L., Devlin, A. S., & Hernandez, B. (2016). Is it the place or the people? Disentangling the effects of hospitals' physical and social environments on well-being. *Environment & Behavior, 48,* 299–323.

Argyle, M. (1988). *Bodily communication* (2nd ed.). London: Methuen.

Armstrong, N., & Wagner, M. (2003). *Field guide to gestures: How to identify and interpret virtually every gesture known to man.* Philadelphia: Quirk Books.

Bailey, A. H., & Kelly, S. D. (2015). Picture power: Gender versus body language in perceived status. *Journal of Nonverbal Behavior, 39,* 317–337.

Banziger, T., Scherer, K. R., Hall, J. A., & Rosenthal, R. (2011). Introducing the MiniPONS: A short multichannel version of the Profile of Nonverbal Sensitivity (PONS). *Journal of Nonverbal Behavior, 35,* 189–204.

Baron-Cohen, S., Wheelwright, S., Hill, J., Raste, Y., & Plumb, I. (2001). The "Reading the Mind in the Eyes" Test Revised Version: A study with normal adults, and adults with Asperger Syndrome or high-functioning autism. *Journal of Child Psychology and Psychiatry, 42,* 241–251.

Bauer, J. C., & Murray, M. A. (2018). "Leave your emotions at home": Bereavement, organizational space, and professional identity. *Women's Studies in Communication, 41,* 60–81.

Beaulieu, C. M. J. (2004). Intercultural study of personal space: A case study. *Journal of Applied Social Psychology, 34,* 794–805.

Beebe, S. A. (1974). Eye contact: A nonverbal determinant of speaker credibility. *Speech Teacher, 23,* 21–25.

Beebe, S. A., & Beebe, S. J. (2017). *Public speaking: An audience-centered approach* (10th ed.). Boston: Pearson.

Beebe, S. A., Beebe, S. J., & Ivy, D. K. (2019). *Communication: Principles for a lifetime* (7th ed.). Boston: Pearson.

Biemiller, L. (2008, July 18). To college employees, the work environment is all-important. *Chronicle of Higher Education*, pp. B12, B14, B17.

Billig, M. (2006). Is my home my castle? Place attachment, risk perception, and religious faith. *Environment & Behavior, 38,* 248–265.

Birdwhistell, R. L. (1960). Kinesics and communication. In E. Carpenter & M. McLuhan (Eds.), *Explorations in communication: An anthology* (pp. 54–64). Boston: Beacon.

Bloom, E., & Heath, N. (2010). Recognition, expression, and understanding facial expressions of emotion in adolescents with nonverbal and general learning disabilities. *Journal of Learning Disabilities, 43*, 180–192.

Bringslimark, T., Hartig, T., & Grindal Patil, G. (2011). Adaptation to windowlessness: Do office workers compensate for a lack of visual access to the outdoors? *Environment & Behavior, 43*, 469–487.

Brown, G., & Robinson, S. L. (2011). Reactions to territorial infringement. *Organization Science, 22*, 210–224.

Brumback, R. A., Harper, C. R., & Weinberg, W. A. (1996). Nonverbal learning disabilities, Asperger's syndrome, pervasive developmental disorder: Should we care? *Journal of Child Neurology, 11*, 427–429.

Buck, R. (1978). The slide-viewing technique for measuring nonverbal sending accuracy: A guide for replication. *Catalog of Selected Documents in Psychology, 8*, 62.

Buck, R. (2005). Measuring emotional experience, expression, and communication: The slide-viewing technique. In V. Manusov (Ed.), *The sourcebook of nonverbal measures: Going beyond words* (pp. 457–470). Mahwah, NJ: Erlbaum.

Buck, R. (2016). *Emotion: A biosocial synthesis.* Cambridge, UK: Cambridge University Press.

Buck, R., Miller, R. E., & Caul, W. F. (1974). Sex, personality, and physiological variables in the communication of emotion via facial expression. *Journal of Personality and Social Psychology, 30*, 587–596.

Buck, R., Savin, V. J., Miller, R. E., & Caul, W. F. (1972). Nonverbal communication of affect in humans. *Journal of Personality and Social Psychology, 23*, 362–371.

Burns, B. (2010, May 21). TSA SPOT program: Still going strong. *TSA Blog.* Retrieved from http://blog.tsa.gov/2010/05/tsa-spot-program-still-going-strong.html

Charles, S. T., & Campos, B. (2011). Age-related changes in emotion recognition: How, why, and how much of a problem? *Journal of Nonverbal Behavior, 35*, 287–295.

Christenfeld, N. (1995). Does it hurt to say um? *Journal of Nonverbal Behavior, 19*, 171–186.

Civile, C., & Obhi, S. S. (2016). Power eliminates the influence of body posture on facial emotion recognition. *Journal of Nonverbal Behavior, 40*, 283–299.

Cole, P. M. (1986). Children's spontaneous control of facial expression. *Child Development, 57*, 1309–1321.

Cornoldi, C., Mammarella, I. C., Goldenring Fine, J., & Siegel, L. S. (2016). *Nonverbal Learning Disabilities.* New York: Guilford.

Costa, M. (2012). Territorial behavior in public settings. *Environment & Behavior, 44*, 713–721.

Darlow, S., & Lobel, M. (2010). Who is beholding my beauty? Thinness ideals, weight, and women's responses to appearance evaluation. *Sex Roles, 63*, 833–843.

Dashtipour, P. (2012). *Social identity in question: Construction, subjectivity, and critique.* New York: Routledge.

Doody, J. P., & Bull, P. (2011). Asperger's syndrome and the decoding of boredom, interest, and disagreement from body posture. *Journal of Nonverbal Behavior, 35*, 87–100.

Douglas, D., & Gifford, R. (2001). Evaluation of the physical classroom by students and professors: A lens model approach. *Educational Research, 43*, 295–309.

Droogsma, R. A. (2007). Redefining hijab: American Muslim women's standpoints on veiling. *Journal of Applied Communication Research, 35*, 294–319.

Dunbar, N. E., & Abra, G. (2010). Observations of dyadic power in interpersonal interaction. *Communication Monographs, 77*, 657–684.

Dunden, L., & Francis, A. (2016). Inking and thinking: Honor students and tattoos. *College Student Journal, 50*, 219–223.

Ekman, P., & Friesen, W. V. (1967). Head and body cues in the judgment of emotion: A reformulation. *Perceptual and Motor Skills, 24,* 711–724.

Ekman, P., & Friesen, W. V. (1968). Nonverbal behavior in psychotherapy research. *Research in Psychotherapy, 1,* 179–216.

Ekman, P., & Friesen, W. V. (1975). *Unmasking the face.* Englewood Cliffs, NJ: Prentice Hall.

Elliott, A. (2013). *Concepts of the self* (3rd ed.). Malden, MA: Polity.

Elliott, A., & du Gay, P. (2009). *Identity in question.* Thousand Oaks, CA: Sage.

Ellis, L. (2006). Gender differences in smiling: An evolutionary neuroandrogenic theory. *Physiology and Behavior, 88,* 303–308.

Erlandson, K. (2012). Stay out of my space. *Journal of College & University Housing, 387,* 46–61.

Farley, S. D. (2014). Nonverbal reactions to an attractive stranger: The role of mimicry in communicating preferred social distance. *Journal of Nonverbal Behavior, 38,* 195–208.

Fassinger, P. A. (2000). How classes influence students' participation in college classrooms. *Journal of Classroom Interaction, 35,* 38–47.

Field, T. (1982). Individual differences in the expressivity of neonates and young infants. In R. S. Feldman (Ed.), *Development of nonverbal behavior in children* (pp. 279–298). New York: Springer-Verlag.

Field, T., Woodson, R., Greenberg, R., & Cohen, D. (1982). Discrimination and imitation of facial expressions of neonates. *Science, 218,* 179–181.

Fischer, A., & LaFrance, M. (2015). What drives the smile and the tear? Why women are more emotionally expressive than men. *Emotion Review, 7,* 22–29.

Floyd, K. (2016a). *The loneliness cure: Six strategies for finding real connections in your life.* Fort Collins, CO: Adams Media.

Floyd, K. (2016b). Affection deprivation is associated with physical pain and poor sleep quality. *Communication Studies, 67,* 379–398.

Frank, M. G., Maroulis, A., & Griffin, D. J. (2013). The voice. In D. Matsumoto, M. G. Frank, & H. S. Hwang (Eds.), *Nonverbal communication: Science and applications* (pp. 53–74). Thousand Oaks, CA: Sage.

Gadea, M., Aliño, M., Espert, R., & Salvador, A. (2015). Deceit and facial expression in children: The enabling role of the "poker face" child and the dependent personality of the detector. *Frontiers in Psychology, 6,* 1089. http://doi.org/10.3389/fpsyg.2015.01089

Galway, T. M., & Metsala, J. L. (2011). Social cognition and its relation to psychosocial adjustment in children with nonverbal learning disabilities. *Journal of Learning Disabilities, 44,* 33–49.

Garland-Thomson, R. (2009). *Staring: How we look.* New York: Oxford University Press.

Giddens, A. (1991). *The consequences of modernity.* Malden, MA: Polity.

Gifford, R. (2014). *Environmental psychology: Principles and practice* (5th ed.). Colville, WA: Optimal Books.

Goberman, A. M., Hughes, S., & Haydock, T. (2011). Acoustic characteristics of public speaking: Anxiety and practice effects. *Speech Communication, 53,* 867–876.

Goffman, E. (1971). *Relations in public: Microstudies of the public order.* New York: Harper Colophon.

Gonzaga, G. C., Keltner, D., & Ward, D. (2008). Power in mixed-sex interactions. *Cognition and Emotion, 22,* 1555–1568.

Gosling, S. D., Ko, S. J., Mannarelli, T., & Morris, M. E. (2002). A room with a cue: Personality judgments based on offices and bedrooms. *Journal of Personality and Social Psychology, 82,* 379–398.

chapter two

Guerrero, L. K., & Floyd, K. (2006). *Nonverbal communication in close relationships.* Mahwah, NJ: Erlbaum.

Guerrero, L. K., Jones, S. M., & Boburka, R. R. (2006). Sex differences in emotional communication. In D. J. Canary & K. Dindia (Eds.), *Sex differences and similarities in communication* (2nd ed., pp. 241–261). Mahwah, NJ: Erlbaum.

Gulabovska, M., & Leeson, P. (2014). Why are women better decoders of nonverbal language? *Gender Issues, 31,* 202–218.

Gurney, D. J., Howlett, N., Pine, K., Tracey, M., & Moggridge, R. (2017). Dressing up posture: The interactive effects of posture and clothing on competency judgments. *British Journal of Psychology, 108,* 436–451.

Hadavi, S. (2017). Direct and indirect effects of the physical aspects of the environment on mental well-being. *Environment & Behavior, 49,* 1071–1104.

Halberstadt, A. G., Dennis, P. A., & Hess, U. (2011). The influence of family expressiveness, individuals' own emotionality, and self-expressiveness on perceptions of others' facial expressions. *Journal of Nonverbal Behavior, 25,* 35–50.

Hall, E. T. (1959). *The silent language.* Garden City, NY: Doubleday.

Hall, E. T. (1966). *The hidden dimension.* Garden City, NY: Doubleday.

Hall, J. A. (1984). *Nonverbal sex differences: Communication accuracy and expressive style.* Baltimore, MD: Johns Hopkins University Press.

Hall, J. A. (2005). Meta-analysis of nonverbal behavior. In V. Manusov (Ed.), *The sourcebook of nonverbal measures: Going beyond words* (pp. 483–492). Mahwah, NJ: Erlbaum.

Hall, J. A. (2006). Women's and men's nonverbal communication: Similarities, differences, stereotypes, and origins. In V. Manusov & M. L. Patterson (Eds.), *The SAGE handbook of nonverbal communication* (pp. 201–218). Thousand Oaks, CA: Sage.

Hall, J. A., Andrzejewski, S. A., & Yopchick, J. E. (2009). Psychosocial correlates of interpersonal sensitivity: A meta-analysis. *Journal of Nonverbal Behavior, 33,* 149–180.

Hall, J. A., Murphy, N. A., & Schmid Mast, M. (2006). Recall of nonverbal cues: Exploring a new definition of interpersonal sensitivity. *Journal of Nonverbal Behavior, 30,* 141–155.

Hart, W., Ottati, V. C., & Krumdick, N. D. (2011). Physical attractiveness and candidate evaluation: A model of correction. *Political Psychology, 32,* 181–203.

Hellmann, J. H., & Jucks, R. (2017). The crowd in mind and crowded minds: An experimental investigation of crowding effects on students' views regarding tuition fees in Germany. *Higher Education, 74,* 131–145.

Hess, U., Adams, R. B., Jr., Grammer, K., & Kleck, R. E. (2009). Face gender and emotion expression: Are angry women more like men? *Journal of Vision, 9,* 1–8.

Hesse, C., & Mikkelson, A. C. (2017). Affection deprivation in romantic relationships. *Communication Quarterly, 65,* 20–38.

Hill, B. M., Ogletree, S. M., & McCrary, K. M. (2016). Body modifications in college students: Considering gender, self-esteem, body appreciation, and reasons for tattoos. *College Student Journal, 50,* 246–252.

Hill, M. C., & Epps, K. K. (2010). The impact of physical classroom environment on student satisfaction and student evaluation of teaching in the university environment. *Academy of Educational Leadership Journal, 14,* 65–79.

Hodges-Simeon, C. R., Gaulin, S. J. C., & Puts, D. A. (2010). Different vocal parameters predict perceptions of dominance and attractiveness. *Human Nature, 21,* 406–427.

Horgan, T. G., Schmid Mast, M., Hall, J. A., & Carter, J. D. (2004). Gender differences in memory for the appearance of others. *Personality and Social Psychology Bulletin, 30*, 185–196.

Hughes, J. L. (2009, June 26). Higher education and Asperger's syndrome. *Chronicle of Higher Education*, p. A27.

Hughes, V., Wood, S., & Foulkes, P. (2016). Strength of forensic voice comparison evidence from the acoustics of filled pauses. *International Journal of Speech, Language & the Law, 23*, 99–132.

Hullman, G. A., Goodnight, A., & Mougeotte, J. (2012). An examination of perceived relational messages that accompany interpersonal communication motivations. *Open Communication Journal, 6*, 1–7.

Hurley, C. M., & Frank, M. G. (2011). Executing facial control during deception situations. *Journal of Nonverbal Behavior, 35*, 119–131.

Imhof, M. (2010). Listening to voices and judging people. *International Journal of Listening, 24*, 19–33.

Israel, K. (2017, February 15). ACLU report on TSA SPOT program overlooks risks for disabled travelers. Retrieved from http://nosmag.org/aclu-report-on-tsa-spot-program-overlooks-risks-for-disabled-travelers/

Ivy, D. K. (2017). *Genderspeak: Communicating in a gendered world* (6th ed.). Dubuque, IA: Kendall Hunt.

Janusik, L. A. (2018). Profile of Nonverbal Sensitivity. In D. L. Worthington & G. D. Bodie (Eds.), *The sourcebook of listening research: Methodology and measures* (pp. 522–529). Malden, MA: John Wiley & Sons.

Jorgenson, J. (2011). Reflexivity in feminist research practice: Hearing the unsaid. *Women & Language, 34*, 115–118.

Jung, M., & Fouts, H. N. (2011). Multiple caregivers' touch interactions with young children among the Bofi foragers in Central Africa. *International Journal of Psychology, 46*, 24–32.

Kabo, F. W. (2017). A model of potential encounters in the workplace: The relationships of homophily, spatial distance, organizational structure, and perceived networks. *Environment & Behavior, 49*, 638–662.

Karpf, A. (2006). *The human voice: How this extraordinary instrument reveals essential clues about who we are.* New York: Bloomsbury.

Kim, Y., Cheon, S-M., Youm, C., Son, M., & Kim, J. W. (2018). Depression and posture in patients with Parkinson's disease. *Gait & Posture, 61*, 81–85.

Koen, J., & Durrheim, K. (2010). A naturalistic observational study of informal segregation: Seating patterns in lectures. *Environment & Behavior, 42*, 448–468.

Kozusznik, M. W., Peiro, J. M., Soriano, A., & Escudero, M. N. (2018). "Out of sight, out of mind?": The role of physical stressors, cognitive appraisal, and positive emotion in employees' health. *Environment & Behavior, 50*, 86–115.

Krendl, A. C., & Ambady, N. (2010). Older adults' decoding of emotions: Role of dynamic versus static cues and age-related cognitive decline. *Psychology & Aging, 25*, 788–793.

Künecke, J., Wilhelm, O., & Sommer, W. (2017). Emotion recognition in nonverbal face-to-face communication. *Journal of Nonverbal Behavior, 41*, 221–238.

Lakens, D., & Stel, M. (2011). If they move in sync, they must feel in sync: Movement synchrony leads to attributions of rapport and entitativity. *Social Cognition, 29*, 1–14.

Lamberg, E. M., & Muratori, L. M. (2012). Cell phones change the way we walk. *Gait & Posture, 35*, 688–690.

Langner, C. A., & Keltner, D. (2008). Social power and emotional expression: Actor and partner effects within dyadic interactions. *Journal of Experimental Social Psychology, 44*, 848–856.

chapter two

Lawson, R. (2015). I just love the attention: Implicit preference for direct eye contact. *Visual Cognition, 23*, 450–488.

Li, S., & Li, Y. (2007). How far is far enough? A measure of information privacy in terms of interpersonal distance. *Environment & Behavior, 39*, 317–331.

Lieberman, D. A., Rigo, T. G., & Campain, R. F. (1988). Age-related differences in nonverbal decoding ability. *Communication Quarterly, 36*, 290–297.

Lohmann, A., Arriaga, X. B., & Goodfriend, W. (2003). Close relationships and placemaking: Do objects in a couple's home reflect couplehood? *Personal Relationships, 10*, 437–449.

Lyman, S. M., & Scott, M. B. (1999). Territoriality: A neglected sociological dimension. In L. K. Guerrero, J. DeVito, & M. L. Hecht (Eds.), *The nonverbal communication reader: Classic and contemporary readings* (2nd ed., pp. 175–183). Prospect Heights, IL: Waveland.

Mamen, M. (2014). *Understanding nonverbal learning disabilities: A common-sense guide for parents and professionals*. London: Jessica Kingsley.

Mann, S., Vrij, A., Leal, S., Granhag, P. A., Warmelink, L., & Forrester, D. (2012). Windows to the soul? Deliberate eye contact as a cue to deceit. *Journal of Nonverbal Behavior, 36*, 205–215.

Mansson, D. H., Marko, F., Bachrata, K., Daniskova, Z., Gajdosikova Zeleiova, J., Janis, V., & Sharov, A. S. (2016). Young adults' trait affection given and received as functions of Hofstede's dimensions of cultures and national origin. *Journal of Intercultural Communication Research, 45*, 404–418.

Martin, H. (2017, February 8). TSA's own files say its program to stop terrorists is unreliable, ACLU says. Retrieved from http://www.latimes.com/business/la-fi-aclu-tsa-20170207-story.html

Martin, M. (2013). *Helping children with Nonverbal Learning Disabilities to flourish: A guide for parents and professionals*. Philadelphia, PA: Jessica Kingsley Publishers.

Matsumoto, D. (2006). Culture and nonverbal behavior. In V. Manusov & M. L. Patterson (Eds.), *The SAGE handbook of nonverbal communication* (pp. 219–235). Thousand Oaks, CA: Sage.

Matsumoto, D., & Hwang, H. (2013). Cultural influences on nonverbal behavior. In D. Matsumoto, M. G. Frank, & H. S. Hwang (Eds.), *Nonverbal communication: Science and applications* (pp. 97–129). Thousand Oaks, CA: Sage.

McClure, E. B. (2000). A meta-analytic review of sex differences in facial expression processing and their development in infants, children, and adolescents. *Psychological Bulletin, 126*, 424–453.

Medved, C. E., & Turner, L. H. (2011). Qualitative research: Practicing reflexivity. *Women & Language, 34*, 109–112.

Mehrabian, A. (1972). *Nonverbal communication*. Chicago: Atherton.

Mehrabian, A. (1981). *Silent messages* (2nd ed.). Belmont, CA: Wadsworth.

Morris, D. (1985). *Bodywatching*. New York: Crown.

Murphy, M. B. (2016). *NLD from the inside out: Talking to parents, teachers, and teens about growing up with Nonverbal Learning Disabilities*. Philadelphia, PA: Jessica Kingsley Publishers.

Napieraliski, L. P., Brooks, C. I., & Droney, J. M. (1995). The effect of duration of eye contact on American college students' attributions of state, trait, and test anxiety. *Journal of Social Psychology, 135*, 273–280.

Nowicki, S., Jr., & Carton, E. (1997). The relation of nonverbal processing ability of faces and voices and children's feelings of depression and competence. *Journal of Genetic Psychology, 158*, 357–363.

Nowicki, S., Jr., & Duke, M. P. (1994). Individual differences in the nonverbal communication of affect: The Diagnostic Analysis of Nonverbal Accuracy Scale. *Journal of Nonverbal Behavior, 18*, 9–35.

Nowicki, S., Jr., & Duke, M. P. (2001). Nonverbal receptivity: The Diagnostic Analysis of Nonverbal Accuracy (DANVA). In J. A. Hall & F. J. Bernieri (Eds.), *Interpersonal sensitivity: Theory and measurement* (pp. 183–198). Mahwah, NJ: Erlbaum.

Nowicki, S., Jr., Glanville, D., & Demertzis, A. (1998). A test of the ability to recognize emotion in the facial expressions of African American adults. *Journal of Black Psychology, 24*, 335–350.

Nowicki, S., Jr., & Mitchell, J. (1998). Accuracy in identifying affect in child and adult faces and voices and social competence in preschool children. *Genetic, Social, and General Psychology Monographs, 124*, 39–59.

Oxford dictionary. Retrieved from www.en.oxforddictionaries.com

Panjwani, N., Chaplin, T. M., Sinha R., & Mayes, C. (2016). Gender differences in emotion expression in low-income adolescents under stress. *Journal of Nonverbal Behavior, 40*, 117–132.

Paul, F. U. J., Mandal, M. K., Ramachandran, K., & Panwar, M. R. (2010). Interpersonal behavior in an isolated and confined environment. *Environment & Behavior, 42*, 707–717.

Peterson, D. R. (1992). Interpersonal relationships as a link between person and environment. In W. B. Walsh, K. H. Craig, & R. H. Price (Eds.), *Person-environment psychology: Contemporary models and perspectives* (pp. 127–155). Hillsdale, NJ: Erlbaum.

Pham, M.-H. T. (2011). If the clothes fit: A feminist takes on fashion. *Ms. Magazine*, 39–42.

Pitterman, H., & Nowicki, S., Jr. (2004). A test of the ability to identify emotion in human standing and sitting postures: The Diagnostic Analysis of Nonverbal Accuracy-2 Posture test. *Genetic, Social, and General Psychology Monographs, 130*, 146–162.

Quintanilla, K. M., & Wahl, S. T. (2016). *Business and professional communication: Keys for workplace excellence* (3rd ed.). Thousand Oaks, CA: Sage.

Rashid, M., & Zimring, C. (2008). A review of the empirical literature on the relationships between indoor environment and stress in health care and office settings. *Environment & Behavior, 40*, 151–190.

Riggio, R. E. (2006). Nonverbal skills and abilities. In V. Manusov & M. L. Patterson (Eds.), *The SAGE handbook of nonverbal communication* (pp. 79–95). Thousand Oaks, CA: Sage.

Rosenthal, R., Hall, J. A., DiMatteo, M. R., Rogers, P. L., & Archer, D. (1979). *Sensitivity to nonverbal communication: The PONS test.* Baltimore, MD: Johns Hopkins University Press.

Rosip, J. C., & Hall, J. A. (2004). Knowledge of nonverbal cues, gender, and nonverbal decoding accuracy. *Journal of Nonverbal Behavior, 28*, 267–286.

Rotter, N. G., & Rotter, G. S. (1988). Sex differences in the encoding and decoding of negative facial emotions. *Journal of Nonverbal Behavior, 12*, 139–148.

Ruark, J. (2010, February 5). Asperger's in the mix. *Chronicle of Higher Education*, p. A4.

Samovar, L. A., Porter, R. E., McDaniel, E. R., & Sexton Roy, C. (2014). Approaches to intercultural communication. In L. A. Samovar, R. E. Porter, E. R. McDaniel, & C. Sexton Roy (Eds.), *Intercultural communication: A reader* (14th ed., pp. 1–3). Boston: Cengage Learning.

Scannell, L., & Gifford, R. (2017). Place attachment enhances psychological need satisfaction. *Environment & Behavior, 49*, 359–389.

Schofield, T. J., Parke, R. D., Castaneda, E. K., & Coltrane, S. (2008). Patterns of gaze between parents and children in European American and Mexican American families. *Journal of Nonverbal Behavior, 32*, 171–186.

Schubert, J. N., Curran, M. A., & Strungaru, C. (2011). Physical attractiveness, issue agreement, and assimilation effects in candidate appraisal. *Politics and the Life Sciences, 30*, 33–49.

Sluzki, C. E. (2016). Proxemics in couple interactions: Rekindling an old optic. *Family Process, 55*, 7–15.

chapter two

Smith, J., LaFrance, M., Knol, K., Tellinghuisen, D., & Moes, P. (2015). Surprising smiles and unanticipated frowns: How emotion and status influence gender categorization. *Journal of Nonverbal Behavior, 39*, 115–130.

Syndicus, M., Weise, B. S., & van Treeck, C. (2018). In the heat and noise of the moment: Effects on risky decision-making. *Environment & Behavior, 50*, 3–27.

Spier, M. (2007). NLD: Nonverbal learning disorder. *Raising Small Souls: Parenting and Guiding Well-Rounded Children*. Retrieved from www.raisingsmallsouls.com/nonverbal-learning-disorder/

Szpak, A., Nicholls, M. E. R., Thomas, N. A., Laham, S. M., & Loetsher, T. (2016). "No man is an island": Effects of interpersonal proximity on spatial attention. *Cognitive Neuroscience, 7*, 45–54.

Tang, D., & Schmeichel, B. J. (2015). Look me in the eye: Manipulated eye gaze affects dominance mindsets. *Journal of Nonverbal Behavior, 39*, 181–194.

Tenner, E. (2004, October 1). Political timber: Glitter, froth, and measuring tape. *Chronicle of Higher Education*, pp. B12–B13.

Termine, N. T., & Izard, C. E. (1988). Infants' responses to their mothers' expressions of joy and sadness. *Developmental Psychology, 24*, 223–229.

Tiemens, R. K. (1978). Television's portrayal of the 1976 presidential debates: An analysis of visual content. *Communication Monographs, 45*, 362–370.

Vilnai-Yavetz, I., Rafaeli, A., & Schneider-Yaacov, C. (2005). Instrumentality, aesthetics, and symbolism of office design. *Environment & Behavior, 37*, 533–551.

Volden, J. (2004). Nonverbal learning disability: A tutorial for speech-language pathologists. *American Journal of Speech-Language Pathology, 13*, 128–141.

Vrij, A., Mann, S., Leal, S., & Fisher, R. (2010). "Look into my eyes": Can an instruction to maintain eye contact facilitate lie detection? *Psychology, Crime, & Law, 16*, 327–348.

Wagner, H. L., MacDonald, C. J., & Manstead, A. S. R. (1986). Communication of individual emotions by spontaneous facial expressions. *Journal of Personality and Social Psychology, 50*, 737–743.

Wang, Z., Huifang, M., Yexin, J., & Fan, L. (2016). Smile big or not? Effects of smile intensity on perceptions of warmth and competence. *Journal of Consumer Research, 43*, 787–805.

Wells, M., & Thelen, L. (2002). What does your workspace say about you? The influence of personality, status, and workspace on personalization. *Environment & Behavior, 34*, 300–321.

Wilt, K., Funkhouser, K., & Revelle, W. (2011). The dynamic relationships of affective synchrony to perceptions of situations. *Journal of Research in Personality, 45*, 309–321.

Winter, J., & Currier, C. (2015, March 27). Exclusive: TSA's secret behavior checklist to spot terrorists. Retrieved from https://theintercept.com/2015/03/27/revealed-tsas-closely-held-behavior-checklist-spot-terrorists/

Woodzicka, J. A. (2008). Sex differences in self-awareness of smiling during a mock job interview. *Journal of Nonverbal Behavior, 32*, 109–121.

Wrench, J. S., & Knapp, J. L. (2008). The effects of body image perceptions and sociocommunicative orientations on self-esteem, depression, and identification and involvement in the gay community. *Journal of Homosexuality, 55*, 471–503.

Zestcott, C. A., Bean, M. G., & Stone, J. (2017). Evidence of negative attitudes toward individuals with a tattoo near the face. *Group Processes & Intergroup Relations, 20*, 186–201.

Zuckerman, M., DePaulo, B. M., & Rosenthal, R. (1981). Verbal and nonverbal communication of deception. In L. Berkowitz (Ed.), *Advances in experimental social psychology* (Vol. 14). New York: Academic Press.

part two

CODES OF NONVERBAL COMMUNICATION

chapter three

ENVIRONMENT AS NONVERBAL COMMUNICATION: OUR PERCEPTIONS AND REACTIONS

chapter outline

After studying this chapter, you should be able to
1. understand how people perceive the environment as a form of nonverbal communication;
2. increase your awareness of the environments you maintain in personal and professional life;
3. identify and define the six ways to perceive an environment;
4. define *chronemics* and give examples of how time affects communication;
5. explain Knapp and Hall's four perceptions of time;
6. understand the impact of color, sound, lighting, smell, and temperature on human communication;
7. explain environmental factors that research has associated with obesity; and
8. define the term *popular culture* and describe two aspects of pop culture that relate to our discussion of environment and nonverbal communication.

case study

ETHNIC ENCLAVES, SAFE SPACES, & SECURITY

You may have heard the term *safe space* before. People have differing opinions on the connotation of *safe space*, but what really makes a *space* feel *safe* to certain groups or individuals? It all comes back to how environment communicates comfort and *safety*. Despite the rhetoric that the United States is a melting pot of cultural identities, we often see members of certain cultural groups segregated in different environments. These environments may be physically created through **ethnic enclaves** in urban areas. Ethnic enclaves are city areas dominated by a certain demographic of people (Hur & Jeffres, 1979; Kim, 2018). For example, an ethnic enclave in St. Louis, Missouri, is the Hill, a predominantly Italian-American community. South of downtown St. Louis, Bevo Mill boasts the largest Bosnian population outside of Bosnia and Herzegovina. The Central West End and Grove neighborhoods of St. Louis are known for LGBTQIA+ inclusivity. Think about how these kinds of environments may create comfort for members of these communities.

Safe spaces may also be created virtually, meaning online. Online communities create spaces for like-minded individuals to communicate regardless of physical distance (Brody, 2013; Döveling, 2015; Ruppel, Burke, & Cherney, 2018). Computer-mediated communication creates safe spaces in which people can discuss politics, gender, race, religion, sexuality, physical and mental health, and more (Clark-Parsons, 2018; Kendal, Kirk, Elvey, Catchpole, & Pryjmachuk, 2017; Maliepaard, 2017).

Paula:	Why are you burning all these candles in your office?
Hunter:	I'm trying to get that creepy smell out of here.
Paula:	What creepy smell?
Hunter:	I've noticed that my office still smells like Charlie's cheap cologne. I'm so glad that pathetic guy moved on to another company. I dunno, just the smell of that guy gives me the creeps.
Paula:	I know what you mean. Your clients may notice that old cheap cologne smell and not want to buy a policy from you. The vanilla candles and your new office arrangement are great!

What does the above interaction teach us? Paula and Hunter's conversation relates to an aspect of nonverbal communication called **environment**—the built or natural surroundings that serve as the contexts in which people interact. Can you think of an environment in your personal or professional life that stands out? Some of us may think of our favorite places to eat or hang out with friends. Pubs, clubs, bars, coffee houses, diners, and restaurants may come to mind as comfortable environments where we like to have downtime or meet others for recreation or friendly conversation. We can also think of environments that are not as comfortable, friendly, or inviting.

Imagine this: You go to interview for a new job. The manager who's going to make the final decision to hire you is extremely late. Meanwhile, you're sitting in her or his office waiting. The temperature in the room is quite warm, so you begin to sweat profusely. You also notice an old pizza box on the manager's desk, with crusted remnants of some past meal inside. Would you be excited to start working for this person? How is this office environment going to influence your interview? Do you now even *want* to interview? Will you verbally and nonverbally communicate differently, because of the environmental effects?

People are significantly influenced by environmental factors such as architecture, design, color, lighting, smell, seating arrangements, temperature, and cleanliness (Chylinski, Northey, & Ngo, 2015; Gang, Feng, Cheng, & Xiaochen, 2017; O'Halloran, Worrall, & Hickson, 2011; TenBrink, Andonova, Schole, & Coventry, 2017). Whether we're satisfied or dissatisfied with the environment in which we're communicating with friends or interviewing for a new job, it's important to realize that environment is a critical code to examine when studying nonverbal communication.

ENVIRONMENT AS NONVERBAL COMMUNICATION ■ ■ ■ ▬

The goal of this chapter is to make you more aware of how people perceive an environment; the control we have over establishing, maintaining, and regulating healthy communication environments; and how these environments influence our communicative decisions in personal and professional life.

The connection between people and environment needs to be made for two reasons: (1) The choices you make about the environment in which you live or work reveal a good deal about who you are, and (2) your nonverbal communication is altered by the environments in which you communicate.

A couple of landmark studies conducted in the 1950s brought our attention to the environment as a nonverbal influence on communication (Maslow & Mintz, 1956; Mintz, 1956). In these experiments, one group of people was placed in a "beautiful" room—a space with adequate lighting, comfortable furniture, and pleasant colors. Another group of people was placed in an "ugly" room—a space with dim lighting, shabby furniture, and dark colors. Each group was asked to rate a series of photographs of people in terms of their attractiveness. In both studies, the results consistently showed that people in the ugly room took longer to complete their ratings, and they rated the people in the photos as significantly less attractive than did people in the beautiful room. Surroundings do make a difference.

Personal surroundings, such as a bedroom, can heavily influence people's perceptions of others.

As we focus on the environment and physical surroundings in this chapter, we want to emphasize that some environments are already built, but other environments we create or adorn for ourselves (e.g., homes, offices, furniture, decorating choices, colors, smells). In fact, many people maintain an entire repertoire that helps them design a unique and personal environment, complete with such things as lighting, pictures, candles, plants, and music (Bringslimark, Hartig, & Grindal Patil, 2011; Perez-Lopez, 2017). Further, the environments we create for ourselves often speak volumes about those relationships we deem most important, such as a highly romantic bedroom that signals the importance of private life with a partner or spouse, or an enlarged office to make room for a coworker (Lohmann, Arriaga, & Goodfriend, 2003).

While it's tempting to think about environment as being solely interior, realize that exterior environments also communicate nonverbally (Lewis, Kerridge, & Jorden, 2009). Let's think first about environments we don't create personally—a state's capitol building or the White House in Washington, D.C., for example. Many college campuses have a central building called Old Main or the Main Building that is connected to student and alumni identity and serves as a focal or historical point for the campus for many generations of students (Biemiller, 2007, 2010). These buildings communicate something before we even walk through their doors, and our verbal and nonverbal communication are affected by those structures when we approach and enter them. While we hate to bring up a sad memory for all of us, the World Trade Center and Pentagon disasters of September 11, 2001 come to mind in this discussion. Horrific crimes were committed against people that day, as well as against important symbols of American prosperity and sovereignty. The image of the two tallest buildings in the country being toppled by a terrorist attack is something we will not soon forget.

Communication scholar Darryl Hattenhauer (1984) helps us understand what he calls the **rhetoric of architecture** by explaining that "architecture not only communicates, but also communicates rhetorically. Churches, shopping malls, doors and stairs—these architectural items not only tell us their meaning and function, but also influence our behavior" (p. 71). One study found that people's motivations to engage in physical activity, such as walking to the grocery store or to work, depended on the condition of sidewalks, roadways, and pedestrian signals on their route (Sallis & Kerr, 2008). Thus, urban planners and transportation specialists attend to the kinds of external environments that impact human behavior (Bishop, 2011).

Have you ever thought about how the built environment on your college campus or in your neighborhood impacts your everyday decisions? Do you walk, drive, or take a shuttle bus to class? Are some routes you use to navigate your campus safer and more attractive than others? Some of you may live on campus, which allows you to walk to class, while others may have to commute and face competition for good parking spaces. All these environmental factors affect our daily experiences, decisions, and communication.

What about interior environments? What do they communicate, nonverbally? Think about banks and financial institutions: A particular air of professionalism is expected since people who work in these kinds of places take care of money. While many people continue to shift their financial management and banking to the Internet, banks in the United States focus on customers who enter local branches wanting a warm and comfortable, yet private environment in which to conduct financial business. In fact, part of establishing a warm environment and enhancing customer satisfaction in some banks and credit unions is achieved using the fresh smell and availability of coffee for any customer who enters the building (Kupritz & Hillsman, 2011; Martin, 2006).

Reflect on your personal experiences in different classrooms. Have you ever had a classroom in which you felt entirely comfortable participating, and then others where you didn't want to speak at all? Fassinger (2000) studied how classroom environments influence students' participation in college classes, finding that students who were in classrooms physically structured to encourage student participation viewed those classes as more cooperative, supportive, respectful, and familiar. High-participation designs that provide less separation and barriers between teachers and students, ones where furniture can be moved and configured to meet an instructional purpose (like circles of seats that encourage group work or informal class discussion) prompt more student participation and less teacher domination. In such designs, students are more confident and professors are more approachable.

Think about environments that you maintain, personally and professionally. What about your bedroom? If someone who didn't know you walked into your bedroom, what perception would she or he have of you? Are your clothes on the floor or put away? Think of other things that may or may not be present in the environment that can serve as nonverbal cues of who you are, what

motivates you, whether you're shy or outgoing, and so on. These environmental factors that you create and control serve as nonverbal messages to others who enter, unintentionally or by invitation.

Just as an awareness of those environments we own and operate is important, we also need to become more aware of environments we don't maintain. Think back to the overly warm office with an old pizza box that we mentioned at the start of this chapter. The manager in this example is responsible for the office in which you're going to interview. This environment communicates something about his or her professionalism, credibility, and organizational skills, a concept termed **impression management**—the formation and maintenance of an impression, perception, or view of a person (Goffman, 1971; Miwa & Hanya, 2006). Environments created in offices, classrooms, and so forth establish comfortable or uncomfortable communication contexts that influence our perceptions of safety and comfort, as well as our perceptions of the attitude, character, and status of the people inhabiting the space (Holley & Steiner, 2005; Kupritz & Hillsman, 2011; Pajo, 2013; Sandberg, 2003).

REMEMBER

Remember!
3.1

Ethnic enclaves	City areas that are dominated by a certain demographic of people
Environment	Built or natural surroundings that influence communication
Rhetoric of architecture	Architectural items (e.g., churches, shopping malls, doors, stairs) that have meaning and influence our behavior
Impression management	Formation of a perception or view of another person

PERCEPTIONS OF ENVIRONMENT ■ ■ ■

Communication scholars Knapp, Hall, and Horgan (2013) suggest that people perceive their environment in six ways: formality, warmth, privacy, familiarity, constraint, and distance. Let's take a look at each of these perceptions in terms of people and environment.

Formality

Have you ever walked into a restaurant and walked right back out again because it was too fancy? Perhaps you've walked into a classroom on the first day and felt extremely nervous. We usually use words like *stuffy* and *serious*, or *relaxed* and *casual* to explain our perception of the **formality** of an environment. Think about your favorite place to eat. Is it formal? casual? relaxed? How does the formality (or lack thereof) influence the way you feel and communicate?

Some of us are church-goers, and people's preferences for church settings vary widely (Herzog, Gray, Dunville, Hicks, & Gilson, 2011). For some of us, a very ornate, spacious, and formal church creates an environment of reverence that allows us to worship. Others want to get away from the formality often associated with church, so we seek a more informal church setting that allows for a less restricted demeanor. Again, remember that the environment serves as a form of nonverbal communication but also influences our nonverbal communication within it. Formality is a perception that people have of environment that relates to how comfortably we can behave, in light of our expectations.

When thinking about formality in an environment, one setting that readily comes to mind is the workplace. For those of you who've worked in professional settings before, think about the tendency for workers to personalize their work spaces. What messages do we get about workers who have lots of personal items in their work spaces, such as photos and knick-knacks? Some companies place strict limitations on the extent to which employees may personalize their workspaces, with some not allowing any personalization whatsoever. However, many American workers do personalize their workspaces, and this type of nonverbal communication can convey a great deal of information, both about the company and its employees (Wells & Thelen, 2002).

Many churches are ornate and spacious, which communicates a significant sense of formality and reverence.

Warmth

In addition to formality, **warmth** is another human perception of environment, meaning that an environment can give off a sense of warmth or coldness. This perception goes beyond temperature. Our sense of warmth is about how we perceive and desire a comfortable, welcoming context that is part of our past or current experience. Can you remember a favorite smell from your childhood? Some of you may think of your grandma's house or a cultural tradition. Smells in an environment certainly contribute to our perception of warmth, as can colors and furnishings.

Reflect for a moment on environments you perceive as providing warmth. While the warmth or welcome feeling of grandma's house might connect with many of us, it's important to consider other environments that people perceive as warm. For example, many hotel/motel chains focus on marketing the warmth of their room features and amenities. For years, Motel 6 used in its advertising the phrase, "We'll leave the light on for you." This phrase (and the "folksy" sound of the voice actor) connected customers to the benefits of an affordable motel room that was ready to welcome guests at any time. Higher-scale hotels have started to emphasize the warmth of their facilities as well. Customers are provided more than "just a room." In fact, many ad spots for these companies feature some of the comforts of home, such as free WiFi and easy Internet access, coffee pots, hair dryers, irons and ironing boards, comfortable bedding, smart TVs, bottled water, mini refrigerators, and high-pressure shower heads to make the room more warm and comfortable for business travelers and families on vacation. People who plan overnight stays sometimes browse pictures on hotel websites to assess how "homey" potential accommodations are (Nguyen, Ruiz-Correa, Schmid Mast, & Gatica-Perez, 2018).

In addition to the warmth of individual rooms, hotels and resorts spend a great deal of money on other aspects of their properties. Many gambling casinos and other tourist-oriented businesses emphasize smell, lighting, color, and sound to create a sense of warmth and comfort for customers who wager money on table games, sports, or slot machines (Åstrøm, 2017; Finlay, Marmurek, Kanetkar, & Londerville, 2010). (Better to lose money in a warm, inviting environment than a stuffy, uncomfortable one!)

Many environments must effectively straddle a line between warmth and formality. One setting of particular importance is health care environments. While it's important for health care offices and facilities to convey a sense of professionalism and formality, they must also convey a sense of warmth for the well-being of their patients and employees. Managing stress is critical for health care workers because it affects their patients' health problems as well as their own satisfaction with their work environment (Andrade, Lima, Devlin, & Hernandez, 2016; Hadavi, 2017; Kozusznik, Peiro, Soriano, & Escudero, 2018; Rashid & Zimring, 2008).

Privacy

People also have a perception of **privacy** when it comes to environment. What type of environment do you prefer if you're meeting someone to talk about something important in your life? Do you prefer a crowded, noisy restaurant, a quiet bar, or someone's personal space, such as a home or apartment? Ask anyone who's ever worked at a restaurant and she or he will tell you that the booths in the restaurant fill up faster than the tables, mainly because booths offer some semblance of privacy.

To further illustrate privacy as a perception people have of environment, let's turn to a very real example in which a private environment is likely needed. Megan identifies as bisexual and has been in a same-sex relationship for a couple of years. She is very selective about whom she shares her personal life with, but she has decided that the time is right for her to come out to her mom and dad. This is an extremely emotional and sensitive experience for Megan, since she has avoided telling her parents about her sexuality and committed relationship for some time now. Megan is an only child and has always been close with her family; one family tradition is to go out to eat for special occasions. Megan believes that the best context in which to break the news to her family will be a restaurant—a place where her mom and dad always bond and share exciting news, as well as discuss serious family matters. So Megan needs to choose a booth in a restaurant where she can reconnect with her parents, have a good dinner, and be provided with a communication context that is relatively private, as she does not know how her mom and dad will respond—whether with happiness or with tears that flow in confusion and sadness.

Can you think of a time when you desired privacy? You can probably think of numerous life situations such as first dates, talking to an important person about a serious issue, and so forth. These are all cases in which we need to have privacy, so we seek environments that will allow us the privacy we perceive we need. In some situations, privacy is not what we desire; we may want to be noticed and at the center of the action in a public place. So with privacy, it's a matter of degree.

Familiarity

A new karaoke bar is opening in town, and your friends want you to meet them there. You enjoy socializing and letting loose with your friends, but this time, you're "going where you've never gone before." Karaoke is something you've always avoided because you don't like to sing in public. What's this place going to be like? What kind of crowd goes there? Will you be pressured to sing? When we meet a new person or encounter an unfamiliar environment, our response is cautionary, anxious, and sometimes mechanical. We've all been in situations where we feel out of place before even entering the front door. We're outside our comfort zone and don't know the rituals and norms associated with this unfamiliar environment.

Our need for familiarity in an environment causes us to ask questions such as, Have I been there before? What kind of crowd usually hangs out there? These questions show us that, while we may be open to experiencing new things, we still like to be clued in about where we're going and what to expect. Our need for familiarity in an environment leads us to develop favorite hangouts, or even to prefer a certain booth or table in our favorite hangout, because we enjoy the certainty of knowing what to expect and how to behave in that environment.

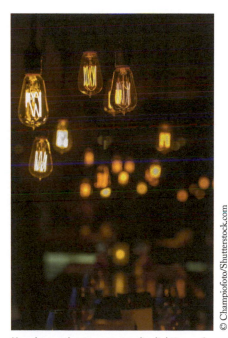

Many bars and restaurants use dim lighting and intimate spaces to create a more familiar and relaxed environment.

© Champiofoto/Shutterstock.com

Constraint

Think of a long car trip with people you don't like. In many instances, we have to gear ourselves up for experiences we don't want to be in. Human perceptions of **constraint** are psychological. Constraint is the "How can I get out of here?" aspect of an environment. Beyond the awkward road trip, we might also dread temporary living arrangements, such as having to share a room with friends, colleagues, or family members during a vacation or business trip. Sometimes, even semi-permanent rooming situations can make us feel constrained, such as living in a university residence hall (Hasan & Fatima, 2018).

We can usually think of ways to cope with temporary confinement, such as escaping the environment whenever we can, going on long walks, listening to music, and so forth. Think about astronauts who spend long stretches of time in space, or people who work for long periods in remote places such as Antarctica; coping with the constraints of such environments is tricky (Paul, Mandal, Ramachandran, & Panwar, 2010). On the other hand, other spaces of confinement are more permanent, such as prisons, rehabilitation clinics, and nursing homes. Most of our perceptions of constraint are shaped by the amount of privacy and space available to us.

Distance

While perceptions of constraint are more psychological in nature, our perceptions of **distance** in an environment pertain to physical arrangements, meaning the measurement or dimensions of a space, how far away from us something is, where furnishings and facilities are located relative to our position, how many people can fit in the space, and so forth. Take a moment to think about a closed area (e.g., an elevator, a crowded airplane). In such a situation, we often want to avoid intimate or personal connections with others. We do what we can to create distance by avoiding eye contact, taking shorter or longer routes to avoid saying hello to people, erecting artificial barriers (such as laptop computers on a plane), and closing doors so people don't think we're present. We may also nonverbally indicate how crowded or intimate an environment is by making jokes, looking at our cell phone, or remaining silent and immobile. All these things serve as part of our repertoire to communicate when space is limited.

KNAPP, HALL, AND HORGAN'S SYSTEM: PERCEPTIONS OF ENVIRONMENT

Formality	Perception of a place as "serious," "stuffy," "relaxed," or "casual"
Warmth	Perception of and desire for a comfortable, welcoming context that is part of our current or past experience
Privacy	Perception of an environment that is protected from others who may overhear what is said
Familiarity	Perception of having been in an environment enough that we know what to expect
Constraint	Psychological perception related to getting out of or away from an environment
Distance	Perception of physical arrangements—the measurement or dimensions of a space

REACTIONS TO ENVIRONMENT ▪ ▪ ▪

Now that we've explored human perceptions of the environment, it's important to consider how people *react* to environment. Remember that, while environment serves as a form of nonverbal communication, it also affects our communication within it. As we first mentioned in Chapter 2, nonverbal scholar Albert Mehrabian (1976) studied people's nonverbal responses to their surroundings. He suggested that people react to environment (which may include the presence of other people in the environment) along three primary dimensions:

1. **Immediacy:** How pleasurable, happy, or satisfied does an environment make you feel? Do you feel positive or negative emotions in the space? Do you want to linger in the space and enjoy yourself, or do you want out of there as soon as possible?
2. **Arousal:** How activated, stimulated, or interested does an environment make you feel? Does an environment make you want to communicate and be social, or to be quiet and enjoy some private time?
3. **Dominance:** How powerful does an environment make you feel? Do you feel in control of the space, or does the space control you?

Before going further with these dimensions, let's consider an example. Think of a course you're currently taking and the classroom where the course is delivered. What color are the walls? Are chalkboards or whiteboards present? What about multimedia elements in the room—are large screens available, along with computer and media equipment on them? How current is the technology? What's the seating like in this classroom? Are seats arranged in a large lecture style, bolted to desks and the floor such that they're fixed, not movable? What sounds or smells are present? What's the lighting like—any windows?

Now let's use Mehrabian's framework to analyze the room: First, does the seating arrangement feel pleasurable and satisfying, or uncomfortable and confining (immediacy)? Second, how aroused—visually, verbally, and nonverbally—are you to learn in this setting? Do white walls, cool or cold temperatures, musty smells, and artificial lighting put you to sleep, meaning low arousal? Or do warm colors, comfortable seating, and effective lighting make you more interested in learning? Do elements in the environment encourage you to interact with fellow students and your professor? Or do these factors make you feel invisible, as though you'd rather do anything but ask a question or offer a comment? Finally, how powerful or dominant (meaning in control) do you feel in this classroom environment? Does the environment make you feel like a speck in a sea of students (which can actually make you feel in control), or are you in such a small space that everything you do is easily seen by everyone in the room? If you changed where you sit in the class, would your perception of dominance (your sense of control) be altered?

Researchers continue to examine classroom environments and how they influence students' learning, level of satisfaction, and evaluations of teaching. Many colleges and universities have made significant investments

Many college classrooms integrate modern design elements and natural lighting to increase student satisfaction and enhance attention.

in upgraded classrooms, lab spaces, and learning centers. In a 2017 study, 918 university students assessed the environment of 30 university classrooms. The students' evaluations were based on nonverbal aspects of classroom temperature, light, and sound, as well as how modern and updated the classrooms were. Students preferred classrooms with more natural light and layouts that reduced psychological distance between professors and students (Castilla, Llinares, Bravo, & Blanca, 2017).

MEHRABIAN'S FRAMEWORK: REACTIONS TO ENVIRONMENT

Remember!
3.3

Immediacy	How happy or satisfied an environment makes us feel
Arousal	How stimulated or energized an environment makes us feel
Dominance	How powerful or in control an environment makes us feel

PERCEPTIONS OF TIME ■ ■ ■

We've established that the environment is communicative, in that people have perceptions of and reactions to their environment. Another part of the communicative environment is time. **Chronemics** is the research term for the communicative aspects of time. Time is something we can't touch—it's intangible, so to speak. However, time is part of that repertoire of furniture, lighting, colors, sounds, smells, and architecture that makes an environment communicative.

In the United States, we try to make time into something that can be touched, meaning that when we spend our time doing something, we believe we should have something to show for it (e.g., products, materials, outcomes). We don't like it when people waste our time. When you've been put on hold on the phone for a long period of time, or have had to wait in a long line for something, you no doubt became acutely aware of the value of time. We do our best to convert time into money. Some employers reward employees with "overtime" and keep track of time by requiring their workforce to "clock in" and "punch out." In fact, many corporations send managers and CEOs to time-management courses so they can be productive with their time at work and train workers to do so as well. Many college students also receive instruction in time management, perhaps during orientation sessions, because quite often what can trip up a student's success is managing time to get things done—not educational ability or intelligence.

Researchers have examined how efficiently people use time, as in one study that found that office workers were interrupted every 3 minutes out of their average 8-hour workday, causing inefficiency (Morgenstern, 2006). Given other research that has determined that people can take as long as 25 minutes to regain their concentration after being interrupted, a significant loss of productivity occurs in many workplaces (Sonnentag, Reinecke, Mata, & Vorderer, 2017).

Our expectations about time influence our professional lives. Jiang, Bazarova, and Hancock (2014) studied chronemics and computer-mediated communication, with results revealing a desire for instant gratification when e-mailing in a professional environment. People who reply to e-mail messages at a slow rate (slower than the sender expects) are perceived as less credible than those who keep their inboxes empty (Kalman & Rafaeli, 2011). Employees have to cope with increasing pressure of handling both electronic and face-to-face communication in the workplace that distracts them from the tasks at hand (Sonnentag, Reinecke, Mata, & Vorderer, 2017). Such expectations aren't limited to just the workplace. Do you feel pressure to communicate quickly with both those people in front of you and those texting you?

Our expectations about time also influence our personal lives and relationships. How much time do you spend talking and texting on your cell phone? If you're in a romantic relationship with someone whose phone time management differs dramatically from yours (e.g., your partner is a speedy and frequent texter who expects quick replies, while you take a more leisurely approach), you could be headed for some conflict over this dimension of your relationship (Duran, Kelly, & Rotaru, 2011; Toma, 2018).

Take a moment to think about the numerous indicators of time in our culture. Clocks, timers, and calendars are integral parts of our daily experience. Cell phones, computers, billboards, and even our cars and home appliances have clocks displaying the time, which shows how much we care about time in American culture. Technology provides us with world clocks to see the time in other countries; do other countries have the same obsession with time as the U.S. does? Like all other nonverbal cues, perceptions of time are culturally rooted (Hall, 1959). Many other countries do not view time the way Americans do, which can lead to cultural misunderstandings (Gonzalez & Zimbardo, 1985/1999). Communication scholar Peter Andersen (2004) explains how perceptions of time can differ in other cultures:

> In the United States and Northern Europe, waiting time for business and social engagements should be kept to a minimum. An American businessman in Latin America might be kept waiting all day for a meeting only to be told to come back tomorrow. This might be a major affront to the American but his Latin American counterpart has no idea this is offensive. (p. 123)

Using a cultural lens, time can be **monochronic** or **polychronic** (Hall & Hall, 1990/1999). In a monochronic view, time is almost tangible, as if it were a commodity that could be bought and sold. This perspective of time dominates most American business, as well as such European regions as Germany, Switzerland, and Scandinavia. A polychronic view of time is the opposite of a monochronic view and is "characterized by the simultaneous occurrence of many things and by a great involvement with people. There is more emphasis on completing human transactions than on holding to schedules" (Hall & Hall, 1990/1999, p. 238).

In U.S. culture, time is often viewed as a commodity. How people spend their time depends greatly on the monetary investment involved in the transaction.

chapter three

spotlight *on research*

Please E-Mail Me Back ASAP!

Online environments, specifically the subset of computer-mediated communication (CMC), take on many forms. CMC channels include e-mail, texting, instant messaging, social media usage, and videochatting using such applications as FaceTime and Skype. Different chronemic expectations exist for each medium or channel, but sometimes expectations regarding speed of reply are blurred, contested, or distorted. For example, with many e-mail delivery systems, a sender can insert an indication of "high importance," often in the form of an exclamation mark attached to a message. The intent behind this nonverbal cue is that precedence should be given to that one message over all others. Because of this and many other features, senders and receivers of CMC messages must negotiate meaning making and impression management.

Tatum, Martin, and Kemper (2018) studied chronemic expectancies and expectancy violations related to instructors' responses to students' e-mails. Because this medium lacks traditional nonverbal cues (e.g., facial expressions, tone of voice, gestures) in comparison to face-to-face (FtF) communication, other nonverbal elements such as speed of response affected students' evaluations of their instructors. Instructors who replied more quickly to student e-mail messages were viewed as more competent, caring, and credible.

Why is this study important to your life? CMC utilization is increasing rapidly, and expectations are still being negotiated and renegotiated. Do you expect someone to reply via e-mail as quickly as via text? Do you view people negatively who don't reply to your texts or e-mails in a timely manner? It's increasingly important to understand how to manage both your online and face-to-face communication by considering such nonverbal cues as chronemics.

Do you want to know more about this study? If so, read Tatum, N. T., Martin, J. C., & Kemper, B. (2018). Chronemics in instructor-student e-mail communication: An experimental examination of student evaluations of instructor response speeds. *Communication Research Reports, 35*, 33-41.

REMEMBER

Chronemics	Study of the communicative aspects of time
Monochronic time	View of time as a tangible commodity
Polychronic time	View of time that places more value on people than schedules

Remember!
3.4

An important nonverbal environmental cue to consider is color. Colors are generally categorized as being either warm (e.g., red, orange, yellow) or cool (e.g., blue, green, purple); warm colors are more arousing and, in some cases, more stress-inducing, than cool colors, which are perceived to be more relaxing.

Three perceptual dimensions of color exist: hue, brightness, and saturation (Amheim, 1954; Mehrabian, 1976). **Hue** refers to the modification of a basic color (e.g., bluish green, reddish orange) in an environment, while **brightness** refers to color intensity. Think of a time when you've been in a really bright room (e.g., bright orange, neon green). Depending on our mood on any given day, we may desire to be in a bright environment. On the other hand, we tend to avoid brightness when we're tired or want to relax. **Saturation** pertains to the amount of color present in an environment. For example, a bright-red door might be used effectively to accent a light-colored house, but an entire environment saturated in bright red might not be as appealing. The effects of color in an environment will vary with its amount and location. Some colors camouflage the small size of a space, actually creating a sense that the room is more spacious than its physical dimensions would suggest (Stamps, 2011).

Scholarly studies have been conducted on the effects of color on human behavior and mood. In older research, prison behavior in response to the wall color of prisoners' holding cells was studied, with the results being that lighter colors, specifically pink, made prisoners weaker and less aggressive (Pellegrini & Schauss, 1980). More recent research has explored the relationship between color in an environment, cognitive performance, and experiencing such emotions as impulsiveness and arousal (Duan, Rhodes, & Cheung, 2018a, 2018b; von Castell, Stelzmann, Obefeld, Welsch, & Hecht, 2018). One study detected a connection between the color red and hostility, in that subjects preferred the color red in situations of rising interpersonal hostility, plus hostile subjects actually detected the color red in an environment significantly more frequently than nonhostile subjects (Fetterman, Tianwei, & Robinson, 2015).

The color choices of a business can affect both employee engagement and customer interest.

© PlusONE/Shutterstock.com

As detailed in Table 3.1, research shows that in the case of some moods, a single color is significantly related, while in other cases, two or more colors promote a particular mood (Murray & Deabler, 1957; Wexner, 1954). Colors present in works of art have been found to influence human mood in health care facilities (Stein, 2006/2008).

chapter three

TABLE 3.1 Colors Associated with Moods

MOOD/TONE	COLOR
Exciting/stimulating	Red
Secure/comfortable	Blue
Distressed/disturbed/upset	Orange
Tender/soothing	Blue
Protective/defending	Brown, blue, black, purple
Despondent/dejected/unhappy/melancholy	Black, brown
Calm/peaceful/serene	Blue, green
Dignified/stately	Purple
Cheerful/jovial/joyful	Yellow
Defiant/contrary/hostile	Red, orange, black
Powerful/strong/masterful	Black

Table adapted and reproduced with permission from Wexner, L. B. (1954). The degree to which colors (hues) are associated with mood-tones. *Journal of Applied Psychology, 38,* 432–435.

Colors in stores, businesses, and even entertainment environments, such as gambling casinos, continue to be the subject of studies (Åstrøm, 2017; Finlay et al., 2010; van Rompay, Tanja-Dijkstra, Verhoeven, & van Es, 2012). Marketing and consumer researchers have found that certain colors match shoppers' expectations and actually enhance sales (Holbrook, 2018; Labrecque & Milne, 2012; Shen, Shi, & Gao, 2018). Is your choice of a shopping environment or your selection of products to purchase influenced by colors in the setting? The next time you're shopping, pay attention to the colors present in your favorite stores, since they're a form of nonverbal communication related to environment.

PERCEPTIONS OF LIGHTING

Lighting also shapes our perceptions of an environment, which in turn influence how we communicate in that environment. Research in the 1970s found that people tend to be less noisy when they're exposed to low lighting and less tired when studying in sunlight compared with artificial light (Maas, Jayson, & Kleiber, 1974; Sanders, Gustanski, & Lawton, 1974). (So much for all those fluorescent bulbs in classrooms!) Recent research indicates a strong connection between lighting in a work environment and employees' well-being, positive mood on the job, and enhanced work behavior (Veitch, Stokkermans, & Newsham, 2011; Vries, Souman, Ruyter, Heynderickx, & Kort, 2018).

PERCEPTIONS OF SOUND

Have you ever been to a restaurant with friends and had a difficult time carrying on a conversation because of all the noise? Dishes clanging, tables being cleared, and a noisy group at a table close by may have been just a few contributors to this noisy environment.

Nonverbal communication researchers have studied the effects of noise on people and their health and creativity, as well as the impact of sound in hospitals, residential buildings, stores, college dorms, and classrooms (Hadavi, 2017; Mehta, Zhu, & Cheema, 2012; Palmer, 1997; Ryu & Jeon, 2011; Syndicus, Weise, & van Treeck, 2018; Weinstein, 1978). Noise impacts environment by affecting the way we feel, what we say, and our desire to stay or leave. Noise in an environment can "make or break" our social experience with family, friends, and significant others. What constitutes "noise" to you? Do you believe that certain sounds are detrimental to your health versus merely annoying? Do some sounds actually improve your health, such as those that relax you or make you laugh?

OUT OF THE CLASSROOM
onto the page

Travis is known by his friends as the guy who has a music playlist for any mood. He likes to listen to different types of music depending on how he currently feels or the mood he wants to be in. Travis has a great workout playlist to get him going at the gym, but he also has a playlist with instrumental music from movie soundtracks to help him focus while doing homework at the library or at his favorite coffee shop.

In class while discussing environment as a form of nonverbal communication, Travis mentioned that he appreciates how music can affect his mood and how his mood can affect his musical choices. When he wants to motivate himself to be active, he tries to play more upbeat music. But he also gets frustrated when he can't choose his own music. His fiancée always takes control of the music while Travis is driving the car. She plays a lot of subtle songs, and that makes it hard for Travis to focus or stay awake on longer drives. This simple example from a class session shows that music can definitely influence environment and environment can have an impact on music and many other factors.

PERCEPTIONS OF SMELL ■ ■ ■

Smell is something many of us spend a good part of our day manipulating. Nonverbal communication scholars use the term **olfaction** to refer to the role of smell in human interaction (Ala , 2017; Hastings, Musambira, & Ayoub, 2011; Mertes, 2018; Winslow, 2017). Each day Americans take baths and showers, deodorize, brush, floss, gargle, wipe, sanitize, and freshen to cover up natural body odors. If smell wasn't important, we wouldn't buy all these products and go through all these routines.

While smells associated with people are important to study (so much so that we take up the topic again in Chapter 5), smells are critical nonverbal environmental cues. Research indicates that smells influence mood (Douce & Janssens, 2013; Krishna, Lwin, & Morrin, 2010; Lin, Cross, & Childers, 2018; Rochet, El-Hage, Richa, Kazour, & Atanasova, 2018). So it tends to follow that we often return to environments that smell pleasing to us, which is part of the draw of successful businesses such as Starbucks and Cinnabon. If a friend's home smells pleasant, we're likely to want to attend gatherings there; if a friend's home smells as though the cat's litter box hasn't been cleaned in decades, we may choose to see our friend in an alternate location. We tend to limit our time in environments that contain smells we don't like, particularly ones that evoke negative emotions. If you've spent time in a hospital or other health care facility, the antiseptic smell is likely a real turn-off, even though it's a smell associated with the positive notion of cleanliness.

Smell can be a form of therapy, relaxation, and cleansing of the mind and body. **Aromatherapy**, which may involve natural products such as eucalyptus or peppermint as well as scented candles or incense, is often used in accord with massage therapy, body wraps, facials, and other services in spas, salons, and resorts to help people relax. Just this term—aromatherapy—reveals the significance of smell in an environment and its effects on people.

Marketers also use smell to help sell their products, since smells have been shown in research to affect human judgment (Bone & Jantrania, 1992; Douce & Janssens, 2013; Gvili, Levy, & Zwilling, 2017; Spangenberg, Crowley, & Henderson, 1996). For example, it's not uncommon to find scented inserts for new colognes tucked between the pages of magazines. Since smell provides marketers with a tool to attract consumers, it's no surprise that brands such as Club Monaco, De Beers, Renaissance Hotels, and Ritz Carlton Resorts and Spas have created their own signature scents as an innovative way to make their concepts and brands stand out (George, 2006).

PERCEPTIONS OF TEMPERATURE ■ ■ ■

The temperature in an environment affects our perceptions and communication, just as the other factors we've considered thus far. Factors that help create temperatures, such as weather, climate, barometric pressure, and seasons, all have an effect (Anderson & Anderson, 1984; Griffit, 1970; Griffit & Veithc, 1971; Guéguen, 2013). An analysis of Major League Baseball games between 1986 and 1988 revealed a strong connection between high temperatures and the number of batters hit by a pitch (Reifman, Larrick, & Fein, 1991). Research into temperature and seasons has examined Seasonal Affective Disorder, finding that individuals with this condition have recurrent episodes of depression during winter, with remission of the symptoms during summer (Kuppili, Selvakumar, & Menon, 2018; Melrose, 2015).

Researchers have paid specific attention to temperature and climate and have generated the following list of related behavioral changes (Knapp, Hall, & Horgan, 2013):

1. Suicide rates increase in the spring and are the highest in the summer.
2. College students break up with their dating partners at the beginnings and ends of semesters.
3. During the summer, people spend more time with friends.
4. During the summer, assault and rape crimes increase.
5. From July to November, people tend to report less happiness but more activity and less boredom.
6. People use their phones less in the summer than in the winter.

One final topic related to temperature warrants brief discussion—that of your own internal or bodily temperature, which can affect your reactions to temperature in an environment. There's

WHAT WOULD *YOU* DO

Amanda is an assistant manager at casual restaurant and has just taken over the responsibility of hiring new employees. She has a hard-working and compatible staff at the restaurant, and she wants to maintain positive morale. Amanda interviewed two applicants, and she is torn on which one to hire. One candidate seemed like an extremely hard worker. One of his references said that he was always timely and a loyal employee. The other candidate was a referral from two of the cashiers at the restaurant. The referral seems like a good worker, but she didn't seem nearly as prepared for the interview as the first candidate.

Amanda is conflicted because she doesn't know who's the right fit for the restaurant's environment. She knows that the first candidate would be an excellent worker, but she overheard some of the employees commenting that he didn't seem to "fit the mold" of the typical employee at the restaurant. The second interviewee seemed like she would fit in very well with the current staff and the "feel" of the place. Amanda doesn't want to jeopardize the morale of the crew; she's a fairly new manager, so she wants to be viewed positively.

What would you do if you were Amanda? Should the environment of a restaurant or other place of business impact hiring decisions? If so, how can a manager communicate this fact to potential new employees?

chapter three

probably no one in the universe hotter than a pregnant woman in her last trimester! Doctors warn expectant mothers not to take overly hot showers or baths or to spend time in hot tubs during their pregnancies, because such environments can overheat the mother and the fetus and cause damage to both. Many women experience hot flashes and night sweats during menopause due to hormonal changes. These kinds of changes, along with simple fevers associated with infections, can affect how you perceive the temperature of an environment.

APPLICATIONS OF RESEARCH ON ENVIRONMENT ■ ■ ■ ▬▬▬▬

In this final section of the chapter, we provide applications of research on the environment as a form of nonverbal communication. We first explore research that documents the connection between health (specifically the problem of obesity) and environment, meaning where we live, work, and study. Next, we devote attention to studies that have examined aspects of popular culture—the restaurants we eat in, the homes we live in, what we purchase to decorate our homes, and how media have capitalized on our interest in improving our home surroundings.

Environment, Health, and Obesity

You've no doubt heard news or seen reports about the "epidemic of obesity" in America. Maybe you've heard about efforts to combat obesity by banning oversized sodas or schools replacing candy and soda machines with ones that offer healthy snacks. It's obvious that we have an obesity problem in our country, but did you ever consider that the environment in which you live, study, and work might play a significant role in the problem?

A good deal of research over the past decade or so documents a connection between environmental features and weight-related health problems (Booth, Pinkston, & Poston, 2005; Campbell et al., 2007; Papas et al., 2007; Trasande et al., 2009). In many of these studies, including a fascinating report by Wells, Ashdown, Davies, Cowett, and Yang (2007), environment is defined as "the space outside of the person" (p. 7). So environmental features include the built environment (i.e., structures) as well as clothing, food packaging and presentation, technology, natural areas, neighborhoods, and urban design. Wells et al. believe that a wider conceptualization of environment is helpful when addressing factors related to the obesity epidemic.

In terms of clothing, Wells et al. (2007) contend that clothing can either provide support for or act as a barrier to physical activity, which is related to health and obesity. Since people used to wear more clothing and that clothing weighed more than today's designs do, the activities of putting on, taking off, laundering, and storing clothing were more physical and calorie burning than they are today. Since people's weight involves a balance of their food consumption and energy expenditure, our culture has evolved to where clothing no longer requires the expenditure of energy it once did. On the other hand, contemporary clothing encourages physical activity more today than in the past, since a good deal of footwear and fashionable clothing is designed for ease of movement and comfort. Think about wearing yoga pants or biking shorts versus sweatpants and sweatshirts and you'll better understand this research team's claims.

Wells et al. (2007) also discuss the food environment and its relationship to obesity. They define "food environment" as "portion sizes and packaging," as well as "patterns of food availability and affordability" (p. 12). We know that dramatic portion expansion significantly contributes to the problem of overeating and obesity, but you may not have thought about how access to healthy foods, both in terms of geographic and economic access, complicates the picture. Teams of researchers have examined the influence of neighborhood food environments on healthy eating and a resulting connection to increased obesity rates (Eckert & Vojnovic, 2017; Laxy, Malecki, Givens, Walsh, & Nieto, 2015; Mellor, Dolan, & Rapoport, 2011; Wong et al., 2018). Results consistently show the following: (1) poorer neighborhoods have significantly fewer supermarkets that offer healthy food choices than wealthy neighborhoods; (2) poorer neighborhoods have more fast food restaurants than restaurants with healthy options on their menus; (3) poorer neighborhoods have up to three times the number of venues for alcohol consumption compared with wealthy neighborhoods; and (4) access (transportation) to supermarkets is limited in poor neighborhoods, thus increasing the likelihood that the poorest among us have the fewest choices, limited access to healthy food, and higher obesity rates (especially among children) than other locales with more options.

These trends led New Orleans native and actor Wendell Pierce to build several grocery stores in some of the poorest neighborhoods in his hometown, in an attempt to cope with what he called the "food desert" in the area (Berkowitz et al., 2018; Black, 2012; Mott, 2013; United Press International, 2013). Pierce and his business associates opened attractive, well-constructed supermarkets that stock healthy food at reasonable prices; they also combat the transportation problem by offering a free shuttle ride home to any customers who spend $50 or more at the market.

Another contributing factor Wells et al. (2007) mention is building design, which fits in nicely with our discussion of environment as a form of nonverbal communication and as affecting how we nonverbally communicate. Wells et al. state, "During the past 100 years, building construction practices along with a wide range of technological developments may have contributed to the obesity epidemic by enabling us to expend less energy" (p. 17). Think about where the stairs are located in most buildings, compared with the elevators; stairwells are often tucked away in dark, secluded areas, while elevators are front and center, inviting us to take the easy way up and down rather than expend more energy taking the stairs. Many college campuses that have grown and sprawled out geographically, out of necessity, offer shuttle buses between buildings or campus sections, rather than encouraging students, faculty, and staff to walk or jog to expend more energy.

Two other obesity-related environmental factors are described in research: (1) increased development of locations for work, study, and home living that require driving versus pedestrian access, again contributing to decreased physical activity, and (2) limited access to natural spaces in which physical activity is possible, also a casualty of building development. Again, all these environmental features can be seen as forms of nonverbal communication that have profound effects on our health and well-being (Ding & Gebel, 2012; Feng, Glass, Curriero, Stewart, & Schwartz, 2010).

POPULAR CULTURE ■ ■ ■

What is "pop culture"? Cultural studies scholar John Fiske (1989) explains that **popular culture** is created by the products of a culture that are owned and made by businesses for the purpose of generating a profit. Examples of pop culture include shopping malls, sporting events, movies, magazines, cell phones, vehicles, virtual communities, furniture, restaurants, amusement parks, and TV shows, to name a few. Pop culture consists of many environments in which we spend leisure time with friends and family. Further, pop culture provides consumers with an array of products that shape everyday experiences, both personally and professionally. Let's consider two examples from pop culture and connect them to our study of nonverbal communication and environment.

RESTAURANT ENVIRONMENTS. Think of the last time you went for fast food and actually entered the restaurant, rather than using the drive-thru. Did you notice the environment? Was it inviting? Did you feel as though it would be okay to pull out your books and study, lingering over your soda? Probably not! Something as everyday and common as a fast-food restaurant serves as a rich example of intentional design driven by the need for customer turnover and corporate profits (Block, Scribner, & DeSalvo, 2004; Eaves & Leathers, 1991; Jeffery, Baxter, McGuire, & Linde, 2006). The next time you want fast food, avoid the drive-thru. Actually go into the restaurant and note the design, seating, colors, lighting, smells, sounds, and temperature, plus the possible presence of "express lines" that get you in and out even faster (Weng, Gotcher, & Kuo, 2017). These carefully calculated environmental elements are forms of nonverbal communication. If you sit down to eat in a fast-food place, you'll likely find that the context you're eating in nonverbally communicates, "Gulp down that burger and get out of here!"

A relaxed dining atmosphere will encourage you to take your time and linger over the meal.

While fast-food settings encourage us to speed through our meals, pricier restaurants create environments that make diners want to linger over a wonderful meal, perhaps ordering more cocktails or another bottle of wine and enjoying conversation over dessert and coffee (and an expensive price tag!). The furnishings—often nicer than those in your own home—make you slow down and take your time, because the seating is likely far more comfortable than that of a fast-food place (and because you want to get your money's worth). The colors, smells, sounds (such as pleasant music), temperature, and lighting all help create the effect of slowing down time and helping customers escape their normal lives. These kinds of effects are carefully researched and executed for repeat business and maximum profits.

HOME IMPROVEMENT SHOWS. After you enjoy your burger and fries or crêpes and lobster, and head to your dorm room, apartment, or home (recognizing that readers of this text have diverse living situations), you might turn on your TV or stream on your phone to find a variety of shows that will teach you how to create a posh home environment or that follow people who struggle with hoarding and the ability to maintain safe living environments (Lepselter, 2011). Many design and home improvement TV shows, such as *Flip or Flop*, *Property Brothers*, and *Fixer Upper*, have seen great success over the past decade. While "extreme" home makeover shows might not appeal to consumers working on a limited budget, home-improvement retailers are using different types of shows to reach consumers based on their income and desired home improvement levels (Steinberg, 2011). The fact that people from home-improvement shows such as Chip and Joanna Gaines can become household names and producers of décor lines at retailers like Target shows the power of what environmental elements nonverbally communicate.

REMEMBER

Remember!
3.5

Hue	Modification of a basic color (e.g., bluish green, red orange) in an environment
Brightness	Intensity of color in an environment
Saturation	Amount of color present in an environment
Olfaction	Role of smell in human interaction
Aromatherapy	Benefits of smell from scented candles or incense used in accord with massage therapy, body wraps, and facials
Popular culture	Products of a culture that are owned and made by businesses for the purpose of generating a profit

UNDERSTANDING ENVIRONMENT: APPLYING THE REFLEXIVE CYCLE OF NONVERBAL COMMUNICATION DEVELOPMENT ■ ■ ■

The first step toward developing your skills and a better understanding of the environment as nonverbal communication is awareness. We encourage you to inventory yourself using the following questions: What are your standards regarding your own environment? What are your needs or preferences for the way other people maintain their environments? Consider your expectations or rules about such things as cleanliness, color, or smell. Are you aware of the impressions others may form about you based on the environments you create and maintain? What environmental factors exist in your life that affect your health and level of physical activity? How is your nonverbal communication affected by environment?

Now that you have engaged in an inventory of self regarding environment, it's time to think about making any appropriate changes to improve how you manage these nonverbal cues in your everyday life. This is Phase 2 in the Reflexive Cycle. Ask yourself: Are there some changes I need to make regarding environment (e.g., dirty car, messy office, lack of lighting in my apartment, the cookie dough candle I burn all the time, taking the elevator instead of the stairs)? If so, how can I make those changes? Perhaps the only thing that needs to change is your awareness of the environments you maintain and how they're perceived by other people.

Beyond engaging in an inventory of self and making appropriate changes, the next step is to inventory others. Can you think of a person who seems to have no awareness of environment? You may be thinking of that "Pig Pen" friend with a messy car or stinky closet. (These are the people who don't get their dorm deposits back when they check out for the summer.) Here's another example: Think of being picked up for a first date. The passenger seat of your date's car is trashy, and empty beer cans cover the floorboard. What kind of first impression does this make? Some people are oblivious to the fact that the environments they maintain communicate who they are. They're not aware enough to perception check with other people for observations and reactions to their environments.

After you've done an inventory of self, changed self, and inventoried others' nonverbal behavior with regard to environment, the fourth phase of the Reflexive Cycle involves interacting with others, trying out the changes you've made or are in the process of making, and observing people as you verbally and nonverbally interact with them. Do people react differently to you as a result of any changes you made? For example, people who are trying to become more organized may draw their coworkers' attention to

the fact that they're straightening up their office and implementing a filing system. It can be interesting to note people's reactions to both subtle and obvious changes in the way we manage environments and how it makes us feel, as well as to gauge our own reactions to changes other people have made related to environment.

In the last part of the cycle, we challenge you to review and assess the whole process, making note of positive and negative aspects, and then begin the cycle again. Remember, the development of communication skills is a never-ending process, as we work to increase our nonverbal abilities on a whole range of topics, not just environment.

SUMMARY ■ ■ ■

In this chapter, we established environment as a nonverbal communication code and emphasized the need to be aware of our own as well as others' perceptions of environment. The control you have over establishing, maintaining, and regulating healthy communication environments influences your communicative decisions in your personal and professional life. For two reasons, you need to give special attention to environment as a nonverbal communication code: (1) The choices you make about the environment in which you live or work reveal a good deal about who you are, and (2) your nonverbal communication is altered by the environments in which you communicate.

Next, we explored six different perceptions people form about environments (formality, warmth, privacy, familiarity, constraint, and distance), followed by ways we react to the environments we choose or find ourselves in. Remember that immediacy (how happy or satisfied an environment can make us feel), arousal (how stimulated or energized an environment can make us feel), and dominance (how powerful and in control an environment can make us feel) are three different ways people react to environments.

In the next section of this chapter, we discussed chronemics—the study of how time and communication work together. We considered the impact of culture on monochronic and polychronic views of time.

Color, sound, and lighting are key nonverbal cues in an environment. Researchers have deemed these nonverbal environmental attributes influential with regard to human behavior; they impact environment by affecting the way we feel, what we say, and our desire to stay or leave.

We next defined olfaction—the role of smell in human interaction. Smell is an important environmental nonverbal cue, as well as a key element in the marketing of products. We explored temperature and seasonal influences on human behavior, noting that people tend to exhibit more aggressive behavior during warmer months than cooler months. Applications of research on the environment as a form of nonverbal communication were discussed, including an examination of the connection between environment and obesity. We then explored two elements of popular culture—restaurants and home improvement shows—to further illustrate how people are affected by environmental factors. Finally, we applied the Reflexive Cycle of Nonverbal Communication Development to our understanding of environment.

DISCUSSION STARTERS

1. Explain how environment is a form of nonverbal communication.
2. What cues does your living environment reveal about your character, upbringing, and culture? Did you ever consider that so much could be revealed in how you maintain your home environment?
3. Review Knapp, Hall, and Horgan's four perceptions of time, and provide an example of each category.
4. Think of how many phrases in American culture relate to time, such as "Time flies when you're having fun" and "It's about time." What does a person's time management nonverbally reveal about her or his character?
5. Do you think the color of a room affects your behavior or mood? What about smells, temperatures, sounds, and lighting? How are your verbal and nonverbal communication affected by these elements?
6. What is your preferred environment for socializing with friends? What kinds of environments are more conducive to friendly conversation? Less conducive? Identify some situations in which you would desire a specific environment for communication.
7. Had you considered the link between environment and obesity in American culture before reading about it in this chapter? Think about the neighborhoods where you grew up—did you notice an association between the economics of the area and access to healthy food or facilities that would encourage physical activity? What does a neighborhood that offers few healthy options communicate to the people living there?

REFERENCES

Alač, M. (2017). We like to talk about smell: A worldly take on language, sensory experience, and the Internet. *Semiotica, 2017,* 143–192.

Amheim, R. (1954). *Art and visual perception.* Berkeley: University of California Press.

Andersen, P. A. (2004). *The complete idiot's guide to body language.* New York: Alpha.

Anderson, C. A., & Anderson, D. C. (1984). Ambient temperature and violent crime: Tests of the linear and curvilinear hypotheses. *Journal of Personality and Social Psychology, 46*, 91–97.

Andrade, C. C., Lima, M. L., Devlin, A. S., & Hernandez, B. (2016). Is it the place or the people? Disentangling the effects of hospitals' physical and social environments on well-being. *Environment & Behavior, 48*, 299–323.

Åstrøm, J. K. (2017). Theme factors that drive the tourist customer experience. *International Journal of Culture, Tourism and Hospitality Research, 11*, 125–141.

Berkowitz, S. A., Karter, A. J., Corbie-Smith, G., Seligman, H. K., Ackroyd, S. A., Barnard, L. S., Atlas, S. J., & Wexler, D. J. (2018). Food insecurity, food "deserts," and glycemic control in patients with diabetes: A longitudinal analysis. *Diabetes Care, 41*, 1188–1195.

Biemiller, L. (2007, June 8). Take me back to old main. *Chronicle of Higher Education,* p. A40.

Biemiller, L. (2010, May 21). Your new buildings need not look old. *Chronicle of Higher Education,* pp.B6–B9.

Bishop, P. (2011). Eating in the contact zone: Singapore foodscape and cosmopolitan timespace. *Continuum: Journal of Media & Cultural Studies, 25*, 637–652.

Black, J. (2012, March 6). In New Orleans, an actor turns grocer. *New York Times.* Retrieved from http://www.nytimes.com/2012/03/07/dining/wendell-pierce-to-open-a-grocery-store-in-new-orleans.html?pagewanted=all&_r=0

Block, J. P., Scribner, R. A., & DeSalvo, K. B. (2004). Fast food, race/ethnicity, and income: A geographic analysis. *American Journal of Preventive Medicine, 27*, 211–217.

Bone, P. F., & Jantrania, S. (1992). Olfaction as cue for product quality. *Marketing Letters, 3*, 289–296.

Booth, K. M., Pinkston, M. M., & Poston, W. S. C. (2005). Obesity and the built environment. *Journal of the American Dietetic Association, 105,* 110–117.

Bringslimark, T., Hartig, T., & Grindal Patil, G. (2011). Adaptation to windowlessness: Do office workers compensate for a lack of visual access to the outdoors? *Environment & Behavior, 43*, 469–487.

Brody, N. (2013). Absence—and mediated communication—makes the heart grow fonder: Clarifying the predictors of satisfaction and commitment in long-distance friendships. *Communication Research Reports, 30*, 323–333.

Campbell, K. J., Crawford, D. A., Salmon, J., Carver, A., Garnett, S. P., & Baur, L. A. (2007). Associations between the home food environment and obesity-promoting eating behaviors in adolescence. *Obesity, 15*, 719–730.

Castilla, N., Llinares, C., Bravo, J. M., & Blanca, V. (2017). Subjective assessment of university classroom environment. *Building & Environment, 122,* 72–81.

Chylinski, M., Northey, G., & Ngo, L. V. (2015). Cross-modal interactions between color and texture of food. *Psychology & Marketing, 32*, 950–966.

Clark-Parsons, R. (2018). Building a digital girl army: The cultivation of feminist safe spaces online. *New Media & Society, 20*, 2125–2144.

Ding, D., & Gebel, K. (2012). Built environment, physical activity, and obesity: What have we learned from reviewing the literature? *Health & Place, 18*, 100–105.

Douce, L., & Janssens, W. (2013). The presence of a pleasant ambient scent in a fashion store: The moderating role of shopping motivation and affect intensity. *Environment & Behavior, 45*, 215–238.

Döveling, K. (2015). "Help me. I am so alone." Online emotional self-disclosure in shared coping-processes of children and adolescents on social networking platforms. *Communications: The European Journal of Communication Research, 40*, 403–423.

Duan, Y., Rhodes, P. A., & Cheung, V. (2018a). The influence of color on impulsiveness and arousal: Part 1—hue. *Color Research & Application, 43,* 396–404.

Duan, Y., Rhodes, P. A., & Cheung, V. (2018b). The influence of color on impulsiveness and arousal: Part 2—chroma. *Color Research & Application, 43,* 405–414.

Duran, R. L., Kelly, L., & Rotaru, T. (2011). Mobile phones in romantic relationships and the dialectic of autonomy versus connection. *Communication Quarterly, 59,* 19–36.

Eaves, M. H., & Leathers, D. G. (1991). Context as communication: McDonald's vs. Burger King. *Journal of Applied Communication Research, 19,* 263–289.

Eckert, J., & Vojnovic, I. (2017). Fast food landscapes: Exploring restaurant choice and travel behavior for residents living in lower eastside Detroit neighborhoods. *Applied Geography, 89,* 41–51.

Fassinger, P. A. (2000). How classes influence students' participation in college classrooms. *Journal of Classroom Interaction, 35,* 38–47.

Feng, J., Glass, T. A., Curriero, F. C., Stewart, W. F., & Schwartz, B. S. (2010). The built environment and obesity: A systematic review of the epidemiologic evidence. *Health & Place, 16,* 175–190.

Fetterman, A. K., Tianwei, L., & Robinson, M. D. (2015). Extending color psychology to the personality realm: Interpersonal hostility varies by red preferences and perceptual biases. *Journal of Personality, 83,* 106–116.

Finlay, K., Marmurek, H. H. C., Kanetkar, V., & Londerville, J. (2010). Casino decor effects on gambling emotions and intentions. *Environment & Behavior, 42,* 525–545.

Fiske, J. (1989). *Understanding popular culture.* Boston: Unwin Hyman.

Gang, H., Feng, L., Cheng, S., & Xiaochen, S. (2017). Effect of workplace environment cleanliness on judgement of counterproductive work behavior. *Social Behavior & Personality: An International Journal, 45,* 599–604.

George, L. (2006, February 13). The sweet smell of shopping. *Maclean's, 55.*

Goffman, E. (1971). *Relations in public: Microstudies of the public order.* New York: Harper Colophon Books.

Gonzalez, A., & Zimbardo, P. G. (1999). Time in perspective. In L. K. Guerrero, J. A. DeVito, & M. L. Hecht (Eds.), *The nonverbal communication reader: Classic and contemporary readings* (2nd ed., pp. 227–236). Prospect Heights, IL: Waveland. (Reprinted from *Psychology Today,* pp. 21–26, 1985)

Griffit, W. (1970). Environmental effects on interpersonal affective behavior: Ambient effective temperature and attraction. *Journal of Personality and Social Psychology, 15,* 240–244.

Griffit, W., & Veithc, R. (1971). Hot and crowded: Influence of population density and temperature on interpersonal affective behavior. *Journal of Personality and Social Psychology, 17,* 92–98.

Guéguen, N. (2013). Weather and smiling contagion: A quasi experiment with the smiling sunshine. *Journal of Nonverbal Behavior, 37,* 51–55.

Gvili, Y., Levy, S., & Zwilling, M. (2017). The sweet smell of advertising: The essence of matching scents with other ad cues. *International Journal of Advertising, 37,* 568–590.

Hadavi, S. (2017). Direct and indirect effects of the physical aspects of the environment on mental well-being. *Environment & Behavior, 49,* 1071–1104.

Hall, E. T. (1959). *The silent language.* Garden City, NY: Doubleday.

Hall, E. T., & Hall, M. R. (1999). Monochronic and polychronic time. In L. K. Guerrero, J. A. DeVito, & M. L. Hecht (Eds.), *The nonverbal communication reader: Classic and contemporary readings* (2nd ed., pp. 237–240). Prospect Heights, IL: Waveland. (Reprinted from *Understanding cultural differences: Germans, French, and Americans,* 1990, Yarmouth, ME: Intercultural Press)

Hasan, S., & Fatima, M. (2018). Factors affecting the academic performance of university students residing in student housing facility. *Khazar Journal of Humanities & Social Sciences, 21*, 83–100.

Hastings, S. O., Musambira, G. W., & Ayoub, R. (2011). Revisiting Edward T. Hall's work on Arabs and olfaction: An update with implications for intercultural communication scholarship. *Journal of Intercultural Communication Research, 40*, 3–20.

Hattenhauer, D. (1984). The rhetoric of architecture: A semiotic approach. *Communication Quarterly, 32*, 71–77.

Herzog, T. R., Gray, L. E., Dunville, A. M., Hicks, A. M., & Gilson, E. A. (2011). Preference and tranquility for houses of worship. *Environment & Behavior, 45*, 504–525.

Holbrook, M. B. (2018). Creating value: The theory and practice of marketing semiotics research. Journal of Marketing Communications, *24*, 212–215.

Holley, L., & Steiner, S. (2005). Safe space: Student perspectives on classroom environment. *Journal of Social Work Education, 41*, 49–64.

Hur, K. K., & Jeffres, L. W. (1979). A conceptual approach to the study of ethnicity, communication and urban stratification. *Communication, 8*, 67–87.

Jeffery, R. W., Baxter, J., McGuire, M., & Linde, J. (2006). Are fast food restaurants an environmental risk for obesity? *International Journal of Behavioral Nutrition and Physical Activity, 3*, 1–6.

Jiang, L. C., Bazarova, N. N., & Hancock, J. T. (2011). From perception to behavior: Disclosure reciprocity and the intensification of intimacy in computer-mediated communication. *Communication Research, 40*, 125–143.

Kalman, Y. M., & Rafaeli, S. (2011). Online pauses and silence: Chronemic expectancy violations in written computer-mediated communication. *Communication Research, 38*, 54–69.

Kendal, S., Kirk, S., Elvey, R., Catchpole, R., & Pryjmachuk, S. (2017). How a moderated online discussion forum facilitates support for young people with eating disorders. *Health Expectations, 20*, 98–111.

Kim, J. (2018). Manhattan's Koreatown as a transclave: The emergence of a new ethnic enclave in a global city. *City & Community, 17*, 276–295.

Knapp, M. L., Hall, J. A., & Horgan, T. G. (2013). *Nonverbal communication in human interaction* (8th ed.). Belmont, CA: Wadsworth/Cengage Learning.

Kozusznik, M. W., Peiro, J. M., Soriano, A., & Escudero, M. N. (2018). "Out of sight, out of mind?": The role of physical stressors, cognitive appraisal, and positive emotion in employees' health. *Environment & Behavior, 50*, 86–115.

Krishna, A., Lwin, M. O., & Morrin, M. (2010). Product scent and memory. *Journal of Consumer Research, 37*, 57–67.

Kuppili, P., Selvakumar, N., & Menon, V. (2018). Sickness behavior and Seasonal Affective Disorder: An immunological perspective of depression. *Indian Journal of Psychological Medicine, 40*, 266–268.

Kupritz, V. W., & Hillsman, T. (2011). The impact of the physical environment on supervisory communication skills transfer. *Journal of Business Communication, 48*, 148–185.

Labrecque, L., & Milne, G. (2012). Exciting red and competent blue: The importance of color in marketing. *Journal of the Academy of Marketing Science, 40*, 711–727.

Laxy, M., Malecki, K. C., Givens, M. L., Walsh, M. C., & Nieto, F. J. (2015). The association between neighborhood economic hardship, the retail food environment, fast food intake, and obesity: Findings from the Survey of the Health of Wisconsin. *BMC Public Health, 15*, 1–10.

chapter three

Lepselter, S. (2011). The disorder of things: Hoarding narratives in popular media. *Anthropological Quarterly, 84*, 919–948.

Lewis, P., Kerridge, I., & Jorden, C. F. (2009). Creating space: Hospital bedside displays as facilitators of communication between children and nurses. *Journal of Child Health Care, 13*, 93–100.

Lin, M-H., Cross, S. N. N., & Childers, T. L. (2018). Understanding olfaction and emotions and the moderating role of individual differences. *European Journal of Marketing, 52*, 811–836.

Lohmann, A., Arriaga, X. B., & Goodfriend, W. (2003). Close relationships and placemaking: Do objects in a couple's home reflect couplehood? *Personal Relationships, 10*, 437–449.

Maas, J., Jayson, J., & Kleiber, D. (1974). Effects of spectral differences in illumination on fatigue. *Journal of Applied Psychology, 59*, 524–526.

Maliepaard, E. (2017). Bisexual safe space(s) on the internet: Analysis of an online forum for bisexuals. *Journal of Economic & Social Geography, 108*, 318–330.

Martin, D. (2006, February 2). Slow down and let 'em smell the coffee. *American Banker,* p. 11.

Maslow, A. H., & Mintz, N. L. (1956). Effects of esthetic surroundings: I. Initial effects of three esthetic conditions upon perceiving "energy" and "well-being" in faces. *Journal of Psychology, 41*, 247–254.

Mehrabian, A. (1976). *Public spaces and private places.* New York: Basic Books.

Mehta, R., Zhu, R., & Cheema, A. (2012). Is noise always bad? Exploring the effects of ambient noise on creative cognition. *Journal of Consumer Research, 39*, 784–799.

Mellor, J. M., Dolan, C. B., & Rapoport, R. B. (2011). Child body mass index, obesity, and proximity to fast food restaurants. *International Journal of Pediatric Obesity, 6*, 60–68.

Melrose, S. (2015). Seasonal Affective Disorder: An overview of assessment and treatment approaches. *Depression Research & Treatment, 2015*, 1–6.

Mertes, M. (2018, June 16). A review of the $30 candle that claims to smell like Nebraska. *Omaha World-Herald.*

Mintz, N. L. (1956). Effects of esthetic surroundings: II. Prolonged and repeated experience in a "beautiful" and "ugly" room. *Journal of Psychology, 41*, 459–466.

Miwa, Y., & Hanya, K. (2006). The effects of interior design on communication and impressions of a counselor in a counseling room. *Environment & Behavior, 38*, 484–502.

Morgenstern, J. (2006, September). We interrupt this magazine.... *O: The Oprah Winfrey Magazine,* 139–140.

Mott, R. (2013, April 2). Food for thought: An actor's new role...in the grocery store. *NBC Nightly News* [Television broadcast]. Retrieved from http://dailynightly.nbcnews.com/_news/2013/04/02/17571711-food-for-thought-an-actors-new-role-in-the-grocery-store?lite

Murray, D. C., & Deabler, H. L. (1957). Colors and mood-tones. *Journal of Applied Psychology, 41*, 279–283.

Nguyen, L., S., Ruiz-Correa, S., Schmid Mast, M., & Gatica-Perez, D. (2018). Check out this place: Inferring ambience from Airbnb photos. *IEEE Transactions on Multimedia, 20*, 1499–1511.

O'Halloran, R., Worrall, L., & Hickson, L. (2011). Environmental factors that influence communication between patients and their healthcare providers in acute hospital stroke units: An observational study. *International Journal of Language & Communication Disorders, 46*, 30–47.

Pajo, K. (2013). The occurrence of "what," "where," "what house," and other repair initiations in the home environment of hearing-impaired individuals. *International Journal of Language and Communication Disorders, 48*, 66–77.

Palmer, C. (1997). Hearing and listening in a typical classroom. *Speech and Hearing Services in Schools, 28,* 213–218.

Papas, M. A., Alberg, A. J., Ewing, R., Helzlsouer, K. J., Gary, T. L., & Klassen, A. C. (2007). The built environment and obesity. *Epidemiologic Reviews, 29,* 129–143.

Paul, F. U. J., Mandal, M. K., Ramachandran, K., & Panwar, M. R. (2010). Interpersonal behavior in an isolated and confined environment. *Environment & Behavior, 42,* 707–717.

Pellegrini, R. F., & Schauss, A. G. (1980). Muscle strength as a function of exposure to hue differences in visual stimuli: An experimental test of kinesoid theory. *Journal of Orthomolecular Psychiatry, 2,* 144–147.

Perez-Lopez, R. (2017). Primary spaces and their cues as facilitators of personal and social inferences. *Journal of Environmental Psychology, 53,* 157–167.

Rashid, M., & Zimring, C. (2008). A review of the empirical literature on the relationships between indoor environment and stress in health care and office settings: Problems and prospects of sharing evidence. *Environment & Behavior, 40,* 151–190.

Reifman, A. S., Larrick, R. P., & Fein, S. (1991). Temper and temperature on the diamond: The heat-aggression relationship in major league baseball. *Personality and Social Psychology Bulletin, 17,* 580–585.

Rochet, M., El-Hage, W., Richa, S., Kazour, F., Atanasova, B. (2018). Depression, olfaction, and quality of life: A mutual relationship. *Brain Sciences, 8,* 80–102.

Ruppel, E. K., Burke, T. J., & Cherney, M. R. (2018). Channel complementarity and multiplexity in long-distance friends' patterns of communication technology use. *New Media & Society, 20,* 1564–1579.

Ryu, J., & Jeon, J. (2011). Influence of noise sensitivity on annoyance of indoor and outdoor noises in residential buildings. *Applied Acoustics, 72,* 336–340.

Sallis, J. F., & Kerr, J. (2008). Physical activity and the built environment. In L. K. Guerrero & M. L. Hecht (Eds.), *The nonverbal communication reader: Classic and contemporary readings* (3rd ed., pp. 270–286). Prospect Heights, IL: Waveland.

Sandberg, J. (2003, March 2). Want to know someone's job status? Look at desk location. *Corpus Christi Caller Times,* p. D4.

Sanders, M., Gustanski, J., & Lawton, M. (1974). Effect of ambient illumination on noise level of groups. *Journal of Applied Psychology, 59,* 527–528.

Shen, M., Shi, L., & Gao, Z. (2018). Beyond the food label itself: How does color affect attention to information on food labels and preference for food attributes? *Food Quality & Preference, 64,* 47–55.

Sonnentag, S., Reinecke, L., Mata, J., & Vorderer, P. (2017). Feeling interrupted—being responsive: How online messages relate to affect at work. *Journal of Organizational Behavior, 39,* 369–383.

Spangenberg, E., Crowley, A., & Henderson, P. (1996). Improving the store environment: Do olfactory cues affect evaluations and behaviors? *Journal of Marketing, 60,* 67–80.

Stamps, A. E., III. (2011). Effects of area, height, elongation, and color on perceived spaciousness. *Environment & Behavior, 43,* 252–273.

Stein, S. (2008). Communicating with color. In L. K. Guerrero & M. L. Hecht (Eds.), *The nonverbal communication reader: Classic and contemporary readings* (3rd ed., pp. 287–288). Prospect Heights, IL: Waveland. (Reprinted from *Women in Business, 58,* p. 14, 2006)

Steinberg, B. (2011). Home-improvement TV still going strong on cable despite soft market. *Advertising Age, 82,* 13.

Syndicus, M., Weise, B. S., & van Treeck, C. (2018). In the heat and noise of the moment: Effects on risky decision-making. *Environment & Behavior, 50,* 3–27.

Tatum, N. T., Martin, J. C., & Kemper, B. (2018). Chronemics in instructor-student e-mail communication: An experimental examination of student evaluations of instructor response speeds. *Communication Research Reports, 35*, 33–41.

TenBrink, T., Andonova, E., Schole, G., & Coventry, K. R. (2017). Communicative success in spatial dialogue: The impact of functional features and dialogue strategies. *Language & Speech, 60*, 318–329.

Toma, C. (2018). Connection, conflict, and communication technologies: How romantic couples use media for relationship management. In Z. Papacharissi (Ed.), *A networked self and love* (pp. 61–85). New York: Routledge.

Trasande, L., Cronk, C., Durkin, M., Weiss, M., Schoeller, D. A., Gall, E. A., et al. (2009). Environment and obesity in the National Children's Study. *Environmental Health Perspectives, 117*, 159–166.

United Press International. (2013, April 7). Actor Wendell Pierce opens food stores. Retrieved from http://www.upi.com/Health_News/2013/04/07/Actor-Wendell-Pierce-opens-food-stores/UPI-48171365314477/

van Rompay, T., Tanja-Dijkstra, K., Verhoeven, J. W. M., & van Es, A. F. (2012). On store design and consumer motivation: Spatial control and arousal in the retail context. *Environment and Behavior, 44*(6), 800–820.

Veitch, J. A., Stokkermans, M. G. M., & Newsham, G. R. (2011). Linking lighting appraisals to work behaviors. *Environment & Behavior, 45*, 198–214.

von Castell, C., Stelzmann, D., Oberfeld, D., Welsch, R., & Hecht, H. (2018). Cognitive performance and emotion are indifferent to ambient color. *Color Research & Application, 43*, 65–74.

Vries, A. D., Souman, J. L., Ruyter, B. D., Heynderickx, I., & Kort, Y. D. (2018). Lighting up the office: The effect of wall luminance on room appraisal, office workers' performance, and subjective alertness. *Building & Environment, 142*, 534–543.

Weinstein, N. D. (1978). Individual differences in reactions to noise: A longitudinal study in a college dormitory. *Journal of Applied Psychology, 63*, 458–466.

Wells, M., & Thelen, L. (2002). What does your workspace say about you? The influence of personality, status, and workspace on personalization. *Environment & Behavior, 43*, 300–321.

Wells, N. M., Ashdown, S. P., Davies, E. H. S., Cowett, F. D., & Yang, Y. (2007). Environment, design, and obesity: Opportunities for interdisciplinary collaborative research. *Environment & Behavior, 39*, 6–33.

Weng, S. J., Gotcher, D., & Juo, C. F. (2017). Lining up for quick service—the business impact of express lines on fast-food restaurant operations. *Journal of Foodservice Business Research, 20*, 65–81.

Wexner, L. B. (1954). The degree to which colors (hues) are associated with mood-tones. *Journal of Applied Psychology, 38*, 432–435.

Winslow, L. (2017). "Not exactly a model of good hygiene": Theorizing an aesthetic of disgust in the Occupy Wall Street movement. *Critical Studies in Media Communication, 34*, 278–292.

Wong, M. S., Chan, K. S., Jones-Smith, J. C., Colantuoni, E., Thorpe, R. J. Jr., & Bleich, S. N. (2018). The neighborhood environment and obesity: Understanding variation by race/ethnicity. *Preventive Medicine, 111*, 371–377.

chapter four

PROXEMICS: OUR USE OF SPACE

chapter outline

After studying this chapter, you should be able to

1. define *proxemics*;
2. identify Hall's four zones of space and the kind of communication that typically occurs within each zone;
3. increase your awareness of the factors influencing people's proxemic behavior;
4. improve your perceptual skills to better appreciate the spatial boundaries of others;
5. define territoriality, identify the three types of territories, and provide examples of each type;
6. explore the various ways people protect and defend their territories from violation, invasion, and contamination;
7. know the difference between crowding and density;
8. outline the various ways people nonverbally cope with high-density, crowded conditions;
9. understand the relationship between privacy and proxemics;
10. identify and define the four dimensions of privacy; and
11. understand the basic components of communication privacy management theory.

case study

WHEN A HOSPITAL ROOM BECOMES A HOME

Most people take their personal space very seriously. Additionally, people feel a sense of ownership when it comes to space and personal property. Even if we aren't at home, we may still claim a space as our own. It could be our office at work, our table at the dining hall, our favorite seat in a classroom, or our car. For some, a sense of ownership over a space comes in one of the most unexpected places—a hospital room, which is what research team Marin, Gasparino, and Puggina (2018) examined.

We tend to consciously and unconsciously structure the space around us. This space may include walls, furniture, décor, or informal space like the personal bubble of space that surrounds each person. When individuals are staying in a hospital, their personal space is usually made vulnerable by hospital staff members' intrusions, for such things as checking vital signs, conducting various tests and procedures, or simply maintaining the room (Marin, Gasparino, & Puggina, 2018). Patients may become uncomfortable if medical staff enters the room without announcing their presence beforehand. (Hospitals are notoriously bad places to get any rest!) Room occupants may experience increasing displeasure if staff moves their personal belongings without consent (Marin, Gasparino, & Puggina, 2018). This study shows how we are often put into situations where we have to negotiate boundaries and ownership of space. We don't own our hospital rooms; in fact, we often have to share them with other patients. But such a situation doesn't negate our tendency to want to delineate and protect a space. By studying proxemics in this chapter, you will learn how to better communicate your needs and respond to the needs of others regarding ownership of the various types of space.

> "I felt dirty! He totally violated my personal bubble."
> "We have a boundary problem, because she invades my space all the time."
> "I still love you, but I just really need some space!"

What do these statements have in common? They all relate to an aspect of nonverbal communication called **proxemics**—the way distance and space play a communicative role in our everyday life. As you've moved through life, you've likely met a wide range of people who either have little awareness of others' personal space needs or who seem distant or hard to get to know. Either way, how we manage our own personal space, our awareness of others' personal space, and, ultimately, how we interact with others in a variety of spaces are important as we continue our study of nonverbal communication.

PROXEMICS AS NONVERBAL COMMUNICATION

The goal of this chapter is to make you more aware of proxemics as a key code of nonverbal communication. The connections among people, space, and distance need to be made for three reasons: (1) Our preferences regarding the distance and space in which we live, work, and play reveal a good deal about who we are as people; (2) our verbal and nonverbal communication is impacted by distance and space; and (3) we use metaphors of distance and space to talk about our relationships as they develop, redefine, or come to an end (Henderson, 2011; Kaminka, 2018; Kim, Zauberman, & Bettman, 2012; Matthews, Derlega, & Morrow, 2006; Sahlstein, 2010; Sanz, 2014).

Physical versus Psychological Space

Imagine that you're standing in line to get coffee, and, while waiting, you check your mobile banking on your phone. You enter your username and password on the app, and you begin to realize that someone behind you is standing way too close; that person could have actually seen what you just typed on your phone. Could your banking get comprised? In a situation such as this, our space is violated, making us feel surveyed, threatened, and unsafe. Has anyone ever stood too close to you in a public space, such as a sporting event or concert? We've all likely had these experiences at one time or another, and they remind us of the powerful force of proxemics. The space within which we communicate, as well as how we feel about that space, influences our communicative decisions.

As we begin to explore this fascinating topic, it's important to contrast physical space with psychological space. **Physical space** refers to where we communicate and how we interact within a given space, as well as how much space is available. We know from the environment chapter that physical spaces serve as a form of nonverbal communication; they also have a profound effect on the people

Others may violate your personal space without your knowledge and compromise your personal information.

who communicate within them. **Psychological space** is the impact of space on our attitude, mood, and emotionality. An easy way to understand psychological space is to consider how you respond or think about particular situations, such as being confined in a small room (for example, trapped in an elevator), being backed into a corner, or having a "space invader" stand close enough to read what's on your phone. Can you think of a situation in which your psychological space got the best of you? How did the experience affect your attitude, mood, and emotions?

Hall's Zones of Space

Anthropologist Edward T. Hall (1959, 1963, 1966, 1968, 1983) has helped us understand proxemics by providing a classification system of four spatial zones, sometimes referred to as conversational distances.

- ZONE 1, Intimate Space: 0 to 1½ feet between communicators. Intimate space is considered the most personal for communication and is usually reserved for those who are emotionally close to us, such as dear friends, partners, and spouses. At times when we get stuck in a crowd or a cramped elevator, we're

We typically allow those who are emotionally close to us into our intimate space.

reminded that people may be in our intimate space by necessity, not invitation.

chapter four

- ZONE 2, Personal Space: 1½ to 4 feet of space between communicators. The conversations we have with our family and friends (and, occasionally, coworkers) usually take place within this zone.
- ZONE 3, Social Space: 4 to 12 feet of space between communicators. Social space is exhibited in professional life and in most educational contexts, although teaching and learning between teachers and young children may involve smaller ranges of space than higher educational levels. Group interactions also tend to take place within social space.
- ZONE 4, Public Space: 12 feet and beyond between communicators. Public space generates communication that usually is not personal in nature. When speakers present in a meeting room or auditorium, the audience is typically at least 12 feet away. Of course, the distance varies according to the physical setting, the occasion, and the speaker's preferences.

An understanding of spatial zones is important to your everyday nonverbal communication competency. Look at the list of zones again and reflect on how your use of spatial zones varies across the many relationships in your life. While proxemics plays a communicative function that helps shape our perceptions of and interactions with others in U.S. culture, we must also remember that expectations and use of space vary as we interact with members of other cultures. In fact, nonverbal scholar Judee Burgoon and colleagues suggest that the distance we manage in our communication with others is based on our cultural and personal expectations (Burgoon, 2016).

REMEMBER

Remember! 4.1

Proxemics	The way distance and space play a communicative role in everyday life
Physical space	Where we communicate and how we interact within a given space, as well as how much space is available
Psychological space	Effect of space on attitude, mood, and emotionality
Intimate space	A distance of 0 to 1½ feet between communicators; considered the most personal range for communication
Personal space	A distance of 1½ to 4 feet between communicators; conversations with family members and friends usually take place within this zone
Social space	A distance of 4 to 12 feet between communicators; used in professional life and many social contexts
Public space	A distance of 12 feet and beyond; usually not personal in nature

FACTORS INFLUENCING THE MANAGEMENT OF SPACE ■ ■ ■ ▬

Why do you stand a certain distance from people in conversation? Are you perfectly comfortable in the middle seat in an airplane, with a stranger on either side of you? Why might you cozy up to one person but keep your distance from another? Why do some people get too close in conversation, while others stay farther away than you're used to? According to research, certain factors influence how we manage our own personal space and how we use proxemics when we relate to other people in everyday life (Gan, 2011; Lewis, Patel, D'Cruz, & Cobb, 2017).

Cultural Background

As we said in Chapter 1, some nonverbal behaviors are innate, such as facial expressions that have universal applications and interpretations, as Charles Darwin (1872/1965) argued. But we learn many more nonverbal cues as we experience life within our cultural settings. Thus, cultural background is a key factor in our understanding and acquisition of nonverbal cues, and space management is no exception (Dong-Hoo, 2010; Gobel, Chen, & Richardson, 2017; Li & Li, 2007; Kemper, 2012; Manusov, 2008; Matsumoto, 2006; Matsumoto & Hwang, 2013; Pearce & Woodford-Smith, 2012). Hall's zones of space are culturally rooted—as are many, if not all, of our beliefs about appropriate nonverbal cues. Hall (1966, 1968, 1983) contended that proxemic behavior was a major distinguishing factor among cultural groups.

Let's consider two interesting studies to help illustrate this point. One line of research examined the use of space in Japan, which contains dense urban areas where space is at a premium (Altman, 1975). In Japanese culture, specific types of space are given specific meanings because of the value placed on space. For example, street intersections are named rather than streets, because intersections are more important than streets in Japanese daily life. Rooms are identified according to their function, with structures such as movable walls and room dividers used to transform a space and enhance a room's functionality. This research also examined the Japanese people's tendency to miniaturize objects because of their cultural sense of space, producing such things as bonsai trees.

As a second example, Hall (1966) observed Arab cultures for their use of proxemics, noting significant differences between how Arabs and Westerners view public space and conversational distance. Arabs do not seek privacy in public spaces, preferring to converse intimately and viewing less-than-intimate conversations as rude. Such intimate conversational behaviors include close distances between people, direct and continuous eye contact, and frequent touch.

Think about all the cultural variations of proxemics within U.S. culture. While someone growing up in the plains states or Texas might prefer wide-open spaces where you can see the entire horizon, someone growing up in New York City might be uncomfortable with all that space, preferring the density and rhythms of a bustling city and tight living conditions that are more familiar. These environments and the cultural customs that come with them affect our proxemic expectations and behavior.

Some cities and communities have large populations of cultural/ethnic groups. Review the example provided in Chapter 3 of ethnic enclaves in St. Louis. Members of such groups may feel a sense of ownership over a certain area, and they may become agitated or uncomfortable when others enter that space (Hur & Jeffres, 1979; Kim, 2018). This same discomfort can emerge when non-minority students attend Historically Black Colleges and Universities or Hispanic Serving Institutions (Jayakumar & Adamian, 2017; Schneeweis, 2016; Zuk, Bierbaum, Chapple, Gorska, & Loukaitou-Sideris 2018).

Gender and Sexuality

Nonverbally, men and women are actually more alike than different. However, when we consider the influence of gender on our personal space management, some distinctive patterns emerge (Anand, Du Bois, Sher, & Grotkowski 2017; Hall, 2006; Jenkins & Finneman, 2018; Li & Li, 2007; Moore, 2017; Morman & Whitely, 2012; Shifman & Lemish, 2011). We talk in more depth about this topic (and a whole range of nonverbal cues) in Chapter 12 on gender, sexuality, and relationships, but for now, consider a few examples. For one, it seems to be socially acceptable in U.S. culture for women to sit next to each other at a movie theater, bar, or restaurant. It would likely seem weird to girls and women to put a seat between them in a public place. Yet, when we shift our focus to men and boys, some social force seems to tell them it's less than appropriate for them to sit right next to each other. They can and do sit next to each other, but it may cause some discomfort or lead them to joke their way through the behavior. One of your authors once saw three boys (probably around 10 years of age) sit on three separate rows in a movie theater, one right in front of each other. In fact, research documents a trend showing that American women's personal space tends to be smaller than that afforded to men, and invaded more frequently than men's (Hall, 2006; Henley, 2001). Studies show that female dyads tend to stand and sit closer together than do male dyads, with the male–female dyad standing and sitting the closest (Hall, 2006; Santilli & Miller, 2011). Sometimes, invasion of personal space results in sexual harassment or sexual assault (Dardis, Kraft, & Gidycz, 2017).

Back to the example of men leaving an empty seat next to or between each other. One explanation we've heard for this behavior is that men are just larger in size than most women and, thus, need more space. It could also be that the extra space tells everyone in the movie theater that these men aren't gay. Their spatial choices may communicate, "Look at us; we're straight." Of course, like we said earlier, some

© MAD_Production/Shutterstock.com

Gender and sexuality may influence our use of space in many settings, such as a movie theater or other public place.

men do sit next to each other at a movie. Does this mean they're more secure with their sexuality? While some cultures are more prohibitive than the United States regarding sexual orientation (such as some Middle Eastern cultures), other cultures are more open. In the United States, homophobia (a fear of being perceived or labeled as gay) isn't as rampant as it once was, but it still exists. The primary explanation we hear for men's spatial behavior relates to homophobia. Most women don't have to deal with this perception, because the latitude of acceptance for women's behavior tends to be wider than for men's. If two women sit close together in a public setting, even moving closer to whisper to each other, most people don't observe this behavior and think, "They must be lesbians." But many men are concerned that their nonverbal behavior will cause people to perceive them as gay (whether they're gay, straight, bisexual, transgender, or queer), and proxemics is one of the most prominent nonverbal clues to such perceptions (Rule, 2017).

Age

Researchers continue to explore the effects of age on a range of nonverbal cues (Feldman & Tyler, 2006; Macchi, Proietti, Gava, & Bricolo, 2015). Age seems to influence the management of space within most cultures (Sahlstein, 2010; Webb & Weber, 2003). Children have a need for affection and typically want to be close to their parents. We hear stories from parents whose children want to sleep in the same bed with mom and dad. Of course, this desire to be around their parents changes with development. For example, toddlers reach an age when they want to venture out from mom's or dad's grasp; it's common to see a parent chasing after some wayward 2-year-old who's enjoying a public adventure. Further along in life, junior high and high school students establish more and more space between themselves and others, particularly family members, as they form and clarify a sense of self. First dates, kisses, sexual experiences, communication with boyfriends and girlfriends, and so on tend to be private experiences for adolescents, occurring at a distance from the family. At times, such exploration can be painful to a parent who misses the hugs and closeness of a child who's now trying to find her or his own way in the world.

As we continue on into adulthood, some of us establish closer proxemics with a partner or spouse than with family members or friends, but for others of us it's the exact opposite—we may feel closer to (and exhibit closer distances when communicating with) our friends than anyone else. In terms of elders and proxemics, research is mixed. While some studies have found that elderly people's space is readily invaded by others, especially by caretakers who help them do things for themselves (much as one would help a child), other research shows that people often avoid touching and put greater distances between themselves and elders, to the elders' physical and psychological detriment (Hjälm, 2012; Murray, 2010; Tank Buschmann, Hollinger-Smith, & Peterson-Kokkas, 1999). While many people give elders a wider berth than they do younger people or their peers, perhaps believing that the

elders' frailty demands more space to maneuver, others assume that elderly people can't take care of themselves and so invade their space to tend to them. Perhaps we should all think about how we behave with our elders, in terms of proxemics and other nonverbal cues, and consider what we'll want when we become elderly.

Status

As we discuss in Chapter 5 on physical appearance, certain physical characteristics communicate messages of status, power, and dominance in U.S. culture—one such characteristic being height. Research has consistently documented a connection between height, credibility, and status, all of which affect the management of space (Galobardes et al., 2012; Osensky, 2017; Valtonen, 2013).

A person's status within society affects proxemic behavior in two ways: (1) A high-status person's use of space tends to differ from that of people with lower status, and (2) differences can be found in how others manage space in a high-status person's presence. In their review of this topic, nonverbal scholars Burgoon and Dunbar (2006) explain:

> Powerful people have access to more space, larger territories, and more private territories, which also afford their occupants or owners greater insulation from intrusion by others and more space in which to display other visible indications of their status and power. They may display more territorial markers, have easy access to others, and may have others' access regulated by gatekeepers—people such as receptionists who can prevent intrusions. In addition to access to space, dominance may also be expressed by taking up more physical space (i.e., a combination of enlarging one's size and occupying more space). (p. 289)

In the first sense we mentioned above, higher-status people tend to operate in larger bubbles of personal space than do lower-status people and also tend to invade others' space more readily (Canagarajah, 2013; Carney, Hall, & Smith LeBeau, 2005; Hall, Coats, & Smith LeBeau, 2005; Kabo, 2017). Think about officials and celebrities you've seen on TV or in person, or bosses you've worked for, especially ones who held a high status or a lot of power within the organization. Compared with people holding less status, those celebs or bosses probably took up more personal space, were less likely to have their space invaded by others, and were more likely to invade the space of lower-status people. In essence, their status made them freer to take and use more space than people with less status. People who are perceived to have a lot of power—and typically the wealth that comes along with power or that helped create their image—often move about in private or concealed transportation that insulates and protects their space (such as limousines with darkened windows or private planes). Many have an entourage—other people who act as buffers to prohibit anyone but a chosen few from entering into the zone of space around the powerful person.

This brings us to the second effect we mentioned, which goes along with the first: Not only do high-status people operate in more personal space, but they're also afforded more space by others

(Hellmann & Jucks, 2017; Prabhu, 2010). Unless you have no manners or are an aggressive reporter trying to get a statement from a public official, you're probably not going to cozy up to a high-status person and get in his or her face. That's considered too aggressive and downright rude in our culture. Most of us back off in the presence of a powerful person. It's fairly easy to spot this trend in action: Go to a courthouse or other public building where city officials work or have offices, and watch a high-ranking public official move about in the lobby of the building. It's common to see a high-status person walk toward an area that's dense with people and then see those people actually pull back from the space, allowing the higher-status person more room. We've seen this happen in situations where professors (whom we don't believe are high status, just typically older!) are given more space by students while waiting for an elevator, as well as inside the elevator compartment.

spotlight *on research*

The Bathroom Privacy Debate

When you think of a place where you expect privacy, a bathroom may come to mind. Bathroom privacy for LGBTQ individuals is a highly contested topic in the United States, related to privacy and ownership of space. Recently, a lot of attention has been paid to transgender individuals' bathroom use, especially those trans persons serving in our military. Some argue that transgender individuals should have full and equal access to the bathroom that aligns with their gender identity or whichever bathroom they're most comfortable using. Others counter that such allowance violates the privacy of non-transgender men and women; thus, transgender individuals should use the bathroom that aligns with their sex assigned at birth.

Scholar Sheila Cavanagh (2013) focused on the narratives of people identifying as queer, to depict the strain and tension they often encounter when using public restrooms. Utilizing performance ethnography (an approach that weaves together communication theory with theatricality, to engage readers), Cavanagh depicted these persons' narratives in an artful and authentic way. She combined the narratives and labeled them Queer Bathroom Monologues. One narrative illustrates the experience of a young trans woman who used the women's restroom at a pub. The trans woman encountered two other women in the restroom who were frightened by her presence, one who screamed that someone should call the police because "there's a boy in the washroom" (Cavanagh, 2013, p. 295).

What impact does Cavanagh's research have on you as a student of nonverbal communication? What do these narratives teach us about proxemics as a nonverbal cue? Our use of space and attitudes about space invasion reflect our beliefs and values, rooted in culture, as well as our gender, sexuality, and identity.

Do you want to know more about this research? If so, read Cavanagh, S. L. (2013). Affect, performance, and ethnographic methods in *Queer Bathroom Monologues*. *Text and Performance Quarterly, 33*, 286-307.

Physical Characteristics

Some of the information in this section may overlap with the previous one, because in U.S. culture as well as other cultures around the world, the physical characteristics of height and weight are connected with status, as are other appearance factors such as clothing, artifacts, and certain aging cues (Burgoon & Dunbar, 2006; Roces, 2013). Research on this topic isn't extensive, but some evidence shows that height affects how people manage space, with shorter people being more likely than taller people to use and invite others into closer interpersonal distances (Caplan & Goldman, 1981; Osensky, 2017). In addition, people who are considered overweight by cultural standards are generally afforded more personal space than people who aren't overweight (Smith & Holm, 2010; Venturini, Castelli, & Tomelleri, 2006).

Do you see evidence of these research trends in your daily life? What happens when a very tall person and a very short person have a conversation—whose approach to space usually rules? Perhaps these people try to adjust to the height difference by sitting down, so that the space in which a conversation takes place becomes more manageable and equitable. What about in the weight arena—do you see evidence of the differences research alludes to? Are you likely to make more space for an overweight or obese person coming toward you? We don't necessarily believe this to be discriminatory or purposeful behavior, although we realize that intentional nonverbal cues of isolation or disapproval are often communicated. But obese people often talk about feeling ostracized by others' reactions to their appearance—from avoiding touch to discontinuing eye gaze to increasing distance.

We talk more about people with disabilities in the privacy management section of this chapter, but research over a couple of decades shows that people who do not have physical disabilities tend to use greater distances when talking to people who do. However, as a conversation progresses over time, the distance generally decreases (Braithwaite, 1991; Grech, 2011; Jeanes & Magee, 2012; Kelly & Carson,

As conversation progresses over time, the distance between a person who has a physical disability and one who does not generally decreases.

2012). Sometimes, people with disabilities are actually given more personal space due to the societal stigma surrounding disability (Hickey-Moody, 2016; Kilbury, Bordieri, & Wong, 1996; Marini, Wang, Etzbach, & Del Castillo, 2013). In one study of space afforded blind people, researchers found that people gave a blind person using a white cane 6 times as much space as they gave a blind person not using a cane (Conigliaro, Cullerton, Flynn, & Rueder, 1989). Some people are cautious when approaching people in wheelchairs, affording them more space because of their disability and means of getting around. Some of this distancing behavior is understandable—if you've ever tried to help someone in a wheelchair maneuver to enter a classroom or exit an elevator, you know what we mean. But some distancing is discriminatory, as though the sight of someone with a disability is unnerving and the added space serves to protect or insulate the able-bodied person from the reality of disabled bodies. Think about your own behavior in this regard and see if you need to make some changes.

Characteristics of the Relationship

Use your common sense and experience to consider these questions: Who tends to exhibit closer interpersonal distances—friends or intimates (such as sexual partners)? Friends or coworkers? Friends or strangers? You've probably decided that the more intimate the relationship, meaning the better the people know each other, the more comfortable they are using closer proxemics when interacting. You're right! Research shows that conversational distances are affected by the type of relationship the interactants have, meaning that friends tend to talk at a more intimate distance than strangers; friends talk more closely than coworkers (unless the coworkers happen also to be friends); and intimate partners, such as dating or married partners, maintain closer interpersonal distances than other combinations of people (Andersen, Guerrero, & Jones, 2006; Fagundes & Schindler, 2012; Okken, van Rompay, & Pruyn, 2012; Sluzki, 2016; Szpak, Nicholls, Thomas, Laham, & Loetsher, 2016).

Subject Matter

Imagine you're having dinner with a close friend. As you shove down the chips and salsa, you chat about your day, what's going on at school and work, and so forth. Then, before your huge platter of fajitas has arrived, your friend leans toward you across the booth, lowers her or his voice to a whisper, opens his or her eyes wide, and says, "Guess what I heard about our friend so-and-so?" In anticipation of a juicy story, you respond by leaning toward your friend, decreasing the distance between the two of you so you can better hear the interesting news. You're "all ears," as the saying goes, and don't really want the food to come until you've heard the "scoop." Your proxemic behavior has just been influenced by the subject matter under discussion.

While this sounds sort of intuitive (kind of "duh"), research has actually examined this very thing—the effects of topic of conversation on proxemic behavior (Lannutti, 2013). In fact, research focused on subject matter and proxemics started many years ago. For instance, scholar Robert Sommer (1961) studied proxemics in conversation but insisted that subjects use impersonal topics, because he knew that the intimacy level of the topic would affect how subjects positioned themselves. Other studies have focused on such elements as proxemic movements (forward and backward lean by people in conversation) that mark critical segments of an interaction, such as beginning and ending phases and topic shifts (Erickson, 1975), as well as the effects on proxemic behavior of receiving positive feedback (such as praise) or negative information (such as an insult). In Leipold's (1963) study, subjects distanced themselves from people who gave negative information, such as an insult, but used shorter distances with people who gave praise. In situations where we're placed in close quarters with people we barely know or have just met, conversation can be sparse or, at best, superficial because of the awkwardness of the situation (Schulz & Barefoot, 1974). That's why people rarely talk on elevators, unless they get on with someone they know.

Setting

This factor is fairly obvious, because we all know that the environment or setting for an interaction affects our behavior. For example, the presence or absence of noise in a setting often affects proxemic behavior, as confirmed by a study that revealed noise to be one of the most common complaints of restaurant patrons in the United States (Daley, 2012). In a social situation such as a club where loud music is playing, we might move closer to someone and lean in to talk, not because we're attracted or interested but simply because we can't hear the person over the roar of the music and other people's conversations. Perhaps you find yourself in a setting where people are whispering, which makes you curious, so you move closer to them so you can overhear their conversation. If there's too much space and interaction is a challenge, we're likely to work to change the physical setting so communication can occur. We see this behavior a lot in the learning environment, where some students will position themselves in the first couple of rows in a lecture hall—not because they want to suck up to the teacher or they're necessarily enraptured by the course topic but simply because they find they can hear and focus better (and learn more) when closer to the front (McKellin, Shahin, Hodgson, Jamieson, & Pichora-Fuller, 2011).

Settings such as a crowded subway can influence your expectations of space.

TERRITORIALITY ■ ■ ■

Another concept related to our study of proxemics is **territoriality**—our sense of ownership of an object, a particular space, a person, or even time. This territory is *ours* (or at least we have come to think of it as ours)—personal, special, and possibly even expensive (e.g., gifts that cost a lot of money, such as jewelry or a new computer). We want our territory to be safe from intrusion by unwelcome outsiders or strangers, and we will use our best verbal and nonverbal means of defending it from those we perceive as invaders.

What territory is *your* territory? Perhaps you're thinking of personal possessions such as purses, book bags, laptop computers, smartphones, or even your room or home. More than likely, you work to protect those objects and prevent those places you regard as your territory from being tarnished or invaded. What about people as territory? Maybe the thought of people as territory is distasteful to you, but we probably all know people who view their boyfriend or girlfriend as their own private territory, and they may become seriously forceful when they believe their territory is being invaded or violated. (Some people are territorial about their pets!) Many of us are protective of our time, defending any hard-fought "private time" to extremes because it's such a precious commodity in our lives. A simple phone call from a solicitor during our personal time can be met with severe frustration. Let's first consider a helpful way of classifying territory, then take up the topic of territorial invasion.

Types of Territory

Communication scholar Irwin Altman (1975) categorized territory into three types: (1) primary, (2) secondary, and (3) public. Extent of ownership is the key factor that separates one type of territory from the other. **Primary territories** (e.g., homes, bedrooms, vehicles) have a clear owner; access by others is limited. Clear rules or barriers such as locks, access codes, and passwords function to protect the territory from invasion or intrusion. Because of unwanted invasion, owners tend to protect their primary territory with intense emotion and, in some cases, aggression.

Secondary territories are important but not as important to the owner or as exclusive as primary territories. A secondary territory generally is not owned by anyone, but people develop a sense of ownership over the space (Erlandson, 2012). Examples include one's dorm room (or side of a shared room), a family pew at a church, someone's parking space (not labeled with a name but seen as owned because a person consistently parks there), a favorite barstool or booth at a routinely frequented restaurant, and a field or court in a gym where teams practice or scrimmage. Since we know we don't really own these spaces, we often use **territorial markers** as nonverbal signals to others that the space is taken or reserved. Markers may include such possessions as notebooks or clothing, other objects in the environment that can be manipulated to "save" a place (such as a chair tilted against a table), or decorations such as ribbons and bows across church pews at weddings, signifying that those rows are reserved for family members. Conflicts often arise over secondary territories because people may have different interpretations of who has the right to enter or occupy the space. If you have a favorite hangout, for example, and a group of visitors from out of town "invades" that hangout, such that you can't sit where you normally sit or do what you normally do there, you may feel some animosity as a result. You have no real right of ownership, but you *feel* that the space is yours.

Public territories are those spaces open to anyone for temporary ownership, and these areas typically do not arouse feelings of invasion. A city bus or subway, a public library, a beach, parks, streets, public buildings such as courthouses, and walkways are all public territories. But these territories can still be invaded, such as when someone turns his or her music up too loud on a public bus, forcing everyone else to "appreciate" their musical tastes, or when someone behaves in an inappropriate or unlawful way, violating the expectations or laws governing a space. An invasion of public space usually has to be extreme for our sense of territoriality to be evoked.

Sociologist Erving Goffman (1971) identified "eight territories of self" as a means of classifying the spaces we experience around us:

1. *Personal space* is territory we reserve as ours and protect and defend vigorously from intrusion. Examples include a home office, closet, or bedroom.

2. *Stalls* are spaces that have designated boundaries for individual use. Study rooms in a university library, public restroom stalls, and parking spaces are examples.

3. *Use space* describes those areas close to our occupied surroundings where we go to perform certain daily tasks. Examples include check-out areas at grocery stores, hotel check-in counters, slot machines in casinos, designated smoking areas, or spaces where people take their turns during a bowling match, golf tournament, or other event.

4. *Turns* represent spaces that are governed by social norms and expectations. We often hear reference to people "waiting for their turn" in line at a hotdog stand or Starbucks. When turns are violated, people tend to get angry and frustrated because they expect their territorial claims to be respected and honored.

5. *Sheaths* pertain to our skin, artifacts, and clothing we use to cover and protect our bodies. While clothing and artifacts (e.g., eyeglasses, makeup) protect and adorn the body and provide privacy, we may choose to forgo that privacy, for example, by wearing clothing that reveals the hard work we put in at the gym.

6. *Possessional territory* refers to the use of personal possessions to mark or claim our surroundings, like those we mentioned when we defined territorial markers. At movie theaters, sporting events, concerts, and picnics, people like to mark their territory with personal possessions such as blankets, handbags, clothing, and water bottles. In a college classroom, students who want to sit near one another often use personal possessions to mark surrounding desks as territory for friends who have not yet arrived to class. You may have a particular spot in the library or student center that you mark and protect so you can limit who comes into that space.

7. *Informational preserves* pertain to a means of protecting information we deem private and that others aren't welcome to view. Personal computers, tablets, smartphones, information posted to our Facebook page or sent to our e-mail account, and traditional mailboxes are examples of information territory.

8. *Conversational preserves* are locations where we talk about intimate or private matters. Some dating or married couples may request a booth when dining out because they want to have conversational preserve for their discussion. You can probably think of times when someone has said, "Let's go someplace where we can talk privately."

REMEMBER

Remember!
4.2

Territoriality	Our sense of ownership of an object, a particular space, a person, or even our time
Primary territories	Territories that have a clear owner and rules or barriers that serve to mark or protect them from invasion
Secondary territories	Territories that are not as important to the owner or as exclusive as primary territories; spaces that one does not own but over which one develops a sense of ownership
Territorial markers	Nonverbal signals to others that a space is taken or reserved
Public territories	Spaces that are open to anyone for temporary ownership

Territorial Violation, Invasion, and Contamination

Another important aspect of understanding our nonverbal behavior with regard for proxemics involves how we protect territory from encroachment (Brown & Robinson, 2011; Costa, 2012). Three types of encroachment are typically viewed as negative: violation, invasion, and contamination (Lyman & Scott, 1967). **Violation** is the most general category of the three, and it means the use of or intrusion into primary territory—usually particular spaces or objects that we view as our personal belongings—without our permission. Parents going through their teenager's room looking for empty beer bottles or drugs exemplifies a violation of territory. Maybe you had an infamous roommate who violated your personal territory by using your expensive shampoo or reading text messages on your phone that you left on. One of our students complained of a roommate who violated their computer by downloading pornographic images and neglecting to remove the images before leaving school!

Invasion is an intense and typically permanent encroachment that is driven by an intention to take over a given territory. The original owner of the territory is often forced out during or after the invasion. Several levels of invasion are important to understand. The first level is large in scale, such as when one country invades another with the intention of expanding its land mass and power. A second level, smaller in scale but still powerful, is exemplified when groups or individuals take over a situation or even a conversation, such as when gangs claim or mark territories with painted symbols, staking out their turf. Yet another level, which is more subtle, can be seen in public places when settings are intruded on. Perhaps you've experienced a situation in

Some groups use graffiti as a way to mark their perceived territories.

which you were enjoying some solitude at a public park or beach, when someone or a group of people arrived and suddenly your solitude was gone.

Contamination is a type of encroachment in which a territory is tarnished with noise or impurity. Maybe you've heard someone complain, "They came to the party late and trashed the place!" Contamination is about doing something to a territory that symbolizes your presence, such as leaving cigarette butts and beer bottles in someone's backyard or wearing someone's sweater and returning it reeking of perfume or smoke. As another example, contamination occurs when neighbors allow their little pack of dogs to come into our yard and leave us fecal presents that we don't find until it's time to mow the lawn.

WHAT WOULD *YOU* DO

Jerikah and Jace are meeting at the library to work on a class project. They've been working on this project for most of the semester, and they always meet at 7pm on Tuesday nights in the library. When they arrive on the second floor, they notice that a sweatshirt has been left on the table in the study nook they use each week. Thinking that someone must have left it behind, Jerikah and Jace move the sweatshirt. If someone doesn't come back for it while they're working, they'll take it to the front desk. After placing their bags at the table, they go around the corner to fill up their water bottles. Upon returning, they notice that their belongings have been moved off the table to a couch nearby. A group of women is sitting at the table, and the infamous sweatshirt is hanging on the back of one of the chairs where the women are sitting.

What would you do if you were Jerikah or Jace? Would you be worried that the people at the table went through your stuff before moving it? What type of territory was that library table? What territorial markers were present? Who should have ownership of that area—the people who got there first or Jerikah and Jace who use that space every week? Is some sort of discussion or confrontation advisable?

Our defense of territory varies in style and intensity. Knapp, Hall, and Horgan (2013) provide the following questions to help us analyze territorial infractions:

1. Who violated our territory?
2. Why did she or he violate our territory?
3. What type of territory was it?
4. How was the violation accomplished?
5. How long did the encroachment last?
6. Do we expect further violations in the future?
7. Where did the violation occur?

We may believe that a violation is severe at first, but when we answer the first question (who did it?), we may find out it was someone we really like or are close to, making the offense more forgivable than if someone else did it. Or we may learn that the person has a really good reason for the invasion, and so we don't feel as violated once we find out why the incident occurred.

VIC, THE LOUSY ROOMMATE

Remember!
4.3

One of our former students, Ian Samples, gave us an easy way to remember the material in this chapter about territorial encroachment. With his permission, we thought we'd pass it along to you. Here's the story of Vic, the lousy roommate.

Imagine you come back to your apartment one night and Vic is using your laptop, working on a paper. Vic has a perfectly good computer of his own in his room, but for some reason, he's using yours. When you ask Vic about this—why he went into your room, got your laptop out of your book bag, and started using it without your permission—Vic explains that he wanted to watch TV in the living room while working on his paper. Since his computer isn't portable, he used your laptop instead. This type of encroachment is a **violation** of primary territory.

But not only is Vic working on your laptop, he's also sitting in your chair while he works and watches TV. You brought that chair from home. It's your favorite chair, and you always sit in it—not Vic, or anyone else for that matter. Yet here Vic is, sitting in your chair and using your laptop. This type of encroachment is an **invasion**.

To make matters worse, Vic decided he was hungry while working on his paper (on your laptop in your favorite chair), so he helped himself to some crackers from the kitchen. The problem is, you now have cracker crumbs in the seat cushion of your favorite chair and all over the keyboard of your laptop, down in some of the cracks between the keys, along with Vic's greasy fingerprints. Strike three for Vic! Not only has he violated your territory, but he's invaded your space and **contaminated** it with his food and greasy fingers.

Vic is the worst kind of roommate, but his name helps us remember the three types of encroachment:

V = violation	The use of someone's primary territory without permission
I = invasion	An intense and typically permanent encroachment of territory that is driven by an intention to take over the territory
C = contamination	The tarnishing of someone's territory with noise or impurity

Classroom Environments as Student Territory

Teachers, particularly those who teach at elementary or secondary school levels, can be territorial about their classrooms. But students can also be protective of their classrooms, which is often surprising to teachers. Some students react negatively when people are in their classrooms who aren't supposed to be there (McLeod, Graham, & Bar, 2013). If you attend the same college for several years and tend to have your major classes in the same rooms, you can view those spaces as your secondary territory and become protective and defensive of them, as if they belong to you, your close friends, and your favorite professors. Students can even become territorial about whole campus buildings, such as the fine arts facility where theatre, music, and art students hang out, or the gym or field house where student athletes work out, practice, and gather. You may come to feel as though a campus area is your "home away from home."

How many of us arrive early for the first day of class to stake out a good seat? Perhaps some of us save a spot close by for a friend, or maybe we use a book bag or laptop to make it look as though someone is sitting in the seat next to us, only to reserve the area for more arm and leg room. Some teachers prefer to assign seats to make roll checking easier, while some will ask students to change their seating arrangements periodically (which usually isn't pretty). Our point is this: Students can be touchy about classroom space and territorial about where they sit.

CROWDING AND DENSITY ▪ ▪ ▪

Have you ever been in a situation where your personal space was violated simply because the crowd at a sporting event or concert was too large? Our individual perceptions of crowding tend to vary from one person to the next. The study of density and crowding gained popularity in the 1960s, as some people became concerned about an increasing world population (Erlich, 1971). For example, one classic study in Norway was conducted with rats to determine how they reacted to the overpopulation of a given space. Over time, the rats responded in negative, dramatic ways to their overcrowded conditions, leading to concerns about how human beings would behave in crowded, overpopulated situations (Calhoun, 1962).

Crowding is a psychological reaction to a perception of spatial restrictions (Judge, 2000). Perhaps you know someone who doesn't like to visit large cities simply because of the number of people and buildings there. When we think about large cities, it's important not to confuse crowding with **density**, defined as the number of people or objects in a space that have the potential to restrict or interfere with people's activities and the achievement of their goals (Machleit, Eroglu, & Powell Mantel, 2008; Phithakkitnukoon, Smoreda, & Olivier, 2012; Wang et al., 2012). Many people who live in high-density areas, such as major cities, learn over time to adjust to the constant invasion and disruption of their personal space.

One way to remember the difference between these two related concepts is to recall our earlier discussion in this chapter about physical and psychological space. Density is a physical dimension, whereas crowding is a psychological reaction based on perception. You may be in a small space with lots of other people (high density), yet not feel crowded because you're comfortable with the place and the people. Conversely, you may be in a wide-open space, but the people you're with, the occasion, or the topic under discussion make you feel crowded and give you the urge to get "outta there." Researchers have studied this distinction, finding that individual perceptions of life in high-density areas have more to do with people's daily experiences than the physical environments within which they live and work (Lomanowska & Guitton, 2012; Sommer, 1969).

How do people cope with high density? According to Knapp, Hall, and Horgan (2013), people cope in the following ways:

1. They spend less time with other people. For example, they engage in shorter exchanges with people because the perception becomes, over time, that there are just too many people to deal with.

2. They ignore or avoid low-priority interactions, such as those that might occur on the street, a city bus, or the subway. Sometimes, avoiding the pleasantries people may exchange in less dense, slower-paced areas (such as small towns) can lead people to make judgments that people in big cities are unfriendly, when actually the density of the setting contributes to the behavior.

3. They shift the responsibility for some transactions. They're aware of the time constraints and complexities of living in a high-density area, and this awareness affects their behavior. For example, they take responsibility for having correct change for the bus, relieving the bus driver of this task so as not to hinder others' entry onto the bus.

4. They simply block others out and become more restrictive about who they choose to connect and interact with. For example, many apartment buildings are guarded by attendants. The high density of an environment can cause people to ignore those who are homeless on the street or generally pay less attention to their surroundings.

© Isantilli/Shutterstock.com

Many upscale neighborhoods and buildings use security guards and cameras to reduce or remove high-density elements in their environment.

Crowding	A psychological reaction to a perception of spatial restrictions
Density	The number of people or objects in a space that have the potential to restrict or interfere with people's activities and the achievement of their goals

PRIVACY MANAGEMENT: AN EXTENSION OF PROXEMICS

Beyond the basics of proxemics as a key nonverbal communication code, let's now turn our attention to privacy, which we all know is an important commodity in everyday life. You may not have thought of it this way, but we use proxemic terms, such as *space* and *distance*, to understand and articulate the status of relationships in our lives. The following statements bear this out: "I feel really close to her." "We've grown apart." "He's been distant over the past few weeks." Beyond using space and distance to talk about and process what happens in our relationships, we also make decisions about boundaries, what private information to reveal and conceal based on how close or connected we feel to a given friend, family member, coworker, or romantic partner.

Privacy is "an interpersonal boundary-control process, which paces and regulates interaction with others" (Altman, 1975, p. 12). Several aspects of privacy are important to understand because of their relevance to our study of nonverbal communication. **Desired privacy** refers to the amount of contact we desire from others, while **achieved privacy** is the actual degree of contact that results from interaction with others. Altman explains that if "the desired privacy is equal to the achieved privacy, an optimum state of privacy exists. If achieved privacy is lower or higher than desired privacy—too much or too little contact—a state of imbalance exists" (pp. 10–11). Can you think of times when you desired to be around your friends and family, and then other times when you didn't want people around you at all? These instances when we restrict and seek interaction can be explained by thinking about privacy as a **dialectic process**, or an interplay between opposing forces, with varying balances of opening and closing the self to others.

Remember!
4.5

Privacy	An interpersonal boundary-control process, which paces and regulates interaction with others
Desired privacy	Amount of contact desired from others at a given point in time
Achieved privacy	Actual degree of contact that results from interaction with others
Dialectic process	Instances when we restrict and seek interaction; an interplay between opposing forces; different balances of opening and closing the self to others

Nonverbal communication scholar Judee Burgoon (1982) categorized dimensions of privacy, because people rarely experience complete privacy or a complete lack of privacy. Instead, people experience various degrees of privacy, described as follows:

1. **Physical privacy** is the degree to which someone is physically inaccessible to others.
2. **Social privacy** occurs when an individual or group opts to withdraw from social interaction.
3. **Psychological privacy** refers to people's ability to exercise control over the expression of their thoughts and feelings.
4. **Information privacy** pertains to people's ability to prevent the collection and distribution of information about themselves or their social networks without their knowledge or permission. (People have increasing concerns about this dimension, given the Internet age we now live in.)

REMEMBER

Remember!
4.6

Physical privacy	Degree to which someone is physically inaccessible to others
Social privacy	When an individual or group opts to withdraw from social interaction
Psychological privacy	People's ability to exercise control over the expression of their thoughts and feelings
Information privacy	People's ability to prevent the collection and distribution of information about themselves or their social networks without their knowledge or permission

chapter four

Communication Privacy Management

Leading privacy scholar in the communication discipline, Sandra Petronio (2000, 2002, 2007, 2013, 2015), developed **communication privacy management (CPM)** theory as a way of better understanding how we establish rules about privacy and manage privacy using spatial metaphors. As you study the information within this chapter on proxemics, it may help to think of privacy as your own little box of personal space—it's not a physical space but an intangible entity you hold dear. You develop rules about your little space, in terms of what you consider private, who has access to you and your private information, how you select those people you want to share private information with, how you actually go about sharing that information, what you expect the sharing of private information to do for (or to) a relationship, how you protect your privacy from intrusion by unwanted others, and so forth. Our privacy rules are in constant motion as we keep things in and let things out, as we draw people in but keep others out. Privacy is important to us all, even those of us who believe ourselves to be fairly open, because without privacy we lose control over who has access to us, who knows what about us, and what they do with that information. Because privacy is so important, we develop rules about how to manage it in our lives and relationships and tend to talk about it in spatial metaphors, like when someone says, "My husband and I have grown apart" or "You're distancing yourself from me. Is something wrong?"

Petronio (2002, 2015) suggests that private information is a form of **self-disclosure**, defined as the sharing of information that people can't learn about us unless we reveal it to them. Self-disclosure is a building block toward intimacy in a relationship, so how we handle the disclosure of private information is critical to the success of any relationship. As we've said, Petronio uses the metaphor of spatial boundaries to delineate the role of private information in relationships. Boundaries act as rules for managing privacy, meaning that we often "draw a line" on what information we will and will not share with people. For example, an instructor may place a symbolic spatial boundary around information about his or her personal life—a boundary that can't be penetrated by students. Many faculty believe that sharing private information with students is inappropriate and can confuse the relationship between teacher and student. Sometimes students attempt to push that boundary, asking inappropriate questions about an instructor's opinions or personal life. As another example, you may think it's perfectly fine to ask people about a medical condition they have or what medications they're taking. You may believe that such questions show your interest in learning more about living with such a condition. But many of us were raised believing that this sort of questioning is intrusive and "none of our business."

CPM theory has been used to examine the management of private information in various contexts (Petronio, 2013). For example, researchers have used CPM theory to better understand the following:

- protection of personal health information (Kordzadeh & Warren, 2017);
- relational bonding between parents and children (Child & Westermann, 2013; Petronio, 2017);
- teacher privacy (Hosek & Presley, 2018);

- efforts to control negative outcomes of private disclosures (Petronio & Bantz, 1991);
- instances of embarrassment (Child, Haridakis, & Petronio, 2012);
- the revelation of private information pertaining to gender and sexuality (Lannutti, 2013; Helens-Hart, 2017);
- how privacy functions in small groups (Plander, 2013);
- privacy issues for people with disabilities (Braithwaite, 1991); and
- self-disclosure via social media (e.g., Facebook, Twitter, Instagram; Baruh, Secinti, & Cemalcilar, 2017; Millham & Atkin, 2018; Worthington & Fitch-Hauser, 2018).

In this body of work, researchers have focused on privacy in face-to-face as well as online relational contexts and have highlighted the concerns of balancing the "private" with the "public." Some of these research applications of CPM theory warrant further discussion.

Teacher Privacy Management

As we've stated, people use space and distance to help them better understand and talk about their relationships; the same is true for teacher–student relationships (Hosek & Presley, 2018; Manca & Ranieri, 2017; McBride & Wahl, 2005; Thompson, Petronio, & Braithwaite, 2012). (By "teacher–student" relationship, we don't mean to imply anything romantic or sexual; we simply mean the connection between teachers and students for the purposes of education.)

In the educational context, instructors deal with privacy issues every day. **Teacher privacy management** pertains to those instances in which teachers make decisions about what private information they want to reveal or conceal in the process of creating a comfortable classroom where learning can take place. These decisions help teachers avoid the negative ramifications of inappropriate revelations and protect their personal lives outside the classroom (McBride & Wahl, 2005). When teachers talk about "boundaries" and establishing appropriate "distances" from their students, they use nonverbal proxemic terms to help guide their behavior and maintain their privacy. We've probably all heard stories in the media about teachers who didn't use good judgment in establishing and maintaining boundaries between themselves and their students. These are the tales of lawsuits and damaged lives.

People with Disabilities

We touched on nonverbal communication and physical disability earlier in this chapter in terms of proxemics; you'll see the topic raised in other chapters in this book as well. We deem it such an important topic that we cover it here as relates to privacy management. Do you have social contact with a person who has a physical disability? (Perhaps you *are* a person with a disability.) Some of us likely have friends and family members who are living with disabilities. Others can think of social situations in which we've avoided making eye contact with a person with a physical disability, maybe at a shopping mall or in an elevator. Or perhaps we've been overly helpful such that we call too much attention to someone's disability and not enough attention to the person *as a person*. Communication scholar Dawn Braithwaite is one of the leading researchers of communication about and among people with disabilities. In one of her early studies (Braithwaite, 1991), she examined the challenges people with disabilities face when it comes to managing private information about their disability. Sometimes people without disabilities ask personal, often embarrassing questions, as though a person's disability were an appropriate topic of conversation—like a shirt one wears or a book one reads. These questions might include how the person became disabled, how the person goes about her or his everyday life, and so forth (Braithwaite & Braithwaite, 2014; Duggan, Bradshaw, & Altman, 2010; Hickey-Moody, 2016; Reynolds, 2017). Have you breached a person's privacy boundary by asking questions or drawing too much attention to a disability?

OUT OF THE CLASSROOM
onto the page

A former student named Amber explained in a class session one day how people treated her differently because of the visible scars she'd received from a bad car accident. Amber felt that, when she sat somewhere in public or even in college classrooms, people would usually sit by her last. She thought that people viewed her differently and opted not to sit by her because of her scars, especially a large one on her face. Amber recounted how people tended to move closer to her when noticing her scars, some asking how she got her scars. Others would move in closer and offer statements of sympathy. Amber explained to the class how much these nonverbal actions and privacy intrusions bothered her. She wanted to be engaged in conversation because she was Amber, not someone with scars.

In this discussion, other students affirmed that they usually have questions about a person's disability before they think about that person's personality. It's unfortunate that disability can be a dehumanizing factor that changes communication and space management. Other students without disabilities revealed that they have difficulty talking to people with disabilities because they want to tread lightly or avoid offending them. Some didn't know if the person wanted their disability to be acknowledged or ignored.

What do you think about Amber's situation? What do you think about the comments from her classmates about communication and disability? Do you have any experiences to share regarding communication, space management, and disability? Have you personally felt like you've communicated differently or been communicated with differently because of disability? Will you approach situations of this type differently in the future after reading about Amber's experience?

Sometimes people without disabilities adjust their communication when interacting with people with disabilities. People with disabilities typically feel that this sort of adjustment isn't necessary because it calls too much attention to the disability and not enough to the *person* with the disability.

REMEMBER

Remember! 4.7

Communication privacy management (CPM)	Theory that explains how we manage privacy using spatial metaphors
Self-disclosure	The sharing of information that people cannot learn about us unless we reveal it to them
Teacher privacy management	Teachers' decisions about what private information they want to reveal or conceal

UNDERSTANDING PROXEMICS: APPLYING THE REFLEXIVE CYCLE OF NONVERBAL COMMUNICATION DEVELOPMENT

Have you ever thought about how you manage space in your own life? The first step to developing your skills and a better understanding of proxemic behaviors as a code of nonverbal communication is awareness. Just as we asked you to do for environment in the previous chapter, we ask you to inventory yourself using the following questions: What standards or expectations do you have regarding space management? What are your needs or preferences regarding the way other people use space? Do you have expectations or rules about such things as a personal bubble or comfort zone? Do these judgments vary depending on who the person is or whether your relationship with that person is personal, intimate, or professional in nature? Are you aware of the impressions others may form about you based on the way you use and manage space?

Now that you've engaged in an inventory of self regarding proxemics, it's time to think about making any appropriate changes, if necessary, to improve how you manage these nonverbal cues in your everyday life. This is Phase 2 in the Reflexive Cycle. Ask yourself: Are there some changes I need to make regarding my own proxemic behaviors (e.g., too close, too distant, space violations, invasions of territory, reactions to encroachment)? If so, how can I make those changes? Perhaps the only thing that needs to change is your level of awareness about how other people perceive and interpret your uses of space.

Beyond engaging in an inventory of self and making any appropriate changes, the next step is to inventory others. Can you think of a person who seems to have no awareness of space and distance? You may be thinking of a friend who gets too close to you in conversation, stands too far away during conversation, or has a restrictive personal bubble. These people may lack self-monitoring skills (the ability to be aware of one's own appropriateness in social situations) or may simply have no realization of how negatively their use of space is viewed by others. Think about a simple social situation, such as a gathering of some friends, as well as the person you are or might be dating. Your significant other doesn't sit next to you at the gathering; when you attempt to get the person to sit by you, he or she blows you off, which embarrasses you in front of your friends. How should you react? Is it time to end this relationship or simply ask your significant other to catch a clue? How might you sensitively find out what's going on?

Some people are oblivious to the fact that their use of space communicates something to other people about their attitude or level of interest. They aren't aware enough to consult with other people about outside observations and resulting interpretations of their use of space. We need to be aware that our use of space sends nonverbal signals to other people. Sometimes we get clues from people who react to our use of space to give us a sense of what message we're sending (e.g., "Back off!"; "Why are you getting so close?"). If someone were uncomfortable with or offended by your use of space, would you notice? What nonverbal signals would the person send? How might you respond?

After you've done an inventory of self, changed self, and inventoried others' nonverbal behavior, the fourth phase of the Reflexive Cycle involves interacting with others, trying out the changes you've made or are in the process of making, and observing people as you verbally and nonverbally interact with them. Do people react differently to you, as a result of any changes you made? For example, some people who tend to distance themselves from others may come to be seen as more friendly if they move closer in conversation. As another example, some people who are trying to become more sensitive to the way they manage space may be recognized for not getting so close or being inappropriate. It can be interesting to note people's reactions to both subtle and obvious changes in your use of space and how that makes you feel, as well as to gauge your own reactions to changes in others' use of space.

In the last part of the cycle, the challenge is to review and assess the whole process, making note of positive and negative aspects, and then begin the cycle again. The Reflexive Cycle of Nonverbal Communication Development is an ongoing process, one that helps us work to develop and improve our nonverbal sending and receiving abilities.

SUMMARY

Proxemics is a fascinating code of nonverbal communication that reveals a lot about how people feel about one another. In this chapter, we defined proxemics as the way distance and space play a communicative role in our everyday lives. Space can be physical or psychological. The different zones of communicative space or conversational distances include intimate, personal, social, and public. As we develop nonverbal communication skills in everyday life, it's important to consider cultural background, gender, sexuality, age, status, physical characteristics (such as having a disability), characteristics of the relationship between interactants, the subject matter of conversation, and the setting for an interaction. All of these factors can influence our proxemic behavior.

Next we discussed territoriality, defined as our sense of ownership of an object, a particular space, a person, or even time. Three major types of territory were examined in this chapter—primary, secondary, and public. We protect and defend our territory from violation (use of territory without permission) and invasion (an intense and typically permanent encroachment driven by an intention to take over territory). The final type of threat we discussed was contamination—a form of encroachment in which someone's territory is tarnished with noise or impurity.

We explored crowding and density as two elements within the study of proxemics that affect our verbal and nonverbal communication. Crowding can be defined as a psychological reaction to a perception of spatial restrictions, while density refers to the number of people or objects in a space that have the potential to restrict or interfere with people's activities and the achievement of their goals.

Then we addressed the fascinating and important topic of privacy, turning to communication privacy management theory to help explain the connection between proxemics and privacy. We often use

chapter four

spatial metaphors to better understand and communicate about our relationships. Managing our privacy by establishing and maintaining boundaries in our relationships is important as we develop connections with people over time. We encourage you to be consciously aware of your and others' nonverbal communication needs, expectations, and desires for privacy. The more we understand ourselves in relation to others regarding distance and space in both personal and professional life, the better prepared we will be to enter new relationships or to strengthen existing ones.

Finally, we applied the Reflexive Cycle of Nonverbal Communication Development to proxemics so that we can become more aware of our own spatial behavior, as well as that of others, to make any changes we deem necessary to help make us more effective communicators. We should keep all phases of the cycle in mind to improve our nonverbal communication. Such a critical assessment enables us to develop more awareness of self in terms of space, distance, and privacy expectations, needs, and desires.

DISCUSSION STARTERS ■ ■ ■

1. Can a space that a person doesn't own be personal? What about the contents of your shopping cart, your favorite table at a restaurant, or a parking space? Provide some examples of physical versus psychological space.

2. What are the three types of territory? What kinds of territorial markers are you likely to use to delineate your space? How do you react when someone invades your space?

3. Explain the three types of encroachment represented by Vic, the lousy roommate. What verbal and nonverbal responses would each type of encroachment trigger in you?

4. What's the difference between crowding and density? Can you feel crowded in a low-density space? Not crowded in a high-density space?

5. We spent a good deal of time discussing privacy in this chapter. Think about your own privacy needs and expectations, and then think of a time when your privacy was violated by someone. Was it an invasion of your private space or private information? How did the invasion make you feel, and how did you react?

REFERENCES ■ ■ ■

Altman, I. (1975). *The environment and social behavior.* Thousand Oaks, CA: Brooks/Cole.

Anand, L., Du Bois, S. N., Sher, T. G., & Grotkowski, K. (2017). Defying tradition: Gender roles in long-distance relationships. *The Family Journal, 26,* 22–30.

Andersen, P. A., Guerrero, L. K., & Jones, S. M. (2006). Nonverbal behavior in intimate interactions and intimate relationships. In V. Manusov & M. L. Patterson (Eds.), *The SAGE handbook of nonverbal communication* (pp. 259–277). Thousand Oaks, CA: Sage.

Baruh, L., Secinti, E., & Cemalcilar, Z. (2017). Online privacy concerns and privacy management: A meta-analytical review. *Journal of Communication, 67,* 26–53.

Braithwaite, D. O. (1991). "Just how much did that wheelchair cost?": Management of privacy boundaries by persons with disabilities. *Western Journal of Speech Communication, 55,* 254–274.

Braithwaite, D. O., & Braithwaite, C. A. (2014). "Which is my good leg?": Cultural communication of persons with disabilities. In L. A. Samovar, R. E. Porter, E. R. McDaniel, & C. Sexton Roy (Eds.), *Intercultural communication: A reader* (14th ed., pp. 162–173). Boston: Cengage Learning.

Brown, G., & Robinson, S. L. (2011). Reactions to territorial infringement. *Organization Science, 22,* 210–224.

Burgoon, J. K. (1982). Privacy and communication. In M. Burgoon (Ed.), *Communication yearbook 6* (pp. 206–249). Beverly Hills, CA: Sage.

Burgoon, J. K. (2016). Expectancy violations theory. In C. R. Berger & M. E. Roloff (Eds.), *The international encyclopaedia of interpersonal communication.* New York: John Wiley & Sons. doi:10.1002/978111 8540190.wbeic0102.

Burgoon, J. K., & Dunbar, N. E. (2006). Nonverbal expressions of dominance and power in human relationships. In V. Manusov & M. L. Patterson (Eds.), *The SAGE handbook of nonverbal communication* (pp. 279–297). Thousand Oaks, CA: Sage.

Calhoun, J. B. (1962). Population density and social pathology. *Scientific American, 206,* 139–148.

Canagarajah, S. (2013). Agency and power in intercultural communication: Negotiating English in translocal spaces. *Language & Intercultural Communication, 13,* 202–224.

Caplan, M. E., & Goldman, M. (1981). Personal space violations as a function of height. *Journal of Social Psychology, 114,* 167–171.

Carney, D. R., Hall, J. A., & Smith LeBeau, L. (2005). Beliefs about the nonverbal expression of social power. *Journal of Nonverbal Behavior, 29,* 105–123.

Cavanagh, S. L. (2013). Affect, performance, and ethnographic methods in *Queer Bathroom Monologues.* Text and Performance Quarterly, *33,* 286–307.

Child, J. T., Haridakis, P. M., & Petronio, S. (2012). Blogging privacy rule orientations, privacy management, and content deletion practices: The variability of online privacy management activity at different stages of social media use. *Computers in Human Behavior, 28,* 1859–1872.

Child, J. T., & Westermann, D. A. (2013). Let's be Facebook friends: Exploring parental Facebook friend requests from a communication privacy management (CPM) perspective. *Journal of Family Communication, 13,* 46–59.

Conigliaro, L., Cullerton, K., Flynn, K., & Rueder, S. (1989). Stigmatizing artifacts and their effect on personal space. *Psychological Reports, 65,* 897–898.

Costa, M. (2012). Territorial behavior in public settings. *Environment & Behavior, 44,* 713–721.

Daley, D. (2012). What? Noise is often the main course at restaurants. *Sound & Communications, 58,* 50–51.

Dardis, C. M., Kraft, K. M., Gidycz, C. A. (2017). "Miscommunication" and undergraduate women's conceptualizations of sexual assault: A qualitative analysis. *Journal of Interpersonal Violence, 32,* 1–29.

Darwin, C. (1965). *The expression of emotion in man and animals.* London: J. Murray. (Original work published in 1872)

chapter four

Dong-Hoo, L. (2010). Digital cameras, personal photography and the reconfiguration of spatial experiences. *Information Society, 26,* 266–275.

Duggan, A., Bradshaw, Y., & Altman, W. (2010). How do I ask about your disability? An examination of interpersonal communication processes between medical students and patients with disabilities. *Journal of Health Communication, 15,* 334–350.

Erickson, F. (1975). One function of proxemic shifts in face-to-face interaction. In A. Kendon, R. M. Harris, & M. R. Key (Eds.), *Organization of behavior in face-to-face interaction* (pp. 175–187). Chicago: Aldine.

Erlandson, K. (2012). Stay out of my space. *Journal of College & University Housing, 387,* 46–61.

Erlich, P. R. (1971). *The population bomb.* New York: Ballantine Books.

Fagundes, C. P., & Schindler, I. (2012). Making of romantic attachment bonds: Longitudinal trajectories and implications for relationship stability. *Personal Relationships, 19,* 723–742.

Feldman, R. S., & Tyler, J. M. (2006). Factoring in age: Nonverbal communication across the life span. In V. Manusov & M. L. Patterson (Eds.), *The SAGE handbook of nonverbal communication* (pp. 181–199). Thousand Oaks, CA: Sage.

Galobardes, B., McCormack, V. A., McCarron, P., Howe, L. D., Lynch, J., Lawlor, D. A., et al. (2012). Social inequalities in height: Persisting differences today depend upon height of the parents. *PLoS ONE, 7,* 1–18.

Gan, Q. (2011). Mobile phone—A specific representation of individual space constructing. *China Media Report Overseas, 7,* 83–86.

Gobel, M. S., Chen, A., & Richardson, D. C. (2017). How different cultures look at faces depends on the interpersonal context. *Canadian Journal of Experimental Psychology, 71,* 258–264.

Goffman, E. (1971). *Relations in public: Microstudies of the public order.* New York: Harper Colophon Books.

Grech, S. (2011). Recolonising debates or perpetuated coloniality? Decentering the spaces of disability, development and community in the global South. *International Journal of Inclusive Education, 15,* 87–100.

Hall, E. T. (1959). *The silent language.* Garden City, NJ: Doubleday.

Hall, E. T. (1963). A system for the notation of proxemic behavior. *American Anthropology, 65,* 1003–1026.

Hall, E. T. (1966). *The hidden dimension.* Garden City, NJ: Doubleday.

Hall, E. T. (1968). Proxemics. *Current Anthropology, 9,* 83–108.

Hall, E. T. (1983). Proxemics. In A. M. Katz & V. T. Katz (Eds.), *Foundation of nonverbal communication: Readings, exercises, and commentary* (pp. 5–27). Carbondale: Southern Illinois University Press.

Hall, J. A. (2006). Women's and men's nonverbal communication: Similarities, differences, stereotypes, and origins. In V. Manusov & M. L. Patterson (Eds.), *The SAGE handbook of nonverbal communication* (pp. 201–218). Thousand Oaks, CA: Sage.

Hall, J. A., Coats, E. J., & Smith LeBeau, L. (2005). Nonverbal behavior and the vertical dimension of social relations: A meta-analysis. *Psychological Bulletin, 131,* 898–924.

Helens-Hart, R. (2017). Females' (non)disclosure of minority sexual identities in the workplace from a communication privacy management perspective. *Communication Studies, 68,* 607–623.

Hellmann, J. H., & Jucks, R. (2017). The crowd in mind and crowded minds: An experimental investigation of crowding effects on students' views regarding tuition fees in Germany. *Higher Education, 74,* 131–145.

Henderson, M.D. (2011). Mere physical distance and integrative agreements: When more space improves negotiation outcomes. *Journal of Experimental Social Psychology, 47,* 7–15.

Henley, N. M. (2001). Body politics. In A. Branaman (Ed.), *Self and society: Blackwell readers in sociology* (pp. 288–297). Malden, MA: Blackwell.

Hickey-Moody, A. (2016). Being different in public. *Continuum: Journal of Media & Cultural Studies, 30,* 531–541.

Hjälm, A. (2012). "Because we know our limits": Elderly parents' views on intergenerational proximity and intimacy. *Journal of Aging Studies, 26,* 296–308.

Hosek, A. M., & Presley, R. (2018). College student perceptions of the (in)appropriateness and functions of teacher disclosure. *College Teaching, 66,* 63–72.

Hur, K. K., & Jeffres, L. W. (1979). A conceptual approach to the study of ethnicity, communication and urban stratification. *Communication, 8,* 67–87.

Jayakumar, U. M., & Adamian, A. S. (2017). The fifth frame of colorblind ideology: Maintaining the comforts of colorblindness in the context of white fragility. *Sociological Perspectives, 60,* 912–936.

Jeanes, R., & Magee, J. (2012). "Can we play on the swings and roundabouts?" Creating inclusive play spaces for disabled young people and their families. *Leisure Studies, 31,* 193–210.

Jenkins, J., & Finneman, T. (2018). Gender trouble in the workplace: Applying Judith Butler's theory of performativity to news organizations. *Feminist Media Studies, 18,* 157–172.

Judge, P. G. (2000). Coping with crowded conditions. In F. Aureli & F. B. M. de Waal (Eds.), *Natural conflict resolution* (pp. 129–154). Berkeley: University of California Press.

Kabo, F. W. (2017). A model of potential encounters in the workplace: The relationships of homophily, spatial distance, organizational structure, and perceived networks. *Environment & Behavior, 49,* 638–662.

Kaminka, G. (2018). Simulating urban pedestrian crowds of different cultures. ACM *Transactions on Intelligent Systems and Technology, 9,* 1–27.

Kelly, C., & Carson, E. (2012). The youth activist forum: Forging a rare, disability-positive space that empowers youth. *Journal of Youth Studies, 15,* 1089–1106.

Kemper, K. R. (2012). Sacred spaces: Cultural hybridity and boundaries for visual communication about the Hopi tribe in Arizona. *Visual Communication Quarterly, 19,* 216–231.

Kilbury, R. Bordieri, J., & Wong, H. (1996). Impact of physical disability and gender on personal space. *Journal of Rehabilitation, 62,* 59–61.

Kim, B., Zauberman, G., & Bettman, J. R. (2012). Space, time, and intertemporal preferences. *Journal of Consumer Research, 39,* 867–880.

Kim, J. (2018). Manhattan's Koreatown as a transclave: The emergence of a new ethnic enclave in a global city. *City & Community, 17,* 276–295.

Knapp, M. L., Hall, J. A., & Horgan, T. G. (2013). *Nonverbal communication in human interaction* (8th ed.). Belmont, CA: Wadsworth/Cengage Learning.

Kordzadeh, N., & Warren, J. (2017). Communicating personal health information in virtual health communities: An integration of privacy calculus model and affective commitment. *Journal of the Association for Information Systems, 18,* 45–81.

Lannutti, P. J. (2013). Same-sex marriage and privacy management: Examining couples' communication with family members. *Journal of Family Communication, 13,* 60–75.

Leipold, W. E. (1963). *Psychological distance in a dyadic interview.* (Unpublished doctoral dissertation). University of North Dakota, Grand Forks, ND.

chapter four

Lewis, L., Patel, H., D'Cruz, M., & Cobb, S. (2017). What makes a space invader? Passenger perceptions of personal space invasion in aircraft travel. *Ergonomics, 60,* 1461–1470.

Li, S., & Li, Y. (2007). How far is far enough? A measure of information privacy in terms of interpersonal distance. *Environment and Behavior, 39,* 317–331.

Lomanowska, A. M., & Guitton, M. J. (2012). Spatial proximity to others determines how humans inhabit virtual worlds. *Computers in Human Behavior, 28,* 318–323.

Lyman, S. M., & Scott, M. B. (1967). Territoriality: A neglected social dimension. *Social Problems, 15,* 237–241.

Macchi Cassia, V., Proietti, V., Gava, L., & Bricolo, E. (2015). Searching for faces of different ages: Evidence for an experienced-based own-age detection advantage in adults. *Journal of Experimental Psychology: Human Perception & Performance, 41,* 1037–1048.

Machleit, K. A., Eroglu, W. A., & Powell Mantel, S. (2008). Perceived retail crowding and shopping satisfaction. In L. K. Guerrero & M. L. Hecht (Eds.), *The nonverbal communication reader: Classic and contemporary readings* (3rd ed., pp. 191–202). Prospect Heights, IL: Waveland.

Manca, S., & Ranieri, M. (2017). Implications of social network sites for teaching and learning: Where we are and where we want to go. *Education and Information Technologies, 22,* 605–622.

Manusov, V. (2008). Stereotypes and nonverbal cues: Showing how we feel about others during cross-cultural interactions. In L. K. Guerrero & M. L. Hecht (Eds.), *The nonverbal communication reader: Classic and contemporary readings* (3rd ed., pp. 314–320). Prospect Heights, IL: Waveland.

Marin, C. R., Gasparino, R. C., & Puggina, A. C. (2018). The perception of territory and personal space invasion among hospitalized patients. *PLoS ONE, 13,* 1–9.

Marini, I., Wang, X., Etzbach, C., & Del Castillo, A. (2013). Ethnic, gender, and contact differences in intimacy attitudes toward wheelchair users. *Rehabilitation Counseling Bulletin, 56,* 135–145.

Matsumoto, D. (2006). Culture and nonverbal behavior. In V. Manusov & M. L. Patterson (Eds.), *The SAGE handbook of nonverbal communication* (pp. 219–235). Thousand Oaks, CA: Sage.

Matsumoto, D., & Hwang, H. S. (2013). Cultural influences on nonverbal behavior. In D. Matsumoto, M. G. Frank, & H. S. Hwang (Eds.), *Nonverbal communication: Science and applications* (pp. 97–120). Thousand Oaks, CA: Sage.

Matthews, A., Derlega, V. J., & Morrow, J. (2006). What is highly personal information and how is it related to self-disclosure decision making? The perspective of college students. *Communication Research Reports, 23,* 85–92.

McBride, M. C., & Wahl, S. T. (2005). "To say or not to say": Teachers' management of privacy boundaries in the classroom. *Texas Speech Communication Journal, 30,* 8–22.

McKellin, W. H., Shahin, K., Hodgson, M., Jamieson, J., & Pichora-Fuller, M. K. (2011). Noisy zones of proximal development: Conversation in noisy classrooms. *Sociolinguistics, 15,* 65–93.

McLeod, S., Daniel, G., & Barr, J. (2013). "When he's around his brothers . . . he's not so quiet": The private and public worlds of school-aged children with speech sound disorder. *Journal of Communication Disorders, 46,* 70–83.

Millham, M. H., & Atkin, D. (2018). Managing the virtual boundaries: Online social networks, disclosure, and privacy behaviors. *New Media & Society, 20,* 50–67.

Moore, J. (2017). Performative face theory: A critical perspective on interpersonal identity work. *Communication Monographs, 84,* 258–276.

Morman, M. T., & Whitely, M. (2012). An exploratory analysis of critical incidents of closeness in the mother/son relationship. *Journal of Family Communication, 12,* 22–39.

Murray, L. L. (2010). Distinguishing clinical depression from early Alzheimer's disease in elderly people: Can narrative analysis help? *Aphasiology, 24,* 928–939.

Okken, V., van Rompay, T., & Pruyn, A. (2012). Exploring space in the consultation room: Environmental influences during patient–physician interaction. *Journal of Health Communication, 17,* 397–412.

Osensky, T. S. (2017). *Shortchanged: Height discrimination and strategies for social change.* Lebanon, NH: University Press of New England.

Pearce, M., & Woodford-Smith, R. (2012). The (dis)location of time and space: Trans-cultural collaborations in Tokyo. *Journal of Media Practice, 13,* 197–213.

Petronio, S. (1991). Communication boundary management: A theoretical model of managing disclosure of private information between marital partners. *Communication Theory, 1,* 311–335.

Petronio, S. (2000). *Balancing the secrets of private disclosures.* Mahwah, NJ: Erlbaum.

Petronio, S. (2002). *Boundaries of privacy: Dialectics of disclosure.* New York: State University of New York Press.

Petronio, S. (2007). Translational research endeavors and the practices of communication privacy management. *Journal of Applied Communication Research, 35,* 218–222.

Petronio, S. (2013). Brief status report on communication privacy management theory. *Journal Family Communication, 13,* 6–14.

Petronio, S. (2017). Communication privacy management theory: Understanding families. In D. O. Braithwaite, E. A. Suter, & K. Floyd (Eds.), *Engaging theories in family communication: Multiple perspectives* (2nd ed., pp. 107–117). New York: Routledge.

Petronio, S., & Bantz, C. (1991). Controlling the ramifications of disclosure: "Don't tell anybody but . . . ." *Journal of Language and Social Psychology, 10,* 263–269.

Petronio, S., & Durham, W. T. (2015). Communication privacy management theory: Significance for interpersonal communication. In D. O. Braithwaite & P. Schrodt (Eds.), *Engaging theories in interpersonal communication: Multiple perspectives* (2nd ed., pp. 335–347). Los Angeles: Sage.

Phithakkitnukoon, S., Smoreda, Z., & Olivier, P. (2012). Socio-geography of human mobility: A study using longitudinal mobile phone data. *PLoS ONE, 7,* 1–9.

Plander, K. L. (2013). Checking accounts: Communication privacy management in familial financial caregiving. *Journal of Family Communication, 13,* 17–31.

Prabhu, T. T. (2010). Proxemics: Some challenges and strategies in nonverbal communication. *IUP Journal of Soft Skills, 4,* 7–14.

Reynolds, J. M. (2017). "I'd rather be dead than disabled"—the ableist conflation and the meanings of disability. *Review of Communication, 17,* 149–163.

Roces, M. (2013). Dress, status, and identity in the Philippines: Pineapple fiber cloth and ilustrado fashion. *Fashion Theory: The Journal of Dress, Body & Culture, 17,* 341–372.

Rule, N. O. (2017). Perceptions of sexual orientation from minimal cues. *Archives of Sexual Behavior, 46,* 129–139.

Sahlstein, E. (2010). Communication and distance: The present and future interpreted through the past. *Journal of Applied Communication Research, 38,* 106–114.

Santilli, V., & Miller, A. N. (2011). The effects of gender and power distance on nonverbal immediacy in symmetrical and asymmetrical power conditions: A cross-cultural study of classrooms and friendships. *Journal of International and Intercultural Communication, 4*, 3–22.

Sanz, E. (2014). The cultural economy of postconsensus television. *International Journal of Communication, 8*, 1596–1614.

Schneeweis, A. (2016). Power, gender, and ethnic spaces. *Journal of Communication Inquiry, 40*, 88–105.

Schulz, R., & Barefoot, J. (1974). Nonverbal responses and affiliative conflict theory. *British Journal of Social and Clinical Psychology, 13*, 237–243.

Shifman, L., & Lemish, D. (2011). "Mars and Venus" in virtual space: Post-feminist humor and the Internet. *Critical Studies in Media Communication, 28*, 253–273.

Sluzki, C. E. (2016). Proxemics in couple interactions: Rekindling an old optic. *Family Process, 55*, 7–15.

Smith, L. H., & Holm, L. (2010). Social class and body management: A qualitative exploration of differences in perceptions and practices related to health and personal body weight. *Appetite, 55*, 311–318.

Sommer, R. (1961). Leadership and group geography. *Sociometry, 24*, 99–110.

Sommer, R. (1969). *Personal space: The behavioral basis of design.* Englewood Cliffs, NJ: Prentice Hall.

Szpak, A., Nicholls, M. E. R., Thomas, N. A., Laham, S. M., & Loetsher, T. (2016). "No man is an island": Effects of interpersonal proximity on spatial attention. *Cognitive Neuroscience, 7*, 45–54.

Tank Buschmann, M. B., Hollinger-Smith, L. M., & Peterson-Kokkas, S. E. (1999). Implementation of expressive physical touch in depressed older adults. *Journal of Clinical Geropsychology, 5*, 291–300.

Thompson, J., Petronio, S., & Braithwaite, D. O. (2012). An examination of privacy rules for academic advisors and college student-athletes: A communication privacy management perspective. *Communication Studies, 63*, 54–76.

Valtonen, A. (2013). Height matters: Practicing consumer agency, gender, and body politics. *Consumption, Markets & Culture, 16*, 196–221.

Venturini, B., Castelli, L., & Tomelleri, S. (2006). Not all jobs are suitable for fat people: Experimental evidence of a link between being fat and "out-of-sight" jobs. *Social Behavior and Personality, 34*, 389–398.

Wang, J., Liao, Y., Wang, J., Fan, J., Chen, T., Gao, X., et al. (2012). Adaptive modeling of the human-environment relationship applied to estimation of the population carrying capacity in an earthquake zone. *Population & Environment, 33*, 233–242.

Webb, J. D., & Weber, M. J. (2003). Influence of sensory abilities on the interpersonal distance of the elderly. *Environment and Behavior, 35*, 695–711.

Worthington, D. L., & Fitch-Hauser, M. (2018). Communication privacy management and mediated communication. In M. Khosrow-Pour (Ed.), *Encyclopedia of Information Science and Technology* (4th ed., pp. 6985–6992). Hershey, PA: IGI Global.

Zuk, M., Bierbaum, A. H., Chapple, K., Gorska, K., & Loukaitou-Sideris, A. (2018). Gentrification, displacement, and the role of public investment. *Journal of Planning Literature, 33*, 31–44.

chapter five

PHYSICAL APPEARANCE: THE BODY AS NONVERBAL COMMUNICATION

chapter outline

chapter objectives

After studying this chapter, you should be able to

1. understand how people perceive physical appearance as a form of nonverbal communication;
2. improve your understanding of how physical appearance impacts your perception of others, as well as your awareness and management of your own physical appearance;
3. explain the difference between attraction and attractiveness;
4. identify and describe Sheldon's body types, along with their corresponding psychological characteristics;
5. understand the role that clothing and artifacts play in nonverbal communication;
6. define homophily; and
7. discuss various forms of body modification and how normalization affects our view of these forms of nonverbal communication.

case study

SERENA'S CATSUIT

In 2017, superstar tennis athlete Serena Williams took on another title: mom. She married Reddit co-founder Alexis Ohanian, then had baby girl Olympia, and then got back on the world tennis tour. Her first outing was at the 2018 French Open, then three weeks later she reached the Wimbledon final, a short 10 months after giving birth. She had serious complications after the birth, mainly connected to her tendency to form blood clots. But with all these accomplishments and changes in her life, what do you imagine made headlines about her comeback? Her clothes.

Serena chose to compete in the French Open in what she termed her "Wakanda-inspired catsuit," an homage to one of her favorite movies, *Black Panther* (*The Australian*, 2018). Each grand slam tournament has rules about players' clothing, so part of the controversy was some people's views that Serena's "onesie" violated the rules. A factor many people didn't realize played into the decision at the time was the health benefits of compression clothing, which helped Serena prevent the formation of blood clots. Sure, she no doubt also wanted the world to see that her body had recovered after pregnancy—let's be honest

Serena Williams' clothing choice made headlines at the 2018 French Open.

about the vanity of the situation, along with the health issues. But with all the topics associated with her extraordinary success as a world class athlete, Serena continues to receive undue attention over nonverbal communication related to physical appearance, specifically her body shape, weight, and clothing choices.

As you work through this chapter, think about times in your life when you have judged (or been judged by) other people for "appearance's sake." Use your personal experiences, as well as the research introduced in this chapter, to consider the power of various aspects of physical appearance in everyday life.

Evelyn:	Have you seen our new boss?
Genie:	No, what does he look like?
Evelyn:	He's really handsome and professional looking.
Genie:	Well, it's about time they hired someone who actually looks good. The other two executives didn't last around here because they just didn't have the image.
Evelyn:	Exactly!

What does the above conversation teach us? Evelyn and Genie reveal the importance of **physical appearance**—the way our bodies and overall appearance nonverbally communicate to others and impact our view of ourselves in everyday life. You may be thinking, *How can the way someone looks be communicative?*

Have you ever thought about how you avoid or are drawn to people who look a certain way? Think about how much time each day you spend grooming yourself. How does my hair look? Does this dress make me look fat? Will people be able to see sweaty armpits if I wear this shirt? Should I use more hair spray? Should I tuck my shirt in or leave it out? Am I wearing too much perfume? Do these jeans make my butt look good? Am I sexy? All these questions relate to **body image**—the view we have of ourselves and the amount of mental energy we invest in our physical appearance.

While how much we care about our appearance varies from person to person, some of us constantly think about how we look. **Image fixation**—a high degree of concern for one's physical appearance—can promote a constant comparison of self with others and an intense desire to look better. Many of us care a great deal about physical appearance, first, because it communicates something about us as people, which other people respond to. Second, while most of us would agree that other qualities of a person are more important, appearance influences our interest in getting to know other people or our motivation to avoid them.

People are significantly influenced by aspects of physical appearance such as body shape, size or weight, height, skin color, smell, hair, clothing, and artifacts (such as makeup or eyeglasses) (Aliakbari & Abdollahi, 2013; Doring & Wansink, 2017; Gurney, Howlett, Pink, Tracey, & Moggridge, 2017; Howlett, Pine, Cahill, Orakcioglu, & Fletcher, 2015; Markley Rountree & Davis, 2011; Palmer-Mehta & Shuler, 2017). Take a moment to reflect on all the products that claim to make your body look better. From grocery store aisles featuring low-fat foods to pop-up Internet ads touting the latest acne remedy, it doesn't take long to realize that physical appearance, as a key nonverbal communication code, is an important aspect of people's lives in the United States and around the world.

PHYSICAL APPEARANCE AS A NONVERBAL COMMUNICATION CODE ■ ■ ■ ■

The goal of this chapter is to make you more aware of physical appearance as a form of nonverbal communication in everyday life. The decisions we make to maintain or alter our physical appearance reveal a great deal about who we are. In addition, the physical appearance of other people impacts our perception of them, how we communicate with them, how approachable they are, how attractive or unattractive they are, and so on.

© Lesterair/Shutterstock.com

In today's world, there are countless products and procedures targeted to our desire to change or improve our appearance.

We don't have to look too hard to find an app, exercise product, skin cream, technological innovation, or surgical procedure tempting us to improve or change our natural body in some way (Larocca, 2017; LaWare & Moutsatsos, 2013; Lee, 2014). We're not advising people *not* to take care of themselves or *not* to work to look good, but it's important to expose and critique some aspects of physical appearance and the pressure to achieve a certain standard that create turmoil in people's lives. Such aftereffects as the rise in eating disorders and elective cosmetic procedures highlight a culture of body customization that goes against our accepting our natural bodies and that can engender low self-esteem (Bissell & Rask, 2010; Brierley, Brooks, Mond, Stevenson, & Stephen, 2016; Cordes, Vocks, Dtising, Bauer, & Waldorf, 2016; DeFeciani, 2016; Kalus & Cregan, 2017; Ura & Preston, 2015).

PHYSICAL ATTRACTIVENESS ■ ■ ■

Before delving further into this topic, an important distinction needs to be made between *attraction* and *attractiveness*. **Attraction** is grounded in the study of interpersonal relationship development. It refers to how we are drawn toward other people interpersonally, spiritually, emotionally, physically, and/or sexually for possible friendship, dating, love, partnership, and marriage (Mulvey, 2006). Attraction is a powerful force in the development of human relationships, but it isn't nonverbal communication per se; it's a psychological variable (Bee & Havitz, 2010; King, 2017; Lilienfield, Lynn, & Namy, 2017). In contrast, **physical attractiveness** is a culturally derived perception of beauty formed by features of our appearance such as height, weight, size, shape, and so on. The distinction between the two terms is this: You may be attracted to someone you believe to be physically attractive, *or not*. Some people are *attractive*, but we're not *attracted* to them—understand the difference? Thus, while attraction is interesting, in this chapter we choose to focus on physical appearance and attractiveness as a form of nonverbal communication, realizing its role in attraction.

In most cultures, including U.S. culture, people have a particular mental picture of physical features (e.g., weight, size, shape) that define beauty, forming into an ideal (Brierley et al., 2016; Poorani, 2012; Stoker, Garretsen, & Spreeuwers, 2016; Trekels & Eggermont, 2017). Perceptions of what constitutes attractiveness vary widely by culture (Barak-Brandes & Lachover, 2016; Chen, 2015; El Jurdi & Smith, 2018; Shuttlesworth & Zotter, 2011). Gender also shapes our views of ideal beauty. Scholars contend that American women feel more pressure than men to be physically attractive (Amon, 2015; Calogero, Pina, & Sutton, 2013; Harrison, Taylor, & Marske, 2006).

How does physical attractiveness (our own and others') affect communication? Do attractive people have an advantage over unattractive people? While these questions would take this whole chapter to address, one aspect of physical attractiveness to mention here is the **halo effect**—people's tendency to attribute positive qualities to physically attractive people (Gibson & Gore, 2016; Guerrero & Floyd, 2006; Lammers, Davis, Davidson, & Hogue, 2016). What this means is that just because someone is perceived as good-looking, he or she is also likely to be perceived as credible, successful, and personable—which might prove to be far from the truth if we were to get to know the person. Nonverbal scholars Guerrero and Floyd (2006) explain that attractiveness is important to individuals and their relationships because "attractive people are benefited in numerous ways and penalized in others" (p. 57).

The Impact of Physical Attractiveness on Our Culture

Reflect on how important physical attractiveness is in your own life. Are there certain decisions you've made based on physical attractiveness? Let's consider an example. J. R. is a manager at a new bar and grille called Perky Perks, opening up close to campus. The establishment will have a sports theme, and the primary investors want to attract a young college crowd. One of the investors has made it clear to J. R. that he wants all young women hired as bartenders and servers to have nice "booties and boobs." While J. R. doesn't publicize this fact, he has decided to hire only attractive young women who will look good in mini-skirts and cut-off tops. While we may find this example disturbing and J. R.'s hiring practice sexist, this kind of hiring practice does exist. In this example, we can see that physical attractiveness will be an advantage for any of the applicants who fit the desired employee look.

GETTING AND KEEPING A JOB. While physical appearance is a focus for J. R. in his hiring process, ethical or not, his example shows us one case in which physical attractiveness does have an effect on hiring. In fact, physical attractiveness often serves as an advantage when applying for a job, especially a high-profile job; in being hired at a higher salary or wage; in being perceived as effective in that job; and actually keeping one's job (Agthe, Sporrle, & Maner, 2010; Cavico, Muffler, & Mujtaba, 2012; Commisso & Finkelstein, 2012; Hamermesh, 2011; Howlett et al., 2015; Quintanilla & Wahl, 2016; Tsai, Huang, & Yu, 2012; Venturini, Castelli, & Tomelleri, 2006).

EDUCATIONAL SETTINGS. Physical attractiveness also affects the educational context. Take the popular website, RateMyProfessors.com; many college students visit the site to evaluate their professors on a range of variables, including physical attractiveness. Users can indicate a teacher's physical attractiveness by inserting a chili pepper next to the instructor's name, signifying her or him as "hot" (Edwards, Edwards, Qing, & Wahl, 2007). More physically attractive professors are rated higher on other attributes as well, such as approachableness, competence, and dynamism in the classroom (Hartman & Hunt, 2013; Miles & Sparks, 2013; Parry, 2011; Soper, 2010; Wilson, 2010). On the downside, however, some studies have found an association between physically attractive teachers and perceptions of sexual misconduct. A highly attractive teacher may be perceived as being more likely to commit sexual misconduct with students, but also likely to receive a less harsh penalty for the misconduct than a less physically attractive teacher (Fromuth, Kelly, Wilson, Finch, & Scruggs, 2013; Geddes, Tyson, & McGreal, 2013).

Now reverse the situation; are teachers' perceptions and evaluations of a student affected by the physical appearance of the student? Research has begun to explore possible connections between such nonverbal cues as weight, clothing, and overall appearance (e.g., neatness, grooming, hygiene) and teachers' assessments of students' personalities and ability to learn, as well as predictions about GPA (Di Domenico, Quitasol, & Fournier, 2015; Shackelton & Campbell, 2014).

DATING, PARTNERING, AND MARRIAGE. Physical attractiveness impacts our dating, partnering, and marital decisions. If you were asked whether you would rather marry, partner with, or date a person who ranks low on physical attributes versus a person who ranks high, what would you say? Nonverbal communication researchers have explored this question over several decades to learn more about the effects of physical attractiveness on dating, partnering, and marriage (Guerrero & Floyd, 2006).

Research shows that we tend to seek out partners we perceive as equal to us in attractiveness—a phenomenon called the **matching hypothesis** (Bar-Tal & Saxe, 1976; Forbes, Adams-Curtis, Rade, & Jaberg, 2001). Think about couples you see each day: Don't most of them "match" in terms of physical attractiveness? While we may think people are attractive when they are more beautiful than we perceive ourselves to be, research shows that we tend to connect with people we perceive to be on our "level." When we see "mismatched" couples, we often make all kinds of inferences about their personalities, financial success, sexual prowess, or motives for being in the relationship. So why do people tend not to seek out the best-looking partners? One explanation is the risk of rejection. To avoid unwanted rejection, people tend to select a person similar to themselves in physical attractiveness (Poulsen, Holman, Busby, & Carroll, 2013).

REMEMBER

Remember!
5.1

Physical appearance	How a person's body and overall appearance communicate a view of self to others
Body image	View of ourselves and the amount of mental energy we invest in our physical appearance
Image fixation	High degree of concern about physical appearance
Attraction	Grounded in the study of interpersonal relationships; how we are drawn toward other people interpersonally, emotionally, physically, sexually, and/or spiritually for possible friendship, dating, love, partnership, and marriage
Physical attractiveness	Culturally derived perception of beauty formed by features such as height, weight, size, shape, and so on
Halo effect	Tendency to attribute positive personality qualities to physically attractive people
Matching hypothesis	Tendency to seek out dating and marital partners we perceive as equal to us in physical attractiveness

THE BODY ▪ ▪ ▪

The appearance of your body helps others form perceptions and stereotypes about you, as well as decisions about how to communicate with you (Brierley et al., 2016; Cordes et al., 2016; Hamermesh, 2011; Oswald & Chapleau, 2010; Trekels & Eggermont, 2017). In this section, we examine how different aspects of our bodies play a role in our overall physical appearance, as a code of nonverbal communication.

Body Type and Shape

Does the type or shape of people's bodies influence communication? Have you ever avoided interaction with another person because of the shape of her or his body? Whether you've thought about this before, the general shape of our bodies does communicate something nonverbally. In fact, scholars developed a system called **somatyping** that classifies people according to their body type (Sheldon, 1940, 1954; Sheldon, Stevens, & Tucker, 1942). While much criticism has been leveled at somatotyping over the years, nonverbal communication researchers typically reference the system in the study of physical appearance and body type.

Refer to Figure 5.1 as we discuss the various body types. Bone structure and muscle mass (or lack thereof) differentiate body types, not how much weight a person carries. The first type is the **ectomorph**. People classified as ectomorphs (ectos) are usually thin, bony (small-boned), and tall. Ectomorphs appear fragile; they usually have flat chests and limited muscular development. The second body type is the **mesomorph**. Mesomorphs (mesos) generally have a triangular body shape with broad shoulders and a tapering at the hip; they are muscular, with a good balance between height and weight, and are usually described as athletic in appearance. The third body type is the **endomorph**. People classified as endomorphs (endos) typically have bodies that are rounded, oval, or pear-shaped; they are usually heavy-set or stocky but not necessarily obese.

Can you think of people or characters in popular culture, media, sports, and so on that reflect the three categories? Abraham Lincoln, Ichabod Crane, and Pee Wee Herman are examples of the ectomorphic or tall and skinny body type—sometimes referred to as lanky or a "tall drink of water." Brad Pitt, Michael Phelps, and Serena Williams are examples of the mesomorphic or athletic body type. Danny Devito, Santa Claus, and Zach Galifianakis have endomorphic characteristics. What about you—what category reflects your body type?

FIGURE 5.1
Body Types

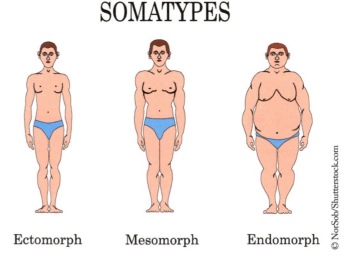

SOMATYPES

Ectomorph   Mesomorph   Endomorph

© NorSob/Shutterstock.com

According to Sheldon's (1940) theory, each body type has a corresponding psychological type. Ectomorphs are typically described as tense, awkward, careful, polite, and detached. Mesomorphs are often described as dominant, confident, energetic, competitive, assertive, enthusiastic, and optimistic. Endomorphs are commonly described as slow, sociable, emotional, forgiving, and relaxed. The connection between body type and psychological profile has fallen out of favor, leaving us with tenuous associations at best, but the somatyping framework has retained its usefulness in research and study.

A highly reliable system for studying body shape, primarily applied to women, is the **waist-to-hip ratio**. Research suggests that an ideal female body has a 0.70 waist-to-hip ratio, meaning for a woman to be considered proportional, her waist size should be 70% of her hip size (Del Zotto & Pegna, 2017; Fitzgerald, Horgan, & Himes, 2016; Scott, 2017; Wilson, Tripp, & Boland, 2005). One study sought to determine if the 0.70 waist-to-hip ratio represented an attractiveness stereotype in other cultures. Male and female subjects from different parts of the world, including the United States, agreed that women with a higher waist-to-hip ratio (above 0.70) were less physically attractive than women with lower waist-to-hip ratios (Singh, 2004). Other research found that congenitally blind men also preferred a low waist-to-hip ratio in women, even though subjects had never seen a woman's figure; through their sense of touch, blind men in this study preferred the "hourglass" shape in women over other body shapes (Karremans, Frankenhuis, & Arons, 2010).

SOMATYPING AND SHELDON'S BODY CLASSIFICATIONS

Remember!
5.2

Somatyping	System that classifies people according to their body type
Ectomorph	Person who is thin, bony, and tall; fragile-looking, with a flat chest and limited muscular development
Mesomorph	Person with a triangular body shape—broad-shouldered and tapered at the hip; muscular and proportioned by height and weight; usually described as athletic
Endomorph	Person with a rounded, oval, or pear-shaped body; usually heavy-set or stocky but not necessarily obese

Preferences for body types vary from culture to culture, especially for women (Bovet & Raymond, 2015; Ciochin, 2013; Furnham, McClelland, & Omer 2003; Sorokowski, Koscinski, Sorokowska, & Huanca, 2014). In cultures where food is abundant (e.g., the United States, where exercise and diet peddling are multibillion dollar industries), people have to work out and watch what they eat to maintain the preferred mesomorphic and ectomorphic body types. In these cultures, being thin and in shape signals that people have the time and money to eat right and keep to a fitness plan. In contrast, in cultures in which the food supply is limited, people tend to prefer endomorphs (especially endomorphic women) because their heft is a sign of wealth and prosperity (Guerrero & Floyd, 2006).

Weight

Body weight is a nonverbal cue, even if you haven't ever thought of it that way. We've established that perceptions about body type vary from culture to culture, but so do perceptions of weight. In many cultures around the world, body weight isn't the obsession it is in the United States. Some years ago, technology giant Hewlett Packard developed a camera with a "slimming feature." The feature actually reduced the middle and enlarged the outside edges of a picture, a technique that removed 10 pounds from people's appearance in photos (MSNBC, 2006).

The media frequently portray young, thin, attractive people doing all kinds of amazing things and finding success, while overweight characters are often ridiculed or the constant butt of jokes. Media provide a barrage of "perfect bodies" with the message that we, the viewers, must do all we can to reach and maintain an ideal weight and stay fit or we will be unlovable or unacceptable in society. The amount of media pressure on this one nonverbal cue is enormous (Dolezal, 2015; Hoffman, 2017; Puhl, Luedicke, & Heuer, 2013; Trekels & Eggermont, 2017; Van Vonderen & Kinnally, 2012). In addition, the growing and very real problem of obesity—the medical designation for being significantly overweight—and its detrimental effects on health lead Americans to spend a lot of time listening to messages or reading websites, articles, and books about weight loss, thinking about how they can lose weight, or attempting to lose weight.

In the United States, the epidemic of obesity has gained national attention, as obesity rates have risen sharply in recent years. According to the Centers for Disease Control and Prevention, 40% of Americans are overweight or obese (Adult Obesity Facts, 2016). (When we published the previous edition of this textbook in 2014, the obesity rate was around 20%.) For adults aged 20–39 (typical college age), the obesity rate is 37%; middle-aged adults have the highest rate among age groups. Members of minority groups are at higher risk than Caucasians, according to the CDC report. With obesity reaching new levels among children as well as adults, various research teams continue to investigate perceptions of obesity, endomorphic body types, and anti-fat prejudice to determine if attitudes have changed over time. Studies consistently show that a significant aversion to endomorphic and obese body types still exists (O'Brien, Latner, Ebneter, & Hunter, 2013; Politano & Politano, 2011). So as more and more children suffer from obesity in U.S. culture, the significant stigma attached to being overweight persists, and perhaps even deepens (Lee, 2014; Puhl et al., 2013; Quick, McWilliams, & Byrd-Bredbenner, 2013).

Height and Status

Physical appearance is important to Evelyn and Genie, as it is to most of us. What does their conversation reveal about preferences for height, as a nonverbal cue? Heterosexual women in American culture tend to like men who are tall and handsome (Re & Perrett, 2012). Tall is still preferable to short, in general, especially when it comes to men in our culture, and that can be a self-esteem downer for men who struggle with their lack of height. Americans' views of and preferences for government leaders, especially presidents, are affected by their height; in fact, voters have elected the taller of the presidential candidates in almost every contest in the 20th and 21st centuries (Tenner, 2004). Author Tanya Osensky (2017), in her book *Shortchanged: Height Discrimination and Strategies for Social Change*, defines "tall privilege" as "the social deference that tall people

receive in our society just because of their height, without their actually doing anything to deserve it" (p. 2). Research over four decades consistently shows that height is equated with credibility, status, power, and dominance (Egolf & Corder, 1991; Galobardes et al., 2012; Stabler, Whitt, Moreault, D'Ercole, & Underwood, 1980; Valtonen, 2013; Vrij, 2001).

Height in American women is a bit of a mixed bag. Some people believe that the same judgments of enhanced credibility and status that apply to tall men also apply to tall

Height has different connotations depending on gender, ethnicity, culture, setting, and many other factors.

women. But some women—especially those who gained above-average height in their puberty years, when they towered over boys their age—see height as a disadvantage, socially and professionally. They may intimidate male bosses, coworkers, and dates simply because of their height advantage. We don't believe this is appropriate, but for some tall women, it's a reality they face.

The Disabled Body

Since we're discussing the body as a nonverbal cue, have you ever considered the communicative properties of the disabled body? Some of you reading this text live with a physical disability every day. Others of you understand the issues from a distance because you have a family member or friend with a disability. Still others have no experience with people who have physical disabilities. Usually, the knowledge or clue that a person is living with a disability is based on physical appearance, but this is not always the case. We remember a student who constantly took flak for having a handicapped sticker on his car and parking in handicapped spots at the university. This student was a very tall man who walked with a confident stride and appeared to have no physical disability. Turns out he had a degenerative joint disease—one that would leave him seriously impaired within a few years—and his doctors said that the shorter the distances he walked, the better.

Nonverbal communication between able-bodied people and people with disabilities has received research attention (Enzinna, 2016/2017; Hickey-Moody, 2016; Scott, 2015). In some social situations, able-bodied people avoid making eye contact with people who have disabilities, such as at a shopping mall, in an elevator, in a college classroom, or at a doctor's office. Many of us were taught that "it's not nice to stare," but it's also not nice to deny someone with a disability the same kind of eye contact we give able-bodied people. One of our students who uses a wheelchair told us that she is frequently ignored in restaurants when she goes out to eat with her friends. Servers look to her dinner companions to provide her order, as if she were mute—not just in a wheelchair—and thus unable to order for herself. On those rare occasions when she is asked for her order, waitpersons make less eye contact with her than with other people at the table, as though they're uncomfortable even looking at her. Another possible explanation she offers is that servers may feel they'll be perceived as staring at a person who is disabled, rather than just giving normal eye contact.

All of us—able-bodied and disabled—need to be more aware of our verbal and nonverbal communication with people who have disabilities. The physical appearance of a person with a disability can lead us to make assumptions about what that person is capable of doing as well as how we should communicate with him or her verbally and nonverbally (Braithwaite, 1990, 1991, 1996; Braithwaite & Braithwaite, 2014; Braithwaite & Thompson, 2000; Marini, Wang, Etzbach, & Del Castillo, 2013; Reynolds, 2017). For example, when you talk to people in a wheelchair (assuming you're not in one yourself), do you tower over them, making them look up the whole time, or do you find a way to stoop or sit down so the conversation can occur on a more parallel level? Do you get louder when you speak to blind people, if you even speak at all? Do you get louder when you speak to deaf persons, or over-enunciate your words (which actually obstructs lip reading)? If you walked to class with someone whose legs were in braces or who relied on permanent crutches, would you slow your pace to match his or hers? Whether we are able-bodied or disabled, an awareness of our nonverbal communication with people who have disabilities enhances our social competence and prepares us for meaningful, inclusive, and respectful relationships.

Skin Color

Skin color is another dimension of physical appearance that has communicative power, much as we might like to downplay it. While we've made some strides in the United States in terms of judging people by skin color, we're not past skin color discrimination. Unfortunately, people in the U.S. and other countries around the world are still categorized, stereotyped, and discriminated against based on the color of their skin (Cowart & Lehnert, 2018; Cuny & Opaswongkarn, 2017; Lerman, McCabe, & Sadin, 2015; Lyngs, Cohen, Hattori, Newson, & Levin, 2016; Martin, Trego, & Nakayama, 2010; Mbure & Aubrey, 2017).

In 2013, the woman who was crowned Miss America was, for the first time in the pageant's history, an Indian American (meaning her roots are in India, not that she's Native American). By Indian standards, Nina Davuluri wasn't considered exceptionally beautiful, because her skin color was too dark to rank her among the most admired of women. One of the most popular cosmetic procedures for women in India is skin whitening; research shows that some Indian women feel pressure to conform to Western beauty standards, which include the lightening of one's skin color (Bakhshi & Baker, 2011; Basu, 2013).

Now let's talk about attempts to modify skin color by tanning—a practice ridiculed by darker-skinned individuals and warned against by dermatologists but still employed by many people. Statistics show that, while rates have decreased in recent years, close to 8 million American women and 2 million American men report regularly using indoor tanning services (Guy, Berkowitz, Holman, & Hartman, 2015). Another study found that 35% of American adults, 59% of college students, and 17% of teenagers admit to having used tanning beds at some time in their lives (Wehner, Chren, Nameth et al., 2014). People who regularly tan (indoors and outdoors) report that, although they understand the risks, they still believe a tan makes them look healthier. One study explored college students' tanning behavior; while students knew the risks of tanning, the practice was still highly popular (Gillen & Markey, 2017). Students who regularly tanned indoors also had more piercings and tattoos, and were more interested in getting cosmetic enhancements than students who did not tan. Clearly, skin color impacts our perceptions of ourselves and other people, and serves as yet another cue of nonverbal communication.

Body Smell

A pleasant body smell is something that many of us spend part of our day attending to and maintaining. Those of us who live in hot climates become especially sensitive to this issue. For women and men alike, it's a balancing act in terms of how much scent, body powder, cologne, or perfume to use, since smell is an integral part of our overall appearance and a powerful nonverbal cue.

Can you think of a neutral smell? We first talked about smell as nonverbal communication in Chapter 3 on environment. Research on **olfaction** (the role of smell in human interaction) indicates that no neutral scents exist (Andersen, 2004; Dimitrius & Mazzarrella, 1999). Each day, Americans, as well as people from other cultures around the world, bathe, shower, deodorize, brush, floss, wipe, sanitize, and freshen to cover up natural body odors. If smell wasn't important, we wouldn't buy so many products and go through so many routines. We use our scent to communicate our personalities, and to attract others and be perceived positively by them, for the purposes of making good impressions, and for developing relationships (Alac, 2017; Lin, Cross, & Childers, 2018; Low, 2006; Sorokowska, 2013; Sorokowska, Sorokowski, & Szmajke, 2012).

While a subtle whiff of perfume might cause someone to be more physically attracted to you, it's that "subtle" part that's important. We encourage students not to wear cologne when interviewing for a job, scholarship, or internship because nervousness or activation in the body can enhance the strength of a scent. You could overwhelm an interviewer and lose a job opportunity, all because your cologne was too strong. This applies to social situations as well; your cologne might increase in effect on a first date due to nerves. At any rate, smell and scent are key nonverbal cues related to physical appearance, so it's important to be mindful of the decisions you make in managing your body smell in both personal and professional situations.

Countless products on the market are designed to produce pleasant-smelling aromas.

As we've mentioned regarding other aspects of physical appearance, culture plays a huge role in forming expectations of smell (Hastings, Musambira, & Ayoub, 2011; Winslow, 2017). In the United States, any trace of natural body odor or sweat is considered bad. That's why we spend so much time and money dousing ourselves with soaps, perfumes, lotions, deodorants, and mouthwashes. In fact, if a bad odor is detected in a room or from a person, communication may come to a stop. But in an increasingly "global village," body odor becomes a complicated issue. You may find yourself working overseas or with people from another country or culture where the emphasis on body smell is not the same as in the United States. In some cultures, the predominant foods people eat cause their skin to emit a smell that people from another country aren't familiar or comfortable with. In these cases, it's not bad body odor; it's just a cultural symptom that an outsider may not understand or adopt.

chapter five

Waist-to-hip ratio	Body measurement of the waist in proportion to the hips
Obesity	Medical term for being significantly overweight
Olfaction	Role of smell in human interaction

Remember!
5.3

Hair

Are you a short-haired, long-haired, or no-haired person? What are your preferences in terms of the length of your own hair? What hair length do you find attractive on other people? Do you like blondes, brunettes, or redheads? These questions introduce another important feature of the body connected to our physical appearance—it's all about the hair.

HAIR COLOR. Many of us have formed perceptions of other people based on the color of their hair. We've heard "blonde jokes" and perhaps made the statement, "She's a dumb blonde." What can we learn from these comments? Right or wrong, we do form impressions of other people based on their hair color. In addition to our perception of other people's attractiveness, hair color tends to influence our evaluation of people's personality and intelligence. People with blonde hair, especially women, are stereotyped as less intelligent or "ditzy," while people with red hair are perceived as hot-tempered or fiery (Beddow, Hymes, & McAuslan, 2011). As we've discussed, people with brown or dark hair, especially men, are included in the more positive description of "tall, dark, and handsome."

Blonde, brown, and red tend to be the most typical colors associated with hair. Ah, but that reflects the youth of many of our readers. What about grey hair—something many of you don't have to think about but will someday? A highly successful industry—one consumed with hair dyeing, streaking, and highlighting—continues to attract consumers who wish to alter or mask this particular nonverbal cue of physical appearance. "Washing away the grey" can take years off a person's appearance, but what does that say about the person and the culture within which she or he lives? Should people feel pressured to cover up their age?

Let's talk about the more "creative" uses of hair dye; times have really changed on this front. Many of our college students view their hair as just another blank canvas on which to display their "art." What nonverbal cues do hair-dyeing processes communicate about a person?

HAIR LENGTH (QUANTITY). Do you like short or long hair, both on yourself and others? Hair length or quantity of hair is another factor to consider as part of our overall physical appearance.

The advice to men about hair and looks is mixed. Some younger men who want to be viewed as more mature are advised by hair stylists to let their hair grow long to conceal a baby face (Masip et al., 2004). While the times continue to change regarding hair length and credibility, still the predominant position or most conservative approach is for men with longer hair (below the collar) to cut or trim it for job interviews so they'll be viewed as professional, serious, and credible. Of course, it depends on the job and the workplace, because some interviewers for high-tech jobs would rather the men look like many of their employees, who often sport long hair, informal clothing, and so forth.

Women with long hair are often perceived as having sex appeal, hence the increased use of hair extensions, for that fuller, longer look. However, many professional women cut their hair to a shorter length to enhance their credibility and downplay their sexuality; some pull their hair up or back while at work and let it down at home. One study examined the "power of the bob," meaning a shorter haircut for women who want to be perceived as powerful and credible (McMurtrie, 2010). As we've said, perceptions about hair length in the workplace are changing, but just be aware that women with long hair in professional settings may still be viewed as incompetent and less intelligent.

As we explore hair length and its influence on physical appearance, it's important to think about hair loss. What impact does hair loss have on physical appearance? Men and women who live with baldness or lose their hair due to medical conditions (such as alopecia) or treatments (such as chemotherapy) may turn to medication, extreme comb-overs, hairpieces or plugs, hair replacement surgery, baseball caps, and so on to hide their hair loss (Cao et al., 2012; Kranz, 2011). Before we judge these efforts, remember

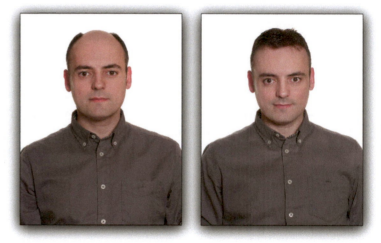

Baldness can have positive or negative impacts on perceptions of physical attractiveness, depending on one's culture and personal preferences.

that having hair may be critical to someone's attempts to regain a sense of self and normalcy, and to recover self-esteem that a serious illness or unexpected medical condition can damage (Thompson, 2009). Hair-loss products and services represent a multimillion-dollar industry in the United States. While some people want to hide their hair loss at all costs, others embrace the bald look, believing it conveys a certain image.

chapter five

BODY HAIR. In U.S. culture, women are expected to shave their armpits and legs. However, in many other cultures around the world, women don't shave these areas and their appearance is positively regarded. In recent years, young women in the United States especially feel a pressure to wax their pubic region—a trend that was unthinkable even a decade ago. Americans also have interesting rules or expectations about men's body hair—chest, arm, leg, and pubic hair are acceptable (to most people), but not back hair. How arbitrary is *that*? Because of such expectations, yet another lucrative industry devoted to altering our physical appearance has developed. Salons and spas offer waxing services and laser removal procedures to keep hair away; do-it-yourself kits are also available in any drugstore, if you're brave enough. Probably one of the best scenes depicting a man caving in to pressure to wax his body hair comes from the movie *The 40-Year-Old Virgin*, in which Steve Carell actually had some of his own chest hair waxed and removed, to add realism (and pain) to the scene. "Manscaping" is now a big business, with statistics showing that in the United States alone, men's hair removal is now a four billion-dollar industry (Le, 2016).

FACIAL HAIR. Medications, hormones, and genetics can cause women to grow facial hair, which is often viewed negatively because facial hair is linked with masculinity. But for men (at least in the United States), the beard is back! People's perceptions of men with facial hair vary, but in general, Americans are much more accepting of male facial hair than in past decades (perhaps with the exception of the 1970s). Many more beard-related products (e.g., oils, combs) are sold and "beard clubs" are popping up (Dixson, Tam, & Awasthy, 2012; Jannuzzi, 2015; Lawson, 2018). However, beards aren't popular with heterosexual women in the United Kingdom; 43% of women surveyed said that they would not sleep with a man with a beard, so once again, culture matters (Davies, 2018).

CLOTHING ■ ■ ■ ■

One of the ways we manage our physical appearance is by making decisions about our clothing. No matter whether you're very clothing-conscious or someone who just makes an effort to be covered, clothing conveys powerful nonverbal messages. Let's first examine the most common functions of clothing, then how clothing is a nonverbal cue related to appearance.

Functions of Clothing

Clothing does communicate something nonverbally to people in our daily interactions (Aliakbari & Abdollahi, 2013; Cundall & Guo, 2017; Gonzalez-Jimenez, 2016). According to communication scholars Knapp, Hall, and Horgan (2013), attire provides the following functions:

1. **Decoration:** We use clothing to decorate our bodies for everyday exhibition, such as wearing a T-shirt that supports a certain cause or group. We also decorate ourselves

with clothing for special occasions, such as costume parties, holidays, weddings, formal outings, and sporting events.

2. **Protection:** Another function of clothing is protection from intrusion or natural elements, such as inclement weather. In some occupations, certain attire is required because it protects the body from harm (e.g., hard hats, back braces, eye protectors, masks, latex gloves, bullet-proof vests, hazardous material suits).

3. **Sexual attraction:** Situations in which we want to be noticed and appear sexually attractive to other people can influence our decisions about clothing. Going out on a romantic date, having a special evening at home with our partner, or going out to a club with friends are a few situations in which our clothing choices may be designed to promote sexual attraction.

4. **Concealment:** We also use clothing as a general means of modesty; in most, if not all, cultures, the body is covered, even if only minimally. The function of concealment also means that we use clothing to hide or mask certain features of the body. During job interviews, applicants may wear long sleeves to hide tattoos, dark-colored clothing to camouflage extra weight, or oversized clothing so that a slender build isn't as evident.

5. **Group identification:** Sporting events, campus gatherings, and political rallies exemplify a few social contexts in which people wear clothing to celebrate and publicize their group identification. Many of us have sports jerseys in our closets because we're proud to be affiliated with and support our favorite teams. Some of us are members of a campus group, political party, or club; when we attend such groups' events, we may be encouraged to wear clothing to indicate our affiliation nonverbally.

6. **Persuasion:** Certain types of clothing, such as uniforms, are persuasive, in that they cause others to comply in ways like following directions, obeying traffic rules, and agreeing to medical staff persons' instructions.

7. **Status:** People respond (usually favorably) to high-status clothing—clothing that communicates achievement, professionalism, or financial success (Gurney et al., 2017; Gurung, Punke, Brickner, & Badalamenti, 2018; Howlett et al., 2015).

OUT OF THE CLASSROOM
onto the page

The clothing we wear reveals a great deal about us; our fashion preferences, income, culture, and profession are only some things our clothing communicates to others. With so many clothing choices out there, why do people make the decisions they do?

During one of our nonverbal communication class sessions, we asked students to discuss the clothes they were wearing and their reasons for wearing them. Many students volunteered to discuss their clothing choices and what they wanted to communicate through those choices.

Matt liked to wear Affliction, Tapout, and Venum clothing. These brands center on the world of mixed martial arts (MMA), of which Matt was both a fan and a competitor. Drianna preferred to wear business casual clothes to class; she was the office manager of a local business, so she wore clothes that communicated her professionalism. Evan favored informal clothing, mainly T-shirts with band logos or musical instrument brands on them. Evan was an aspiring musician, so his clothing choices were a show of solidarity for fellow musicians. Angelique preferred a funky, vintage look, which she could find at reasonable prices at thrift and second-hand shops. Jason was in to the cutting-edge approach, acclaiming the virtues of investing in clothing enhanced by technology, such as a vest with outlets for powering up his cell phone or headphones, and even a solar-powered jacket he'd recently purchased. At the end of the class discussion, it was apparent that most students had widely different reasons for picking their clothes.

Do you intend for your clothes to communicate something about you and your personality? What types of judgments do you make about others based on their clothing? In both your social and professional life, it's important to remember that clothing usually serves a purpose beyond necessity; clothing communicates status, social class, cultural background, and so forth. As a subset of your overall physical appearance, clothing is one of the most significant nonverbal cues people notice about you before any verbal information is exchanged.

Expressions of Personality and Culture

Clothing is also a nonverbal expression of our personality and culture. What type of personality is someone trying to express by wearing a T-shirt that says, "Spank Me," "For Sale," "I Taste Good," or "I'm out of estrogen and I have a gun!"?

Beyond expressions of personality, clothing also communicates and celebrates our cultural beliefs. The brightly colored gowns and matching headpieces worn by some African women, the beautiful saris (draped dresses) many Indian women wear, and the beaded outfits and elaborate feather headdresses displayed by leaders of Native American tribes are but a few examples of cultural expressions of clothing. In some cultures, women are expected to keep their heads covered, while in the Jewish culture, the men traditionally wear kipot (Jewish hats). One of the most extreme examples of cultural clothing comes from news footage of women in Afghanistan during the Taliban rule, forced to cover themselves in public from head to toe; the images of those blue burkas are seared in our minds.

Dressing to Connect with Others

Some of us dress a certain way because we feel that other people are going to like us more because of our clothing selection. Can clothing influence popularity? In fact, clothing can be beneficial to our interpersonal relationships. When we achieve **homophily** with others, or a perceived similarity in appearance, background, and attitudes, our relationships and level of popularity in other people's eyes are enhanced. We tend to like people whom we perceive to be similar to us, and this includes similarity in the clothes we wear. But the need for homophily can create pressure—peer pressure to conform and be trendy, seeking clothing that reflects current fashion trends (which can put pressure on the pocketbook as well). Some level of social appropriateness or fitting in is understandable, but we also encourage the "different drummer" in each of us.

One example of homophily and appearance comes from the world of work, where we see wide acceptance of the casual Friday approach (i.e., dressing down at work on Fridays; Goodman, 2015; TenBrink & Gelb, 2017) Even in recent presidential campaigns, candidates adhered to a casual Friday tradition by dressing more casually for their Friday public appearances (Givhan, 2011). While the trend toward more casual dress in the workplace is popular, casual Friday is not without its controversies. Some believe that if people can function effectively at work in casual clothing on Fridays, what's to say they can't be effective in such attire the rest of the workweek? Others believe that casual Friday or dressing down erodes a professional person's credibility, so it's a trend that should go away (Leszcz, 2013).

Many businesses have adopted a casual Friday dress code.

REMEMBER

Remember!
5.4

Decoration	How we decorate our bodies for celebrations and special occasions
Protection	How we use clothing to protect our bodies from intrusion or harm
Sexual attraction	Ways clothing helps draw sexual attention from others
Concealment	How clothing helps us conceal features of our body we don't want others to see
Group identification	How clothing allows us to communicate or celebrate a group we identify with or connect to
Persuasion	Ways clothing influences others' behavior
Status	How clothing communicates social and professional class
Homophily	Perceived similarity in people's appearance, background, and attitudes that benefits relationships

ARTIFACTS

In addition to clothing, **artifacts** such as jewelry, eyeglasses, cologne, and makeup are temporary or mobile aspects of physical adornment that provide clues about our personalities, attitudes, and behaviors and that nonverbally communicate something about us to other people (Crymble, 2012;

Netchaeva & Ress, 2016). You might think of a piercing or tattoo as an artifact or form of body decoration; however, we prefer to think of it this way: Artifacts are temporary—you can take off your jewelry or wash makeup off your face. While tattoo removal is a more available and affordable option these days, most tattoos remain (in some form) on the body. Most piercings are permanent, unless a hole goes without jewelry long enough that it heals shut. Since, in most situations, piercings and tattoos are permanent, we prefer to view them as body modifications and will discuss them in the next section of this chapter. For now, let's consider a few categories of artifacts and how they communicate nonverbally.

Jewelry

The most common artifact that comes to mind is jewelry. How many of us are wearing jewelry this very second, as we explore this topic? Rings, bracelets, anklets, watches, cufflinks, necklaces, earrings, nose rings, pins, and so on are examples of jewelry many of us wear on a daily basis. What nonverbal message does jewelry send? Wedding rings serve as a great example of how jewelry can inform us nonverbally about other people. If we're out on the town with friends for a fun evening and notice an attractive person across the room, one clue to figure out his or her availability is to look for a ring. If we notice a ring, we're led to believe that our person of interest isn't available. On the other hand, if we don't see a ring, it may be okay to approach, buy the person a drink, and ask for a phone number. However, we suggest caution here, in that some married men in the United States don't own or wear wedding rings, while many, if not most, married women do.

Take a moment to think about how jewelry communicates nonverbally. How does jewelry communicate status? Does a Rolex watch communicate a different image than a Swatch? A different message is certainly sent by diamonds versus rhinestones. What does too much jewelry communicate—possible compensation for insecurity about attractiveness? Some people in U.S. culture and in other parts of the world like to wear crosses, typically as necklaces or lapel pins. Should you assume that everyone who wears a cross is a member of the Christian faith? Was this the image Madonna wanted to communicate when she wore multiple crosses while singing "Like a Virgin"?

Eyeglasses

In addition to jewelry, eyeglasses (including sunglasses) also send nonverbal messages. For example, people who wear glasses are often perceived as being more intelligent and honest but also more nerdy than those without glasses. You've probably heard the old rhyme, "Boys don't make passes at girls who wear glasses," but is this still the case? Women with glasses may be viewed as brainy or studious, but glasses are also a fashion statement. Popular eyeglass styles and shapes seem to change constantly. For a while, large-framed eyeglasses were in style, then it wasn't long before the skinnier frames and no-rim glasses began to be seen as hip and cool.

chapter five

The way people use and wear eyeglasses also sends nonverbal signals. For example, people who chew on their glasses may be perceived as nervous and tense. People who push their eyeglasses up into their hair or onto their forehead may send a signal that they're willing to be approached—they attempt to make direct eye contact without the distraction of glasses. Just as we mentioned about hair color, eyeglasses can be seen as an artifact of the aging process. Many people with perfect eyesight in their youth find themselves needing glasses, contacts, or reading glasses when they reach their 40s or 50s. People who wear reading glasses are interesting to watch; they often use their glasses when trying to articulate or emphasize an important point, in conversation as well as in public speaking situations.

Then there are those who wear sunglasses indoors (such as rapper Lil John and actor Jack Nicholson). What nonverbal message does this behavior send? One possibility is that the wearer doesn't want anyone to see how bloodshot his or her eyes are, which could be an indication of alcohol or substance use. Another interpretation is that the wearer is covering up a black eye, which is often a telltale sign of physical abuse. Yet another view is that it allows wearers control over other people—they can see your eyes, but you can't see theirs. Or perhaps they simply believe it makes them look cool. Some people have medical conditions (like U2's Bono) that make their eyes extremely sensitive to light; so they aren't trying to send a nonverbal message at all—they're just trying to see! There's something unsettling about not being able to see someone's eyes, at least in American culture, but be careful not to rush to judgment before you know someone's reasons for shielding his or her eyes.

Makeup

Speaking of billion-dollar industries, we could go on forever about the cosmetics industry—but we won't. Instead, let's take a moment to examine cosmetics and the nonverbal messages sent by people wearing them.

Makeup is a common artifact, worn primarily by women and increasingly by men in American culture. Applications of makeup follow trends in our culture and other cultures around the world. While wearing bright blue lipstick might have been unthinkable a few years ago, we are witnessing more openness to nontraditional applications of all kinds of makeup. It seems that people are less judgmental about a person's choice of makeup, but one stereotype persists: Overdone makeup is, to many people, reminiscent of prostitutes.

While more acceptable now than in the past, men's use of makeup is still a controversial subject. Clinique was one of the first companies to develop a line of men's cosmetics, but men were slow to embrace these products. For some reason, bronzers are pretty well accepted, but, illogically enough, they're typically not viewed as a form of makeup by the men who wear them. If you can easily tell that a man is wearing makeup, what nonverbal signal does that send?

MODIFYING THE BODY ■ ■ ■

In this chapter, our purpose was to cover the reality of physical appearance; we said upfront, "Looks do matter." We've explored some aspects of physical appearance, as well as their effects on human behavior. But we do have some fears or reservations associated with the complex topic of **body modification**, meaning the more permanent methods of changing the way we look (Hill, Ogletree, & McCrary, 2016; Park, 2016; Rowsell, Kress, & Street, 2013; Wegenstein, 2012).

Fitness Post Envy

A lot of college students work out regularly, but are you one of those people who posts your workout, diet, and health gains on social media? While it's just as understandable to want to share fitness accomplishments as it is to share making good grades, getting a hoped-for job, or other positive things in life, can we agree that it can be annoying to see photo after photo with posts about how much weight someone is losing, how many reps someone got in that day, or how healthily someone is eating?

The research team of Analisa Arroyo and Steven Brunner (2016) explored some unintended consequences of social media posts on people's perceptions of their bodies and negative talk about their bodies. Close to 500 college students responded to a survey asking for the most frequent posts about health, fitness, and diet they typically saw or read on such social networking sites as Facebook, Twitter, Instagram, and Pinterest. The six most-reported posts were as follows: (1) pictures of healthy food, cooked or eaten; (2) pictures of oneself working out; (3) posts about one's workout; (4) inspirational fitness quotations or images; (5) before and after pictures of oneself; and (6) statistics on one's workout, like how many calories were burned or miles were run. Subjects also reported on how often they viewed or read such social media posts. Then subjects responded to scales assessing negative body talk (how often and in what ways did they talk negatively about their body) and satisfaction with their body.

The results showed that the more these college students saw or read health, diet, and fitness photos and posts by their friends on social media, the more they compared themselves negatively to others, talked about their body negatively, and were dissatisfied with their body. These results were more pronounced in women than men in the study. So while you might think it's fun or motivating (to you as well as your friends on social media) to share your experiences with fitness, diet, and health, and improvements you're making to your body, consider the nonverbal signals such activity sends and the possible effects on others. Your accomplishments may not be as encouraging or motivating as you might think.

Do you want to know more about this study? If so, read Arroyo, A., & Brunner, S. R. (2016). Negative body talk as an outcome of friends' fitness posts on social networking sites: Body surveillance and social comparison as potential moderators. *Journal of Applied Communication Research, 44*, 216-235.

Cosmetic procedures are more popular than ever. In 2017, the rate of cosmetic surgical procedures being performed in the United States was up 11% over the previous year, with breast augmentation being the most prevalent (American Society for Aesthetic Plastic Surgery, 2018). Women still outpace men in opting for cosmetic procedures; the fastest-growing surgical procedures from 2012 to 2017 were eyelid surgery (to lift droopy eyelids or to create a crease to make the eyes look larger) and buttock augmentation. The practice of injecting materials like Botox, primarily into the face, increased 40% over the same five-year period (American Society for Aesthetic Plastic Surgery, 2018).

We're not suggesting that people should *not* care about how they look or *not* strive for good health. Instead, we want to talk about the *need* to modify ourselves, this process of customizing our bodies to match up to some idealized beauty standard. We know our readers are adults and can make up their own minds about body modification, but the constant pressure to improve our physical appearance can take a toll on our emotional stability and warp our priorities in life. A barrage of persuasive messages from the media and the Internet create an expectation to transform ourselves, bringing the process of modifying our bodies into a normal part of conversation. **Normalization**—the process of making a viewpoint or action about something such a normal and everyday part of reality that it can't be questioned—benefits cosmetic, fitness, and food industries, among others. Normalization destigmatizes cosmetic surgery, procedures, piercing, and tattooing, making these choices a more acceptable part of daily life and less the exception than the rule (Brooks, 2004; Calogero et al., 2013; Kalus & Cregan, 2017). The more something becomes accepted or normalized, the less we question it or think to ask: Is this good for me? Why am I even considering doing this? Not reflecting in this way can lead to some hasty decisions; some choices pan out over time, but some decisions are regrettable (and irreversible) down the road.

You've probably seen or read about people, mostly women, who are addicted to cosmetic surgery—those people who have multiple surgeries but are still never happy with the way they look. There's actually a term for this problem: Body Dysmorphic Disorder, a preoccupation with a bodily defect and a propensity toward cosmetic surgery (Ehsani et al., 2013; Phillips, 2018). Our concerns about body modifications don't stem from worries about "going under the knife" or a fear of botched medical procedures. The concern centers around an increasing dissatisfaction with our natural selves, fostered by the constant talk about enlarging, reducing, buffing, bulking, filling, piercing, whitening, suctioning, tattooing, and tightening various parts of the body. As we explore this important topic, consider how normalized body modification has become in your life. Think about the pros and cons of body modification, examining about what you believe you'll gain if you change your body in these ways.

Piercings

Very simply, **piercings** are holes in the skin created for the purposes of wearing jewelry and expressing oneself. They are an ancient yet increasingly popular form of body modification, sometimes viewed as body art, that can send nonverbal messages (Hong & Young Lee, 2017; Lim, Ting, Leo, & Jayanthy, 2013). One extension of the piercing phenomenon is **stretching**, the practice of expanding a piercing by wearing larger and larger gauges to widen the hole in the ear lobe. While stretching is a popular form of self-expression (even rebellion) for some people, others cringe at the sight of the large, gaping holes in people's ear lobes once the gauges are removed.

Researchers have attempted to learn college students' motivations for getting piercings as well as their sources of influence. Multiple studies indicate that a majority of students hold a positive image of body art, view piercings as a form of self-expression and a way to be unique, and report that friends (not family) are major influences on their piercing decisions (Hong & Young Lee, 2017; Johncock, 2012). To some people, body modification is a rite of passage, whether social or cultural. Other research into piercing has examined the following connections: piercing and a higher rate of suicide attempts (Hicinbothem, Gonsalves, & Lester, 2006); the relationship between engaging in healthy behaviors and the likelihood of getting tattoos and piercings (Gillen & Markey, 2017; Huxley & Grogan, 2005); the correlation between piercing and mental health (Stim, Hinz, & Brahler, 2006); how piercing relates to masculine development (Denness, 2005); and tattooing and body piercing as risk-taking behaviors and self-harm, just as eating disorders are considered risky behavior and a means of harming oneself (Claes, Vandereycken, & Vertommen, 2005; Holbrook, Minocha, & Laumann, 2012; King & Vidourek, 2013; Preti, Pinna, Nocco, & Mulliri, 2006).

For some people, there's no limit to the location of the piercing. One study distinguished non-intimate piercing locations (e.g., ears, eyebrows, lips, bellybutton, nose, tongue) from intimate locations (e.g., nipples, penis, vagina) and explored characteristics of people choosing to receive intimate piercings (Caliendo, Armstrong, & Roberts, 2005). People with intimate piercings described themselves as young; well-educated; less likely to get married; of sexual orientations that included heterosexual, homosexual, and bisexual; and having initiated sexual activity at an earlier age than the average person in the U.S. population. Their purposes for getting intimate piercings include uniqueness, self-expression, and sexual expression.

Other research explored a possible link between piercings and tattoos and the sexual behaviors of young adults. A total of 120 young adults (some with body modifications, some without) were surveyed regarding their sexuality. The findings indicated that subjects with body modifications had their first intercourse statistically earlier, were more sexually active, and held more liberal attitudes toward sexual behavior than subjects who did not modify their bodies (Nowosielski, Sipiski, Kuczerawy, Kozłowska-Rup, & Skrzypulec-Plinta, 2012).

How are body modifications perceived by potential employers? In 2006, scholar Nancy Swanger examined the perceptions of college recruiters and human resource managers toward interviewees who had visible body modifications; almost 90% of recruiters and managers viewed the tattoos and piercings of interviewees negatively. But times have changed (somewhat). While more recent research affirms the tendency for employers to hold negative views of employee body modifications, attitudes vary depending on the location of the modification on an employee's body (visible versus hidden) and how close-ly the employee works with customers (Timming, 2014). So we understand that you want to be true to yourself on a job interview, but you can still do that while camouflaging, rather than flaunting, your tattoos and removing jewelry from some of your piercings (including earrings on men), given the potential for employers to view these body modifications negatively.

What are the possible nonverbal messages sent by someone with a piercing or multiple piercings?

Tattoos

In addition to piercings, **tattoos**—temporary or permanent ink messages, symbols, and art placed on the body—are also a popular form of body modification (Dunden & Francis, 2016; Pfeifer, 2012; Rowsell et al., 2013). The number of people getting tattoos has increased dramatically in recent years, leading one research team to call tattoos "common, accepted, and mainstream" (Hill et al., 2016, p. 251). While tattooing used to be viewed as an act of deviance (something only soldiers, sailors, convicts, bikers, and drunken people did), today's tattoos are often planned in advance and well thought out in terms of both design and body location (Dickson, Dukes, Smith, & Strapko, 2014, 2015; Strubel & Jones, 2017). All sorts of people now get tattoos—people you might not expect to have them. Even Barbie got a tattoo in 2009, to the horror of some parents (*NBC Nightly News*, 2009). Some people get tattoos in tribute to other people, but here's one piece of advice: Avoid tattooing the name of your current love interest on your body; we hate to be pessimists, but you might live to regret that decision. TV shows such as TLC's *America's Worst Tattoos* showcase people who regret a poorly drawn or ill-conceived tattoo and seek out tattoo artists to fix their "mistakes."

Studies have found some negative trends about people who choose to get tats, particular-ly multiple tats, such as increased alcohol consumption, earlier-than-expected sexual activity, sui-cide ideation, rate of suicide attempts, and depression (Guégen, 2012a, 2012b; Koch, Roberts, Armstrong, & Owen, 2015; Nowosielski et al., 2012). While tats are much more common now-adays, negative perceptions persist about tats and the people who get them. Location matters, as many people are negative about face tattoos and those close to the face, like on the neck area (Zestcott, Bean, & Stone, 2017). The genre of a tattoo (e.g., tribal, traditional, Japanese) can also cause perceptions to vary (Timming, 2014).

What nonverbal messages are sent by someone who has a visible tattoo? Is the person an ex-hibitionist, a risk taker, a masochist (a lover of pain), or just a free spirit who views her or his body as a blank canvas, primed for artistic expression? Conversely, what's conveyed nonverbally when someone gets a tattoo on a part of the body that she or he can't see—that only others can see? A few years back, a friend had a large sunflower (about 6 by 6 inches) tattooed on her lower back. (Yes, we know this is fondly called a "tramp stamp.") We found this interesting because obviously she could see the tattoo only in a mirror—why get a tattoo mainly for other people to see? What nonverbal signal does this send?

WHAT WOULD *YOU* DO?

Bianca is proud of her colorful, multiple tattoos. She was scared to get her first one—mostly worried about the pain and what her parents might think—but she never regretted any of her decisions to get the tats. But an odd thing started happening: She got lots of comments (mostly compliments like, "Nice tattoo!") from men—men she didn't know, complete strangers who chose to speak to her about her tats. Some asked "Where'd you get that?" The frequency of this happening started to irritate and then alarm her. She told a friend about it and they Googled tattoo harassment, just to see if there was anything written on the subject. Lo and behold, they found an article posted by Melissa Fabello, frequent contributor to everydayfeminism.com, in which Fabello coined the term "tatcalling." Like Bianca, Fabello tired of constant comments about her tats, such as one guy at an airport Starbucks asking her to turn so he could see fully the tats on her legs. Bianca hadn't viewed the comments as a form of street harassment, similar to "catcalling," because to her this form of body art was her choice, a point of pride. She now struggled to cope with all the attention, wondering if covering up her tats was the right thing to do or a cop out. Was she being overly sensitive to male attention? Should she just suck it up or should she call out the behavior when it happened again?

If you were Bianca, *what would you do*? Would you stand your ground, enjoy your tats being visible, and work to change your response to people's comments about your tattoos? Would you tell people their comments were unwanted, unappreciated, and a form of "tatcalling"? Or would you cover up your tats to avoid uncomfortable attention about them?

Cosmetic Surgery and Procedures

Have you ever thought about getting cosmetic surgery? AMC's popular series *Freakshow* showcases a wide variety of unique body modifications, often ones that require extensive procedures or even surgery. If you're someone who would never get a full-on surgery, what about cosmetic procedures such as Botox injections, varicose vein or stretch mark removals, or collagen injections in your lips? Beyond having fat sucked from your hips or getting breast implants, a whole series of procedures are now advertised by cosmetic surgeons, laser spas, and salons across the world (Cook & Dwyer, 2017; Lee, 2014). Below are the top five body modification surgeries performed in 2017, according to the American Society for Aesthetic Plastic Surgery (2018):

chapter five

1. *Breast augmentation:* Most common cosmetic procedure in the United States, a process of enlarging the breasts through the insertion of implants
2. *Liposuction:* A process of suctioning fat from the body
3. *Eyelid blepharoplasty:* Altering the appearance of eyelids, either because of drooping (that impairs vision) or a desire to have larger, more Western-looking eyes
4. *Breast lift:* Raising the position of the breasts so as to correct and prevent sagging
5. *Tummy tuck:* Surgery to remove excess skin around the stomach area, typically caused by being overweight or pregnancy

Certainly, there are pros and cons to body modification procedures and treatments. Here's our question: What nonverbal signals are sent when someone alters his or her physical appearance in such ways? Some people who have liposuction or a tummy tuck may be criticized because they didn't attempt to lose weight or tighten fatty places the "old-fashioned way" (through diet and exercise). But many people *have* tried repeatedly to lose weight or tone up after losing considerable weight, and results just aren't possible for them. Like most things in life, it's wise to get as much information as possible and resist the urge to critique before knowing the facts and circumstances behind people's choices.

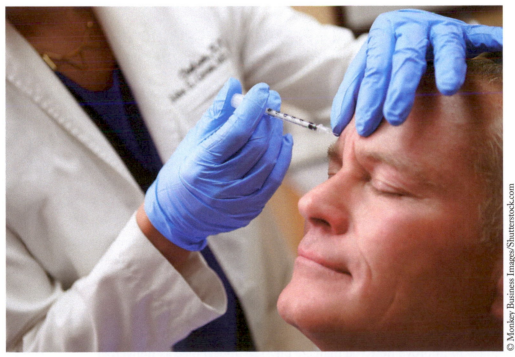

© Monkey Business Images/Shutterstock.com

Botox injections are an increasingly popular form of cosmetic procedure in the United States. What's your view of such a procedure? Is it just another useful beauty tool or a crazy thing to do, to get injected with a toxic substance, to camouflage a wrinkle?

Artifacts	Temporary aspects of physical adornment other than clothing (e.g., jewelry, eyeglasses, cologne, makeup) that provide clues about our personalities, attitudes, and behaviors and that nonverbally communicate something about us to other people
Body modification	More permanent methods of changing physical appearance (e.g., piercings, tattoos, cosmetic procedures)
Normalization	Process of making a viewpoint or action such a normal and everyday part of reality that it can't be questioned
Piercings	Form of body modification created by putting holes into the skin for the purpose of wearing jewelry
Stretching	Practice of expanding a healed piercing by wearing larger and larger gauges to widen the hole in the ear lobe
Tattoos	Form of body modification involving temporary or permanent ink messages or images placed on the body

UNDERSTANDING PHYSICAL APPEARANCE: APPLYING THE REFLEXIVE CYCLE OF NONVERBAL COMMUNICATION DEVELOPMENT

Have you ever thought about how you manage physical appearance in your own life? How much time do you spend thinking about your physical appearance? Recall our discussion of the Reflexive Cycle of Nonverbal Development in Chapter 2. The first step to developing your skills and a better understanding of nonverbal communication is awareness. In the realm of physical appearance, we ask you to inventory yourself using the following questions: What standards do you have regarding your own appearance? What are your needs or preferences regarding the physical appearance of other people? Do you have expectations or rules about looks? Do these judgments vary depending on who the person is or whether the relationship is personal or professional? Are you aware of the impressions others may have about you based on your physical appearance?

Now that you have engaged in an inventory of self in relation to physical appearance, it's time to think about making, if necessary, any appropriate changes to improve how you manage physical appearance as nonverbal communication in everyday life. This is Phase 2 in the Reflexive Cycle. Ask yourself: Are there some changes I need to make in my physical appearance, perhaps with regard to cleanliness, attire, jewelry, hair, or weight? If so, how can I make those changes? Perhaps the only thing that needs to change is your attitude about your physical appearance; perhaps you need to work on being less self-critical and accepting yourself more as you are physically.

Beyond engaging in an inventory of self and making appropriate changes, the next step is to inventory others. Can you think of a person who seems to have no awareness of his or her physical appearance? Images of a sloppy friend who wears wrinkled clothes (the same ones for days in a row) and practices bad hygiene may come to mind. These people may lack self-aware-ness or maybe they just couldn't care less about how they look. The problem is, most of us live in a culture where looks matter. While we agree that U.S. culture's overemphasis on appearance is a problem, we acknowledge the im-portance of learning to live effectively in a social context. We need to be aware that the physical appearance we maintain (or not) sends nonverbal signals to other people.

After you have done an inventory of self, changed self, and inventoried others' nonverbal behavior, the fourth phase of the Reflexive Cycle involves interacting with others, trying out the changes you've made or are in the process of making, and observing people as you verbally and nonverbally interact with them. Do people have different re-actions to you as a result of any changes you made? For example, some peo-ple who've lost a lot of weight can't handle the different way people respond to them; sometimes this effect is so pronounced and uncomfortable that it drives them to regain the weight. As another example, some men decide to shave their beards and mustaches, just for a change; when they interact with people after changing this aspect of their appearance, most people notice that something is different (e.g., "You look younger"; "Have you lost weight?"), but they can't put their finger on what has changed. It can be interesting to note people's reactions to both subtle and obvious changes in your physical appearance and how that makes you feel, as well as to gauge your own reactions to changes in others' appearance.

In the last part of the cycle, we challenge you to review and assess the whole process, making note of positive and negative aspects, and then to begin the cycle again. Remember, the development of communication skills is a never-ending process as we work to develop our nonverbal abilities on a whole range of topics, not just physical appearance.

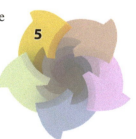

SUMMARY ■ ■ ■

In this chapter, we established physical appearance as a nonverbal communication code and emphasized the need to be aware of our physical appearance, as well as how we respond to the physical appearance of other people. For two reasons, we need to give special attention to physical appearance as a nonverbal communication code: (1) The decisions we make to maintain or alter our physical appearance reveal a great deal about who we are, and (2) the physical appearance of other people impacts our perceptions of them, how we communicate with them, how approachable they are, how attractive or unattractive they are, and so on.

Next, we defined physical attractiveness—a culturally derived perception of beauty, formed by such bodily features as height, weight, size, shape, and so on—and explored the effects of physical attractiveness in contexts such as interviews and hiring decisions, educational settings, and dating and marriage. We also introduced the matching hypothesis, which explains our tendency to seek romantic partners whom we perceive to be equal to us in physical attractiveness.

We then discussed somatyping, meaning the classification of people according to three different body types—ectomorphs, mesomorphs, endomorphs. The next few sections on physical appearance examined weight, height as related to status, and the disabled body for their ability to communicate something about us nonverbally. We then explored other features of the body (skin color, body smell, and hair) for the important role they play in physical appearance, and we re-introduced olfaction as the role of smell in human interaction. Next, we studied clothing, and its various functions, as a form of nonverbal communication. We then defined *homophily* as a perceived similarity in appearance, background, and attitudes that enhances our interpersonal relationships, and we discussed how clothing can serve to connect us to others. The last topic in this section was an examination of artifacts (jewelry, eyeglasses, cologne, makeup) and what they nonverbally communicate about us to other people.

The final section explored the complex topic of body modification, including discussions of the nonverbal messages sent by piercings, tattoos, and cosmetic surgery and procedures. We presented the problem of normalization—making something in society so everyday and commonplace that it goes without question—in relation to people's motivations for modifying their bodies. Finally, we closed the chapter by applying the Reflexive Cycle of Nonverbal Communication Development to our understanding of physical appearance.

DISCUSSION STARTERS ■ ■ ■

1. Explain how physical appearance is a form of nonverbal communication. What does your overall physical appearance communicate about you to others?

2. What is the difference between physical attraction and attractiveness? Do you believe that you can find people physically attractive but not be attracted to them?

3. Review Sheldon's three body types and relate them to figures in popular media. Do you think knowledge of body types is useful?

4. Think about how many self-improvement products exist in the United States related to physical appearance, especially to weight loss or gain. Make a list of these products and discuss the ones that might actually help someone, versus those that are bogus. Do you feel compelled or pressured to use these products?

5. What do you think about the discussion of the disabled body presented in this chapter? Have you ever thought about this aspect of nonverbal communication? How might your nonverbal cues change with persons who have disabilities, now that you know more about this topic?

6. Looking at the various functions of clothing provided in this chapter, consider your own strategies or preferences for the way you dress in various social situations. Are you more likely to dress for comfort and protection, rather than to express your personality? How is your clothing a form of nonverbal communication about you?

7. We talked a good deal in this chapter about body modification, in specific, piercings, tattoos, cosmetic surgery and procedures, and the problem of normalization. Have your views on body modification changed as you've gotten older and been exposed to different kinds of situations? What nonverbal cues do you receive about people who have piercings and/or tattoos?

REFERENCES ■ ■ ■

Adult obesity facts. (2016). Retrieved from www.cdc.gov/obesity/data

Agthe, M., Sporrle, M., & Maner, J. K. (2010). Don't hate me because I'm beautiful: Anti-attractiveness bias in organizational evaluation and decision making. *Journal of Experimental Social Psychology, 46*, 1151–1154.

Alac, M. (2017). We like to talk about smell: A worldly take on language, sensory experience, and the Internet. *Semiotica, 2017,* 143–192.

Aliakbari, M., & Abdollahi, K. (2013). Does it matter what we wear? A sociolinguistic study of clothing and human values. *International Journal of Linguistics, 5,* 34–45.

American Society for Aesthetic Plastic Surgery. (2018). Cosmetic surgery national data bank statistics, 2018. Retrieved from www.asaps.org

Amon, M. J. (2015). Visual attention in mixed-gender groups. *Frontiers in Psychology, 5,* 1–10.

Andersen, P. A. (2004). *The complete idiot's guide to body language.* New York: Alpha.

Arroyo, A., & Brunner, S. R. (2016). Negative body talk as an outcome of friends' fitness posts on social networking sites: Body surveillance and social comparison as potential moderators. *Journal of Applied Communication Research, 44,* 216–235.

Australian, The. (2018, May 30). French Open: Serena Williams returns to grand slam in black body suit. Retrieved from https://www.theaustralian.com.au/sport/tennis/french-open-serena-williams-returns-to-grand-slam-in-black-body-suit/news-story/55538bbf35376eb209ba1616b8cc8463

Bakhshi, S., & Baker, A. (2011). "I think a fair girl would have better marriage prospects than a dark one": British Indian adults' perceptions of physical appearance ideals. *Europe's Journal of Psychology, 7,* 458–486.

Barak-Brandes, S., & Lachover, E. (2016). Branding relations: Mother-daughter discourse on beauty and body in an Israeli campaign by Dove. *Communication, Culture, & Critique, 9,* 379–394.

Bar-Tal, D., & Saxe, L. (1976). Perceptions of similarity and dissimilarity of attractive couples and individuals. *Journal of Personality and Social Psychology, 33,* 772–781.

Basu, M. (2013, September 26). "White is beautiful": Why India needs its own Oprah Winfrey. *CNN.* Retrieved from http://www.cnn.com/2013/09/25/world/asia/indian-ideal-of-beauty/

Beddow, M., Hymes, R., & McAuslan, P. (2011). Hair color stereotypes and their associated perceptions in relationships and the workplace. *Psi Chi Journal of Undergraduate Research, 16,* 12–19.

Bee, C. C., & Havitz, M. E. (2010). Exploring the relationship between involvement, fan attraction, psychological commitment and behavioral loyalty in a sports spectator context. *International Journal of Sports Marketing & Sponsorship, 11,* 140–157.

Bissell, K., & Rask, A. (2010). Real women on real beauty: Self-discrepancy, internalization of the thin ideal, and perceptions of attractiveness and thinness in Dove's Campaign for Real Beauty. *International Journal of Advertising, 29,* 643–668.

Bovet, J., & Raymond, M. (2015). Preferred women's waist-to-hip ratio variation over the last 2500 years. *PLoS ONE, 10:* e0123284.

Braithwaite, D. O. (1990). From majority to minority: An analysis of cultural change from able bodied to disabled. *International Journal of Intercultural Relations, 14,* 465–483.

Braithwaite, D. O. (1991). "Just how much did that wheelchair cost?": Management of privacy boundaries by persons with disabilities. *Western Journal of Speech Communication, 55,* 254–274.

Braithwaite, D. O. (1996). "I am a person first": Different perspectives on the communication of persons with disabilities. In E. B. Ray (Ed.), *Communication and disenfranchisement: Social health issues and implications* (pp. 257–272). Mahwah, NJ: Erlbaum.

Braithwaite, D. O., & Braithwaite, C. A. (2014). "Which is my good leg?": Cultural communication of persons with disabilities. In L. A. Samovar, R. E. Porter, E. R. McDaniel, & C. Sexton Roy (Eds.), *Intercultural communication: A reader* (14th ed., pp. 162–173). Boston: Cengage Learning.

Braithwaite, D. O., & Thompson, T. L. (2000). *Handbook of communication and people with disabilities: Research and application.* Mahwah, NJ: Erlbaum.

Brierley, M-E., Brooks, K. R., Mond, J., Stevenson, R. J., & Stephen, I. D. (2016). The body and the beautiful: Health, attractiveness and body composition in men's and women's bodies. *PLoS ONE, 11:* e0156722.

chapter five

Brooks, A. (2004). Under the knife and proud of it: An analysis of the normalization of cosmetic surgery. *Critical Sociology, 30*, 207–239.

Caliendo, C., Armstrong, M. L., & Roberts, A. E. (2005). Self-reported characteristics of women and men with intimate body piercings. *Journal of Advanced Nursing, 49*, 474–484.

Calogero, R., Pina, A., & Sutton, R. (2013). Cutting words: Priming self-objectification increases women's intention to pursue cosmetic surgery. *Psychology of Women Quarterly, 38*, 197–207.

Cao, T. W., Mauro, L. M., Tabas, I. A., Chen, A. L., Lianes, I. C., & Jiminez, J. J. (2012). Cross-section trichometry: A clinical tool for assessing the progression and treatment response of alopecia. *International Journal of Trichology, 4*, 259–264.

Cavico, F. J., Muffler, S. C., & Mujtaba, B. G. (2012). Appearance discrimination, "lookism" and "lookphobia" in the workplace. *Journal of Applied Business Research, 28*, 791–802.

Chen, J-Y. (2015). Female college students' attitudes toward non-surgical cosmetic procedures. *Intercultural Communication Studies, 24*, 116–130.

Ciochin, R. (2013). The body perceived. The body shown. *Annals of Spiru Haret University, Journalism Studies, 14*, 19–25.

Claes, L., Vandereycken, W., & Vertommen, H. (2005). Self-care versus self-harm: Piercing, tattooing, and self-injuring in eating disorders. *European Eating Disorders, 13*, 11–18.

Commisso, M., & Finkelstein, L. (2012). Physical attractiveness bias in employee termination. *Journal of Applied Social Psychology, 42*, 2968–2987.

Cook, P. S., & Dwyer, A. (2017). No longer raising eyebrows: The context and domestication of Botox as a mundane medical and cultural artefact. *Journal of Consumer Culture, 17*, 887–909.

Cordes, M., Vocks, S., Dtising, R., Bauer, A., & Waldorf, M. (2016). Male body image and visual attention towards oneself and other men. *Psychology of Men & Masculinity, 17*, 243–354.

Cowart, K. O., & Lehnert, K. D. (2018). Empirical evidence of the effect of colorism on customer evaluations. *Psychology & Marketing, 35*, 357–367.

Crymble, S. B. (2012). Contradiction sells: Feminine complexity and gender identity dissonance in magazine advertising. *Journal of Communication Inquiry, 36*, 62–84.

Cundall, A., & Guo, K. (2017). Women gaze behaviour in assessing female bodies: The effects of clothing, body size, own body composition and body satisfaction. *Psychological Research, 81*, 1–12.

Cuny, C., & Opaswongkarn, T. (2017). "Why do young Thai women desire white skin?" Understanding conscious and nonconscious motivations of young women in Bangkok. *Psychology & Marketing, 34*, 556–568.

Davies, H. J. (2018, June 4). To beard or not to beard: Is facial hair really a turnoff? Retrieved from https://www.theguardian.com/fashion/shortcuts/2018/jun/04/to-beard-or-not-to-beard-is-facial-hair-really-a-turn-off

Defeciani, L. (2016). Eating disorders and body image concerns among male athletes. *Clinical Social Work Journal, 44*, 114–123.

Del Zotto, M., & Pegna, A. J. (2017). Electrophysiological evidence of perceived sexual attractiveness for human female bodies varying in waist-to-hip ratio. *Cognitive, Affective, & Behavioral Neuroscience, 17*, 577–591.

Denness, B. (2005). Tattooing and piercing: Initiation rites and masculine development. *British Journal of Psychotherapy, 22*, 21–36.

Dickson, L., Dukes, R., Smith, H., & Strapko, N. (2014). Stigma of ink: Tattoo attitudes among college students. *The Social Science Journal, 51*, 268–276.

Dickson, L., Dukes, R., Smith, H., & Strapko, N. (2015). To ink or not to ink: The meaning of tattoos among college students. *College Student Journal, 49*, 106–120.

Di Domenico, S. I., Quitasol, M. N., & Fournier, M. A. (2015). Ratings of conscientiousness from physical appearance predict undergraduate academic performance. *Journal of Nonverbal Behavior, 39*, 339–353.

Dimitrius, J., & Mazzarella, M. (1999). *Reading people: How to understand people and predict their behavior—anytime, anyplace.* New York: Ballantine.

Dixon, B. J., Tam, J. C., & Awasthy, M. (2013). Do women's preferences for men's facial hair change with reproductive status? *Behavioral Ecology, 24*, 708–716.

Dolezal, L. (2015). *The body and shame: Phenomenology, feminism, and the socially shaped body.* Lanham, MD: Lexington.

Doring, T., & Wansink, B. (2017). The waiter's weight: Does a server's BMI relate to how much food diners order? *Environment & Behavior, 49*, 192–214.

Dunden, L., & Francis, A. (2016). Inking and thinking: Honor students and tattoos. *College Student Journal, 50*, 219–223.

Edwards, C., Edwards, A., Qing, Q., & Wahl, S. T. (2007). The influence of computer-mediated word-of-mouth communication on student perceptions of instructors and attitudes toward learning course content. *Communication Education, 56*, 255–277.

Egolf, D. B., & Corder, L. E. (1991). Height differences of low and high job status female and male corporate employees. *Sex Roles, 24*, 365–373.

Ehsani, A., Fakour, Y., Gholamali, F., Mokhtari, L., Sadat Hosseini, M., Khosrovanmehr, N., et al. (2013). Prevalence of body dysmorphic disorder in patients referred to Razi hospital cosmetic clinic with complaints of cosmetic disorders. *Tehran University Medical Journal, 71*, 164–170.

El Jurdi, H., & Smith, S. (2018). Mirror, mirror: National identity and the pursuit of beauty. *Journal of Consumer Marketing, 35*, 40–50.

Enzinna, M. N. (2016/2017). Reconsidering nonverbal communication among children with mental and physical disabilities. *Journal of the Communication, Speech, and Theatre Association of North Dakota, 29*, 56–70.

Fabello, M. A. (2015, June 30). My tats aren't an invitation for harassment—so please stop "tatcalling" me. Retrieved from https://everydayfeminism.com/2015/06/tattoos-are-not-invitations/

Fitzgerald, C. J., Horgan, T. G., & Himes, S. M. (2016). Shaping men's memory: The effects of a female's waist-to-hip ratio on men's memory for her appearance and biographical information. *Evolution & Human Behavior, 37*, 510–516.

Forbes, G. B., Adams-Curtis, L. E., Rade, B., & Jaberg, P. (2001). Body dissatisfaction in women and men: The role of gender-typing and self-esteem. *Sex Roles, 44*, 461–484.

Fromuth, M. E., Kelly, D. B., Wilson, A. K., Finch, L. V., & Scruggs, L. (2013). An exploratory study of the effects of teacher attractiveness on undergraduates' perceptions of teacher-student sexual involvement. *Journal of Child Sexual Abuse, 22*, 341–357.

Furnham, A., McClelland, A., & Omer, L. (2003). A cross-cultural comparison of ratings of perceived fecundity and sexual attractiveness as a function of body weight and waist-to-hip ratio. *Psychology, Health and Medicine, 8*, 219–230.

chapter five

Galobardes, B., McCormack, V. A., McCarron, P., Howe, L. D., Lynch, J., Lawlor, D. A., et al. (2012). Social inequalities in height: Persisting differences today depend upon height of the parents. *PLoS ONE, 7,* 1–18.

Geddes, R. A., Tyson, G. A., & McGreal, S. (2013). Gender bias in the education system: Perceptions of teacher-student sexual relationships. *Psychiatry, Psychology and the Law, 20,* 608–618.

Geller, S. (2006). The anatomy of casual Friday. *DNR: Daily News Record, 36,* 42–45.

Gibson, J., & Gore, J. (2016). Is he a hero or a weirdo? How norm violations influence the halo effect. *Gender Issues, 33,* 299–310.

Gillen, M. M., & Markey, C. H. (2017). Beauty and the burn: Tanning and other appearance-altering attitudes and behaviors. *Psychology, Health & Medicine, 22,* 1271–1277.

Givhan, R. (2011, August 15). The casual-Friday campaign. *Newsweek, 158,* 161.

Gonzalez-Jimenez, H. (2016). Associations between cosmopolitanism, body appreciation, self-esteem and sought functions of clothing. *Personality & Individual Differences, 101,* 110–113.

Goodman, E. N. (2015). Master casual Fridays. *Ebony, 70,* 48–49.

Guégen, N. (2012a). Tattoos, piercings, and alcohol consumption. *Alcoholism: Clinical & Experimental Research, 36,* 1253–1256.

Guégen, N. (2012b). Tattoos, piercings, and sexual activity. *Social Behavior and Personality, 40,* 1543–1548.

Guerrero, L. K., & Floyd, K. (2006). *Nonverbal communication in close relationships.* Mahwah, NJ: Erlbaum.

Gurney, D. J., Howlett, N., Pine, K., Tracey, M., & Moggridge, R. (2017). Dressing up posture: The interactive effects of posture and clothing on competency judgments. *British Journal of Psychology, 108,* 436–451.

Gurung, R. A. R., Punke, E., Brickner, M., & Badalamenti, V. (2018). Power and provocativeness: The effects of subtle changes in clothing on perceptions of working women. *The Journal of Social Psychology, 158,* 252–255.

Guy, G. P., Berkowitz, Z., Holman, D., & Hartman, A. (2015). Recent changes in the prevalence and factors associated with frequency of indoor tanning among U.S. adults. *JAMA Dermatol, 151,* 1256–1259.

Hamermesh, D. (2011). *Beauty pays: Why attractive people are more successful.* Princeton, NJ: Princeton University Press.

Harrison, K., Taylor, L., & Marske, A. (2006). Women's and men's eating behavior following exposure to ideal-body images and text. *Communication Research, 33,* 507–529.

Hartman, K. B., & Hunt, J. B. (2013). What ratemyprofessor.com reveals about how and why students evaluate their professors: A glimpse into the student mind-set. *Marketing Education Review, 23,* 151–161.

Hastings, S. O., Musambira, G. W., & Ayoub, R. (2011). Revisiting Edward T. Hall's work on Arabs and olfaction: An update with implications for intercultural communication scholarship. *Journal of Intercultural Communication Research, 40,* 3–20.

Hicinbothem, J., Gonsalves, S., & Lester, D. (2006). Body modification and suicidal behavior. *Death Studies, 30,* 351–363.

Hickey-Moody, A. (2016). Being different in public. *Continuum: Journal of Media & Cultural Studies, 30,* 531–541.

Hill, B. M., Ogletree, S. M., & McCrary, K. M. (2016). Body modifications in college students: Considering gender, self-esteem, body appreciation, and reasons for tattoos. *College Student Journal, 50,* 246–252.

Hoffman, L. (2017, Spring). Body by Kardashian? Khloe's revenge body and the strict demands of the family business. *Bitch*, 12–13.

Holbrook, J., Minocha, J., & Laumann, A. (2012). Body piercing: Complications and prevention of health risks. *American Journal of Clinical Dermatology, 13,* 1–17.

Hong, B-K., & Young Lee, H. (2017). Self-esteem, propensity for sensation seeking, and risk behaviour among adults with tattoos and piercings. *Journal of Public Health Research, 6,* 158–163.

Howlett, N., Pine, K. J., Cahill, N., Orakcioglu, I., & Fletcher, B. C. (2015). Unbuttoned: The interaction between provocativeness of female work attire and occupational status. *Sex Roles, 72,* 105–116.

Huxley, C., & Grogan, S. (2005). Tattooing, piercing, healthy behaviours and health value. *Journal of Health Psychology, 10,* 831–841.

Jannuzzi, J. (2015, August 20). See how popular beards have been since forever. Retrieved from www.gq.com

Johncock, W. (2012). Modifying the modifier: Body modification as social incarnation. *Journal for the Theory of Social Behaviour, 42,* 241–259.

Kalick, S. M., Zebrowitz, L. A., Langlois, J. H., & Johnson, R. M. (1998). Does human facial attractiveness honestly advertise health? Longitudinal data on an evolutionary question. *Psychological Science, 9,* 8–13.

Kalus, A., & Cregan, C. (2017). Cosmetic facial surgery: The influence of self-esteem on job satisfaction and burnout. *Asia Pacific Journal of Human Resources, 55,* 320–336.

Karremans, J. C., Frankenhuis, W. E., & Arons, S. (2010). Blind men prefer a low waist-to-hip ratio. *Evolution & Human Behavior, 31,* 182–186.

King, K. A., & Vidourek, R. A. (2013). Getting inked: Tattoo and risky behavioral involvement among university students. *The Social Science Journal, 50,* 540–546.

King, P. (2017). *The science of attraction: Flirting, sex, and how to engineer chemistry and love.* New York: CreateSpace Independent Publishing Platform.

Knapp, M. L., Hall, J. A., & Horgan, T. G. (2013). *Nonverbal communication in human interaction* (8th ed.). Belmont, CA: Wadsworth/Cengage Learning.

Koch, J. R., Roberts, A. E., Armstrong, M. L., & Owen, D. C. (2015). Tattoos, gender, and well-being among American college students. *The Social Science Journal, 52,* 536–541.

Kranz, D. (2011). Young men's coping with androgenetic alopecia: Acceptance counts when hair gets thinner. *Body Image, 8,* 343–348.

Lammers, W. J., Davis, S., Davison, O., & Hogue, K. (2016). Impact of positive, negative, and no personality descriptors on the attractiveness halo effect. *Psi Chi Journal of Psychological Research, 21,* 239–344.

Larocca, A. (2017, August 7–20). Political peroxide. *New York,* 44–46.

LaWare, M. R., & Moutsatsos, C. (2013). "For skin that's us, authentically us": Celebrity, empowerment, and the allure of antiaging advertisements. *Women's Studies in Communication, 36,* 189–208.

Lawson, J. (2018, April 23). Top 21 best beard styles and how to rock them with pride. Retrieved from https://www.beardbrand.com/blogs/urbanbeardsman/beard-styles

Le, V. (2016, April 12). Why the multi-billion dollar hair-removal business is aboutt to get even bigger. Retrieved from https://www.inc.com/vanna-le/why-the-billion-dollar-hair-removal-industry-is-about-to-see-an-even-bigger-boom.html

Lee, S-Y. (2014). The effects of cosmetic surgery reality shows on women's beliefs of beauty privileges, perceptions of cosmetic surgery, and desires for cosmetic enhancements. *American Communication Journal, 16,* 1–14.

chapter five

Lerman, A. E., McCabe, K. T., & Sadin, M. L. (2015). Political ideology, skin tone, and the psychology of candidate evaluations. *Public Opinion Quarterly, 79*, 53–90.

Leszcz, B. (2013, April 15). The casual Friday lie. *Canadian Business*, 66.

Lilienfeld, S. O., Lynn, S. J., & Namy, L. L. (2017). *Psychology: From inquiry to understanding* (4th ed.). Boston: Pearson.

Lim, W., Ting, D., Leo, E., & Jayanthy, C. (2013). Contemporary perceptions of body modifications and its acceptability in the Asian society: A case of tattoos and body piercings. *Asian Social Science, 9*, 37–42.

Lin, M-H., Cross, S. N. N., & Childers, T. L. (2018). Understanding olfaction and emotions and the moderating role of individual differences. *European Journal of Marketing, 52*, 811–836.

Low, K. E. Y. (2006). Presenting the self, the social body, and the olfactory: Managing smells in everyday life experiences. *Sociological Perspectives, 49*, 607–631.

Lyngs, U., Cohen, E., Hattori, W. T., Newson, M., & Levin, D. T. (2016). Hearing in color: How expectations distort perception of skin tone. *Journal of Experimental Psychology: Human Perception and Performance, 42*, 2068–2076.

Mahoney, J. L., Lord, H., & Carryl, E. (2005). Afterschool program participation and the development of child obesity and peer acceptance. *Applied Developmental Science, 9*, 202–215.

Marini, I., Wang, X., Etzbach, C., & Del Castillo, A. (2013). Ethnic, gender, and contact differences in intimacy attitudes toward wheelchair users. *Rehabilitation Counseling Bulletin, 56*, 135–145.

Markley Rountree, M., & Davis, L. (2011). A dimensional qualitative research approach to understanding medically unnecessary aesthetic surgery. *Psychology & Marketing, 28*, 1027–1043.

Martin, J. N., Trego, A. B., & Nakayama, T. K. (2010). College students' racial attitudes and friendship diversity. *Howard Journal of Communications, 21*, 97–118.

Masip, J., Garrido, E., & Herrero, C. (2004). Facial appearance and impressions of credibility: The effects of facial babyishness and age on person perception. *International Journal of Psychology, 39*, 276–289.

Mbure, W. G., & Aubrey, J. S. (2017). A transnational analysis of skin tone ideals in cosmetics advertisements in women's lifestyle magazines. *Howard Journal of Communications, 28*, 339–355.

McMurtrie, R. J. (2010). Bobbing for power: An exploration into the modality of hair. *Visual Communication, 9*, 399–424.

Miles, A. D., & Sparks, W. (2013). Examining social media and higher education: An empirical study on ratemyprofessor.com and its impact on college students. *International Journal of Economy, Management, & Social Sciences, 2*, 513–524.

MSNBC. (2006, June 7). [Television broadcast].

Mulvey, K. (2006, January 23). Love and the laws of attraction: Express yourself. *The Express,* p. 31.

NBC Nightly News. (2009, April 30). Barbie turns 50. [Television broadcast]. New York: National Broadcasting Company.

Netchaeva, E., & Ress, M. (2016). Strategically stunning: The motivations behind the lipstick effect. *Psychological Science, 27*, 1157–1168.

Nowosielski, K., Sipiski, A., Kuczerawy, I., Kozłowska-Rup, D., & Skrzypulec-Plinta, V. (2012). Tattoos, piercing, and sexual behaviors in young adults. *Journal of Sexual Medicine, 9*, 2307–2314.

O'Brien, K. S., Latner, J. D., Ebneter, D., & Hunter, J. A. (2013). Obesity discrimination: The role of physical appearance, personal ideology, and anti-fat prejudice. *International Journal of Obesity, 37*, 455–460.

Osensky, T. S. (2017). *Shortchanged: Height discrimination and strategies for social change.* Lebanon, NH: University Press of New England.

Oswald, D. L., & Chapleau, K. M. (2010). Selective self-stereotyping and women's self-esteem maintenance. *Personality & Individual Differences, 49,* 918–922.

Palmer-Mehta, V., & Shuler, S. (2017). Rising against the third shift: Reclaiming the postpartum body in "A Beautiful Body Project." *Women's Studies in Communication, 40,* 359–378.

Park, J. (2016). Signs of social change on the bodies of youth in Korea. *Visual Communication, 15,* 71–92.

Parry, M. (2011, December 2). Researchers find RateMyProfessors.com useful, if not chili-pepper hot. *Chronicle of Higher Education,* p. A4.

Pfeifer, G. M. (2012). Attitudes toward piercings and tattoos: Does body modification suggest a lack of professionalism, or is it simply freedom of expression? *American Journal of Nursing, 112,* 15.

Phillips, K. A. (2018). Body dysmorphic disorder. In K. D. Brownell & T. B. Walsh (Eds.), *Eating disorders and obesity: A comprehensive handbook* (pp. 141–151). New York: Guilford.

Politano, G. M., & Politano, P. M. (2011). The obesity epidemic and current perceptions of somatotypes by children. *North American Journal of Psychology, 13,* 349–359.

Poorani, A. A. (2012). Who determines the ideal body? A summary of research findings on body image. *New Media & Mass Communication, 2,* 1–12.

Poulsen, F. O., Holman, T. B., Busby, D. M., & Carroll, J. S. (2013). Physical attraction, attachment style, and dating development. *Journal of Social & Personal Relationships, 30,* 301–319.

Preti, A., Pinna, C., Nocco, S., & Mulliri, E. (2006). Body of evidence: Tattoos, body piercing, and eating disorder symptoms among adolescents. *Journal of Psychosomatic Research, 61,* 561–566.

Puhl, R. M., Luedicke, J., & Heuer, C. A. (2013). The stigmatizing effect of visual media portrayals of obese persons on public attitudes: Does race or gender matter? *Journal of Health Communication, 18,* 805–826.

Quick, V., McWilliams, R., & Byrd-Bredbenner, C. (2013). Fatty, fatty, two-by-four: Weight-teasing history and disturbed eating in young adult women. *American Journal of Public Health, 103,* 508–515.

Quintanilla, K. M., & Wahl, S. T. (2016). *Business and professional communication: Keys for workplace excellence* (3rd ed.). Thousand Oaks, CA: Sage.

Re, D. E., & Perrett, D. I. (2012). Concordant preferences for actual height and facial cues to height. *Personality & Individual Differences, 53,* 901–906.

Reynolds, J. M. (2017). "I'd rather be dead than disabled"—the ableist conflation and the meanings of disability. *Review of Communication, 17,* 149–163.

Rich, S. S., Essery, E. V., Sanborn, C. F., DiMarco, N. M., Morales, L. K., & LeClere, S. M. (2008). Predictors of body size stigmatization in Hispanic preschool children. *Obesity, 16,* 11–17.

Rowsell, J., Kress, G., & Street, B. (2013). Visual optics: Interpreting body art, three ways. *Visual Communication, 12,* 97–122.

Scott, J-A. (2015). Almost passing: A performance analysis of personal narratives of physically disabled femininity. *Women's Studies in Communication, 38,* 227–249.

Scott, J. R. (2017, October 13). How to calculate and understand your waist to hip ratio. Retrieved from https://www.verywellfit.com/waist-to-hip-ratio-and-examples-3496140

Shackelton, N. L., & Campbell, T. (2014). Are teachers' judgments of pupils' ability influenced by body shape? *International Journal of Obesity, 38,* 520–524.

Sheldon, W. H. (1940). *The varieties of human physique: An introduction to constitutional psychology.* New York: Harper.

Sheldon, W. H. (1954). *Atlas of men.* New York: Harper.

Sheldon, W. H., Stevens, S. S., & Tucker, S. (1942). *The varieties of temperament: A psychology of constitutional differences.* New York: Harper & Row.

Shuttlesworth, M. E., & Zotter, D. (2011). Disordered eating in African American and Caucasian women: The role of ethnic identity. *Journal of Black Studies, 42,* 906–922.

Singh, D. (2004). Mating strategies of young women: Role of physical attractiveness. *Journal of Sex Research, 41,* 43–54.

Soper, K. (2010, September 17). RateMyProfessors'appearance.com. *Chronicle Review,* p. B24.

Sorokowska, A. (2013). Assessing personality using body odor: Differences between children and adults. *Journal of Nonverbal Behavior, 37,* 153–163.

Sorokowska, A., Sorokowski, P., & Szmajke, A. (2012). Does personality smell? Accuracy of personality assessments based on body odour. *European Journal of Personality, 26,* 496–503.

Sorokowski, P., Koscinski, K., Sorokowska, A., & Huanca, T. (2014). Preference for women's body mass and waist-to-hip ratio in Tsimane men of the Bolivian Amazon: Biological and cultural determinants. *PLoS ONE, 10*: e105468.

Stabler, B., Whitt, K., Moreault, D., D'Ercole, A., & Underwood, L. (1980). Social judgments by children of short stature. *Psychological Reports, 46,* 743–746.

Stim, A., Hinz, A., & Brahler, E. (2006). Prevalence of tattooing and body piercing in Germany and perception of health, mental disorders, and sensation seeking among tattooed and body pierced individuals. *Journal of Psychosomatic Research, 60,* 531–534.

Stoker, J. I., Garretsen, J., & Spreeuwers, L. J. (2016). The facial appearance of CEOs: Faces signal selection but not performance. *PLoS ONE, 11*: e0159950.

Strubel, J., & Jones, D. (2017). Painted bodies: Representing the self and reclaiming the body through tattoos. *Journal of Popular Culture, 50,* 1230–1253.

Swanger, N. (2006). Visible body modification (VBM): Evidence from human resource managers and recruiters and the effects on employment. *Journal of Hospitality Management, 25,* 154–158.

TenBrink, C., & Gelb, B. (2017). When firms mature: Keeping the ho-hum at bay and embracing change. *Journal of Business Strategy, 38,* 12–17.

Tenner, E. (2004, October 1). Political timber: Glitter, froth, and measuring tape. *Chronicle of Higher Education,* pp. B12–B13.

Thompson, S. (2009). Do you know why it's not just hair to me? The importance of eliciting breast-cancer survivors' explanatory models throughout the cancer continuum. *Journal of Communication in Healthcare, 2,* 148–158.

Timming, A. R. (2014). Visible tattoos in the service sector: A new challenge to recruitment and selection. *Work, Employment and Society, 29,* 60–78.

Trekels, J., & Eggermont, S. (2017). Beauty is good: The appearance culture, the internalization of appearance ideals, and dysfunctional appearance beliefs among tweens. *Human Communication Research, 43,* 173–192.

Tsai, W., Huang, T., & Yu, H. (2012). Investigating the unique predictability and boundary conditions of applicant physical attractiveness and non-verbal behaviours on interviewer evaluations in job interviews. *Journal of Occupational & Organizational Psychology, 85*, 60–79.

Ura, M., & Preston, K. S. J. (2015). The influence of thin-ideal internalization on women's body image, self-esteem, and appearance avoidance: Covariance structure analysis. *American Communication Journal, 17*, 15–26.

Valtonen, A. (2013). Height matters: Practicing consumer agency, gender, and body politics. *Consumption, Markets & Culture, 16*, 196–221.

Van Vonderen, K. E., & Kinnally, W. (2012). Media effects on body image: Examining media exposure in the broader context of internal and other social factors. *American Communication Journal, 14*, 41–57.

Venturini, B., Castelli, L., & Tomelleri, S. (2006). Not all jobs are suitable for fat people: Experimental evidence of a link between being fat and "out-of-sight" jobs. *Social Behavior and Personality, 34*, 389–398.

Vrij, A. (2001). Credibility judgments of detectives: The impact of nonverbal behavior, social skills, and physical characteristics on impression formation. *Journal of Social Psychology, 133*, 601–610.

Wegenstein, B. (2012). *The cosmetic gaze: Body modification and the constructions of beauty.* Cambridge, MA: MIT Press.

Wehner, M. R., Chren, M., Nameth, D., et al. (2014). International prevalence of indoor tanning: A systematic review and meta-analysis. *JAMA Dermatol, 150*, 390–400.

Wilson, J. M. B., Tripp, D. A., & Boland, F. J. (2005). The relative contributions of waist-to-hip ratio and body mass index to judgements of attractiveness. *Sexualities, Evolution and Gender, 7*, 245–267.

Wilson, R. (2010, August 13). Being hot leaves some professors cold. *Chronicle of Higher Education*, pp. A1, A9.

Winslow, L. (2017). "Not exactly a model of good hygiene": Theorizing an aesthetic of disgust in the Occupy Wall Street movement. *Critical Studies in Media Communication, 34*, 278–292.

Zestcott, C. A., Bean, M. G., & Stone, J. (2017). Evidence of negative implicit attitudes toward individuals with a tattoo near the face. *Group Processes & Intergroup Relations, 20*, 186–201.

chapter six

KINESICS: BODY MOVEMENT, GESTURES, AND POSTURE

chapter outline

chapter objectives

After studying this chapter, you should be able to

1. define kinesics;
2. identify Scheflen's three dimensions of body movement related to posture and the primary nonverbal cues related to each dimension;
3. contrast self-synchrony, interactive synchrony, and mimicry;
4. describe the relationship between posture, height, and status/dominance;
5. understand how factors such as culture, sex/gender, and status contribute to the development of an individual style of walking;
6. discuss research findings related to female and male sitting behavior;
7. identify, define, and provide examples of each of Ekman and Friesen's five kinesic categories;
8. overview primary cultural differences related to the use of gestures;
9. discuss major findings related to kinesic research on flirting and the communication of attraction; and
10. discuss major findings related to kinesic research on prelinguistic children's acquisition of gestures, a form of sign language between parents and children.

case study

ATHLETES' BODY MOVEMENTS: CONSISTENCY AND CONTROVERSY

What did French soccer players do upon winning the 2018 World Cup? They did the typical thing soccer players do when scoring goals and winning matches: They ran, then dropped to their knees and slid until teammates jumped on top of them to celebrate. What does Rafael Nadal do when he wins a tennis match? He drops his racket, puts his arms straight up in the air, and tosses his head back with his eyes closed—every time, same drill. Such images of world-class athletes are iconic because many athletes consistently use gestures and body positions to convey their emotions of joy, gratitude, relief, triumph, and even anger (Butterworth, 2013; Furley, Dicks, & Memmert, 2012; Furley & Schweizer, 2014; Matsumoto & Hwang, 2012; Merola, 2007; Wortman, 2013). Some of these nonverbal cues have caused controversy; one situation in particular has cost a professional athlete a great deal of money and perhaps his career.

At the time this book went to print, the National Football League was still embroiled in a controversy that started when then-San Francisco 49ers player Colin Kaepernick sat and then knelt during the playing of the national anthem at a 2016 preseason game (Mindock, 2017). Kaepernick explained that the body positions were in protest of racial inequality and police brutality in the United States. Soon, other athletes and a few team owners joined Kaepernick's silent protest during the anthem at their own games. Many players, owners, coaches, and fans (as well as the U.S. president at the time) believed the nonverbal positioning was disrespectful of our country, its military, and its police forces. Others believed that free speech, in this instance in the form of sitting or kneeling during the anthem, is a cherished and protected American right (Hafner, 2017). In May of 2018, the NFL commissioner and team owners approved a new policy requiring all players to stand during the national anthem or be given the option of staying in the locker room during the anthem; however, a few months later the policy was challenged by the NFL Players Association (Knoblauch, 2018).

Athletes often use body positions at sporting events that later become iconic, or instantly recognized, universally interpreted, and thereafter associated with the athlete.

You may or may not have an opinion about this situation; some of our students have very strong opinions on both sides of the controversy. But this situation exemplifies the power of nonverbal body positions and gestures, as symbolic and attention-getting cues of communication.

DO THE LOCOMOTION

Have you ever heard someone's footsteps coming down the hall and thought to yourself, "Oh, good. That's Mary coming this way. I need to talk to her"? Or perhaps you have thought, "Uh-oh. That's Bob coming, and if I'm not busy, he'll talk my head off for an hour. Better get on the phone quickly." We may not readily think of them this way, but our footsteps are a form of nonverbal communication that others can detect and interpret. If we're having a bad day, our footsteps can sound heavy, as though we're carrying the weight of the world on our shoulders. Conversely, if we're having a great day, we will probably walk with a "spring in our step."

In Chapter 2, we defined **kinesics** as the study of human movement, gestures, and posture (Birdwhistell, 1960). As we explained in that chapter, technically, movements of the face and eyes are considered kinesics, but because your face and eyes can produce a vast amount of information, we discuss them as separate codes in the next chapter. Raymond Birdwhistell (1960, 1967, 1970, 1974) is considered the "father of kinesics"; his work forms the foundation for how kinesics has been studied and is still studied today.

Body movement is a fundamental behavior of human beings; sighted people as well as those who are blind from birth communicate through gestures before they learn to speak (Iverson, Tencer,

Lany, & Goldin-Meadow, 2000). Research shows that sensitivity to body movement and the ability to decode kinesics can emerge as early as 4 to 6 months of age, so it's clear that an understanding of kinesics is important (Feldman & Tyler, 2006). The way our body moves; the way we gesture with our hands, arms, shoulders, and, occasionally, torso, legs, and feet; as well as how we walk, stand, and carry ourselves are powerful nonverbal clues about us (Floyd, 2018; Richmond, McCroskey, & Hickson, 2011). Based on genetics, physiological development, psychological characteristics, and upbringing, within the context of the culture into which we were born and in which we live, we develop certain patterns in our walk, stance or posture, and use of gestures. These patterns become easily recognizable by others who come to know us, but they can be affected by our mood and emotions (Halovic & Kroos, 2018; Reschke, Knothe, & Walle, 2017).

STAND UP FOR YOURSELF ■ ■ ■

Ever heard one of your parents say, "Stand up straight!"? As annoying as that command may be, our parents are right. In American culture as well as many other cultures, an upright yet relaxed body posture is attached to many attractive attributes, such as confidence, positivity, relaxation, and high self-esteem (Bailey & Kelly, 2015; Cuddy, 2018; Wilkes, Kydd, Sagar, & Broadbent, 2017). Our moods and emotions are revealed through our body posture, whether or not we realize it or consciously intend it. If you're feeling upbeat and positive, your posture is likely to be straighter; if you're feeling stressed, bored, or sad, those emotions register in your body and affect how you stand, sit, and move (Civile & Sukhvinder, 2016; Doody & Bull, 2011). How aware are you of your posture? Do you tend to stand in a dominant position, or does your stance typically give off signs of weakness, timidity, or low self-esteem? How is your posture affected by your mood and emotions?

Scheflen's Dimensions of Posture

Nonverbal scholar Albert Scheflen has contributed significantly to our understanding of the role of posture and other kinesic behaviors in human interaction (Scheflen, 1974; Scheflen & Scheflen, 1972). This line of research identified three dimensions of posture: (1) inclusiveness/noninclusiveness; (2) face-to-face/parallel; and (3) congruence/incongruence. These are dimensions, which means they represent a range of behavior or postural tendencies.

Inclusiveness/noninclusiveness is the degree to which a person's body posture includes or excludes one person, relative to other people. Imagine you're at a party, observing a man and woman sitting on a couch. If the woman exhibits highly inclusive nonverbal cues, she will arrange her body and posture in such a way as to focus her attention on the man, to the exclusion of other people on

WHAT WOULD *YOU* DO ?

Your friend has *terrible* posture. He doesn't actually *walk*; he sort of shuffles. Most of the time his head's down, his shoulders slump to the ground such that you marvel at how he manages to keep his book bag from sliding right off them. His hair is always in his eyes, blocking people's view of his face, and his clothes are beyond baggy, blocking people's view of his body. In general, non-verbally he's sort of shut off. You—his good friend—know that he's a really great guy and could be a great friend to lots of people. He's just unaware of the nonverbal vibe he gives off to other people. And he's not one of those "I-don't-care-what-other-people-think" kinds of people either; he honestly struggles with making friends and dating. Most people simply think he's weird.

What would you do in this situation? Are you your brother's keeper—in other words, do you take it on yourself to help your friend become more aware of, and possibly change, his non-verbal communication? We're not suggesting you make this a humanitarian project in which you perform a makeover just to make yourself feel good for "saving" some poor schmoe. But what's the appropriate response when you see your friend puzzled or possibly hurting over his own isolation?

the couch or in the near vicinity. These moves indicate a high degree of liking and interest. Conversely, if she's not interested in or dislikes the man, she'll arrange her posture in such a way as to exclude him, but not the other people on the couch or nearby. Maybe you've seen someone carry on a conversation with people on a couch or in a crowded booth at a restaurant, skipping the person right next to them, talking over him or her to the people at the other end of the couch or table. Talk about sending a negative signal!

The second dimension is **face-to-face/parallel,** the degree to which two people face each other directly versus orienting themselves side by side, with their shoulders in a line (a parallel position). Back to the man and woman sitting on the couch: If they like each other, they're more likely to assume a face-to-face position, turning their bodies toward each other, even though a couch is more conducive to side-by-side seating than face-to-face. If the two people are unfriendly or dislike each other, they're more likely to assume a parallel posture than a face-to-face one. (They probably wouldn't be on the couch together at all, but you get the point.) Face-to-face body postures tend to indicate mutual involvement and some level of intimacy. Sometimes the nature of a task is more the cause for body postures, rather than liking or showing interest; for example, playing videogames or watching TV involves more parallel positioning than face-to-face. In such instances, posture may not tell us much about the relationship between the people we're observing.

Scheflen's third dimension is termed **congruence/incongruence,** which refers to the degree of mirroring or imitation of the behavior between two or more people. When the woman on the couch oriented her body posture directly toward the man, what if the man didn't adjust his posture to match hers? If you were observing such an interaction, you might conclude that the woman was interested and attracted but the man wasn't. In a high-congruence situation, one person's behavior is imitated by another; in a low-congruence (or incongruent) situation, behaviors won't be mirrored. Scheflen reminds us that the wise interpreter of nonverbal communication will observe a range of behaviors over time to get the fullest possible picture of a situation. We can make interpretive mistakes (and social blunders) if we jump too quickly to a conclusion about a situation or person's behavior based on nonverbal cues in isolation and out of context.

Scholars have described Scheflen's third dimension in terms of **synchrony** (Beavin Bavelas & Chovil, 2006; Lakens & Stel, 2011; Wilt, Funkhouser, & Revelle, 2011). Synchrony comes in two forms: First, **self-synchrony** refers to a person's coordination of speech and body movement or how coordinated a person is in her or his own behavior, meaning that verbal messages and nonverbal cues work together in synch to produce a fluid outcome. Perhaps you've seen someone who can't "walk and chew gum." The problem might be a case of poor self-synchrony.

A second form is **interactive synchrony,** which focuses on the coordination of speech and body movement between at least two people (Alda, 2018; Baimel, Birch, & Norenzayan, 2018; Brambilla, Sacchi, Menegatti, & Moscatelli, 2016; Lozza et al., 2018; Schmidt, Morr, Fitzpatrick, & Richardson, 2012). Interactive synchrony has also been termed "the chameleon effect" (Chartrand & Bargh, 1999, p. 893), "social rhythm" (Knapp, Hall, & Horgan, 2013, p. 222), and "postural echo" ("Do You Know?" 2006, p. 40). This type of synchrony is a particularly fascinating phenomenon for the keen eye to observe when people appear to be in rhythm, mirroring one another's movements unknowingly. Have you ever been in conversation with someone and the person took a sip of his or her drink? If you also had a drink in your hand, you likely took a sip at that moment as well. This is an example

of the lure of nonverbal interactive synchrony, or our desire to be in rhythm with other people. British psychologist and former commentator for the UK's *Big Brother* TV show Peter Collett reported for Sky News on the obvious synchrony in the nonverbal cues of Prince Harry and American Meghan Markle, who wed in London in May of 2018 (Collett, 2018). Collett contrasted the new royal couple's cues with the obviously not-in-synch Prince Charles and Princess Diana.

© I've shit/Shutterstock.com

According to Scheflen's second dimension of posture, these two people exhibit a high level of congruence in their body positions on the bench.

A related phenomenon is **mimicry**, which looks a lot like synchrony, but is a bit different (Lakin, Jefferis, Cheng, & Chartrand, 2003). French scholar Nicolas Guéguen (2011) defines mimicry as "the imitation of postures, facial expressions, mannerisms, and other verbal and nonverbal behaviors" (p. 725). Typically, mimicry occurs when one person intentionally copies or mirrors the behavior of another, in terms of such cues as body position, gestures, facial expressions, eye contact, spatial positioning, and even tone of voice.

As a persuasive technique, salespersons are often trained to detect nonverbal cues of customers, then work to mimic those cues to convey a sense of solidarity or rhythm, thus increasing the chances of a sale. With synchrony, less intentionality is involved and people find themselves in nonverbal rhythm (or really know when they are *not* in synch with someone). With mimicry, typically one party intentionally mirrors the behavior of the other, for a variety of reasons (e.g., to show liking or attraction, to achieve a desired outcome like getting a job or landing a sale). One application of what we've learned about mimicry can be found in the food service industry, where wait staff are often trained to lean down or squat by diners' tables, in an effort to put themselves more on the level of their customers. (Scheflen would call this behavior congruence.) A study conducted by the Center for Hospitality Research at Cornell University's School of Hotel Administration found that wait staff who introduced themselves to diners while squatting down by the table or booth increased their tips by 3%, on average (Rush, 2006). Even strangers sitting on a subway may demonstrate mimicry; if one person shifts a position, either sitting or standing, several other people around her or him are likely to shift as well.

Guéguen and other researchers have studied various effects and properties of mimicry in social situations (Dijk, Fischer, Morina, van Eenwijk, & van Kleef, 2018; Guéguen, 2012). Findings show that mimicry leads to increased compliance with a request (Guéguen, Martin, & Meineri, 2011), heightened comprehension of a message in face-to-face interaction (Holler & Wilkin, 2011), perceptions of romantic interest (Farley, 2014), and increased self-consciousness and decreased social anxiety on the part of the person being mimicked (Guéguen, 2011).

Power, Status, and Dominance

The relationship between posture and perceptions of power, dominance, and status has also been the subject of much research (Arnette & Pettijohn, 2012; Burgoon & Dunbar, 2006; Dunbar & Abra, 2010; Gonzaga, Keltner, & Ward, 2008; Hullman, Goodnight, & Mougeotte, 2012; Toscano, Schubert, & Glessner, 2018). Social psychologist David Johnson (2012) contends,

> individuals with high status and power may engage in a dominance display by puffing themselves up to full size, stiffening their backs, tightening their brows, thrusting their chins forward, and leaning toward the challenger in an attempt to convince others of their power. (p. 199)

A common posture often connected to dominance is a spread-legged stance with the hands on the hips, called the **arms akimbo** position (Andersen, 2004; Armstrong & Wagner, 2003; Panjwani, Chaplin, Sinha, & Mayes, 2016). Hands on the hips may indicate frustration or anger rather than dominance. A variation of this position involves the arms crossed across the chest, which is a comfortable position for many people but can signal irritation and inapproachability. Interestingly, the high-status stance we describe tends to be more of a male position than a female one, because a spread-legged stance on a woman would send a different signal than when enacted by a man. However, as communication scholar Peter Andersen (2004) points out, reversing the hand position such that the thumbs point forward and the fingers go backward on the hips, along with a bit of a frontal pelvic tilt, changes the message significantly. This simple change in placement of the hands is more indicative of a woman's position than a man's, at least in American culture (and we can *never* forget the effects of culture on all nonverbal behavior), and it tends to soften the sense of dominance in this stance.

However, dominant nonverbal cues aren't always correlated with high-status behaviors. Consider the job interview situation, in which an interviewer tends to be much more relaxed than a job applicant, who is putting herself or himself on the line to get hired. Consultants Audrey Nelson and Susan Golant (2004) explain:

> The more restricted, tight, pulled in, and tense, the less power we have. This is evident during a job interview. The interviewer is in a power position, relaxed and at ease; the interviewee looks like a private in the military, sitting in a straight-backed, full-attention position. (p. 171)

One position that illustrates a relaxed yet dominant style and conveys self-confidence is called "the cape and crown," which is performed by lifting up the arms and placing the hands on the back of one's head, sometimes in conjunction with a hip tilt. People can enact this kinesic behavior in a seated position, perhaps leaning back in a chair or with their feet elevated. The position is considered more of a male behavior than a female one; however, it is quite common among female celebrities such as Beyoncé because it conveys an "I'm in charge; I'm royalty" message (Soll, 2007, p. 18). It can also accentuate a person's head, making the person look larger or more dominant than other people, with the sharp angles of the elbows acting as cues of aggression.

We discussed height in Chapter 5 on physical appearance. As we suggested there, since height is associated with confidence, extroversion, and high status in American culture, it's important to make the most of our height by standing as

© landmarkmedia/Shutterstock

Beyoncé often takes a "cape and crown" stance when being photographed. The kinetic cue conveys relaxation, but also dominance and self-confidence.

chapter six

erect as possible, without looking like we're in a body cast (Galobardes et al., 2012; Osensky, 2017; Re & Perrett, 2012; Valtonen, 2013). This is particularly important when we're in a public situation in which an audience (live or mediated) is looking at us and judging our credibility. When making a presentation, remember the positive impressions people form related to nonverbal cues. An effective presenter will evidence good posture while at the same time incorporating body movement into the presentation. Standing completely still can make a speaker look rigid, boring, and detached from the situation at hand. While a minimal level of forward body lean conveys confidence and interest, a backward lean may indicate nervousness or a fear of the audience (Beebe & Beebe, 2018; Beebe, Beebe, & Ivy, 2018). Try to avoid leaning too much on a podium or resting your body on a tabletop (if seated while speaking) unless such a move is done sparingly to create drama or for some other intended effect. Most microphones on stands are adjustable, and mics are sophisticated enough now to pick up a voice without the speaker's having to stoop to be heard.

REMEMBER

Remember!
6.1

Kinesics	Study of human movement, gestures, and posture
Inclusiveness/noninclusiveness	Degree to which a person's body posture includes or excludes people relative to others
Face-to-face/parallel	Degree to which two people face each other directly versus orienting themselves side by side, with their shoulders in a line (a parallel position)
Congruence/incongruence	Degree of mirroring or imitation of the behavior between two or more people
Self-synchrony	Coordination of speech and body movement enacted by one person
Interactive synchrony	Coordination of speech and body movement between at least two speakers
Mimicry	Intentional mirroring of another person's nonverbal cues
Arms akimbo	A spread-legged stance with the hands on the hips, often indicating dominance or frustration

What celebrities or historical figures have memorable walks? Marilyn Monroe's walk, with her famous sashay of the hips, is certainly memorable. Actor Daniel Day Lewis, in response to a question about how he so successfully "inhabited" the character of Abraham Lincoln for his role in the movie *Lincoln* explained that once he nailed Lincoln's iconic world-weary walk, the rest of the character took shape. How we walk is one of the most personal and long-lasting elements within our nonverbal repertoire, but it's often overlooked (Harper, 2006).

While adults don't typically retain memories from infancy, we know from research and observation that the vast majority of babies crawl before they learn to walk. As Andersen (2004) explains, crawling is a "milestone in a baby's development," in that it's the "baby's new window to the world" (p. 92). This first level of body movement exploration is critical. Andersen recommends that parents get down on all fours and crawl with their babies as a way to create rapport and see the world from their baby's perspective.

Before most children begin to walk, they pull themselves upright with the help of stationary objects. In other words, they "cruise," which Andersen describes as the behavior of standing while holding onto furniture or other structures (or sometimes a parent's leg), as a means of steadying themselves in an upright position (p. 92). Andersen suggests that cruising marks a transition from infancy into childhood. And we've all probably witnessed—in person or on TV—those all-important first steps a child takes. The wobbly steps and lurching arms, often resembling Frankenstein or zombies, are comical and thrilling to watch, as well as highly significant in a child's development. The word *toddler* is derived from the toddling from side to side that most children exhibit as they learn to walk.

While less is known or written about how we evolve from a childhood style into an adult style of walking, a good deal of research exists on the subject of adult walking style, or *gait* as it's termed in scientific studies. There's even an

Actor Gary Oldman's superb portrayal of the character of Winston Churchill in the 2017 movie *Darkest Hour* was enhanced by his mastery of the prime minister's unique posture and walk.

The child's "cruising" behavior will soon give way to walking with that side-to-side motion that gives children around this age the name "toddler."

academic journal called *Gait & Posture*, mostly containing studies about medical conditions, running, aging, and walking ability. For most people, walking ability declines with age (Robertson, Savva, King-Kallimanis, & Kenney, 2015; Verlinden et al., 2013).

Consider the idiosyncratic nature of walking—meaning each person has his or her own unique walk. Some commonalities emerge in walking behavior because the movements are more obvious and prevalent, such as someone who walks with slumped shoulders and feet—more shuffling than taking steps. Some people bounce when they walk, while others seem to glide as though gravity doesn't apply to them. Still others sort of schlep from side to side when they walk, creating an inefficient but easily recognizable gait. Some people move their arms a lot when they walk; others walk as though their upper body and arms aren't attached to their lower body.

Our culture, as well as genetic profile, physiological features, upbringing, psychological characteristics, and emotions shape the way we walk and stand (Halovic & Kroos, 2017). An upright carriage, with the head held high and shoulders squared, and a wide stride and quick pace convey confidence, positivity, and happiness in American culture, but in some cultures this style of walking may convey arrogance, a lack of politeness and respect for others, and lower status. For example, Montepare and Zebrowitz (1993) observed the gait of people in the United States and Korea. In their research, older Americans walking with a slow gait were not perceived as being dominant, but older Koreans walking with the same slow gait were perceived as being dominant in Korean culture. The researchers attributed the difference, in part, to the higher level of esteem placed on elders in Korean culture compared with American culture.

Some generalizations have been made about the sexes and their ways of walking, such that some believe a person's sex can be determined simply by observing that person's walk. Andersen (2004) suggests that men's bodies are somewhat motionless while walking, with the hips and torso firmly facing frontward, the feet moving about one foot apart in stride, and the arms swinging significantly. In contrast, women tend to keep their arms closer to their sides and "add motion to their locomotion," in that they have more swing or side-to-side motion in their walks (p. 92). Part of this phenomenon is physiological, in that women's pelvic areas are configured differently than men's because women are the baby birthers in our species. Women's hips move more than men's when walking, mostly because women tend to put one foot in front of the other, which engages the hip action.

The way this woman walks may be connected to her cultural background, but may have more to do with the activity of checking her cell phone than her culture.

Weaving While You Walk/Talk/Text

The evidence about the dangers of driving while talking on a cell phone (even a hands-free device) is clear; driving and texting is especially unsafe—often lethal. But did you know that talking or texting makes you a dangerous *walker*?

We've watched students head out of our classes with that immediate grab-the-phone, check-the-messages behavior, as though the pope or the president texted them while they were in class. We've had our share of near collisions with students who don't look up from their phones while navigating the campus. Granted, fostering a social network correlates with college success, and tapping in to that social network multiple times a day is typical of college students (Nathan, 2006). But is it unreasonable to ask you to *not* walk while you talk or text?

Physical therapists and professors Eric Lamberg and Lisa Muratori (2012) of Stony Brook University in New York studied the walking behavior of students on their cell phones. Here's how the study was set up: Students were first asked to visually locate a target ahead of them; then their vision was compromised (partially blocked), and they were asked to walk to the remembered target while researchers noted various aspects of their movement. A week later, the same students were asked to (1) walk; (2) walk while talking on a cell phone; or (3) walk while texting toward that same target from the week prior. Again, researchers measured several aspects of the walking behavior for later analysis.

You know how people who talk or text on their cell phones while driving tend to drive slowly, often without realizing it? A similar effect happens when we're walking. Lamberg and Muratori (2012) found that students using their cell phones (either talking or texting) walked significantly more slowly than those subjects not using their cells; in addition, these students had a 61% increase in lateral deviation, meaning they walked more sideways than straight toward a target. The result of such a deviation is that it takes people longer to reach a destination because they veer off and make less forward progress. The findings were more pronounced for texting than talking but the group who merely talked and walked were also impaired. Lamberg and Muratori concluded, "The dual-task of walking while using a cell phone impacts function and working memory and influences gait to such a degree that it may compromise safety" (p. 688).

Will the results of this study affect your nonverbal behavior, in terms of how you walk while talking or texting? Maybe not, but try to be on the lookout for your poor, aging professors who are trying to get across campus just as you are; if they're also on their cell phones, steer clear!

Care to know more about this study? If so, check out Lamberg, E. M., & Muratori, L. M. (2012). Cell phones change the way we walk. *Gait & Posture, 35,* 688–690.

The pace at which we walk is also a fascinating nonverbal aspect to observe and study, because some people believe that pace correlates with power and status. However, the verdict is out on this phenomenon. Consider your own experience. Do higher-status or "power" people tend to walk faster, as though they've got many places to be, lots to do, and tons of people waiting to meet them? Or do higher-status people tend to move more leisurely because, simply put, they *can*? Their time is more their own; they can control the pace of their movement because much in their lives is in their control. If you watch a busy office complex, you'll likely see the employees lower on the totem pole scurrying around to retrieve things for their bosses, while their bosses wouldn't be caught dead "scurrying." With this behavior, as well as many others we describe in this book, the higher-status person calls the nonverbal shots; lower-status people are expected to adapt their nonverbals to parallel or remain subordinate to the higher-status person's.

Research has also examined nonverbal behaviors associated with victimization and being targeted for sexual advances and attack (Fulham et al., 2017; Gunns, Johnston, & Hudson, 2002; Ritchie, Blais, Forth, & Book, 2018; Sakaguchi & Hasegawa, 2006). Social scientific experiments, as well as interviews with inmates, reveal that a weak walking style sends a cue of vulnerability to a would-be mugger or attacker. A weak walking style involves a lack of arm swing, short steps, and a slow pace, while a strong walking style involves longer strides, swinging arms, and a quickened pace. The latter style conveys confidence, and this line of research has found that confident walkers rank near the bottom as potential targets of crime.

How do you tend to walk in a group? Granted, it depends on where you're walking and how much space you have. If you're on a crowded sidewalk in Times Square, you can't walk abreast with three of your best buddies. Research has explored people's patterns when walking in groups, especially groups of three (triads), finding that the most common formation is two people positioned laterally (side by side) in front and the third person behind them (Costa, 2010). If this is a consistent pattern for a triad, that third person may feel as though "three's a crowd." People walking in a group of four tend to split themselves into pairs, but, again, the setting affects the pattern.

Research shows that the most common walking pattern for groups of three is V-shaped, like this one: two people in front and one person behind.

We include sitting behavior in this chapter because people tend to do a lot of sitting (some more than others). You can tell a lot about people and their relationships simply by observing where and how they sit (Guerrero & Floyd, 2006; Nelson & Golant, 2004). Sex differences in sitting behavior are easily detectable in American culture. Typically, men assume open sitting positions, meaning that their legs are often extended and spread apart rather than close together. A man is more likely to cross one leg over his other knee at a 90-degree angle to the floor, while a woman is more likely to cross her legs at the knee with the crossed leg hanging down, or to cross her legs at the ankles (Andersen, 2004; Hall, 2006).

Perhaps you're familiar with Young Life, a Christian ministry prevalent in American high schools. Many Young Life meetings involve sitting on the floor, since they often take place in halls or open spaces without chairs. Plus, chairs can make a setting too formal—something Young Life tries to avoid. If you have been in such a setting or find yourself sitting on the floor with a large group of people, note the sex differences in sitting behavior. Oftentimes, men will stretch themselves out to the point that they may actually lie on the floor, perhaps with their heads resting on their elbows, whereas women tend to sit straight up on the floor, often cross-legged or on their knees so they take up less space and look "ladylike."

While another nonverbal cue related to sitting isn't new, the attention it's receiving is quite new. The behavior occurs when men sit with their legs spread wide, feet typically angled out, and with a forward torso lean. This sitting style causes men to often take up two seats, or at least more than the usual one. Terms for this behavior include "manspreading" (recently included in the Oxford Dictionary), "man-sitting," or (coarsely) "ballrooming" (Petter, 2017; Schuler, 2017). Explanations for why this occurs range from physiological to a power play (seeking status and dominance). As for physiology, the position does allow a man to avoid testicular compression from thigh muscles, but may also relate to male hip joint configuration (McGill & Carroll, 2017). In

New York City, the Metro Transportation Authority recently began a campaign with posters in subway cars and stations, trying to heighten awareness of the problem. Some posters include the message, "Dude...Stop the Spread. It's a space issue" (Petter, 2017). In 2017, the transit authority in Madrid, Spain, outlawed the behavior altogether on public transportation (Ahluwalia, 2017). However, some men are fighting back, citing how many women for years have taken up extra seats with the multiple bags they carry (Schuler, 2017).

© Cihan Terian/Shutterstock.com

MORE THAN A GESTURE ■ ■ ■

In Chapter 1 we defined nonverbal communication and mentioned one exception to the definition, in particular reference to hand and arm gestures. Here's a quick review: When communicating through sign language with people who are deaf, the signs look like nonverbal gestures to people who can hear. But to people who are deaf (and those hearing people who know sign language) these gestures, and the accompanying body posture and facial and eye expressions, are actually language. They are either individual words or phrases that have direct meanings for receivers of such signs. Sign language is verbal communication in exchanges with persons who are deaf. Here we examine gestures—movements of the head, arms, hands, fingers, torso, legs, and feet—as nonverbal expressions.

Ekman and Friesen's Kinesic Categories

Various researchers have proposed models for analyzing and coding kinesics, just as exist for spoken or written language (Leathers & Eaves, 2008; Novack & Goldin-Meadow, 2017). In one of their most comprehensive contributions to nonverbal research, Ekman and Friesen (1969) developed five categories of movement and gestures according to how they function in human interaction.

EMBLEMS. Nonverbal cues that have specific, widely understood meanings in a given culture and that may actually substitute for a word or phrase are called **emblems.** What are some famous nonverbal gestures that have become emblematic over time? One is the index and middle finger extended upward, palm facing out, which could be interpreted as the number 2, a symbol for peace, or the letter *V* as in victory (famous with cheerleaders and politicians). In the 1970s, the contradictions surrounding this gesture were obvious, in that President Nixon vigorously used the "V for Victory" sign—even as he boarded a helicopter on the White House lawn after resigning the presidency—while Vietnam War protestors used the sign as an emblem of peace.

As we said, emblems have widely understood meanings, but note that we didn't say *universally*

Not that long ago, this guy was the norm on college campuses. If he was a "child of the '60s," does his gesture likely indicate "V for victory," the number 2, or "peace"?

© Mazzzur/ Shutterstock.com

understood meanings. Only a few gestures have virtually the same meaning for members of any culture, anywhere, across time (Givens, 2016; Hasler, Salomon, Tuchman, Lev-Tov, & Friedman, 2017; Matsumoto & Hwang, 2013a, 2013b; Vennekens-Kelly, 2012). Three gestures that have the widest generalizability cross-culturally include the pointing gesture, in which one uses the index finger of a hand in a motion to draw attention in a certain direction (Flack, Naylor, & Leavens, 2018). Another is a "come here" gesture, and the third is its opposite, the "stay away" gesture. We have no way of knowing that members of every culture throughout history have used these basic gestures and interpreted them the same way, but they're presumed to be the closest to universal that researchers have uncovered.

Gestures can also become emblematic for a co-culture (a group within a larger culture); consider the many hand and arm signals colleges and universities develop in conjunction with their mascots and athletic teams. One of the most well-known is the "Hook 'em Horns" gesture at the University of Texas. This gesture is made by extending the arm away from the body, turning the palm outward, and sticking only the index and little finger upward, to resemble the shape of long-horns. Occasionally, this sign is confused with a similar one in American Sign Language, which adds an extension of the thumb outward to mean "I love you." Take the index finger out of this configuration and we have a sign many surfers and rockers use. Officials at sporting events, choral and orchestral conductors, and traffic cops are examples of individuals who must rely on carefully negotiated and learned sets of emblematic gestures to accomplish their duties.

Use emblematic gestures with caution because, as we've warned with regard to other forms of kinesics, emblems emerge or are negotiated within cultures (Samovar, Porter, McDaniel, & Sexton Roy, 2014). Without cultural sensitivity, our nonverbal behaviors may offend whole groups of people unintentionally; some gestures have a positive meaning in one culture and a negative meaning in another. For example, a thumbs-up sign can simply mean "okay" or "all's well"; from a water skier, it usually means "more speed," and from a pilot onboard an aircraft carrier, it means "ready for takeoff" (Armstrong & Wagner, 2003). It's a gesture commonly used by hitchhikers, not just in the United States but in other countries around the world. But use the thumbs-up gesture in Greece and you might not get a welcome reception; some translations of the gesture are obscene, with a message (sanitized for our readers) of "get stuffed" (Morris, Collett, Marsh, & O'Shaughnessy, 1979, p. 195).

ILLUSTRATORS. We frequently use nonverbal **illustrators** to complement, contradict, repeat, substitute for, or accent a verbal message (Beattie, Ross, & Webster, 2010; Gunter & Weinbrenner, 2017; Hassemer & Williams, 2016). (We refer you to Chapter 1 for our explanation of each of these functions.) Illustrators are simple, everyday movements, including facial expressions, that we often enact without really thinking about them. As with all things nonverbal, culture has an impact on illustrator usage (Smithson, Nicoladis, & Marentette, 2011).

Have you seen someone give directions over the phone? With the prevalence of cell phones nowadays, it's easy to spot people in all kinds of locales giving directions, mainly because they often use complementing gestures. If the person says, "You'll go down a big hill, then turn onto the first street on the right," the person most likely will make the arm movement for downhill, then move her or his arm toward the right, even though the person at the other end of the conversation can't see these movements.

Studies show that illustrating gestures enhance people's comprehension and recall of a message (Cook, Yip, & Goldin-Meadow, 2010; Smithson & Nicoladis, 2014; Stevanoni & Salmon, 2005). Think about trying to get a child to remember something: If you want a child to be home at a certain time, for instance, she or he is more likely to remember your instruction if you tap your watch dramatically and hold up four fingers while saying, "Be home by 4," rather than simply telling the child what you want. Same goes for the effective public speaker, who will select gestures to correspond with key passages or words in a speech, making audience members more likely to remember those moments. In contrast, a communicator who uses too many illustrators reduces recall and learning (Dargue & Sweller, 2018; Hupp & Gingras, 2016; Matthews-Saugstad, Raymakers, & Kelty-Stephen, 2017; Wray, Saunders, McGuire, Cousins, & Norbury, 2017). Overdone or repetitive gestures become tiring and distracting (even comical), such that you may remember the odd, overuse of gestures but not someone's message.

AFFECT DISPLAYS. Nonverbal gestures, postures, and facial expressions that communicate emotion are called **affect displays**. Beginning in 1872, when Charles Darwin systematically studied the expression of emotion in both humans and animals, and continuing through decades of research, scientists have been learning that we primarily communicate emotion through nonverbal cues (ten Brinke, Porter, & Baker, 2012; Darwin, 1872/1965; Gagnon, Gosselin, Hudon-ven der Buhs, Larocque, & Milliard, 2010; Schug, Matsumoto, Horita, Yamagishi, & Bonnet, 2010). If you've just broken up with a romantic partner and are sad about the relationship ending, are you more likely to reveal the sadness you feel through your nonverbal cues or to walk up to a group of friends and say, "I just broke up with so-and-so and I'm really sad about it"? Granted, you might make such a statement, but the nonverbal cues typically arrive first and are then accompanied by the verbal message.

Our face tends to express which *kind* of emotion we're feeling, while our body reveals the intensity or how *much* of the emotion we're feeling. If we're happy, for example, our face may telegraph our joy to others. The movement of our hands, the openness of our posture, and the speed with which we move tell others just how happy we are. Likewise, if we're depressed, our face likely reveals our sadness or dejection, unless we're very adept at masking our emotions. Slumped shoulders and a lowered head may indicate the intensity of our despair.

The smile shows he's happy; other nonverbal cues show he's REALLY happy.

© Aaron Amat/Shutterstock.com

Research suggests two factors (among many) that affect your ability to encode and decode affect displays: (1) your general level of self-expressiveness, meaning how much you express emotionally through your nonverbal cues, and (2) the level of expressiveness of your family of origin. In Halberstadt, Dennis, and Hess's (2011) study, people who were more "naturally" expressive were more accurate in detecting and interpreting others' emotional cues. In addition, people from highly expressive families were *less* accurate decoders of emotional nonverbal cues (affect displays), because they'd grown up with so much emotional display that the cues were lost on them. In contrast, people from less expressive families were more accurate decoders because they had to sharpen their skills; the nonverbal cues in their families were less obvious, and so more effort was needed and more decoding skills developed as a result.

REGULATORS. **Regulators** control the interaction or flow of communication between people. When we're eager to respond to a message, we're likely to make eye contact, raise our eyebrows, open our mouth, take in a breath, and lean forward slightly. When we don't want to be part of the conversation, we do the opposite: We tend to avert our eyes, close our mouth, cross our arms, and lean back in our seats or away from the verbal action.

Next time you have a staff meeting at your job or a meeting for a student club where one person—typically the president or chair of the club—runs the meeting, note both the subtle and more obvious nonverbal regulators present in the meeting. Typically, the lead person, highest-ranking officer, or boss begins the meeting by virtue of his or her status (Dunbar & Abra, 2010; Toscano et al., 2018). At more formal gatherings or with larger groups, people tend to look to the group's leader, attempt to make eye contact, use an open facial expression, and offer the nonverbal gesture of raising a hand to be given a chance to speak; all these nonverbal behaviors regulate or control the interaction in the room. An unspoken but generally known rule is operating in such a setting, but we've probably all participated in situations where people didn't know the rule. These people may blurt out their contributions without using any nonverbal indications that they want to participate, often to the dismay of others present and sometimes to their own embarrassment. When approaching such a setting, especially as a new member, watch and learn. If we observe other people's nonverbal cues to learn the informal, unspoken rules that govern the interaction *before* we verbally participate, we'll fit in with the group more effectively and make a more positive impression on the people there.

Some people believe that regulators are the glue that holds conversations together—the little head nods, vocal expressions (such as "um" and "uh-huh"), facial expressions, body postures (especially leaning in), and eye contact that people come to expect when they engage in conversation. When we don't receive these sorts of nonverbal cues from a conversational partner, we may have a negative reaction and believe that our listener isn't listening to us at all. Research shows that candidates who receive favorable responses in job interviews, as well as those who actually *land* the job, use more nonverbal regulators in their interviews—direct eye contact, smiling, head nodding, and head shaking—than do other interviewees (DeGroot & Gooty, 2009; Krumhuber, Manstead, Cosker, Marshall, & Rosin, 2009; Tsai, Huang, & Yu, 2012).

ADAPTORS. Test anxiety is a very real thing; most of our students exhibit some sort of test anxiety. If professors pay attention to students taking exams in class, they'll no doubt see examples of nervous tension in students' bodies—frequent shifts in posture, hair twirling, pencil chewing or tapping, running hands through the hair repeatedly, and staring up at the ceiling (hoping for a vision of the right answer) Then there's the thigh shaker. Some people can make one of their legs quiver up and down at a very high speed, and they don't usually realize they're doing it. These are examples of **adaptors**—nonverbal behaviors that help us satisfy a personal need, cope with emotions, and adapt to the immediate situation (Fujiwara & Daibo, 2014; Zywiczynski, Wacewicz, & Orzechowski, 2017).

Perhaps part of our clothing is cutting off circulation; what do we do? Announce to the people around us that we have a clothing issue or adapt to the situation with some sort of nonverbal behavior? Many women will agree that bras are a pain—always creeping up in the back, falling off the shoulders, or pinching in a variety of important places. We've never seen a woman stand up and announce that she needs a bra adjustment, but we've seen plenty who correct these situations nonverbally. These behaviors—adjusting our clothes, makeup, hair, eyeglasses, and so forth; fidgeting nervously with our hands and feet; and interacting nonverbally with our environment—reveal our attempts to normalize situations and make ourselves feel more comfortable and able to function effectively.

Gestures and Culture

A variety of scholars and writers over past decades have written about cultural effects on nonverbal kinesic behavior, offering some advice that we've already touched on in this chapter and elsewhere in this book (Armstrong & Wagner, 2003; Axtell, 1998; Gruber, King, Hay, & Johnston, 2016; Matsumoto & Juang, 2017; Morris et al., 1979). But here are a few other research findings and observations that might help you become a more effective "global" communicator. Consider the simple greeting ritual, which is enacted quite differently across the globe. Americans tend to think that everyone shakes hands in greeting, but this is not the case. In India and Thailand, people place their hands in a praying position in front of their chests and bow to the person they are greeting, with the translation being, "I pray to God for you." This gesture can also mean "thank you" and "I'm sorry," which can be confusing for nonnatives. Older generations in some Middle Eastern countries perform a greeting in which the right hand sweeps upward, touching first the heart and then the forehead, and then up and outward, accompanied by a slight head nod—known as the *salaam* (Axtell, 1998).

Some greetings are more physical than others: Eskimos bang each other on the head or shoulders, while Polynesian men who don't know each other embrace and rub each other's backs. Maori tribespeople in New Zealand rub noses as a sign of friendship; some East African tribes'

greetings consist of spitting at each other's feet, while Tibetan tribesmen stick their tongues out at each other. The bow, evidenced in many Asian countries, isn't a common behavior for most Americans, but when Westerners visit most Asian countries, a slight bow is recommended as a sign of courtesy and respect for the customs of the country. The higher the status of the person we're bowing to, the lower the bow should be. The person of lower status (the visitor to the country, in this case) bows first. And interpreting the bow as a sign of subservience is incorrect; to the Japanese, a bow signals respect and humility, not lowered status (Axtell, 1998). Again, when moving to another culture or traveling across the globe, we should do our homework. It's wise to research the customs and traditions of the countries we're moving to or visiting, to pay attention to nonverbal differences in particular, and to adapt our behavior appropriately so that we can communicate effectively.

In some cultures, this greeting gesture is enacted instead of a handshake.

REMEMBER

Remember! 6.2

Ekman and Friesen's Categories of Movements and Gestures		
Category	**Definition**	**Example**
Emblems	Behaviors that have specific, generally understood meanings	A hitchhiker's raised thumb
Illustrators	Cues that accompany verbal messages and provide meaning	Someone pointing while giving directions to a location
Affect displays	Expressions of emotion	Leaning toward someone to indicate attraction
Regulators	Cues that control and manage the flow of communication	Nodding your head while listening
Adaptors	Behaviors that help you adjust to your environment	Chewing your fingernails when nervous

APPLICATIONS OF KINESICS RESEARCH ■ ■ ■

Many applications of the basic research on kinesics have emerged in past decades, and work is still being done in this area. In this section, we overview two areas of research that couldn't be more different.

Such a Flirt

What do you look like when you're attracted to someone? How do you behave if you want the other person to know you're attracted? Even if you're married or in another form of committed relationship, perhaps you find it interesting to think about how people flirt or show attraction and interest in each other. Decades of research into the phenomenon of flirting has produced some intriguing findings (Abrahams, 1994; Grammer, Kruck, Juette, & Fink, 2000; Hall, 2016; Hall & Xing, 2015; Hall, Xing, & Brooks, 2015; Renninger, Wade, & Grammer, 2004; Singh, 2004; Speer, 2017; Weber, Goodboy, & Cayanus, 2010). A study done in the '80s found 52 gestures and nonverbal behaviors that heterosexual women use to signal their interest in men, many of which are still prevalent today (Knox & Wilson, 1981). Among the top nonverbal flirting cues were smiling, surveying a crowded room with one's eyes, using more forward body lean, and moving closer to the person of interest.

Here's an interesting and consistent research finding: Heterosexual men tend to view flirting as a more sexual behavior than women do, and men often misinterpret women's friendly behaviors as signs of sexual attraction and interest (Abbey, 1982; Farris, Treat, Viken, & McFall, 2008; Henningsen, Henningsen, & Valde, 2006; Henningsen, Kartch, Orr, & Brown, 2009; LaFrance, Henningsen, Oates, & Shaw, 2009). The likelihood of this kind of misinterpretation increases as alcohol consumption increases (Abbey, Zawacki, & Buck, 2005; Delaney & Gluade, 1990). We're reminded of that old country and western song "The Girls All Look Prettier at Closin' Time."

Online flirting is now a popular research subject, given the significant growth in romantic connections made through online dating services, over Facebook, through the placement of video advertisements on sites such as YouTube, and so forth (Henningsen, Henningsen, McWorthy, McWorthy, & McWorthy, 2011; Meenagh, 2015). Arguably, the most significant body of work on this topic comes from Irish psychologist and professor Monica Whitty, who, along with various colleagues, has investigated such topics as the evolution of online romantic relationship development, how women and men connect online, how people sell themselves online, how that selling often involves minor and sometimes major deceptions, how relationships progress from online to face-to-face formats, and some abuses related to online connections, such as cyber-stalking (surveillance) and the online dating romance scam (Buchanan & Whitty, 2014; Whitty, 2003, 2004, 2007, 2015; Whitty & Carr, 2003).

OUT OF THE CLASSROOM
onto the page

When the subject of flirting comes up in class, along with research that consistently finds that, heterosexually speaking, men tend to misperceive women's nonverbal cues by reading more sexual intent into their actions than women actually intend, it *always* gets interesting. A discussion on this topic went like this:

Guy #1: You girls go on and on about how guys are animals and how we miss the point, that you don't want anything more than to have fun with your friends when you go out to a club, blah, blah. But then you'll let us buy you drinks all night. I think that makes you feel powerful or something, and that thing about guys misreading stuff, it's just not true—not with me and my buddies anyway.

Guy #2: Yeah, I agree. Don't tell me women don't want us to pay them attention and flirt. If you don't flirt with them, you catch hell for that. The way some girls dress when they go out, it's ridiculous to think that a guy isn't gonna look at them and try to make something happen.

Woman #1: But that's *exactly* the problem—you think we want you because we're dressed a certain way, but can't we just dress to look good and have fun without you guys thinking we want you? Who's to blame here? It's like we can't even make eye contact or smile at you without you thinking it's an invitation to hook up.

Sound familiar? It seems as though this particular "battle of the sexes" is far from over. Women still seem to be struggling to find a way to express a healthy sexuality and enjoy men's company without leading men on or—going the opposite direction—being too prudish or just plain rude. Men still seem to be trying to figure out exactly what women want, what their nonverbal cues mean, and how to react accordingly. One thing's for sure: Nonverbally communicating our attraction to another person is still complicated.

Another body of research along these lines has examined the difference between **courtship** and **quasi-courtship behavior,** with the primary difference being the "end game" (desired outcome or goal; Grammer, Kruck, & Magnusson, 1998; Scheflen, 1965). Courtship behavior involves those nonverbal actions we consciously and unconsciously exhibit when we're attracted to someone, someone with whom we possibly want to establish a relationship or connection, typically for the purposes of sexual activity (Hall, 2016). Quasi-courtship behavior differs from courtship behavior, although many of the nonverbal cues are the same (Henningsen, 2004; Yeomans, 2009). Think about the word *quasi*, which means "resembling" or "seeming." According to Scheflen's vision of this set of behaviors (first observed in family therapy sessions where some wives would flirt with their therapists, even with their husbands in the room), quasi-courtship cues also signal attraction or interest, but the goal or motive behind the behavior differs. As Guerrero and Floyd (2006) explain, "Whereas the courtship process has eventual copulation as its intended outcome, quasi-courtship does not. Rather, people engaging in quasi-courtship behaviors are being flirtatious with no actual goal of achieving sexual contact" (p. 80).

Quasi-courtship behavior is most prevalent in a first stage of **courtship readiness**, in which we tend to alter our normal pattern of eye contact (engaging in more direct eye gaze with the person we're interested in), suck in our stomach, tense our muscles, and stand up straighter in the presence of someone we're either attracted to or want to flirt with. The second stage includes **preening** behaviors, which include such actions as combing our hair, reapplying makeup, straightening our tie, pulling up our socks, and double-checking our appearance in the mirror. In the third stage, we demonstrate **positional cues**, using our posture and body orientation to be seen and noticed by another person, as well as to orient ourselves in such a way as to prevent invasion by a third party. We intensify these cues in the fourth stage, termed **appeals to invitation**, using close proximity, exposed skin, open body positions, and direct eye contact to signal our availability and interest. In this last stage, quasi-courtship behaviors may transform into courtship behaviors, and the "end game" may shift. The next time you're in a social setting, watch for these subtle and not-so-subtle nonverbal cues and try to detect who's *toying* with whom versus who's *into* whom.

Courtship behavior	Nonverbal actions we consciously and unconsciously exhibit when we are attracted to someone, someone with whom we possibly want to establish a relationship, typically for the purposes of sexual activity
Quasi-courtship behavior	Nonverbal actions we consciously and unconsciously exhibit when we are attracted to someone but the motive is not to establish a relationship or make sexual contact
Courtship readiness	First stage, in which we begin to alter our normal nonverbal patterns
Preening	Second stage, in which we attend to our appearance and make adjustments
Positional cues	Third stage, in which we use posture and body orientation to draw the attention of another person
Appeals to invitation	Fourth stage, in which we use more obvious and direct nonverbal cues to signal availability and interest

Remember! 6.3

Kids and Kinesics

While many of you do not yet have children of your own, some of you are parents, and you may be aware of the extraordinary work that has been accomplished with very young children and gesturing to communicate. One organization, Kindermusik, helps children develop musical abilities, but an important offshoot of the organization's work is an educational program designed to teach parents to sign with their hearing children who have not yet acquired language skills. Two such programs are Sign and Sing and Signing Smart, which combine song and playful interaction for parents and children (aged six months to three years) in an effort to help children learn 50 signs from American Sign Language. These programs build on finger plays related to songs and rhymes children typically learn, such as "This Little Piggy," and parents begin to substitute signs in other songs, as well as in interactions with their children.

As the Kindermusik website suggests, these activities "speed a child's language development, ease frustration, enhance long-term learning abilities," and improve motor skills—more specifically, they "strengthen fingers for zipping zippers and using scissors" (Kindermusik, 2018). Various signs, such as the gesture for "more" (as in "I want more food"), "all done" (as in "I'm done eating"), "ball," and "book," are taught by the parent to the young child. The goal is for children to be able to communicate their wants and needs prior to the age when they start developing spoken or written language. Hearing children who learn sign language put sentences together twice as fast as non-signing children (West, 2007; Sansavini et al., 2010).

More and more parents these days are teaching their very young children a few hand signals or signs, to help foster communication.

UNDERSTANDING KINESICS: APPLYING THE REFLEXIVE CYCLE OF NONVERBAL COMMUNICATION DEVELOPMENT

Have you thought about your own kinesic behavior, including your walk, stance, posture, and use of gestures? As you will no doubt recognize by now, the Reflexive Cycle begins with an inventory of self. The first step to develop your skills and a better understanding of the role of kinesic behavior in human interaction is to look at yourself. What tendencies do you have in terms of kinesics? Do you move and gesture just like one of your parents? Were you taught anything specific about hand gestures or movement in general? Do you use certain gestures because your friends use them?

    One of your authors remembers a situation that arose in a public speaking class, in which a male student seemed very "tight" in front of an audience. This particular student barely moved during a speech performance and used few, if any, gestures. When asked about his lack of movement, he explained that when he was growing up, especially in his middle school years, he became self-conscious about his physicality and the possibility of looking clumsy. (He grew tall quickly and lacked coordination.) His parents told him not to move too much and to try to keep his arms by his sides so he wouldn't risk appearing clumsy in front of his peers and teachers. While his well-meaning parents believed this advice would help their son's confidence and smoothness when communicating with other people, the advice had a more long-lasting and pronounced effect than they could have realized. Once this young man grew into his body and matured, he needed to learn how to loosen up and move and gesture freely, especially because movement in a public speaking situation (or even conversationally) helps reduce nerves and creates more visual interest for listeners.

Once you've surveyed your own behavior and decided if you have some changes to make, it's time to inventory others' kinesic behaviors. The next time you're in a social situation with lots of people, do some keen nonverbal observation. How do people stand, move, and gesture in social settings? Note the variation in these behaviors across people, because some people move a lot, while others move very little.

Your next step in the Reflexive Cycle is to transact with others, enacting any kinesic changes you've decided are appropriate, and to detect how your nonverbal behaviors transact with others' behaviors in everyday conversation. Do the kinesic behaviors you exhibit coordinate with others' or are they in opposition? How do the kinesics reveal or express what is transpiring in conversation?

After you've inventoried yourself, begun to make changes in your kinesic behavior, inventoried others' kinesics, and engaged in mutual transaction of behavior (such that your nonverbal cues affect other people and theirs affect you), your final step is to evaluate the whole process. What did you learn about your own and others' body movements that you believe makes you a better communicator? Again, the reflexive process takes an honest assessment of yourself, the willingness to change, keen observational skills, and a sense of "communicator adventure," as you put your new behaviors into action, transact with others, note the results, and reevaluate.

SUMMARY ■ ■ ■

In this chapter, we explored kinesics—the study of human movement, gestures, and posture. First, we examined posture for what it reveals nonverbally about a person. Scheflen's research identified three dimensions of posture: (1) inclusiveness/noninclusiveness, (2) face-to-face/parallel, and (3) congruence/incongruence. These dimensions help us observe nonverbal behavior and analyze people's attitudes and feelings about others as they interact. In related research, we also explored nonverbal synchrony, a coordination of speech and movement within one person (self-synchrony)

and across people in an interaction (interactive synchrony), which we contrasted with mimicry. This section concluded with an examination of nonverbal kinesic cues of power, status, and dominance.

The second major topic of study was walk, in terms of how our walk is influenced by our culture, genetic profile, physiological features, upbringing, psychological characteristics, and emotions. Specific attention was paid to cultural and sex differences regarding walking behavior. We include sitting behavior in this chapter because it's a common position for people across various cultures. Plus, we can tell a lot about people and their relationships simply by observing where and how they sit.

In the third major section of this chapter, we explored gestures, first by reviewing Ekman and Friesen's kinesic categories as a system for organizing and understanding kinesic behavior. Then we examined how gestures vary according to culture, with suggestions about studying native customs when traveling or relocating outside of our home culture. Two applications of kinesics research were provided to help us better understand how research enhances our understanding of the role of kinesics in our overall nonverbal behavior. First, flirting behavior was described in nonverbal terms, supported by research. Second, programs helping parents and prelinguistic children learn sign language were discussed, once again as evidence of the powerful role of nonverbal communication in human development. Finally, we worked through the Reflexive Cycle as it applies to kinesics, encouraging students to carefully inventory their own kinesics as well as keenly observe the kinesics of others to better understand transactions in which they engage on a daily basis.

DISCUSSION STARTERS ▪ ▪ ▪

1. What cues does your posture provide about your character, upbringing, culture, and specific emotions and mood? Did you ever consider that so much could be revealed in how you carry yourself?

2. Think of how many phrases in American culture relate to walking, such as "walk the walk; talk the talk" and "walk on the wild side." What makes a person's walk memorable and worthy of imitation?

3. What's your preferred sitting position, and what does it reveal about you to others? How can we detect emotions, such as nervousness and anxiety, through people's sitting behavior? How is the kinesic behavior of sitting related to proxemics (the use of space)?

4. Review Ekman and Friesen's kinesic categories and provide examples of each of the five categories of gesture.

5. How are gestures and culture related? What can you tell about a given culture by studying its gestures? How can you go about learning gestures in another culture?

6. What are some of the pitfalls related to kinesic behaviors and flirting? How easily can some kinesics be misperceived in a flirtatious context?

REFERENCES ■ ■ ■

Abbey, A. (1982). Sex differences in attributions for friendly behavior: Do males misperceive females' friendliness? *Journal of Personality and Social Psychology, 42,* 830–838.

Abbey, A., Zawacki, T., & Buck, P. O. (2005). The effects of past sexual assault perpetration and alcohol consumption on reactions to women's mixed signals. *Journal of Social and Clinical Psychology, 24,* 129–157.

Abrahams, M. F. (1994). Perceiving flirtatious communication: An exploration of the perceptual dimensions underlying judgments of flirtatiousness. *Journal of Sex Research, 31,* 283–292.

Ahluwalia, R. (2017, June 8). Madrid bans manspreading on public transport. Retrieved from https://www.independent.co.uk/travel/news-and-advice/mandspreading-madrid-spain-ban-public-transport-bus-metro-behaviour-etiquette-a7779041.html

Alda, A. (2018). *If I understood you, would I have this look on my face?: My adventures in the art and science of relating and communicating.* New York: Random House.

Andersen, P. A. (2004). *The complete idiot's guide to body language.* New York: Alpha.

Armstrong, N., & Wagner, M. (2003). *Field guide to gestures: How to identify and interpret virtually every gesture known to man.* Philadelphia: Quirk Books.

Arnette, S. L., & Pettijohn, T. F. II. (2012). The effects of posture on self-perceived leadership. *International Journal of Business and Social Science, 3,* 8–12.

Axtell, R. E. (1998). *Gestures: Do's and taboos of body language around the world.* New York: Wiley.

Bailey, A. H., & Kelly, S. D. (2015). Picture power: Gender versus body language in perceived status. *Journal of Nonverbal Behavior, 39,* 317–337.

Baimel, A., Birch, S. A. J., & Norenzayan, A. (2018). Coordinating bodies and minds: Behavioral synchrony fosters mentalizing. *Journal of Experimental Social Psychology, 74,* 281–290.

Beattie, G., Ross, J., & Webster, K. (2010). The fixation and processing of the iconic gestures that accompany talk. *Journal of Language and Social Psychology, 29,* 194–213.

Beavin Bavelas, J., & Chovil, N. (2006). Nonverbal and verbal communication: Hand gestures and facial displays as part of language use in face-to-face dialogue. In V. Manusov & M. L. Patterson (Eds.), *The SAGE handbook of nonverbal communication* (pp. 97–115). Thousand Oaks, CA: Sage.

Beebe, S. A., & Beebe, S. J. (2018). *Public speaking: An audience-centered approach* (10th ed.). Boston: Pearson.

Beebe, S. A., Beebe, S. J., & Ivy, D. K. (2019). *Communication: Principles for a lifetime* (7th ed.). Boston: Pearson.

Birdwhistell, R. L. (1960). Kinesics and communication. In E. Carpenter & M. McLuhan (Eds.), *Explorations in communication: An anthology* (pp. 54–64). Boston: Beacon.

Birdwhistell, R. L. (1967). Some body motion elements accompanying spoken American English. In L. Thayer (Ed.), *Communication: Concepts and perspectives* (pp. 53–76). Washington: Spartan.

Birdwhistell, R. L. (1970). *Kinesics and context: Essays on body motion communication.* Philadelphia: University of Pennsylvania Press.

Birdwhistell, R. L. (1974). The language of the body: The natural environment of words. In A. Silverstein (Ed.), *Human communication: Theoretical explorations* (pp. 203–220). New York: Wiley.

Brambilla, M., Sacchi, S., Menegatti, M., & Moscatelli, S. (2016). Honesty and dishonesty don't move together: Trait convent information influences behaioral synchrony. *Journal of Nonverbal Behavior, 40,* 171–186.

Buchanan, T., & Whitty, M. T. (2014). The online dating romance scam: Causes and consequences of victimhood. *Psychology, Crime and Law, 20.* http://doi.org/10.1080/1068316x.2013.772180

Burgoon, J. K., & Dunbar, N. E. (2006). Nonverbal expressions of dominance and power in human relationships. In V. Manusov & M. L. Patterson (Eds.), *The SAGE handbook of nonverbal communication* (pp. 279–297). Thousand Oaks, CA: Sage.

Butterworth, M. L. (2013). The passion of the Tebow: Sports media and heroic language in the tragic frame. *Critical Studies in Media Communication, 30*, 17–33.

Chartrand, T. L., & Bargh, J. A. (1999). The chameleon effect: The perception–behavior link and social interaction. *Journal of Personality and Social Psychology, 76*, 893–910.

Civile, C., & Sukhvinder, S. O. (2016). Power eliminates the influence of body posture on facial emotion recognition. *Journal of Nonverbal Behavior, 40*, 284–299.

Collett, P. (2018, May 16). What can we learn from the body language of the royals? Retrieved from https://news.sky.com/video/what-can-we-learn-from-body-language-of-the-royals-11374745

Cook, S. W., Yip, T. K., & Goldin-Meadow, S. (2010). Gesturing makes memories that last. *Journal of Memory and Language, 63*, 465–475.

Costa, M. (2010). Interpersonal distances in group walking. *Journal of Nonverbal Behavior, 34*, 15–26.

Cuddy, A. (2018). *Presence: Bringing your boldest self to your biggest challenges.* New York: Back Bay Books/Little, Brown and Company.

Dargue, N., & Sweller, N. (2018). Not all gestures are created equal: The effects of typical and atypical iconic gestures on narrative comprehension. *Journal of Nonverbal Behavior, 42*, 1–19.

Darwin, C. (1965). *Expression of emotions in man and animals.* Chicago: University of Chicago Press. (Original work published 1872)

DeGroot, T., & Gooty, J. (2009). Can nonverbal cues be used to make meaningful personality attributions in employment interviews? *Journal of Business Psychology, 24*, 179–192.

Delaney, H. J., & Gluade, B. A. (1990). Gender differences in perception of attractiveness of men and women in bars. *Journal of Personality and Social Psychology, 16*, 378–391.

Dijk, C., Fischer, A. H., Morina, N., van Eenwijk, C., & van Kleef, G. A. (2018). Effects of social anxiety on emotional mimicry and contagion: Feeling negative, but smiling politely. *Journal of Nonverbal Behavior, 42*, 81–99.

Do you know? (2006, June). *Martha Stewart Living,* 40.

Doody, J. P., & Bull, P. (2011). Asperger's syndrome and the decoding of boredom, interest, and disagreement from body posture. *Journal of Nonverbal Behavior, 35*, 87–100.

Dunbar, N. E., & Abra, G. (2010). Observations of dyadic power in interpersonal interaction. *Communication Monographs, 77*, 657–684.

Ekman, P., & Friesen, W. V. (1969). The repertoire of nonverbal behavior: Categories, origins, usage, and coding. *Semiotica, 1*, 49–98.

Farley, S. D. (2014). Nonverbal reactions to an attractive stranger: The role of mimicry in communicating preferred social distance. *Journal of Nonverbal Behavior, 38*, 195–208.

Farris, C., Treat, T. A., Viken, R. J., & McFall, R. M. (2008). Perceptual mechanisms that characterize gender differences in decoding women's sexual intent. *Psychological Science, 19*, 348–354.

Feldman, R. S., & Tyler, J. M. (2006). Factoring in age: Nonverbal communication across the life span. In V. Manusov & M. L. Patterson (Eds.), *The SAGE handbook of nonverbal communication* (pp. 181–199). Thousand Oaks, CA: Sage.

Flack, Z. M., Naylor, M., & Leavens, D. A. (2018). Pointing to visible and invisible targets. *Journal of Nonverbal Behavior, 42*, 221–236.

Floyd, K. (2018). *Communication matters* (3rd ed.). New York: McGraw-Hill.

Fujiwara, K., & Daibo, I. (2014). The extraction of nonverbal behaviors: Using video images and speech-signal analysis in dyadic conversation. *Journal of Nonverbal Behavior, 38*, 377–388.

Fulham, L., Book, A. S., Blais, J., Ritchie, M. B., Gauthier, N. Y., & Costello, K. (2017). The effect of hypervigilance on the relationship between sexual victimization and gait. *Journal of Interpersonal Violence.* http://doi-org./10.1177/0886260517713714

Furley, P., Dicks, M., & Memmert, D. (2012). Nonverbal behavior in soccer: The influence of dominant and submissive body language on the impression formation and expectancy of success of soccer players. *Journal of Sport & Exercise Psychology, 34*, 61–82.

Furley, P., & Schweizer, G. (2014). The expression of victory and loss: Estimating who's leading or trailing from nonverbal cues in sports. *Journal of Nonverbal Behavior, 38*, 13–29.

Gagnon, M., Gosselin, P., Hudon-ven der Buhs, I., Larocque, K., & Milliard, K. (2010). Children's recognition and discrimination of fear and disgust facial expressions. *Journal of Nonverbal Behavior, 34*, 27–42.

Galobardes, B., McCormack, V. W., McCarron, P., Howe, L. D., Lynch, J., Lawlor, D. A., et al. (2012). Social inequalities in height: Persisting differences today depend upon height of the parents. *PLoS ONE, 7*, 1–8.

Givens, D. B. (2016). Reading palm-up signs: Neurosemiotic overview of a common hand gesture. *Semiotica, 210*, 235–250.

Gonzaga, G. C., Keltner, D., & Ward, D. (2008). Power in mixed-sex interactions. *Cognition & Emotion, 22*, 1555–1568.

Grammer, K., Kruck, K. B., & Magnusson, M. S. (1998). The courtship dance: Patterns of nonverbal synchronization in opposite sex encounters. *Journal of Nonverbal Behavior, 22*, 3–25.

Grammer, K., Kruck, K., Juette, A., & Fink, B. (2000). Nonverbal behavior as courtship signals: The role of control and choice in selecting partners. *Evolution and Human Behavior, 21*, 371–390.

Gruber, J., King, J., Hay, J., & Johnston, L. (2016). The hands, head, and brow. *Gesture, 15*, 1–36.

Guéguen, N. (2011). The mimicker is a mirror of myself: Impact of mimicking on self-consciousness and social anxiety. *Social Behavior and Personality, 39*, 725–728.

Guéguen, N. (2012). The effects of incidental similarity with a stranger on mimicry behavior. *Open Behavioral Science Journal, 6*, 15–22.

Guéguen, N., Martin, A., & Meineri, S. (2011). Mimicry and helping behavior: An evaluation of mimicry on explicit helping request. *Journal of Social Psychology, 15*, 1–4.

Guerrero, L. K., & Floyd, K. (2006). *Nonverbal communication in close relationships.* Mahwah, NJ: Erlbaum.

Gunns, R. E., Johnston, L., & Hudson, W. M. (2002). Victim selection and kinematics: A point-light investigation of vulnerability to attack. *Journal of Nonverbal Behavior, 26*, 129–158.

Gunter, T. C., & Weinbrenner, J. E. (2017). When to take a gesture seriously: On how we use and prioritize communicative cues. *Journal of Cognitive Neuroscience, 29*, 1355–1367.

Hafner, J. (2017, September 27). Anthem kneeling isn't aimed at veterans, and other NFL protest misconceptions. Retrieved from https://www.usatoday.com/story/news/nation-now/2017/09/25/anthem-kneeling-isnt-aimed-veterans-and-other-nfl-protest-misconceptions/701409001/

Halberstadt, A. G., Dennis, P. A., & Hess, U. (2011). The influence of family expressiveness, individuals' own emotionality, and self-expressiveness on perceptions of others' facial expressions. *Journal of Nonverbal Behavior, 35*, 35–50.

Hall, J. [Judith] A. (2006). Women's and men's nonverbal communication: Similarities, differences, stereotypes, and origins. In V. Manusov & M. L. Patterson (Eds.), *The SAGE handbook of nonverbal communication* (pp. 201–218). Thousand Oaks, CA: Sage.

chapter six

Hall, J. [Jeffrey] A. (2016). Interpreting social-sexual communication: Relational framing theory and social-sexual communication, attraction, and intent. *Human Communication Research, 42*, 138–164.

Hall, J. [Jeffrey] A., & Xing, C. (2015). The verbal and nonverbal correlates of the five flirting styles. *Journal of Nonverbal Behavior, 39*, 41–68.

Hall, J. [Jeffrey] A., Xing, C., & Brooks, S. (2015). Accurately detecting flirting: Error management theory, the traditional sexual script, and flirting base rate. *Communication Research, 42*, 939–958.

Halovic, S., & Kroos, C. (2018). Not all is noticed: Kinematic cues of emotion-specific gait. *Human Movement Science, 57*, 478–488.

Harper, V. B., Jr. (2006). Walking the walk: Understanding nonverbal communication through walking. *Communication Teacher, 20*, 61–64.

Hasler, B. S., Salomon, O., Tuchman, P., Lev-Tov, A., & Friedman, D. (2017). Real-time gesture translation in intercultural communication. *Artificial Intelligence & Society, 32*, 25–35.

Hassemer, J., & Williams, B. (2016). Producing and perceiving gestures conveying height or shape. *Gesture, 15*, 404–424.

Henningsen, D. D. (2004). Flirting with meaning: An examination of miscommunication in flirting interactions. *Sex Roles, 50*, 481–489.

Henningsen, D. D., Henningsen, M. L. M., McWorthy, E., McWorthy, C., & McWorthy, L. (2011). Exploring the effects of sex and mode of presentation in perceptions of dating goals in video-dating. *Journal of Communication, 61*, 641–658.

Henningsen, D. D., Henningsen, M. L. M., & Valde, K. S. (2006). Gender differences in perceptions of women's sexual interest during cross-sex interactions: An application and extension of cognitive valence theory. *Sex Roles, 54*, 821–829.

Henningsen, D. D., Kartch, F., Orr, N., & Brown, A. (2009). The perceptions of verbal and nonverbal flirting cues in cross-sex interactions. *Human Communication, 12*, 371–381.

Holler, J., & Wilkin, J. (2011). Co-speech gesture mimicry in the process of collaborative referring during face-to-face interaction. *Journal of Nonverbal Behavior, 35*, 133–153.

Hullman, G. A., Goodnight, A., & Mougeotte, J. (2012). An examination of perceived relational messages that accompany interpersonal communication motivations. *Open Communication Journal, 6*, 1–7.

Hupp, J. M., & Gingras, M. C. (2016). The role of gesture meaningfulness in word learning. *Gesture, 15*, 340–356.

Iverson, J. M., Tencer, H. L., Lany, J., & Goldin-Meadow, S. (2000). The relation between gesture and speech in congenitally blind and sighted language-learners. *Journal of Nonverbal Behavior, 24*, 105–130.

Johnson, D. W. (2012). *Reaching out: Interpersonal effectiveness and self-actualization* (11th ed.). Boston: Pearson.

Kindermusik. (2018). Retrieved from www.kindermusik.com

Knapp, M. L., Hall, J. A., & Horgan, T. G. (2013). *Nonverbal communication in human interaction* (8th ed.). Belmont, CA: Wadsworth/Cengage Learning.

Knoblauch, A. (2018, May 23). NFL expected to enact national anthem policy for '18. Retrieved from NFL.com

Knox, D., & Wilson, K. (1981). Dating behaviors of university students. *Family Relations, 30*, 255–258.

Krumhuber, E., Manstead, A. S. R., Cosker, D., Marshall, D., & Rosin, P. L. (2009). Effects of dynamic attributes of smiles in human and synthetic faces: A simulated job interview setting. *Journal of Nonverbal Behavior, 33*, 1–15.

LaFrance, B. H., Henningsen, D. D., Oates, A., & Shaw, C. M. (2009). Social–sexual interactions? Meta-analyses of sex differences in perceptions of flirtatiousness, seductiveness, and promiscuousness. *Communication Monographs, 76*, 263–285.

Lakens, D., & Stel, M. (2011). If they move in sync, they must feel in sync: Movement synchrony leads to attributions of rapport and entitativity. *Social Cognition, 29*, 1–14.

Lakin, J. L., Jefferis, V. W., Cheng, C. M., & Chartrand, T. L. (2003). The chameleon effect as social glue: Evidence for the evolutionary significance of nonconscious mimicry. *Journal of Nonverbal Behavior, 27*, 145–161.

Lamberg, E. M., & Muratori, L. M. (2012). Cell phones change the way we walk. *Gait & Posture, 35*, 688–690.

Leathers, D. G., & Eaves, M. H. (2008). *Successful nonverbal communication: Principles and applications* (4th ed.). Boston: Pearson.

Lozza, N., Spoerri, C., Ehlert, U., Kesselring, M., Hubmann, P., Tschacher, W., & La Marca, R. (2018). Nonverbal synchrony and complementarity in unacquainted same-sec dyads: A comparison in a competitive context. *Journal of Nonverbal Behavior, 42*, 179–197.

Matsumoto, D., & Hwang, H. S. (2012). Evidence for a nonverbal expression of triumph. *Evolution and Human Behavior, 33*, 520–529.

Matsumoto, D., & Hwang, H. S. (2013a). Body and gestures. In D. Matsumoto, M. G. Frank, & H. S. Hwang (Eds.), *Nonverbal communication: Science and applications* (pp. 75–96). Thousand Oaks, CA: Sage.

Matsumoto, D., & Hwang, H. S. (2013b). Cultural similarities and differences in emblematic gestures. *Journal of Nonverbal Behavior, 37*, 1–27.

Matsumoto, D., & Juang, L. (2017). *Culture and psychology* (6th ed.). Boston: Cengage Learning.

Matthews-Saugstad, K. M., Raymakers, E. P., & Kelty-Stephen, D. (2017). Gesturing more diminishes recall of abstract words when gesture is allowed and concrete words when it is taboo. *Quarterly Journal of Experimental Psychology.* https://doi.org/10.1080/17470218.2016.1263997

McGill, S., & Carroll, B. (2017). *Gift of injury.* Ontario, Canada: Backfitpro Inc.

Meenagh, J. (2015). Flirting, dating, and breaking up within new media environments. *Sex Education, 15*, 458–471.

Merola, G. (2007). Emotional gestures in sport. *Language Resources and Evaluation, 41*, 233–254.

Mindock, C. (2017, September 26). Taking a knee: Why are NFL players protesting and when did they start kneeling? Retrieved from https://www.independent.co.uk/news/world/americas/us-politics/taking-a-knee-national-anthem-nfl-trump-why-meaning-origins-racism-us-colin-kaepernick-a8521741.html

Montepare, J. M., & Zebrowitz, L. A. (1993). A cross-cultural comparison of impressions created by age-related variations in gait. *Journal of Nonverbal Behavior, 17*, 55–68.

Morris, D., Collett, P., Marsh, P., & O'Shaughnessy, M. (1979). *Gestures: Their origins and distribution.* London: Jonathan Cape.

Nathan, R. (2006). *My freshman year: What a professor learned by becoming a student.* New York: Penguin.

Nelson, A., & Golant, S. K. (2004). *You don't say: Navigating nonverbal communication between the sexes.* New York: Prentice Hall.

Novack, M. A., & Goldin-Meadow, S. (2017). Gesture as representational action: A paper about function. *Psychonomic Bulletin & Review, 24*, 652–665.

Osensky, T. S. (2017). *Shortchanged: Height discrimination and strategies for social change.* Lebanon, NH: University Press of New England.

Panjwani, N., Chaplin, T. M., Sinha, R., & Mayes, L. C. (2016). Gender differences in emotion expression in low-income adolescents under stress. *Journal of Nonverbal Behavior, 40*, 117–132.

Petter, O. (2017, July 27). Revealed: The scientific explanation behind "Manspreading." Retrieved from https://www.independent.co.uk/life-style/manspreading-scientific-explanation-revealed-men-behaviour-public-transport-etiquette-a7862771.html

Re, D. E., & Perrett, D. I. (2012). Concordant preferences for actual height and facial cues to height. *Personality & Individual Differences, 53*, 901–906.

Renninger, L. A., Wade, T. J., & Grammer, K. (2004). Getting that female glance: Patterns and consequences of male nonverbal behavior in courtship contexts. *Evolution and Human Behavior, 25*, 416–431.

Reschke, P. J., Knothe, J. M., & Walle, E. A. (2017). Postural communication of emotion: Perception of distinct poses of five discrete emotions. *Frontiers in Psychology, 8*, 710. https://doi.org/10.3389/fpsyg.2017.00710

Richmond, V. P., McCroskey, J. C., & Hickson, M. L., III. (2011). *Nonverbal behavior in interpersonal relations* (7th ed.). Boston: Pearson.

Ritchie, M. B., Blais, J., Forth, A. E., & Book, A. S. (2018). Identifying vulnerability to violence: The role of psychopathy and gender. *Journal of Criminal Psychology, 8*, 125–137.

Robertson, D. A., Savva, G. M., King-Kallimanis, B. L., & Kenny, R. A. (2015). Negative perceptions of aging and decline in walking speed: A self-fulfilling prophecy. *PLoS ONE, 10*, 1–17.

Rush, C. (2006). *The mere mortal's guide to fine dining.* New York: Broadway Books.

Sakaguchi, K., & Hasegawa, T. (2006). Person perception through gait information and target choice for sexual advances: Comparison of likely targets in experiments and real life. *Journal of Nonverbal Behavior, 30*, 63–85.

Samovar, L. A., Porter, R. E., McDaniel, E. R., & Sexton Roy, C. (2014). Approaches to intercultural communication. In L. A. Samovar, R. E. Porter, E. R. McDaniel, & C. Sexton Roy (Eds.), *Intercultural communication: A reader* (14th ed., pp. 1–3). Boston: Cengage Learning.

Sansavini, A., Bello, A., Guarini, A., Savini, S., Stefanini, S., & Caselli, M. C. (2010). Early development of gestures, object-related-actions, word comprehension and word production, and their relationships in Italian infants. *Gesture, 10*, 52–85.

Scheflen, A. E. (1965). Quasi-courtship behavior in psychotherapy. *Psychiatry, 28*, 245–257.

Scheflen, A. E. (1974). *How behavior means.* New York: Gordon & Breach.

Scheflen, A. E., & Scheflen, A. (1972). *Body language and the social order.* Englewood Cliffs, NJ: Prentice Hall.

Schmidt, R. C., Morr, S., Fitzpatrick, P., & Richardson, M. J. (2012). Measuring the dynamics of interactional synchrony. *Journal of Nonverbal Behavior, 36*, 263–279.

Schug, J., Matsumoto, D., Horita, Y., Yamagishi, T., & Bonnet, K. (2010). Emotional expressivity as a signal of cooperation. *Evolution and Human Behavior, 31*, 87–94.

Schuler, L. (2017, July 18). There's a reason why men take up so much room when they sit. Retrieved from https://tonic.vice.com/en_us/article/evdkwm/manspreading-is-an-anatomical-necessity

Singh, D. (2004). Mating strategies of young women: Role of physical attractiveness. *Journal of Sex Research, 41*, 43–54.

Smithson, L., & Nicoladis, E. (2014). Lending a hand to imagery? The impact of visuospatial working memory interference upon iconic gesture production in a narrative task. *Journal of Nonverbal Behavior, 38*, 247–258.

Smithson, L., Nicoladis, E., & Marentette, P. (2011). Bilingual children's gesture use. *Gesture, 11*, 330–347.

Soll, L. (2007, February 9). The best of bad pits. *Entertainment Weekly*, 18.

Speer, S. A. (2017). Flirting: A designedly ambiguous action? *Research on Language & Social Interaction, 50*, 128–150.

Stevanoni, E., & Salmon, K. (2005). Giving memory a hand: Instructing children to gesture enhances their event recall. *Journal of Nonverbal Behavior, 29*, 217–233.

ten Brinke, L. T., Porter, S., & Baker, A. (2012). Darwin the detective: Observable facial muscle contractions reveal emotional high-stakes lie. *Environment and Human Behavior, 33*, 411–416.

Toscano, H., Schubert, T. W., & Giessner, S. R. (2018). Eye gaze and head posture jointly influence judgments of dominance, physical strength, and anger. *Journal of Nonverbal Behavior.* http://doi.org/10.1007/s10919-018-0276-5

Tsai, W., Huang, T., & Yu, H. (2012). Investigating the unique predictability and boundary conditions of applicant physical attractiveness and nonverbal behaviours on interviewer evaluations in job interviews. *Journal of Occupational & Organizational Psychology, 85*, 60–79.

Valtonen, A. (2013). Height matters: Practicing consumer agency, gender, and body politics. *Consumption, Markets & Culture, 16*, 196–221.

Vennekens-Kelly, E. (2012). *Subtle differences, big faux pas: Test your cultural competence.* Scottsdale, AZ: Summertime.

Verlinden, V. J. A., van der Geest, J. N., Hoogendam, Y. Y., Hofman, A., Breteler, M. M. B., & Ikram, M. A. (2013). Gait patterns in a community-dwelling population aged 50 years and older. *Gait & Posture, 37*, 500–505.

Weber, K., Goodboy, A. K., & Cayanus, J. L. (2010). Flirting competence: An experimental study on appropriate and effective opening lines. *Communication Research Reports, 27*, 184–191.

West, M. (2007, September 9). Learning to communicate: Babies may talk sooner if they learn to sign. *Corpus Christi Caller Times*, p. 6B.

Whitty, M. T. (2003). Cyber-flirting: Playing with love on the Internet. *Theory and Psychology, 13*, 339–357.

Whitty, M. T. (2004). Cyber-flirting: An examination of men's and women's flirting behaviour both offline and on the Internet. *Behaviour Change, 21*, 115–126.

Whitty, M. T. (2007). Introduction. In M. T. Whitty, A. Baker, & J. A. Inman (Eds.), *Online m@tchmaking* (pp. 1–14). New York: Palgrave Macmillan.

Whitty, M. T. (2015). Anatomy of the online dating romance scam. *Security Journal, 28*, 443–455.

Whitty, M. T., & Carr, A. N. (2003). Cyberspace as potential space: Considering the web as a playground to cyber-flirt. *Human Relations, 56*, 861–891.

Wilkes, C., Kydd, R., Sagar, M., & Broadbent, E. (2017). Upright posture improves affect and fatigue in people with depressive symptoms. *Journal of Behavior Therapy and Experimental Psychiatry, 54*, 143–149.

Wilt, K., Funkhouser, K., & Revelle, W. (2011). The dynamic relationships of affective synchrony to perceptions of situations. *Journal of Research in Personality, 45*, 309–321.

Wortman, J. (2013). Victory gestures: Science discovers a new emotion. *Breaking Muscle.* Retrieved from http://breakingmuscle.com/sports-psychology/victory-gestures-science-discovers-a-new-emotion

Wray, C., Saunders, N., McGuire, R., Cousins, G., & Norbury, C. F. (2017). Gesture production in language impairment: It's quality, not quantity, that matters. *Journal of Speech, Language & Hearing Research, 60*, 969–982.

Yeomans, T. (2009, November). *Communicating initial interest and attraction: Quasi-courtship versus courtship behaviors.* Paper presented at the meeting of the National Communication Association, Chicago, IL.

Zywiczynski, P., Wacewicz, S., & Orzechowski, S. (2017). Adaptors and the turn-taking mechanism: The distribution of adaptors relative to turn borders in dyadic conversation. *Interaction Studies, 18*, 276–298.

chapter seven

FACE AND EYES: REVEALING, MODIFYING, AND DECEIVING

chapter outline

chapter objectives

After studying this chapter, you should be able to

1. understand facial and eye behavior as key codes of nonverbal communication;
2. identify contrasting elements between the innate versus the learned perspective, in terms of the acquisition and development of facial expressions;
3. list and describe four facial management techniques;
4. identify and explain Ekman and Friesen's eight categories of facial expressions;
5. review the Facial Action Coding System and explain its use in assessing emotion in each region of the face;
6. discuss common procedures of facial modification;
7. identify three influences of eye behavior and explain how each nonverbally operates in everyday conversation;
8. provide 10 purposes of eye behavior and explain how each nonverbally operates in everyday conversation;
9. list and explain six forms of eye behavior;
10. review common procedures of eye modification; and
11. identify key research findings regarding facial and eye behavior and deception. case study

case study

WHO'S RIGHT? PERSONAL EXPRESSION VS. CUSTOMER SATISFACTION

Megan has worked in the hospitality industry for a couple of years. She enjoys working with guests who visit her hotel. In the past, Megan was commended for her outstanding customer service. She has a chipper demeanor; she smiles and maintains eye contact with guests to let them know she's genuinely interested in making their stay great. Her previous manager, Shelley, promoted her to the front desk manager a couple of months ago. But then Shelley moved to a different location and the company hired a new guy, Thomas, to be the general manager of the hotel.

Megan has some difficulty with Thomas because he gives negative feedback about things not associated with her job performance. For example, Thomas told Megan that she doesn't wear enough makeup, which he thinks makes her look unprofessional. Additionally, Thomas told her that she must wear her hair down to cover the tattoo behind her ear. Thomas thinks some guests might be offended by her tattoo, but Megan doesn't think it's that big of a deal because her small tattoo is art, not words or any particular message. Megan also has a nose piercing, which Thomas says she shouldn't wear at work, again citing non-professionalism. Megan has become increasingly frustrated because she doesn't believe her personal choices about her appearance should influence people's perceptions of how well she performs in her job. Megan is now trying to figure out how to best vocalize her concerns and respond to these recent critiques. Is Megan right, in that nonverbal cues like smiling and making eye contact are more important in customer service than having a tattoo or piercing? Or does Thomas have a point, that the tattoo and nose ring are also important nonverbal signals that might affect customer satisfaction?

FACIAL AND EYE BEHAVIOR AS NONVERBAL COMMUNICATION ■ ■ ■ ■ ▬

Wanda:	Did you see the look on her face?
Jackie:	Yeah, she was totally offended by Ruben's comment.
Wanda:	You could tell by the look in her eye, she was about to explode.
Jackie:	Oh, I know!

This brief conversation illustrates how facial and eye behaviors influence our perceptions of others' emotions, attitudes, and desires. We rely on facial and eye behavior to alert us to what other people are thinking or, more important, feeling (Courbalay, Deroche, & Descarreaux, 2017; Lobmaier, 2012; Mendolia, 2007).

We emphasize the emotional aspect because many people trudge through life hurting others' feelings by using lackluster facial and eye responses that communicate the following messages: "I don't care about what you're saying," "I'm not listening to you," "I think you're stupid," and "You're not important." Obviously, violations or misuses of the other nonverbal communication codes you're studying in class and reading about in this book can also lead to hurt feelings and relational tensions with friends, partners, and even social acquaintances. Yet there's a special power of the human face and eyes to send positive messages of joy and affirmation, which is why we rely on them so much in our everyday communication (Houston, Grandey, & Sawyer, 2018; Paulmann, Titone, & Pell, 2012).

Perhaps you've heard the expression, "The eyes are the windows to the soul" or "Nice to see a familiar face." Even in everyday service encounters at coffee shops, pubs, grocery stores, and restaurants, we evaluate facial and eye behavior as part of the customer service we experience, as we referenced in the opening case study (Keh, Ren, Hill, & Li, 2013; Houston et al., 2018). Facial and eye behaviors, within the larger category of kinesics (discussed in Chapter 6), are critical to the study of nonverbal communication; so in this chapter, we focus on them as significant nonverbal codes.

SIGNIFICANCE OF FACIAL BEHAVIOR ■ ■ ■

By some estimates, attributed primarily to nonverbal scholar Ray Birdwhistell (1974), the human face is capable of producing more than 250,000 expressions. What an incredible ability! Computer-generated imaging technology, a rapidly growing trend in film, theatre, and video gaming, continues to evolve in its potential to emulate this human ability (Farrar, Krcmar, & McGloin, 2013; Parker, 2014). The human face is so important in communication that it has become, according to communication theorists Domenici and Littlejohn (2006), "a symbol of close personal interaction" (p. 10). They point out that "we use expressions such as 'face to face,' 'face time,' 'in your face,' and 'saving face.' In other words, the metaphor of face is powerful in bringing many aspects of personal communication to the fore" (p. 10).

Your face is connected to your public identity; it's the *you* presented to others in everyday encounters. Scholar Erving Goffman (1967) wrote about this presentation of self in everyday life, explaining how face can be "lost," "maintained," "protected," or "enhanced." This approach has been incorporated by communication scholars into a concept known as **facework**, defined as "a set of coordinated practices in which communicators build, maintain, protect, or threaten personal dignity, honor, and respect" (Domenici & Littlejohn, 2006, pp. 11–12). Consider the times when you've thought about how you or someone else could "save face" in an embarrassing or awkward situation.

ACQUISITION AND DEVELOPMENT OF FACIAL EXPRESSION ■ ■ ■

Nonverbal communication scholars have debated for many years about the origins of facial expressions. The main point in the debate has been whether facial expressions are innate, learned, or both. **Innate behavior**, as related to the face, means that facial expression is biological, or an ability that comes to humans at birth. In contrast, if facial expressions are **learned behavior**, that means they are acquired through cultural, social, and family experiences over time.

© Muh/ Shutterstock.com.

Many different expressions can be used to communicate feelings about an awkward or embarrassing situation.

Evolution and Natural Selection: The "Born" Perspective

Charles Darwin (1872/1965) is famous for his theory of **evolution,** or how species change and adapt over time. From Darwin's perspective, facial expressions are acquired through evolution and **natural selection,** meaning that the organisms best suited to survival in an environment will thrive and pass on their genetic advantages to future generations. Darwin was interested in how facial expressions of animals served as primary survival mechanisms that evolved along with other physical characteristics. He contended that higher-order primates also used facial expressions to communicate emotions, feelings, and attitudes.

While Darwin's observations of facial expressions in animals are interesting and important to consider, our focus is on the nonverbal dimensions of the *human* face. Decades of research observing children has found evidence that most human facial behaviors are inborn or genetically derived (Eibl-Eibesfeldt, 1970, 1972; Grossman & Kegl, 2007; Spackman, Fujiki, Brinton, Nelson, & Allen, 2005). The six basic facial expressions of emotion (sadness, anger, disgust, fear, surprise, and happiness) produced by children without disabilities can also be observed in children who are born deaf and blind. Since children with these disabilities aren't able to see or hear, the chances of them learning how to express emotions from family or social experiences are minimal or nonexistent, since humans learn primarily through auditory and visual channels (Gagnon, Gosselin, Hudon-ven der Buhs, Larocque, & Milliard, 2010; Grossman & Kegl, 2007; Matsumoto & Willingham, 2009; Spackman et al., 2005).

The ultimate nonverbal communication assignment would be to travel the globe and document facial expressions across cultures. Do you think you would find universal facial expressions, or do you think culture influences facial expressions in humans? Studies provide evidence that facial expressions are, in fact, similar (if not universal) across cultural boundaries, thus strengthening the "nonverbal cues as innate" stance (Elfenbein, 2006; Hess, Blaison, & Kafetsios, 2016; Jack, Garrod, Yu, Caldara, & Schyns, 2012; Boas, Ferreira, de Moura, Maia, & Amaral, 2016).

External Factors: The "Learned" Perspective

In addition to evolution and natural selection, another aspect of our study of the nonverbal dimensions of the face is **external factors**—influences on our facial expressions that come from environment, social norms, and culture. While a great deal of research suggests that human facial expressions are innate characteristics, we can probably all agree that we learn how to act in relation to social contexts. For example, one of the authors of this text recently observed parents instructing their young child to "act like a big girl" during the screening process at an airport security check point. The little girl stood up straight and shifted her smiling facial expression into a serious one, reminding us all that "security is no laughing matter." As children develop, they're often coached by family members and teachers about what facial expression is appropriate for a particular emotion and situation (Ekman & Friesen, 1967; Gosselin, Maassarani, Younger, & Perron, 2011; Grossard et al., 2018). Children can learn at very early ages to mask disappointment and other emotions that register in their facial expressions to appear more socially appropriate or to comply with what an adult desires or expects. In one study, one group of preschool and elementary children were presented with new toys, while another group of children were presented with broken, used toys. The children (some of whom were as young as 2 1/2 years old) who got the disappointing toys registered disappointment and confusion on their faces but quickly masked those emotions, put smiles on their little faces, and thanked the researchers for the presents (Cole, 1986).

Innate and Learned

A final perspective on the acquisition of facial expression that is important to review is a combined perspective—that is, that facial behavior is both innate and learned. For many decades, nonverbal communication scholars have agreed with this position (Ekman & Friesen, 1969a, 1969b, 1975; Ekman, Friesen, & Ellsworth, 1972). Some of the facial expressions we're born with are closely associated with those six primary emotions we mentioned earlier: sadness, anger, disgust, fear, surprise, and happiness. We may be born able to express these emotions on our faces, but with experience we learn different facial expressions or more nuanced ways of communicating (and sometimes masking) what we feel (Minotte, 2017). We often feel combinations of emotions, like fear and anger, anger and disgust, joy and surprise, and so forth; our facial expressions can reveal these combinations as well (Shichuan, Yong, & Martinez, 2014).

When a baby is born into the world, he or she feels free to express emotions without management or holding back. But over time, as the person grows into adulthood, she or he becomes socialized and trained to control the expression of emotions based on the context. We learn what is socially appropriate and accepted in terms of expressive behavior. For example, a teacher may get irritated at students who are talking in the back of a classroom. Rather than expressing that irritation facially, the teacher may mask the emotion and choose to ignore the disruption until after class, thinking that an emotional outburst will throw off the rhythm of the class and only make the situation worse. Put simply, people are born with an ability to express emotions through facial and bodily expressions. But as we mature, we're expected to adapt our nonverbal expressions and mold them to what is appropriate for a given communication and cultural context (Puccinelli, Motyka, & Grewal, 2010; Grossard et al., 2018).

One of the most heavily researched facial cues is the smile, in terms of how we produce smiles and how people receive and interpret them (Brisini, 2017; Fischer & LaFrance, 2015; Forgas & East, 2008; Guéguen, 2008, 2013; Wang, Mao, Li, & Liu, 2017). The popularity of smiling as a research topic likely corresponds to the fact that the smile is one of a very few culturally universal nonverbal cues (Szarota, 2010). One could argue that a smile is an innate behavior, given evidence that sensory-deprived children produce smiles comparable to those of children who do not have such impairments. But different types of smiles exist, including genuine and forced or faked smiles; some of these expressions are learned as adaptations of the basic smile (Hugenberg & Sczesny,

2006; Schmidt, 2006). **Genuine smiles** are unconscious and uncontrolled—the kind a photographer will try to capture so a picture reflects who we really are (Krumhuber & Kappas, 2005). One form of genuine smile is the **Duchenne smile** (named after a French specialist in anatomy), also termed a **felt smile,** which engages the muscles around the eyes as well as those around the lips that cause the corners of the mouth to move upward. These smiles send the following positive messages: "Good to see you," "Let's play," or "Let's be friends" (Ekman, Davidson, & Friesen, 1990; Fridlund & Russell, 2006; Gunnery & Hall, 2014; Gunnery, Hall, & Ruben, 2013; Ilicic, Kulczynski, & Baxter, 2018; Krumhuber, Likowski, & Weyers, 2014).

Smiling is said to make people feel better. So when we're smiling, we may feel happier, which in turn communicates happiness to other people; the same goes for frowning, which to most people signals a negative emotion like anger (Yoo & Noyes, 2016). But when our smiles are forced and conscious, we often plaster a **fake smile** on our faces, which involves a less wide expression than a genuine smile (generally speaking), with possibly a forced baring or gritting of the teeth (Ekman & Friesen, 1982). Fake smiles can damage how others view us in social situations, while genuine smiles promote social relationships and convey honest emotions to other people (Ilicic et al., 2018; Okubo, Kobayashi, & Ishikawa, 2012; Yamamoto & Suzuki, 2006). Nonverbal psychology professor Marianne LaFrance (2011) wrote an entire book about smiling; she explores five primary kinds of smiles (genuine, angry, sad, relieved, and embarrassed) for their communicative power.

The genuineness of our smiles can significantly influence our personal relationships.

©CREATISTA/Shutterstock.com

Facework	A set of coordinated practices in which communicators build, maintain, protect, or threaten personal dignity, honor, and respect
Innate behavior	A biological activity or trait that comes to human beings at birth
Learned behavior	Nonverbal expressions acquired through cultural, social, and family experiences over time
Evolution	How species change and adapt over time
Natural selection	Darwin's theory that the organisms best suited to survival in an environment will thrive and pass on their genetic advantages to future generations
External factors	Influences on facial expressions such as environment, social norms, and culture
Genuine smile	An unconscious and uncontrolled smile that promotes social relationships and conveys honest emotions
Duchenne (felt) smile	A form of genuine smile that communicates positive messages
Fake smile	A forced and conscious smile that can damage how others view us in social situations

MANAGING FACIAL EXPRESSIONS

We've established that the face communicates basic human emotions. The question we explore in this section is, How do people manage their facial expressions? You may not have ever thought of facial expressions as something needing to be "managed," but what we mean is that we have some degree of control over what we express on our faces. While some expressions happen quickly and innately (like opening the eyes wide and raising the eyebrows when surprised), for other expressions we have a choice. In some situations and for some emotions, facial expression is purposeful. Because of social norms and communication expectations, it's important to understand emotional expression and how it varies situationally (Buck, 1994; Grossard et al., 2018; Holler & Wilkin, 2011; Sato & Yoshikawa, 2007).

Stemming from the work of nonverbal scholars Paul Ekman and Wallace Friesen (1969a, 1969b, 1975), facial management techniques are categories of behavior that help us determine the appropriate facial response for any given situation. The four most common techniques are: neutralization, masking, intensification, and deintensification.

NEUTRALIZATION. Neutralization is the process of using facial expressions to erase or numb how we really feel. People who neutralize their facial expressions are often referred to as having a poker face. If you watch *The World Series of Poker* on TV, you don't have to look too hard to find players engaged in the neutralization of facial expressions. Many poker players use caps, sunglasses, and costumes as part of their attempt to neutralize their true emotions cued by the face.

MASKING. The next facial management technique we use in certain social contexts is **masking**—concealing the expressions connected to a felt emotion and replacing them with expressions more appropriate to the situation. Here's an example: Over the past few weeks, Cindy and Ashley have studied hard for a huge history exam. They share the goal of earning at least a B on the exam. When their professor passes out the exam scores, Cindy's face lights up and she immediately bursts with joy in response to her A. When Ashley receives her grade and realizes that she has earned only a D, she's extremely disappointed and initially feels anger and envy toward Cindy, since they studied together. When Cindy expresses happiness about her good grade, Ashley masks her facial expression of disappointment, thus suppressing her feelings about her own grade, and congratulates Cindy.

INTENSIFICATION. The next facial management technique is called **intensification**—the use of a facial expression that reveals an exaggeration of how we feel about something. For example, Joel is really nervous about meeting the parents of his partner, Sam. Joel isn't used to disclosing his sexual orientation to people he doesn't know well, so meeting his partner's family is causing a lot of anxiety. When Joel is introduced to Sam's parents, he intensifies his smile to send a message of happiness and pleasure. He's glad to meet them, as a turning point in his relationship with Sam, but feels a pressure to intensify his smile since he's meeting them for the first time and the situation feels awkward. Perhaps you can think of other situations in which social pressure requires or leads to an exaggerated facial expression.

DEINTENSIFICATION. The final facial management technique is **deintensification**—the reduction of intensity of our facial expression related to a particular emotion due to social or cultural expectations. In U.S. culture, men are not conditioned to express intense feelings of sadness, fear, or worry. Televised sporting events such as football, baseball, and basketball games often show close-up shots of members of the losing team sitting on the bench looking forlorn, to capture a sense of their emotion. While some athletes deintensify what they're feeling during a game, match, or meet, others simply "let it all hang out" for the cameras. Men in U.S. culture are allowed some emotion, but not too much, since their role is often to keep it together so they can maintain their toughness—a key element often associated with masculinity (Fischer & LaFrance, 2015). Thus, many men tend to deintensify their facial expressions of sadness or grief, as well as joy, to meet perceived social expectations.

Deintensification is also exemplified by people in leadership positions (Huovinen & Weselius, 2015; Trichas, Schyns, Lord, & Hall, 2017). People in charge of businesses, classrooms, governments, crisis response teams, and the like are expected to keep their emotions in check so they can protect others and continue to do their jobs. In states hard hit by hurricanes in recent years, often the state's governor and other officials worked to deintensify their facial expressions and other nonverbal cues in TV appearances and briefings, so as to convey a controlled, calm demeanor and reassure the public (Claeys & Cauberghe, 2014; De Waele & Claeys, 2017). When a Category 5 tornado ripped through Moore, Oklahoma, in 2013, video footage showed the heroism of schoolteachers who, as the tornado approached, deintensified facial expressions of their own fear, told stories, and led their students in song. Good communicators know what face to wear given the constraints of a communicative situation.

People who brief the public in crisis situations must be especially careful to maintain professional facial expressions during times of high stress.

EKMAN AND FRIESEN'S FACIAL MANAGEMENT TECHNIQUES

Remember! 7.2

Neutralization	Using facial expressions that erase or numb how we really feel
Masking	Concealing the expressions connected to a felt emotion and replacing them with expressions more appropriate to the situation
Intensification	Use of a facial expression that reveals an exaggeration of how we feel about something
Deintensification	Reduction of intensity of a facial expression related to a particular emotion due to social or cultural expectations

Ekman and Friesen's Classification of Facial Expressions

In addition to facial management techniques, Ekman, Friesen, and colleagues created a classification system that reflects eight different styles of facial expressions (Ekman & Friesen, 1969a, 1969b; Ekman, Friesen, & Tompkins, 1971). Let's review them, understanding that many, if not all, of these styles are subconscious to the communicator, and people may use a combination of styles, not just one style all the time.

1. *The withholder:* With this style of facial expression, the face does not exhibit any states of emotion (the ultimate poker face). Facial movement is restricted.
2. *The revealer:* Opposite of the withholder, the face tells all, with little doubt as to how the person feels.
3. *The unwitting expressor:* A person tries to mask an emotion but "unwittingly" reveals the emotion through facial expressions, which may surprise the communicator.
4. *The blanked expressor:* In this style, the communicator believes an emotion is being conveyed, but no one else can see it.
5. *The substitute expressor:* This style of facial expression displays an emotion other than what the communicator thinks is being portrayed. The substitute expressor thinks a message of sadness is being sent, for example, while others interpret the facial expression as related to a different emotion.
6. *The frozen-affect expressor:* In this style, part of an emotion is displayed at all times, meaning that a characteristic or feature of the face translates to an emotion in the minds of viewers. For example, someone whose mouth naturally turns down at the corners can be perceived to be frowning and sad all the time.
7. *The ever-ready expressor:* In this style, a communicator tends to display one general facial expression as a response to almost any situation, no matter the emotion felt. For example, the ever-ready expressor smiles whether receiving good or bad news.
8. *The flooded-affect expressor:* When these communicators feel a particular emotion, that emotion "floods" their face with a certain expression; they rarely look neutral when they're emotional. For example, if a person has registered anger on her or his face, a situation that might evoke a different emotion doesn't cause the look of anger to go away.

What's your primary style of facial expression? While this list is useful in the general classification of styles of facial expressions, it's important to remember that we rarely display only one emotion at a time on our faces. In other words, our emotions aren't one-dimensional; we may register several emotions and express them simultaneously on our faces. These multiple facial expressions are called **affect blends**. In addition, in some situations, we may try to be neutral in our expression but one portion of our face reveals how we feel. This phenomenon is known as a **partial**—an emotion that registers in a single area of the face while other facial areas are controlled.

One other form of facial expression is interesting, while we're on the subject of styles and controlled versus spontaneous expressions. In a classic study, researchers Haggard and Isaacs (1966) detected dramatic, rapid changes of expressions flashing across their subjects' faces, which they termed **micromomentary facial expressions,** sometimes called **microexpressions** in research. These expressions can be at odds with other nonverbal cues and what a person says, but researchers believe they are truer indicators of an emotion before that emotion is masked. Observers have to be quick enough to detect them or use technology that can detect them in micro-seconds (Demetrioff, Porter, & Baker, 2017; Ekman, 2009; Matsumoto & Hwang, 2011; Yan, Wu, Liang, Chen, & Fu, 2013).

Facial Action Coding System

Ekman and Friesen designed a process called the **Facial Action Coding System (FACS)** that separates the face into three regions (see Figure 7.1): eyebrows and forehead; eyes and eyelids; and lower face, including the cheeks, nose, and mouth. When researchers study human faces, they focus in microscopic detail on the face and its myriad movements in an effort to better understand how our faces communicate what we think and feel.

FIGURE 7.1
Three Regions of the Face

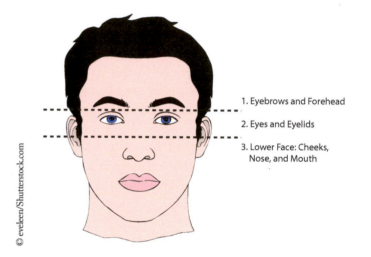

© eveleen/Shutterstock.com

1. Eyebrows and Forehead

2. Eyes and Eyelids

3. Lower Face: Cheeks, Nose, and Mouth

In the past, studies utilizing FACS generally had researchers relying on shared sets of photos or videos, often using actor portrayals. However, this standardized material has been criticized as lacking flexibility, control, and realism. Advances in computer technology now allow scholars to study and manipulate facial expressions by using computer-generated models. Roesch and colleagues (2011) developed FACSGen, a tool that allows for the creation of realistic synthetic 3-D facial stimuli, based on FACS. This tool gives researchers control over facial action units, allowing for more dynamic interactions within a research setting.

Using Ekman's six primary emotions (see Table 7.1), researchers over several decades have learned to classify particular emotions in terms of where they emerge on the face (Atkinson, Tipples, Burt, & Young, 2005; D'Acremont & Van der Linden, 2007; Ekman & Friesen, 1975; Fernández-Dols, Carrera, & Crivelli, 2011; Johnson, Ekman, & Friesen, 1975; Mendolia, 2007). Let's explore each region of the face to see what's communicated nonverbally.

TABLE 7.1 Ekman and Friesen's Six Basic Emotions Revealed by the Face

EMOTION	FACIAL LOCATION
Sadness	Eyes and eyelids
Anger	Forehead, mouth, brows, and cheeks
Disgust	Multiple areas of face, including bridge of the nose
Fear	Eyes and eyelids
Happiness	Lower facial region; eyes and eyelids
Surprise	All facial regions (brows/forehead, eyes/eyelids, and lower face)

EYEBROWS AND FOREHEAD. The first region of the face includes the eyebrows and forehead, which can communicate a variety of messages. For example, lowering the brows can be viewed as a frown, a signal of disappointment or anger. In contrast, raising the brows can signal interest or surprise. At the more extreme level, brow raises can communicate amazement, surprise, or fear (Flecha-Garcia, 2010; Zhengrui & Hongqiang, 2018). Raising one brow, also known as the **cocked eyebrow,** can be a sign of questioning or confusion. **Knitted eyebrows** (both brows lowered toward the nose and eyes) can signal pain, illness, anxiety, or frustration. **Flashing eyebrows** (both brows raised and lowered quickly) can signal flirtation (sometimes sexual) or a friendly greeting, depending on the situation.

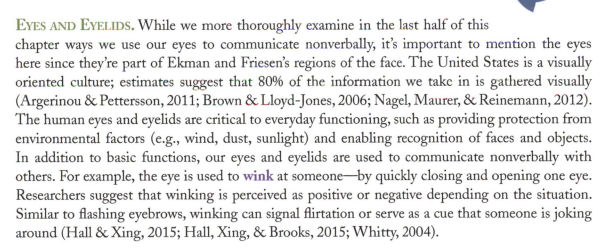

EYES AND EYELIDS. While we more thoroughly examine in the last half of this chapter ways we use our eyes to communicate nonverbally, it's important to mention the eyes here since they're part of Ekman and Friesen's regions of the face. The United States is a visually oriented culture; estimates suggest that 80% of the information we take in is gathered visually (Argerinou & Pettersson, 2011; Brown & Lloyd-Jones, 2006; Nagel, Maurer, & Reinemann, 2012). The human eyes and eyelids are critical to everyday functioning, such as providing protection from environmental factors (e.g., wind, dust, sunlight) and enabling recognition of faces and objects. In addition to basic functions, our eyes and eyelids are used to communicate nonverbally with others. For example, the eye is used to **wink** at someone—by quickly closing and opening one eye. Researchers suggest that winking is perceived as positive or negative depending on the situation. Similar to flashing eyebrows, winking can signal flirtation or serve as a cue that someone is joking around (Hall & Xing, 2015; Hall, Xing, & Brooks, 2015; Whitty, 2004).

CHEEKS. Do you have a friend or loved one with a light complexion whose face turns red in response to embarrassment? Nonverbal behaviorist Desmond Morris (1985) explains that the lower facial region typically reveals the true emotions people experience. The flushing of the cheeks you've likely observed on other people or may display yourself, primarily triggered by shame, embarrassment, or self-consciousness, is explored in nonverbal communication research (de Jong &

Dijk, 2013; Drummond & Bailey, 2013; Kiho, Sungkun, & Jang-Han, 2012). The pattern of blood rushing into the cheeks varies, depending on whether an emotion of anger or embarrassment is felt. Specifically, reddening associated with anger tends to spread throughout the face, while reddening from embarrassment is more subtle and confined to a smaller region of the face.

NOSE. Another important region of the human face is the nose. Take a moment to think about life without a nose. It's hard to imagine, isn't it? You wouldn't be able to smell, and breathing would be extremely difficult. Some view the nose as a protector of the eyes and a filter against dust and debris. You may not think your nose communicates much, but its size and shape send signals to others, warranted or not. Some people have a perky "button" nose, often conveying youthfulness; others have a large, bulbous nose, which may send a different kind of signal to an onlooker. Plus, the bridge of the nose is integral to facial expression; it's a primary area for conveying the emotion of disgust, as we typically wrinkle the bridge of the nose when we confront a disgusting stimulus.

MOUTH. The human mouth is used for a wide variety of actions, such as talking, smiling, laughing, frowning, kissing, singing, screaming, eating, drinking, and even smoking. Clearly, the human mouth is one of the most active body parts, and, at the same time, it's used to express a variety of emotions. In fact, since the mouth is so important in terms of location on the face, as well as the functions it serves, members of cultural and ethnic groups often modify the appearance of the mouth, which we discuss in more detail in the next section.

REMEMBER

Remember! 7.3

Affect blends	Expressing several emotions simultaneously on the face
Partial	An emotion that registers in a single area of the face while other facial areas are controlled
Micromomentary facial expressions (microexpressions)	Dramatic, rapid changes of facial expressions
Facial Action Coding System (FACS)	A research coding system that examines the face in three regions: eyebrows and forehead, eyes and eyelids, and lower face (including cheeks, nose, and mouth)
Cocked eyebrow	One brow raised
Knitted eyebrows	Both brows lowered toward the nose and eyes
Flashing eyebrows	Both brows raised and lowered quickly
Wink	Quickly closing and opening one eye, usually directed toward another person

MODIFYING THE FACE ▪ ▪ ▪ ▪

Because the face is so important to people across cultures and ethnicities, we continue to see increases in the amounts of money spent on facial modification so people can achieve what their culture views as ideal (Holliday & Cairnie, 2007; Rossion, 2013). Procedures are more common and normalized today, as people alter their faces with tattoos, piercings, color, makeup, and cosmetic procedures, such as collagen and Botox injections (Cook & Dwyer, 2017; Davis, 1995, 2003; Guéguen, 2012; Kalus & Cregan, 2017; Wegenstein, 2012; Zestcott, Bean, & Stone, 2017). In Chapter 5 on physical appearance, we discussed some personal and social consequences of **body modification**, meaning the more permanent methods of changing the way we look. Here, we refine our focus to **facial modification**—that is, more permanent methods of changing the face. To be clear, we're not talking about people who seek remedies from disfigurement from birth defects or such catastrophes as car wrecks or fires. Our focus is the alteration of the face for which the key motivation is to enhance perceptions of attractiveness.

Similar to body modification, the cosmetic surgery industry offers an array of procedures and products that enable people to change each region of the face, including the nose, cheeks, chin, eyes, and forehead (Davis, 2003; Holliday & Cairnie, 2007; Luo, 2012). One basic perception of attractiveness relates to **facial symmetry**, meaning a face that is equally proportioned in size and shape. Research shows that in U.S. culture, as well as many other cultures around the world, equally proportioned or symmetrical faces are viewed as highly attractive (Cunningham, Barbee, & Philhower, 2002; Ewing, Rhodes, & Pellicano, 2010; Grammer & Thornhill, 1994). Some cosmetic procedures are aimed at simply achieving greater symmetry in the face.

You've no doubt heard or read stories of celebrities and non-celebrities alike who attempt to correct a facial flaw (as they perceive it) or try to "turn back the hands of time" by modifying their faces, either through surgery or cosmetic procedures. Some procedures do enhance appearance and possibly even health, such as facial peels and laser techniques that reverse the effects of sun damage. But you've probably also heard the tragic outcomes of some of these surgeries and procedures, such as the people who become addicted to facial and body modification, such that after multiple procedures, they end up looking less than human, or people who die from complications of surgery.

Below we list some of the most common facial modification procedures. While more women than men in the United States undergo facial modification procedures, the number of men seeking to alter their facial features is on the rise (American Society for Aesthetic Plastic Surgery, 2018). Surgical procedures were up 11% in 2017; injectable nonsurgical procedures increased by 40% over the past decade. In 2017, the rate of eyelid surgery increased by 26% over the previous five-year period. Below we list the top five cosmetic procedures performed in the United States.

1. *Rhinoplasty:* This is the technical term for nose surgery. Originally developed to correct breathing problems in youth, the nose is broken and reshaped to a preferred size.
2. *Botox:* This procedure consists of an injection of a toxic substance that temporarily paralyzes muscles and skin tissues, typically applied to the forehead and around the

eyes, for the purposes of tightening the skin on the face, reducing wrinkles, and making people look younger. According to the American Society for Aesthetic Plastic Surgery (2018), Americans spent around $1.75 billion on injectables in 2017.

3. *Laser treatments:* Lasers are applied to the face or other areas of the body marred by acne or skin discolorations, to produce a more consistent skin tone. Americans spent nearly $4 million on "skin rejuvenation procedures" in 2017.

4. *Facelift:* This is a complex surgical procedure in which the skin on the face (and sometimes the neck) is surgically detached, lifted up, and reattached to defy the natural aging effects of gravity and to create a tighter, more youthful-looking face.

5. *Collagen injections:* Some people, especially women, wish to create more fullness in their lips, which have a tendency to thin and flatten with age. They undergo this procedure, in which collagen is injected into the lips, to achieve a fuller, more youthful look (at least for the few months the effect lasts).

6. *Chin implants:* Some people believe they have a "weak chin" (a chin that recedes or doesn't balance their nose), or they simply don't like their profiles. To correct this, they opt for a procedure in which material or a "bridge" of sorts is implanted into their existing chin to make the chin more prominent.

Procedures designed to make ethnic minorities look more Caucasian or members of other cultures appear more American or Western are controversial but occur with such frequency that they actually have a categorical label now—**ethnic cosmetic surgery** (Davis, 2003b). Feminist scholar Kathy Davis (2003b) discusses this issue, suggesting that "while a white person may be free to experiment with her or his appearance—and this includes indulging in the surgical fix—the same experiment takes on a different meaning when undertaken by people of color or the ethnically marginalized" (pp. 83–84). Davis contends that "cosmetic surgery for people of color or the ethnically marginalized is about 'race,' while cosmetic surgery for white Anglos is about beauty" (p. 84). Whether any sort of facial feature is a point of cultural pride or something one desires to change depends on the individual.

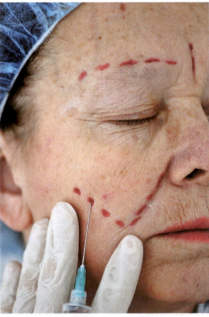

Cosmetic surgeries, such as Botox injections, are motivated by social perceptions of attractiveness.

Remember!
7.4

Body modification	More permanent methods of changing the way the body looks
Facial modification	More permanent methods of changing the face
Facial symmetry	A face that's equally proportioned in size and shape
Ethnic cosmetic surgery	Medical procedures that make members of other cultures or ethnic minority groups look more Western or Caucasian

WHAT WOULD *YOU* DO

Your friend recently started working as a server at a popular restaurant in town. She was excited about the job because she was told that people tipped well there. Your friend has now been serving for about a month, and she's discouraged about the tips she's receiving. She mentions to you that she's always attentive and quick with her service, so she's unsure about why her tips aren't as good as her coworkers'.

Later that week, you decide to go visit your friend at work. You friend lights up when she sees you sitting in her section. She smiles and makes pleasant facial expressions to greet you. But you soon notice that she's not using the same nonverbal cues at her other tables. When taking orders, her face is rather expressionless. She spends more time looking down, writing orders, than making eye contact with her customers. You noticed that she even rolled her eyes when people complained about the accuracy of their order.

Based on what you've learned from this chapter about the importance of engaging others with facial expression, would you opt to provide feedback to your friend about her nonverbal customer service? What advice would you give her, regarding how should she use her face and eyes to provide customers with a better experience?

SIGNIFICANCE OF EYE BEHAVIOR ■ ■ ■

In this section, we review the study of eye behavior, also known as **oculesics**, which includes eye contact, eye movement, and other functions of the eyes. As stated earlier, estimates indicate that 80% of the information in our everyday surroundings is taken in visually, despite other human communicative behaviors such as talking, listening, moving, and touching (Morris, 1985). In American culture, we feel connected to other people if eye contact with them is established, believing that the eyes truly are "the windows to the soul." That's why eye contact is emphasized in most basic communication courses and has been a central topic within the study of nonverbal behavior for decades (Argyle & Cook, 1976; Beebe & Beebe, 2018; Beebe, Beebe, & Ivy, 2018; Lamer, Reeves, & Weisbuch, 2015; Tang & Schmeichel, 2015; Weick, McCall, & Blasovich, 2017). Communication scholar Steve Beebe (1974) studied the influence of eye contact on judgments of speaker credibility and found that the best speakers connect with their audiences in a variety of ways, the primary one being through eye contact.

Influences of Eye Behavior

It's helpful to think of eye behavior in terms of its influence on social interaction. The first influence of eye behavior is its powerful ability to stimulate **arousal**—a positive or negative reaction in response to another person. To clarify, we don't mean *sexual* arousal here but, rather, in the sense scholar Albert Mehrabian (1971, 1972, 1981) developed, meaning activation or a reaction to stimuli. We all experience some degree of arousal when we see another person. The arousal may be extremely positive in response to someone we like and haven't seen for a while. On the other hand, we may experience negative arousal if we cross paths with someone who gets on our nerves.

© Andrey Popov/Shutterstock.com

Appropriate eye contact is considered a critical aspect of the job interview process.

Another influence of eye behavior relates to **salience**, meaning that what we do with our eyes is more noticeable than other actions of the face and body. Simply put, the eyes really matter in social interaction and are critical to our study of nonverbal communication. Our eyes play a central role in developing relationships with others, as well as managing everyday communicative needs such as attention getting, listening, and showing interest (Guéguen & Jacob, 2002; Guerrero & Floyd, 2006; Horstmann, Becker, & Ernst, 2016; Lachat, Conty, Hugueville, & George, 2012). Take a moment to reflect on the power of eye behavior in your everyday life. Even in the most mundane social encounters, such as those at the grocery store, eye behavior helps us manage politeness and common courtesy. For example, think of that awkward moment when you almost run over another person with your shopping cart. As you hold the cart back, you make quick eye contact, squeeze out a smile, and mumble a quick "excuse me." This approach works most of the time and gets us out of social predicaments. Of course, some of us may practice a more intense, second option: avoid eye contact, don't smile, get that cart out of the way, and move on to the dairy section.

spotlight *on research*

Eye Contact = Better Teachers and Students?

Have you ever been in class and your attention starts to drift? Perhaps you start to stare blankly at your notes, check your phone or laptop, or watch the clock. On occasion some people get called out by the instructor for not paying enough attention. Many of these students are likely not making eye contact with the professor, or even looking at the white board or PowerPoint slides. Eye contact provides the instructor with feedback that students are actually engaged and listening to the material or discussion.

Your college or university probably offers online courses; maybe you've already had the opportunity to take an online course. Something odd about an online course is the absence of that instructor standing in front of you in real-time, explaining the information. Scholars Beege, Schneider, Nebel, and Rey (2017) studied the importance of nonverbal communication in instructing and facilitating online courses. Just because students aren't present for a live class session doesn't mean the instructor has no way to engage students.

Beege et al. suggest that instructors post video lectures for their online courses to a website or educational technology like Blackboard, to better engage learners. The immediacy provided by nonverbal behaviors in videos, especially eye contact, engages viewers with the professor and course content. It's likely that you enjoyed online courses more and learned more when instructors incorporated technology and nonverbal cues, such as eye contact in videos, to better connect to you and other students.

Want to know more about this study? If so, read Beege, M., Schneider, S., Nebel, S., & Rey, G. D. (2017). Look into my eyes! Exploring the effect of addressing in educational videos. *Learning & Instruction, 49*, 113-120.

The third influence of eye behavior is **involvement**—the need to interact with other people, even if just with a simple acknowledgement of eye contact or a head nod. A good example of this is when we pass by a stranger on campus. We don't know the person and haven't had class with him or her before, but as we approach there's some form of energy that leads us to get involved, even if only for a second or two. Some of us may view ourselves as shy and perhaps even avoidant when it comes to strangers; yet we usually still participate in some sort of involvement, if only a head nod or grunt, promoted by the briefest moment of eye contact. It's quite common to see students, particularly male students, acknowledge each other by making brief eye contact and slightly lifting their chins, which translates into the ever-popular "What's up?" greeting.

REMEMBER

Remember!
7.5

Oculesics	Study of eye behavior, including eye contact, eye movement, and other functions of the eyes
Arousal	A positive or negative reaction to another person
Salience	The fact that what we do with our eyes is more noticeable than other actions of the face and body
Involvement	The need to interact with other people, even if just with a simple acknowledgement of eye contact or a head nod

Purposes of Eye Behavior

In addition to influences of eye behavior, nonverbal communication researchers have explored its various purposes (Kendon, 1967). As we review 10 purposes of eye behavior below, reflect on how you use your eyes and if the purposes connect with your personal experience.

1. *Recognizing others:* One of the most basic functions of the eye is to help us recognize other people, objects, places, and so forth. Those of us who have the privilege of sight often take this ability for granted, until we find ourselves groping about in a suddenly dark room, we emerge into the sunlight from a dark location, or we experience an injury or illness that takes away our sight. Medical research has detected a rare condition that prevents sighted people from recognizing others, termed *prosopagnosia* or, more commonly, *face blindness* (Diaz, 2008; Hewitt, 2007; Sellers, 2010). People who suffer from this malady have no problems with their eyesight, but their brains are impaired such that they can't remember what people look like, even family members.

chapter seven

2. *Scanning:* Another primary function of eye behavior is to scan the environment and social situations, typically checking for physical safety and social comfort (Palancia & Itier, 2012). You scan a busy movie theater to find an open seat or hunt through a crowd for an open area where you'll be more comfortable. Another more social use of the scanning function relates to flirting. When we come into a social setting, such as a club or party, we're likely to scan the area and the people in it with our eyes, whether or not we go to the event alone. Such scanning helps us get "the lay of the land," as well as identify interesting people to talk to, where refreshments are located, whether anyone has noticed our arrival, and so forth. Scanning is typically a precursor to flirting (Collett, 2004; Renninger, Wade, & Grammer, 2004; Speer, 2017).

3. *Thinking (cognitive activity):* Eye behavior reflects **cognitive activity**—the use of the brain for memory recall and information processing (Bakan, 1971; Hietanen & Hietanen, 2017). Researchers measure **conjugate lateral eye movements**—involuntary eye movements to the left or right that reveal brain activity or thought processes—while asking subjects thought-provoking questions that require them to use different parts of their brain (Armstrong, Bilsky, Zhao, & Olatunji, 2013; Bakan & Strayer, 1973; Leigh & Zee, 2015; Sedgwick & Festinger, 2017; Theeuwes, Kramer, Hahn, & Irwin, 1998). When people move their eyes to the left, it's thought to reflect activity in the right hemisphere of the brain, and vice versa. So by tracking eye behavior, you get a "window" into brain activity.

4. *Decreasing physical and psychological distance:* As we've discussed elsewhere in this book, **nonverbal immediacy cues** communicate approachability, availability, closeness, and warmth (Kraft-Todd et al., 2017; McCroskey, Richmond, & McCroskey, 2006; Mehrabian, 1971, 1972, 1981). Eye contact is a key immediacy behavior, in that it can decrease the physical and psychological distance between people, such as often occurs between speakers and audiences in a public communication setting (Beebe, 1974; Beebe & Beebe, 2018).

5. *Regulating interaction:* Eyes also function to **regulate** interaction, meaning that we send nonverbal cues with our eyes to let another person know whether a conversation is going to start, continue, or come to an end (Duncan, 1972). People generally take turns at talk in a conversation (termed, logically, **turn-taking**), and eye contact, along with other nonverbal cues, helps cue the behavior. This process is a subset of **interaction management,** or how people use verbal and nonverbal communication to conduct or manage their conversations (Guerrero & Floyd, 2006). We examine turn-taking more thoroughly in Chapter 9 on vocal nonverbal cues, but it's also pertinent to our study of eye behavior. The eyes help us manage interaction by letting us know when it's okay to speak or respond. Further, broken eye contact usually cues that a conversation is over. Trying to continue a conversation after eye contact is broken can be annoying to or perceived as negative by the person wanting to move on to another appointment or to someone more interesting.

6. *Establishing and defining relationships:* We use eye gaze to connect with others, and then to help define and manage those relationships. If we make eye contact and connect, a relationship is likely to be initiated. If we avoid eye contact and don't connect, a relationship has less chance of forming. While eye gaze is critical to establishing and maintaining relationships, it's important to avoid staring—giving too much eye contact or looking at another person in a way that is viewed as socially inappropriate (Garland-Thomson, 2009). If you're interested in establishing a relationship with someone, you're likely to make a lot of eye contact with that person, but if the eye contact isn't returned, indicating that the feeling isn't mutual, you may be accused of staring.

7. *Displaying power:* In addition to regulating interaction, eye behavior can be used as a **power display**—a nonverbal means of indicating dominance over another person or even an animal (Dunbar & Abra, 2010; Tang & Schmeichel, 2015; Weick et al., 2017). You've probably heard of the "stare-down" or "staring match" that can be a fun game for children, but it can also cause conflict among adults striving for interpersonal superiority. The **power stare** occurs when a person narrows the eyelids (almost into a squint) and maintains eye contact with someone without blinking, as an assertion of authority (Tannen, 2006). You often see two boxers at a pre-bout press conference or just before a match engaged in a mutual power stare in an attempt to psych each other out and establish dominance. People who are being stared at usually respond in one of two ways: (1) They either stare back to send a signal that the power stare from the other person isn't working and they're not going to back down, or (2) they avoid eye contact altogether to escape potential conflict.

   Another phenomenon related to power displays is termed the **visual dominance ratio,** or the amount of eye contact we make when we're talking to someone versus when we're listening to that person (Ellyson, Dovidio, & Fehr, 1981; Hall, 2006; Koch, Baehne, Kruse, Zimmermann, & Zumbach, 2010). In face-to-face conversation, the general expectation is to engage in mutual eye gaze, with brief breaks away, when both speaking and listening. But some people make steady eye contact only when they're talking and break eye contact and look elsewhere the majority of the time someone else is talking; this behavior can communicate dominance. It can also be quite irritating if you're the person giving steady eye contact, which signals your attention, while your conversational partner is looking everywhere but at you. It can make you feel undervalued and invisible.

8. *Expressing emotions:* The eyes also function to express emotions and to detect the emotions of others (Campbell, Murray, Atkinson, & Ruffman, 2017; Lea, Qualter, Davis, Perez-Gonzalez, & Bangee, 2018; Widman, Schroger, & Wetzel, 2018). In fact, some experts suggest that emotions are most readily detected from eye behavior, meaning that if you want to know how someone's feeling, you should watch his or her eyes. When people have lost a loved one and are mourning, their eyes usually have a

certain tired or watery look from crying and exhaustion as a byproduct of the grieving process. It's likely hard for them to maintain eye contact, because the body just won't respond as it normally does. Or perhaps you see a friend at some distance and can tell that something's up, but you can't determine what emotion the person is feeling until he or she gets closer and you can focus on the eyes. As we said in Chapter 6 on body movement, the face and eyes will tell you *which* particular emotions are being felt, while the body will tell you *how much* of the emotion is being felt.

9. *Excluding:* Eye behavior can be used for **exclusion**—the process of closing others out from the action or from conversation. If you've ever intentionally focused on a person but been aware that someone else is waiting to speak with you or attempting to join the conversation, then you've likely used eye gaze that prevented or excluded that other person from the conversation. Closing others out isn't always done with mean intention or disrespect. Sometimes our conversations are personal in nature or related to business—contexts that make it awkward to include another person.

10. *Monitoring feedback:* You're at a staff meeting and a coworker tells an off-color joke. He or she looks around the room, trying to detect what other people thought of the joke, because no one's laughing. An uncomfortable silence fills the room, and people avoid making eye contact with the coworker who told the joke. What's going on here? We use our eyes to monitor the feedback we receive from other people, which is an important function. In this example, people's lack of eye gaze with the jokester, in tandem with the absence of vocalizations (laughter) and presence of negative facial expressions, should signal to the person that her or his joke was not well received.

Cognitive activity	Use of the brain for memory recall and information processing
Conjugate lateral eye movements	Involuntary eye movements to the left or right that reveal brain activity or thought processes
Nonverbal immediacy cues	Nonverbal cues of approachability, availability, closeness, and warmth that decrease psychological and physical distance between people
Regulating	Eye behavior that lets another person know whether a conversation will begin, continue, or come to an end
Turn-taking	A structure for conversation, and a means of studying or tracking conversations for the purpose of analysis
Interaction management	How people use verbal and nonverbal communication to conduct or manage their conversations with others
Power display	A nonverbal means of indicating dominance over another person
Power stare	A narrowing of the eyelids (almost into a squint) and the maintenance of eye contact without blinking, as a means of establishing dominance
Visual dominance ratio	Amount of eye contact made when talking to someone versus listening to that person
Exclusion	The use of eye behavior to close others out of a conversation

Remember!
7.6

FORMS OF EYE BEHAVIOR ■ ■ ■

Various forms of eye behavior have been studied and defined by many nonverbal communication scholars (Argyle & Cook, 1976; Brône, Oben, Jehoul, Vranjes, & Feyaerts, 2017; Callahan, 2000; Evitts & Gallop, 2011; Exline & Fehr, 1982; Garner & Iba, 2017; Ijuin, Umata, Kato, & Yamamota, 2018). While the common term for looking at people or things is *eye contact*, the research term is **gaze,** defined as looking at someone or something in any given context. A subset of gaze is **mutual gaze,** which occurs when two people look at each other, either in the eyes or within the region of the face (Monk & Gale, 2002). In the United States and many other countries, parents teach their children to "look people in the eye," encouraging mutual gaze as an eye behavior reflective of respect and confidence (Lawson, 2015). But for some cultures, mutual eye gaze is a sign of disrespect, such as in some Asian cultures where greeting rituals involve bowing, lowering the head, and eye gaze avoidance.

Another form of eye behavior is the **one-sided look,** a gaze or look toward another person that's not reciprocated. In other words, you may look in the direction of another person to get her or his attention or initiate conversation; if he or she doesn't look back, your eye gaze is one-sided and **gaze aversion** has occurred. Gaze aversion is usually *intentional,* in the sense that the person who avoids eye contact is typically aware of the behavior (Doherty-Sneddon & Phelps, 2005). A variety of factors can influence people to avert their eye gaze, including low self-esteem, embarrassment, and discomfort over potential conflict (Bowers, Crawcour, Saltuklaroglu, & Kalinowski, 2010; Lamer et al., 2015). Gaze aversion is sometimes confused with **gaze omission**—an *unintentional* avoidance of eye contact. Gaze aversion usually comes with a reason, such as deceit, disinterest, dislike, embarrassment, conflict avoidance, and so forth. But gaze omission can reflect shyness, being preoccupied or distracted by thought, or simply being raised without lessons about the importance of eye contact or role models who enacted it appropriately.

Another interesting phenomenon related to the eyes is **civil inattention**, which occurs when two people share the same space or cross paths but acknowledge each other with only a quick look or glance, without starting a conversation (Goffman, 1967; Zuckerman, Miserandino, & Bernieri, 1983/2008). Perhaps you've seen this behavior in elevators, in crowded school hallways, or on trains, buses, or other forms of public transportation.

Our gaze behavior influences others' perceptions of us. In fact, those of you preparing for job interviews should take note of your eye behavior. If you exhibit gaze aversion or omission in an interview, your credibility and hire-ability may be harmed (Lobmaier, 2012; Quintanilla & Wahl, 2016). Likewise, if you stare at someone who's interviewing you, rather than making and breaking eye contact in succession (typical of interactions in the United States), you may also be perceived negatively (Garland-Thomson, 2009). Sometimes it's difficult to manage our gaze behavior when we're nervous, but the more we think about it and prepare ahead of the event, the better we're likely to behave (Callahan, 2000). Whether rehearsing a presentation or holding a simple conversation, be aware of eye behavior that may cause your listeners to perceive you as untrustworthy, incompetent, lacking in confidence, or just downright boring (Beebe & Beebe, 2018; Beebe et al., 2019).

Gaze	Looking at someone or something in any given context
Mutual gaze	Occurs when two people look at each other, either in the eyes or within a region of the face
One-sided look	A gaze or look toward another person that's not reciprocated
Gaze aversion	Occurs when someone intentionally doesn't return another person's gaze
Gaze omission	Unintentional avoidance of eye contact
Civil inattention	When people share the same space or cross paths but acknowledge each other with only a quick look or glance, without starting a conversation

Pupil Dilation: Size Matters

Pupil dilation occurs when the pupils of the eyes increase in size or open more widely. This phenomenon can actually tell us something nonverbally about another person. Communication researchers have studied human pupil dilation under a variety of conditions for several decades and have reported some interesting findings (Bakan, 1971; Goldwater, 1972; Hess, 1968, 1975a, 1975b; Hess & Petrovich, 1987; Hess & Polt, 1964; Kramer et al., 2013; Lick, Cortland, & Johnson, 2016; Pettijohn & Tesser, 2005; Widman, Schroger, & Wetzel, 2018). In general, positive visual images stimulate pupil dilation, as if the eyes try to take in more of a positive stimulus. In the 1960s, when research on pupil dilation was a hot topic, in one study, men's pupils dilated when they looked at pictures of women and women's pupils dilated when they viewed pictures of men; however, women's pupils also dilated upon seeing pictures of newborn babies (Hess & Polt, 1960). Research with gay men found that their pupils dilated when they looked at pictures of men (Hess, Seltzer, & Shlien, 1965).

When some of this research hit the popular press in the 1960s and 1970s, advertisers attempted to make use of the findings by enlarging the appearance of models' pupils in ads. The approach didn't produce increased ad sales (models looked stoned), so the fad fell out of favor quickly. In addition, relationship experts at the time suggested that if you wanted to find out if someone was attracted to you, you should watch their pupils for dilation. This was really hard to do, since it required that people get up in someone's face to check out her or his pupils; plus, it turned out to be an unreliable predictor of attraction. It's important to remember that environmental conditions such as the brightness of lighting also affect pupil size. Watch jumping to a conclusion that someone is attracted to you just because her or his pupils dilate during conversation; it could be dim lighting.

MODIFYING THE EYES

Certain parts of the face and eyes are so important to people across cultures that we've started to see increases in the amount of money spent on cosmetic surgery and other procedures to accomplish **eye modification**—permanent and temporary changes to the eyes (Patel & Itani, 2018; Roscoe, 2018; Ueda & Koyama, 2011).

Just as for body and facial modification, the cosmetic alteration industry offers a menu of surgeries, procedures, and products that enable people to change the appearance of their eyes. The American Society of Aesthetic Plastic Surgery (2018) reports that eyelid surgery was third on the list of the top five cosmetic surgical procedures performed on Americans in 2017. As we described in Chapter 5 on physical appearance, for Asians and Asian Americans (predominantly women), the fastest-growing and most common cosmetic surgery is a process that creates a crease over the eye, since most Asians do not have extra skin or creases that make their eyes look more prominent (McCurdy & Lam, 2005). Double eyelid surgery, or **upper blepharoplasty,** on people of Asian descent makes their eyes look wider and more Western, providing another example of ethnic cosmetic surgery, discussed earlier in this chapter (Davis, 2003b; Kaw, 1993, 1994). While the popularity of eyelid surgery among Asian Americans is often attributed to Western influence, it's important to note that many Asians and Asian Americans view an alert and bright-eyed look as aesthetically desirable (McCurdy & Lam, 2005; Patel & Itani, 2018). While eyelid surgery is an increasingly popular procedure, other methods of enhancing or modifying the eye area have been developed over time and are still available; we describe some of them below.

1. *Eyelift:* In this surgical procedure, skin around the eyes (and sometimes forehead) is detached, lifted up, and reattached to reduce wrinkles, swelling, and appearance of bags under the eyes.

2. *Eye cosmetics:* Most students are familiar with eye makeup, but you might be surprised to learn that more men (not just rock stars) are drawn these days to eye cosmetics such as mascara, eyeliner, eye shadow, and eyebrow definer. The process of tattooing permanent makeup, such as eyeliner and brow color, is still available and popular.

3. *Eye creams:* History is replete with miracle creams that are said to naturally or chemically make the eyes look younger and more rested. The effectiveness of these products varies, but expensive eye creams (as well as inexpensive cucumbers) are readily available and commonly used at spas.

4. *Fake eyelashes:* Fake eyelashes are an enormously profitable product within the cosmetic industry; such lashes can be attached as an extension of or replacement for the natural eyelash. But before you assume that only stage actors, drag queens, and Kim Kardashian use these, it's important to realize that such a product can be helpful in enhancing the self-esteem of people whose eyelashes (as well as other facial and body hair) have fallen out due to chemotherapy or a medical condition known as alopecia, which causes hair loss.

5. *Eyeglasses:* We all know that eyeglasses (including sunglasses) are primarily used to enhance vision, but they also modify the overall appearance of the face and eyes. People who wear glasses are often perceived as highly intelligent and honest, but also more "nerdy" or "bookish" than those who don't wear glasses. Sunglasses can be an effective way to cover up bloodshot, blackened, or crying eyes and to protect the eyes from sunlight, but we all know their primary uses: to make a fashion statement and to look cool.

6. *LASIK surgery:* This is one of the most popular and effective laser techniques that helps correct human vision so eyeglasses or contact lenses aren't needed.

7. *Colored contacts:* Contact lens companies a few decades ago began producing dramatically colored soft contact lenses that could temporarily modify eye color, allowing people to experiment and express different parts of their personalities. This innovation was quite a fad, but like many fads, it isn't seen much anymore because, as good a product as the contacts were, people still saw them as fake and sometimes formed negative perceptions of the people wearing them.

8. *Eyebrow piercings:* We cover the topic of piercings thoroughly in Chapter 5, but suffice it to say here that piercing the eyebrow and even the sensitive skin around the eye, as a form of body adornment and personal expression, is more commonly seen today than in past decades.

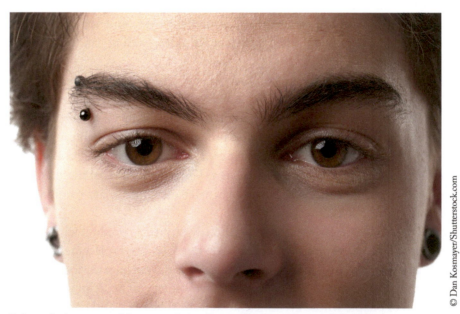

Eyebrow piercings are one of the many varieties of eye modification gaining popularity today.

chapter seven

OUT OF THE CLASSROOM
onto the page

The ways we decorate or alter our appearance can nonverbally communicate a great deal of information about us. From the amount of piercings, tattoos, makeup, and cosmetic surgeries in the United States and other places around the world, it's obvious that the human face and eyes are important to members of many different cultures.

In a recent class discussion about facial and eye modification, some students (mostly the female students) talked about how they utilized makeup to modify their faces. Students revealed that they typically used cosmetics to cover imperfections, sun damage, or pimples, especially before a social occasion. While some preferred the "natural look," most admitted to wearing at least some level of makeup each day to class. More students than in years past shared that they had male friends who wore makeup every day, but many male students in the class were still averse to men wearing cosmetics.

Anthony revealed that he wore glasses without prescriptions because he'd been told by others that he looked smarter with glasses. Jenny had a different view, saying that she'd never be caught in public with her glasses on unless she was sick or hungover. Otherwise, she made sure to always wear her contact lenses because she thought glasses made her "look like a librarian."

Several students had face and eyebrow piercings, and were quite open about why they chose to get them, how much pain was involved (not much), and what nonverbal messages they thought the piercings sent. Paris talked about her choice to get a piercing through the septum of her nose rather than through a nostril. She thought a nose ring (also called a horseshoe or circular barbell) would make her look fierce, which was what she wanted. Some people didn't care for septum piercings, believing that it was hard to make eye contact with people who had them because the eye was always so drawn to the nose ring.

Mindy talked about wearing green colored contacts most of the time, noting how people were surprised upon seeing her actual eye color because they believed her natural color was green. Some students, like Anthony and Mindy, described how people sometimes gave them negative feedback about altering their appearance "for no reason." Anthony said some people were actually offended by his wearing glasses when he didn't need them, saying that it might create a perception that he was fake or manipulative. (This was a lively discussion!)

What do you think of the modifications these students talked about? Why are some people so critical of the choices others make regarding their faces and eyes?

LYING EYES (AND FACES): NONVERBAL CUES OF DECEPTION ■ ■ ■ ▬▬

One of the more fascinating areas of research on facial and eye behavior is their association with deception. Think for a moment about some stereotypical behaviors associated with lying: avoiding eye contact, looking down at the floor, shuffling the feet, fidgeting, clearing the throat, stammering to get words out, and using lots of filled pauses such as "um" and "er." We explore vocal cues of deception in Chapter 9, but here we focus on facial and eye cues that research has connected to deception.

Before we begin this section, keep a few things in mind: First, deception is a complex business that involves a multitude of verbal and nonverbal cues, so it's important not to use this information as a surefire way of catching people in lies. It's not that simple. Another complicating factor is that, when information about deception cues becomes public and well-known, many liars will change their behavior. For example, remember the old adage about liars not being able to look people in the eye when lying? Once that information became readily known as a dead giveaway that someone was lying, people who were intent on deceiving others changed that behavior. People who are good at getting away with deception can look you straight in the eye and lie to your face. Finally, deception cues are idiosyncratic, meaning people exhibit deceptive behavior in unique ways within their cultural contexts. Deception will manifest itself differently across cultural groups, so be careful in generalizing too much from the research.

Communication and pyschology researchers have identified a range of **deception cues**, defined as nonverbal indications of dishonesty (Carson, 2012; Cohen, Beattie, & Shovelton, 2010; De Waele & Claeys, 2017; Ekman, 2001; Novotny et al., 2018; Park, Levine, McCornack, Morrison, & Ferrara, 2002; Vrij, 2000). These deception cues exist within a larger framework known as **interpersonal deception theory**, which helps identify and explain the verbal and nonverbal behavior of deceivers (Buller & Burgoon, 1996; Burgoon, Schuetzler, & Wilson, 2015; Jensen & Burgoon, 2008; Wise & Rodriguez, 2013).

Research shows that deceptive communicators are prone to **leakage**, meaning their deception makes itself known nonverbally, typically in a manner beyond control (Doody, 2017; Ekman & Friesen, 1969a; Frank & Hurley, 2011; Frank & Svetieva, 2013; Funkhouser & Barnett, 2016; Knapp, McGlone, Griffin, & Earnest, 2015; Porter, ten Brinke, & Wallace, 2012). Studies on deception leakage have focused on the sending of deceptive verbal and nonverbal messages, as well as how receivers detect deception in others (Dunbar, Jensen, Tower, & Burgoon, 2014; Hamlin, Wright, van der Zee, & Wilson, 2018; Paik & van Swol, 2017; Stromwall, Hartwig, & Granhag, 2006; Vrij, 2006b).

Deceptive Facial Behavior

One facial behavior that has been the subject of study regarding deception is smiling, but studies have produced inconsistent results. While DePaulo et al.'s (2003) review of many studies on the topic found no relationship between smiling and deception, in other studies deceivers smiled less than truth tellers (Granhag & Stromwall, 2002; Vrij, 2006a). Ekman and Friesen (1982) suggest that truth tellers are more likely to evidence Duchenne (or felt) smiles, whereas deceivers will use fake smiles.

Adaptors in the form of self-touches and fidgeting have also been linked to deception (Caso, Maricchiolo, Bonaiuto, Vrij, & Mann, 2006; Caso, Vrij, Mann, & De Leo, 2006). One such facial adaptor occurs when a deceiver covers her or his mouth with the hand while talking, as if to say, "This is only half true" or "I'm not proud of what's coming out of my mouth." It may also be an irrational attempt to muffle what's being said, so as to somehow mute the lies. In other instances, deceivers will cover their eyebrows or other parts of their face, perhaps in an effort to create a barrier between themselves and their receivers or to shield themselves from someone's wrath when they've been caught in a lie.

Deceptive Eye Behavior

Like we said, breaking or being unable to sustain eye gaze is commonly believed to indicate deception, but research hasn't determined a consistent pattern. Some studies have detected decreased eye contact (gaze aversion) when people lie (Hirsch & Wolf, 2001; McCarthy & Lee, 2009), but others have found an increase in eye gaze, possibly due to deceivers' trying to compensate for their deception by making more eye contact than expected (DePaulo et al., 2003; Mann et al., 2012). Our best advice is this: While most chronic liars will develop the ability to engage in mutual gaze while lying to someone, most of us aren't able to pull this off. So one eye behavior to watch for or consider when we wonder about someone's truthfulness is gaze avoidance.

While some sources have suggested that rapid or frequent eye blinking is associated with deception, research is also mixed on this front. Some studies have found that eye blinking slows or is suppressed during deceptive attempts, because of all the brain activity occurring at the time (Marchak, 2013; Vrij, 2004). However, other studies have found that the rate of blinking increases among people attempting to deceive (DePaulo et al., 2003; Zuckerman & Driver, 1985).

Here's a useful generalization regarding detecting deception in another person: Compare what you see and hear from a person against what is normal behavior for him or her. It's important to get a baseline of behavior, meaning a sense of how someone typically behaves, and then look for aberrations—the odd facial expression, a strange tone in the voice, a change in patterns of eye contact, and so forth. Again, you don't necessarily know for sure that deception is occurring in these instances, but it's a possibility, one that you can pursue further to find out what's happening.

Familiarity, Suspicion, and Deception Detection

Since deception can be deadly for a relationship, most of us are motivated to understand how our coworkers, friends, family members, and intimate partners view deception, as well as what verbal and nonverbal behaviors they tend to use when they deceive, *if* they deceive. Start with yourself—are you aware of your own behavior when you try to deceive someone? Maybe you consider yourself a truthful person, but there are different levels of lies, beginning with the "little white lie" and ranging up to the "big whopper." Most of us are taught that lying isn't right; so if and when we choose to lie, we register some sort of activation in the body, meaning that the added energy it takes to be untruthful reveals itself somewhere (what we earlier called leakage).

Then think about others' behavior, particularly the behavior of those who are emotionally closest to you. If the person you love the most in the world deceived you, would that deception more likely be enacted verbally, nonverbally, or through a combination of behaviors? Granted, it depends on the lie. For example, if you came into the room wearing the most horrible outfit possible and asked your best friend how you looked, if your friend chose to lie and said that you looked great, that level of lie probably wouldn't take much effort, nor would it be readily detectable from nonverbal cues. But in those instances when the "big whopper" of a lie is told, how do people you know behave? What nonverbal cues emerge?

Research has examined the impact of familiarity and suspicion on deception detection, finding two interesting, yet competing trends: First, we may be better able to detect deception in someone we know well, because we know what to look for. That relates back to what we said earlier about getting a baseline of information. As we continue to know someone better, we learn how she or he typically behaves, so we can compare normal behavior with behavior we think might be deceptive and go from there. Once our suspicion has been aroused, research says that intimate partners or friends are fairly accurate detectors of deception (McCornack & Parks, 1990; Stiff, Kim, & Ramesh, 1992). However, a second view is that familiarity hampers our ability to detect deception because we presume that people are telling us the truth (often called a "truth bias"; Elaad, 2010; Street & Masip, 2015; van Swol, Braun, & Kolb, 2015). We may also wish to remain "blissfully ignorant," as one scholar puts it (Collett, 2004, p. 287). We don't want to think about someone we love deceiving us, so we presume truthfulness, don't notice cues to the contrary, or attempt to distract ourselves from deception cues. We may attribute a change in behavior to *any other possible thing* (e.g., "he must be tired," "she's had a bad day") so as to avoid thinking that someone we care about is lying to us (Millar & Millar, 1995). In these cases, our familiarity and trust blinds us to the reality of deception.

Pupil dilation	An increase in size or widening of the pupils in the eyes
Eye modification	Permanent or temporary methods of changing the eyes
Upper blepharoplasty	A surgical procedure that modifies the eyelids
Deception cues	Nonverbal indications of dishonesty
Interpersonal deception theory	Theory that helps explain verbal and nonverbal behavior of deceivers
Leakage	Nonverbal cues outside of a deceiver's control that signal dishonesty

UNDERSTANDING FACIAL AND EYE BEHAVIOR: APPLYING THE REFLEXIVE CYCLE OF NONVERBAL COMMUNICATION DEVELOPMENT

Have you thought much about how you use your face and eyes to communicate with others? The first step to developing your skills and a better understanding of these behaviors as nonverbal communication is awareness. Again, we ask you to inventory yourself using the following questions: How do you use your eyes and facial nonverbal cues in communication with others? What are your needs or preferences regarding other people's facial and eye cues? Do you have expectations or rules about such things as smiling or staring? Are you aware of the impressions others may form about you based on your facial and eye behavior?

Now that you have engaged in an inventory of self regarding facial and eye signals, it's time to think about making any appropriate changes to improve how you manage these nonverbal cues in your everyday life. This is Phase 2 in the Reflexive Cycle. Ask yourself, Are there some changes I need to make regarding my facial and eye behavior (e.g., frowning, smiling, eye rolling, gaze aversion, staring)? If so, how can I make those changes? Perhaps the only thing you need to change is your awareness of how your facial and eye behaviors are perceived by other people.

Beyond engaging in an inventory of self and making appropriate changes, the next step is to inventory others. Some people are oblivious to the fact that their facial and eye behaviors communicate something to other people about their attitude or level of interest. Can you think of people who lack awareness of what they do with their face or eyes? You may be thinking of a friend who rolls her or his eyes all the time, a coworker who avoids eye contact, or a classmate who puts on a fake smile. These people may lack self-monitoring skills (awareness of their appropriateness in social situations) or the ability to honestly assess their own nonverbal communication. In addition, they aren't aware enough to perception check with other people for outside observations and resulting interpretations of their facial and eye cues. Other people are well aware of how they come across to others, in terms of facial and eye behavior; perhaps they've actually worked on these cues. These are the people we can learn from.

After you have done an inventory of self, changed self, and inventoried others' nonverbal behavior, the fourth phase of the Reflexive Cycle involves interacting with others, trying out the changes you've made or are in the process of making, and observing people as you verbally and nonverbally interact with them. Do people have different reactions to you, as a result of any changes you made? For example, some of you who don't smile much may appear to other people as being more friendly if you try to smile more or just generally maintain a more positive facial expression. As another example, some of you who are trying to become better listeners by working on your eye contact may get feedback from others that they appreciate how well you listen to them, or that they appreciate your empathy. It can be interesting to note people's reactions to both subtle and obvious changes in your facial and eye behavior and how that makes you feel, as well as to gauge your own reactions to changes in others' behavior.

In the last part of the cycle, we challenge you to review and assess the whole process, making note of positive and negative aspects, and then to begin the cycle again. We've said it before, and we'll say it again: The development of nonverbal communication skills is a continuous process, as we work to develop and hone our nonverbal abilities in an effort to become more effective communicators.

SUMMARY ■ ■ ■

In this chapter, we established facial and eye behaviors as nonverbal communication and emphasized the need to be aware of these important nonverbal cues, as well as how we respond to the facial and eye cues of other people. The first part of the chapter reviewed the significance of facial behavior. We explored different viewpoints on facial expression acquisition and development, including evolution, natural selection, external factors, and innate versus learned perspectives. We also reviewed facial management with a focus on Ekman and Friesen's four management techniques of neutralization, masking, intensification, and deintensification.

Next we examined the Facial Action Coding System (FACS)—a technique that separates the face into three regions for study: eyebrows and forehead; eyes and eyelids; and lower face, including the cheeks, nose, and mouth. We discussed facial modification, which refers to more permanent methods of altering the appearance of the face.

In the next section of this chapter, we explored the significance of eye behavior in nonverbal communication and the influences on eye behavior, including arousal, salience, and involvement. Further, we overviewed 10 purposes of eye behavior: recognizing others, scanning, thinking, decreasing physical and psychological distance, regulating interaction, establishing and defining relationships, displaying power, expressing emotions, excluding, and monitoring feedback.

The next few sections focused on different forms of eye behavior, beginning with key terms related to gaze behavior. We explored research findings on pupil dilation, which occurs when the pupils dilate or widen in response to stimuli. This section closed with a discussion of the complex topic of eye modification, in which we provided a listing of cosmetic procedures and products that enable people to modify their eyes. We provided research results regarding common facial and eye behaviors associated with deception. Research has produced mixed findings regarding ways to detect deception through attention to facial and eye behavior, but some common deception cues include fake smiling, facial adaptors, avoiding eye contact, and frequent and rapid blinking. This chapter ended with a brief discussion of the effects of familiarity and suspicion on the ability to detect deception among people who are close to us emotionally.

DISCUSSION STARTERS ■ ■ ■

1. Explain how facial and eye behavior is a form of nonverbal communication. What do your facial and eye cues nonverbally communicate to others?

2. Take a moment to think about how we use the metaphor of face in everyday life. What are some other common uses of facial metaphors that come up in conversation?

3. Review the difference between innate and learned behavior, with regard to facial expressions. Do you think your facial expressions are innate, learned, or a combination?

4. Looking at the various eye behaviors presented in this chapter, what's the most interesting to you? Take a moment to review the section on gaze. What experiences have you had with gaze aversion, gaze omission, and civil inattention?

5. In both of the primary sections of this chapter, we explored various methods of modifying the face and eyes. What reactions do you have to these techniques or processes? Have you ever thought about undergoing a cosmetic procedure to modify your face or eyes? If so, what's the reasoning behind your decision? Have you ever viewed this kind of process as something that could affect your nonverbal communication?

6. We explored the role of facial and eye cues in the communication of deception. What are the most central facial and eye behaviors that deceivers exhibit? How skilled do you think you are at detecting deception in other people? Does your ability change when it comes to people who are emotionally close to you?

REFERENCES ■ ■ ■

American Society for Aesthetic Plastic Surgery. (2018). Cosmetic surgery national data bank: Statistics. Retrieved from https://www.surgery.org/media/statistics

Argerinou, M. D., & Pettersson, R. (2011). Toward a cohesive theory of visual literacy. *Journal of Visual Literacy, 30,* 1–19.

Argyle, M., & Cook, M. (1976). *Gaze and mutual gaze.* Cambridge, UK: Cambridge University Press.

Armstrong, T., Bilsky, S. A., Zhao, M., & Olatunji, B. (2013). Dwelling on potential threat cues: An eye movement marker for combat-related PTSD. *Depression and Anxiety, 30,* 497–502.

Atkinson, A. P., Tipples, J., Burt, D. M., & Young, A. W. (2005). Asymmetric interference between sex and emotion in face perception. *Perception and Psychophysics, 67,* 1199–1213.

Bakan, P. (1971). The eyes have it. *Psychology Today, 4,* 64–69.

Bakan, P., & Strayer, F. F. (1973). On reliability of conjugate lateral eye movements. *Perceptual and Motor Skills, 36,* 429–430.

Beebe, S. A. (1974). Eye contact: A nonverbal determinant of speaker credibility. *Speech Teacher, 23,* 21–25.

Beebe, S. A., & Beebe, S. J. (2018). *Public speaking: An audience-centered approach* (10th ed.). Boston: Pearson.

Beebe, S. A., Beebe, S. J., & Ivy, D. K. (2019). *Communication: Principles for a lifetime* (7th ed.). Boston: Pearson.

Beege, M., Schneider, S., Nebel, S., & Rey, G. D. (2017). Look into my eyes! Exploring the effect of addressing in educational videos. *Learning & Instruction, 49,* 113–120.

Birdwhistell, R. L. (1974). The language of the body: The natural environment of words. In A. Silverstein (Ed.), *Human communication: Theoretical explorations* (pp. 203–220). New York: Wiley.

Boas, D. C., Ferreira, L., de Moura, M. C., Maia, S., & Amaral, I. (2016). Analysis of interaction and attention processes in a child with congenital deaf-blindness. *American Annals of the Deaf, 161,* 327–341.

Bowers, A. L., Crawcour, S. C., Saltuklaroglu, T., & Kalinowski, J. (2010). Gaze aversion to stuttered speech: A pilot study investigating differential visual attention to stuttered and fluent speech. *International Journal of Language & Communication Disorders, 45,* 133–144.

Brisini, T. (2017). The practice of smiling: Facial expressions and repertory performance in Professor Palmai's "School of Smiles." *Text and Performance Quarterly, 37,* 1–19.

Brône, G., Oben, B., Jehoul, A., Vranjes, J., & Feyaerts, K. (2017). Eye gaze and viewpoint in multimodal interaction management. *Cognitive Linguistics, 28,* 449–483.

Brown, C., & Lloyd-Jones, T. J. (2006). Beneficial effects of verbalization and visual distinctiveness on remembering and knowing faces. *Memory and Cognition, 34,* 277–286.

Buck, R. (1994). Social and emotional functions in facial expression and communication: The readout hypothesis. *Biological Psychology, 38,* 95–115.

Buller, D. B., & Burgoon, J. K. (1996). Reflections on the nature of theory building and the theoretical status of interpersonal deception theory. *Communication Theory, 6,* 311–328.

Burgoon, J. K., Schuetzler, R., & Wilson, D. W. (2015). Kinesic patterning in deceptive and truthful interactions. *Journal of Nonverbal Behavior, 39,* 1–24.

Callahan, P. E. (2000). Indexing resistance in short-term dynamic psychotherapy (STDP): Change in breaks in eye contact during anxiety (BECAS). *Psychotherapy Research, 10,* 87–99.

chapter seven

Campbell, A., Murray, J. E., Atkinson, L., & Ruffman, T. (2017). Face age and eye gaze influence older adults' emotion recognition. *Journal of Gerontology, 72*, 633–636.

Carson, T. L. (2012). *Lying and deception: Theory and practice.* Oxford, UK: Oxford University Press.

Caso, L., Maricchiolo, F., Bonaiuto, M., Vrij, A., & Mann, S. (2006). The impact of deception and suspicion on different hand movements. *Journal of Nonverbal Behavior, 30*, 1–19.

Caso, L., Vrij, A., Mann, S., & De Leo, G. (2006). Deceptive responses: The impact of verbal and nonverbal countermeasures. *Legal and Criminological Psychology, 11*, 99–111.

Claeys, A-S., & Cauberghe, V. (2014). Keeping control: The importance of nonverbal expressions of power by organizational spokespersons in times of crisis. *Journal of Communication, 64*, 1160–1180.

Cohen, D., Beattie, G., & Shovelton, H. (2010). Nonverbal indicators of deception: How iconic gestures reveal thoughts that cannot be suppressed. *Semiotica, 182*, 133–174.

Cole, P. M. (1986). Children's spontaneous control of facial expression. *Child Development, 57*, 1309–1321.

Collett, P. (2004). *The book of tells.* London: Bantam.

Cook, P. S., & Dwyer, A. (2017). No longer raising eyebrows: The context and domestication of Botox as a mundane medical and cultural artefact. *Journal of Consumer Culture, 17*, 887–909.

Courbalay, A., Deroche, T., & Descarreaux, M. (2017). Estimating pain and disability in virtual patients with low back pain: The contribution of nonverbal behaviors. *Journal of Nonverbal Behavior, 41*, 289–304.

Cunningham, M. R., Barbee, A., & Philhower, C. L. (2002). Dimensions of facial physical attractiveness: The intersection of biology and culture. In G. Rhodes & L. A. Zebrowitz (Eds.), *Facial attractiveness* (pp. 193–238). Westport, CT: Ablex.

D'Acremont, M., & Van der Linden, M. (2007). Memory for angry faces, impulsivity, and problematic behavior in adolescence. *Journal of Abnormal Child Psychology, 35*, 313–324.

Darwin, C. (1965). *The expression of emotion in man and animals.* Chicago: University of Chicago Press. (Original work published 1872)

Davis, K. (1995). *Reshaping the female body: The dilemma of cosmetic surgery.* New York: Routledge.

Davis, K. (2003). *Dubious equalities and embodied differences: Cultural studies on cosmetic surgery.* Lanham, MD: Rowman & Littlefield.

de Jong, P. J., & Dijk, C. (2013). Social effects of facial blushing: Influence of context and actor versus observer perspective. *Social & Personality Psychology Compass, 7*, 13–26.

Demetrioff, S., Porter, S., & Baker, A. (2017). I know how you feel: The influence of psychopathic traits on the ability to identify micro-expressions. *Psychology, Crime & Law.* doi.org/10.1080/106831 6x.2016.1247159

De Waele, A., & Claeys, A-S. (2017). Nonverbal cues of deception in audiovisual crisis communication. *Public Relations Review, 43*, 680–689.

DePaulo, B. M., Lindsay, J. L., Malone, B. E., Muhlenbruck, L., Charlton, K., & Cooper, H. (2003). Cues to deception. *Psychological Bulletin, 129*, 74–118.

Diaz, A. L. (2008). Do I know you? A case study of prosopagnosia (face blindness). *The Journal of School Nursing.* doi.org/1177/1059840508322381

Doherty-Sneddon, G., & Phelps, F. G. (2005). Gaze aversion: A response to cognitive or social difficulty? *Memory and Cognition, 33*, 727–733.

Domenici, K., & Littlejohn, S. W. (2006). *Facework: Bridging theory and practice.* Thousand Oaks, CA: Sage.

Doody, P. (2017). Is there evidence of robust, unconscious self-deception? A reply to Funkhouser and Barrett. *Philosophical Psychology, 30*, 657–676.

Drummond, P. D., & Bailey, T. (2013). Eye contact evokes blushing independently of negative affect. *Journal of Nonverbal Behavior, 37*, 207–216.

Dunbar, N. E., & Abra, G. (2010). Observations of dyadic power in interpersonal interaction. *Communication Monographs, 77*, 657–684.

Dunbar, N. E., Jensen, M. L., Tower, D. C., & Burgoon, J. K. (2014). Synchronization of nonverbal behaviors in detecting mediated and non-mediated deception. *Journal of Nonvrebal Behavior, 38*, 355–376.

Duncan, S. D., Jr. (1972). Some signals and rules for taking speaking turns in conversations. *Journal of Personality and Social Psychology, 23*, 283–292.

Eibl-Eibesfeldt, I. (1970). *Ethology: The biology of behavior.* New York: Rinehart & Winston.

Eibl-Eibesfeldt, I. (1972). Similarities and differences between cultures in expressive movement. In R. A. Hinde (Ed.), *Nonverbal communication* (pp. 207–283). Lincoln: University of Nebraska Press.

Ekman, P. (2001). *Telling lies* (3rd ed.). New York: W. W. Norton.

Ekman, P. (2009). Lie catching and microexpressions. In C. Martin (Ed.), *The philosophy of deception* (pp. 118–133). Oxford, UK: Oxford University Press.

Ekman, P., Davidson, R. J., & Friesen, W. V. (1990). The Duchenne smile: Emotional expression and brain physiology: II. *Journal of Personality and Social Psychology, 58*, 342–353.

Ekman, P., & Friesen, W. V. (1967). Head and body cues in the judgment of emotion: A reformulation. *Perceptual and Motor Skills, 24*, 711–724.

Ekman, P., & Friesen, W. V. (1969a). Nonverbal leakage and clues to deception. *Psychiatry, 32*, 88–106.

Ekman, P., & Friesen, W. V. (1969b). The repertoire of nonverbal behavior: Categories, origins, usage, and coding. *Semiotica, 1*, 49–98.

Ekman, P., & Friesen, W. V. (1975). *Unmasking the face: A guide to recognizing emotions from facial cues.* Englewood Cliffs, NJ: Prentice Hall.

Ekman, P., & Friesen, W. V. (1982). Felt, false, and miserable smiles. *Journal of Nonverbal Behavior, 6*, 238–252.

Ekman, P., Friesen, W. V., & Ellsworth, P. (1972). *Emotion in the human face: Guidelines for research and an integration of findings.* New York: Pergamon Press.

Ekman, P., Friesen, W. V., & Tompkins, S. S. (1971). Facial affect scoring technique: A first validity study. *Semiotica, 3*, 37–58.

Elaad, E. (2010). Truth bias and regression toward the mean phenomenon in detecting deception. *Psychology Reports, 106*, 641–642.

Elfenbein, H. A. (2006). Learning in emotion judgments: Training and the cross-cultural understanding of facial expressions. *Journal of Nonverbal Behavior, 30*, 21–36.

Ellyson, S. L., Dovidio, J. F., & Fehr, B. J. (1981). Visual behavior and dominance in women and men. In C. Mayo & N. M. Henley (Eds.), *Gender and nonverbal behavior.* New York: Springer-Verlag.

Ewing, L., Rhodes, G., & Pellicano, E. (2010). Have you got the look? Gaze direction affects judgments of facial attractiveness. *Visual Cognition, 18*, 321–330.

Exline, R. V., & Fehr, B. J. (1982). The assessment of gaze and mutual gaze. In K. R. Scherer & P. Ekman (Eds.), *Handbook of methods in nonverbal behavior research* (pp. 91–135). Cambridge, UK: Cambridge University Press.

chapter seven

Farrar, K. M., Krcmar, M., & McGloin, R. P. (2013). The perception of human appearance in video games: Toward an understanding of the effects of player perceptions of game features. *Mass Communication & Society, 16*, 299–324.

Fernández-Dols, J., Carrera, P., & Crivelli, C. (2011). Facial behavior while experiencing sexual excitement. *Journal of Nonverbal Behavior, 35*, 63–71.

Fischer, A., & LaFrance, M. (2015). What drives the smile and the tear? Why women are more emotionally expressive than men. *Emotion Review, 7*, 22–29.

Flecha-Garcia, M. (2010). Eyebrow raises in dialogue and their relation to discourse structure, utterance function, and pitch accents in English. *Speech Communication, 52*, 542–554.

Forgas, J. P., & East, R. (2008). How real is that smile? Mood effects on accepting or rejecting the veracity of emotional facial expressions. *Journal of Nonverbal Behavior, 32*, 157–170.

Frank, M. G., & Hurley, C. M. (2011). Executing facial control during deception situations. *Journal of Nonverbal Behavior, 35*, 119–131.

Frank, M. G., & Svetieva, E. (2013). Deception. In D. Matusomo, M. G. Frank, & H. S. Hwang (Eds.), *Nonverbal communication: Science and application* (pp. 121–144). Thousand Oaks, CA: Sage.

Fridlund, A. J., & Russell, J. A. (2006). The functions of facial expressions. In V. Manusov & M. L. Patterson (Eds.), *The SAGE handbook of nonverbal communication* (pp. 299–319). Thousand Oaks, CA: Sage.

Funkhouser, E., & Barrett, D. (2016). Robust, unconscious self-deception: Strategic and flexible. *Philosophical Psychology, 29*, 682–696.

Gagnon, M., Gosselin, P., Hudon-ven der Buhs, I., Larocque, K., & Milliard, K. (2010). Children's recognition and discrimination of fear and disgust facial expressions. *Journal of Nonverbal Behavior, 34*, 27–42.

Garland-Thomson, R. (2009). *Staring: How we look.* New York: Oxford University Press.

Garner, J. T., & Iba, D. L. (2017). Why are you saying that? Increases in gaze duration as responses to group member dissent. *Communication Studies, 68*, 353–367.

Goffman, E. (1967). *Interaction ritual: Essays on face-to-face behavior.* New York: Pantheon.

Goldwater, B. C. (1972). Psychological significance of pupillary movements. *Psychological Bulletin, 77*, 340–355.

Gosselin, P., Maassarani, R., Younger, A., & Perron, M. (2011). Children's deliberate control of facial action units involved in sad and happy expressions. *Journal of Nonverbal Behavior, 35*, 225–242.

Grammer, K., & Thornhill, R. (1994). Human (homo sapiens) facial attractiveness and sexual selection: The role of symmetry and averageness. *Journal of Comparative Psychology, 108*, 233–242.

Granhag, P. A., & Stromwall, L. A. (2002). Repeated interrogations: Verbal and nonverbal cues to deception. *Applied Cognitive Psychology, 16*, 243–257.

Grossard, C., Chaby, L., Hun, S., Pellerin, H., Bourgeois, J., Dapogny, A., Ding, H., Serret, S., Foulon, P., Chetouani, M., Chen, L., Bailly, K., Grunszpan, O., & Cohen, D. (2018). Children's facial expression production: Influence of age, gender, emotion subtype, elicitation condition and culture. *Frontiers in Psychology, 9*, 446.

Grossman, R. B., & Kegl, J. (2007). Moving faces: Categorization of dynamic facial expressions in American Sign Language by deaf and hearing participants. *Journal of Nonverbal Behavior, 31*, 23–38.

Guéguen, N. (2008). The effect of a woman's smile on men's courtship behavior. *Social Behavior & Personality: An International Journal, 36*, 1233–1236.

Guéguen, N. (2012). Does red lipstick really attract men? An evaluation in a bar. *International Journal of Psychological Studies, 4,* 206–209.

Guéguen, N. (2013). Weather and smiling contagion: A quasi experiment with the smiling sunshine. *Journal of Nonverbal Behavior, 37,* 51–55.

Guéguen, N., & Jacob, C. (2002). Direct look versus evasive glance and compliance with a request. *Journal of Social Psychology, 142,* 393–396.

Guerrero, L. K., & Floyd, K. (2006). *Nonverbal communication in close relationships.* Mahwah, NJ: Erlbaum.

Gunnery, S. D., & Hall, J. A. (2014). The Duchenne smile and persuasion. *Journal of Nonverbal Behavior, 38,* 181–194.

Gunnery, S. D., Hall, J. A., & Ruben, M. (2013). The deliberate Duchenne smile: Individual differences in expressive control. *Journal of Nonverbal Behavior, 37,* 29–41.

Haggard, E. A., & Isaacs, F. S. (1966). Micromomentary facial expressions as indicators of ego mechanisms in psychotherapy. In L. A. Gottschalk & A. H. Auerback (Eds.), *Methods of research in psychotherapy* (pp. 154–165). New York: Appleton-Century-Crofts.

Hall, J. [Judith] A. (2006). Women's and men's nonverbal communication: Similarities, differences, stereotypes, and origins. In V. Manusov & M. L. Patterson (Eds.), *The SAGE handbook of nonverbal communication* (pp. 201–218). Thousand Oaks, CA: Sage.

Hall, J. [Jeffrey] A., & Xing, C. (2015). The verbal and nonverbal correlates of the five flirting styles. *Journal of Nonverbal Behavior, 39,* 41–68.

Hall, J. [Jeffrey] A., Xing, C., & Brooks, S. (2015). Accurately detecting flirting: Error management theory, the traditional sexual script, and flirting base rate. *Communication Research, 42,* 939–958.

Hamlin, I., Wright, G. R. T, van der Zee, S., & Wilson, S. (2018). The dimensions of deception detection: Self-reported deception cue use is underpinned by two broad factors. *Applied Cognitive Psychology.* doi.org/10.1002/acp.3402

Hess, E. H. (1968). Pupillometric assessment. In J. M. Shlien (Ed.), *Research in psychotherapy.* Washington, DC: American Psychological Association.

Hess, E. H. (1975a). The role of pupil size in communication. *Scientific American, 233,* 110–112, 116–119.

Hess, E. H. (1975b). *The tell-tale eye.* New York: Van Nostrant Reinhold.

Hess, E. H., & Petrovich, S. B. (1987). Pupillary behavior in communication. In A. W. Siegman & S. Feldstein (Eds.), *Nonverbal behavior and communication* (2nd ed., pp. 327–348). Hillsdale, NJ: Erlbaum.

Hess, E. H., & Polt, J. M. (1960). Pupil size as related to interest value of visual stimuli. *Science, 132,* 349–350.

Hess, E. H., & Polt, J. M. (1964). Pupil size in relation to mental activity during simple problem solving. *Science, 143,* 1190–1192.

Hess, E. H., Seltzer, A. L., & Shlien, J. M. (1965). Pupil response of hetero- and homosexual males to pictures of men and women: A pilot study. *Journal of Abnormal Psychology, 70,* 165–168.

Hess, U., Blaison, C., & Kafetsios, K. (2016). Judging facial emotion expressions in context: The influence of culture and self-construal orientation. *Journal of Nonverbal Behavior, 40,* 55–64.

Hewitt, B. (2007, December 24). When every face is unfamiliar. *People,* 107–110.

Hietanen, J. O., & Heitanen, J. K. (2017). Genuine eye contact elicits self-referential processing. *Consciousness and Cognition, 51,* 100–115.

Hirsch, A. R., & Wolf, C. J. (2001). Practical methods for detecting mendacity: A case study. *Journal of the American Academy of Psychiatry and the Law, 29*, 438–444.

Holler, J., & Wilkin, K. (2011). Co-speech gesture mimicry in the process of collaborative referring during face-to-face dialogue. *Journal of Nonverbal Behavior, 35*, 133–153.

Holliday, R., & Cairnie, A. (2007). Man made plastic: Investigating men's consumption of aesthetic surgery. *Journal of Consumer Culture, 7*, 57–78.

Horstmann, G., Becker, S., & Ernst, D. (2016). Perceptual salience captures the eyes on a surprise trial. *Attention, Perception & Psychophysics, 78*, 1889–1900.

Houston, L., Grandey, A., & Sawyer, K. (2018). Who cares if "service with a smile" is authentic? An expectancy-based model of customer race and differential service reactions. *Organizational Behavior and Human Decision Processes, 144*, 85–96.

Hugenberg, K., & Sczesny, S. (2006). On wonderful women and seeing smiles: Social categorization moderates the happy face response latency advantage. *Social Cognition, 24*, 516–539.

Huovinen, A., & Weselius, H. (2015). "No smiling, please, Ms. Prime Minister!" Constructing a female politician on the cover of a news magazine. *Catalan Journal of Communication & Cultural Studies, 7*, 3–20.

Ijuin, K., Umata, I., Kato, T., & Yamamoto, S. (2018). Difference in eye gaze for floor apportionment in native- and second-language conversations. *Journal of Nonverbal Behavior, 42*, 113–128.

Ilicic, J., Kulczynski, A., & Baxter, S. (2018). How a smile can make a difference: Enhancing the persuasive appeal of celebrity endorsers. *Journal of Advertising Research, 58*, 41–64.

Jack, R. E., Garrod, O. G. B., Yu, H., Caldara, R., & Schyns, P. G. (2012). Facial expressions of emotion are not culturally universal. *Proceedings of the National Academy of Sciences of the USA, 109*, 7241–7244.

Jensen, M. L., & Burgoon, J. K. (2008). Interpersonal deception theory. In L. K. Guerrero & M. L. Hecht (Eds.), *The nonverbal communication reader* (3rd ed., pp. 421–431). Long Grove, IL: Waveland.

Johnson, H. G., Ekman, P., & Friesen, W. V. (1975). Communicative body movements: American emblems. *Semiotica, 15*, 335–353.

Kalus, A., & Cregan, C. (2017). Cosmetic facial surgery: The influence of self-esteem on job satisfaction and burnout. *Asia Pacific Journal of Human Resources, 55*, 320–336.

Kaw, E. (1993). Medicalization and racial features: Asian American women and cosmetic surgery. *Medical Anthropology Quarterly, 7*, 74–89.

Kaw, E. (1994). Opening faces: The politics of cosmetic surgery and Asian American women. In N. Sault (Ed.), *Many mirrors: Body image and social relations* (pp. 241–265). New Brunswick, NJ: Rutgers University Press.

Keh, H., Ren, R., Hill, S., & Li, X. (2013). The beautiful, the cheerful, and the helpful: The effects of service employee attributes on customer satisfaction. *Psychology & Marketing, 30*, 211–226.

Kendon, A. (1967). Some functions of gaze-direction in social interaction. *Acta Psychologica, 26*, 22–63.

Kiho, K., Sungkun, C., & Jang-Han, L. (2012). The influence of self-focused attention on blushing during social interaction. *Social Behavior & Personality: An International Journal, 40*, 747–753.

Knapp, M. L., McGlone, M. S., Griffin, D. L., & Earnest, W. (2015). *Lying and deception in human interaction* (2nd ed.). Dubuque, IA: Kendall Hunt.

Koch, S. C., Baehne, C. G., Kruse, L., Zimmermann, F., & Zumbach, J. (2010). Visual dominance and visual egalitarianism: Individual and group-level influences of sex and status in group interactions. *Journal of Nonverbal Behavior, 34*, 137–153.

Kramer, S. E., Lorens, A., Coninx, F., Zekveld, A. A., Piotrowska, A., & Skarzynski, H. (2013). Processing load during listening: The influence of task characteristics on the pupil response. *Language & Cognitive Processes, 28*, 426–442.

Krumhuber, E. G., & Kappas, A. (2005). Moving smiles: The role of dynamic components for the perception of the genuineness of smiles. *Journal of Nonverbal Behavior, 29*, 3–24.

Krumhuber, E. G., Likowski, K. U., & Weyers, P. (2014). Facial mimicry of spontaneous and deliberate Duchenne and non-Duchenne smiles. *Journal of Nonverbal Behavior, 38*, 1–11.

Kraft-Todd, G. T., Reinero, D. A., Kelley, J. M., Heberlein, A. S., Baer, L., & Riess, H. (2017). Empathic nonverbal behavior increases ratings of both warmth and competence in a medical context. *PLoS ONE, 12*, 1–16.

Lachat, F., Conty, L., Hugueville, L., & George, N. (2012). Gaze cueing effect in a face-to-face situation. *Journal of Nonverbal Behavior, 36*, 177–190.

LaFrance, M. (2011). *Lip service: Smiles in life, death, trust, lies, work, memory, sex, and politics.* New York: W. W. Norton.

Lamer, S. A., Reeves, S. L., & Weisbuch, M. (2015). The nonverbal environment of self-esteem: Interactive effects of facial-expression and eye-gaze on perceivers' self-evaluations. *Journal of Experimental Social Psychology, 56*, 130–138.

Lawson, R. (2015). I just love the attention: Implicit preference for direct eye contact. *Visual Cognition, 23*, 450–488.

Lea, R. G., Qualter, P., Davis, S. K., Perez-Gonzalez, J-C., & Bangee, M. (2018). Trait emotional intelligence and attentional bias for positive emotion: An eye tracking study. *Personality & Individual Differences, 128*, 88–93.

Leigh, R. J., & Zee, D. R. (2015). *The neurology of eye movements.* Oxford, UK: Oxford University Press.

Lick, D. J., Cortland, C. I., & Johnson, K. L. (2016). The pupils are the windows to sexuality: Pupil dilation as a visual cue to others' sexual interest. *Evolution and Human Behavior, 37*, 117–124.

Lobmaier, J. S. (2012). Facial expression and eye gaze direction: Are they combined when processing emotionally relevant facial information? *Journal of Communication Research, 4*, 89–101.

Luo, W. (2012). Selling cosmetic surgery and beauty ideals: The female body in the web sites of Chinese hospitals. *Women's Studies in Communication, 35*, 68–95.

Mann, S., Vrij, A., Leal, S., Granhag, P., Warmelink, L., & Forrester, D. (2012). Windows to the soul? Deliberate eye contact as a cue to deceit. *Journal of Nonverbal Behavior, 36*, 205–215.

Marchak, F. M. (2013). Detecting false intent using eye blink measures. *Frontiers in Psychology.* doi:10.3389/fpsyg.2013.00736

Matsumoto, D., & Hwang, H. (2011). Evidence for training the ability to read microexpression of emotion. *Motivation and Emotion.* https://doi.org/10.1007/s11031-011-9212-2

Matsumoto, D., & Willingham, B. (2009). Spontaneous facial expressions of emotion of congenitally and noncongenitally blind individuals. *Journal of Personality and Social Psychology, 96*, 1–10.

McCarthy, A., & Lee, K. (2009). Children's knowledge of deceptive gaze cues and its relation to their actual lying behavior. *Journal of Experimental Child Psychology, 103*, 117–134.

McCornack, S. A., & Parks, M. R. (1990). What women know that men don't: Sex differences in determining the truth behind deceptive messages. *Journal of Social and Personal Relationships, 7*, 107–118.

McCroskey, J. C., Richmond, V. P., & McCroskey, L. L. (2006). Nonverbal communication in instructional contexts. In V. Manusov & M. L. Patterson (Eds.), *The SAGE handbook of nonverbal communication* (pp. 421–436). Thousand Oaks, CA: Sage.

McCurdy, J. A., & Lam, S. M. (2005). *Cosmetic surgery of the Asian face* (2nd ed.). New York: Theime.

Mehrabian, A. (1971). *Silent messages.* Belmont, CA: Wadsworth.

Mehrabian, A. (1972). *Nonverbal communication.* Chicago: Atherton.

Mehrabian, A. (1981). *Silent messages* (2nd ed.). Belmont, CA: Wadsworth.

Mendolia, M. (2007). Explicit use of categorical and dimensional strategies to decode facial expressions of emotion. *Journal of Nonverbal Behavior, 31*, 57–75.

Millar, M. G., & Millar, K. (1995). Detection of deception in familiar and unfamiliar persons: The effects of information restriction. *Journal of Nonverbal Behavior, 19*, 69–84.

Minotte, K. L. (2017). Integrative and masking emotion work: Marital outcomes among dual-earner couples. *Marriage & Family Review, 53*, 88–104.

Monk, A. F., & Gale, C. (2002). A look is worth a thousand words: Full gaze awareness in video-mediated conversation. *Discourse Processes, 33*, 257–278.

Nagel, F., Maurer, M., & Reinemann, C. (2012). Is there a visual dominance in political communication? How verbal, visual, and vocal communication shape viewers' impressions of political candidates. *Journal of Communication, 62*, 833–850.

Novotny, E., Carr, Z., Frank, M. G., Dietrich, S. B., Shaddock, T., Cardwell, M., & Decker, A. (2018). How people really suspect and discover lies. *Journal of Nonverbal Behavior, 42*, 41–52.

Okubo, M., Kobayashi, A., & Ishikawa, K. (2012). A fake smile thwarts cheater detection. *Journal of Nonverbal Behavior, 36*, 217–225.

Paik, J. E., & van Swol, L. M. (2017). Justifications and questions in detecting deception. *Group Decision and Negotiation, 26*, 1041–1060.

Palancia, A., & Itier, R. J. (2012). Attention capture by direct gaze is robust to context and task demands. *Journal of Nonverbal Behavior, 36*, 123–134.

Park, H. S., Levine, T. R., McCornack, S. A., Morrison, K., & Ferrara, M. (2002). How people really detect lies. *Communication Monographs, 69*, 144–157.

Parker, J. R. (2014). Theater as virtual reality. In J. Tanenbaum, M. S. El-Nasr, & M. Nixon (Eds.), *Nonverbal communication in virtual worlds* (pp. 151–174). Pittsburgh, PA: ETC Press.

Patel, S. Y., & Itani, K. (2018). Review of eyelid reconstruction techniques. *Seminars in Plastic Surgery, 32*, 95–102.

Paulmann, S., Titone, D., & Pell, M. D. (2012). How emotional prosody guides your way: Evidence from eye movements. *Speech Communication, 54*, 92–107.

Pettijohn T., II, & Tesser, A. (2005). Threat and social choice: When eye size matters. *Journal of Social Psychology, 145*, 547–570.

Porter, S., ten Brinke, L., & Wallace, B. (2012). Secrets and lies: Involuntary leakage in deceptive facial expressions as a function of emotional intensity. *Journal of Nonverbal Behavior, 36*, 23–37.

Puccinelli, N. M., Motyka, S., & Grewal, D. (2010). Can you trust a customer's expression? Insights into nonverbal communication in the retail context. *Psychology & Marketing, 27*, 964–988.

Quintanilla, K. M., & Wahl, S. T. (2016). *Business and professional communication: Keys for workplace excellence.* (3rd ed.). Thousand Oaks, CA: Sage.

Renninger, L. A., Wade, T. J., & Grammer, K. (2004). Getting that female glance: Patterns and consequences of male nonverbal behavior in courtship contexts. *Evolution and Human Behavior, 25,* 416–431.

Roesch, E. B., Tamarit, L., Reveret, L., Grandjean, D., Sander, D., & Scherer, K. R. (2011). FACSGen: A tool to synthesize emotional facial expressions through systematic manipulation of facial action units. *Journal of Nonverbal Behavior, 35,* 1–16.

Roscoe, L. A. (2018). I feel pretty. *Health Communication, 33,* 1055–1057.

Rossion, B. (2013). The composite face illusion: A whole window into our understanding of holistic face perception. *Visual Cognition, 21,* 139–253.

Sato, W., & Yoshikawa, S. (2007). Enhanced experience of emotional arousal in response to dynamic facial expressions. *Journal of Nonverbal Behavior, 31,* 119–135.

Schmidt, K. L. (2006). Movement differences between deliberate and spontaneous facial expressions: Zygomaticus major action in smiling. *Journal of Nonverbal Behavior, 30,* 37–52.

Sedgwick, H. A., & Festinger, L. (2017). Eye movements, efference, and visual perception. In R. A. Monty & J. W. Senders (Eds.), *Eye movements and psychological processes* (5th ed., pp. 221–230). New York: Routledge.

Sellers, H. (2010). *You don't look like anyone I know: A true story of family, face blindness, and forgiveness.* New York: Penguin Books.

Shichuan, D., Yong, T., & Martinez, A. M. (2014). Compound facial expressions of emotion. *Proceedings of the National Academy of Sciences, 111,* 1454–1462.

Spackman, M. P., Fujiki, M., Brinton, B., Nelson, D., & Allen, J. (2005). The ability of children with language impairment to recognize emotion conveyed by facial expression and music. *Communication Disorders Quarterly, 26,* 131–143.

Speer, S. A. (2017). Flirting: A designedly ambiguous action? *Research on Language & Social Interaction, 50,* 128–150.

Stiff, J. B., Kim, H. J., & Ramesh, C. (1992). Truth biases and aroused suspicion in relational deception. *Communication Research, 19,* 326–345.

Street, C. N. H., & Masip, J. (2015). The source of the truth bias: Heuristic processing? *Scandinavian Journal of Psychology, 56,* 254–263.

Stromwall, L. A., Hartwig, M., & Granhag, P. A. (2006). To act truthfully: Nonverbal behavior and strategies during a police interrogation. *Psychology, Crime, and Law, 12,* 207–219.

Szarota, P. (2010). The mystery of the European smile: A comparison based on individual photographs provided by Internet users. *Journal of Nonverbal Behavior, 34,* 249–256.

Tannen, D. (2006, August). Every move you make. *O: The Oprah Winfrey Magazine,* 175–176.

Tang, D., & Schmeichel, B. J. (2015). Look me in the eye: Manipulated eye gaze affects dominance mindsets. *Journal of Nonverbal Behavior, 39,* 181–194.

Theeuwes, J., Kramer, A. F., Hahn, S., & Irwin, D. E. (1998). Our eyes do not always go where we want them to go: Capture of the eyes by new objects. *Psychological Science, 9,* 379–385.

Trichas, S., Schyns, B., Lord, R., & Hall, R. (2017). "Facing" leaders: Facial expression and leadership perception. *The Leadership Quarterly, 28,* 317–333.

Ueda, S. S., & Koyama, T. T. (2011). Influence of eye make-up on the perception of gaze direction. *International Journal of Cosmetic Science, 33*, 514–518.

van Swol, L. M., Braun, M. T., & Kolb, M. R. (2015). Deception, detection, demeanor, and truth bias in face-to-face and computer-mediated communication. *Communication Research, 42*, 1116–1142.

Vrij, A. (2000). *Detecting lies and deceit: The psychology of lying and its implications for professional practice.* Chichester, UK: Wiley.

Vrij, A. (2004). Why professionals fail to catch liars and how they can improve. *Legal and Criminological Psychology, 9*, 159–181.

Vrij, A. (2006a). Challenging interviewees during interviews: The potential effects on lie detection. *Psychology, Crime, and Law, 12*, 193–206.

Vrij, A. (2006b). Nonverbal communication and deception. In V. Manusov & M. L. Patterson (Eds.), *The SAGE handbook of nonverbal communication* (pp. 341–359). Thousand Oaks, CA: Sage.

Wang, Z., Mao, H., Li, Y. J., & Liu, F. (2017). Smile big or not? Effects of smile intensity on perceptions of warmth and competence. *Journal of Consumer Research, 43*, 787–805.

Wegenstein, B. (2012). *The cosmetic gaze: Body modification and the constructions of beauty.* Cambridge, MA: MIT Press.

Weick, M., McCall, C., & Blascovich, J. (2017). Power moves beyond complementarity: A staring look elicits avoidance in low power perceivers and approach in high power perceivers. *Personality and Social Psychology Bulletin, 43*, 1188–1201.

Whitty, M. T. (2004). Cyber-flirting: An examination of men's and women's flirting behavior both offline and on the Internet. *Behavior Change, 21*, 115–126.

Widman, A., Schroger, E., & Wetzel, N. (2018). Emotion lies in the eye of the listener: Emotional arousal to novel sounds is reflected in the sympathetic contribution to the pupil dilation response and the P3. *Biological Psychology, 133*, 10–17.

Wise, M., & Rodriguez, D. (2013). Detecting deceptive communication through computer-mediated technology: Applying interpersonal deception theory to texting behavior. *Communication Research Reports, 30*, 342–346.

Yamamoto, K., & Suzuki, N. (2006). The effects of social interaction and personal relationships on facial expressions. *Journal of Nonverbal Behavior, 30*, 167–179.

Yan, W.-J., Wu, Q., Liang, J., Chen, Y.-H., & Fu, X. (2013). How fast are the leaked facial expressions? The duration of micro-expressions. *Journal of Nonverbal Behavior, 37*, 217–230.

Yoo, S., & Noyes, S. (2016). Recognition of facial expressions of negative emotions in romantic relationships. *Journal of Nonverbal Behavior, 40*, 1–12.

Zestcott, C. A., Bean, M. G., & Stone, J. (2017). Evidence of negative implicit attitudes toward individuals with a tattoo near the face. *Group Processes & Intergroup Relations, 20*, 186–201.

Zhengrui, H., & Hongqiang, Z. (2018). Stance markers in television news presentation: Expressivity of eyebrow flashes in the delivery of news. *Semiotica, 2018*, 279–300.

Zuckerman, M., & Driver, R. E. (1985). Telling lies: Verbal and nonverbal correlates of deception. In A. W. Siegman & S. Feldstein (Eds.), *Multichannel integrations of nonverbal behavior* (pp. 129–148). Hillsdale, NJ: Erlbaum.

Zuckerman, M., Miserandino, M., & Bernieri, F. (2008). Civil inattention exists—in elevators. In L. K. Guerrero & M. L. Hecht (Eds.), *The nonverbal communication reader* (3rd ed., pp. 130–138). Long Grove, IL: Waveland. (Original work published 1983)

chapter eight

TOUCH: OUR BODIES IN CONTACT

chapter outline

chapter objectives

After studying this chapter, you should be able to

1. define haptics as a nonverbal communication code;
2. understand the touch ethic, in terms of how it is formed and how it affects our everyday nonverbal communication with others;
3. describe touch deprivation and explain the importance of touch for infants and the elderly;
4. identify Heslin's five categories of touch and provide examples of touches that apply to each category;
5. identify Jones and Yarbrough's six meanings of touch and provide examples of touches that apply to each category;
6. review expectancy violation theory as applicable to touch;
7. define location, duration, and intensity as three ways to gauge the appropriateness of a touch; and
8. describe current applications of haptics research.

case study

LEARNING TO TOUCH

*Y*ou've lived long enough to know that touch is powerful. A touch can convey much more than words, but a touch given inappropriately or received in way that's unintended or unwelcome can destroy a relationship. Touch is powerful, but also volatile because, unlike the other codes of nonverbal communication, touch involves bodies coming into contact. Think for a moment about how you learned how to touch other people; you likely learned from your parents, other family members, friends, and romantic partners. You likely also learned from the media and the Internet (a good *and* a bad thing).

None of us has avoided the occasional "touch gone wrong," either out of ignorance, a lack of forethought, or simply because we had to confront a new circumstance and didn't know how to behave. This is part of the learning curve of life. Perhaps you extended a handshake to someone, only to be met with a much firmer one, leaving you feeling like you'd like a "take two" on that exchange. Maybe your first ever passionate kiss didn't go as well as you would've liked—most everyone has "been there, done that."

As we approach this important topic of touch as a powerful nonverbal cue, think about how you learned to touch others, mistakes you made, and also leaps in learning that you've taken along the way. Think about those people who taught you the most on this topic—like professors who made you practice a professional handshake in nonverbal communication class (your authors are both guilty!), a parent or friend who wrapped their arms around you and comforted you when you were scared or sad, or your buddies who high-fived you in triumph. These are powerful experiences that have shaped who you are.

> "That guy had a really weak handshake—that 'wet fish' kind. I wouldn't hire him to work here."
> "I went on a first date with this girl and she was all over me. Sometimes that's okay, but this time it bugged me."
> "My husband's family is very affectionate. It was awkward for me at first, since my family isn't all that 'touchy,' but now I'm used to it."

What do these comments have in common? They're about the most powerful, yet most misunderstood, nonverbal communication code of all—touch. The study of touch among humans is often referred to as **haptics** (Fulkerson, 2011; Lederman & Klatzky, 2009); less often, you may hear a reference to **tactile behavior, tactics,** or **zero proxemics.** In this chapter, we explore this important code of nonverbal communication, beginning with an examination of its power.

Touch is a powerful form of nonverbal communication.

THE POWER OF TOUCH ■ ■ ■

A baby is crying in a back room of a house; what happens? The parents may decide that letting the baby cry itself to sleep is the best thing, but most parents will go into the room, touch or pick up the baby, and try to calm it so it can sleep. Your friend has just learned that a family member is seriously ill; how do you comfort your friend? You might sit with the person, let her or him cry it out, and possibly extend a hug for support and sympathy. A team has just won a championship; what are you likely to see? Probably you'll see lots of high-fives, hugs, and slaps on the back or rear end. What's common to these examples is that each illustrates the significant role of touch in everyday human interaction.

Out of the five human senses, touch develops first (Hertenstein, Keltner, App, Bulleit, & Jaskolka, 2006). We'll say it again: Touch is the most powerful of all the codes, yet also the most misunderstood among the realm of nonverbal behavior. Think about it: The other codes (e.g., facial expressions, eye gaze, vocalics) don't involve physical contact. Touch is accomplished when one person's body comes into contact with something or with another person's body.

Touch is the most misunderstood code of nonverbal communication because a sender's meaning behind a touch may not correspond with a receiver's interpretation of the touch. This kind of incongruence happens frequently, in all kinds of settings and within all kinds of relationships. Sometimes a misunderstanding is of relatively minor consequence. For example, two men shake hands and one places a hand on the forearm of the other. From the first man's perspective (sender of the touch), the forearm touch simply adds warmth or emphasis to the handshake. But from the second man's perspective, the forearm touch might be interpreted as a dominance cue, as though the first man intends to convey his status. At other times, a misunderstanding about touch can cause a major offense or rift, such as in cases where a coworker or boss thinks his or her touch is a sign of friendliness, while the recipient of the touch deems it sexual harassment.

Of the five human senses, touch is the first to develop. Touch is critical to the health and development of infants.

© Oksana Kuzmina/Shutterstock.com

Consider how many relationships have either not gotten off the ground or ended, simply because of a misunderstanding over touch or the lack of touch. Some people have cold, distant fathers, and the lack of touch they received growing up causes them to be cautious around men in both adolescence and adulthood. Other people have doting mothers—those who touch, protect, or cradle their children too much—which can also lead to negative consequences later in life. These are just a couple of examples that illustrate the contention that more misunderstandings between people are possible with respect to the touch nonverbal code than other codes.

TOUCH ETHIC ■ ■ ■

What purpose do you believe touch serves in human interaction, in general? Think about your "philosophy of touch," meaning rules or expectations you have about your own touching behavior toward others, as well as how others can touch you. Think about touches you *don't* like—those you find inappropriate, irritating, or distracting. Does a negative judgment depend on the person offering the touch? On the situation? Your mood?

These questions all pertain to something we call the **touch ethic**, meaning people's beliefs about and preferences for touch. The touch ethic encompasses our rules about appropriate and inappropriate touch, our expectations for how people will receive our touch and extend touch to us, whether we are "touchy" people or not (how much touch we're comfortable with), and how we actually behave regarding touch. The touch ethic develops early in life and remains fairly constant; however, it can change during our life span because of our relationships and experiences.

The primary influence on our touch ethic is our culture, in that we learn the "rights and wrongs" of touch, along with other nonverbal behaviors, from our culture's standards and traditions (Andersen, 2011; Mansson et al., 2016; Matsumoto & Hwang, 2013). But within that larger framework of culture, our family of origin has the most powerful impact. Secondary influences include extended family members, friends, and romantic partners. What did you observe, experience, and learn about touch while growing up? If you grew up in a two-parent family, you most likely observed your parents' touch—how often they touched; where they touched (environment as well as body location); what parts of their bodies they used; if touch from one parent to another was accepted, reciprocated, or rejected; and so forth. You registered how your parents and siblings touched you and how you touched them. Our earliest experiences with touch—even touch as infants—impact the touch ethic in the most profound way (Jung & Fouts, 2011; Moszkowski & Stack, 2007). If you grew up fighting, wrestling, or rough-housing with parents or siblings, these forms of aggressive touch are components of your touch ethic as well.

Our touch ethic may change over time, meaning that if you grew up in circumstances involving touch that you later, as an adult, deem inappropriate or not preferable, your touch ethic will likely evolve to accommodate that change of view. Perhaps you accepted some forms of touch as a kid, but those touches seemed inappropriate, unwelcome, or just physically infeasible as you got a bit older, such as sitting on a parent's lap. Parents often lament the day when their children and adolescents decide they're too old for goodnight kisses or hugs. The kids would rather *die* than be kissed or touched by their parents in front of their friends. Heterosexually speaking, we can probably remember a time when kissing or touching a member of the opposite sex was gross (because they had "cooties"). But as our bodies and emotions evolved and hormones began to rage, we started to change our views about contact with members of the opposite sex—contact that we began to see as interesting or wonderful. Gays and lesbians sometimes describe this same process, but with a different result: Kissing or touching an opposite-sex person may have continued to seem gross or simply didn't feel to the homosexual person the way it seemed to feel to heterosexuals. Same-sex touching during childhood and adolescence was, for a lot of people, confusing and turbulent territory.

Our touch ethic may change because we fall in love. If our romantic partner's touch ethic differs from ours, we may find that our rules or expectations evolve to match our partner's, or vice versa. Sometimes, "unnatural" or dramatic events cause a shift in the touch ethic. For example, a child who grew up in a loving home but was physically or sexually abused by an extended family member or family friend is likely to seriously alter his or her touch ethic because of the experience. Tragedies or sad situations, such as a loved one's serious illness, can alter the touch ethic as well, as people use touch to comfort one another. Someone who isn't that comfortable with touch may suddenly seek the comfort of someone else's shoulder, as a way of coping with a difficult or traumatic experience.

Change may happen in the other direction, too, in that people who were once comfortable with touch experience a trauma or encounter a circumstance that causes them to reduce physical contact with others, typically termed **touch avoidance** (Hielscher & Mahar, 2017; Johansson, 2013; Kashdan, Doorley, Stiksma, & Hertenstein, 2016; Peck & Webb, 2011). Some people are generally touch avoidant, with most everyone across most circumstances; the term for this is **trait touch avoidance.** A primary care physician who is trait touch avoidant will find her or his profession challenging, since touch to patients is commonly required and is perceived by patients as helpful, empathic, and related to their improved health (Cocksedge, George, Renwick, & Chew-Graham, 2013; Montague, Chen, Xu, Chewning, & Barrett, 2013). In contrast, some people experience **state touch avoidance** because their profession may cause them to avoid touching others, such as is often the case for psychologists and social workers, whose touch with clients or patients could be viewed as inappropriate or unprofessional (Green, 2017; Harrison, Jones, & Huws, 2012; Lynch & Garret, 2010).

TOUCH AND HUMAN DEVELOPMENT

We heard somewhere that human beings need at least 12 hugs each day to remain psychologically stable. If that's true, we know a lot of unstable people out there, because many of us don't get 12 hugs a day. Psychologist Sidney Jourard believes that the United States is a touch-starved country; he cites examples such as going out of our way not to bump into people and being embarrassed when we accidentally touch someone, such as might happen in a crowded environment (Jourard, 1964, 1966; Martin & Nuttall, 2017). Compared with other parts of the world, such as Europe and Latin America, U.S. culture is restrictive in its approach to and beliefs about touch (Andersen, 2011). Anthropologist Desmond Morris (1967, 1969) has long critiqued the way Americans hire "licensed touchers," such as massage therapists and beauticians, to provide human contact.

But the United States is not alone on this front: A study reported in a Canadian newspaper suggested that Canadians suffer from "touch deficit" because a third of the population regularly goes an entire day without any human contact (Harris, 2005). The explanation for the Canadian lack of touch was an increased emphasis on social boundaries, changes in sex roles, and more reliance on electronic communication. Whether you're a Canadian or an American who doesn't get

chapter eight

your 12 hugs a day, the point is this: Human beings need physical contact with one another to survive and thrive. Affection is important to the success of our relationships; it also plays a powerful role in our physical and mental health (Floyd, 2015; Hesse & Mikkelson, 2017; Jakubiak & Feeney, 2016a, 2016b; Koole, Sin, & Schneider, 2014; Triscoli, Croy, Olausson, & Sailer, 2017). Since most of what we discuss in this chapter relates to touch in adulthood, in the next section we examine the importance of touch in the human development of infants and children, and then at the end of life, among the members of American society who are the most touch deprived.

Infancy and Childhood

When we hear of abandoned babies or abused children, we're reminded of some of the worst aspects of our society. We're emotionally moved by the thought of a helpless infant or child being denied human contact or given the wrong kind of contact, because we know how important touch is to the development and well-being of the most vulnerable among us. Research shows that depriving infants and children of touch can retard their mental, physical, and emotional development; can cause them to be sickly, socially maladjusted, quiet, and overweight; and can even kill them (Cekaite & Kvist, 2017; Feldman, 2011; Stack & Jean, 2011). Touching premature infants who undergo incubation in the early hours of their lives is critical to their development and to the establishment of a successful parent–child relationship (Feldman, Eidelman, Sirota, & Weller, 2002; Lappin, 2005). Research shows that children who experience abundant positive touch as they grow up tend to be warm, affectionate, socially adept, and confident adults (Jones & Brown, 1996; Reece, Ebstein, Cheng, Ng, & Schirmer, 2016; Weiss, 1990).

While it is beyond our scope to review the vast literature on touch and infant/child development, one area of research is particularly interesting. Have you heard of infant massage? It's been around awhile but has been steadily gaining popularity as an effective parenting technique and a way to enhance parent–child bonding. A leading scholar in this area is Tiffany Field (2011), who researches the positive relationship between infant massage and health. We know the benefits of general touch between parents and infants, but a purposeful massage goes beyond simple holding, cradling, or touching of a baby. Caressing a baby's skin using

Parent-child touch is very important. Depriving infants and children of touch can slow their mental, physical, and emotional development.

appropriate pressure has been shown to assist in premature infant weight gain, mental development, and motor coordination (Field, 1998, 2000, 2011; Vicente, Veríssimo, & Diniz, 2017). It also serves as an expression of love; provides meaningful parent–child exchanges, particularly for fathers who might not normally touch their babies as often as mothers do; and can actually help mothers who suffer from postnatal depression (Aznar & Tenenbaum, 2016; Cordes, Egmose, Smith-Nielsen, Koppe, & Vaever, 2017; Onzawa, Glover, Adam, Modi, & Kumar, 2001; Waters, West, Karnilowicz, & Mendes, 2017).

Touch Deprivation and the Elderly

While touch to infants and children has been studied, especially the effects of **touch deprivation** (lack of physical contact between people), the role of touch in adult development is also the subject of research. Touch deprivation has been studied cross-culturally; research has linked it with alienation, depression, aggression, violence, and poor physical and mental health (Field, 2002, 2005; Floyd, 2016; Floyd & Hesse, 2017; Punyanunt-Carter & Wrench, 2009). These findings underscore the importance of human contact to our basic well-being as we develop into adults. But what about the end of the age spectrum?

It's a fact: Unless we die at an early age, we're all going to be elderly someday. Unfortunately, in U.S. culture, elderly people aren't revered as they are in other cultures, such as many Asian cultures in which the elder members of society are held in high esteem and respected for their wisdom and experience. It's sad, but true, that elderly people tend to be the most alienated and touch-deprived segment of American society. Psychotherapist Maggie Turp (2000) explains:

> As we move into late adulthood, our "tactile" circumstances change. We are less likely to have young children to attend to. We are less likely than previously to be in a sexual relationship. If we lose a longstanding and affectionate partner, we lose the touch experiences that were a part of that relationship and they are not easy to replace. Activities involving vigorous movement, which, because of the overlaps between touch and movement, might to some degree substitute for touch experience, are also likely to diminish. And if we experience a narrowing of our social world, then touch equivalents such as gaze will also be less available to compensate for deficits of physical touching. (p. 68)

While elders may need more touch from others, such as being helped out of a chair or attended to medically, these touches tend to be functional, not affectionate. Elders may be granted latitude when they extend touch to others—few of us would reject the handshake or hug of an elderly person, even someone we don't know—but they tend to receive less touch, other than what is necessary to help them function physically.

Part of the reason for the touch deprivation is our perception of elderly people as frail (Sehlstedt et al., 2016; Vieira et al., 2016). Perhaps we fear touching or hugging them because we think we might hurt them. In some cases, our fears are reasonable, because many elderly are frail, but do we

chapter eight

forget that light hugs or other types of touches are possible? A more honest explanation for touch deprivation is this: Some people are put off by the physical appearance of elderly folks. For some, it's related to their own fear of aging and becoming infirm, which leads people to distance themselves from elderly people and avoid physical contact with them. What's more interesting is that this is a *learned* behavior. Children, for the most part, aren't put off by the appearance of the elderly; they're just as likely to approach an elder as they are anyone else.

More research is being done on touch deprivation among the elderly. Not surprisingly, a good deal of this work focuses on improved physical and mental health of elder patients who receive touch from health care providers. Nurses, physical and occupational therapists, counselors, and other caregivers who provide tactile contact with elder patients have a profound effect on the patients' relaxation level, recovery time, general stress level, adherence to instructions about medication, and ability to heal (Bundgaard & Nielsen, 2011; Coakley & Duffy, 2010; Guéguen, Meineri, & Charles-Sire, 2010; Hart, 2012; Jakubiak & Feeney, 2017). A caring touch from a health care provider can also help an elderly patient and her or his family members handle difficult situations, such as receiving bad news about prognosis or coping with end-of-life issues (Kozlowska & Doboszynska, 2012; Papathanassoglou & Mpouzika, 2012; Villagran, Goldsmith, Wittenberg-Lyles, & Baldwin, 2010).

One interesting attempt to reduce elderly people's touch deprivation is pet therapy, sometimes termed animal-facilitated or animal-assisted therapy (Cherniak & Cherniak, 2014; Ernst, 2013; Phung et al., 2017; Sollami, Gianferrari, Alfieri, Artioli, & Taffurelli, 2017). Animals, particularly therapy dogs in such programs as Paws With a Cause, are loaned to elder-care facilities so the patients can have contact with the animals. Animals in nursing homes and other elder-care facilities generate many positive effects, including the lowering of elder patients' blood pressure, decreased anxiety and depression, and enhanced attitude and mood (Allen, 2003; Sollami et al., 2017).

© Sue McDonald/Shutterstock.com

Pet therapy has proven effective, in that the presence of and contact with animals helps fulfill the touch needs of elderly people who may be socially isolated.

Coaching and Touching: What Do Parents Think?

We've said that touch is powerful and can also be misunderstood, making it a volatile nonverbal code. Affection from the right person can lift our spirits, but touch can also be abusive. Touch can be weaponized and can destroy lives.

Perhaps you read or heard news accounts in 2018 of Olympian and university gymnasts' court cases over abuse they suffered by a one-time USA Gymnastics' team doctor. The doctor was convicted on multiple counts of sexual abuse and was sentenced in January of 2018 to 175 years in prison. A few months later, some of these gymnasts filed lawsuits against both the International Gymnastics Federation and Michigan State University, where some of them trained and where the doctor in question was employed (Freiss, 2018; Thorbecke, 2018). The lawsuits were aimed at a swath of people who either knew or should have known that the abuse was happening—people like coaches, trainers, and other officials.

The coach-athlete relationship has been researched extensively, as people try to better understand and navigate these important relationships and the nonverbal cues that go with them. However, little research exists on coach-athlete physical contact, which is surprising given how fraught the topic can be. In some situations, a coach must touch an athlete to get the person into a correct position, enhance the athlete's ability to successfully perform a skill, or to extend affection when triumphs are made and support over losses or setbacks. How do coaches navigate touch with their athletes so that they aren't accused of abuse or, worse, cross over a boundary into actual abuse? What are parents' roles in all of this?

The research team of Thomas Gleaves and Melanie Lang (2017) investigated how sports are becoming a "no-touch zone," meaning the trend for coaches to adopt a defensive, no-physical contact policy with their athletes, lest they be accused of abuse. Gleaves and Lang specifically focused on competitive youth swimming and parents' perspectives on appropriate physical contact. Think about when you learned to swim, likely from an adult; you probably received some sort of touch from your instructor, as you learned to form your arms into a stroke and kick your feet to navigate through water. Sometimes swim instructors touch the backs of kids' heads to lower them into position; this contact can be necessary because of the natural human tendency to not want to go below the surface of water. Did you or your parents ever deem any of these touches inappropriate?

Gleaves and Lang interviewed parents of competitive youth swimmers, believing parents to be important "stakeholders in the athletic triangle" (p. 192). After compiling interview data, the researchers found three themes or circumstances in which parents believed coach-athlete touch was appropriate: "(a) to prevent, minimize, or treat physical harm to a child; (b) to teach a child a sport-specific technique or skill; and (c) for pastoral care or moral support" (p. 200). From a parent's point of view, a coach's primary responsibility is the safety, protection, and welfare of any athlete, especially since in a sporting context a coach steps into the role of parent. Touch is a tool in teaching and coaching sports, but any touch must be appropriate for the sporting context.

Want to know more about this study? If so, check out Gleaves, T., & Lang, M. (2017). Kicking "no-touch" discourses into touch: Athletes' parents' constructions of appropriate coach-child athlete physical contact. *Journal of Sport & Social Issues, 41*, 191-211.

Haptics (tactile behavior, tactics, zero proxemics)	Study of touch among people
Touch ethic	Beliefs about and preferences for touch
Touch avoidance	Reduction or lack of physical contact with people
Trait touch avoidance	Tendency to avoid physical contact with most people across most circumstances
State touch avoidance	Tendency to avoid physical contact only with certain people or in certain circumstances
Touch deprivation	Lack of physical contact between people

Remember!
8.1

TYPES OF TOUCH

Several different systems for categorizing touch have been developed to help us better understand this complex code of nonverbal communication. We've selected a couple to review with you so you can better gauge your own touch behavior toward others, as well as their contact with you.

Heslin's Categories

Social psychologist Richard Heslin (1974) classified touch into categories ranging from distant and impersonal to close and intimate.

1. **Functional/professional:** These touches serve a specific function, usually within the context of a professional relationship, and are generally low in intimacy (even if the contact is with an intimate part of the body). Examples include a doctor giving a patient a physical exam, a massage therapist working out the kinks in someone's neck, and a beautician giving a customer a makeup demonstration.

2. **Social/polite:** Touches associated with cultural norms, such as handshakes, hugs, and kisses as greeting and departure rituals, fall under this category. Like the first category, these touches indicate fairly low intimacy within a relationship.

3. **Friendship/warmth:** People use touch to show their nonromantic emotion and affection toward each other. Close friends may hug, exchange kisses on the cheek, or pat each other on the back to show their liking and connection. As in other categories, friendship/warmth touches are enacted differently across cultures.

How would you classify the touch in this photo, according to Heslin's categories? Is this a touch of friendship/warmth or love/intimacy? Sometimes it's hard to gauge the significance and meaning of touches without knowing more about the relationship and context.

© Plume Photography/Shutterstock.com

4. **Love/intimacy:** These touches are highly personal and intimate, used to communicate strong feelings of affection. Hugs may last longer or may involve more of the body in contact than hugs between friends; kisses may last longer and be placed on the lips rather than on the cheek. While typically thought of within the context of romantic relationships, other loving relationships, such as those between family members, may involve these touches as well.

5. **Sexual arousal:** These touches are extremely intimate and typically target the sexual zones and organs of the body for the purpose of sexual arousal. If people engaged in this kind of touching also love each other, then touches in the love/intimacy and sexual arousal categories often overlap.

HESLIN'S CATEGORIES OF TOUCH

Remember!
8.2

Functional/professional	Non-intimate touches that serve a specific function, usually within the context of a professional relationship
Social/polite	Touches associated with cultural norms that indicate fairly low intimacy within a relationship
Friendship/warmth	Touches that show nonromantic emotion and affection
Love/intimacy	Highly personal and intimate touches that communicate feelings of romantic affection
Sexual arousal	Extremely intimate touches that typically target the sexual zones or organs of the body for the purpose of sexual arousal

Jones and Yarbrough's Meanings of Touch

Communication scholars Jones and Yarbrough (1985) provide a system that helps us understand the various meanings behind a touch. The six most meaningful categories of touch are as follows:

1. **Positive affect (affectionate) touches:** These touches indicate a degree of liking or positivity toward another person. Such touches can convey messages of support, appreciation, inclusion, sexual interest, and affection. When college roommates reunite after not seeing each other over the summer, they're likely to hug, even if it's the brief "bro hug."

2. **Playful touches:** These touches include both playful affection and playful aggression subcategories. They convey teasing or joking between people, and may include mildly aggressive touch such as wrestling or rough-housing, tickling, grabbing, pinching, and so forth. Parents and children often engage in this form of touch as a means of expressing affection.

3. **Control touches:** These touches are used to gain compliance from someone, to get someone's attention, or to engender a response. The touch is persuasive, meaning that it conveys a person's influence or attempt to control a situation or others' behavior. Someone may have a forceful grip or a vigorous shake when shaking hands, which can communicate dominance or power.

4. **Ritualistic touches:** Touch is an important component of many everyday rituals. We generally think of these kinds of touches as being associated with greeting and departure rituals, such as you're likely to see at an airport or family gathering.

5. **Task-related touches:** To accomplish a specific task, touch often is required, so these touches serve an instrumental function. For example, a dentist has to come into contact with the client's face and mouth area to examine the teeth. A limo driver or bellhop may offer a hand of assistance to someone exiting a car.

6. **Accidental touches:** These touches are unintentional and, thus, meaningless, according to Jones and Yarbrough. However, accidental touch can be embarrassing and can generate anxiety (Martin & Nuttall, 2017). Think of a crowded airplane with narrow seats, where it's likely that passengers' arms or hips will come into contact during a flight. When people get on an already crowded elevator, people at the back may bump into one another as everyone adjusts to the cramped conditions.

Jones and Yarbrough's categories of touch can overlap. Let's use the dentist example again: A dentist will likely touch your face and mouth during an examination of your teeth, but what if you feel some pain as a result and lift up off the exam chair? The dentist may gently touch your shoulder or arm to try to settle you back down into the chair so the exam can continue. Is this touch task-related or controlling? The point is that it doesn't really matter which category a touch fits into; the categories should be used to better understand common meanings behind touches you see and experience in everyday life.

Remember!
8.3

Positive affect (affectionate) touches	Touches that indicate a degree of liking or positivity toward another person
Playful touches	Touches that convey teasing, joking, or mild aggression between people
Control touches	Touches used to gain compliance, get someone's attention, or generate a response
Ritualistic touches	Touches typically associated with rituals, such as greetings and departures
Task-related touches	Touches that serve an instrumental function, meaning those that help accomplish a task
Accidental touches	Unintentional and meaningless touches

GAUGING THE APPROPRIATENESS OF TOUCH

This is a tricky topic, because we all have our own standards or rules about the appropriateness or inappropriateness of touch. To tackle this subject, let's first revisit a theory that helps us understand nonverbal communication in everyday life.

Expectancy Violations Theory

Communication scholar Judee Burgoon and various colleagues developed **expectancy violations theory** to help explain how nonverbal communication functions in everyday interaction (Afifi & Burgoon, 2000; Burgoon, 1978, 1983, 1993, 1995; Burgoon & Hale, 1988). We introduced this theory in Chapter 1, but it has particular relevance for our discussion of touch. You may remember that, according to the theory, we develop expectations for appropriate nonverbal behaviors in ourselves and others, based on our cultural backgrounds, personal experiences, and knowledge of those with whom we interact. When those expectations are violated, we become more engaged in what's happening and the nature of our relationship with the violator becomes a critical factor as we attempt to interpret and respond to the violation.

You can see how this theory involves appropriateness because it pertains to actions people believe adhere to or violate a rule or expectation for both private and public behavior. But the ramifications for a violation in the realm of touch are more serious than for other nonverbal codes. It's one thing to stand too close to someone when talking; it's another thing to touch someone in the

chapter eight

wrong place on his or her body or to touch inappropriately in a given situation. Bodily contact is more intrusive and personal than a proxemic violation, an inappropriate gesture, or staring.

Tie signs are nonverbal behaviors that not only express affection but also signal the status of the relationship to other people (Morris, 1977). Making out is an extreme example of a tie sign; others include holding hands, walking arm in arm or with one person's arm around the other's shoulders, touching each other's faces, and so forth. Some people claim that they engage in this form of touching simply to convey affection, but they shouldn't forget that their behavior exists in a social context, one in which the touch communicates volumes to onlookers about the nature of the relationship, as well as about their touch ethic. Many of us are uncomfortable with PDAs (public displays of affection).

According to expectancy violations theory, we register nonverbal violations and react to adapt to the circumstances. If the violating person is what Burgoon terms a "rewarding" communicator, meaning the person has high credibility, status, and attractiveness (in personality or physicality), we may view the behavior as less of a violation and simply adjust our expectations. We may even reciprocate or mimic the behavior. However, if the violator is not a rewarding communicator, we're likely to use reactive nonverbal behaviors in an effort to compensate for or correct the situation. Our tendency in a rules-violation situation is to attempt to correct the violation nonverbally before resorting to verbal communication. We're more likely to try to disregard or ignore a minor inappropriate touch, such as an overly enthusiastic handshake, than to say to someone, "Please don't grip my hand so hard when you shake it."

Appropriateness: Location, Duration, and Intensity

Besides using expectancy violation theory to help you understand how nonverbal communication functions, three aspects related to touch can help you gauge its appropriateness. The first is **location**, which we mean in two senses: First, the location on the body where contact is made has a significant impact on whether we deem a touch appropriate or inappropriate. At some point in your life, you've probably heard the unfortunate comparison of touch exploration to the game of baseball (i.e., getting to first or second base, scoring a home run), but the metaphor does help illustrate our point about the importance of body location in a judgment of touch appropriateness. Socially speaking, you have rules about who can touch you, when, where on your body, and in what setting. Maybe you're involved in a romantic relationship but believe abstinence is best for you right now; to you—at this point in your life and development—sexual activity with your partner may involve only kissing and petting, not intercourse or oral sex. That's considered a rule or expectation about intimate touch—who can touch you when and where on your body. Such a rule must be respected and adhered to by your intimate partner(s).

The second sense of location with regard to touch means the setting or context within which the touch occurs. We mentioned PDAs earlier; many of us were raised to believe that intimate touching, such as making out or petting, should be done only in private—never in public, not even at a party. Others of us have different rules, meaning any form of touch is okay, anytime and any-place. But think of other examples: When you meet a date's or partner's parents for the first time, should you merely shake hands with them or hug them? Does this vary, depending on the cultural background of the family, or whether it's the mother or the father you're meeting? If you extend a touch that's received as inappropriate, should you say something or just remember never to do that again?

WHAT WOULD *YOU* DO

Marisa works part-time at the campus library and, for the most part, she likes her job. It's quiet, of-fers flexible hours, and she gets to catch up on studying during slow times. Well, she likes her job except for one thing: her supervisor. He's a graduate student who works at the library while finishing his master's degree, and he's only a few years older than Marisa. She cringes when he comes near her while she's working, because she just knows he's going to circle around her desk, reach for her shoulders, and give her the old inappropriate backrub.

Her boss must think a backrub is appropriate between a supervisor and an employee because he does it all the time, never wondering if Marisa appreciates the touch. Marisa knows he's married, so she doesn't think the backrubs are flirta-tious or sexual—they're just weird. His actions embarrass Marisa and make her feel disrespected. Sometimes when she sees her boss coming toward her, she gets up from her desk and makes herself busy so she can avoid the unwanted touch.

What would you do in Marisa's situation? Would you continue the diversionary tactics, such as getting up from your desk before the supervisor moves closer, or would you just quit the job? Would you report the unwanted touch to your supervisor's supervisor? Would you say something right to your supervisor's face, explaining that you find the backrubs inappropriate and asking him or her to refrain from touching you, or would that just be too weird or scary? Do you deem the supervisor's backrubs a form of sexual harassment?

The next aspect related to appropriateness is **duration**, meaning how long a touch lasts. Touches can be fleeting or long-lasting, but you have rules about this, too. Gy-necological or prostate exams can seem to take *forever*, as though you're in a time warp. These situations pose a paradox—non-intimate touches ex-tended to our most intimate areas of the body—so they can be confusing and uncomfortable. If doctors are wise and well trained, they'll do all they can to reduce the discomfort their unwelcome touch causes and get these exams over with quickly. As a less awkward example, consider the basic embrace: A long hug communicates more emotion or intense affection than a short hug (Guerrero & Floyd, 2006; Harjunen, Spapé, Ahmed, Jacucci, & Ravaja, 2017).

When we refer to the **intensity** of a touch, we mean the power, force, or concentration of bodily contact. If you're anxious about a job interview, you might grip a bit harder when you shake hands with your potential employer. If you're nervous about kissing your date good night on a first date, you might miscalculate the amount of pressure to apply to the lips. Our emotions influence the amount of intensity we put into a touch (Hertenstein, Holmes, McCullough, & Keltner, 2009; Katsumi, Dolcos, Kim, Sung, & Dolcos, 2017; Thompson & Hampton, 2011).

When judging the appropriateness of a touch, consider location (on the body and also the physical setting), duration, and intensity.

REMEMBER

Remember! 8.4

Expectancy violations model	Model that suggests that we develop expectations for appropriate nonverbal behaviors in ourselves and others; when expectations are violated, we experience heightened arousal and the nature of our relationships becomes critical
Tie sign	Nonverbal behaviors that express affection between people and also signal the status of the relationship to others
Location	Area of the body where physical contact is made; setting or context within which a touch occurs
Duration	How long a touch lasts
Intensity	Power, force, or concentration of bodily contact

APPLICATIONS OF HAPTICS RESEARCH ■ ■ ■

Many interesting applications of the research on haptics continue to emerge as we seek to better understand this powerful, yet complicated code of nonverbal communication. Here, we briefly overview some provocative topics of research on touch.

Culture and Touch

As we've said, like other nonverbal communication codes, touch is culturally rooted, which means that we should interpret the meaning of a touch within its appropriate cultural context. Much was made of the public "bromance" between U.S. President Donald Trump and France's President Emmanuel Macron when they met at the White House in April of 2018. The two men showed remarkable touch between them, in terms of frequency and intimacy, with lots of hand holding and embracing. Trump at one point even

Trump and Macron touched often during their visit at the White House.

picked dandruff off of Macron's suit at a photo shoot, which many thought odd and inappropriate (Hirschfeld Davis & Rogers, 2018).

Nonverbal communication scholar Edward T. Hall (1966, 1981) believed that cultures can be distinguished according to two categories of nonverbal behavior: the distances at which members of a given culture interact and the touch that occurs between members (haptics). You may recall our discussion of Hall's zones of space in Chapter 4 on proxemics. With regard for haptics, Hall terms those cultures exhibiting frequent touch **contact cultures**, while those exhibiting infrequent touch are called **noncontact cultures**. Over time, these labels have evolved into **high-contact cultures** and **low-contact cultures**, given no evidence to suggest that a culture exists without any physical contact among its members. High-contact cultures include Latin America, India, France, and Arab countries (Andersen, 2011; Kras, 1989); low-contact cultures include Germany and Northern European nations, North America (which, of course, includes the United States), and many Asian countries, such as China, Japan, Korea, Indonesia, and Malaysia (Barnlund, 1989; Kim, 1977). Other research supports Hall's cultural categories; Morris (1971, 1977) observed that people in low-contact cultures engage in far less everyday, casual touch and are more restrictive in their public touching than are people in Mediterranean and Latin cultures.

Cultural distinctions can be easily noted in the greetings members of different cultural groups give one another (Axtell, 1999). French Canadian greetings look a lot like those Americans use (handshakes for men, brief hugs for women); Puerto Rican and Italian women often grasp each other's shoulders and kiss both cheeks when greeting. Saudi Arabian men shake right hands to greet each other, and may also place their left hands on each other's shoulders while kissing both cheeks (Moore, Hickson, & Stacks, 2013).

Offering Comfort

As hard as it is, think of a time when you grieved the death of someone—someone close enough that you attended the funeral or memorial service, then gathered at someone's home or other location after the service. (If you haven't had this experience, think of something comparable.) What do you recall seeing? Most likely, you saw a lot of touch, even if you didn't consciously register it as such at the time. Were people hugging, holding each other and crying, patting hands or backs, or extending other kinds of comforting touches? When emotions run high, people tend to reach out to each other and make bodily contact, *but not everyone*. Some people don't want to be physically close or in contact with other people when they're grieving, and we have to be sensitive to this and not impose our will or needs on such people (Floyd & Ray, 2016).

One of the most prolific scholars to study the communication of emotional support was Brant Burleson, whose research over decades and with various colleagues explored verbal and nonverbal means of offering comfort to people in emotional distress (Bodie, Burleson, & Jones, 2012; Burleson, 1982, 1985, 1994; Burleson, Albrecht, & Sarason, 1994; Burleson et al., 2005; Burleson et al., 2011; Burleson & Goldsmith, 1998; Burleson & Samter, 1985; MacGeorge, Feng, & Burleson, 2011). Since Burleson's untimely death, his work on comfort and support has been extended by family members, colleagues, and students (MacGeorge et al., 2016). Burleson (2003) contended that the communication of comfort and emotional support is critical to relationships, and that such behavior can help people establish, maintain, and even repair close relationships. This body of research shows that people who are able to provide emotional support for others are perceived as more likable, popular, and socially attractive than people who cannot extend this kind of support to others.

Touch is an important way we express comfort and emotional support (Floyd, 2015; Guerrero & Floyd, 2006). One team of researchers in the 1980s interviewed women who had recently given birth, to find out their views on touch during labor (Stolte & Friedman, 1980). Overwhelmingly, the women viewed touches they received during labor positively. They reported supportive feelings from being touched on the hand by their husbands, family members, and nurses, but negative feelings from being touched by physicians on their abdomen or pelvic area (understandably!). Related research shows that people's brain activity, specifically their fear response, revealed by an MRI is altered when they hold the hand of a medical staff member or a loved one during a scan (Case et al., 2016; Coan, Schaefer, & Davidson, 2006). Physical affection alters our hormone levels and reduces the stress we feel in our bodies (Floyd et al., 2018; Floyd, Pauley, & Hesse, 2010; Floyd & Riforgiate, 2008). Again,

© Antonio Guillem/Shutterstock.com

Simple closeness and touches can offer comfort and support to people who are grieving, but not everyone who grieves views touch the same way.

as we've said for all the topics within this chapter, the appropriateness of extending a touch depends on the situation and the people involved. Sensitivity and a keen awareness of the power of nonverbal cues are important in situations where an offer of comfort could make a lot of difference.

Biological Sex, Relationships, and Touch

Over several decades of research on touch and **biological sex** (meaning one's sex typically assigned at birth), results are consistent: Touch seems to be more a woman's "realm" than a man's (Guerrero & Floyd, 2006). As one team of researchers put it, women have a "greater theoretic bandwidth of appropriate affectionate behaviors" than do men (Floyd & Morman, 1997, p. 292). Research findings have consistently revealed the following:

1. Women express more nonverbal affection than men.
2. Women receive more touch, from both men and other women, than do men.
3. Women engage in more frequent and more intimate same-sex touch than do men.
4. Women are more comfortable with touch in general, and same-sex touch in specific, than are men.
5. Women in heterosexual stable or married relationships are more likely to initiate touch than are their male partners.
6. Women perceive themselves as being more affectionate than men (Floyd, 1997, 2000; Hall & Veccia, 1990; Hanzal, Segrin, & Dorros, 2008; Harjunen, Spapé, Ahmed, Jacucci, & Ravaja, 2017; Harrison & Shortall, 2011; Jones, 1986; Major, Schmidlin, & Williams, 1990).

Some of these same researchers have tried to determine what's at the root of the differing touch behavior of men and women, with most agreeing that **homophobia** (a fear of being labeled homosexual or a general dislike of homosexual people) is the primary culprit. Yes, things have changed dramatically over the past decade, but it's a stretch to say that homophobia isn't still affecting people's perceptions in the United States and other countries around the world (Dolinski, 2010). Let's say, for example, that you see two women holding hands as they walk through a shopping mall somewhere in the United States. Are you likely to jump to the conclusion that they're lesbians, or might you simply think they're good friends or sisters, comfortable with expressing their affection and connection in public? Now picture two men doing the same thing—holding hands as they window-shop. What interpretation comes to mind first? Homophobia leads men—straight, gay, bisexual, trans, and queer—to seek covert means of expressing affection and affiliation with one another, because the negative sanctions associated with more overt expressions are serious (Bowman & Compton, 2014; Knofler & Imhof, 2007; Morman & Floyd, 1998; Puckett et al., 2017). So before assuming that women are just better than men at expressing their emotions and affection through touch, consider the societal constraints that have operated for a very long time and that continue to affect this form of nonverbal communication.

chapter eight

An interesting line of research documents sex differences in perceptions of touch. Scholar Antonia Abbey's (1982, 1987, 1991; Abbey, Zawacki, & Buck, 2005) multidecade research consistently shows that, among heterosexuals, men tend to misinterpret women's touches as being more intimate than the women intend. In terms of Heslin's categories, the biggest discrepancy occurs between the friendship/warmth and love/intimacy categories. Abbey found that men often interpret women's touches as indications of love and intimacy (or general romantic interest and attraction), leading to sexual arousal, rather than as friendship or warmth, as intended. However, some men believe that women send mixed signals regarding intimacy. Women may intend to be flirtatious, but when men read more serious intent into the touches and other nonverbal behaviors and want to pursue the encounter, women may back off and contend that they were just "being friendly." These are complicated relational waters.

OUT OF THE CLASSROOM
onto the page

Hugging is *everywhere* these days. Are we a less uptight culture than we used to be? Are people so touch deprived that everybody hugs everybody nowadays? Only a few short decades ago, American men rarely hugged other men. Chalk it up to homophobia or cultural evolution, but the "bro hug" is a relatively new development (Bowman & Compton, 2014). The bro hug starts with a hand clasp (not a traditional handshake), continues with the clasped hands moving up between the participants' chests as they draw toward each other, and culminates with one arm around each other's shoulders, palm to back. It's usually a very quick exchange and concludes with a pat or slap on the back but it's common and tends to be very different from the female-to-female or male-to-female hug. What's the main difference? Breasts.

In a recent class session, one of your authors and her students discussed sex differences and the bro hug, realizing that men tend not to hug women this way because the clasped hands would land on the woman's breasts during the hug, which would likely be perceived as inappropriate. Women rarely clasp hands before hugging, probably for the same reason. But why are so many men more comfortable with hugging as a sign of liking and affection these days compared with the past? Perhaps, as we said, fears about being perceived as homosexual have lessened over time; it's more common to see men hugging than it used to be, which some people view as a positive sign that things have loosened up, that behavior isn't so restrictive, and that men can show affection for their buddies without being teased or criticized (or worse).

Nonverbal cues of touch and affection are fascinating to note, because they reveal volumes about the nature of people's relationships. Next time you're out at a social event, watch the touches that pass between people. Can you tell if people are friends or "more than friends"? Can you tell from people's touch if they're on a first date or if they've been together a long time? If a couple has been together awhile, the need or desire to touch publicly usually diminishes. Partners are more likely to sit across from each other at a booth or table, rather than side by side, and not spend as much time together at a party or other social gathering.

Today men can show affection for each other without fear of being criticized.

Physical affection is critical to the formation and continuance of successful romantic relationships, the development of intimacy, and satisfaction with one's partner (Andersen, Guerrero, & Jones, 2006; Bello, Brandau-Brown, Zhang, & Ragsdale, 2010; Floyd, 2016; Floyd & Hesse, 2017; Horan & Booth-Butterfield, 2010, 2013; Miller, Denes, Diaz, & Buck, 2014; Rancourt, MacKinnon, Snowball, & Rosen, 2017). In the case of marriage, studies have produced interesting findings. In the 1970s, Heslin and colleagues used his touch categories to better understand married partners' interpretations of touches

What kind of touch is operating in this photo that clues you about the nature of the relationship between these two people?

from their partners (Nguyen, Heslin, & Nguyen, 1975, 1976). In general, married people in these studies held a positive view of touch but associated touch more with sexual activity than did unmarried subjects. Other studies showed that people in long-term relationships, including marriages, touched each other less frequently and less intimately than did people who were working to establish a romantic relationship or to repair one that was in trouble (Guerrero & Andersen, 1991, 1994; Patterson, Gardner, Burr, Hubler, & Roberts, 2012). Scholars explain that *quantity* of touch appears to be more important when trying to get a relationship off the ground or back on track, while *quality* of touch becomes more important over the long haul of a relationship.

Contact (high-contact) cultures	Cultures exhibiting frequent touch
Noncontact (low-contact) cultures	Cultures exhibiting infrequent touch
Biological sex	One's sex typically assigned at birth
Homophobia	A fear of being labeled homosexual or a general dislike of homosexual people

Remember!
8.5

Power, Status, and Touch

In other codes chapters of this book, we describe nonverbal cues that communicate power and status. For example, in Chapter 3 we explore several status cues related to the environment (e.g., corner offices, expensive furniture, the presence of gatekeepers to buffer the boss from subordinates and the public), the physical appearance cue of height in Chapter 5, kinesic cues of stance and posture in Chapter 6, and ways people use their voices to command attention and influence others in Chapter 9. It follows, then, that certain touch behaviors work in tandem with other cues to communicate power and status (Hall, 2011; Sekerdej, Simao, Waldzus, & Brito, 2018).

Research shows that powerful people tend to initiate touch toward others, but generally they don't receive touch from lower-status people unless it comes in the form of reciprocation or a formalized greeting, such as a handshake (Ames, 2018; Burgoon & Dunbar, 2006; Dunbar & Abra, 2010; Hall, 1996). Say an employee enters her or his boss's office for a meeting. If the boss extends his or her hand for a handshake with the employee, the employee should reciprocate because that's expected and proper behavior in American culture. But if the boss also places his or her free hand on the employee's shoulder, should the employee do the same—put her or his free hand on the boss's shoulder? In general, the answer is no, because, as we've said elsewhere in this chapter, placing a hand on someone's shoulder can be viewed as a dominance behavior, so the employee most likely should not reciprocate this touch.

Typically, higher-status people are afforded more liberty in initiating touch; lower-status people are advised to wait for nonverbal cues from those of higher status. It's hard to imagine a situation in which a lower-status person would initiate an unprovoked touch toward a boss—such as giving a boss a hug or a slap on the back. Such nonverbal actions would not likely go over well, but of course it depends on the situation and the organizational climate. It's commonplace in many organizations for bosses to initiate touch with employees. But these days, more than ever, that touch has to be appropriate, professional, and non-intimate, or else you could be looking at a charge of sexual harassment (Boddy, 2017; Bernstein, 2018; Paludi, 2015).

High-status people also have more prerogative to violate nonverbal expectations, because it's less likely that their actions will be perceived negatively than if a low-status person does the same thing (Bailey & Kelly, 2015; Brey & Shutts, 2015; Wiltermuth, Raj, & Wood, 2018). For example, what if your boss came into the workplace one day looking disheveled and upset, suddenly started crying, and reached out to you for comfort? Would you provide your boss with a supportive embrace or arm around the shoulder? While the situation would no doubt be startling

Who's the more dominant guy in this photo? Can you tell by a touch if power, status, and dominance is being conveyed?

and awkward, such behavior would likely evoke different responses and interpretations if a low-status person did the same thing—crumpling into a sobbing heap in the boss's arms. Powerful people are afforded more benefit of the doubt, verbally and nonverbally, than are less powerful people.

UNDERSTANDING HAPTICS: APPLYING THE REFLEXIVE CYCLE OF NONVERBAL COMMUNICATION DEVELOPMENT

Applying the Reflexive Cycle to your touch behavior can be eye-opening, because you likely haven't thought all that much about how, when, and where you touch other people, or about how you view or process the touch you receive. It's important to work through the cycle because touch is such a powerful nonverbal cue, with significant rewards when extended appropriately and serious sanctions when done inappropriately.

Since the first step in the cycle is self-awareness, let's address some questions: What's your touch ethic? What kinds of touch do you like and dislike giving, as well as receiving? For example, you may not be a massage person; paying someone to rub your neck may seem like the last thing you want to do. How much of your touch ethic comes from what you observed and experienced with your parents and siblings? How comfortable are you with touching other people? Perhaps you're comfortable touching only those people you know well, keeping touch ritualized with strangers or new people you meet. Or perhaps you're fairly "touchy" with people in general. What rules do you have about appropriate touch across situations, locations, and people? This inventory of your touch ethic should take some time, because it affects all the other steps in the cycle.

Once you've inventoried your touch ethic and behavior, you may have identified some areas you want to improve or change. Maybe you're nervous about job interviewing, fearing that your handshake and other nonverbal cues will hurt your chances of getting a job. In several of our communication courses, we have students practice professional handshakes with one another, because this simple form of touch often gets overlooked. Students just assume they know how to shake someone's hand properly, but a weak handshake, at least in American culture, sends negative signals. It's surprising but often the case that many college men haven't had much experience shaking hands with a woman, so practicing this important nonverbal cue in the safety of the classroom is generally appreciated by our students. The last thing anyone wants to do is communicate disrespect by offering what career services staff call the "fingerella"—that limp, weak-fingered, half-handed touch—instead of a robust handshake.

The third phase of the Reflexive Cycle involves inventorying others' touch behavior. If you really want to become savvy when it comes to touch, become more of a people watcher, because you'll learn a lot from observing other people. You've no doubt seen this in movies: The suave guy approaches a woman or a group of women in a social scene while his buddies look on, noting the smooth way he makes connections, especially physical ones. (Ryan Gosling comes to mind.) We're not suggesting that you observe people and merely copy what they do, because touch is more complex than that, but you can get some pointers from watching other people, noting things that work as well as the negative consequences of inappropriate touch.

Your next step in the Reflexive Cycle is to interact with others, enacting any haptic changes you've decided are appropriate, and gauge how your nonverbal behaviors transact with others'. If you change your handshake, for instance, do people notice? Do potential employers react any differently because of such a change? We've seen some of our students decide to start shaking hands with more professors and classmates because they like the mature tone such a touch sets. This behavior almost always receives a positive response. Just remember that a purposeful change in touch behavior, because it involves bodily contact, is likely to register significantly with people, so be prepared for this.

So you've inventoried yourself, begun to make changes in your touch behavior, inventoried others' approaches to touch, and engaged in mutual transaction of behavior (such that your touch impacts other people and theirs impacts you). Now the final phase of the Reflexive Cycle involves an evaluation of the whole process. What did you learn about your own and others' touch behavior that makes you a better communicator? We've said it before and we'll say it again: The reflexive process includes a courageous inventory of yourself (your background and upbringing, behavior, and attitudes), a willingness to experiment and attempt some change, keen observational skills of others' behavior, and more social experience, as you put your new behaviors into action, transact with others, note the results, and reevaluate.

SUMMARY ■ ■ ■

This chapter was devoted to haptics—the study of human touch—as a powerful code of nonverbal communication. We began by discussing how touch is a complex and powerful nonverbal cue, because, unlike other codes, touch involves bodily contact between people. We then explored the touch ethic, meaning our beliefs about and preferences for touch, because the touch ethic affects how we touch other people, as well as how we interpret their touches toward us.

Next, we delved into the topic of the role of touch in human development, beginning with research on the importance of touch to infants and children. We then discussed the detrimental effects of being deprived of touch, especially for elder adults in American society, who tend to be the most touch deprived among us.

Because touch is such a complicated nonverbal code, category systems have been developed to help us understand and study it. We first overviewed Heslin's categories, which include functional/professional, social/polite, friendship/warmth, love/intimacy, and sexual arousal types of touch. Research indicates that problems arise when men view women's touches as indications of love/intimacy or sexual arousal but women intend these touches to indicate merely friendship. A second category system helps us understand the meanings behind certain touches; Jones and Yarbrough offer six primary meanings for touch: positive affect (affectionate), playful, control, ritualistic, task-related, and accidental touches.

In the next section of this chapter, we examined ways we can gauge the appropriateness of touch, including touches we extend to other people and touches we receive from them. Expectancy violations theory helps us understand this phenomenon, because violating someone's expectations regarding bodily contact can have serious consequences. We also explored location, duration, and intensity of touch, which offer clues about appropriateness.

We outlined some of the many applications of haptics research, beginning with a discussion of touch as a culturally rooted nonverbal behavior. We then explored the communicative power of touches such as hugs, pats on the hand or back, and pats on the arm near the shoulder, which are often used to comfort or show support for people in need. Another topic studied over decades by communication scholars is sex differences in touch behavior. Findings indicate that women touch people in general more often and more intimately than do men; women also receive more touches from both men and women. One explanation for this phenomenon that has consistently received support in research is that homophobia in society affects men's touching behavior, causing them to look for covert means of conveying affection for fear that their masculinity and sexuality will be called into question.

We examined the complicated topic of touch within ongoing, committed relationships, because behavioral patterns of touch seem to change depending on the stage of a relationship a couple is experiencing. Research shows that quality of touch appears to be more critical for marriage, as opposed to quantity of touch, which is important in new relationships.

Our final application of haptics research pertained to touches that reveal a person's power or status. Powerful, high-status people have more free rein regarding touch than do low-status people, but all touch in professional settings needs to be expressed carefully because of the potential for such actions to be interpreted as sexual harassment. Finally, we applied the Reflexive Cycle of Nonverbal Communication Development to the code of touch, in terms of inventorying your own touch behavior, making any necessary changes, observing and inventorying others' use of touch, transacting with other people and understanding how touch operates within interaction, and, finally, reexamining the whole process so you can become a more effective communicator.

DISCUSSION STARTERS ■ ■ ■ ■

1. Think of ways that touch has power. Why do we suggest that bodily contact is the most powerful code of nonverbal communication, compared with eye contact or proxemics?
2. When we asked the question, "What is your touch ethic?" in this chapter, were you able to respond? What lessons did you learn from your parents and siblings regarding appropriate touch as you were growing up? Have you ever been in a romantic relationship that changed your touch ethic?
3. Discuss some causes of touch deprivation among elderly members of our society, and then inventory your own behavior regarding touch you extend to your elders. Do you have some changes to make?
4. How can people get the meanings of touch confused, such as interpreting someone's friendship/warmth touch (one of Heslin's categories) as an indication of love or romantic interest? Can category confusion alter a person's touch ethic?
5. Why do people seem to have such varying views on the appropriateness of touch? Recall a situation in which either you or a friend viewed someone's touch as inappropriate, because of location, duration, or intensity, but the other person thought the touch was perfectly acceptable. How can this kind of perceptual difference exist?
6. Does your experience match studies that have found that touch among intimate partners changes over time, meaning that touch becomes more about quality than quantity the

longer two people are in a relationship? Is this trend a "relationship downer" or just something to be expected and coped with?

7. From either your travels or knowledge of other cultures, describe some cultural differences in touch behavior. If someone makes a cultural gaffe in the form of an inappropriate touch, what's the best way to handle the situation?

8. Have you worked with people who use touch as a means of conveying their power or status? How do you cope with workplace touches that can best be interpreted as "power plays"? How might inappropriate touches in the workplace be construed as sexual harassment?

REFERENCES

Abbey, A. (1982). Sex differences in attributions for friendly behavior: Do males misperceive females' friendliness? *Journal of Personality and Social Psychology, 42*, 830–838.

Abbey, A. (1987). Misperception of friendly behavior as sexual interest: A survey of naturally occurring incidents. *Psychology of Women Quarterly, 11*, 173–194.

Abbey, A. (1991). Misperception as an antecedent of acquaintance rape: A consequence of ambiguity in communication between men and women. In A. Parrot & L. Bechhofer (Eds.), *Acquaintance rape: The hidden crime* (pp. 96–111). New York: Wiley.

Abbey, A., Zawacki, T., & Buck, P. O. (2005). The effects of past sexual assault perpetration and alcohol consumption on reactions to women's mixed signals. *Journal of Social and Clinical Psychology, 25*, 129–157.

Afifi, W. A., & Burgoon, J. K. (2000). The impact of violations on uncertainty and the consequences for attractiveness. *Human Communication Research, 26*, 203–233.

Allen, K. (2003). Are pets a healthy pleasure? The influence of pets on blood pressure. *Current Directions in Psychological Science, 12*, 236–239.

Ames, M. F. (2018). *A good firm handshake (and other essential business tips).* Hilton, NY. Retrieved from michelle@agoodfirmhandshake.com

Andersen, P. A. (2011). Tactile traditions: Cultural differences and similarities in haptic communication. In M. J. Hertenstein & S. J. Weiss (Eds.), *The handbook of touch: Neuroscience, behavioral, and health perspectives* (pp. 351–371). New York: Springer.

Andersen, P. A., Guerrero, L. K., & Jones, S. M. (2006). Nonverbal behavior in intimate interactions and intimate relationships. In V. Manusov & M. L. Patterson (Eds.), *The SAGE handbook of nonverbal communication* (pp. 259–277). Thousand Oaks, CA: Sage.

Axtell, R. E. (1999). Initiating interaction: Greetings and beckonings across the world. In L. K. Guerrero, J. A. DeVito, & M. L. Hecht (Eds.), *The nonverbal communication reader: Classic and contemporary readings* (2nd ed., pp. 395–405). Prospect Heights, IL: Waveland.

Aznar, A., & Tenenbaum, H. R. (2016). Parent-child positive touch: Gender, age, and task differences. *Journal of Nonverbal Behavior, 40*, 317–333.

Bailey, A. H., & Kelly, S. D. (2015). Picture power: Gender versus body language in perceived status. *Journal of Nonverbal Behavior, 39*, 317–337.

Barnlund, D. C. (1989). *Communicative styles of Japanese and Americans: Images and realities.* Belmont, CA: Wadsworth.

Bello, R. S., Brandau-Brown, F. E., Zhang, S., & Ragsdale, J. D. (2010). Verbal and nonverbal methods for expressing appreciation in friendships and romantic relationships: A cross-cultural comparison. *International Journal of Intercultural Relations, 34*, 294–302.

Bernstein, A. (2018). Preventing sexual harassment in the workplace. *Nursing and Residential Care.* https://doi.org/10.12968/nrec.2018.20.7.344

Boddy, C. R. (2017). Harassment in the workplace. In D. Poff & A. Michalos (Eds.), *Encyclopedia of business and professional ethics.* New York: Springer.

Bodie, G. D., Burleson, B. R., & Jones, S. M. (2012). Explaining the relationships among supportive message quality, evaluations, and outcomes: A dual-process approach. *Communication Monographs, 79*, 1–22.

Bowman, J. M., & Compton, B. L. (2014). Self-presentation, individual differences, and gendered evaluations of nonverbal greeting behaviors among close male friends. *The Journal of Men's Studies, 22*, 207–221.

Brey, E., & Shutts, K. (2015). Children use nonverbal cues to make inferences about social power. *Child Development, 86*, 276–286.

Bundgaard, K., & Nielsen, K. B. (2011). The art of holding hand: A fieldwork study outlining the significance of physical touch in facilities for short-term stay. *International Journal for Human Caring, 15*, 34–41.

Burgoon, J. K. (1978). A communication model of personal space violations: Explication and an initial test. *Human Communication Research, 4*, 129–142.

Burgoon, J. K. (1983). Nonverbal violations of expectations. In J. M. Weimann & R. P. Harrison (Eds.), *Nonverbal interaction* (pp. 77–111). Beverly Hills, CA: Sage.

Burgoon, J. K. (1993). Interpersonal expectations, expectancy violations, and emotional communication. *Journal of Language and Social Psychology, 12,* 30–48.

Burgoon, J. K. (1995). Cross-cultural and intercultural applications of expectancy violations. In R. L. Wiseman (Ed.), *Intercultural communication theory* (Vol. 19, pp. 194–214). Thousand Oaks, CA: Sage.

Burgoon, J. K., & Dunbar, N. E. (2006). Nonverbal expressions of dominance and power in human relationships. In V. Manusov & M. L. Patterson (Eds.), *The SAGE handbook of nonverbal communication* (pp. 279–297). Thousand Oaks, CA: Sage.

Burgoon, J. K., & Hale, J. L. (1988). Nonverbal expectancy violations: Model elaboration and application to immediacy behaviors. *Communication Monographs, 55*, 58–79.

Burleson, B. R. (1982). The development of comforting communication skills in childhood and adolescence. *Child Development, 53*, 1578–1588.

Burleson, B. R. (1985). The production of comforting messages: Social-cognitive foundations. *Journal of Language and Social Psychology, 4*, 253–273.

Burleson, B. R. (1994). Comforting messages: Features, functions, and outcomes. In J. A. Daly & J. M. Wiemann (Eds.), *Personality and interpersonal communication* (pp. 305–349). Newbury Park, CA: Sage.

Burleson, B. R. (2003). Emotional support skills. In J. O. Greene & B. R. Burleson (Eds.), *Handbook of communication and social interaction skills* (pp. 551–594). Mahwah, NJ: Erlbaum.

Burleson, B. R., Albrecht, T., & Sarason, I. G. (1994). *The communication of social support: Messages, interactions, relationships, and community.* Thousand Oaks, CA: Sage.

Burleson, B. R., & Goldsmith, D. J. (1998). How the comforting process works: Alleviating emotional distress through conversationally induced reappraisals. In P. A. Andersen & L. K. Guerrero (Eds.), *Handbook of communication and emotion: Research, theory, applications, and contexts* (pp. 246–280). San Diego, CA: Academic Press.

Burleson, B. R., Hanasono, L. K., Bodie, G. D., Holmstrom, A. J., McCullough, J. D., Rack, J. J., et al. (2011). Are gender differences in responses to supportive communication a matter of ability, motivation, or both? Reading patterns of situation effects through the lens of a dual-process theory. *Communication Quarterly, 59*, 37–60.

Burleson, B. R., & Samter, W. (1985). Consistencies in theoretical and naive evaluations of comforting messages. *Communication Monographs, 52*, 103–123.

Burleson, B. R., Samter, W., Jones, S. M., Kunkel, A., Holmstrom, A. J., Morenson, S. T., et al. (2005). Which comforting messages *really* work best? A different perspective on Lemieux and Tighe's "receiver perspective." *Communication Research Reports, 22*, 87–100.

Case, L. K., Laubacher, C. M., Olausson, H., Wang, B., Spagnolo, P. A., & Bushnell, M. C. (2016). Encoding of touch intensity but not pleasantness in human primary somatosensory cortex. *The Journal of Neuroscience, 36*, 5850–5860.

Cekaite, A., & Kvist, M. H. (2017). The comforting touch: Tactile intimacy and talk in managing children's distress. *Research on Language and Social Interaction, 50*, 109–127.

Cherniak, E. P., & Cherniak, A. R. (2014). The benefit of pets and animal-assisted therapy to the health of older individuals. *Current Gerontology and Geriatrics Research, 2014*. https://dx.doi.org/10.1155/2014/623203

Coakley, A. B., & Duffy, M. E. (2010). The effect of therapeutic touch on postoperative patients. *Journal of Holistic Nursing, 28*, 193–200.

Coan, J. A., Schaefer, H. S., & Davidson, R. J. (2006). Lending a hand: Social regulation of the neural response to threat. *Psychological Science, 17*, 1032–1039.

Cocksedge, S., George, B., Renwick, S., & Chew-Graham, C. A. (2013). Touch in primary care consultations: Qualitative investigation of doctors' and patients' perceptions. *British Journal of General Practice, 63*, e283–e290.

Colombo, G., Dello Buono, M., Smania, K., Raviola, R., & De Leo, D. (2006). Pet therapy and institutionalized elderly: A study on 144 cognitively unimpaired subjects. *Archives of Gerontology and Geriatrics, 42*, 207–216.

Cordes, K., Egmose, I., Smith-Nielsen, J., Koppe, S., & Vaever, M. S. (2017). Maternal touch in caregiving of mothers with and without postpartum depression. *Infant Behavior and Development, 49*, 182–191.

DiBiase, R., & Gunnoe, J. (2004). Gender and culture differences in touching behavior. *Journal of Social Psychology, 144*, 49–62.

Dolinski, D. (2010). Touch, compliance, and homophobia. *Journal of Nonverbal Behavior, 34*, 179–192.

Dunbar, N. E. (2004). Dyadic power theory: Constructing a communication-based theory of relational power. *Journal of Family Communication, 4*, 235–248.

Dunbar, N. E., & Abra, G. (2010). Observations of dyadic power in interpersonal interaction. *Communication Monographs, 77*, 657–684.

Ernst, L. S. (2013). Animal-assisted therapy: Paws with a cause. *Nursing Management, 44*, 16–20.

Feldman, R. (2011). Maternal touch and the developing infant. In M. J. Hertenstein & S. J. Weiss (Eds.), *The handbook of touch: Neuroscience, behavioral, and health perspectives* (pp. 373–408). New York: Springer.

chapter eight

Feldman, R., Eidelman, A. L., Sirota, L., & Weller, A. (2002). Comparison of skin-to-skin (kangaroo) and traditional care: Parenting outcomes and preterm infant development. *Pediatrics, 110*, 16–26.

Field, T. (1998). Touch therapy effects on development. *International Journal of Behavioral Development, 22*, 779–797.

Field, T. (2000). Infant massage therapy. In C. H. Zeanah (Ed.), *Handbook of infant mental health* (2nd ed., pp. 494–500). New York: Guilford.

Field, T. (2002). Violence and touch deprivation in adolescents. *Adolescence, 37*, 735–749.

Field, T. (2005). Touch deprivation and aggression against self among adolescents. In D. M. Stoff & E. J. Susman (Eds.), *Developmental psychobiology of aggression* (pp. 117–140). New York: Cambridge University Press.

Field, T. (2011). Massage therapy: A review of recent research. In M. J. Hertenstein & S. J. Weiss (Eds.), *The handbook of touch: Neuroscience, behavioral, and health perspectives* (pp. 455–468). New York: Springer.

Fine, A. (Ed.). (2010). *Handbook on animal-assisted therapy: Theoretical foundations and guidelines for practice* (3rd ed.). London: Elsevier.

Floyd, K. (1997). Communicating affection in dyadic relationships: An assessment of behavior and expectancies. *Communication Quarterly, 45*, 68–80.

Floyd, K. (2000). Affectionate same-sex touch: The influence of homophobia on observers' perceptions. *Journal of Social Psychology, 140*, 774–788.

Floyd, K. (2015). *The loneliness cure: Six strategies for finding real connections in your life.* Fort Collins, CO: Adams Media.

Floyd, K. (2016). Affection deprivation is associated with physical pain and poor sleep quality. *Communication Studies, 67*, 379–398.

Floyd, K., & Hesse, C. (2017). Affection deprivation is conceptually and empirically distinct from loneliness. *Western Journal of Communication, 81*, 446–465.

Floyd, K., & Morman, M. T. (1997). Affectionate communication in nonromantic relationships: Influences of communicator, relational, and contextual factors. *Western Journal of Communication, 61*, 279–298.

Floyd, K., Pauley, P. M., & Hesse, C. (2010). State and trait affectionate communication buffer adults' stress reactions. *Communication Monographs, 77*, 618–636.

Floyd, K., Pauley, P. M., Hesse, C., Eden, J., Veksler, A. E., & Woo, N. T. (2018). Supportive communication is associated with markers of immunocompetence. *Southern Journal of Communication.* https://doi.org/10.1080/1041794X.2018.1488270

Floyd, K., & Ray, C. D. (2016). Thanks, but no thanks: Negotiating face threats when rejecting offers of unwanted social support. *Journal of Social & Personal Relationships, 34*, 1260–1276.

Floyd, K., & Riforgiate, S. (2008). Affectionate communication received from spouses predicts stress hormone levels in healthy adults. *Communication Monographs, 75*, 351–368.

Freiss, S. (2018, January 24). Ex-USA Gymnastics doctor gets up to 175 years as abuse victims applaud. Retrieved from https://www.reuters.com/article/us-gymnastics-usa-nassar/ex-usa-gymnastics-doctor-gets-up-to-175-years-as-abuse-victims-applaud-idUSKBN1FD1B9

Fulkerson, M. (2011). The unity of haptic touch. *Philosophical Psychology, 24*, 493–516.

Gleaves, T., & Lang, M. (2017). Kicking "no-touch" discourses into touch: Athletes' parents' constructions of appropriate coach-child athlete physical contact. *Journal of Sport & Social Issues, 41*, 191–211.

Green, L. (2017). The trouble with touch? New insights and observations on touch for social work and social care. *British Journal of Social Work, 47,* 773–792.

Guéguen, N., Meineri, S., & Charles-Sire, V. (2010). Improving medication adherence by using practitioner nonverbal techniques: A field experiment on the effect of touch. *Journal of Behavioral Medicine, 33,* 466–473.

Guerrero, L. K., & Andersen, P. A. (1991). The waxing and waning of relational intimacy: Touch as a function of relational stage, gender, and touch avoidance. *Journal of Social and Personal Relationships, 8,* 147–165.

Guerrero, L. K., & Andersen, P. A. (1994). Patterns of matching and initiation: Touch behavior and touch avoidance across romantic relationship stages. *Journal of Nonverbal Behavior, 18,* 137–153.

Guerrero, L. K., & Floyd, K. (2006). *Nonverbal communication in close relationships.* Mahwah, NJ: Erlbaum.

Hall, E. T. (1966). *The hidden dimension* (2nd ed.). Garden City, NY: Anchor/Doubleday.

Hall, E. T. (1981). *Beyond culture.* New York: Doubleday.

Hall, J. A. (1996). Touch, status, and gender at professional meetings. *Journal of Nonverbal Behavior, 20,* 23–44.

Hall, J. A. (2011). Gender and status patterns in social touch. In M. J. Hertenstein & S. J. Weiss (Eds.), *The handbook of touch: Neuroscience, behavioral, and health perspectives* (pp. 329–350). New York: Springer.

Hall, J. A., & Veccia, E. M. (1990). More "touching" observations: New insights on men, women, and interpersonal touch. *Journal of Personality and Social Psychology, 59,* 1155–1162.

Hanzal, A., Segrin, C., & Dorros, S. M. (2008). The role of marital status and age on men's and women's reactions to touch from a relational partner. *Journal of Nonverbal Behavior, 32,* 21–35.

Harjunen V. J., Spapé, M., Ahmed, I., Jacucci, G., & Ravaja, N. (2017). Individual differences in affective touch: Behavioral inhibition and gender define how an interpersonal touch is perceived. *Personality and Individual Differences, 107,* 88–95.

Harris, M. (2005, September 27). Survey finds Canadians increasingly out of touch: 44% want more physical contact in their lives. *Can West News Service,* for *National Post,* p. A2.

Harrison, C., Jones, R. S. P., & Huws, J. C. (2012). "We're people who don't touch": Exploring clinical psychologists' perspectives on their use of touch in therapy. *Counseling Psychology Quarterly, 25,* 277–287.

Harrison, M., & Shortall, J. (2011). Women and men in love: Who really feels it and says it first? *Journal of Social Psychology, 151,* 727–736.

Hart, J. (2012). Healing touch, therapeutic touch, and Reiki: Energy medicine advances in the medical community. *Alternative & Complementary Therapies, 18,* 309–313.

Hertenstein, M. J., Holmes, R., McCullough, M., & Keltner, D. (2009). The communication of emotion via touch. *Emotion, 9,* 566–573.

Hertenstein, M. J., & Keltner, D. (2011). Gender and the communication of emotion via touch. *Sex Roles, 64,* 70–80.

Hertenstein, M. J., Keltner, D., App, B., Bulleit, B. A., & Jaskolka, A. R. (2006). Touch communicates distinct emotions. *Emotion, 6,* 528–533.

Heslin, R. (1974). *Steps toward a taxonomy of touching.* Paper presented at the meeting of the Midwestern Psychological Association, Chicago, IL.

Hesse, C., & Mikkelson, A. C. (2017). Affection deprivation in romantic relationships. *Communication Quarterly, 65,* 20–38.

chapter eight

Hielscher, E., & Mahar, D. (2017). An exploration of the interaction between touch avoidance and the pleasant touch (C-tactile afferent) system. *Perception, 46*, 18–30.

Hirschfeld Davis, J., & Rogers, K. (2018, April 24). Le bromance: Trump and Macron, together again. Retrieved from https://www.nytimes.com/2018/04/24/us/politics/trump-macron-bromance.html

Horan, S., & Booth-Butterfield, M. (2010). Investigating affection: An investigation of affection exchanges theory and relational qualities. *Communication Quarterly, 58*, 394–413.

Horan, S., & Booth-Butterfield, M. (2013). Understanding the routine expression of deceptive affection in romantic relationships. *Communication Quarterly, 61*, 195–216.

Jakubiak, B. K., & Feeney, B. C. (2016a). A sense of security: Touch promotes state attachment security. *Social Psychological and Personality Science, 7*, 745–753.

Jakubiak, B. K., & Feeney, B. C. (2016b). Keep in touch: The effects of imagined touch support on stress and exploration. *Journal of Experimental Social Psychology, 65*, 59–67.

Jakubiak, B. K., & Feeney, B. C. (2017). Affectionate touch to promote relational, psychological, and physical well-being in adulthood: A theoretical model and review of the research. *Personality and Social Psychology Review, 21*, 228–252.

Johansson, C. (2013). Views on and perceptions of experiences of touch avoidance: An exploratory study. *Current Psychology, 32*, 44–59.

Jones, S. E. (1986). Sex differences in touch communication. *Western Journal of Speech Communication, 50*, 227–241.

Jones, S. E., & Brown, B. C. (1996). Touch attitudes and touch behaviors: Recollections of early childhood touch and social self-confidence. *Journal of Nonverbal Behavior, 20*, 147–163.

Jones, S. E., & Yarbrough, A. E. (1985). A naturalistic study of the meanings of touch. *Communication Monographs, 52*, 19–56.

Jourard, S. (1964). *The transparent self.* New York: Van Nostram-Reinhold.

Jourard, S. (1966). An exploratory study of body-accessibility. *British Journal of Social and Clinical Psychology, 5*, 221–231.

Jung, M., & Fouts, H. N. (2011). Multiple caregivers' touch interactions with young children among the Bofi foragers in Central Africa. *International Journal of Psychology, 46*, 24–32.

Kashdan, T. B., Doorley, J., Stiksma, M. C., & Hertenstein, M. J. (2016). Discomfort and avoidance of touch: New insights on the emotional deficits of social anxiety. *Cognition & Emotion, 31*, 1638–1646.

Katsumi, Y., Dolcos, S., Kim, S., Sung, J., & Dolcos, F. (2017). When nonverbal greetings "make it or break it": The role of ethnicity and gender in the effect of handshake on social appraisals. *Journal of Nonverbal Behavior, 41*, 345–365.

Kim, K. (1977). Misunderstanding in nonverbal communication: America and Korea. *Papers in Linguistics, 10*, 1–22.

Klopf, D. W., Thompson, C. A., Ishii, S., & Sallinen-Kuparinen, A. (1991). Nonverbal immediacy differences among Japanese, Finnish, and American university students. *Perceptual and Motor Skills, 73*, 209–210.

Knofler, T., & Imhof, M. (2007). Does sexual orientation have an impact on nonverbal behavior in interpersonal communication? *Journal of Nonverbal Behavior, 31*, 189–204.

Koole, S. L., Sin, M. T. A., & Schneider, I. K. (2014). Embodied terror management: Interpersonal touch alleviates existential concerns among individuals with low self-esteem. *Psychological Science, 25*, 30–37.

Kozlowska, L., & Doboszynska, A. (2012). Nurses' nonverbal methods of communicating with patients in the terminal phase. *International Journal of Palliative Nursing, 18*, 40–46.

Kras, E. S. (1989). *Management in two cultures: Bridging the gap between U.S. and Mexican managers.* Yarmouth, ME: Intercultural Press.

Lappin, G. (2005). Using infant massage following a mother's unfavorable neonatal intensive care unit experiences: A case study. *RE:view, 37*, 87–95.

Lederman, S. J., & Klatzky, R. L. (2009). Haptic perception: A tutorial. *Attention, Perception, & Psychophysics, 71*, 1439–1459.

Lynch, R., & Garret, P. M. (2010). More than words: Touch practices in child and family social work. *Child and Family Social Work, 15*, 389–398.

MacGeorge, E. L., Feng, B., & Burleson, B. R. (2011). Supportive communication. In M. L. Knapp & J. A. Daly (Eds.), *The SAGE handbook of interpersonal communication* (pp. 317–354). Thousand Oaks, CA: Sage.

MacGeorge, E. L., Guntzviller, L. M., Brisini, K. S., Bailey, L. C., Salmon, S. K., Severen, K., Branch, S. E., Lillie, H. M., Lindley, C. K., Pastor, R. G., & Cummings, R. D. (2016). The influence of emotional support quality on advice evaluation and outcomes. *Communication Quarterly, 65*, 80–96.

Major, B., Schmidlin, A., & Williams, L. (1990). Gender patterns in social touch: The impact of setting and age. *Journal of Personality and Social Psychology, 58*, 634–643.

Mansson, D. H., Marko, F., Bachrata, K., Daniskova, Z., Zeleiova, J. G., Janis, V., & Sharov, A. S. (2016). Young adults' trait affection given and received as functions of Hofstede's dimensions of cultures and national origin. *Journal of Intercultural Communication Research, 45*, 404–418.

Martin, B. A. S., & Nuttall, P. (2017). Tense from touch: Examining accidental interpersonal touch between consumers. *Psychology & Marketing, 34*, 946–955.

Matsumoto, D., & Hwang, H. S. (2013). Cultural influences on nonverbal behavior. In D. Matsumoto, M. G. Frank, & H. S. Hwang (Eds.), *Nonverbal communication: Science and applications* (pp. 97–120). Thousand Oaks, CA: Sage.

Miller, M. J., Denes, A., Diaz, B., & Buck, R. (2014). Attachment style predicts jealous reactions to viewing touch between a romantic partner and close friend: Implications for Internet social communication. *Journal of Nonverbal Behavior, 38*, 451–476.

Montague, E., Chen, P-Y., Xu, J., Chewning, B., & Barrett, B. (2013). Nonverbal interpersonal interactions in clinical encounters and patient perceptions of empathy. *Journal of Participatory Medicine, 5*, e33.

Moore, N-J., Hickson, M., III, & Stacks, D. W. (2013). *Nonverbal communication: Studies and applications* (6th ed.). Oxford, UK: Oxford University Press.

Morman, M. T., & Floyd, K. (1998). "I love you, man": Overt expressions of affection in male–male interaction. *Sex Roles, 38*, 871–881.

Morris, D. (1967). *The naked ape: A zoologist's study of the human animal.* London: Jonathan Cape.

Morris, D. (1969). *The human zoo: A zoologist's classic study of the urban animal.* New York: Random House.

Morris, D. (1971). *Intimate behavior.* New York: Random House.

Morris, D. (1977). *Man watching: A field guide to human behavior.* New York: Abrams.

Moszkowski, R. J., & Stack, D. M. (2007). Infant touching behaviour during mother-infant face-to-face interactions. *Infant and Child Development, 16*, 307–319.

chapter eight

Nguyen, T., Heslin, R., & Nguyen, M. L. (1975). The meanings of touch: Sex differences. *Journal of Communication, 25*, 92–103.

Nguyen, T., Heslin, R., & Nguyen, M. L. (1976). The meaning of touch: Sex and marital status differences. *Representative Research in Social Psychology, 7*, 13–18.

Onzawa, K., Glover, V., Adam, D., Modi, N., & Kumar, R. C. (2001). Infant massage improves mother–infant interaction for mothers with postnatal depression. *Journal of Affective Disorders, 63*, 201–207.

Paludi, M. A. (2015). Introduction. In M. A. Paludi, J. L. Martin, J. E. Gruber, & S. Fineran (Eds.), *Sexual harassment in education and work settings: Current research and best practices for prevention* (pp. xix-lii). Santa Barbara, CA: Praeger.

Papathanassoglou, E. D. E., & Mpouzika, M. D. A. (2012). Interpersonal touch: Physiological effects in critical care. *Biological Research for Nursing, 14*, 431–443.

Patterson, J., Gardner, B. C., Burr, B. K., Hubler, D. S., & Roberts, M. K. (2012). Nonverbal behavioral indicators of negative affect in couple interaction. *Contemporary Family Therapy, 34*, 11–28.

Peck, J., & Webb, A. (2011). Individual differences in interpersonal touch: Development of the "Comfort with Interpersonal Touch Scale." *Advances in Consumer Research, 39*, 771–772.

Phung, A., Joyce, C., Ambutas, S., Browning, M., Fogg, L., Christopher, B-A., & Flood, S. (2017). Animal-assisted therapy for inpatient adults. *Nursing, 47*, 63–66.

Puckett, J. A., Newcomb, M. E., Ryan, D. T., Swann, G., Garofalo, R., & Mustanski, B. (2017). Internalized homophobia and perceived stigma: A validation study of stigma measures in a sample of young men who have sex with men. *Sexuality Research and Social Policy, 14*, 1–16.

Punyanunt-Carter, N. M., & Wrench, J. S. (2009). Development and validity testing of a measure of touch deprivation. *Human Communication, 12*, 67–76.

Rancourt, K. M., MacKinnon, S., Snowball, N., & Rosen, N. O. (2017). Beyond the bedroom: Cognitive, affective, and behavioral responses to partner touch in women with and without sexual problems. *Journal of Sex Research, 54*, 862–876.

Reece, C., Ebstein, R., Cheng, X., Ng, T., & Schirmer, A. (2016). Maternal touch predicts social orienting in young children. *Cognitive Development, 39*, 128–140.

Sehlstedt, I., Ignell, H., Backlund Wasling, H., Ackerley, R., Olausson, H., & Croy, I. (2016). Gentle touch perception across the lifespan. *Psychology and Aging, 31*, 176–184.

Sekerdej, M., Simao, C., Waldzus, S., & Brito, R. (2018). Keeping in touch with context: Non-verbal behavior as a manifestation of communality and dominance. *Journal of Nonverbal Behavior.* https://doi.org/10.1007/s10919-018-0279-2

Sollami, A., Gianferrari, E., Alfieri, M., Artioli, G., & Taffurelli, C. (2017). Pet therapy: An effective strategy to care for the elderly? An experimental study in a nursing home. *Acta Bio Medica, 88*. https://doi.org/10.23750/abm.v88i%20-s.6281

Stack, D. M., & Jean, A. D. L. (2011). Communicating through touch: Touching during parent–infant interactions. In M. J. Hertenstein & S. J. Weiss (Eds.), *The handbook of touch: Neuroscience, behavioral, and health perspectives* (pp. 273–298). New York: Springer.

Stolte, K., & Friedman, H. (1980). Patients' perceptions of touch during labor. *Journal of Applied Communication Research, 8*, 10–21.

Thompson, E. H., & Hampton, J. A. (2011). The effect of relationship status on communicating emotions through touch. *Cognition and Emotion, 25*, 295–306.

Thorbecke, C. (2018, April 20). Disgraced gymnastics doctor's alleged victims file new lawsuits. Retrieved from https://abcnews.go.com/GMA/News/disgraced-gymnastics-doctors-alleged-victims-file-lawsuits/story?id=54597592

Triscoli, C., Croy, I., Olausson, H., & Sailer, U. (2017). Touch between romantic partners: Being stroked is more pleasant than stroking and decelerates heart rate. *Physiology & Behavior, 177*, 169–175.

Turp, M. (2000). Touch, enjoyment and health: In adult life. *European Journal of Psychotherapy and Counseling, 3*, 61–76.

Vieira, A. I., Nogueira, D., de Azevedo Reis, E., da Lapa Rosado, M., Nunes, M. V., & Castro-Caldas, A. (2016). Hand tactile discrimination, social touch and frailty criteria in elderly people: A cross sectional observational study. *Archives of Gerontology and Geriatrics, 66*, 73–81.

Villagran, M., Goldsmith, J., Wittenberg-Lyles, E., & Baldwin, P. (2010). Creating COMFORT: A communication-based model for breaking bad news. *Communication Education, 59*, 220–234.

Vincente, S., Veríssimo, M., & Diniz, E. (2017). Infant massage improves attitudes toward childbearing, maternal satisfaction and pleasure in parenting. *Infant Behavior and Development, 49*, 114–119.

Waters, S. F., West, T. V., Karnilowicz, H. R., & Mendes, W. B. (2017). Affect contagion between mothers and infants: Examining valence and touch. *Journal of Experimental Psychology, 146*, 1043–1051.

Weiss, S. J. (1990). Parental touching: Correlates of a child's body concept and body sentiment. In K. E. Barnard & B. T. Brazelton (Eds.), *Touch: The foundation of experience* (pp. 425–459). Madison, CT: International Universities Press.

Wiltermuth, S. S., Raj, M., & Wood, A. (2018). How perceived power influences the consequences of dominance expressions in negotiations. *Organizational Behavior and Human Decision Processes, 146*, 14–20.

chapter nine

VOCALICS: OUR VOICES SPEAK NONVERBAL VOLUMES

chapter outline

chapter objectives

After studying this chapter, you should be able to

1. define vocalics (paralanguage) as a nonverbal communication code;
2. understand the difference between verbal and vocal communication;
3. identify the major anatomical contributors to voice production and explain their primary functions;
4. list and describe five properties and three qualities of the voice;
5. define vocalizations and explain how they serve as nonverbal communication;
6. identify three types of pauses and give examples of how each emerges in conversation, as well as public speaking situations;
7. discuss positive and negative uses of silence, including self-silencing;
8. identify four categories of turn-taking and explain how each nonverbally operates in everyday conversation;
9. contrast interruptions with overlaps in conversation and explain how each can reflect dominance; and
10. provide the four most common types of vocal cues associated with deception and offer examples of each.

case study

FRYING YOUR VOCALS

*H*ave you heard young women drop the pitch of their voices to produce a creaky, croaking sound? Britney Spears used the technique to sing lower pitches when performing (Fessenden, 2011). Celebrities like Zooey Deschanel and Kim Kardashian often use this vocal cue when speaking, as do many young American women. As one columnist put it, it's like "Ke$ha woke up in the morning feeling like P-Diddy" (Khazan, 2014). It's called vocal fry (technical name glottalization) and occurs when air generates irregular vibrations of the vocal cords, producing a popping sound. It's an affectation, meaning a nonverbal choice to manipulate the voice in this way. What's the point, you wonder?

Researchers have tried to determine the point of such a shift in voice, with subjects in studies saying it's just something fun and trendy to do, to generate more interest in what you say and how you say it. Men can produce the sound too, but tend to use it less than women (Anderson, Klofstad, Mayew, & Venkatachalam, 2014; Yuasa, 2010). Problem is, it's really bad for your throat. Another problem is, it's not winning you points with people who hear it.

Anderson et al.'s (2014) research found that American women using vocal fry are perceived as less competent, less educated, less trustworthy, less attractive, and less hireable; women receive more negative reactions to vocal fry than do men. Perhaps women use the technique believing that a lowered pitch will enhance how they're perceived, but it often backfires. However, Higdon (2016) suggests that sexism underlies people's perceptions of vocal fry; men using lowered pitch may be perceived as more masculine, but when women do the same thing, they're "masculinized" and criticized. As we study in this chapter the power of the voice as a nonverbal cue, think about how you manipulate such things as your voice pitch, in order to achieve some effect or goal.

[Ring tone . . .]
"Hello?"
"Hey, what's up?"
"Hey, you. Nothin's up. What's up with you?"
"Same old boring stuff. [Sigh] Nothing to report. [Pause] Just thought I'd see what you were doin'. Talk to you later."
"Okay, later."

This is an excerpt from a typical phone conversation, but how did the person answering the phone know who was calling (without looking at the screen)? No names were mentioned, but the exchange indicates obvious familiarity.

Most of us don't have a voiceprint machine (spectrogram) handy, which creates a visual image of a person's speech. Human beings (those who aren't hearing impaired) have the capability to learn to recognize people by the sounds of their voices (Maguinness, Roswandowitz, & von Kriegstein, 2018; Stevenage, Neil, Parsons, & Humphreys, 2018). This happens in particular when we're infants and our eyes can't quite focus on people's faces yet; we rely on sounds more than visual images in those early days of development. What's funny, however, is that often we don't recognize our own voices when we hear them on recordings, or we may feel that the recording is distorted. That's because the voice we hear inside our own head isn't the voice others hear. Our true voice is the one we project to others; so with the sophistication of today's technology, recordings accurately capture and reproduce our true voices.

© Mangostar.Shutterstock.com

Even with external distractions and using a cell phone, most of us easily learn to recognize people through the unique sounds of their voices.

What voices do you like to hear? Rihanna's? Or do you prefer Kelly Clarkson's powerful tone? What about Bruno Mars's high-energy sound? Thinking more personally, are there people in your life whose voices evoke certain emotions in you? Are there some politicians' voices that make you cringe when you hear them on TV?

Rihanna, Kelly Clarkson, and Bruno Mars have distinctive, memorable singing voices. Politicians like Senator Cory Booker and former Secretary of State Hillary Clinton have powerful speaking voices, ones that have served them well in public life.

The voice is a miraculous mechanism, one we explore in this chapter as a code of nonverbal communication. Now don't get confused: This chapter focuses on *vocal* aspects, not *verbal* ones—and there's a difference. Verbal means words, either written or spoken. Vocal means the sounds we make that accompany words or nonwords (such as "uh-huh") that have communicative power. You've no doubt heard the phrase, "It's not *what* you say but *how* you say it." When you study *how* people express themselves through their voices, you study **vocalics**, sometimes referred to as **paralanguage**.

Besides being able to identify someone from his or her voice, you can also come to detect physical, emotional, and attitudinal states through **tone of voice** (sometimes referred to as **prosody** or the "music of speech"), meaning all the elements of sound that the human voice can produce and manipulate (Frank, Maroulis, & Griffin, 2013, p. 54). That's another subject we explore in this chapter—how we vary aspects of our voices to create tone, which alerts people to what we're thinking and feeling (Kalathottukaren, Purdy, & Ballard, 2917; Paquette-Smith & Johnson, 2016; Weinstein, Zougkou, & Paulmann, 2018). For example, you've probably heard a parent say, "Don't use that tone of voice with me"—perhaps as you were growing up and testing the boundaries of your parents' patience. Or maybe you can tell if someone isn't feeling well, if they're sad or angry, or if they're expressing sarcasm, just by paying attention to that all-important tone of voice.

If you have the physical ability to hear and speak, you use your voice (as well as a whole host of other nonverbal cues) to help convey the meaning behind what you say. When you think about it, we would all be in big trouble as communicators if our voices didn't have the capacity to shape our words. How would we convey a question, if not for our ability to raise our pitch at the end of a series

chapter nine

of words? When we teach children to do things, we tend to slow down the rate of our instructions, to give them time to comprehend the meaning of our messages. If someone tends to interrupt us too often, we increase our volume and rate of speaking, hoping to communicate to the interrupter, "Hey, don't break in; I'm talking here!" Sarcasm and irony are all about tone (Katz & Hussey, 2017; Woodland & Voyer, 2011). So you can see how important a function vocalics play in everyday interaction. Let's begin our coverage of this important nonverbal code with a brief discussion of the anatomical mechanism that produces the voice.

PRODUCTION OF VOICE ■ ■ ■

We rely primarily in this section on the work of communication scholar Lynn Wells (2004), author of *The Articulate Voice: An Introduction to Voice and Diction*, and sociologist Anne Karpf (2006), who wrote *The Human Voice: How This Extraordinary Instrument Reveals Essential Clues about Who We Are*. You may not tend to think of your voice as an instrument, but it's something capable of producing sound, just like a tuba or guitar. Karpf and Wells both explain that voice production isn't accomplished by a single organ but, rather, by a process of combining different body parts into a sequence. As you'll note in Figure 9.1, the primary vocal organs are the trachea, larynx (including vocal folds or cords), pharynx, nose, jaw, and mouth (including the soft palate, hard palate, teeth, tongue, and lips). Our lungs are critical to voice production as well, since the voice is "audible air." As Karpf puts it, "the process by which we breathe in order to live also, with minor changes, provides the energy for speech" (p. 23).

FIGURE 9.1
Anatomy of the voice

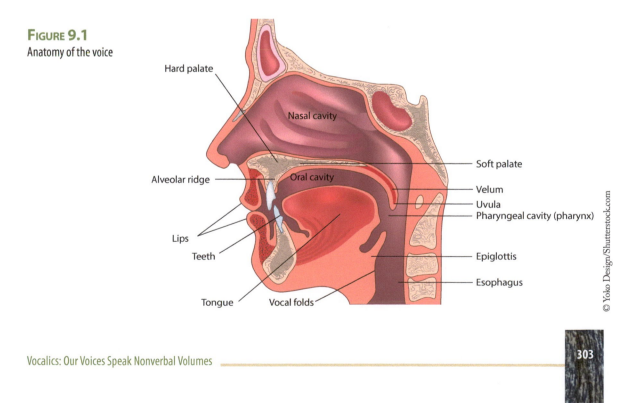

© Yoko Design/Shutterstock.com

Our breathing is altered when we speak; we breathe in quickly and exhale slowly so that the breath will carry our statements. As we take in air through the pharynx (throat), down into the trachea (windpipe), and into our lungs, we then expel that air by contracting our diaphragms. The air goes back up the trachea to the larynx (colloquially referred to as the voice box), which controls the flow of air between the lungs and the throat. At this point, the air meets an obstacle—the vocal folds (cords). The central space or slit between the folds, through which air passes, is termed the glottis. These elastic vocal folds act like a pair of curtains, opening and closing as they control the flow of air. In the closed position, the folds operate to prevent the passage of foreign matter, such as food and drink, into the trachea (Lessac, 1997). When air meets the folds rushing through the glottis, the folds vibrate and sound is produced. That sound is a succession of bursts of air, more like a buzz or a hiss.

Once air has made the vocal folds vibrate, the jaw, tongue, teeth, lips, and nasal and oral cavities take over and contort the process to produce sound. So there you have it—a brief explanation of voice production. The process of producing sound is more complicated than this of course, but for our interests, we at least now understand the basic mechanism. More important to our discussion is the role of voice production in human communication.

REMEMBER

Remember! 9.1

| Vocalics (paralanguage) | Study of how people express themselves through their voices |
| Tone of voice (prosody) | All the qualities that the human voice can produce and manipulate |

PROPERTIES AND QUALITIES OF THE VOICE

Some aspects of the voice are anatomical and therefore basically unchangeable, such as the physical dimensions of the vocal folds, which control the range of pitches a person can produce. In general, women cannot physically produce the same low notes as most men. There are limits to what the voice can do, because of our anatomy and physiology. But many aspects of voice production are changeable; these vocal properties give us variety as speakers.

Vocal Properties

Vocal properties are aspects of the voice that can be purposefully altered to create meaning within our nonverbal communication repertoire. What do you sound like when you're mad? Do you get loud? Do you speed up your rate of speech when you argue? If you're asked a question in class by a professor and you're unsure of the answer, how differently do the sounds come out of your mouth as you try to answer, compared with times when you answer with confidence? You probably speak more quietly and with some hesitation when unsure, possibly throwing in an "um" or "er" along the way. These are examples of the five vocal properties that can be controlled and manipulated.

PITCH. **Pitch** is the "falling or rising tone heard in the voice: It creates our voice's melody" (Karpf, 2006, p. 35). As young children, when our bodies and voices are developing, we produce higher pitches. But as we age and our hormones change, our voices also change (Dabbs & Mallinger, 1999; Feinberg et al., 2006). If you're male, do you remember battling the change in your voice during puberty, most likely in your middle school years? Those unpredictable moments when your voice could suddenly go into a yodel are but one of myriad embarrassments boys experience during puberty. The vocal effects of puberty are more subtle for girls, but girls' and women's voices, specifically the control of pitch, are affected by their menstrual cycles, when hormones are in flux (Banai, 2017). Many professional female singers try to schedule performances around their periods, to maximize voice production and control. Menopausal women typically experience a deepening of the voice, again due to hormonal and other physiological changes (Eichorn, Kent, Austin, & Vorperian, 2017). Men's and women's voices deepen with age; our voice capacity diminishes over the years (Davidson, 2016; Stathopoulos, Huber, & Sussman, 2011).

You have an average pitch to your voice, sometimes referred to as habitual or usual pitch (Wells, 2004). If you want to know what it is, just say "mm-hmm" (the equivalent of yes) out loud. The normal or typical way you say "mm-hmm" reveals the most comfortable or average pitch of your voice, termed the **fundamental frequency** (Gelfer & Bennett, 2013; Riding, Lonsdale, & Brown, 2006). We all have a pitch range, meaning that we can produce low pitches (slowly vibrating vocal folds) to high pitches (quickly vibrating vocal folds), and some people have a wider pitch range than others. For example, pop singer Mariah Carey is known for her tremendous range, including such high pitches that it almost sounds as though an orchestral instrument made the sound instead of a human voice. If you're familiar with the song "Ol' Man River" from the classic musical *Showboat*, you know that only a man with a deep bass voice can accomplish that song (as it was meant to be sung).

In general, men can produce more low pitches than can women, and women can produce more high pitches than can men (Evans, Neave, Wakelin, & Hamilton, 2008; Krolokke & Sorensen, 2006). Low voice pitch in men and high pitch in women are associated with perceptions of attractiveness, trustworthiness, and credibility (Belin, Boehme, & McAleer, 2017; Jones, Feinberg, DeBruine, Little, & Vukovic, 2008, 2010; Montano, Tigue, Isenstein, Barclay, & Feinberg, 2017; Oleszkiewicz, Pisanski, Lachowicz-Tabaczek, & Sorokowska, 2017; Rezlescu et al., 2015). But scholarly evidence suggests that vocal sex differences may be more about what's acceptable in society than physiology (Albert et al., 2018; Bruckert, Lienard, Lacroix, Kreutzer, & Leboucher, 2006; O'Connor & Barclay, 2018). Research indicates that women and men have equal abilities to produce high pitches but many men have been socialized not to use higher pitches, lest they sound feminine (Cartei & Reby, 2012; Henley, 2001).

While you have limitations in the range of pitches your voice can produce, you can extend your range with practice (Hughes, Mogilski, & Harrison, 2014; Wells, 2004). Voice teachers will help you find your ideal pitch range—pitches you can hit the best and with ease—and then they will work to extend your range upward and downward on the scale, to help you develop more flexibility in what you can sing or say. Actress and model Kathy Ireland got tired of being perceived as ditzy or unintelligent because of her high-pitched, baby-like voice, and so she hired a vocal coach and worked to lower her speaking voice.

You may hear a shift in pitch from low to high when adults talk to infants, children, the elderly, romantic partners, and even pets, commonly called baby talk. The shifting pitch may represent an expression of affection or an offer of care or comfort, and has been detected cross-culturally (Farley, Hughes, & LaFayette, 2013; Guerrero & Floyd, 2006; Trainor, Austin, & Desjardin, 2000; Yamamoto & Haryu, 2018). However, particularly in communication with elderly people, baby talk can be interpreted as condescending, patronizing, and disrespectful (Andersen, 2004; Hehman, Corpuz, & Bugental, 2012).

Patterns of pitch are termed **intonation**, described by sociolinguist Sally McConnell-Ginet (1983) as "the tune to which we set the text of our talk" (p. 70). It's important to develop intonation that's interesting to listeners, that conveys your personality, and that accommodates the speech styles of others, if that's your goal (Gijssels, Casasanto, Jasmin, Hagoort, & Casasanto, 2016; Hughes, Farley, & Rhodes, 2010). For example, in U.S. culture, we associate seriousness, confidence, and credibility with lower intonation, and flightiness and insecurity with higher intonation (Imhof, 2010; Nelson & Golant, 2004). So if you want to be taken seriously when you speak, you'll want to work on using the lower pitches available to you and not letting your voice rise too high, lest you be seen as nervous, overemotional, erratic, or deceptive.

However, using a pattern of low pitches or one consistent pitch can be problematic as well because this reflects a lack of **vocal variety**, also termed **inflection**. Research shows that monotone voices are generally perceived as unpleasant, while vocal variety is received more positively (Andre, Petr, Andre, Hausberger, & Lemasson, 2016; Jones et al., 2008, 2010; Shen & Souza, 2017). In our teaching of public speaking over the years, we've noticed that many students—particularly the men—tend to go monotone during presentations. A monotone voice occurs most often because of nervousness, but it belies an inflection problem, meaning that the speaker isn't varying her or his pitches to create vocal interest (Feinberg, Jones, Little, Burt, & Perrett, 2005; Goberman, Hughes, & Haydock, 2011). One of the best ways to increase your vocal variety is to read to children. Most children will insist that you "do the voices" when you read out loud to them, and this can be a great way to experiment with your pitch range.

A final pitch-related vocal cue is called **upspeak** or **uptalk**, which occurs when every statement ends with an upward pitch shift, as though all sentences are turned into questions (Warren,

2016). Upspeakers sound unsure, as though their every statement needs affirmation from others. One study found that listeners perceived statements delivered in upspeak as unfinished (Tyler, 2015). Women tend to use more upspeak than men, often causing them to be perceived as lacking in assertiveness and competence. Men who upspeak are typically viewed as lacking in confidence (Lebowitz, 2015).

spotlight *on research*

Transgender Voice

We don't know how educated you are on transgender identity, but you've likely heard, read, or seen information about the process some people go through to align their internal and external gender. Many of these folks have suffered because their physical attributes and hormonal systems reflect one sex, but their psychology and emotions correspond to a different sex. The discrepancy can be agony. But now people have more options; new information helps us all become more educated about transgender identity.

It's likely that some of you reading this information are transgender, or are contemplating or questioning your identity. The good news is, people have more resources to turn to and utilize as they think about and pursue a transition (Spencer & Capuzza, 2014). As we continue to witness more societal acceptance of trans persons, our understanding of this form of identity will no doubt deepen. But make no mistake: We may be more accepting than in years past, but trans persons still receive a great deal of discrimination, abuse, and interrogation about their identities, bodies, and experiences.

If a person chooses to transition, either by utilizing hormone therapies, undergoing surgical procedures, or a combination of methods currently available, one of the more difficult challenges involves the voice. One obstacle trans persons have to confront is an ages-long tradition in many societies of equating low pitches with masculinity and high pitches with femininity, a rather arbitrary distinction (Zimman,

2018). Nevertheless, trans women (men transitioning into women) often struggle with their voices, feeling like every time they open their mouths to speak, their voices betray them because of the generally lower pitch range they possess. Trans men (women transitioning into men) are challenged as well, but many have experienced success in lowering their pitch range through testosterone therapy (Ziegler, Henke, Wiedrick, & Helou, 2018).

Speech pathologists and voice therapists are now more educated and equipped to help transgender individuals develop vocal cues that enhance their transitions (Hancock, Childs, & Irwig, 2017; Hancock & Haskin, 2015; Mills, Stoneham, & Georgiadou, 2017; Oates & Dacakis, 2015; Sawyer, Perry, & Dobbins-Scaramelli, 2014). One approach is producing promising results; it's called Wendler glottoplasty and involves surgically altering the vocal folds to produce a wider range of pitches, upward or downward (Mastronikolis, Remacle, Biagini, Kiagiadaki, & Lawson, 2013). While this surgery may seem serious or drastic, it's been successful for many patients undergoing transition (Meister, Kuhn, Shehata-Dieler, Hagen, & Kleinsasser, 2017).

Do you want to know more about transgender identity? All of the sources cited in this spotlight box appear in the reference list at the end of the chapter, but for a general understanding, we recommend this book, especially Jennifer Finney Boylan's Introduction (pp. xv-xvii), *Trans Bodies, Trans Selves: A Resource for the Transgender Community*, edited by Laura Erickson-Schroth.

Vocal properties	Aspects of the voice that can be purposefully altered to create meaning
Pitch	Falling or rising tone heard in the voice
Fundamental frequency	Most comfortable or often-used pitch of the voice
Intonation	Patterns of pitch
Vocal variety (inflection)	Varying the pitches used in speaking
Upspeak/uptalk	Ending every statement with an upward pitch shift, as though all sentences are turned into questions

RATE. Speech **rate** simply means the pace at which sounds are uttered. According to Karpf (2006), the average speaking rate (which she calls **tempo**) of an American or British adult is 120 to 150 words per minute, or around six syllables per second. Primarily, your rate of speech reflects your culture and your upbringing, meaning what you heard and patterned after at home. Genetics plays a role in this phenomenon, but having similar vocal patterns as family members has more to do with nurture (the environment within which you were raised) than nature (genetics) (Karpf, 2006). Just as our pitch range shifts, our speaking rate often slows as we age (Waller, Eriksson, & Sorqvist, 2015).

Our voices (and ears) are highly adaptable. Ever traveled somewhere, heard the locals speak, and picked up properties of their way of speaking, only to be laughed at when you returned home and talked to your friends? What you hear often transfers to how you speak, and this is true of speech rate (Bosker, 2017a; Schultz et al., 2016). For example, if one of your friends comes up to you and excitedly starts spilling his or her good news, you're likely to adopt that same rate when you respond, just because speech properties are "catching." Likewise, if you're speaking normally or hurriedly and a friend is sad or down, when that person speaks to you in a slower rate of speech (a telltale sign of negative emotion), you'll likely slow your rate to correspond with your friend's. Sometimes this tendency is referred to as **synchrony**—as we discussed in Chapter 6 in relation to bodily synchrony—which occurs when people's nonverbal cues mirror each other (Lozza et al., 2018; Maslowski, Meyer, & Bosker, 2018).

Speech rate is significantly affected by emotion, and this effect is often hard to control (Banziger, Patel, & Scherer, 2014; Juslin, Laukka, & Banziger, 2018; Kuhn, Wydell, Lavan, McGettigan, & Garrido, 2017; Morningstar, Dirks, & Huang, 2017; Morningstar, Ly, Feldman, & Dirks, 2018).

When nervous, you're more likely to speak faster than normal, which reveals your emotional state. If you're aware that this tends to happen to you and you don't want your nerves revealed, then you'll need to practice controlling this tendency so that listeners (e.g., job interviewers, audiences, would-be dates) don't detect your nerves (Frauendorfer, Schmid Mast, Nguyen, & Gatica-Perez, 2014; Laukka et al., 2008). Karpf (cited in Fuller, 2006) suggests that, when people are angry, their speech rates max out at 200 vibrations per second. She describes how, according to historical experts, Adolph Hitler's average rate while giving speeches was 228 vibrations per second. In fact, his vocal aggression was so closely associated with his power that American spies tried to find ways to slip female hormones into his food, in an attempt to slow him down and diminish perceptions of his powerfulness.

Research shows that people with slower speaking rates are often judged as being colder, weaker, less truthful, less credible and less persuasive than faster speakers (Feldstein, Dohm, & Crown, 2001; Limbu, Jayachandran, Babin, & Peterson, 2016; Novak-Tot, Niebuhr, & Chen, 2017). Effective vocalics are especially critical to politicians, leaders, and crisis spokespersons, whose ability to persuade, reassure, and inspire is crucial to their success (Bosker, 2017b; Claeys & Cauberghe, 2014; De Waele & Claeys, 2017; De Waele, Claeys, & Cauberghe, 2017; Goethals, 2005).

How fast do you think this angry, frustrated worker is talking? Our emotions affect our speech rate, among other vocal properties.

VOLUME. Simply defined, **volume** (sometimes called **intensity**) refers to the softness or loudness of your voice. Karpf (2006) suggests that the average conversational volume for speakers standing about 3 feet apart is 60 decibels. Quiet speech ranges from 35 to 40 decibels, while shouting rises to about 75 decibels. As a way to gauge these amounts, since you're not likely to have a decibel meter handy, Karpf explains that rustling leaves average 10 decibels of sound and loud music averages 80 decibels. If you're exposed to 120 decibels of sound, it will create a sensation in your body that is like a touch; beyond 120 decibels, you will feel physical pain. These facts beg the question: Just how loudly do you play your music through headphones?

Volume is another vocal property you can vary to your advantage, unless you have hearing loss. Some people who experience hearing loss—whether they know they have or not—speak loudly in order to hear themselves, but this can be offputting to listeners who feel as though people are barking at them (Rasetshwane et al., 2018). In general, louder voices are associated with confidence, assertiveness, and boldness, while softer voices are associated with low self-esteem, timidity, and passivity (Nelson & Golant, 2004; Wells, 2004). However, softer voices can also indicate a calm self-assurance, suggesting that someone doesn't feel the need to get loud to control a conversation; the hushed tones dominate because of their sheer contrast with other people's volume (Hartmann & Mast, 2017).

As we said for other vocal properties, for most of us, volume is affected by our emotions and attitudes (Karpf, 2006). While we tend to associate raising one's voice or shouting with dominance and displays of anger, some of us get very, very quiet when

How loud is this crowd? Besides our rate of speaking, our vocal volume is affected by our emotions.

we're angry (Andersen, 2004; Guerrero & Floyd, 2006; Pavlich, Rains, & Segrin, 2017).

One of the functions of nonverbal communication covered in Chapter 1 was **accenting**—the use of nonverbal cues to emphasize or draw special attention to a verbal message (Ekman, 1965). An extreme increase or decrease in volume will accent a verbal message. While volume is controllable, it takes a lot of work to alter volume because, first, people are often unaware that they speak too softly or loudly and, second, many people won't take the time and energy to break a long-term habit. But you can work to achieve a louder voice for those occasions that demand it (such as making speeches when there are no microphones or the equipment fails) or a softer voice when needed (such as when you want privacy). Parents often work with children to develop their "inside voices" versus "outside voices" so they can function appropriately in social settings.

ARTICULATION AND PRONUNCIATION. **Articulation** (also called **enunciation**) refers to how *distinctly* you speak, while **pronunciation** refers to how *correctly* you speak, according to a dictionary's indication of proper pronunciation (Wells, 2004). If you have trouble understanding what someone says, the problem may be that she or he slurs words, drops syllables, emphasizes the wrong syllables, or mumbles—articulation errors. It might also be that the person doesn't speak words correctly—pronunciation errors. For example, some people say "pasketti" instead of "spaghetti" and "sim-yoo-lar" instead of "similar," which are pronunciation problems. If they say "pasketti" and "sim-yoo-lar" crisply and cleanly, they articulate just fine but pronounce these words incorrectly. Someone who mumbles "spaghetti" when asked what he or she wants for dinner pronounces the word correctly but articulates it poorly. Both are nonverbal vocalic problems that can cause confusion in listeners and a breakdown in communication.

As with other vocal cues, our physical health and emotions come into play in this area. When we don't feel well, are fatigued, or are in a bad mood, our articulation may be affected, causing us to speak softly, slur sounds, or mumble. Articulation and pronunciation are the easiest to change of all the vocal properties, but, like other changes, they take concentrated effort. You may simply not know that you pronounce certain words incorrectly until someone points it out to you.

Rate (tempo)	Pace at which sounds are uttered
Synchrony	When people's nonverbal cues mirror each other
Volume (intensity)	Softness or loudness of the voice
Accenting	The use of nonverbal cues to emphasize or draw special attention to a verbal message
Articulation (enunciation)	How distinctly a person speaks
Pronunciation	How correctly a person speaks, according to a dictionary's indication of proper pronunciation

Vocal Qualities

Some qualities of the voice are physiologically based and a challenge to change, such as the condition of your vocal folds or your ability to breathe to assist your voice production. But other qualities can be invoked (or faked) to achieve a certain communication goal, or they become habit because you've spoken that way over time. In this section, we explore three **vocal qualities**, characteristics of the voice that develop subtly and more as habits than as conscious choices.

BREATHINESS. No matter your age or what movies you grew up watching, no voice in U.S. culture is more recognizable for its breathiness than Marilyn Monroe's. If you've seen footage of Monroe's tribute to President Kennedy at his birthday celebration, when she sang "Happy Birthday," it looks as though she might have passed out on each phrase, so much breath escaped her body. The physiological explanation for **breathiness** in the voice is this: The glottis (space between the vocal folds) narrows but lets through more air than we normally use to make sounds, and, as a result, the vocal folds vibrate but don't fully close (Eddins, Anand, Camacho, & Shrivastav, 2016; Latoszek, Maryn, Gerrits, & De Bodt, 2017). In essence, breathiness has to do with an overabundance of air moving through almost-closed vocal folds. Breathiness is associated with femininity in American culture, and with other stereotypical traits such as helplessness, sexiness, and childishness. However, Karpf (cited in Fuller, 2006) suggests that men and women alike exhibit breathiness in the voice when sexually aroused, because hormones alter the amount and form of mucus in the larynx, which leads to that out-of-breath sound.

Just as we've seen for other aspects of the voice, our emotions and attitudes can be conveyed through how much or how little breath escapes when we speak. For example, have you ever had a nightmare and tried to scream or cry out, only to feel as though you couldn't get any breath to pass through your throat? Sometimes, when we're really excited, it's hard to "catch our breath," meaning that our anatomical functioning associated with producing the breath we need to make sound is impaired. As we struggle for air and to get the mechanism going, we may make breathy vocalizations until we're more fully functional.

RASPINESS. We most often think of the vocal quality of **raspiness** as hoarseness or a gravelly sound in the voice. Some experts call it a throaty or guttural quality, which works well if you're speaking German but not so well when speaking English (Wells, 2004). One famous raspy voice belongs to actor Harvey Fierstein, probably most notable for his role on Broadway as the mother(!) of the central character in the musical *Hairspray*.

Raspiness in the voice involves an overabundance of friction on the vocal folds caused by forcing too much air through the mechanism, and it can be created for dramatic effect. Some cheerleaders develop raspiness due to constant abuse of their voices, but these conditions tend to be fleeting. If raspiness persists, it's likely due to reflux or other gastric problems, excessive phlegm, dryness because of an illness, or the presence of nodes (inflamed, roughened tissue) that may develop on the folds over time (Fujiki, Chapleau, Sundarrajan, McKenna, & Sivasankar, 2017; Narasimhan & Vishal, 2017). Constant

© Bettmann/Contributor/Getty Images

Marilyn Monroe, shown here singing "Happy Birthday," is still the epitome of the breathy, sexy voice.

© Miro Vrlik Photography/Shutterstock.com

Actor Harvey Fierstein is known for his deep, raspy voice.

chapter nine

inflammation of the vocal folds because of illness, smoking, straining, repeated vomiting (bulimia-related), or other irritations can engender raspiness in the voice over the long haul. Professional singers who overtire their voices (e.g., Adele) or whose style involves straining to reach high notes (e.g., Aerosmith's Steven Tyler) can develop voice problems, which can force some of them out of the business, prompt some to have surgery to repair the damage, and cause some to lower the key of their songs as they age (Davidson, 2016).

NASALITY. The punch line to a certain joke goes, "Would you like some *whine* with that cheese?" When we refer to **nasality** in the voice, we mean when air is trapped or heavily contained in the nasal cavities, instead of resonating through all the vocal structures, and then is pushed or squeezed out to form a whiny sound (Wells, 2004). Nasality can also be caused by a physical defect, such as a deviated septum or cleft palate. Perhaps the actress Fran Drescher (formerly of the TV show *The Nanny*) best embodies what we call a nasal or whiny voice. Nasality is similar to a quality termed *twang* in research on vocal disorders, which voice experts Lombard and Steinhauer (2007) describe as the "bright, brassy, ringing voice quality commonly heard in country-western singing, witch-cackling, a child's 'nya, nya' taunt, and is equated often with duck quacking" (p. 295). However, some languages require that people be able to produce a nasal sound for the language to be spoken correctly; European Portuguese is one example of such a language (Freitas, Teixeira, Silva, Oliveira, & Dias, 2015).

Actress Fran Drescher is know for her nasal or whiny voice.

Research on perceptions of people with nasal voices isn't extensive, but in American culture, as well as many other cultures around the globe, nasal voices aren't typically deemed attractive. Over several decades, psychologist Miron Zuckerman and various colleagues have studied what makes voices attractive. This line of research has determined that attractive voices are more varied (meaning non-monotone), more resonant, lower in pitch (for men only), and less nasal (Zuckerman & Driver, 1989; Zuckerman, Hodgins, & Miyake, 1990; Zuckerman & Miyake, 1993). Zuckerman and Sinicropi (2011) examined people's reactions when someone's voice and physicality don't match. Previous research had determined that people responded negatively when someone was vocally attractive but physically unattractive (or the reverse). Zuckerman and Sinicropi investigated further and discovered that the negativity doesn't arise because of the discrepancy between vocal and physical attractiveness, but has more to do with a general disappointment over the less attractive element. Said more simply, if someone is physically great-looking but has a terrible voice, your lowered perception of that person has more to do with disappointment over the bad voice than with the fact that the voice and looks don't match. As an extension of Zuckerman's line of research, Klofstad (2017) found that voters' selection of political leaders was influenced by a perceived match in the attractiveness level of candidates' faces and voices.

Vocalizations

You're coming to realize that the human voice is a marvelous mechanism, capable of producing a multitude of nonverbal sounds to help generate meaning. Another category of sounds is **vocalizations**, meaning nonwords or sounds not tied to speech, including those that can substitute for speech (Anikin, Baath, & Persson, 2018; Argyle, 1988/1999; Vasconelos, Dias, Soares, & Pinheiro, 2017). Consider the examples below:

Questioner:	"Hey, are you hungry? Want something to eat?"
Responder:	"Mm-hmm."
Questioner:	"Man, that test was HARD. Did you think so?"
Responder:	"Unh-uh. Guess I studied more than you."
Questioner:	"That guy is HOT."
Responder:	"Hmmmm. I don't know, maybe."
Questioner:	"I wiped out on that last wave. Check out my foot—is it swollen?"
Responder:	"Geeeeez. That looks painful."

In each of these examples, the responder uses a nonword or vocalization that has a fairly universal interpretation (at least among English speakers). We learn these vocalizations and the inflections that accompany them fairly easily growing up, recognizing that they help get our point across. Nonverbal communication scholar Peter Andersen (2004) terms these vocalizations "linguistic shortcuts" because they're often used as responses to others' communication (p. 202). Mehrabian (1981) calls them "verbal reinforcers" (p. 45). Most of the time, vocalizations are heard as supportive responses that aren't commonly interpreted as interruptions. Speaking them in rapid succession can signal people to speed up what they're saying or to stop so the other person can say something. Vocalizations can stand alone, but they often accompany words, as evidenced in the examples above.

Other vocalizations are individualistic and can have nonverbal communicative power for listeners. Knapp, Hall, and Horgan (2013) provide the following list: "laughing, crying, whispering, snoring, yelling, moaning, yawning, whining, sighing, and belching" (p. 330). Argyle (1988/1999) would add grunting to the list. These are sounds the voice can produce that have meaning for listeners but aren't verbal communication.

Do people tell you that you have a great laugh? We tend to remember people with distinctive laughs. Some people laugh with their mouths open, but no sound comes out or they wheeze as air escapes; some people snort when they laugh. Other people produce "belly laughs," which sound robust and hearty and generally make everyone around them burst into laughter as well. Each of us is capable of producing different kinds of laughs, meaning that laughter is versatile. While something might make you roar with side-splitting laughter, other stimuli will elicit high-pitched giggles. Then there's the snicker. There's really no way to explain or write out the snicker, but we all know what it sounds like, right? It's mostly accomplished by releasing air through the nose, but it involves the throat as well, and it sends a message.

It probably won't surprise you to know that scholars have researched the communicative properties of laughter. Laughter has been studied for its specific rhythms, duration, and changes in fundamental frequency (Kipper & Todt, 2003); for the way shared laughter impacts relationships (Kurtz & Algoe, 2017); for its impact on attitudes and emotions of listeners (Vlahovic, Roberts, & Dunbar, 2012); and to determine if laughter evoked by media occurs differently than laughter that erupts in social contexts (Vettin & Todt, 2004).

What kind of sound do you think this woman's laugh would produce? Deep and hearty? High and giggly? Is she a snorter?

Have you noticed that we seem to have lost the art of the whisper these days? We notice this the most when we're in a movie theater, irritated by the loud conversations all around us, the people answering and *actually talking* on their cell phones while the film is showing, and those who have to comment on everything coming across the screen. (Especially irritating are those people who see a movie for the second time and have to alert everyone around them when the "good" or "scary parts" are coming.) Is whispering considered a female-appropriate behavior only? Some of our male students say that whispering isn't manly.

What really isn't manly (or womanly, for that matter) is talking too loudly when you should be whispering.

Vocal qualities	Characteristics of the voice that develop subtly, more as habits than as conscious choices
Breathiness	Overabundance of air rushing through the vocal folds
Raspiness	Hoarseness or a gravelly sound in the voice
Nasality	Whiny sound produced when air is trapped or too heavily contained in the nasal cavities, instead of resonating through all the vocal structures
Vocalization	A nonword or sound not tied to speech, including those that can substitute for speech

APPLICATIONS OF VOCALICS RESEARCH ■ ■ ■

Many interesting applications of the research on vocalics continue to emerge, as social scientists and music scholars try to better understand the fascinating mechanism of the voice. Here we briefly overview some provocative topics of research on this code of nonverbal communication.

Pausing

A **pause** is a temporary stop in speech, sometimes referred to as a **vocal hesitation**. The more all-encompassing term for this aspect of vocalics is **fluency**, meaning how continuously we produce sound as communicators (Bosker, Pinget, Quene, Sanders, & deJong, 2012). Spontaneous speech is a disfluent activity, meaning it's discontinuous and fragmented. We may have moments when our vocalizations flow—and those are the moments we remember the most, when we sound impressive, glib, and convincing. But even in those flowing moments, we pause between statements. We need pauses to get the intake of breath necessary to produce speech, and we use them before, during, and after speech. Pauses vary in length; some are very brief and almost undetectable, while others are lengthy and unbearable. Ever heard of the "pregnant pause," the long pause filled with emotion or suspense?

Research suggests that pausing behavior may be related to (1) emotions, because people who are depressed tend to pause in their speech more than people who aren't depressed (Karpf, 2006),

chapter nine

and (2) the complexity of a message, meaning that pausing may be more necessary when delivering a complex message compared with a simple one (Greene & Ravizza, 1995). Pausing and silence are culturally rooted nonverbal behaviors. A judgment of how short or long a pause should be depends on one's culture. For example, a typical pause in Japanese culture can last as long as eight seconds, compared with about one second on average for Americans (Karpf, as cited in Fuller, 2006). In general, Americans have little tolerance for silence (Remland, 2016).

At least three different types of pauses are at your disposal as a communicator. The first is the **filled pause**, which occurs when we use nonwords or sounds like "um" and "er" when we pause to take a breath. A filled pause can cover silence, give us time to think about what to say next, help us maintain our turn at talk and ward off interrupters, create an opening to let someone else speak, or give us time to be convincingly deceptive (Hughes, Wood, & Foulkes, 2016; Ruhlemann, Bagout-dinov, & O'Donnell, 2011; Tian, Maruyama, & Ginzburg, 2017). While filled pauses are common, they're much more acceptable in conversation than in public speaking. In everyday conversation, usually we don't focus on or register the number of fillers we or someone else uses. But when ours is the only voice a group of listeners hears, as in a presentation or broadcast, an "uh" or "er" becomes obvious and can distract listeners, undermine our credibility, and detract from our overall effect. One study examined filled pauses in presentations and found that listeners perceive them as indications of anxiety and a lack of preparation on a speaker's part (Christenfeld, 1995). While filled pauses create better impressions on listeners than do silent pauses, a style that uses no pauses at all (except between sentences, where short pauses are expected) is received the most positively by listeners.

Silent pauses (sometimes called **unfilled pauses**) are breaks in speech that carry no sound; sometimes they're used on purpose but sometimes not. Sometimes they may emerge because we're stumped, flabbergasted, emotional, or reluctant to say anything (Etehadieh & Rendle-Short, 2016). We occasionally pause unintentionally when our brains are heavily engaged or working overtime (a phenomenon termed *cognitive load*); the pause allows our brains time to catch up so we can produce effective communication (Frank et al., 2013).

A third type of pause is the **audible pause** (sometimes known as an audible gasp), in which air is taken in and speech is disrupted. In some instances, the audible pause may substitute for speech. For example, what if a total stranger came up to you and asked your weight? You might draw in a quick breath, revealing your shock or surprise at the question, and then stumble out some kind of response. When speech is disrupted by a sigh, that sigh can also be viewed as a form of audible pause, but with air being expelled rather than drawn in.

A pause is often purposeful; it can be used as a stall tactic when the receiver of a request doesn't want to comply with the request (Roberts, Francis, & Morgan, 2006). Pauses can create dramatic effect in a presentation or set up a punch line for a joke. Many politicians and actors learn to use pauses effectively. In fact, trained stage actors are taught to "pause for applause" or "hold for laughs," because if they continue with dialogue over an audience's reaction, they'll ruin the enjoyment of the laughter, cut the applause short, or cause the audience to miss the next few lines.

Silence

While pauses tend to be fairly short, if you've ever received the "silent treatment" from a loved one, you know that silence can seem to last forever. Very simply, **silence** is the absence of sound. Some people feel that they need lots of words and nonverbal messages to communicate, while others think "silence is golden." People have long been fascinated with silence: A classic Simon and Garfunkel song refers to "The Sound of Silence"; you've probably heard of "suffering in silence" and a reference to a police or military "code of silence." Karpf (2006) suggests that silence is the "most culturally bound aspect of communication" (p. 189). She provides multiple examples of cultural uses of silence, which can cause difficulties when members of different cultures attempt to communicate and interpret one another's silence.

You may never have thought of silence as a form of nonverbal communication, but it's one of the most powerful ways to communicate a message nonverbally (Acheson, 2008; Bruneau, 2008; Ephratt, 2008; Jaworski, 1999; Wagner, 2010). In their book on nonverbal communication in intimate relationships, Guerrero and Floyd (2006) describe the downside of silence, those instances when it is "intimidating and threatening," such as in response to conflict (p. 158). A couple can be in the heat of an argument when one partner simply stops talking *and* listening. While silence may seem like the best thing to do in the heat of battle, it can be used as a power play or stall tactic, which can bring conflict resolution to a screeching halt. Guerrero and Floyd discuss common ways silence manifests in close relationships: "failing to acknowledge a relational partner's presence, giving a partner the silent treatment, failing to respond to a partner's question, or ignoring someone's suggestions or requests" (p. 158). Relational silence can heighten frustration, and generate feelings of disrespect, resentment, and neglect (Knapp, Vangelisti, & Caughlin, 2013). However, avoidance and silence as conflict management strategies aren't necessarily negative; silence can effectively promote peace in relationships that experience conflict (Cheng & Tardy, 2009; Georgakopoulos, 2004).

Educators have studied silence in elementary- to college-level classrooms, focusing on such behaviors as the "hushing" technique some teachers use with students, why some students choose to be silent in the classroom, and the effects of student silence on a teacher's emotions and development (Rendle-Short, 2005; Smith & King, 2018; Thornberg, 2006). English professor Mary Reda (2010a, 2010b) explains that college students often weigh such factors as instructor expectations, the importance of classmates' impressions of them if they speak up in class, and their own levels of self-esteem when deciding to speak in class or stay silent.

What goes through your mind when you make a decision to put your hand up and ask a question in class rather than remaining silent?

chapter nine

Positive uses of silence certainly exist. In *Quiet: The Power of Introverts in a World That Can't Stop Talking*, Susan Cain (2012) discusses many people's need for silence, in both their personal and professional lives. She explains that

> some companies are starting to understand the value of silence and solitude and are creating "flexible" open plans that offer a mix of solo workspaces, quiet zones, casual meeting areas, cafés, reading rooms, computer hubs, and even "streets" where people can chat casually with each other without interrupting others' workflow. (p. 94)

Silence has been studied for its role in therapeutic conversations, meaning the ways therapists use silence in their counseling sessions, as well as how they respond to silence from their patients (Ladany, Hill, Thompson, & O'Brien, 2004; MacDonald, 2005). In some contexts, silence can communicate respect for authority, such as in a meeting with your boss when you let the higher-status person speak first and break the silence (Burgoon, Buller, & Woodall, 1996). Sometimes it can be really nice to find someone you can just *be* with, without talking; silence can indicate comfortability between people.

One of the more interesting lines of research into silence as nonverbal communication explores **self-silencing**, defined as the inhibition of self-expression (Schuessler Harper, 2006, 2007). Self-silencing theory first emerged from research with clinically depressed adult women, who reported that they constantly refrained from expressing their beliefs and opinions to their husbands or significant others. As a result, they experienced depression, low self-esteem, a morphing of identity into the kind of wife or partner they believed to be socially and culturally acceptable, and a lack of trust in their own opinions (Jack, 1991). Psychologist Schuessler Harper (2007) suggests that self-silencing can become necessary in some relationships out of a sheer need for preservation. Schuessler Harper's research focused on adolescent self-silencing. Adolescents who revealed that they frequently self-silenced in their dating relationships, particularly during times of conflict, evidenced the following, compared with non-self-silencers: (1) greater levels of depression, (2) greater sensitivity to rejection by a dating partner, (3) earlier ages of transitioning into their first experience with sexual intercourse, (4) greater discomfort when they tried to refuse offers of sexual activity from their partners, and (5) poor overall communication with their partners.

Pause (vocal hesitation)	A break or change in the production of sound
Fluency	How continuously we produce sound
Filled pause	A vocalization such as "um" or "er" that fills a pause, typically as a way of covering silence and giving the communicator time to think of what to say, or to encourage others to speak
Silent pause	Breaks in speech that carry no sound
Audible pause	A pause in which air is taken in and speech is disrupted
Silence	The absence of sound
Self-silencing	The inhibition of self-expression

Turn-Taking in Conversation

For the most part, ordinary, everyday conversations occur in turns: One person speaks or takes a turn, then another person responds (takes a turn), and the back and forth continues (Corps, Gambi, & Pickering, 2018; Sacks, Schegloff, & Jefferson, 1978). The turns at talk aren't always clean, meaning that turns often overlap, statements are incomplete, people may try to talk at the same time, and so on. But for the purpose of analysis, it's helpful to view conversation as a series of turns—that is, unless someone dominates the conversation and changes it into a monologue. Turn-taking, as a structure for conversation and a means of studying or tracking conversation for the purpose of analysis, is a subset of interaction management, or how people use verbal and nonverbal communication to conduct or manage their conversations (Guerrero & Floyd, 2006). Even a conversation that seems chaotic involves a set of informal, culturally-based rules that most people tend to learn over time and through social experience, even though speakers may violate those rules (Bolden, 2018; Roberts & Levinson, 2017). Research on this topic emerged when scholars tried to determine those features of conversation that regularly appear and give interaction its form (Cappella, 1985; Duncan, 1972, 1973; Duncan & Fiske, 1977; Wiemann & Knapp, 1975; Wilson, Wiemann, & Zimmerman, 1984). Like many other aspects of nonverbal communication, turn-taking cues accompany other nonverbal cues (e.g., eye contact, head nodding, forward or backward lean, facial expressions) to help accomplish the desired outcome. Four types of turn-taking cues help us understand how conversations are managed. Try to learn these terms as they apply to how a *speaker* behaves, not how a *listener* or *receiver* behaves.

TURN-REQUESTING CUES. How do you let others know that you'd like to speak? Do you simply butt into a conversation, saying, "Excuse me, but I'd like a turn at talk"? We doubt it, although you might say something like that if you're having particular difficulty getting the floor. We typically use **turn-requesting cues** to signal that we'd like to engage in conversation, usually beginning with an intake of breath. This intake may or may not cue others that we want to talk, or others may ignore this cue and continue right over us, but turns at talk begin with an intake of breath necessary to carry speech. Another

In many cultures around the world, conversation occurs through a series of turns taken at talk.

method of requesting a turn at talk is to use a **stutter start**, meaning a repetition of the first word or the first letter of the word that starts the statement we want to make—such as, "Well, . . . well, . . . w . . . w . . ."—or the use of a filled pause, such as "ah" or "um," as a means of being recognized as a conversational participant. We also use **back-channel cues**, such as "hmmm" and "uh-huh," which are responses to others' statements that can encourage them to continue speaking and signal our interest and attentiveness in the conversation while also indicating that we'd like a turn at talk. Some conversationally impatient people will use rapid-fire back-channel cues in succession, to hurry along someone who's talking and thus gain a turn.

TURN-MAINTAINING CUES. If you're talking and someone obviously wants to say something or respond to you but you don't want to stop talking, what are you likely to do? Put your hand up in the air and say, "Please be patient. I haven't yet finished my turn at talk"? We doubt it; most people prefer nonverbal cues to verbal statements when trying to correct what they perceive as inappropriate behavior (Burgoon, 2016). When speakers sense that someone wants to interrupt or take a turn but they want to maintain the floor or simply haven't finished what they want to say, they typically get louder and faster. These vocal strategies are **turn-maintaining cues**. Filled pauses can help us maintain our turn at talk; they keep our sound and turn going, helping us ward off interruptions.

TURN-YIELDING CUES. How do you indicate that you've finished a turn at talk—throw your arms up in the air and yell, "ta da!"? We doubt it, but you're likely to use a subtle **turn-yielding cue** to indicate that you wish to relinquish the floor, at least for the time being. The most common form of this cue is simply to drop your pitch, meaning to use a diminishing pattern of intonation as you near the end of your turn (Walker, 2017). Another yielding cue involves rising intonation, such as ending your turn as a question, which invites others to respond. You can also give up your turn and encourage others to engage through the use of a tag line or filled pause, such as "you know" or "and, um . . . ." Finally, a tactic often used by teachers when they want students to respond to their questions or participate in class discussion is simple silence. If instructors are patient enough to endure a short silence, usually a student will bail them out and offer a comment.

TURN-DENYING CUES. What if you don't want to engage in conversation, or you just want to listen but not talk? Do you blurt out, "I pass"? We doubt it; you're more likely to use **turn-denying cues** to indicate to people that you want them to continue talking or don't want to converse at all. Mentioned earlier, back-channel cues spoken slowly can reinforce speakers and indicate that their turn at talk should continue. Another common way to avoid taking a turn at talk is simply to be silent, although this can be awkward, especially if only two people are involved in the conversation. Long silent pauses give others the opportunity to take a turn, thus relieving you of having to take a turn when you don't want to.

Interruptions and Overlaps

Besides turn-taking cues, interruptions and overlaps emerge frequently in conversation. **Interruptions** are abrupt intrusions into someone's speech—they're obvious and disrupt the flow of speech (West & Zimmerman, 1983). Typically, when one person interrupts another, the first person's speech is halted and the interrupter's speech takes over. However, sometimes interruptions aren't acknowledged or accepted, meaning that the first speaker continues to speak, usually faster and louder, to stave off the intrusion. The second speaker either has to reassert the interruption more forcefully or wait for another opportunity to seek a turn.

In contrast, **overlaps** tend to occur just as one speaker finishes a turn at talk and another begins a turn. Overlaps are considered less offensive than interruptions, because overlapping may be seen as enthusiastic and supportive—as trying to reinforce or dovetail with someone's idea. However, be aware that some people aren't forgiving about overlaps; they view them as interruptions (Heldner & Edlund, 2010). Perhaps they grew up with the rule that a listener waits for someone to stop talking completely before taking a turn.

Scholars have examined the role of power or dominance in interaction management, looking specifically at how speakers establish turns at talk; protect, maintain, and lengthen them; and use interruptions and overlaps to dominate others (Cusen, 2017; Dethlefs, et al., 2016; Dunbar & Abra, 2010; Farley, 2008; Hodges-Simeon et al., 2010; Youngquist, 2009). Interruptions indicate dominance and power play more often than overlaps, because they cut a speaker off midstream or prevent a speaker from making another comment, suggesting that the interrupter's contribution is somehow more important or insightful. One study found that the more frequently a person interrupted, the more negatively that person is perceived (Gnisci, Sergi, DeLuca, & Errico, 2012). We've stressed throughout this book the importance of placing all judgments of appropriateness within a cultural context; views about interrupting and overlapping are culturally rooted as well. Speakers interrupting

chapter nine

OUT OF THE CLASSROOM
onto the page

Ever interrupted a professor mid-lecture? This was the subject of a recent class session in one of our nonverbal communication classes. While discussing vocalics as powerful nonverbal cues, Mindy raised her hand to signal to the professor that she had a question, then asked: "If a professor is lecturing and a student has a question, what's the best way to handle that? Lots of teachers will tell you to be sure and ask questions when you have them, but then they get on a roll with their lecture, so you wonder if you should interrupt them to ask a question."

We grant that some professors are inconsistent; they tell students to ask questions but then don't seem to "come up for air" during lectures. So students are put in the awkward position of interrupting the professor, breaking her or his flow of information, and risking feeling embarrassed in front of classmates. Throwing your hand up in the air to ask a question isn't the easiest thing to do, particularly if the teacher is "on a roll," as Mindy described.

From the professor's side of the equation, yes, we can "get on a roll" and forget to monitor what's going on with our students. Simply asking at the end of a class session, "Are there any questions?" is often an ineffective strategy, because students are mentally checking out of that class and transitioning into their next experience, like heading home, off to a job, or out to another class.

You've probably seen effective and ineffective student methods for posing questions to profs, as well as effective and ineffective prof responses to such moments; so what's the best approach? As professors, we suggest that instructors need to be better communicators, not getting so caught up in delivering information that they forget about or ignore listeners. Students need to be assertive (but polite and respectful at the same time) in slowing down a professor or getting him or her to pause for a question, because rolling past a student's question or creating an environment where students simply won't ask questions defeats the whole purpose of being there—learning.

and overlapping one another's remarks might be judged as chaotic in one cultural context, but in another, such conversational energy might be typical, reflective of merely a lively exchange.

Given rising travel costs, crunched schedules, and the ease of use and increased quality of videoconferencing, it's not surprising that many professional meetings now take place through a mediated channel rather than face to face. Many college students tell us that they now expect job interviews to be accomplished via Skype, FaceTime, or other such applications on computers or cell phones. The technology is much improved, but it's still the case that when people in different locations try to converse, the vocalics can get tricky (Shin, Liu, Jang, & Bente, 2017; Sindoni, 2014). Conversational dynamics require careful attention to ensure that questions and comments aren't "lost in translation." One researcher studied vocalics during conference calls, finding that interruptions, overlaps, and pauses occurred with less frequency than in face-to-face meetings, mainly because of a concentrated effort to help all parties hear and be heard clearly (Halbe, 2012).

3

REMEMBER

Remember!
9.6

Turn-taking	When one person speaks or takes a turn in conversation, then another person responds (takes a turn), and so forth
Interaction management	How we use verbal and nonverbal messages to conduct or manage our communication with others
Turn-requesting cues	Vocal nonverbal cues that signal that we would like to engage in conversation
Stutter start	Repetition of the first word or first letter or sound of the first word of a statement we want to make
Back-channel cues	Vocal nonverbal cues that can encourage others to continue speaking and signal our interest in a conversation while also indicating that we'd like a turn at talk
Turn-maintaining cues	Vocal nonverbal cues that indicate that we want to maintain the floor or our turn at talk
Turn-yielding cues	Vocal nonverbal cues that indicate that we want to relinquish the floor
Turn-denying cues	Vocal nonverbal cues that indicate that we want other people to continue talking or don't want to converse at all
Interruptions	Obvious and abrupt vocal intrusions into someone's speech that disrupt the flow
Overlaps	Vocalizations that tend to occur just as one speaker finishes a turn at talk and another begins a turn

chapter nine

Vocal Indications of Deception

When you think about detecting deception, you probably think of lie detector machines that conduct polygraph tests—sophisticated devices that measure all kinds of physiological responses in humans to determine if someone is being truthful or deceptive (Knapp, McGlone, Griffin, & Earnest, 2015; Levine, Blair, & Carpenter, 2018; Vrij, Fisher, & Blank, 2017). While the technology of lie detection has advanced, the results of polygraph tests are still not legally admissible in most U.S. courts of law. For our purposes, we're more interested in human lie detectors.

One of the most heavily researched topics within the field of nonverbal communication is deception, or the study of how people use their bodies and voices to deceive others. Research has focused on deceivers' behavior (termed **leakage** in research), as well as on how receivers detect de-

ception in others (Carson, 2012; De Waele & Claeys, 2017; Frank & Svetieva, 2013; Hamlin, Wright, van der Zee, & Wilson, 2018; Vrij, 2006). People "leak" their deception in a variety of ways. No one behavioral cue is a dead giveaway of deception (DePaulo et al., 2003; Novotny et al., 2018; Paik & van Swol, 2017). While we might wish deception revealed itself as simply as a nose growing with the telling of a lie, deception and its detection is complicated, with multiple cues attached.

The use of lie detector machines is still controversial, even with advances in the technology that helps us detect deception.

Before we explore four primary vocal indicators of deception, we need to repeat something mentioned in Chapter 5 when we discussed facial and eye behaviors related to deception: Once information gets publicized as to how deceivers tend to act, people who deceive *change* that behavior so they won't be caught in their lies. People intent on lying or who get caught in a lie may or may not exhibit the vocal cues we discuss here.

In general, the best way to detect deception in someone you know fairly well is to compare the behavior you think reveals deception to how the person usually acts or speaks, meaning her or his baseline of normal behavior. Watch and listen for behaviors that are out of the ordinary for that person. These altered behaviors could be outgrowths of anxiety or extra energy in the body, usually present when someone is being deceptive. Altered nonverbal cues have multiple causes, but deception is one thing to consider as you try to interpret what's going on. Again, the nonverbal cues should outweigh the verbal ones, because nonverbal cues carry the truer meaning behind a message. But, as you'll see, deception detection is a tricky endeavor.

Researchers estimate that most people's ability to detect deception accurately is around 50% (Frank & Svetieva, 2013). When people such as TSA agents, police officers, Secret Service personnel, and therapists, who are trained to deal with deception, are tested for their detection abilities, their accuracy rates are higher than the average person's (Elaad, 2009; O'Sullivan, Frank, & Hurley, 2010; Wachi et al., 2017). And then there are the "wizards," those people who have been studied by researchers because they have extremely high and unusual lie-detecting abilities, as accurate as 90% when tested. The primary distinguishing characteristic of wizards compared with the rest of us is that they pay closer attention to the presence and absence of nonverbal cues, especially micro cues that many of us miss (O'Sullivan, 2005; O'Sullivan & Ekman, 2004). People who attend to vocal cues are more accurate detectors of deception than people who attend to other cues, such as eye contact, facial expressions, and movements (Bond & DePaulo, 2006; Burgoon, Blair, & Strom, 2008; DePaulo et al., 2003).

Read this typical exchange between a mother and child, and then we'll analyze it for deceptive elements.

> **Mother:**   Jeffrey, come here this instant and tell me what happened to this cookie jar. It's on the kitchen floor and broken into pieces! Did you break this jar while I was outside talking to the neighbors?
>
> **Jeffrey:**   [After a long pause and in a very high-pitched voice] Uh, NO, Mom. I didn't break the cookie jar. I didn't go near it 'cuz you told me not to, so I dunno what happened. I'm not 'posed to have cookies before dinner, so I didn't get up there. The jar must've fallen off the counter all by itself, 'cuz I sure didn't do it.

HIGH PITCH. One reliable indicator of deception is unusually high pitch (Anolli & Ciceri, 1997; O'Sullivan, 2005; Warren, Schertler, & Bull, 2009). Children, such as Jeffrey in our cookie jar example, often produce high pitches in their speech or vocalizations when trying to deceive. Adults do this, too. In fact, it's interesting to watch courtroom testimony when, in the heat of emotion, witnesses, defendants, and plaintiffs may exhibit unusually high pitches as they testify. Pitch variation, with higher than usual peaks, can belie a deceiver's intentions. Most explanations for this phenomenon point to increased tension in the body, and thus in the voice, due to anxiety related to deception. The more stressful the act of deception, the greater the increases in pitch (Andersen, 2004; DePaulo et al., 2003).

RESPONSE LATENCY. Jeffrey paused a few seconds before answering his mother's questions—a common nonverbal cue when people are challenged, feel cornered, or know they're about to lie. The amount of time it took Jeffrey to answer is termed **response latency** (Mapala, Warmelink, & Linkenauger, 2017). Again, what you want to listen for if you think you're being deceived is a change in behavior. If someone typically maintains a fast or normal pace of responding, then that person takes longer than usual to respond to a question or comment, deception is a possibility. Again, we say *possibility*; we urge caution when interpreting nonverbal cues you believe indicate deception—detection is an imprecise activity. Often, the response isn't complete silence; it can be masked by a filled pause, meaning that a deceiver may use vocalizations during the pause before she or he responds, usually for the purpose of buying time to come up with something to say.

MESSAGE DURATION. Look back at the conversation between Jeffrey and his mother; note how short the mother's questions were, compared with the length of Jeffrey's answer. One vocal cue of deception is message duration, or the length of a verbal message. To repeat, when attempting to determine deception in someone you know, use your baseline of information about the person, and then watch and listen for aberrant nonverbal behaviors. If someone tends to be verbose (takes lengthy turns at talk), then listen for unusually short, curt statements or answers to questions. Limiting how much you engage in conversation can be an indication of deception. Conversely, if someone typically gives moderate or short answers to questions but exhibits out-of-character behavior in conversation by offering unusually long turns at talk, the person might be trying to deceive.

WHAT WOULD YOU DO?

You're working on a massive group project for a course in your major field of study—a huge chunk of your grade is riding on this project. Three other members of your group meet with you in the student center to work on the project, but one person (the friend you know the best among the group) is a no-show. Not showing up, not even texting or calling to say you can't make it, is really out of the norm for this person, so you start to worry. The next day you see your friend in another class and ask what happened. The person hems and haws, finally mumbling out a long and lame tale about car trouble and a dead phone. You don't buy it; something's fishy.

All the vocal cues are odd for this person, who's normally a conscientious student. Other nonverbal cues besides the vocalics are screaming, making you increasingly suspicious that you're being deceived. *What would you do* in this situation? Would you interrogate the person until you get a true explanation? Would you let it go, for the sake of keeping the peace and progressing on the group project? Would you feel less friendship for the person, as a result?

SPEECH DISFLUENCIES AND ERRORS. Remember that most of us were taught that lying is wrong; so when we attempt to deceive, we experience some sort of heightened activation in the body, some extra energy. That energy must travel somewhere, and, as we've said, for many people the nervousness or activation manifests itself or "leaks" through the voice. We overviewed speech fluency in earlier sections on pausing and silence, but realize that speech disruptions (disfluencies) can be evidence of anxiety, possibly generated by or created in anticipation of deception (Frank & Svetieva, 2013; Harrigan, Suarez, & Hartman, 1994; Hughes, Wood, & Foulkes, 2016; Knapp et al., 2015; Tian, Maruyama, & Ginzburg, 2017).

If you suspect someone is lying to you, listen for disfluencies—sometimes referred to as **speech errors**, meaning vocalizations that disrupt the flow of speech. Guerrero and Floyd (2006) explain:

> Although the term speech errors may seem to imply a verbal behavior, the markers that are typically measured are vocalic but not verbal. These include vocal disfluencies such as filled pauses (e.g., "um" or "uh") and false starts, excessively long pauses, and long response latencies (the time lapse between when a question is posed and when the recipient begins to answer it). (pp. 178–179)

Speech errors have all kinds of causes—being in a hurry; being tired or not feeling well, such that you slur your words or pause in odd places; or being so frustrated that the words just don't come out right. Many things can cause speech errors, but deception is one of them (Andersen, 2004; Feeley & de Turck, 1998; Vrij & Heaven, 1999).

REMEMBER

Remember!
9.7

Leakage	Ways people nonverbally reveal deception
Response latency	A deception cue; the amount of time someone takes to respond to another person's communication
Message duration	A deception cue; the length of someone's message or response to another person's communication
Speech errors	A deception cue; incorrect uses of grammar, mispronounced words, and so forth

UNDERSTANDING VOCALICS: APPLYING THE REFLEXIVE CYCLE OF NONVERBAL COMMUNICATION DEVELOPMENT ▪ ▪ ▪ ▪▪▪▪▪▪

By now you know what we're going to ask you to do—walk yourself through the Reflexive Cycle with regard to how you use your voice to communicate nonverbally with others, as well as how you perceive others' voices. You may not think much about your voice unless you make a lot of presentations or are a singer, but each of us needs to think about this important channel of nonverbal information. How would you characterize your voice? Low and loud? Raspy, breathy, or nasal? Do you like the sound of your own voice, either in your head or on a recording? What feedback have you received about your voice and speech production? Answering these kinds of questions is the first step in the cycle, inventorying your own nonverbal communication.

But this personal inventory goes beyond a mere description of your voice, from your own perspective. How does your voice reveal your emotions? Think of a time when you were really down, sad, or depressed; how did your voice give you away? It's important to become more aware of situations that put your voice under duress or cause you to vary from your normal way of speaking.

Once you've inventoried yourself in terms of your voice and speech patterns, you may have identified some areas you want to improve or change. Perhaps you need to work with a vocal coach to overcome disfluencies or learn to breathe differently so you gain more vocal power. Perhaps you need to take a public speaking or voice and diction course, or other communication courses that will require you to work on your vocal production. Still another technique is to work with a recording device—summoning up the courage to record yourself and listen to the playback, noting elements you want to affect or change, working diligently to make the changes, re-recording yourself, and continuing the work. Changing your voice and the way you deliver your verbal communication, both in everyday conversation and presentations, takes time and effort, because you've learned habits over your lifetime that will be hard to alter.

The third phase of the Reflexive Cycle involves inventorying others' vocalic behavior. When you're in professional, educational, and social settings, sharpen your listening skills to attend to the vocal nonverbal behaviors of others, noting things you want to emulate as well as avoid. Perhaps you admire the fluidity with which your boss speaks, or how a teacher's words seem to command attention. Specifically, what contributes to those effects? Pausing? Volume? Rate? Pitch? Articulation? Note people's uses of pauses and hesitations—do they create interest or bog down the message? Do you detect any deception from the way people use high pitches, response latencies, message durations, or speech errors? You can learn a great deal about vocalics from all this listening and observation.

Your next step in the Reflexive Cycle is to interact with others, enacting any vocalic changes you've decided are appropriate and gauging how your nonverbal behaviors transact with others' behaviors. Do you find that your vocalic changes heighten other people's interest in and attention to you? Do you feel that you have more vocalic options at your disposal now?

After you've inventoried yourself, begun to make changes in your vocalic behavior, inventoried others' vocalics, and engaged in mutual transaction of behavior (such that your vocal nonverbal communication affects other people and theirs affects you), the final phase of the Reflexive Cycle involves an evaluation of the whole process. What did you learn about your own and others' voices that makes you a better communicator? As we've said in other chapters and reiterate here, the reflexive process requires an honest assessment of yourself, the willingness to change, keen observational skills, and a sense of "communicator adventure," as you put your new behaviors into action, transact with others, note the results, and reevaluate.

SUMMARY ■ ■ ■

This chapter was devoted to vocalics—the study of the voice as a code of nonverbal communication and how we use our voices to produce messages. We began with an overview of the anatomical and physiological functioning of the voice, to gain an understanding of how the mechanism works to produce voice.

Five properties were explored for their unique contributions to vocal production: pitch, rate, volume, articulation, and pronunciation. We also discussed how our emotions are revealed by the pitches we use, the rate with which we speak, and the varying levels of volume we produce. While vocal properties are easily changeable, vocal qualities are harder to vary. These qualities include breathiness, raspiness, and nasality. The final topic in this section was vocalizations, defined as nonwords or sounds that accompany speech or stand alone, as forms of nonverbal communication.

Pausing and silence are vocal nonverbal cues that are often overlooked, but they carry communicative power. We explored three types of pauses and their functions in conversation and presentations, then examined silence for its nonverbal clues. We discussed silence as a reaction or strategy in conflict situations, as well as positive and negative uses of silence. Self-silencing theory refers to the way people inhibit their self-expression, producing a negative impact on self-esteem and communication in relationships.

We then explored interaction management, in terms of how turn-taking operates to organize conversation. Nonverbal cues associated with four types of turns were provided: turn-requesting, turn-maintaining, turn-yielding, and turn-denying cues. We contrasted interruptions with overlaps, and investigated how these vocal nonverbal cues can affect people's perceptions of our communication and us, as communicators.

Finally, we delved into the provocative topic of deception, in terms of vocal nonverbal cues deceivers tend to use. Four common vocalic cues are high pitch, response latency, message duration, and speech disfluencies and errors. We discussed the complex process of detecting deception in others' communication, including tips for what to consider when attempting to discover if someone is lying or not. In general, the mechanism that enables us to produce vocal nonverbal communication is complex, but understanding how vocalics operate can give average communicators an edge as we interact with others. The chapter closed with an examination of how the Reflexive Cycle of Nonverbal Communication Development can help you enhance your use of vocal cues.

DISCUSSION STARTERS ■ ■ ■

1. How do verbal and vocal communication differ? How do we separate out the vocal nonverbal cues from the verbal, for purposes of analysis?

2. Review the five major properties of the voice, and then assess your own voice versus the "ideal" voice in terms of these properties. What changes would you like to make in vocal properties to enhance these important nonverbal cues?

3. What's the best laugh you ever heard? Can you describe it in terms of pitch, duration, or odd noises? Why do you think laughter is contagious? What kind of messages can laughter send to listeners?

4. Recall the three vocal qualities we explored in this chapter. Think of some famous people—celebrities, politicians, musicians, athletes—whose voices correspond with the three qualities.

5. What role do you think pausing and silence should play in conflict? When people in a romantic, intimate relationship argue, what positive uses can they make of pausing and silence? What are some negative uses of pausing and silence?

6. What rules did you learn growing up about interruptions and overlaps? Have you strayed from those rules as you've become an adult and participated in your own social situations?

7. Deception among people is tough; we know it exists, but we wish it didn't. Think about instances when you were deceived by others—from little white lies to real whoppers. Then analyze those instances for elements of deceivers' voices and speech production that might have been clues that they were deceiving you. If you didn't pick up on those clues then, do you think you will now, if there are future attempts to deceive you?

REFERENCES ■ ■ ■

Acheson, K. (2008). Silence as gesture: Rethinking the nature of communicative silences. *Communication Theory, 18*, 535–555.

Albert, G., Pearson, M., Arnocky, S., Wachowiak, M., Nicol, J., & Murphy, D. R. (2018). Effects of masculinized and feminized male voices on men and women's distractibility and implicit memory. *Journal of Individual Differences 39*, 151–165.

Andersen, P. A. (2004). *The complete idiot's guide to body language.* New York: Alpha.

Anderson, R. C., Klofstad, C. A., Mayew, W. J., & Venkatachalam, M. (2014). Vocal fry may undermine the success of young women in the labor market. *PLoS ONE.* doi.org/10.1371/journal.pone.0097506

Andre, V., Petr, C., Andre, N., Hausberger, M., & Lemasson, A. (2016). Voice features of telephone operators predict auditory preferences of consumers. *Interaction Studies, 17*, 77–97.

Anikin, A., Baath, R., & Persson, T. (2018). Human non-linguistic vocal repertoire: Call types and their meaning. *Journal of Nonverbal Behavior, 42*, 53–80.

Anolli, L., & Ciceri, R. (1997). The voice of deception: Vocal strategies of naive and able liars. *Journal of Nonverbal Behavior, 21*, 259–284.

Argyle, M. (1999). *Bodily communication*. In L. K. Guerrero, J. A. DeVito, & M. L. Hecht (Eds.), *The nonverbal communication reader: Classic and contemporary readings* (2nd ed., pp. 135–148). Prospect Heights, IL: Waveland. (Original work published 1988)

Banai, I. P. (2017). Voice in different phases of menstrual cycle among naturally cycling women and users of hormonal contraceptives. *PLoS ONE, 12*. e0183462.

Banziger, T., Patel, S., & Scherer, K. R. (2014). The role of perceived voice and speech characteristics in vocal emotion communication. *Journal of Nonverbal Behavior, 38*, 31–52.

Belin, P., Boehme, B., & McAleer, P. (2017). The sound of trustworthiness: Acoustic-based modulation of perceived voice personality. *PLoS ONE, 12*, e0185651.

Bolden, G. B. (2018). Speaking "out of turn": Epistemics in action in other-initiated repair. *Discourse Studies, 20*, 142–162.

Bond, C. F., Jr., & DePaulo, B. M. (2006). Accuracy of deception judgments. *Review of Personality and Social Psychology, 10*, 214–234.

Bosker, H. R. (2017a). How our own speech rate influences our perception of others. *Journal of Experimental Psychology: Learning, Memory, & Cognition, 43*, 1225–1238.

Bosker, H. R. (2017b). The role of temporal amplitude modulations in the political arena: Hillary Clinton vs. Donald Trump. *Proceedings of Interspeech, 2017*, 2228–2232.

Bosker, H. R., Pinget, A.-F., Quene, H., Sanders, T., & deJong, N. H. (2012). What makes speech sound fluent? The contributions of pauses, speed, and repairs. *Language Testing, 30*, 159–175.

Bruckert, L., Lienard, J., Lacroix, A., Kreutzer, M., & Leboucher, G. (2006). Women use voice parameters to assess men's characteristics. *Proceedings of the Royal Society of London, Series B, 273*, 83–89.

Bruneau, T. J. (2008). How Americans use silence and silences to communicate. *China Media Research, 4*, 77–85.

Burgoon, J. K. (2016). Expectancy violations theory. In C. R. Berger & M. E. Roloff (Eds.), *The international encyclopaedia of interpersonal communication*. New York: John Wiley & Sons. https://doi:10.1002/9781118540190.wbeic0102

Burgoon, J. K., Blair, J. P., & Strom, R. E. (2008). Cognitive biases and nonverbal cue availability in detecting deception. *Human Communication Research, 34*, 572–599.

Burgoon, J. K., Buller, D. B., & Woodall, W. G. (1996). *Nonverbal communication: The unspoken dialogue* (2nd ed.). New York: McGraw-Hill.

Cain, S. (2012). *Quiet: The power of introverts in a world that can't stop talking.* New York: Crown.

Cappella, J. N. (1985). Controlling the floor in conversation. In A. W. Siegman & S. Feldstein (Eds.), *Multichannel integrations of nonverbal behavior* (pp. 69–104). Hillsdale, NJ: Erlbaum.

Carson, T. L. (2012). *Lying and deception: Theory and practice.* Oxford, UK: Oxford University Press.

Cartei, V., & Reby, D. (2012). Acting gay: Male actors shift the frequency components of their voices towards female values when playing homosexual characters. *Journal of Nonverbal Behavior, 36*, 79–93.

Cheng, C.-C., & Tardy, C. (2009). A cross-cultural study of silence in marital conflict. *China Media Research, 5*, 35–44.

Christenfeld, N. (1995). Does it hurt to say um? *Journal of Nonverbal Behavior, 19*, 171–186.

Claeys, A-S., & Cauberghe, V. (2014). Keeping control: The importance of nonverbal expressions of power by organizational spokespersons in times of crisis. *Journal of Communication, 64*, 1160–1180.

Corps, R. E., Gambi, C., & Pickering, M. J. (2018). Coordinating utterances during turn-taking: The role of prediction, response preparation, and articulation. *Discourse Processes, 55*, 230–240.

Cusen, G. (2017). On interruptions in doctor-patient interactions: Who is the stranger here? *Philologica, 9*, 81–92.

Dabbs, J. M., Jr., & Mallinger, A. (1999). High testosterone levels predict low voice pitch among men. *Personality and Individual Differences, 27*, 801–804.

Davidson, J. (2016, October 3-16). Where the top notes go: Why do voices deepen and thin over time? *New York*, 113–118.

DePaulo, B. M., Lindsay, J. L., Malone, B. E., Muhlenbruck, L., Charlton, K., & Cooper, H. (2003). Cues to deception. *Psychological Bulletin, 129*, 74–118.

Dethlefs, N., Hastie, H., Cuayahuitl, H., Yu, Y., Rieser, V., & Lemon, O. (2016). Information density and overlap in spoken dialogue. *Computer Speech & Language, 37*, 82–97.

De Waele, A., & Claeys, A-S. (2017). Nonverbal cues of deception in audiovisual crisis communication. *Public Relations Review, 43*, 680–689.

De Waele, A., Claeys, A-S., & Cauberghe, V. (2017). The organizational voice: The importance of voice pitch and speech rate in organizational crisis communication. *Communication Research.* https://doi.org/10.1177/0093650217692911

Dunbar, N. E., & Abra, G. (2010). Observations of dyadic power in interpersonal interaction. *Communication Monographs, 77*, 657–684.

Duncan, S. (1972). Some signals and rules for taking speaking turns in conversations. *Journal of Personality and Social Psychology, 23*, 283–292.

Duncan, S. (1973). Toward a grammar for dyadic conversation. *Semiotica, 9*, 24–46.

Duncan, S., & Fiske, D. W. (1977). *Face-to-face interaction.* Hillsdale, NJ: Erlbaum.

Eddins, D. A., Anand, S., Camacho, A., & Shrivastav, R. (2016). Modeling of breathy voice quality using pitch-strength estimates. *Journal of Voice, 30*, 774.e1-774.e7.

Eichorn, J. T., Kent, R. D., Austin, D., & Vorperian, H. K. (2017). Effects of aging on vocal fundamental frequency and vowel formants in men and women. *Journal of Voice, 31.* https://doi.org/10.1016/j.jvoice.2017.08.003

Ekman, P. (1965). Communication through nonverbal behavior: A source of information about an interpersonal relationship. In S. S. Tomkins & C. E. Izard (Eds.), *Affect, cognition, and personality* (390–442). New York: Springer.

Elaad, E. (2009). Lie-detection biases among male police interrogators, prisoners, and laypersons. *Psychological Reports, 1005*, 1047–1056.

Ephratt, M. (2008). The functions of silence. *Journal of Pragmatics, 40*, 1909–1938.

Erickson-Schroth, L. (Ed.). (2014). *Trans bodies, trans selves: A resource for the transgender community.* New York: Oxford University Press.

Etehadieh, E., & Rendle-Short, J. (2016). Intersubjectivity or preference: Interpreting student pauses in supervisory meetings. *Australian Journal of Linguistics, 36*, 172–188.

Evans, S., Neave, M., Wakelin, D., & Hamilton, C. (2008). The relationship between testosterone and vocal frequencies in human males. *Physiology & Behavior, 93*, 783–788.

Farley, S. D. (2008). Attaining status at the expense of likeability: Pilfering power through conversational interruptions. *Journal of Nonverbal Behavior, 32*, 241–260.

Farley, S. D., Hughes, S. M., & LaFayette, J. N. (2013). People will know we are in love: Evidence of differences between vocal samples directed toward lovers and friends. *Journal of Nonverbal Behavior, 37,* 123–128.

Feeley, T. H., & de Turck, M. A. (1998). The behavioral correlates of sanctioned and unsanctioned deceptive communication. *Journal of Nonverbal Behavior, 22,* 189–204.

Feinberg, D. R., Jones, B. C., Law Smith, M. J., Moore, F. R., DeBruine, L. M., Cornwall, R. E., et al. (2006). Menstrual cycle, trait estrogen level, and masculinity preferences in the human voice. *Hormones and Behavior, 46,* 215–222.

Feinberg, D. R., Jones, B. C., Little, A. C., Burt, D. M., & Perrett, D. I. (2005). Manipulations of fundamental and formant frequencies influence the attractiveness of human male voices. *Animal Behaviour, 69,* 561–568.

Feldstein, S., Dohm, F. A., & Crown, C. L. (2001). Gender and speech rate in the perception of competence and social attractiveness. *Journal of Social Psychology, 141,* 785–808.

Fessenden, M. (2011, December 9). "Vocal fry" creeping into U.S. speech. Retrieved from https://www.sciencemag.org/news/2011/12/vocal-fry-creeping-us-speech

Frank, M. G., Maroulis, A., & Griffin, D. J. (2013). The voice. In D. Matusomo, M. G. Frank, & H. S. Hwang (Eds.), *Nonverbal communication: Science and application* (pp. 53–74). Thousand Oaks, CA: Sage.

Frank, M. G., & Svetieva, E. (2013). Deception. In D. Matusomo, M. G. Frank, & H. S. Hwang (Eds.), *Nonverbal communication: Science and application* (pp. 121–144). Thousand Oaks, CA: Sage.

Frauendorfer, D., Schmid Mast, M., Nguyen, L., & Gatica-Perez, D. (2014). Nonverbal social sensing in action: Unobtrusive recording and extracting of nonverbal behavior in social interactions illustrated with a research example. *Journal of Nonverbal Behavior, 38,* 231–245.

Freitas, J., Teixeira, A., Silva, S., Oliveira, C., & Dias, M. S. (2015). Detecting nasal vowels in speech interfaces based on surface electromyography. *PLoS ONE, 10,* e0127040.

Fujiki, R. B., Chapleau, A., Sundarrajan, A., McKenna, V., & Sivasankar, M. P. (2017). The interaction of surface hydration and vocal loading on vocal measures. *Journal of Voice, 31,* 211–217.

Fuller, W. (2006, August). Talking points: Five facts about the human voice. *O: The Oprah Winfrey Magazine,* 76.

Gelfer, M. P., & Bennett, Q. E. (2013). Speaking fundamental frequency and vowel formant frequencies: Effects on perception of gender. *Journal of Voice, 27,* 556–566.

Georgakopoulos, A. (2004). The role of silence and avoidance in interpersonal conflict. *Peace and Conflict Studies, 11,* 85–95.

Gijssels, T., Casasanto, L. S., Jasmin, K., Hagoort, P., & Casasanto, D. (2016). Speech accommodation without priming: The case of pitch. *Discourse Processes, 53,* 233–251.

Gnisci, A., Sergi, I., DeLuca, E., & Errico, V. (2012). Does frequency of interruptions amplify the effect of various types of interruptions? Experimental evidence. *Journal of Nonverbal Behavior, 36,* 39–57.

Goberman, A. M., Hughes, S., & Haydock, T. (2011). Acoustic characteristics of public speaking: Anxiety and practice effects. *Speech Communication, 53,* 867–876.

Goethals, G. R. (2005). Nonverbal behavior and political leadership. In R. E. Riggio & R. S. Feldman (Eds.), *Applications of nonverbal communication* (pp. 95–115). Mahwah, NJ: Erlbaum.

Greene, J. O., & Ravizza, S. M. (1995). Complexity effects on temporal characteristics of speech. *Human Communication Research, 21,* 390–421.

Guerrero, L. K., & Floyd, K. (2006). *Nonverbal communication in close relationships.* Mahwah, NJ: Erlbaum.

Halbe, D. (2012). "Who's there?" Differences in the features of telephone and face-to-face conferences. *Journal of Business Communication, 49,* 48–73.

chapter nine

Hamlin, I., Wright, G. R. T, van der Zee, S., & Wilson, S. (2018). The dimensions of deception detection: Self-reported deception cue use is underpinned by two broad factors. *Applied Cognitive Psychology*. https://doi.org/10.1002/acp.3402

Hancock, A. B., Childs, K. D., & Irwig, M. S. (2017). Trans male voice in the first year of testosterone therapy: Make no assumptions. *Journal of Speech, Language, and Hearing Research, 60*, 2472–2482.

Hancock, A. B., & Haskin, G. (2015). Speech-language pathologists' knowledge and attitudes regarding lesbian, gay, bisexual, transgender, and queer (LGBTQ) populations. *American Journal of Speech-Language Pathology, 24*, 206–221.

Harrigan, J. A., Suarez, I., & Hartman, J. S. (1994). Effect of speech errors on observers' judgments of anxious and defensive individuals. *Journal of Research in Personality, 28*, 505–529.

Hartmann, M., & Mast, F. W. (2017). Loudness counts: Interactions between loudness, number magnitude, and space. *Quarterly Journal of Experimental Psychology, 70*, 1305–1322.

Hehman, J. A., Corpuz, R., & Bugental, D. (2012). Patronizing speech to older adults. *Journal of Nonverbal Behavior, 36*, 249–261.

Heldner, M., & Edlund, J. (2010). Pauses, gaps, and overlaps in conversations. *Journal of Phonetics, 38*, 555–568.

Henley, N. M. (2001). Body politics. In A. Branaman (Ed.), *Self and society: Blackwell readers in sociology* (pp. 288–297). Malden, MA: Blackwell.

Higdon, M. J. (2016). Oral advocacy and vocal fry: The unseemly, sexist side of nonverbal persuasion. *Legal Communication & Rhetoric, 13*, 209–219.

Hodges-Simeon, C. R., Gaulin, S. J. C., & Puts, D. A. (2010). Different vocal parameters predict perceptions of dominance and attractiveness. *Human Nature, 21*, 406–427.

Hughes, S. M., Farley, S. D., & Rhodes, B. (2010). Vocal and physiological changes in response to the physical attractiveness of conversational partners. *Journal of Nonverbal Behavior, 34*, 155–167.

Hughes, S. M., Mogilski, J., & Harrison, M. (2014). The perception and parameters of intentional voice manipulation. *Journal of Nonverbal Behavior, 38*, 107–127.

Hughes, V., Wood, S., & Foulkes, P. (2016). Strength of forensic voice comparison evidence from the acoustics of filled pauses. *International Journal of Speech, Language and the Law, 23*, 99–132.

Imhof, M. (2010). Listening to voices and judging people. *International Journal of Listening, 24*, 19–33.

Jack, D. C. (1991). *Silencing the self: Women and depression*. Cambridge, MA: Harvard University Press.

Jaworski, A. (1999). The power of silence in communication. In L. K. Guerrero, J. A. DeVito, & M. L. Hecht (Eds.), *The nonverbal communication reader: Classic and contemporary readings* (2nd ed., pp. 156–162). Prospect Heights, IL: Waveland.

Jones, B. C., Feinberg, D. R., DeBruine, L. M., Little, A. C., & Vukovic, J. (2008). Integrating cues of social interest and voice pitch in men's preferences for women's voices. *Biology Letters, 4*, 192–194.

Jones, B. C., Feinberg, D. R., DeBruine, L. M., Little, A. C., & Vukovic, J. (2010). A domain-specific opposite-sex bias in human preferences for manipulated voice pitch. *Animal Behaviour, 79*, 57–62.

Juslin, P. N., Laukka, P., & Banziger, T. (2018). The mirror to our soul? Comparisons of spontaneous and posed vocal expression of emotion. *Journal of Nonverbal Behavior, 42*, 1–40.

Kalathottukaren, R. T., Purdy, S. C., & Ballard, E. (2017). Prosody perception and production in children with hearing loss and age- and gender-matched controls. *Journal of the American Academy of Audiology, 28*, 283–294.

Karpf, A. (2006). *The human voice: How this extraordinary instrument reveals essential clues about who we are.* New York: Bloomsbury.

Katz, A. N., & Hussey, K. (2017). Do people hear a sarcastic tone of voice when silently reading sarcastic text? *Metaphor and Symbol, 32,* 84–102.

Khazan, O. (2014, May 29). A speech trend called vocal fry could be hurting your chances of getting hired. Retrieved from https://www.businessinsider.com/vocal-fry-may-hurt-chance-of-getting-hired-2014-5

Kipper, S., & Todt, D. (2003). The role of rhythm and pitch in the evaluation of human laughter. *Journal of Nonverbal Behavior, 27,* 255–272.

Klofstad, C. A. (2017). Looks and sounds like a winner: Perceptions of competence in candidates' faces and voices influences vote choices. *Journal of Experimental Political Science, 4,* 229-240.

Knapp, M. L., Hall, J. A., & Horgan, T. G. (2013). *Nonverbal communication in human interaction* (8th ed.). Belmont, CA: Wadsworth/Cengage Learning.

Knapp, M. L., McGlone, M. S., Griffin, D. L., & Earnest, W. (2015). *Lying and deception in human interaction* (2nd ed.). Dubuque, IA: Kendall Hunt.

Knapp, M. L., Vangelisti, A. L., & Caughlin, J. (2013). *Interpersonal communication and human relationships* (7th ed.). Boston: Pearson.

Krolokke, C., & Sorensen, A. S. (2006). *Gender communication theories and analyses: From silence to performance.* Thousand Oaks, CA: Sage.

Kuhn, L. K., Wydell, T., Lavan, N., McGettigan, C., & Garrido, L. (2017). Similar representations of emotions across faces and voices. *Emotion, 17,* 912–937.

Kurtz, L. E., & Algoe, S. B. (2017). When sharing a laugh means sharing more: Testing the role of shared laughter on short-term interpersonal consequences. *Journal of Nonverbal Behavior, 41,* 45–65.

Ladany, N., Hill, C. D., Thompson, B. J., & O'Brien, K. M. (2004). Therapist perspectives on using silence in therapy: A qualitative study. *Counseling and Psychotherapy Research, 4,* 80–89.

Lakin, J. L., Jefferis, V. W., Cheng, C. M., & Chartrand, T. L. (2003). The chameleon effect as social glue: Evidence for the evolutionary significance of nonconscious mimicry. *Journal of Nonverbal Behavior, 27,* 145–161.

Latoszek, B., Maryn, Y., Gerrits, E., & De Bodt, M. (2017). The Acoustic Breathiness Index (ABI): A multivariate acoustic model for breathiness. *Journal of Voice, 31,* 511e.11-511.e27.

Laukka, P., Linnman, C., Ahs, F., Pissiota, A., Frans, O., Faria, V., et al. (2008). In a nervous voice: Acoustic analysis and perception of anxiety in social phobics' speech. *Journal of Nonverbal Behavior, 32,* 195–214.

Lebowitz, S. (2015). A speech pathologist says men use upspeak and vocal fry, too—and it can make them look less confident at work. Retrieved from https://www.businessinsider.com/men-use-upspeak-and-vocal-fry-too-2015-8

Lessac, A. (1997). *The use and training of the human voice: A bio-dynamic approach to vocal life* (3rd ed.). New York: McGraw-Hill.

Levine, T. R., Blair, J. P., & Carpenter, C. J. (2018). A critical look at meta-analytic evidence for the cognitive approach to lie detection: A re-examination of Vrij, Fisher, & Blank (2017). *Legal & Criminological Psychology, 22,* 1–21.

Limbu, Y. B., Jayachandran, C., Babin, B., & Peterson, R. T. (2016). Empathy, nonverbal immediacy, and salesperson performance: The mediating role of adaptive selling behavior. *Journal of Business & Industrial Marketing, 31,* 654–667.

Lombard, L. E., & Steinhauer, K. M. (2007). A novel treatment for hypophonic voice: Twang therapy. *Journal of Voice, 21,* 294–299.

Lozza, N., Spoerri, C., Ehlert, U., Kesselring, M., Hubmann, P., Tschacher, W., & La Marca, R. (2018). Nonverbal synchrony and complementarity in unacquainted same-sex dyads: A comparison in a competitive context. *Journal of Nonverbal Behavior, 42,* 179–197.

MacDonald, F. F. (2005). Why do we talk so much? The art of silence in psychotherapy. *Annals of the American Psychotherapy Association, 8,* 43.

Maguinness, C., Roswandowitz, C., & von Kriegstein, K. (2018). Understanding the mechanisms of familiar voice-identity recognition in the human brain. *Neuropsychologia.* https://doi.org/10.1016/j.neuro psychologia.2018.03.039

Mapala, T., Warmelink, L., & Linkenauger, S. A. (2017). Jumping the gun: Faster response latencies to deceptive questions in a realistic scenario. *Psychonomic Bulletin & Review, 24,* 1350–1358.

Maslowski, M., Meyer, A. S., & Bosker, H. R. (2018). How the tracking of habitual rate influences speech perception. *Journal of Experimental Psychology: Learning, Memory, & Cognition.* https://doi:10.1037/ xlm0000579

Mastronikolis, N. S., Remacle, M., Biagini, M., Kiagiadaki, D., & Lawson, G. (2013). Wendler glottoplasty: An effective pitch raising surgery in male-to-female transsexuals. *Journal of Voice, 27,* 516–522.

McConnell-Ginet, S. (1983). Intonation in a man's world. In B. Thorne, C. Kramarae, & N. Henley (Eds.), *Language, gender, and society* (pp. 69–88). Rowley, MA: Newbury.

Mehrabian, A. (1981). *Silent messages* (2nd ed.). Belmont, CA: Wadsworth.

Meister, J., Kuhn, H., Shehata-Dieler, W., Hagen, R., & Kleinsasser, N. (2017). Perceptual analysis of the male-to-female transgender voice after glottoplasty. *Laryngoscope, 127,* 875–881.

Mills, M., Stoneham, G., & Georgiadou, I. (2017). Expanding the evidence: Developments and innovations in clinical practice, training and competency within voice and communication therapy for trans and gender diverse people. *International Journal of Transgenderism, 18,* 328–342.

Montano, K. J., Tigue, C. C., Isenstein, S. G. E., Barclay, P., & Feinberg, D. R. (2017). Men's voice pitch influences women's trusting behavior. *Evolution and Human Behavior, 38,* 293–297.

Morningstar, M., Dirks, M. A., & Huang, S. (2017). Vocal cues underlying youth and adult portrayals of socio-emotional expressions. *Journal of Nonverbal Behavior, 41,* 155–183.

Morningstar, M., Ly, V. Y., Feldman, L., & Dirks, M. A. (2018). Mid-adolescents' and adults' recognition of vocal cues of emotion and social intent: Differences by expression and speaker age. *Journal of Nonverbal Behavior, 42,* 237–251.

Narasimhan, S. V., & Vishal, K. (2017). Spectral measures of hoarseness in persons with hyperfunctional voice disorder. *Journal of Voice, 31,* 57–61.

Nelson, A., & Golant, S. K. (2004). *You don't say: Navigating nonverbal communication between the sexes.* New York: Prentice Hall.

Novak-Tot, E., Niebuhr, O., & Chen, A. (2017). A gender bias in the acoustic-melodic features of charismatic speech? *Proceedings of Interspeech, 2017,* 2248–2252.

Novotny, E., Carr, Z., Frank, M. G., Dietrich, S. B., Shaddock, T., Cardwell, M., & Decker, A. (2018). How people really suspect and discover lies. *Journal of Nonverbal Behavior, 42,* 41–52.

Oates, J., & Dacakis, G. (2015). Transgender voice and communication: Research evidence underpinning voice intervention for male-to-female transsexual women. *S163 Perspectives on Voice and Voice Disorders, 25,* 48–58.

O'Connor, J. J. M., & Barclay, P. (2017). The influence of voice pitch on perceptions of trustworthiness across social contexts. *Evolution and Human Behavior, 38,* 506–512.

O'Connor, J. J. M., & Barclay, P. (2018). High voice pitch mitigates the aversiveness of antisocial cues in men's speech. *British Journal of Psychology.* https://doi.org:10.1111/bjop.12310

Oleszkiewicz, A., Pisanski, K., Lachowicz-Tabaczek, K., & Sorokowska, A. (2017). Voice-based assessments of trustworthiness, competence, and warmth in blind and sighted adults. *Psychonomic Bulletin Review, 24,* 856–862.

O'Sullivan, M., & Ekman, P. (2004). The wizards of deception detection. In P. A. Granhag & L. A. Stromwall (Eds.), *The detection of deception in forensic contexts* (pp. 269–286). New York: Cambridge University Press.

O'Sullivan, M., Frank, M. G., & Hurley, C. M. (2010). Training for individual differences in lie detection accuracy. In J. G. Voeller (Ed.), *Handbook of science and technology for homeland security.* New York: Wiley.

Paik, J. E., & van Swol, L. M. (2017). Justifications and questions in detecting deception. *Group Decision and Negotiation, 26,* 1041–1060.

Paquette-Smith, M., & Johnson, E. K. (2016). I don't like the tone of your voice: Infants use vocal affect to socially evaluate others. *Infancy, 21,* 104–121.

Pavlich, C. A., Rains, S. A., & Segrin, C. (2017). The nonverbal bully: Effect of shouting and conversational distance on bystanders' perceptions. *Communication Reports, 30,* 129–141.

Rasetshwane, D. M., High, R. R., Kopun, J. G., Neely, S. T., Gorga, M. P., & Jesteadt, W. (2018). Influence of suppression on restoration of spectral loudness summation in listeners with hearing loss. *Journal of the Acoustical Society of America, 143,* 2994–3008.

Reda, M. M. (2010a). *Between speaking and silence: A study of quiet students.* New York: SUNY Press.

Reda, M. M. (2010b, September 10). What's the problem with quiet students? Anyone? Anyone? *Chronicle of Higher Education,* p. A68.

Remland, M. S. (2016). *Nonverbal communication in everyday life* (4th ed.). Thousand Oaks, CA: Sage.

Rendle-Short, J. (2005). Managing the transitions between talk and silence in the academic monologue. *Research on Language and Social Interaction, 38,* 179–218.

Rezlescu, C., Penton, T., Walsh, V., Tsujimura, H., Scott, S. K., & Banissy, M. J. (2015). Dominant voices and attractive faces: The contribution of visual and auditory information to integrated person impressions. *Journal of Nonverbal Behavior, 39,* 355–370.

Riding, D., Lonsdale, D., & Brown, B. (2006). The effects of average fundamental frequency and variance of fundamental frequency on male vocal attractiveness to women. *Journal of Nonverbal Behavior, 30,* 55–61.

Roberts, F., Francis, A. L., & Morgan, M. (2006). The interaction of inter-turn silence with prosodic cues in listener perceptions of "trouble" in conversation. *Speech Communication, 48,* 1079–1093.

Roberts, S. G., & Levinson, S. C. (2017). Conversation, cognition and cultural evolution: A model of the cultural evolution of word order through pressures imposed from turn taking in conversation. *Interaction Studies, 18,* 402–429.

Ruhlemann, C., Bagoutdinov, A., & O'Donnell, M. B. (2011). Windows on the mind: Pauses in conversational narrative. *International Journal of Corpus Linguistics, 16,* 198–230.

Sacks, H., Schegloff, E. A., & Jefferson, G. (1978). A simplest systematics for the organization of turn taking for conversation. In J. Schenkein (Ed.), *Studies in the organization of conversational interaction* (pp. 7–55). New York: Academic.

Sawyer, J., Perry, J. L., & Dobbins-Scaramelli, A. (2014). A survey of the awareness of speech services among transgender and transsexual individuals and speech-language pathologists. *International Journal of Trans-genderism, 15,* 146–163.

Schuessler Harper, M. (2007). Keeping quiet: Self-silencing and its association with relational and individual functioning among adolescent romantic couples. *Journal of Social and Personal Relationships, 24,* 99–116.

Schuessler Harper, M., Dickson, J. W., & Welsh, D. P. (2006). Self-silencing and rejection sensitivity in adolescent romantic relationships. *Journal of Youth and Adolescence, 35,* 435–443.

Schultz, B. G., O'Brien, I., Phillips, N., McFarland, D. H., Titone, D., & Palmer, C. (2016). Speech rates converge in scripted turn-taking conversations. *Applied Psycholinguistics, 37,* 1201–1220.

Shen, J., & Souza, P. E. (2017). The effect of dynamic pitch on speech recognition in temporally modulated noise. *Journal of Speech, Language, and Hearing Research, 60,* 2725–2739.

Shin, S. Y., Liu, W., Jang, J-W., & Bente, G. (2017). The benefits of distance and mediation: How people react to conflicts in video chat vs. FtF. *Computers in Human Behavior, 73,* 1–8.

Sindoni, M. G. (2014). Through the looking glass: A social semiotic and linguistic perspective on the study of video chats. *Text & Talk, 34,* 325–347.

Smith, L., & King, J. (2018). Silence in the foreign language classroom: The emotional challenges for L2 teachers. In J. D. M. Agudo (Ed.), *Emotions in second language teaching: Theory, research, and teacher education* (pp. 323–339). New York: Springer.

Spencer, L. G., & Capuzza, J. C. (Eds.). (2015). *Transgender communication studies: Histories, trends, and trajectories.* New York: Lexington.

Stathopoulos, E. T., Huber, J. E., & Sussman, J. E. (2011). Changes in acoustic characteristics of the voice across the life span: Measures from individuals 4–93 years of age. *Journal of Speech, Language, and Hearing Research, 54,* 1011–1021.

Stevenage, S. V., Neil, G. J., Parsons, B., & Humphreys, A. (2018). A sound effect: Exploration of the distinctiveness advantage in voice recognition. *Applied Cognitive Psychology.* https://dx.doi.org/10.1002.acp.3424

Thornberg, R. (2006). Hushing as a moral dilemma in the classroom. *Journal of Moral Education, 35,* 89–104.

Tian, Y., Maruyama, T., & Ginzburg, J. (2017). Self addressed questions and filled pauses: A cross-linguistic investigation. *Journal of Psycholinguistic Research, 46,* 905–922.

Trainor, L. J., Austin, C. M., & Desjardin, R. N. (2000). Is infant-directed speech prosody a result of the vocal expression of emotion? *Psychological Science, 11,* 188–195.

Tyler, J. C. (2015). Expanding and mapping the indexical field. *Journal of English Linguistics, 43,* 284–310.

Vasconcelos, M., Dias, M., Soares, A. P., & Pinheiro, A. P. (2017). What is the melody of that voice? Probing unbiased recognition accuracy with the Montreal affective voices. *Journal of Nonverbal Behavior, 41,* 239–267.

Vettin, J., & Todt, D. (2004). Laughter in conversation: Features of occurrence and acoustic structure. *Journal of Nonverbal Behavior, 28,* 93–115.

Vlahovic, T. A., Roberts, S., & Dunbar, R. (2012). Effects of duration and laughter on subjective happiness within different modes of communication. *Journal of Computer-Mediated Communication, 17,* 436–450.

Vrij, A. (2006). Nonverbal communication and deception. In V. Manusov & M. L. Patterson (Eds.), *The SAGE handbook of nonverbal communication* (pp. 341–359). Thousand Oaks, CA: Sage.

Vrij, A., Fisher, R. P., & Blank, H. (2017). A cognitive approach to lie detection: A meta-analysis. *Legal and Criminological Psychology, 23,* 7–19.

Vrij, A., & Heaven, S. (1999). Vocal and verbal indicators of deception as a function of lie complexity. *Psychology, Crime, and Law, 4,* 401–413.

Wachi, T., Kuraishi, H., Watanabe, K., Otsuka, Y., Yokota, K., & Lamb, M. E. (2017). Police officers' ability to detect lies within a deception paradigm. *Psychology, Public Policy, and Law, 23*, 301–311.

Wagner, K. (2010, April 10). HALT! *Lies Young Women Believe.* Retrieved from http://www.liesyoungwomenbelieve.com/index.php?id=480

Walker, G. (2017). Pitch and the projection of more talk. *Research on Language and Social Interaction, 50*, 206–225.

Waller, S. S., Eriksson, M., & Sorqvist, P. (2015). Can you hear my age? Influences of speech rate and speech spontaneity on estimation of speaker age. *Frontiers in Psychology.* doi.org/10.3389/fpsyg.2015.00978

Warren, G., Schertler, E., & Bull, P. (2009). Detecting deception from emotional and unemotional cues. *Journal of Nonverbal Behavior, 33*, 59–69.

Warren, P. (2016). *Uptalk: The phenomenon of rising intonation.* Cambridge, UK: Cambridge University Press.

Weinstein, N., Zoughou, K., & Paulmann, S. (2018). You "have" to hear this: Using tone of voice to motivate others. *Journal of Experimental Psychology: Human Perception and Performance, 44*, 898–913.

Wells, L. K. (2004). *The articulate voice: An introduction to voice and diction* (4th ed.). Boston: Allyn & Bacon.

West, C., & Zimmerman, D. H. (1983). Small insults: A study of interruptions in cross-sex conversations between unacquainted persons. In B. Thorne, C. Kramarae, & N. Henley (Eds.), *Language, gender, and society* (pp. 102–117). Rowley, MA: Newbury.

Wiemann, J. M., & Knapp, M. L. (1975). Turn-taking in conversations. *Journal of Communication, 25*, 75–92.

Wilson, T. P., Wiemann, J. M., & Zimmerman, D. H. (1984). Models of turn-taking in conversational interaction. *Journal of Language and Social Psychology, 3*, 159–184.

Woodland, J., & Voyer, D. (2011). Context and intonation in the perception of sarcasm. *Metaphor & Symbol, 26*, 227–239.

Yamamoto, H. W., & Haryu, E. (2018). The role of pitch pattern in Japanese 24-month-olds' word recognition. *Journal of Memory and Language, 99*, 90–98.

Youngquist, J. (2009). The effect of interruptions and dyad gender combination on perceptions of interpersonal dominance. *Communication Studies, 60*, 147–163.

Yuasa, I. P. (2010). Creaky voice: A new feminine voice quality for young urban-oriented upwardly mobile American women? *American Speech, 85*, 315–337.

Ziegler, A., Henke, T., Wiedrick, J., & Helou, L. B. (2018). Effectiveness of testosterone therapy for masculinizing voice in transgender patients: A meta-analytic review. *International Journal of Transgenderism, 19*, 25–45.

Zimman, L. (2018). Transgender voices: Insights on identity, embodiment, and the gender of the voice. *Language and Linguistics Compass.* https://doi.org/10.1111/Inc3.12284

Zuckerman, M., & Driver, R. E. (1989). What sounds beautiful is good: The vocal attractiveness stereotype. *Journal of Nonverbal Behavior, 13*, 67–82.

Zuckerman, M., Hodgins, H., & Miyake, K. (1990). The vocal attractiveness stereotype: Replication and elaboration. *Journal of Nonverbal Behavior, 14*, 97–112.

Zuckerman, M., & Miyake, K. (1993). The attractive voice: What makes it so? *Journal of Nonverbal Behavior, 17*, 119–135.

Zuckerman, M., & Sinicropi, V. (2011). When physical and vocal attractiveness differ: Effects on favorability of interpersonal impressions. *Journal of Nonverbal Behavior, 35*, 75–86.

part three

APPLICATIONS OF NONVERBAL COMMUNICATION

chapter ten

NONVERBAL COMMUNICATION, TECHNOLOGY, AND SOCIAL MEDIA

chapter outline

chapter objectives

After studying this chapter, you should be able to

1. provide three traditional nonverbal communication codes and explain how they function in cell phone usage;
2. discuss nontraditional nonverbal communication codes, specifically the use of emoticons, emojis, acronyms, textisms, grammar, spelling, and punctuation, and explain how they function;
3. describe how nonverbal cues operate in a video chat and how video chatting differs from face-to-face interaction;
4. discuss the impact of cell phone usage, both calling and texting, on the development and maintenance of romantic relationships;
5. understand the role of nonverbal cues in the development of an online persona;
6. describe how nonverbal chronemics function online versus offline;
7. recognize nonverbal cues associated with computer-mediated communication (CMC); and
8. explain the differences between the physical body and the virtual body, including nonverbal cues associated with each.

case study

SWIPE RIGHT

ave you gone on a date recently? Where did you meet the person? Online? Face to face? **Computer-mediated communication (CMC)** is defined as human communication facilitated by technology. No matter what means you use to connect with others, it's likely that CMC plays a part in how you initiate and maintain relationships of all types, including romantic or intimate ones. Lately, online dating sites and apps have become a primary way people search for relationships, dates, or hook-ups. Online dating websites from match.com to ChristianMingle.com make romantic CMC available to anyone with a computer and Internet access. Additionally, dating apps such as Tinder, Bumble, and Grindr provide diverse users the opportunity to meet others online. Some people openly admit to using dating apps to find love while others see it as taboo or unnatural. What's your stance? Can lifelong relationships be successfully built through CMC?

CMC is becoming increasingly present in our day-to-day interactions; it's almost unavoidable (Chang, 2016). Therefore, we must observe and analyze the similarities and differences between CMC and traditional face-to-face (FtF) communication. Much of a message is communicated nonverbally (Floyd, 2016), so how does CMC influence our ability to send nonverbal cues?

chapter ten

Think about those nonverbal cues that are present when using CMC, versus which cues are absent and cause communication challenges in this medium. How has technology changed how you nonverbally communicate?

Online dating and dating apps have gained significant popularity in the past decade.

Daughter: John and I just broke up.

Mother: When did this happen? Did you talk on the phone?

Daughter: No. He texted me.

Mother: What did he say?

Daughter: Nothing, except that he thought we should break up! Can you believe it? That sure shows how much he cares.

What does this brief conversation reveal about how we communicate when using technology? In the not-so-distant past, breaking up with a romantic partner was something most people did face to face, out of respect for the other person's feelings and simply because it was the right thing to do. Giving bad news over the phone, through a text message, or via a social networking site happens more frequently today, as people take advantage of the convenience and impersonality of mediated communication and the comfort of not having to deliver disappointing news or risk conflict face to face (Gershon, 2010; Ishii, 2010; Raacke & Bonds-Raacke, 2011; Starks, 2007; Tagg, Seargeant, & Brown, 2017; Weisskirch & Delevi, 2012). Another trend is to break up by simply disappearing and allowing no contact—not answering one's phone, not responding to texts or e-mails, and so forth—a phenomenon known as **ghosting** (Davidson, Joinson, & Jones, 2018; LeFebvre, 2017). A person's absence or refusal of contact is also a nonverbal cue!

Mechanisms such as phones, e-mail systems, or text messaging reduce or filter out many nonverbal channels that would be present in a face-to-face situation. Nonverbal cues of being hurt, dejected, or outraged (e.g., angry facial expressions, tears, emotional vocalizations, increased distance, lack of touch or, worse, violent touch), such as in our breakup example, can be mediated, saving people from having to experience these behaviors "in the flesh."

Breaking up is just one aspect of relating to others that has changed because of increased accessibility to and affordability of technology. Our ways of communicating with one another continue to change almost daily, such that it's hard to keep up with all the innovation. Do you think technology has helped or hurt communication? While some think all this technology use is making people dumber or less critical thinkers, others such as Clive Thompson (2013), author of the book *Smarter Than You Think*, believe that technology is actually making us smarter, boosting our memory and renewing our interest in writing. One thing is clear: Technological innovation regarding communication isn't going away; it's only going to increase as newer, faster, more convenient, and more affordable approaches continue to be developed for our use.

Many people think that communication facilitated by such systems as e-mail, social networking, and texting pales in comparison with face-to-face communication because of the loss of nonverbal cues. You may remember that in Chapter 1 we discussed how nonverbal communication experts suggest that about 65% of the meaning in our messages is conveyed through nonverbal channels, leaving only 35% to be accomplished verbally (Birdwhistell, 1970).

So is all online communication hampered in this way, or do other nonverbal cues emerge or operate that we don't typically think of as nonverbal cues? Your textbook authors argue the latter, suggesting that we need to change our thinking on this topic to consider how various elements within texting, e-mailing, creating and maintaining web pages or social networking profiles, and other means of relating to people in mediated contexts are forms of nonverbal communication. As smartphones, laptops, tablets, and social media have become a part of everyday life, it's not too surprising that the nature of our communication, especially our nonverbal communication, has changed (Lew, Walther, Pang, & Shin, 2018; Montepare, 2014; Pöschl & Döring, 2017; Walther, Loh, & Granka, 2005; Youngvorst & High, 2018). We invite you to explore this chapter with an open mind as to what constitutes nonverbal communication in this age of technology.

NONVERBAL COMMUNICATION AND THE EVER-PRESENT CELL PHONE ■ ■ ■

A few years ago, one of your authors conducted a radical experiment with her nonverbal communication class: She gathered students' cell phones, put them all in a box, and stored them under her desk until the entire 2 1/2-hour class session was over. Some students were so freaked out at the removal of their phones that they fibbed to the professor, claiming they didn't bring them to class that night. (These fibs were exposed, and each and every student surrendered a phone.)

For about the first 10 minutes of class, many students were so distracted that their phones weren't within their reach or control that all they could do was stare at the area where the box of confiscated phones was stored. After another 10 minutes, however, most students adjusted to the absence of their phones and were able to concentrate on the subject and the class discussion. At the start of the second half of class, the professor asked students what they did during their break; some said, "We actually *talked* to each other." Others said that they were very uncomfortable without their phones during the break, so they sort of shut down.

One interesting point about this experiment is that the professor wouldn't even try it today, because most students would simply refuse to surrender their phones—the experiment just wouldn't work. Even though research shows that students who text during class sessions don't learn as much as students who stay off their phones in class (Bolkan & Griffin, 2017; Kuznekoff & Titsworth, 2013), confiscating a student's cell phone—even temporarily—would likely be seen as a violation today. Studies show that students experience moderate to severe anxiety when separated from their phones or forced into restricted phone use (Cheever, Rosen, Carrier, & Chavez, 2014; Clayton, Leshner, & Almond, 2015). Compared with only a few short years ago, we now carry so much more personal data in our phones, access so much more information, and connect with so many more people that privacy and security concerns alone would make the classroom experiment a nonstarter for most students.

Just how much are you affected by that cell phone you carry everywhere with you? Is more of your life in it now than even just a few short years ago? More specifically, think about how your nonverbal cues are different because of your connection to your phone. Maybe you're one of those people who prefers hands-free phone usage, meaning you have Bluetooth or a wireless headphone so you don't have to hold your device. If you have to wait in line, even just a few minutes for your daily Starbucks fix, do you immediately get on your phone to pass the time? What have cell phones done to our patience levels? If you lose your phone for even a few minutes or hours, does it feel as though your life is ruined?

Traditional Nonverbal Cues Affected by Cell Phone Usage

On April 3, 2018, the cell phone officially turned 45! Now some 5 billion mobile phones are in use worldwide. While many aspects of our nonverbal communication repertoire are affected by cell phone usage, three traditional nonverbal cues stand out: (1) kinesics—more specifically, how we move when talking or texting on our phones; (2) eye contact, in that our focus on our phones diminishes our eye contact with people and the world around us; and (3) vocalics, in terms of the use of our own voices when we're on our cells, plus sophisticated innovations (such as voiced assistance and voice-recognition software on smartphones).

KINESICS. Are you one of those students who walks across campus with your head bent over your phone screen? Ever trip or run into a solid object or another person because you were focused on your phone? The evidence is clear when it comes to the dangers of driving while talking on a cell phone (even a hands-free device); driving and texting is especially unsafe—many times lethal. But did you know that talking or texting on your cell phone makes you a dangerous *walker*?

We explored this topic in Chapter 6 on kinesics, but it bears summarizing here. Physical therapists Lamberg and Muratori (2012) studied students' cell phone and walking behavior. You know how people who text or talk on their cells while driving tend to drive slowly, often without realizing it, and sometimes wander into an adjacent lane? Same thing happens to our walking. Lamberg and Muratori found that students who engaged in cell phone use (either talking or texting) walked significantly more slowly than did those subjects not using their cells; in addition, students showed a 61% increase in lateral deviation, meaning they walked more sideways toward a target than straight at it. The result of such a deviation is that it takes people longer to reach a destination because they veer off and make less forward progress; plus, they're more likely to run into people and objects. Lamberg and Muratori concluded that people's memory and gait are compromised by cell phone usage, such that they become safety hazards.

Did you know that using your cell phone while walking could be dangerous?

EYE CONTACT. In terms of eye contact, it doesn't take too long to register the impact of this technological innovation: Just go to any restaurant and you'll see people sitting together awaiting the arrival of their food, using their phones to talk, text, play games, or watch videos. They ignore the people they're with, giving preference to the phone over their face-to-face companions. Question: Is this a rude nonverbal cue, or is it becoming so commonplace that we don't think about it anymore? What message does it send if you prioritize a texting partner over someone sitting across from you? Research has found that the mere presence of a cell phone in a social setting negatively impacts people's satisfaction with face-to-face conversations in those settings (Allred & Crowley, 2017).

VOCALICS. Are you one of those people who talk too loudly on their cells, to the annoyance of people around them? Airports are common settings for this nonverbal communication violation. You're trapped there, waiting for your flight to board, when someone decides to carry on a personal conversation within earshot of everyone at your gate, oftentimes oblivious to listeners nearby. Is this irritating or no big deal? In 2013, a debate emerged after the Federal Aviation Administration lifted the cell phone ban on airplanes, leaving it up to individual airlines to develop their own policies. Many frequent flyers, as well as airline employees, weighed in heavily against allowing cell phone usage during flight, while others said they would be glad to see the ban lifted so they could conduct business in the air and make better use of valuable time. Currently, a few airlines allow travelers to use their cells during flights, only having to turn them to airplane mode during take offs and landings. Many other airlines ban them until after landing. The main thing is to realize that there's no need to shout when you're on a cell phone; we can *all* hear you.

Another vocalic aspect related to our phones and other devices surrounds voice-recognition software and programmed voices, such as Siri on iPhones or Alexa on Amazon Echoes. **Voice-recognition software/talk to text** is becoming increasingly popular and accessible. We know from Chapter 9 on vocalics that each human voice has unique qualities, but you must admit that artificial intelligence having a voice can be kind of creepy. Most new computers and smartphones today come with voice-recognition software that can be programmed to recognize and respond to your voice. Perhaps some of you saw the 2013 Spike Jonze movie *Her*, in which a man falls in love with a sophisticated computer program that speaks in a woman's voice.

Another feature of this technology is that you can speak into a computer microphone or smartphone, and the device will process your words and post them on the screen or in a text message. For people with carpal tunnel syndrome, bad backs, numbness in their hands, or other physical conditions that make constant computer work or texting difficult, this technology is invaluable. Many people simply find it faster than tapping out a text. One of your authors is such a lousy texter that she experimented with a voice-recognition app on her iPhone, but she found that it involved just as many errors in translation as her manually written texts did. (Perhaps her Southern accent is partly to blame.)

Nontraditional Nonverbal Cues and Mediated Communication

As communication continues to converge with existing and new technologies, our nonverbal communication must also adapt to these new media. While some people claim that nonverbal communication barely exists in mediated communication, technological advances have made it easier to convey more information nonverbally. Although face-to-face communication still offers a richer experience of nonverbal cues, people have found creative ways to express emotions or "color" their messages on mobile devices. Emoticons; emojis; acronyms and textisms; grammar, spelling, and punctuation in mediated messages; and video chat applications such as Skype and FaceTime expand the ways we can express nonverbal cues in mediated contexts.

EMOTICONS/EMOJIS. **Emoticons** (short for "emotion icons") and **emojis** are some of the best tools available to convey emotions and attitudes nonverbally in mediated contexts (Blair, 2017; Dresner & Herring, 2010; Garrison, Remley, Thomas, & Wierszewski, 2011; Jibril & Abdullah, 2013; Kaye, Malone, & Wall, 2017; Riordan, 2017). Beginning with simple creative uses of symbols and punctuation marks available on the common keyboard, Internet users over the years have devised new and clever emoticons that enhance communication. Emojis are defined by the online Merriam-Webster dictionary as "images, symbols, or icons used in text fields in electronic communication to express the emotional attitude of the writer, convey information succinctly, and communicate a message playfully without using words." They're commonly used in texting, e-mailing, and on social media. Some people also text using Bitmojis, which include a personal avatar, to inject emotion into a mediated message.

Think about a message you might send online or via text that could be misconstrued as mean or hurtful; adding the commonly used smiley face emoji can nonverbally communicate that you're being sarcastic or playful or that you're joking. Mediated sarcasm is hard to convey without emojis. Along with nonverbal functions, some scholars argue that emoticons and emojis are now so commonplace that they've become part of verbal language itself. Think about how you use emojis or other methods to convey emotion in a mediated context. Have you ever sent a text or online message that was nothing but an emoji, perhaps the "thumbs up" icon instead of typing "okay" or "goodbye"? As emoticons and emojis receive more use from all branches of society, as well as cross-culturally, they have the ability to form stand-alone meanings. They may soon be viewed more as verbal communication than as nonverbal cues that enhance or clarify a verbal message.

Emojis can express emotions and attitudes that would otherwise be hard to convey in a mediated format.

ACRONYMS AND TEXTISMS. Acronyms (abbreviations for longer terms or phrases, typically formed using the first letter of each word) may seem like a form of verbal communication since they're strings of letters, but they have nonverbal functions. Using an acronym versus full words is a nonverbal choice in your communication style; plus, such use conveys a certain familiarity—an assumption that the receiver of a message will know what you mean. It's a form of shorthand that has some degree of intimacy to it. We all now know most of the standard acronyms, such as *lol* (laughing out loud) and *omg* (oh my God) (both of which the Webster's dictionary people added to the English lexicon), and *smh* (shaking my head). Occasionally, a new acronym will make its way through the culture, sometimes puzzling receivers until they figure it out or ask the sender of the message for clarification.

You're certainly familiar with **textisms** or **textese** (writing in textisms), even if you didn't know there was a term for the phenomenon; textisms are abbreviated, nonstandard forms of language that create a shorthand for communicators (Rosen, Chang, Erwin, Carrier, & Cheever, 2010). Often, these linguistic shortcuts involve a combined use of letters, numbers, and punctuation marks, such as *CUl8tr* (see you later), *by4now*, *2nite*, and *4ever*. Enhanced speed and a desire to create a unique language are both motivations for the use of textese, but interestingly enough, research is divided on whether frequent use of textisms affects kids' and adults' ability to spell and use grammar correctly (Powell & Dixon, 2011; van Dijk, van Witteloostuijn, Vasic, Avrutin, & Blom, 2016).

GRAMMAR, SPELLING, AND PUNCTUATION. One of the major ways we communicate nonverbally in mediated contexts is through the grammar, spelling, and punctuation included (or not) in our messages. Similar to online forums, comment areas, and gaming, cues related to grammar, spelling, and punctuation can be communicated to convey our feelings and clarify short messages. A nonverbal cue is embedded in the choice to type "nice" in a text message, rather than "niiiiiiiice!!!" (Steinmetz, 2013).

Researchers Carr and Stefaniak (2012) investigated the impact of punctuation and grammatical accuracy on perceived professionalism. Their research revealed that grammatical accuracy influenced a receiver's perception of a sender's credibility but that people altered their level of negativity depending on the device or mechanism used to send the mediated message. Grammatical errors, misspellings, and absent or incorrect punctuation are typical of texting, given that speed and convenience are key. So people are less likely to judge harshly an error or purposeful deviation in a text message compared with one in an e-mail or online post, where the implication is that the crafting of the e-mail message or post is more deliberate and the author has the time to do so more leisurely.

Errors or deviations in messages sent via tablets, such as iPads or Kindle Fires, seem to fall somewhere in between the judgment levels for infractions via phones and computers. Some users of such devices include a standard caveat, such as "Sent from my iPhone (or iPad), so please excuse my grammar and spelling," with each message that goes out. One of our colleagues uses this message: "Sent from my iPad, so message may appear curt or may contain grossly inappropriate autocorrections." Ever sent a text quickly, only to realize later that the autocorrect feature on your phone distorted the message or changed certain words into something you didn't intend? What if the receiver of that miscommunication was a potential employer you were trying to impress? Some of us have been embarrassed by such a situation and decided to turn off the autocorrect feature on our phones or tablets. While aspects pertaining to words or verbal communication are important, how the words appear or their various features, including the time involved in sending and responding to texts, are all critical nonverbal aspects associated with mediated communication.

Studies suggest that women text more than men, and are more likely than men to use first-person language and repeated exclamation points in text messages and tweets, while men typically share more links and include more technologically related language (Ogletree, Fancher, & Gill, 2014; Steinmetz, 2013). In one study, girls thought boys' texts were "short and brisk," while boys thought that girls' texts were "overly long, prying, and containing unneeded elements" (Ling, Baron, Lenhart, & Campbell, 2014, p. 423). What sense do you get about someone who uses proper capitalization, punctuation, grammar, and spelling in a text versus someone who abbreviates everything, includes frequent textisms, uses only lowercase letters, and would never think of putting a period at the end of a line?

VIDEO CHATS, VIDEOS, & PHOTOS AS CMC. One of the most profound technological innovations in recent years, in terms of nonverbal communication, is the visual phone conversation or **video chat**. Some of us are old enough to remember how cool it was when cartoon character George Jetson could have a video chat with his boss at work or when detective Dick Tracy video-chatted with the police commissioner through his watch. Now such means of connecting are commonplace, with more and more people using video chats as an important vehicle of communication with others.

Advances in multimedia technology have allowed smartphone interactions to take on this whole new level of nonverbal immediacy. Most new phones and tablets allow video interactions that closely simulate face-to-face conversation—interactions that became available on computers only in recent years, usually in the form of group videoconferencing (Taylor, Hester, & Wilson, 2011). Current video chat incarnations such as Skype, FaceTime, Snapchat, and Google Hangouts, among others being developed as we speak, allow users to interact regardless of physical location. Although the richness of video chat cues can't compare to an authentic face-to-face interaction, people now have the ability to observe the facial expressions, eye behavior, gestures, and even environment of the other person through the camera on their phone, tablet, or computer.

Being able to see the people you're communicating with via phones and CMC can increase a feeling of immediacy even though you may be physically far away from them. Photos sent through Snapchat and Instagram provide users with a way to keep their friends "in the loop" with what they're doing. Through such apps, users may contact each other individually or create group chats. The tendency to communicate nonverbally by sending photos and videos through one's phone or computer is more pronounced in younger women than in other age- and sex-related groups (Barker, 2018). The perception that people are still close to you emotionally, if not physically, can aid in creating and maintaining long-distance friendships and romantic relationships (Taylor & Bazarova, 2018; Tong & Walther, 2010).

Probably no other segment of American society has enjoyed this technological innovation more than members of the armed forces and their families. Military personnel, with their lengthy and often-repeated deployments overseas, are enjoying with unprecedented frequency the ability to video chat with loved ones, an activity made even more meaningful if one has infants and small

Technological innovations such as video chat and social media help us stay connected to those who aren't physically close to us.

children in the family (Maguire, Heinemann-LaFave, & Sahlstein, 2013; McClure & Barr, 2017). Obviously, when more nonverbal cues are available than just the sound of someone's voice or the length of a text message or e-mail, the potential for richer, more meaningful interaction expands significantly.

Cell Phones and Romantic Relationships

It's challenging under the best of circumstances to make a romantic relationship work, right? So, does a cell phone, with its immediacy and ease of use, enhance or detract from a relationship? Especially in a new relationship, it can be difficult for people to pick up on and accurately interpret nonverbal cues from a significant other; this challenge is only compounded by the reduced traditional nonverbal cues inherent in most mediated communication. What role should cell phones play in a romantic relationship?

Multiple studies have examined this question, seeking to better understand the impact of phone usage (talking, texting, and sending videos and photos) on the development of a relationship (Halpern & Katz, 2017; Kelly, Miller-Ott, & Duran, 2017; Spencer, Lambertsen, Hubler, & Burr, 2017). In Duran, Kelly, and Rotaru's (2011) study, students were asked to self-report their rules, if any, concerning phone usage in a relationship, as well as their perceived impressions of conflict or connection with their significant others. One of the most heavily researched tensions in romantic relationships is termed *autonomy–connection*, meaning the push–pull of how connected people are as a couple versus how independent or autonomous they are as individuals (Baxter & Montgomery, 1996, 2000). Duran and colleagues' results indicated that cell phone usage in a romantic relationship could be a source of autonomy–connection conflict, with higher levels of tension related to the quantity of calling and texting. In simpler terms, one partner in a relationship might prefer to exchange numerous text messages every day with her or his partner, as a means of feeling connected and staying in touch with day-to-day happenings. But the other partner might feel that such a high level of contact is suffocating or intrusive; thus, conflict will likely result from this disparate view of the role of phone usage. One person's connectedness can be another's source of irritation, leading to a feeling of being controlled or smothered (Hall & Baym, 2011).

Satisfaction with cell phone communication with one's relational partner has been strongly and positively correlated with relational certainty and satisfaction with the overall relationship (Halpern & Katz, 2017; Jin & Pena, 2010; Miller-Ott, Kelly, & Duran, 2012). Believing that one's romantic partner should be instantly and always accessible via cell phone and that texts should be quickly responded to can cause conflict in a relationship, so partners should negotiate appropriate rules guiding cell phone usage that will make them both comfortable.

Computer-mediated communication (CMC)	Human communication facilitated by technologies such as chat rooms, e-mail systems, social networking sites, and online gaming
Ghosting	Ending a relationship by disappearing and refusing to respond to phone calls, texts, or e-mail messages
Voice-recognition software/ talk to text	Technology that allows computers/smartphones/tablets to recognize voices, respond to commands, and post one's words on a screen or in a text message
Emoticons/Emojis	Electronic symbols, images, and icons that convey a sender's emotions and attitudes to an intended receiver
Acronyms	Abbreviations for longer terms or phrases, typically formed using the first letter of each word
Textisms	Abbreviated, nonstandard forms of language that create a shorthand for communicators
Textese	Writing in textisms
Video chat	Visual conversations accomplished using technology, such as computers and smartphones, by participants in different geographical locations

NONVERBAL COMMUNICATION AND SOCIAL MEDIA ■ ■ ■ ■ ▬

Social media are increasingly important forums for verbal and nonverbal communication. Research shows that having a social network correlates with college success; tapping into that social network multiple times a day is typical for today's college student (Kim & Kim, 2017; Saha & Karpinski, 2018).

Although Facebook and Twitter have been the dominant social media platforms for several years, other options continue to surface, such as Snapchat, Instagram, Google+, LinkedIn, Tumblr, Instagram, and Pinterest.

Social media, at its core, attempts to foster social interaction similar to how face-to-face interaction occurs. Just as in face-to-face contexts, people try to convey the best possible image of themselves and create favorable interactions with others through social networking (Zuckerberg, 2013). Think about all the nonverbal cues on a Facebook page: the profile picture, cover photo, personal information, favorite books, favorite quotations, relationship status. When people look at your social media profile, they may learn information about you that you never disclosed personally to them (Chen & Li, 2017; Lueders, Hall, Pennington, & Knutson, 2014). All these elements convey information about you and your personal and professional life. Whether we realize it or not, much of what people observe from our Facebook profile and postings includes nonverbal cues that impact others' perceptions of us.

Cody texted some of his friends about going downtown to get dinner and drinks after work on Friday. Sydney, Roger, and Donovan all replied to the group text saying that they might be able to go. Cody has been really busy with work, so he's looking forward to finally going out with some friends to relax and have a good time. On Friday, Cody texted his friends again just to double-check about their plans. Roger and Donovan didn't reply. Sydney sent a Snapchat of her at home with the caption, "not feeling so well—think I'm going to stay home." Cody was discouraged that his plans fell through, but he decided just to have a relaxing night at home too.

Later that evening, Cody went on Snapchat and opened the SnapMap. He noticed that Sydney and Donovan were at the same location, but he assumed it was a glitch. The next morning, Donovan noticed that Roger posted to his Instagram a story from his time at the bars. In the story that Roger posted, Sydney and Donovan can be seen in the background. Cody now knows his friends ditched him, but he doesn't know how to respond.

If you were Cody, *what would you do*? Does the ability to investigate others' trustworthiness via social media seem ethical and understandable, or downright creepy? Do you allow friends to see your location on social media? Do you feel like you have to be careful about what you post?

The Online Persona

Scholar Ervin Goffman's (1959) research on how people present or represent themselves in everyday life is applicable to the online or mediated context. Goffman suggests that "the expressiveness of the individual (and therefore his capacity to give impressions) appears to solve two radically different kinds of sign activity: the expression that he *gives,* and the expression that he *gives off* " (p. 2). What people *give* refers to our verbal communication, typically occurring in face-to-face settings. However, since mediated communication relies more heavily on verbal text than on nonverbal cues, what people *give* takes on more significance. The *giving off* part is nonverbal, which involves such things as facial expressions, gestures, body movements, and attire (Martey & Stromer-Galley, 2007). What we typically think of as nonverbal cues may be altered in online formats, but we still *give off* these cues to assist in the transmission of the verbal message and to represent ourselves to our online partners (Li et al., 2008; Lueders et al., 2014).

Social media researchers are fascinated with the ways people present themselves online (Kashian, Jang, Shin, Dai, & Walther, 2017; Liang, Fu, & Shen, 2017; Tsay-Vogel, Shanaham, & Signorielli, 2018; Walther et al., 2011). In the 1990s, as research into online identity was exploding, scholar Mark Poster (1990) observed that in computer-mediated contexts, individuals were affected in the following ways: (1) New possibilities for playing with identities emerged, (2) sex/gender cues were removed, and (3) the subject was dispersed and dislocated in space and time.

We know you've heard or read this before, but it bears repeating: Give careful consideration to creating your online persona, meaning the image of yourself you want to convey to others in an online format. As in offline life, first impressions are huge; they can significantly help or hinder any form of relationship. So it's important to tailor your online profile in a way that appeals to the people who are important to you. Nonverbal cues such as the environments depicted in photos (e.g., bars, parties, classrooms, offices), gestures used (e.g., symbols, obscene gestures), physical appearance (e.g., bad hair and/or makeup, costumes others won't understand), and facial expressions (e.g., happy, belligerent, silly) can all affect how others view you without actually meeting you face to face. Have you ever noticed how some people act differently online than they do in person?

Remember, when others view a profile, they critique the profile owner and see how her or his values, behaviors, and experiences match up with their own. In fact, there's even a phenomenon termed "Facebook envy," in which skimming through other people's accomplishments and photos posted on Facebook can lead to feelings of jealousy, envy, and misery (Arroyo & Brunner, 2016; Cohen, Bowman, & Borchert, 2014; Fleuriet, Cole, & Guerrero, 2014; Krasnova, Wenninger, Widjaja, & Buxmann, 2013; Pera, 2018; Yuen et al., 2018). In addition, others' responses to your online information affect how you're perceived—fair or not. Research shows that others' public postings to or about you and the physical attractiveness of your online friends affect people's perceptions of you (Walther, Van Der Heide, Kim, Westerman, & Tong, 2008). While it can be tempting to cater to close friends when creating and communicating your online persona, keep in mind that your information is there for anyone to see, no matter how safe and secure your social networking site makes you feel. How people respond to your online presence also influences how you're viewed. Many potential employers begin their hiring process by researching an applicant's social media profile to see if the person fits within the company culture.

Another aspect of online persona development that warrants discussion is the lure of anonymity online. **Anonymity** refers to the ability to communicate, participate, and maintain a presence online without revealing one's true identity. While many social networking sites reflect actual profiles of users, other online forums allow people to engage, yet remain anonymous, often creating alternate identities for themselves so they can explore behaviors and aspects of their personalities too risky to experiment with in offline life. Like many things in life, there's an upside and a downside to the anonymity that online communication affords.

Avatars are extensions of the self online, ways that people express themselves using embodiments or manifestations, most often as characters in interactive games (Martey & Consalvo, 2011; Turkay & Kinzer, 2017; You, Kim, & Lee, 2017). Some avatars use one's actual name and are created to look similar to how the person looks in offline life, but many are given creative aliases and appearances that extend the user's personality (or are sometimes radical departures from the user's "real" self). Increasingly, students create avatars for their online college classes so as to facilitate distance learning and to accommodate those students who have disabilities (Adamo-Villani & Anasinga-raju, 2017; De Martino et al., 2017; Mørch, Caruso, Hartley, & Ludlow, 2018; Murphy, Cash, & Kellinger, 2018). Avatars allow people to visually and nonverbally express human characteristics and emotions (Bernal & Maes, 2017). Avatars, as well as screen names and aliases, give online communicators the ability to play with their sex and gender identity—a phenomenon termed **gender swapping** (Chou, Lo, & Teng, 2017; Hussain & Griffiths, 2008; Whitty & Buchanan, 2010).

Perhaps you've created an avatar to play Fortnite or some other video game where you're allowed to assume a different identity or create a visual representation of yourself. In the 1990s, communication scholar Tim Jordan (1999) used the term **identity fluidity** to articulate how our online identity may change at any moment with a simple change of screen name, online format, or avatar. While some identity exploration and experimentation is understandable and can be fun online, taking it too far, such that it deceives and hurts others, is certainly a problem.

When given a chance to select an online avatar, would you select one physically similar or different from you?

The nonverbal appearance and behaviors of avatars are impacted by culture, just as culture significantly affects our face-to-face nonverbal communication. One study explored differences between members of Asian and European cultures regarding spatial behavior (proxemics) in online avatar interactions. Observations indicated that Asian dyads interacted at greater virtual distances than did European dyads, which is consistent with patterns observed in face-to-face interactions (Hasler & Friedman, 2012). Further analysis indicated that Asians were more tolerant of invasions of their personal (virtual) space than were Europeans in the study.

OUT OF THE CLASSROOM
onto the page

Social media can be a place to share knowledge and things you're passionate about with others, but sometimes not all that you encounter online is accurate or genuine. Maybe you've seen a "friend" post on social media an exaggerated story or pass along a conspiracy theory as though it was fact. Perhaps you've read some "fake news." Such nonverbal cues as misspellings, bad grammar, overused punctuation (like repeated exclamation points), putting certain words in all caps for emphasis, and multiple re-posts can be telltale signs of an overwrought or false piece of information.

When we teach public speaking and cover persuasion and ethics, we often challenge students to find potential fallacies on social media. A student in one public speaking class shared a tweet from someone who generalized and stereotyped based on racial profiling. Another student found a GoFundMe campaign claiming to help pay someone's funeral arrangements, but it turned out the campaign was just a scheme to get money, capitalizing on the emotions and generosity of others.

Other students found political figures and celebrities using fallacious reasoning in their tweets and posts. Authors of the posts made argumentative claims and offered opinions, but didn't cite any data to substantiate such claims or back up their views. Additionally, students were concerned with some companies' advertisements. Ads were flashy and distracting, which frustrated students who wanted the ads simply to discuss the company's brand values, mission, or products.

In these classes, after we discuss the problems created by unethical or uninformed social media users, we debrief about the ramifications of online postings. Because social media is an increasingly common place to receive and digest news, it's important to be information literate, using our critical thinking skills as we take care with what we believe to be factual or fake.

spotlight *on research*

Privacy vs. Online Surveillance: The Problem of Cyberstalking

Are you aware of how someone can "creep" on someone's social media or "stalk" someone's profile? This kind of proxemic surveillance may sound a bit innocent at first, like it stems from just being generally curious. But persistent cyberstalking gets into a whole other level of offense. With increased use of and reliance on social media and CMC in our daily lives, cyberstalking is becoming more common. Researchers Smoker and March (2017) investigated cyberstalking among former and current intimate partners.

Cyberstalking is the practice of accessing (sometimes via hacking) another person's social media pages to discover personal or private information. Sometimes cyberstalkers can gain access to all the information they wish to learn because of a target's or victim's weak privacy settings. In their research, Smoker and March found that partners of all sexual orientations and gender identities reported participating in cyberstalking behaviors. How would you feel if this sort of intrusion happened to you? *Has* it happened to you?

Imagine that you're going on a blind date. A week prior to the date, you post on Facebook that a relative of yours is undergoing surgery. During the blind date, your date slips and asks how your relative is doing after your surgery. You never told your date this information. Were you cyberstalked or was the person just doing his or her "homework" before your date?

According to Smoker and March, cyberstalking can lead to physical, emotional, or financial abuse toward the target of the stalking. For most people, the idea that a current or ex-partner is "checking up on them" causes serious tension and stress. People may block the cyberstalker on their social media to bar the person from accessing their page; however, cyberstalkers may create new profiles or fake profiles to regain access. Often, victims never notice they're being stalked online.

Some downsides definitely exist to using the tools that CMC provides us with. No wonder some people wish to "unplug" or go on a social media cleanse! How does this make you feel about your privacy online? How does social media affect your level of trust in romantic as well as platonic relationships?

Want to know more about this study? If so, check out Smoker, M., & March, E. (2017). Predicting perpetration of intimate partner cyberstalking: Gender and the dark tetrad. *Computers in Human Behavior, 72*, 390-396.

Anonymity	Ability to communicate, participate, and maintain a presence online without revealing one's true identity
Flaming	Aggressive online communication that intentionally disrupts, heckles, and harasses others
Avatars	Ways people express themselves online and convey emotions through embodiments and manifestations that resemble human characteristics
Gender swapping	Use of screen names, aliases, and avatars that allow participants to experiment with gender identity
Shouting	Typing words in all caps in e-mails, text messages, and online postings
Identity fluidity	How online identities can change at any moment with a simple change of screen name, online format, or avatar

Time Matters: Mediated Chronemics

In Chapter 3 on environment as a form of nonverbal communication, we defined **chronemics** as the communicative aspects of time. Our sense of time can play a role in mediated contexts as well as face-to-face situations (Kalman, Scissors, Gill, & Gergle, 2013; Lew et al., 2018; Tatum, Martin, & Kemper, 2018). Face-to-face interactions are **dynamic**, in that they typically involve no interruption of time between message formation, sending, receiving, and feedback. However, technology allows for **static** communication, in which the turn-taking process of communication can take place over a greater length of time. For example, a friend invites you out for dinner via text or e-mail. You have the opportunity to ask others if they want to join or to make other plans before you respond. In a face-to-face setting, you don't have the luxury of time to gather more information. Instead, you're expected to give a response to your friend immediately. The ability to frame your responses on your own terms without violating another person's time expectations is yet another reason why people prefer to engage in communication through text and e-mail instead of verbal dialogues.

Although mediated communication does allow for greater chronemic freedom than face-to-face interaction, it's still possible to violate a person's time expectations in a mediated format. Say you're texting with a friend; messages are flowing and communication seems effective. But then, when you ask for specifics, such as setting a time to have dinner or see a movie, all of a sudden your friend's messages stop. What are you left thinking in a situation such as this? As another example, ever get an e-mail or text message at what you consider an inappropriate hour? A conservative Christian student of ours not too long ago told the class about an instance when she realized she was e-mailing a friend's husband at a very late hour about a church project they were both working on. The verbal content of the e-mail was harmless, but she felt as though e-mailing someone's husband about any subject at an hour when the man would likely be in bed was inappropriate. These are examples of **chronemic expectancy violations**, in which a person's use of time violates what another deems polite or appropriate.

Researchers Kalman and Rafaeli (2011) examined how online pauses and silence in computer-mediated communication can violate chronemic expectancy norms. In the study, managers were asked to evaluate job candidates who varied in the length of time they took to respond to an e-mail message (response latency). As defined in Chapter 9 on vocalics, **response latency** is the amount of time someone takes to respond to a message, both in face-to-face and online contexts. Kalman and Rafaeli's findings reinforced traditional expectancy violations theory, with managers reacting more favorably to job applicants who provided prompt e-mail feedback compared with those who took longer to respond. Applicants who met the chronemic expectancies of managers had higher evaluations, perceived credibility, and overall attractiveness compared with other responders. So, although mediated communication does allow for a greater tolerance of pauses and silence, it's still important to evaluate chronemic expectancies depending on the situation and perceived appropriateness.

Within the context of social networking, have you ever been criticized for not posting enough or not responding quickly enough to another person's post or shared photo? Some people expect that if they've messaged or tweeted you, you'll drop everything and respond immediately—laptop, pad, or phone permanently in hand. If you don't, what's the result of this nonverbal chronemic cue that forces someone to wait? Do you view professors who Facebook with their students differently than those who don't or who won't accept friend requests from students? What perceptions are formed of teachers who make it a policy not to Facebook with students until after they've graduated and are no longer their students? It may be a bit of a stretch to term this behavior *online chronemics*, but "to friend or not to friend" is a form of nonverbal response latency that contributes to perceptions about a person.

REMEMBER	
Chronemics	Communicative aspects of time
Dynamic time	Form of time that usually involves no interruptions between message formation, sending, receiving, and feedback; typical of face-to-face interaction
Static time	Form of time that may involve interruptions between message formation, sending, receiving, and feedback; typical of mediated or online interaction
Chronemic expectancy violations	Instances when one person's use of time violates what another person deems polite or appropriate
Response latency	How long it takes someone to formulate a response to a statement or question in interaction

Remember! **10.3**

NONVERBAL DIMENSIONS OF COMPUTER-MEDIATED COMMUNICATION (CMC) ■ ■ ■ ■

Nonverbal communication codes covered in previous chapters are important to examine when our interaction shifts from face-to-face communication to CMC (i.e., computer-mediated communication, defined earlier as human communication facilitated by technology). When human communicators rely on computers as a key vehicle for communicating with friends, family members, colleagues, clients, and even strangers, it's important to realize how nonverbal cues emerge on this channel (Kashian et al., 2017; Lew et al., 2018). Understanding the presence or absence of nonverbal communication codes in face-to-face versus computer-mediated communication can be confusing, so we provide Table 10.1 for clarity.

TABLE 10.1 Nonverbal Codes in Face-to-Face (FtF) vs. Computer-Mediated Communication (CMC)

NONVERBAL CODE	FACE-TO-FACE COMMUNICATION (FTF)	COMPUTER-MEDIATED COMMUNICATION (CMC)
Environment	Our surroundings communicate who we are and influence how we behave and interact.	Virtual communities, such as Facebook, create webs of personal relationships in cyberspace. Surroundings depicted in photos posted to webpages can create a constant or variant sense of self, just like physical environments maintained offline.
Proxemics/territoriality	Territoriality and our use of personal space influence our communication and reveal our thoughts, attitudes, and emotions.	Response time in CMC creates a feeling of distance or closeness. Video chatting allows traditional nonverbal cues to emerge. Online journals are private spaces for users. Avatar placement brings attention to space.
Physical appearance	Clothing, artifacts, weight, height, tattoos, piercings, and skin color are elements of physical appearance that people observe and judge us by.	We can post digitally modified pictures of ourselves online. We can also describe our idealized, fantasized virtual body. Gender swapping and avatars alter the appearance of the virtual body.
Kinesics (body movement, gestures, and posture)	Gestures can substitute for or accent verbal communication.	Avatars convey emotion by mimicking human movement. Emoticons and punctuation communicate emphasis, like an accenting gesture.

(Continued)

chapter ten

Face/eye behavior	The face and eyes are instrumental in regulating interaction. Facial features send unintended messages.	Emoticons and emojis represent facial expressions, which indicate the emotions of the user.
Touch (haptics)	Touch is the most powerful and misunderstood nonverbal code, and can convey an array of emotions and meanings.	Immediacy in e-mails and social media postings creates a sense of touch, as if the receiver were with us. As with the physical body, the virtual body can be abused and sexualized online.
Vocalics (paralanguage)	Vocal characteristics such as pitch, rate, and volume influence how others interpret our verbal messages.	Voice-recognition/talk-to-text technology enables online communication. Typed punctuation and formatting indicate inflection, as well as emotion.

While smartphones and pads/tablets are probably only a step away from being the equivalent of computers, in this section of the chapter we focus on nonverbal cues in those messages generated by computers. You'll detect some overlap with previous sections, because computer-generated messages may also contain emojis, grammar mistakes, or textisms. Many of us access our social networking sites through our computers as well as other devices; many of us receive e-mail messages via our phones. We recognize the overlap of areas here—mapping the technological terrain is challenging.

Nonverbal Cues and CMC

As technology continues to advance, communication scholars witness its widening effects on how we communicate. Computer-mediated communication (CMC) changes the way we maintain and form personal and professional relationships; we continue to adapt our communication as the medium evolves (Blair, 2017; Bryant & Sheldon, 2017; Chen & Li, 2017; DeAndrea, Tong, Levine, & Walther, 2012; Kashian et al., 2017; Quintanilla & Wahl, 2016; Walther et al., 2005). Common CMC methods include texting, e-mailing, instant messaging, and social media use. Let's review a few features of CMC for their nonverbal impact.

CHANNEL & FORMALITY. A **channel** is the specific medium through which a message is sent. Computer-mediated messages may be sent through multiple channels (e.g., Facebook post, tweet, Snapchat, text message). These channels often have different practices based on **formality**, meaning the etiquette (netiquette, or proper use) and normative rules of a specific channel. For example, Facebook users typically use less curse words than they use on Twitter. One reason for this trend is because more parents, family members, and older people in general utilize Facebook than younger people (Miller, 2013). Font selection as well as the length of an online message (termed **message duration** in Chapter 9) are nonverbal cues within CMC. Tweets have certain character counts (even though this restriction changed in 2017), whereas Facebook posts aren't restricted in length (Larson, 2017). The frequency with which you post, tweet, or engage in other online formats is also a nonverbal cue.

Sometimes a violation of expectations occurs due to the breaking of these rules or someone being unaware that rules or common patterns of engagement exist. As we discussed earlier in this chapter, people often use acronyms and textisms to send messages more quickly via CMC. Would you send an e-mail that included acronyms, textisms, and emojis to a professor or potential employer like you might in a text to your best friend? We hope not, but research shows that many people don't adapt their messages when changing channels; thus, they may send inappropriately informal messages through a more formal channel such as e-mail (Beer, 2017; Semingson & Owens, 2017).

EMOTION. Have you ever sent a text message and the receiver totally misunderstood you? You're not alone! In fact, a good deal of research has explored how computer-mediated messages may be misinterpreted or misconstrued due to reduced nonverbal cues (Edwards, Bybee, Frost, Harvey, & Navarro, 2017; Hautasaari, Yamashita, & Gao, 2017; Riordan, 2017). Sure, emojis and emoticons can help you communicate some of your message nonverbally, but emotions such as grief and anxiety are still difficult to convey via icons or words typed on a screen (Riordan, 2017). Conflict and the emotions that go with it aren't easily handled through CMC. "Okay," "ok," and "k" may communicate different emotions associated with the word. At other times, message senders don't mean anything by their spelling of words or when they replace a word like "okay" with a thumbs-up emoji (Edwards et al., 2017). Experts suggest that emotional communication is better handled face to face, even if it's difficult; online emotion is a challenge to convey as well as interpret down the line, when nonverbal cues are missing or compromised (Quintanilla & Wahl, 2016).

People may use CMC for ill-will. **Aggressive communication**, which serves the sender at the receiver's emotional expense, is common online, sadly. You may have heard that people are "bolder behind a screen." Online attackers and trolls use their screens to shield their personal identities and spew their venom at will. Without having to deal with face-to-face fallout, a malicious communicator is able to reap the benefits of aggressive communication without any responsibility (Ferrara, Ianniello, Villani, & Corsello, 2018; Quintanilla & Wahl, 2016; Tagg et al., 2017). Aggressive nonverbal cues may include continuous or repeated rapid-fire postings, tweets, or other messages; dramatic use of punctuation marks or fonts, like exclamation points and boldface; and the use of all caps (known as shouting) for certain words, to draw attention to aggressive or hostile meanings.

PERSONALIZATION. Computer-mediated platforms provide ways for users to nonverbally communicate their identity. Think about ways you personalize mediated platforms to show your personality and passions. Do you have cover and thumbnail photos on Facebook? Perhaps your profile picture on Twitter communicates that you like hiking, animals, or cooking. Frequent posts to Snapchat or Instagram of you at various restaurants may communicate to others that you're a foodie (or simply have a healthy appetite and an active social life!). You may select a specific username or e-mail address that communicates something about you. An email address such as DrImanXAmple@University.Edu has actual nonverbal ramifications. You'd think differently of gamerY@RPG.com or sexybabeonthebeach@hotmail.com than Dr. Iman. Ultimately, the way you manage your CMC affects the way people view you (Quintanilla & Wahl, 2016; Toma, 2017; Toma & D'Angelo, 2017).

THE VIRTUAL BODY

One of the most interesting nonverbal codes that has significant impact on the face-to-face context but is diminished or nonexistent in the CMC context is physical appearance. As we mentioned in Chapter 5, U.S. culture (as well as many other cultures around the world) places a great deal of emphasis on looks. One important aspect within the larger category of physical appearance is the body, a topic increasing in significance in communication research (Brierley, Brooks, Mond, Stevenson, & Stephen, 2016; Corey, 2007; Trekels & Eggermont, 2017).

Researchers have long debated the importance of the **physical body** (the body that isn't mediated but exists in face-to-face communication) in human impression formation and relationship development. The impact of the **virtual body** (the body that is mediated, represented, or constructed through pictures, descriptions, avatars, emojis, etc.) on CMC has been and continues to be the subject of research (Bernal & Maes, 2017; Chou et al., 2017 McRae, 1996; Villani, Gatti, Confalonieri, & Riva, 2012; Whitty & Carr, 2003).

Our bodies and the way we talk about and portray them are important, given the increasing frequency of online relationships (Bryant & Sheldon, 2017; Ellison, Hancock, & Toma, 2012; Finkel, Eastwick, Karney, Reis, & Sprecher, 2012; Guadagno, Okdie & Kruse, 2012; Smith, 2016; Smith & Anderson, 2016; Strubel & Petrie, 2017; Toma & D'Angelo, 2017). Probably most of us know someone who has initiated a relationship online. (Maybe you *are* that someone; it's quite common now.) The typical first questions potential romantic partners ask online are about age, sex,

Many people take "selfies" to post on social media or dating apps.

appearance, and location (Whitty & Gavin, 2001). So it seems that one of the first things that interests people who seek a romantic partner is the body. One important difference between face-to-face and CMC encounters is the lack of restriction in the way the virtual body looks, since the Internet allows a person to create a new and improved body through text, avatar, or icon (Bryant & Sheldon, 2017; Whitty, 2003, 2004). This new and improved body can have an ideal weight, perfect skin, a good job, confidence—a whole array of characteristics and attributes that may or may not be the reality. What seems contradictory about this is, while CMC has the benefit of reducing the importance of physical characteristics and beauty, people still seem to elevate appearance when relating online.

Cyber-Flirting and Online Deception

One aspect of CMC that is particularly interesting to think about is **cyber-flirting**—representing the body online to attract others (Hobbs, Owen, & Gerber, 2017; Mortensen, 2017; Whitty, 2003, 2004). Some of you may be experienced in the art and skill of online flirting; others of you may just now be ready to step up to the keyboard and give it a try. Still others of you will never engage in this activity. (Play at your own risk is our best advice.) In flirting situations that involve primarily text rather than photos, the body may be represented through descriptions of how attractive one appears. For example, instead of preparing to look good for a face-to-face date, individuals online may create a first impression by describing through text their attractiveness. Another approach is to use emojis that convey flirtation and interest, often called "flirtmojis" (Gregory, 2016; King-Slutzky, 2017).

Cyber-flirting and online dating give people an alternative to more traditional ways to meet (e.g., bars, coffee shops, parties, set-ups). But it's important to realize some drawbacks to this form of connecting, mainly the potential for deception (Burgoon, 2005; DeAndrea et al., 2012; Ellison et al., 2012; Guadagno et al., 2012; Hall, Park, Hayeon, & Michael, 2010; Toma, 2017; Toma &

D'Angelo, 2017; Zhou, 2005; Zhou, Twitchell, Qin, Burgoon, & Nunamaker, 2003). **Catfishing** (posing online as someone you're not) is a serious problem; the ease of communicating a false identity to online partners is intoxicating for some people who care little about the damage they do to others (McHugh, 2013; Smith, Smith, & Blazka, 2017). A lesser offense occurs when people post photos of their younger, thinner, full-head-of-hair selves on dating sites. These deceivers may believe that doing so is harmless, given the remote possibility of meeting online partners face to face. It's understandable to want to look one's best when flirting online, but representing oneself ideally, not realistically, is still a form of deception. One study of Internet relationships revealed that a substantial number of men and women lie online about their age and physical appearance (McCown, Fisher, Page, & Homant, 2001). Men in the study revealed a higher rate of lying (77%) compared with women (46%). Many online dating sites have taken pains to diminish the possibility of deception on the part of users.

Cybersex: Getting "Virtually" Physical

As online relationships develop, it's more common today than it used to be for people to have virtual sexual experiences, despite many people's beliefs that such activity, even between committed, monogamous partners, is amoral, wrong, or just weird (Goldsmith & Byers, 2017; Hobbs et al., 2017; Lee & Wahl, 2007). **Cybersex**—sexual experiences, fantasies, and interactions exchanged in real time online—is a topic important to the study of online relational development, even though many online relationships develop successfully without sexual activity. Cybersex is very personal and intimate for people in online relationships; it can serve an important maintenance function for those in committed relationships who are geographically separated (i.e., in long-distance relationships) or cross-residential (i.e., residing in different areas, usually for employment or educational reasons) (Cole, 2017; Goldsmith & Byers, 2017). Many people who participate in cybersex consider it just as satisfying and essential as face-to-face sexual activity. For some, it's preferable because of the view that cybersex lacks the complications that face-to-face sex may evoke. Others use cybersex or sexting on dating or hookup apps as precursors to face-to-face sexual experiences (Duguay, Burgess, & Light, 2017; Macapagal et al., 2018). However, many people who participate in cybersex don't use their real names and view it as entertainment; others view it as a form of pornography (Dines, 2010). This topic is controversial, to say the least.

If a person is in a face-to-face, monogamous relationship and has cybersex online with someone other than her or his partner, would you consider that cheating, meaning **cyber-infidelity**? Interestingly, research reveals varying reactions to cybersex with someone other than one's partner (Sahni & Jain, 2018; Viano, 2018; Vossler, 2016). Some people term it "emotional infidelity," viewing online sexual activity as adultery and fair grounds for divorce when it occurs outside of one's marriage (Fiely, 2003; Meyers, 2012). Others view cybersex as relatively harmless and not a real problem, an activity akin to watching porn or reading a sexy novel (Sahni & Swasti, 2018; Turkle, 1995). The physical body versus the virtual body comes into play here. Nonverbal communication codes, such as physical appearance and touch, are important in making a distinction between sexual experiences with the physical body in face-to-face settings versus such experiences with the virtual body online.

REMEMBER	
Physical body	The body that is not mediated but real and existing in face-to-face communication
Virtual body	The body that is mediated, represented, or constructed through e-mail messages, pictures, descriptions, avatars, and emoticons/emojis
Cyber-flirting	Representing the body online to attract others
Catfishing	Posing online as someone you're not
Cybersex	Sexual experiences, fantasies, interactions, and descriptions that are exchanged in real time through the Internet
Cyber-infidelity	Having an online sexual relationship with someone other than one's face-to-face sexual, monogamous partner

SUMMARY

In this chapter, we explored how nonverbal communication functions in the context of technology and social media. We began the chapter by examining three traditional nonverbal codes (kinesics, eye contact, and vocalics) as mediated by technology. Next we explored some nonverbal cues unique to cell phone and pad/tablet usage, including emoticons, emojis, acronyms, textisms, grammar, spelling, and punctuation in text messages. While video chatting has been available for a few decades, primarily through computer usage, the ability to video-chat on one's phone or tablet is relatively new; certain nonverbal cues are more present in video chatting, although still not to the level of the face-to-face conversation. We concluded this section with a review of research on cell phone usage and the development and maintenance of romantic relationships.

We then shifted from cell phone usage to nonverbal cues and social media, beginning with a discussion of nonverbal cues important to consider when developing one's online persona. We reviewed research that shows that a profile owner's online friends and their nonverbal cues, primarily physical attractiveness and behaviors described in postings and depicted in photos, affect perceptions of that profile owner. Online chronemics should be considered as well, because how one uses time in sending, posting, receiving, and responding to online messages is a form of nonverbal communication.

chapter ten

Computer-mediated communication (CMC) is an umbrella term for an area of research that launched this topic of study. In this chapter, we contrasted nonverbal codes in the face-to-face and CMC arenas, then examined nonverbal dimensions of CMC. The chapter concluded with a contrast between nonverbal cues of the physical body and the virtual body, then an exploration of nonverbal cues surrounding cyber-flirting, cybersex, and cyber-infidelity. We trust that your reading of this chapter has provided you with a better understanding of some of the more important aspects of nonverbal communication and how they influence both our online and offline lives.

DISCUSSION STARTERS ■ ■ ■

1. What are the most critical nonverbal cues in online settings or when using technology to communicate? How has the explosion of technology and social media affected how you communicate nonverbally?

2. How do you feel when you send an e-mail or text message and get no response? What nonverbal impression do you get about the person you contacted? What if the person takes a long time to reply to your message (response latency)—might your feelings or impressions be altered by the delay?

3. Do you think emojis help you communicate your feelings when e-mailing or texting, or have these elements become expected now? Is it easier for you to communicate your personal feelings when using technology and social media as opposed to face to face? Why or why not?

4. Think about your own important relationships and the role your cell phone plays in the maintenance of those relationships. Do you have set guidelines for phone usage with your friends or romantic partners? Have you ever been misunderstood during or as a result of a mediated exchange? If so, was the culprit some aspect of nonverbal communication related to the online exchange? Did you or the other person change your online behavior to avoid future misunderstandings?

5. What are the primary differences between face-to-face communication and computer-mediated communication (CMC)? What nonverbal cues are missing or altered in CMC, and how do they affect interaction?

6. What's the difference between the physical body and the virtual body? Does your physical body differ from your virtual body? How are these elements related to our study of nonverbal communication?

REFERENCES

Adamo-Villani, N., & Anasingaraju, S. (2017). Holographic signing avatars for deaf education. In G. Vincenti, A. Bucciero, M. Helfert, & M. Glowatz (Eds.), *E-Learning, e-education, and online training* (pp. 54–61). New York: Springer.

Allred, R. J., & Crowley, J. P. (2017). The "mere presence" hypothesis: Investigating the nonverbal effects of cell-phone presence on conversation satisfaction. *Communication Studies, 68*, 22–36.

Arroyo, A., & Brunner, S. R. (2016). Negative body talk as an outcome of friends' fitness posts on social networking sites: Body surveillance and social comparison as potential moderators. *Journal of Applied Communication Research, 44*, 216–235.

Barker, V. (2018). Text you pictures: The role of group belonging, race identity, race, and gender in older adolescents' mobile phone use. *Social Sciences, 7*, 1–16.

Baxter, L. A., & Montgomery, B. M. (1996). *Relating: Dialogues and dialectics*. New York: Guilford.

Baxter, L. A., & Montgomery, B. M. (2000). Rethinking communication in personal relationships from a dialectical perspective. In K. Dindia & S. Duck (Eds.), *Communication and personal relationships* (pp. 31–53). New York: Wiley.

Beer, A. (2017). From business letters to email and mobile communication. In G. Mautner & F. Rainer (Eds.), *Handbook of business communication: Linguistic approaches* (pp. 153–173). Berlin: De Gruyter Mouton.

Bernal, G., & Maes, P. (2017). Emotional beasts: Visually expressing emotions through avatars in VR. In *Proceedings of the 2017 CHI Conference Extended Abstracts on Human Factors in Computing Systems* (pp. 2395–2402). New York: ACM Publications.

Birdwhistell, R. L. (1970). *Kinesics and context*. Philadelphia: University of Pennsylvania Press.

Blair, J. R. (2017). *Emojis used as nouns, verbs, and adjectives* (Doctoral dissertation, Northeastern Illinois University). Retrieved from ProQuest. (10618423)

Bolkan, S., & Griffin, D. J. (2017). Students' use of cell phones in class for off-task behaviors: The indirect impact of instructors' teaching behaviors through boredom and students' attitudes. *Communication Education, 66*, 313–329.

Brierley, M-E., Brooks, K. R., Mond, J., Stevenson, R. J., & Stephen, I. D. (2016). The body and the beautiful: Health, attractiveness and body composition in men's and women's bodies. *PLoS ONE, 11*: e0156722.

Burgoon, J. K. (2005, November). *Truth, lies and virtual worlds* (The Carroll C. Arnold Distinguished Lecture, National Communication Association). Boston: Allyn & Bacon.

Bryant, K., & Sheldon, P. (2017). Cyber dating in the age of mobile apps: Understanding motives, attitudes, and characteristics of users. *American Communication Journal, 19*, 1–15.

Carr, C. T., & Stefaniak, C. (2012). Sent from my iPhone: The medium and message as cues of sender professionalism in mobile telephony. *Journal of Applied Communication Research, 40*, 403–424.

Chang, C. (2016). Responses to conflicting information in computer-mediated communication: Gender difference as an example. *New Media & Society, 18*, 5–24.

Cheever, N. A., Rosen, L. D., Carrier, M., & Chavez, A. (2014). Out of sight is not out of mind: The impact of restricting wireless mobile device use on anxiety levels among low, moderate and high users. *Computers in Human Behavior, 37*, 290–297.

Chen, H. T., & Li, X. (2017). The contribution of mobile social media to social capital and psychological well-being: Examining the role of communicative use, friending and self-disclosure. *Computers in Human Behavior, 75*, 958–965.

Chou, Y. J., Lo, S. K., & Teng, C. I. (2017). Reasons for avatar gender swapping by online game players: A qualitative interview-based study. In Information Resources Management Association (Ed.), *Discrimination and diversity: Concepts, methodologies, tools, and applications* (pp. 202–219). Hershey, PA: IGI Global.

Clayton, R. B., Leshner, G., & Almond, A. (2015). The extended iSelf: The impact of iPhone separation on cognition, emotion, and physiology. *Journal of Computer-Mediated Communication, 20*, 119–135.

Cohen, E. L., Bowman, N. D., & Borchert, K. (2014). Private flirts, public friends: Understanding romantic jealous responses to an ambiguous social networking site message as a function of message access exclusivity. *Computers in Human Behavior, 35*, 533–541.

Cole, C. (2017). *Type dirty to me: An analysis of sexting as a form of communication in long-term romantic relationships* (Honors thesis). Retrieved from Digital Commons@EMU. (532)

Corey, A. M. (2007). Body politics in online communication. *Texas Speech Communication Journal, 32*, 21–32.

Davidson, B., Joinson, A., & Jones, S. (2018). Technologically enhanced dating: Augmented human relationships, robots, and fantasy. In Z. Papacharissi (Ed.), *A networked self and love* (pp. 145–171). Abingdon, UK: Routledge.

DeAndrea, D. C., Tong, S. T., Liang, Y. J., Levine, T. R., & Walther, J. B. (2012). When do people misrepresent themselves to others? The effects of social desirability, ground truth, and accountability on deceptive self-presentations. *Journal of Communication, 62*, 400–417.

De Martino, J. M., Silva, I. R., Bolognini, C. Z., Costa, P. D. P., Kumada, K. M. O., Coradine, L. C., da Silva Brito, P. H., do Amaral, W. M., Benetti, A. B., Poeta, E. T., Angare, L. M. G., Ferreira, C. M., & Angare, L. M. G. (2017). Signing avatars: Making education more inclusive. *Universal Access in the Information Society, 16*, 793–808.

Dines, G. (2010). *Pornland: How porn has hijacked our sexuality.* Boston: Beacon.

Dresner, E., & Herring, S. C. (2010). Functions of the nonverbal in CMC: Emoticons and illocutionary force. *Communication Theory, 20*, 249–268.

Duguay, S., Burgess, J., & Light, B. (2017). Mobile dating and hookup app culture. In L. Humphreys & P. Messaris (Eds.), *Digital media: Transformations in human communication* (pp. 213–221). New York: Peter Lang.

Duran, R. L., Kelly, L., & Rotaru, T. (2011). Mobile phones in romantic relationships and the dialectic of autonomy versus connection. *Communication Quarterly, 59*, 19–36.

Edwards, R., Bybee, B. T., Frost, J. K., Harvey, A. J., & Navarro, M. (2017). That's not what I meant: How misunderstanding is related to channel and perspective-taking. *Journal of Language and Social Psychology, 36*, 188–210.

Ellison, N. B., Hancock, J. T., & Toma, C. L. (2012). Profile as promise: A framework for conceptualizing veracity in online dating self-presentations. *New Media & Society, 14*, 45–62.

Ferrara, P., Ianniello, F., Villani, A., & Corsello, G. (2018). Cyberbullying, a modern form of bullying: Let's talk about this health and social problem. *Italian Journal of Pediatrics, 44*. https://doi.org/ 10.1186/ s13052-018-0446-4

Fiely, D. (2003). Cyber-infidelity: Internet access implicated in growing number of divorces. *Columbus Dispatch*, p. B1.

Finkel, E. J., Eastwick, P. W., Karney, B. R., Reis, H. T., & Sprecher, S. (2012). Online dating: A critical analysis from the perspective of psychological science. *Psychological Science in the Public Interest, 13*, 3–66.

Fleuriet, C., Cole, M., & Guerrero, L. K. (2014). Exploring Facebook: Attachment style and nonverbal message characteristics as predictors of anticipated emotional reactions to Facebook postings. *Journal of Nonverbal Behavior, 38*, 429–450.

Floyd, K. (2016). *Interpersonal communication* (3rd ed.). New York: McGraw-Hill.

Garrison, A., Remley, D., Thomas, P., & Wierszewski, E. (2011). Conventional faces: Emoticons in instant messaging discourse. *Computers & Composition, 28*, 112–125.

Gershon, I. (2010). *The breakup 2.0: Disconnecting over new media.* Ithaca, NY: Cornell University Press.

Goffman, E. (1959). *The presentation of self in everyday life.* Garden City, NJ: Doubleday Anchor Books.

Goldsmith, K. M., & Byers, E. S. (2017). Perceived and reported romantic and sexual outcomes in long-distance and geographically close relationships. *The Canadian Journal of Human Sexuality.* https://doi.org/10.3138/cjhs.2018-0016

Gregory, A. (2016, Fall). Flirtmoji. *Bitch*, 14.

Guadagno, R. E., Okdie, B. M., & Kruse, S. A. (2012). Dating deception: Gender, online dating, and exaggerated self-presentation. *Computers in Human Behavior, 28*, 642–647.

Hall, J. A., & Baym, N. K. (2011). Calling and texting (too much): Mobile maintenance expectations, (over) dependence, entrapment, and friendship satisfaction. *New Media & Society, 14*, 316–331.

Hall, J. A., Park, N., Hayeon, S., & Michael, J. C. (2010). Strategic misrepresentation in online dating: The effects of gender, self-monitoring, and personality traits. *Journal of Social & Personal Relationships, 27*, 117–135.

Halpern, D., & Katz, J. E. (2017). Texting's consequences for romantic relationships: A cross-lagged analysis highlights its risks. *Computers in Human Behavior, 71*, 386–394.

Hasler, B. S., & Friedman, D. A. (2012). Sociocultural conventions in avatar-mediated nonverbal communication: A cross-cultural analysis of virtual proxemics. *Journal of Intercultural Communication Research, 41*, 238–259.

Hautasaari, A., Yamashita, N., & Gao, G. (2017). How non-native English speakers perceive the emotional valence of messages in text-based computer-mediated communication. *Discourse Processes.* https://doi.org/10.1080/0163853X.2017.1323184

Hobbs, M., Owen, S., & Gerber, L. (2017). Liquid love? Dating apps, sex, relationships and the digital transformation of intimacy. *Journal of Sociology, 53*, 271–284.

Hussain, Z., & Griffiths, M. D. (2008). Gender swapping and socializing in cyberspace: An exploratory study. *CyberPsychology & Behavior, 11*, 47–53.

Ishii, K. (2010). Conflict management in online relationships. *Cyberpsychology, Behavior, and Social Networking, 13*, 365–370.

Jibril, T., & Abdullah, M. (2013). Relevance of emoticons in computer-mediated communication contexts: An overview. *Asian Social Science, 9*, 201–207.

chapter ten

Jin, B., & Pena, J. F. (2010). Mobile communication in romantic relationships: Mobile phone use, relational uncertainty, love, commitment, and attachment styles. *Communication Reports, 23*, 39–51.

Jordan, T. (1999). *Cyberpower: The culture and politics of cyberspace and the Internet.* London: Routledge.

Kalman, Y. M., & Rafaeli, S. (2011). Online pauses and silence: Chronemic expectancy violations in written computer-mediated communication. *Communication Research, 38*, 54–69.

Kalman, Y. M., Scissors, L. E., Gill, A. J., & Gergle, D. (2013). Online chronemics convey social information. *Computers in Human Behavior, 29*, 1260–1269.

Kaye, L. K., Malone, S. A., & Wall, H. J. (2017). Emojis: Insights, affordances, and possibilities for psychological science. *Trends in Cognitive Sciences, 21*, 66–68.

Kashian, N., Jang, J. W., Shin, S. Y., Dai, Y., & Walther, J. B. (2017). Self-disclosure and liking in computer-mediated communication. *Computers in Human Behavior, 71*, 275–283.

Kelly, L., Miller-Ott, A. E., & Duran, R. L. (2017). Sports scores and intimate moments: An expectancy violations theory approach to partner cell phone behaviors in adult romantic relationships. *Western Journal of Communication, 81*, 619–640.

Kim, B., & Kim, Y. (2017). College students' social media use and communication network heterogeneity: Implications for social capital and subjective well-being. *Computers in Human Behavior, 73*, 620–628.

King-Slutzky, J. (2017). An emoji guide for the text message clueless. Retrieved from www.nerve.com

Krasnova, H., Wenninger, H., Widjaja, T., & Buxmann, P. (2013, February). *Envy on Facebook: A hidden threat to users' life satisfaction?* Paper presented at the International Conference on Wirtschaftinformatik, Leipzig, Germany.

Kuznekoff, J. H., & Titsworth, S. (2013). The impact of mobile phone usage on student learning. *Communication Education, 62*, 233–252.

Lamberg, E. M., & Muratori, L. M. (2012). Cell phones change the way we walk. *Gait & Posture, 35*, 688–690.

Larson, S. (2017, November 7). Welcome to a world with 280-character tweets. Retrieved from https://money.cnn.com/2017/11/07/technology/twitter-280-character-limit/

Lee, R., & Wahl, S. T. (2007). Justifying surveillance and control: An analysis of the media framing of pedophiles and the Internet. *Texas Speech Communication Journal, 32*, 1–15.

LeFebvre, L. (2017). Phantom lovers: Ghosting as a relationship dissolution strategy in the technological age. In N. M. Punyanunt-Carter & J. S. Wrench (Eds.), *The impact of social media in modern romantic relationships* (pp. 219–235). Lanham, MD: Lexington.

Lew, Z., Walther, J. B., Pang, A., & Shin, W. (2018). Interactivity in online chat: Conversational contingency and response latency in computer-mediated communication. *Journal of Computer-Mediated Communication, 23*, 201–221.

Liang, H., Fu, K., & Shen, F. (2017). Privacy protection and self-disclosure across societies: A study of global Twitter users. *New Media & Society, 19*, 1476–1497.

Ling, R., Baron, N. S., Lenhart, A., & Campbell, S. W. (2014). "Girls text really weird": Gender, texting and identity among teens. *Journal of Children and Media, 8*, 423–439.

Lueders, A., Hall, J. A., Pennington, N. R., & Knutson, K. (2014). Nonverbal decoding on Facebook: Applying the IPT-15 and the SSI to personality judgments. *Journal of Nonverbal Behavior, 38*, 413–427.

Macapagal, K., Moskowitz, D. A., Li, D. H., Carrión, A., Bettin, E., Fisher, C. B., & Mustanski, B. (2018). Hookup app use, sexual behavior, and sexual health among adolescent men who have sex with men in the United States. *Journal of Adolescent Health*, *62*, 708–715.

Maguire, K. C., Heinemann-LaFave, D., & Sahlstein, E. (2013). "To be so connected, yet not at all": Relational presence, absence, and maintenance in the context of a wartime deployment. *Western Journal of Communication*, *77*, 249–271.

Martey, R., & Consalvo, M. (2011). Performing the looking-glass self: Avatar appearance and group identity in Second Life. *Popular Communication*, *9*, 165–180.

Martey, R. M., & Stromer-Galley, J. (2007). The digital dollhouse: Context and social norms in The Sims Online. *Games and Culture*, *2*, 314–334.

McClure, E., & Barr, R. (2017). Building family relationships from a distance: Supporting connections with babies and toddlers using video and video chat. In R. Barr & D. N. Linebarger (Eds.), *Media exposure during infancy and early childhood: The effects of content and context on learning and development* (pp. 227–248). New York: Springer.

McCown, J. A., Fisher, D., Page, R., & Homant, M. (2001). Internet relationships: People who meet people. *CyberPsychology & Behavior*, *4*, 593–596.

McHugh, M. (2013, August 23). It's catfishing season! How to tell lovers from liars online, and more. Retrieved from https://www.digitaltrends.com/web/its-catfishing-season-how-to-tell-lovers-from-liars-online-and-more/

McRae, S. (1996). Coming apart at the seams: Sex, text, and the virtual body. In L. Cherny & L. R. Weise (Eds.), *Wired women: Gender and new realities in cyberspace* (pp. 242–263). Seattle: Seal.

Meyers, S. (2012). *Chatting or cheating: How to detect infidelity, rebuild love, and affair-proof your relationship* (Amazon Kindle ed.). Tarzana, CA: From the Heart.

Miller, D. (2013, December 20). Facebook's so uncool, but it's morphing into a different beast. Retrieved from http://theconversation.com/facebooks-so-uncool-but-its-morphing-into-a-different-beast-21548

Miller-Ott, A. E., Kelly, L., & Duran, R. L. (2012). The effects of cell phone usage rules on satisfaction in romantic relationships. *Communication Quarterly*, *60*, 17–34.

Montepare, J. M. (2014). Nonverbal behavior in the digital age: Meanings, models, and methods. *Journal of Nonverbal Behavior*, *38*, 279–281.

Mørch, A. I., Caruso, V., Hartley, M. D., & Ludlow, B. L. (2018). Creating contexts for collaborative learning in a 3D virtual world for distance education. In Y. Qian (Ed.), *Integrating multi-user virtual environments in modern classrooms* (pp. 137–164). Hershey, PA: IGI Global.

Mortensen, K. K. (2017). Flirting in online dating: Giving empirical grounds to flirtatious implicitness. *Discourse Studies*, *19*, 581–597.

Murphy, K. M., Cash, J., & Kellinger, J. J. (2018). Learning with avatars: Exploring mixed reality simulations for next-generation teaching and learning. In J. Keengwe (Ed.), *Handbook of research on pedagogical models for next-generation teaching and learning* (pp. 1–20). Hershey, PA: IGI Global.

Ogletree, S. M., Fancher, J., & Gill, S. (2014). Gender and texting: Masculinity, femininity, and gender role ideology. *Computers in Human Behavior*, *37*, 49–55.

Pera, A. (2018). Psychopathological processes involved in social comparison, depression, and envy on Facebook. *Frontiers in Psychology*, *9*. https://doi.org/10.3389/fpsyg.2018.00022

Pöschl, S., & Döring, N. (2010). Nonverbal cues in mobile phone text messages: The effects of chronemics and proxemics. In R. Ling & S. W. Campbell (Eds.), *The reconstruction of space and time* (pp. 109–135). New York: Routledge.

Powell, D., & Dixon, M. (2011). Does SMS text messaging help or harm adults' knowledge of standard spelling? *Journal of Computer Assisted Learning, 27*, 58–66.

Quintanilla, K. M., & Wahl, S. T. (2016). *Business and professional communication: Keys for workplace excellence* (3rd ed.). Thousand Oaks, CA: Sage.

Raacke, J., & Bonds-Raacke, J. (2011). An investigation of the dimensions of SMS communication use by college students. *Individual Differences Research, 9*, 210–218.

Riordan, M. A. (2017). Emojis as tools for emotion work: Communicating affect in text messages. *Journal of Language and Social Psychology, 36*, 549–567.

Rosen, L. D., Chang, J., Erwin, L., Carrier, L. M., & Cheever, N. A. (2010). The relationship between "textisms" and formal and informal writing among young adults. *Communication Research, 37*, 420–440.

Saha, N., & Karpinski, A. C. (2018). The influence of social media on international students' global life satisfaction and academic performance. In Information Resources Management Association (Ed.), *Student engagement and participation: Concepts, methodologies, tools, and applications* (pp. 1255–1275). Hershey, PA: IGI Global.

Sahni, S. P., & Jain, G. (2018). An overview: Internet infidelity. In S. P. Sahni & G. Jain (Eds.), *Internet infidelity: An interdisciplinary insight in a global context* (pp. 1–12). New York: Springer.

Sahni, S. P., & Swasti, S. (2018). Myths associated with Internet infidelity: Is it a real problem? In S. P. Sahni & G. Jain (Eds.), *Internet infidelity: An interdisciplinary insight in a global context* (pp. 175–184). New York: Springer.

Semingson, P., & Owens, D. (2017). Beyond netiquette guidelines: Best practices for proactively fostering professional communication behaviors in e-learning. In J. Dron & S. Mishra (Eds.), *E-learn: World conference on e-learning in corporate, government, healthcare, and higher education* (pp. 467–471). Vancouver, BC: Association for the Advancement of Computing in Education.

Smith, A. (2016, March 1). 15% of American adults have used online dating sites or mobile dating apps. Retrieved from http://www.pewinternet.org/2016/02/11/15-percent-of-american-adults-have-used-online-dating-sites-or-mobile-dating-apps/

Smith, A., & Anderson, M. (2016, February 29). 5 facts about online dating. Retrieved from http://www.pewresearch.org/fact-tank/2016/02/29/5-facts-about-online-dating/

Smith, L. R., Smith, K. D., & Blazka, M. (2017). Follow me, what's the harm? Considerations of catfishing and utilizing fake online personas on social media. *Journal of Legal Aspects of Sport, 27*, 32–45.

Smoker, M., & March, E. (2017). Predicting perpetration of intimate partner cyberstalking: Gender and the dark tetrad. *Computers in Human Behavior, 72*, 390–396.

Spencer, T. A., Lambertsen, A., Hubler, D. S., & Burr, B. K. (2017). Assessing the mediating effect of relationship dynamics between perceptions of problematic media use and relationship satisfaction. *Contemporary Family Therapy, 39*, 80–86.

Starks, K. M. (2007). Bye bye love: Computer-mediated communication and relational dissolution. *Texas Speech Communication Journal, 32*, 11–20.

Steinmetz, K. (2013, September 9). The linguist's mother lode: What Twitter reveals about slang, gender and no-nose emoticons. *Time*, 56–57.

Strubel, J., & Petrie, T. A. (2017). Love me Tinder: Body image and psychosocial functioning among men and women. *Body Image, 21*, 34–38.

Tagg, C., Seargeant, P., & Brown, A. A. (2017). *Taking offence on social media.* Basingstoke, UK: Palgrave Macmillan.

Tatum, N. T., Martin, J. C., & Kemper, B. (2018). Chronemics in instructor–student e-mail communication: An experimental examination of student evaluations of instructor response speeds. *Communication Research Reports, 35*, 33–41.

Taylor, S. H., & Bazarova, N. N. (2018). Social media and subjective well-being: A relational perspective. In Z. Papcharissi (Ed.), *A networked self and love* (pp. 102–128). Abingdon, UK: Routledge.

Taylor, T., Hester, E., & Wilson, L. S. (2011). Video conferencing vs. talking face-to-face: Is video suitable for supportive dialogue? *International Journal of Therapy and Rehabilitation, 18*, 392–403.

Thompson, C. (2013). *Smarter than you think: How technology is changing our minds for the better.* New York: Penguin Press.

Toma, C. L. (2017). Developing online deception literacy while looking for love. *Media, Culture & Society, 39*, 423–428.

Toma, C. L., & D'Angelo, J. D. (2017). How people self-present and form impressions of others through online dating profiles. In N. Punyanunt-Carter & J. Wrench (Eds.), *The impact of social media in modern romantic relationships* (pp. 147–162). Lanham, MD: Lexington.

Tong, S. T., & Walther, J. B. (2010). Just say "no thanks": Romantic rejection in computer-mediated communication. *Journal of Social and Personal Relationships, 28*, 488–506.

Trekels, J., & Eggermont, S. (2017). Beauty is good: The appearance culture, the internalization of appearance ideals, and dysfunctional appearance beliefs among tweens. *Human Communication Research, 43*, 173–192.

Tsay-Vogel, M., Shanahan, J., & Signorielli, N. (2018). Social media cultivating perceptions of privacy: A 5-year analysis of privacy attitudes and self-disclosure behaviors among Facebook users. *New Media & Society, 20*, 141–161.

Turkay, S., & Kinzer, C. K. (2017). The relationship between avatar-based customization, player identification, and motivation. In B. Dubbels (Ed.), *Transforming gaming and computer simulation technologies across industries* (pp. 48–79). Hershey, PA: IGI Global.

Turkle, S. (1995). *Life on the screen: Identity in the age of the Internet.* New York: Simon & Schuster.

van Dijk, C. N., van Witteloostuijn, M., Vasic, N., Avrutin, S., & Blom, E. (2016). The influence of texting language on grammar and executive functions in primary school children. *PLoS ONE, 11*. e0152409

Viano, E. C. (2018). Technology and virtual sex: Online infidelity in the U.S. In S. P. Sahni & G. Jain (Eds.), *Internet infidelity: An interdisciplinary insight in a global context* (pp. 69–84). New York: Springer.

Vossler, A. (2016). Internet infidelity 10 years on: A critical review of the literature. *The Family Journal, 24*, 359–366.

Villani, D., Gatti, E., Confalonieri, E., & Riva, G. (2012). Am I my avatar? A tool to investigate virtual body image representation in adolescence. *CyberPsychology, Behavior & Social Networking, 15*, 435–440.

Walther, J. B., Liang, Y., DeAndrea, D. C., Tong, S., Carr, C. T., Spottswood, E. L., et al. (2011). The effect of feedback on identity shift in computer-mediated communication. *Media Psychology, 14*, 1–26.

chapter ten

Walther, J. B., Loh, T., & Granka, L. (2005). Let me count the ways: The interchange of verbal and nonverbal cues in computer-mediated and face-to-face affinity. *Journal of Language and Social Psychology, 24,* 36–65.

Walther, J. B., Van Der Heide, B., Kim, S., Westerman, D., & Tong, S. (2008). The role of friends' appearance and behavior on evaluations of individuals on Facebook: Are we known by the company we keep? *Human Communication Research, 34,* 28–49.

Weisskirch, R. S., & Delevi, R. (2012). Its ovr b/n u n me: Technology use, attachment styles, and gender roles in relationship dissolution. *CyberPsychology, Behavior & Social Networking, 15,* 486–490.

Whitty, M. T. (2003). Cyber-flirting: Playing at love on the Internet. *Theory and Psychology, 13,* 339–357.

Whitty, M. T. (2004). Cyber-flirting: An examination of men's and women's flirting behavior both offline and on the Internet. *Behavior Change, 21,* 115–126.

Whitty, M. T., & Buchanan, T. (2010). What's in a screen name? Attractiveness of different types of screen names used by online daters. *International Journal of Internet Science, 5,* 5–19.

Whitty, M. T., & Carr, A. N. (2003). Cyberspace as potential space: Considering the web as a playground to cyber-flirt. *Human Relations, 56,* 861–891.

Whitty, M. T., & Gavin, J. K. (2001). Age/sex/location: Uncovering the social cues in the development of on-line relationships. *CyberPsychology & Behavior, 4,* 623–630.

You, S., Kim, E., & Lee, D. (2017). Virtually real: Exploring avatar identification in game addiction among massively multiplayer online role-playing games (MMORPG) players. *Games and Culture, 12,* 56–71.

Youngvorst, L. J., & High, A. C. (2018). "Anyone free to chat?" Using technological features to elicit quality support online. *Communication Monographs, 85,* 203–223.

Yuen, E. K., Koterba, E. A., Stasio, M. J., Patrick, R. B., Gangi, C., Ash, P., Barakat, K., Greene, V., Hamilton, W., & Mansour, B. (2018). The effects of Facebook on mood in emerging adults. *Psychology of Popular Media Culture.* https://doi.org/10.1037/ppm0000178

Zhou, L. (2005). An empirical investigation of deception behavior in instant messaging. *IEEE Transactions on Professional Communication, 48,* 147–160.

Zhou, L., Twitchell, D., Qin, T., Burgoon, J. K., & Nunamaker, J. F., Jr. (2003). An exploratory study into deception detection in text-based computer-mediated communication. In *Proceedings of the 36th Hawaii International Conference on System Sciences.* Los Alamitos, CA: IEEE.

Zuckerberg, R. (2013). *Dot complicated: Untangling our wired lives.* New York: HarperOne.

chapter eleven

NONVERBAL COMMUNICATION IN PROFESSIONAL AND EDUCATIONAL CONTEXTS

chapter outline

379

After studying this chapter, you should be able to

1. understand the importance of nonverbal communication in professional life;
2. distinguish between direct and indirect nonverbal communication with regard to the job search process;
3. identify and describe key nonverbal communication codes to be aware of in job interviews;
4. apply nonverbal communication codes to the superior–subordinate relationship in professional settings;
5. understand the importance of coworker nonverbal communication;
6. describe nonverbal behaviors most important to customer relations personnel;
7. identify the nonverbal essentials of leadership;
8. define emotional intelligence as an essential quality of leaders and describe its similarities to nonverbal communication sensitivity;
9. understand the importance of nonverbal communication in educational settings;
10. apply nonverbal communication codes to learning environments and teacher behavior;
11. define teacher nonverbal immediacy and offer examples of immediate teacher nonverbal behavior in the college classroom; and
12. describe the most common student nonverbal cues, including adapting behavior, misbehavior, and cues related to students with disabilities.

case study

NONVERBAL PROFESSIONALISM

Darrien recently changed departments at work, and he was excited to have new supervisor. His former supervisor, Norman, was extremely overbearing. When Norman ran video conference calls with employees, he rolled his eyes and sighed (audibly) when people shared their ideas. Face to face, Norman talked very loudly and got in the faces of employees when communicating with them. Darrien felt that Norman's nonverbal approach to communicating with employees was bad for company culture, given that Norman intimidated employees and made them fearful to engage in interaction. Darrien was relieved to learn that Norman left the company, and he's ready to work with his new supervisor, Brayden.

Before Brayden became his supervisor, Darrien and he were pretty good friends at work. They didn't hang out after work, but they always got along well. But now, Brayden acts weirdly—differently than he did when Darrien and Brayden were on the same level in the company. It's as if

"Norman's ghost" inhabits Brayden's body. In meetings, Brayden openly displays his dislike of others' ideas by making faces, sighing, avoiding eye contact with a speaker, and shifting in his chair until the person stops speaking. On occasion, he outright laughs at others' contributions, causing them embarrassment and resentment. Is there something about ascending to positions of authority that can make some bosses complete nonverbal jerks?

In the world of work, the way people nonverbally communicate says a lot about their work ethic, drive, and professionalism. In this case, we see how people can let authority go to their heads, as they become nonverbally aggressive and unsupportive, rather than using nonverbal communication to reinforce and inspire coworkers and subordinates.

NONVERBAL COMMUNICATION IN TWO EVERYDAY CONTEXTS

In this chapter, we explore nonverbal communication that occurs in two settings we commonly encounter in our lives. We begin with a discussion of critical nonverbal cues in *professional settings*, such as organizations and companies in which nonverbal cues are important to getting a job as well as succeeding in a job. In addition, we examine the role of nonverbal communication in developing leadership abilities. Then we overview nonverbal communication in *educational settings* such as the ones you experience almost every day.

THE IMPORTANCE OF NONVERBAL COMMUNICATION IN PROFESSIONAL CONTEXTS

We've all heard our parents, teachers, friends, and neighbors ask the daunting question, "What are you going to do with your degree?" This question can be really annoying. But coming from the right person at the right time in the right place, any question about our future, our occupation, or what we dream about is open for discussion. While it can be challenging and emotional to think about what we're going to do when we get out of school, it's important to think about communication skills, especially our nonverbal communication skills, as we approach any professional context.

One of the first professional situations in which we can use our nonverbal communication skills is the job search. Hunting for a job *is* a job; so once you start the hunt, be steadfast and patient, because it may take some time before you get an offer. The popular online job-hunting website CareerBuilder.com (2018) reports that it takes 17 interviews, on average, to get one job offer.

While some people approach a job search with little self-confidence, others make the mistake of entering the job search with too much confidence, as though the hunt were simple or a good job easy to land right after graduation. After all, they have their degree in a given area of study, have technical skills and competencies, and feel as though they can get the job done better than their competition. While many people have certifications, undergraduate degrees, and professional training, many also struggle with job placement. We wonder, "Why can't Bobby Joe get a job? He's such a smart guy." Sure, Bobby Joe *is* a smart guy, but what if Bobby Joe is inept when it comes to verbal and nonverbal communication skills? Bobby Joe may have no awareness of how he comes across in job interviews. Let's help out all the Bobby Joes of the world by looking at some nonverbal communication skills that are important in any professional setting.

GETTING THE JOB ■ ■ ■

Nonverbal communication is critical to job applicants in any hiring situation (Beebe & Mottet, 2016; Eaves & Leathers, 2016; Olszewski, Panorska, & Gillam, 2017; Peck & Levashina, 2017; Quintanilla & Wahl, 2016). You may think that nonverbal cues related to the hiring process occur only face to face or in a direct manner; however, nonverbal communication in a job search is both direct and indirect, in terms of the impression we establish in professional situations and the impact of nonverbal behavior on the hiring process (Beebe, Beebe, & Ivy, 2019; Remland, 2006). **Direct nonverbal communication** refers to what we do during a live interview with a hiring committee, manager, or business owner, whether it's accomplished through face-to-face interaction, telephone communication, or online via webcam. In contrast, **indirect nonverbal communication** refers to those job interviewing decisions or actions that tend not to occur face to face. In other words, indirect nonverbal communication comes before or after the actual interview, but it's just as important as the direct cues. We explore both of these forms in the sections to follow.

Direct Nonverbal Communication

Direct nonverbal communication can best be understood by applying many of the nonverbal communication codes we've examined in previous chapters to the job interview context. One primary code is **physical appearance**—the way our bodies and overall appearance communicate to others and impact our view of ourselves in everyday life. Physical appearance has a direct impact because it communicates something about us to people in hiring

Nonverbal cues play a critical role in the job interview process.

© Mangostar/Shutterstock.com

chapter eleven

positions (Hammermesh, 2011; O'Brien, Latner, Ebneter, & Hunter, 2013; Peck & Levanshina, 2017). With an increasing emphasis on physical attractiveness and communicating a professional image in the job-search process, more and more employers are searching for people who have "the look" that will build business (Baert, 2018; Barth & Wagner, 2017; Milkman, 2018; Sims, 2017; Thornbory & White, 2006; Timming, 2014; Tsai, Huang, & Yu, 2012).

Appearance in a job interview is important for two reasons: (1) Our physical appearance, as well as the decisions we make to maintain or alter our appearance, communicates powerful nonverbal signals to other people; and (2) the physical appearance of other people impacts our perceptions of them (and, in this case, the organization with which we interview), how we communicate with them, how approachable they are, and so on. The nonverbal code of coworkers' and bosses' physical appearance directly clues us in on such things as workplace culture, what to wear in terms of clothing or a uniform, and what types of people work in that setting.

A central component of physical appearance is clothing. We all know that clothing communicates something to people, so it's no surprise that it's a critical nonverbal signal in a job interview (Antonellis, Berry, & Silsbee, 2017; Chandor, Hargie, & Crute, 2017; Gurung, Punke, Brickner, & Badalamenti, 2018; Saiki, 2013). Before going further, we need to mention something that students constantly ask us about when this topic comes up in class: They often believe that, because people who work at a certain business or organization dress casually, applicants should also dress casually for job interviews. They think that doing so will show they've researched the company and are dressed casually for the interview so they'll be perceived as fitting in. This viewpoint couldn't be more wrongheaded, but we understand that sometimes it's also a justification for lacking the funds to purchase proper interviewing attire. We're sympathetic to student economics, but remember this: An applicant for a job is on the *outside* looking in and wanting in. Job candidates don't work at the business or for the organization yet but, rather, are selling themselves to land a position. It's not a good idea to try to match workers' style of dress until you land the job, because *you aren't one of them yet*. You need to look as though you want the job, you're competing for the job, and you care enough about getting the job to go out of your way to look impressive.

In terms of apparel, buzzwords such as "business casual," "professional attire," or "dressing down" give us a sense of what's expected, but we don't always get those clues prior to a job interview. Can clothing help us get a job? The answer is, "You bet" (Eaves & Leathers, 2016; Gurney, Howlett, Pine, Tracey, & Moggridge, 2017; Peluchette, Karl, & Rust, 2006). While we're not the fashion police or judges on *Project Runway,* we do want to mention a few nonverbal cues related to appearance that potential employers look for.

1. In general, go for a conservative look: As we said, even if the company environment is a casual one, don't dress casually until you get the job. Conservative for men means a dark suit, white shirt, a serious tie (no stains, no cartoon characters), dark socks (that match the color of the suit), and dress shoes (polished and clean). For women, a dark suit with a skirt is still preferable, although pantsuits are much more acceptable than

they used to be. (Watch the hemlines of skirts; sit down in them before you purchase them. Some skirts don't work well or show more than you want when you sit.) A light-colored blouse under the suit works best; avoid bright colors. Hose and nice dress shoes (clean and polished, with a low heel) are still preferred, even though standards have changed a good deal regarding the wearing of hose.

2. Pay attention to **artifacts** (temporary aspects of physical adornment other than clothing—e.g., jewelry, piercings, fingernail polish, makeup, bags, cologne) so you don't wear or carry too much of anything that might be distracting to an interviewer. Classic leather or microfiber accessories (portfolios, briefcases) make a good impression. Never take a bookbag to an interview, no matter how casual the job. It'll brand you a student, not a professional.

3. Think about basic hygiene. This may sound sort of "duh," but you'd be surprised how many people don't consider basic cleanliness, such as that of their fingernails, in terms of the negative impression an unkempt appearance can make on a potential employer.

4. The best guideline is to find out ahead of the interview what is standard or typical dress at the organization you're interviewing with, and then to go one step higher or more professional than that. You can tone it down once you get the job.

Hair length is another factor to consider as a nonverbal cue related to physical appearance. Young men who want to be viewed at job interviews as more mature and seasoned are often advised by stylists to let their hair grow out to a traditional length, to avoid showing a baby face (Masip, Garrido, & Herrero, 2004). Men with longer hair (below the shirt collar) are advised to cut or trim their hair for interviews so they will be viewed as professional, serious, and credible. We do recognize that hair length and style may not be important in certain industries, so you can do what you want with your hair *once you land a job*. But when you're *wanting* the job, again, as we've said, your best bet is to go conservative. If you're male and have long hair, at least pull it back for the interview.

What about men's facial hair? Job interviewers' perceptions of facial hair vary, so it can depend on the situation whether facial hair will work for or against you in an interview (Davies, 2018). The most conservative look is clean-shaven.

Body smell during a job interview is another form of direct nonverbal communication. As we mentioned in Chapter 5 on physical appearance, nonverbal communication scholars use the term **olfaction** to refer to the role of smell in

A more conservative appearance is the norm for many professionals.

human interaction (Hastings, Musambira, & Ayoub, 2011; Sorokowska, 2013; Sorokowska, Sorokowski, & Szmajke, 2012). For both women and men, it's a balancing act in terms of how much scent, body spray, or cologne to use, since smell is closely connected to our overall appearance (Lin, Cross, & Childers, 2018; Low, 2006). We suggest to students that they wear very little to no cologne when interviewing for a job, because nervousness or chemical activation in the body enhances the strength of a scent. You could overwhelm an interviewer and lose a job opportunity, all because your cologne was too strong. Many interviewers have allergies that could be negatively impacted by an interviewee's scent.

In addition to physical appearance, **kinesics** (defined as human movement, gestures, and posture), in particular our body posture, are forms of direct nonverbal communication. Posture is attached to many attractive attributes in U.S. culture, such as confidence, positivity, and high self-esteem (Guerrero & Floyd, 2006; Osensky, 2017). We make personality judgments based on something as subjective as posture, so it's worth thinking about. How aware are you of your posture? Do you tend to stand in a dominant position, or does your stance typically give off signs of weakness, timidity, or low self-esteem? In a job interview, an interviewer tends to be much more relaxed than an applicant, who is putting herself or himself on the line to get hired. So even if the interviewer looks relaxed, maintain your professional, erect body posture. The level of relaxation or tension you feel will tend to show up in your body posture and movement, which can be clues to potential employers (Gurney et al., 2017).

What about your tone of voice and how well you articulate during an interview? Remember that when we study how people express themselves through their voices, we're studying **vocalics**, sometimes referred to as paralanguage. Besides being able to identify someone from his or her voice, we can also come to detect physical, emotional, and attitudinal states through **tone of voice**, which is a nontechnical term for all the elements of sound the human voice can produce and manipulate (Frank, Maroulis, & Griffin, 2013). Think about the direct impact your tone of voice can have in an interview setting. What does your voice say about you to potential employers? Vocalics are particularly critical in telephone interviews, which these days are often precursors to face-to-face interviews. Phone interviews save employers money and time, and they're often used as a weeding-out tool. That means you have the use of only one nonverbal code—vocalics—to help you make a positive impression.

Many job interviews, at least initial screening interviews, are conducted today via webcam or apps like Skype and FaceTime. If you're asked to use this type of technology for a job interview, you may find that more volume and enhanced articulation are necessary to ensure you can be easily heard through the technology, especially if a group of people is conducting the interview. Watch out for filled pauses (e.g., "uh," "er," "um"), even if you're trying to come up with an answer to an interview question. Pauses are exaggerated in a phone or webcam situation where there are no other or reduced nonverbal cues (such as physical appearance or facial expressions) to accompany the voice. In phone, webcam, and face-to-face interviews alike, be careful not to interrupt the interviewers (another vocalic cue). While interrupting may be your general style in interpersonal settings, it'll likely be seen as rude behavior in an interview.

One very important aspect of direct nonverbal communication to consider within the category of **haptics** (i.e., touch) is the **professional handshake**, which can be distinguished from the social handshake (Hiemstra, 1999). In professional settings in the United States, the handshake is critical to making a good first impression (Ames, 2018; Chaplin, Phillips, Brown, Clanton, & Stein, 2000). Poor handshakes can be deal breakers.

An informal handshake in a professional setting can damage business relationships.

In the professional handshake, here's what needs to happen: The hands need to meet fully, firmly, and equally (meaning palm-to-palm, locked or hooked around the space between the thumb and forefinger, and with no turn of the hands—i.e., hands stay straight up and down), with definite but brief shaking. Social handshakes don't usually turn out this way; they often aren't equal, meaning that people may take only the time to grab part of the hand or a few fingers. They're often accomplished with a quick touch and no shake, and this may or may not create a negative impression. However, giving a social handshake when a professional one is expected will not serve you well. And don't assume that a good handshake is "natural" or something everyone can do, because we've received some pretty lousy handshakes in our years of interviewing people for faculty and administrative positions. Especially avoid the dreaded "fingerella"—that weak, limp, half-hearted handshake that communicates a whole host of negative messages.

One final form of direct nonverbal communication critical to successful job interviewing is **eye gaze** (commonly referred to as eye contact), defined as looking at the general eye area of another person. Eye gaze is extremely important in U.S. culture because we make all kinds of judgments about people—particularly about trustworthiness and sincerity—on the basis of whether they make or avoid eye contact. In fact, research has found that of all the nonverbal cues, eye contact is the most critical to judgments of credibility (Beebe, 1974). So if you want to make a positive impression within the first few seconds of meeting a potential employer, you will stand with good posture, extend your hand to give a firm, professional handshake, and at the same time make good eye contact.

Regarding eye contact, it's important to recognize its relationship with other nonverbal cues we project in a job interview. Researcher Janek Lobmaier (2012) investigated the relationship between facial expressions and eye gaze, finding that these two important nonverbal codes actually combine to communicate impressions to others. Since facial expressions can be critical indicators of mood, they have the ability to influence whether interactions with others take place or not. People with angry scowls on their faces might project the impression that they don't wish to be disturbed, whereas people who make eye contact while projecting positive facial expressions can send the opposite message.

Imagine how these research findings might be important to the context of the job interview; consider how your facial expressions and eye behaviors should work in tandem to generate the impression you wish to convey to potential employers. What exactly is *good* eye contact in a job interview? As we discussed in Chapter 7, in U.S. culture, good eye contact occurs when one person looks in the general eye area of another person, then breaks to briefly look elsewhere—up, down, around the room, or other areas of the person's face (such as the forehead)—then returns to the eyes. But you have to reach a balance here: Too little eye contact (not meeting someone's gaze) is perceived negatively, as though you have something to hide; too much eye contact is an invasion we call staring in this culture, and it's definitely viewed negatively (Garland-Thomson, 2009; Weick, McCall, & Blascovich, 2017). The best approach is to mirror the eye contact you receive from the interviewer.

REMEMBER

Remember! **11.1**

Direct nonverbal communication	Nonverbal cues related to face-to-face, telephone, or online communication, as in a live interview with a hiring committee, manager, or business owner
Indirect nonverbal communication	Decisions or actions that tend not to occur face to face but, rather, before or after a job interview
Physical appearance	How our bodies and appearance communicate to others and impact our view of ourselves
Artifacts	Temporary aspects of physical adornment other than clothing
Olfaction	Role of smell in human interaction
Kinesics	Human movement, gestures, and posture
Vocalics	How people express themselves through their voices
Tone of voice	Elements of sound that the human voice can produce and manipulate
Haptics	Human touch
Professional handshake	Full, firm, and equal handshake that makes a good first impression as a professional
Eye gaze (eye contact)	Looking at the general eye area of another person

Indirect Nonverbal Communication

In review, many of the nonverbal communication codes discussed in previous chapters, such as physical appearance, vocalics, kinesics, touch, and so on, are *direct* forms of nonverbal communication that impact the professional interview. What about more subtle, *indirect* nonverbal communication? We tell our students that indirect nonverbal communication can make all the difference when it comes to standing out among other applicants. As we said earlier, **indirect nonverbal communication** refers to decisions or actions that tend not to occur face to face; these are nonverbal cues that speak volumes about you before or after the actual interview, and they're just as important as the direct cues.

PRE-INTERVIEW ACTIVITY. Nonverbal communication is a central part of several activities that job applicants need to accomplish prior to actually interviewing. Let's begin with the **cover letter** (letter of introduction to a potential employer) and **résumé** (a document that details your educational and professional experience). You've probably not thought of it this way before, but cover letters and résumés serve as nonverbal reflections of who you are and what you have to offer. We know that many job applications nowadays are conducted entirely online, but some companies and organizations still prefer receiving hard copies of documents. Plus, it's wise to take hard-copy backups of documents with you to interviews so that if your interviewer misplaced your materials, you have extras on hand.

Plenty of books on résumés and cover letters offer tips, such as Richard Walsh's (2008) *The Only Résumé and Cover Letter Book You'll Ever Need,* Michael Farr's (2011) *The Quick Résumé and Cover Letter Book,* and Scott Bennett's (2014) *The Elements of Résumé Style.* Besides introducing yourself, expressing your interest in the job, and listing your education, career goals, experience, references, and so on, think about what your documents communicate nonverbally about you. Given that a cover letter and résumé are just a bunch of words on paper, how can they communicate something nonverbally? Here are some nonverbal aspects of cover letters and résumés that you need to consider so that you can communicate yourself to potential employers in the best manner possible.

Résumés should be neat and professional, containing only information relevant to the position.

1. *Paper quality:* People who submit cover letters and résumés on traditional white (cheap) printer paper run the risk of having their documents look like everyone else's. In contrast, documents printed on high-quality paper

in a light color, such as cream or grey, say something about the applicant's interest in establishing a positive first impression. This trend can vary from year to year; if everyone is using nice colored paper, use nice white paper to make your documents stand out.

2. *Print quality, font, and ink color:* In addition to the quality of the cover letter and résumé paper, it's also important to consider print quality, font, and color. Poorly printed documents can send a message that an applicant is sloppy or doesn't care about details. The font you choose sends nonverbal signals as well, or attributes about the words you use that shape people's impressions of you (Bringhurst, 2013). Think also about ink color for your cover letter and résumé. We recommend staying with traditional black ink because of the potential indirect nonverbal messages other colors might send. In addition, it's unwise to try to squeeze out the last bit of ink from a cartridge to print interview documents; if your typeface is too faint to be easily read, your papers will most likely wind up in File 13 (aka the trash can), so make sure your print is dark and readable.

3. *Typos and misspellings:* While words are verbal, **typos** (mistakes in typing) and **misspellings** (mistakes in spelling) speak volumes nonverbally. These are probably the most common mistakes students make with their cover letters and résumés. Résumés with even a single typo can get sent to the garbage can so fast your head will spin. Don't rely solely on a computer spell-checking program; get a second set of eyes to proof your résumé before copying it, and certainly before sending it out.

4. *Length:* The general rule used to be—and still is to a great extent—to keep your cover letter short and sweet and your résumé to a single page (Beebe et al., 2019). However, for some of us who have years of experience, a one-page résumé is hard to manage and doesn't really sell us in the best way. You may find it necessary to create a more extended résumé, but just realize that some potential employers will hurl your résumé on the trash heap without reading it, just because it's longer than one page.

What are some other factors that serve as indirect nonverbal communication? Since so much pre-interview communication takes place via e-mail, it's important to think about nonverbal elements of e-mail exchanges. While we address nonverbal cues and technology in more depth in Chapter 10, let's explore a few features of online communication that serve as nonverbal cues about us.

For starters, have you ever thought about how your e-mail address can communicate aspects of your personality, interests, occupation, and even your deviances? Granted, the address itself is verbal, but the image it communicates makes it a nonverbal cue. The typical e-mail address for a professor might look like this: richard.prof@university.edu.

The first part of the e-mail address designates the owner's or recipient's name; the last part of the address points to the server or location where the recipient can be found.

As e-mail has become more widely utilized as a preferred communication channel at work, people have moved away from providing their real names in their e-mail addresses (Esfehani, 2011; Flynn & Flynn, 2003). Instead, now many people select something about themselves to produce a more creative e-mail address. While there is a sense of play or freedom in setting up an e-mail address, think about the impressions others will form about you based on such a simple thing as your e-mail address (Kingsley Westerman & Westerman, 2010). As another tip, be mindful of your social media presence when you're job hunting, especially photos and comments you post online. Employers are very likely to conduct Internet searches on potential applicants. Google yourself and see what comes up; would you hire you?

POST-INTERVIEW ACTIVITY. Once you've interviewed, you may think that all you have to do is wait to hear from the people who interviewed you, but there's more to it than that if you want to be successful. Nonverbal communication is a critical part of what we call your post-interview activity. Business etiquette specialists and personal effectiveness consultants advise that people should always send a thank-you note after professional encounters such as job interviews (Chandor et al., 2017; Eaves & Leathers, 2016). If you're interviewed by a group of people, it's best if you thank each person individually, not just the chair or head of the group.

Does an e-mail message of thanks suffice? Many people have moved away from sending hand-written thank-you notes via traditional mail, since e-mail is faster and cheaper. After all, isn't an e-mail message sent just hours or the day after a job interview more impressive than a handwritten card received days or weeks later? While sending a thank-you e-mail is indeed faster, it doesn't take much time or effort, and employers know that (because they use e-mail a lot, too). What nonverbal signal about you and your professionalism is conveyed when a potential employer receives a nice-looking, handwritten thank-you note within a few days of your interview? Such attention to detail and the care involved can communicate many positive things about you and set you apart from your competitors.

Handwritten thank-you notes can strengthen impressions of courteousness and professionalism after an interview.

Indirect nonverbal communication	Decisions or actions that tend not to occur face to face but, rather, before or after an interview
Cover letter	Letter of introduction to a potential employer
Résumé	Document indicating educational and professional experience that serves as a reflection of who people are and what they can offer a potential employer
Typos	Mistakes in typing
Misspellings	Mistakes in spelling

ON THE JOB ■ ■ ■

Congratulations, you've landed a job! This section of the chapter focuses on the important role of nonverbal communication with bosses, coworkers, and the customers or clients you're expected to impress. After all, your successful verbal and nonverbal skills are what got you here in the first place!

Superior–Subordinate Nonverbal Communication

How does nonverbal communication impact employer–employee interaction? One way to prepare for this interaction is by understanding **status**—a person's rank or position in an organization. In most situations, those people who hold higher status have more years of experience, training, education, and rank. In the language of the workplace, the **superior** (supervisor/employer) is typically the higher-status person, and the **subordinate** (employee) is the lower-status person (Hynes & Veltsos, 2018; Khan & Omar, 2018; Lybarger, Rancer, & Lin, 2017; Merkin, 2018; Paramasivam & Subramaniam, 2018; Quintanilla & Wahl, 2016). Let's apply some of the nonverbal communication codes from previous chapters to the superior–subordinate relationship.

ENVIRONMENT. One of the first nonverbal codes that impacts employer–employee relationships is **environment**—the built or natural surroundings that serve as the contexts in which people interact. We know from Chapter 3 on environment as a form of nonverbal communication that people are influenced by such factors as office architecture, design, colors, lighting, smell, seating arrangements, temperature, and cleanliness (Gang, Feng, Cheng, & Xiaochen, 2017; Kupritz & Hillsman, 2011; Tenbrink, Andonova, Schole, & Coventry, 2017).

What might a person in a leadership or high-status role have in his or her professional environment or office, compared with subordinates? The professional environment is important because it communicates status, credibility, and organizational skills, all of which impact **impression management**—the formation of an impression, perception, or view of a person (Goffman, 1971; Peck & Levashina, 2017). Names on the door; diplomas, awards, and plaques on the wall; and the presence of expensive office furnishings provide nonverbal reinforcement that the occupant of that office is in charge. In addition, professional environments are important to employers because job interviews, important meetings, and private conversations often take place in the bosses' offices. These offices are usually situated in the most status-oriented locations within the larger company environment, such as a corner section of the building that has large windows and private elevators, flanked by assistants' desks that protect the boss from foot traffic. In contrast, the lowest-ranking workers tend to have offices, cubicles, or desks located near restrooms and high-traffic areas, usually with no buffer from noise or people (Haynes, Suckley, & Nunnington, 2017).

PROXEMICS. Proxemics, defined as the way distance and space play a communicative role in everyday life, also applies to superior–subordinate communication (Quintanilla & Wahl, 2016). Superiors can more readily invade their subordinates' space and privacy (called a **violation**, the use of people's territory without their permission, which we studied in Chapter 4) than the reverse (Kabo, 2017). In many organizational settings, subordinates have their own desks, cubicles, or offices where they keep personal belongings and other professional items. It can be unsettling to realize that the boss has

The amount of personal space an employee has in a workplace may depend on the person's status in the organization.

access to subordinates' offices and can choose to relocate employees or take over or violate their spaces because of higher status. (This isn't good management style, but it happens.) On the other hand, if subordinates violate their superiors' space without permission, a reprimand or termination may follow.

PHYSICAL APPEARANCE. As we discussed previously in this chapter, physical appearance serves as direct nonverbal communication in professional settings; our appearance can also convey our status within an organization. For superiors (higher-status people), conservative, solid-colored, well-fitting, and well-made clothing often communicates power and success. It's not uncommon to see supervisors "dress the part" of their position. For example, executives of large corporations tend to dress in expensive business suits with the best-looking accessories, such as high-quality leather shoes. Perhaps you've heard male professionals talk about wearing a "power" tie and looking sharp. This isn't a hard-and-fast rule, but higher-status employers typically dress better (more formally and expensively) than their employees, to stand out and convey their dominance (Gurney et al., 2017; Howlett, Pine, Cahill, Orakcioglu, & Fletcher, 2015). Clothing is often an indicator of rank, because at some places of business, organizational standards communicate to employees and customers alike who does what. For example, you often see counter and kitchen employees at fast-food restaurants dressed alike but the manager is dressed differently—usually more conservatively or formally—so she or he is recognizable.

KINESICS. The pace at which a person walks is also a fascinating nonverbal aspect to observe and study, because some people believe that pace correlates with power and status (as we first mentioned in Chapter 6 on kinesics). Do higher-status people tend to walk faster, as though they've got many places to be, lots to do, and tons of people wanting to meet them, and they're cutting their arrival at every meeting too closely? Or do higher-status people tend to move at a more leisurely pace because, simply put, they *can*? Their time is more their own; they can control the pace of their movement because much in their lives is in their control. Watch a busy workplace sometime, noting the movement among employees. Try to pick out the higher status people in the situation, because they are likely moving to a different rhythm than lower status employees. In general, in workplace settings, higher-status people call the nonverbal shots; lower-status people are expected to adapt their nonverbals to parallel or remain subordinate to the cues of higher-status people (Beebe & Mottet, 2016; Hall, 2001; Hynes & Veltsos, 2018; Quintanilla & Wahl, 2016).

VOCALICS. Another nonverbal code applied to our study of superiors and subordinates is **vocalics** or **paralanguage**, defined as the study of how people express themselves through their voices. Higher-status professionals tend to sound authoritative, using pitch, rate, and volume properties of the voice to convey status and dominance (Weiss & Morrison, 2018). In addition, vocal behaviors of higher-status people include a less anxious tone, little disfluency, and the use of silence to communicate authority. In contrast, subordinates may sound submissive, yet engaged in what their superiors say. Subordinates usually have more anxious tones of voice and filled pauses, and may use silence to protect themselves if their superiors "call them on the carpet." As we explored in Chapter 9 on vocalics, nonverbal communication scholars have examined the role of power or dominance in interaction management (how conversation gets accomplished), looking specifically at how higher-status speakers establish turns at talk; protect, maintain, and lengthen them; and use interruptions and overlaps to dominate other communicators (Dunbar & Abra, 2010; Farley, 2008; Gnisci, Sergi, DeLuca, & Errico, 2012; Hodges-Simeon, Gaulin, & Puts, 2010; Youngquist, 2009).

Michael is interning at a law firm. He has to balance many e-mails from his superiors, and sometimes he finds it overwhelming. Michael experiences the most anxiety when e-mailing with his direct supervisor, Teigen. Teigen's e-mails are usually short and to the point, so Michael has difficulty interpreting Teigen's tone. He likes Teigen as a person and tries to engage her in conversation when they meet face to face, but Teigen seems to be all business.

Michael is worried that Teigen doesn't like him and fears he might be doing something wrong. When Tiegen doesn't respond to an e-mail within a couple of hours, Michael usually follows up with "Didn't know if you saw my last e-mail, but might you address it now?" Other times, Michael asks for more direction; Teigen always refers him back to a previous e-mail by responding "per my last e-mail," rather than giving him any clarification. Michael is definitely uncomfortable with Teigen's e-mail etiquette, but he's fearful about bringing it up. After all, he's just an intern at the firm; he doesn't know if Teigen will take offense or respond positively to his concerns.

What would you do if you were in Michael's situation? Perhaps you're someone who likes detailed, longer e-mails, like Michael. Maybe you'd see it from Teigen's point of view, believing that e-mail communication should be terse and direct to accomplish efficiency in the workplace. Do you have any pet peeves when it comes to professional communication through e-mail or other mediated channels? What would you do if you had to write a blurb about e-mail etiquette or netiquette for a company's handbook?

TOUCH. What role does touch play in the superior–subordinate relationship? People with higher status tend to initiate more touch with subordinates (rather than the reverse), control how touch occurs in professional settings, and in general have more freedom to express themselves through touch than do subordinates (Hall, 2011). Subordinates usually receive touch from superiors and are inclined to accept the touch. Typically, a subordinate will not initiate touch toward a higher-status person and will reciprocate touch only if it seems appropriate (Sekerdej, Simao, Waldzus, & Brito, 2018).

Now, we grant that this is a "touchy" topic—more difficult now than in years past. While some touches, such as a handshake or pat on the back (we said back, not backside), may convey respect from bosses to employees, we all know by now that touch can be misused. One boss's affectionate or appreciative touch is one employee's sexual harassment, so this is a difficult area to handle. Many employers walk on eggshells around the office because the nonverbal power of touch evokes such individualized interpretations of what a touch means. Today's supervisors are leery of touch toward subordinates due to a fear of lawsuits and sexual harassment claims (Bernstein, 2018; Boddy, 2017; Paludi, 2015; Powell, 2018; Roehling & Huang, 2018; Scarduzio, Wehlage, & Lueken, 2018). While today's climate may seem restrictive, think about it: An office climate that's a bit more restrictive in terms of how bosses and employees treat one another is preferable to one in which boundaries about touch and proxemics are violated on a daily basis, with no repercussions.

spotlight
on research

Nonverbal Immediacy and Your Boss

As the baby boomer generation moves closer to retiring from the workforce, it's the responsibility of colleges and universities to educate today's students on how to lead and supervise in the professional workplace. However, many students are under the false impression that they will learn everything they need to know from their program of focus, whether it's computer science, business, health care, or something else. Because graduates from all fields enter the workforce, it's important for students to learn positive communication strategies for interacting with coworkers, subordinates, bosses, and clients.

Jia, Cheng, and Hale (2017) studied the relationship between supervisors' nonverbal immediacy behaviors (Mehrabian, 1966) and subordinate satisfaction. The researchers hypothesized that supervisor nonverbal immediacy cues, such as smiling, using a pleasant tone of voice, making eye contact, etc., would be positively correlated with subordinates' perceptions that they received adequate emotional support from their supervisors. Essentially, researchers thought that a more immediate supervisor would be viewed as more competent and caring by their workers.

After analyzing their data, Jia and colleagues concluded that supervisor nonverbal immediacy is extremely important to subordinates. Supervisors who take the time to make small talk, greet employees, make eye contact, and have pleasant facial expressions are able to engage their employees more effectively. Employees are more likely to view a nonverbally immediate supervisor as caring and someone they can talk to regarding work or life events that influence their quality of work.

Want to know more about this study? If so, read Jia, M., Cheng, J., & Hale, C. L. (2017). Workplace emotion and communication: Supervisor nonverbal immediacy, employees' emotion experience, and their communication motives. *Management Communication Quarterly, 31*, 69-87.

Status	A person's rank or position in an organization
Superior	Supervisors or employers in professional situations who typically rank higher than others in terms of hierarchy
Subordinate	Employees in professional situations who typically rank lower than others in terms of hierarchy
Environment	Built or natural surroundings that serve as the context in which people interact
Impression management	Formation of an impression, perception, or view of another person
Proxemics	The way distance and space play a communicative role in everyday life, such as in the development of coworker relationships
Violation	Use of people's territory without their permission
Vocalics (paralanguage)	Study of how people express themselves through their voices

Coworker Nonverbal Communication

We'll be the first to admit it—communication with bosses is important. But we can't forget the importance of interpersonal relationships with our colleagues. Nonverbal cues play a huge role in making impressions on others, which underlies the formation of relationships in both personal and professional life. In fact, research suggests that we quickly make judgments about other people based on nonverbal information, even as quickly as the first 10 seconds after meeting them (Petrician, Todorov, & Grady, 2014; Ryan, 2016). You may decide whether you like a fellow employee just as quickly, before your colleague has had time to utter more than "hello." Nonverbal cues are important not only in the early stages of relationships but also as we maintain, deepen, and sometimes terminate those relationships. This is true for our personal relationships *at* as well as *away* from work.

Just as with other types of relationships, the more we understand and perceive about our colleagues' nonverbal communication, the more likely it is that we will build positive relationships with them (Bonaccio, O'Reilly, O'Sullivan, & Chiocchio, 2016; Re & Rule, 2016). The more we get to know our colleagues, the more likely we will use nonverbal cues to convey negative emotions and messages, rather than announcing our explicit dislike of something or someone (Yoo & Noyes, 2016). In fact, it's safer to use

nonverbal cues to let our friends at work know of our disagreement with a decision or policy or our dislike of another person, especially the boss; we wouldn't want to risk being overheard by the wrong person. Most of the nonverbal cues we've discussed with regard to other types of relationships pertain also to the coworker relationship. Nonverbal cues related to one's work environment, proximity to coworkers and bosses, physical appearance (in terms of maintaining an appearance that conveys professionalism relevant to the particular job and organization), kinesics (including facial and eye behavior), touch, and vocalics all play critical roles in getting to know and getting along with one's colleagues (Kuzmenko, 2017; Quintanilla & Wahl, 2016).

Nonverbal Communication with Customers and Clients

Nonverbal communication is critical to interacting successfully with customers, clients, or potential business contacts (Lin & Lin, 2017; Sohn & Lee, 2018). **Customer relations**, also known as customer service, is the interaction between employees or representatives of an organization or business and the people the organization sells to or serves. Retail centers, restaurants, banks, insurance companies, movie theaters, and so on are but a few examples of locations where we experience service. Nonverbal communication helps professionals fine-tune their relations with customers who expect and demand excellent service (Krapels, 2000; Yuksel, 2008). In today's competitive business environment, consumers expect to be served by professionals who are knowledgeable about their products and services, and who communicate with dignity, respect, and courtesy. Sad to say, many times that's not what we experience.

Let's explore some basic functions of nonverbal cues, relating them to the customer service arena. Remember from Chapter 1 that nonverbal cues can work independently or in tandem with verbal language to convey meaning. First, nonverbal cues can *substitute* for verbal messages. Say you're at a baseball game and see a guy going up and down the aisles of the stadium, selling hot dogs. (The hot dog salesperson is actually a customer service rep.) He gets near your row and your hunger kicks in, but you know he can't hear you from where he is. You simply call on your nonverbal powers, wave to get his attention, make eye contact, and hold up one or two fingers (depending on how hungry you are). In customer relations, nonverbal cues often substitute for verbal messages, so it is important for customer service reps to develop and improve their nonverbal sending and receiving abilities.

We often use nonverbal cues in connection with words, to *complement* our communication or to clarify or extend the meaning of our words. This complementary function allows us to convey more information, leading to a more accurate interpretation by receivers of our communication. Complementary cues also help color our expressed emotions and attitudes. For example, a long, heavy sigh may reveal how tired or bored we are—something we definitely want to avoid if we work in customer relations.

On occasion, our nonverbal cues *contradict* rather than complement our verbal cues. Have you ever dealt with someone behind the returns counter when you have a real problem with something you bought? While the employee's verbal communication might be acceptable or rote, the nonverbal facial expressions, body postures, vocalic indications of exasperation, and other cues belie the verbal message. Sometimes customer service reps get frustrated or sick of dealing with complainers all day, but that doesn't mean their behavior as professionals shouldn't be at its best. Those of us who work in customer relations, either part-time while in college or as a career, need to remember that our nonverbal and verbal communication should coordinate so as to represent our organization professionally.

Nonverbal behaviors may also serve a *repeating* function. Say you're working as a flight attendant and your airline allows only one carry-on item per passenger (as most airlines do now). A passenger has violated the carry-on rule, made it past the ticket-counter workers, and now wants to stow all his or her stuff. The first time you speak to the person, you (the customer service rep) explain that she or he needs to check extra bags at the gate. When you realize that the passenger is too far away from you or too wrapped up in the "stowing" activity and can't hear you, you hold up baggage claim tickets and point to the excessive bags. In this example, your verbal communication comes first, followed by a nonverbal signal that repeats the message, thus clarifying the communication exchanged between the two of you. Customer service personnel often use this repeating function, because many times customers won't understand or accept a verbal message alone.

One of the more fascinating functions of nonverbal communication in customer relations is its ability to *regulate* conversation. As we know from the chapter on vocalics, most conversations occur in a series of turns at talk by the interactants, and this is true of the customer service rep/customer exchange as well. Those turns are negotiated by a series of regulator cues. For example, the customer service rep may lean toward the customer, make eye contact, raise the eyebrows, and take in a breath—all before uttering a word. These nonverbal cues are important, because when customers perceive positive conversational regulators—bodily, facial, and vocal cues of patience and con-

cern—the entire exchange is affected in the right direction. But when customers are belligerent (as we sometimes are), our negative nonverbal conversational regulators may rouse the same kind of behavior in the employee. The whole point of the exchange is likely defeated as a result.

Finally, nonverbal behaviors in customer relations often *accent* or provide emphasis for a verbal message. Customer relations professionals have to be very careful on this point, because certain accenting cues can be perceived negatively

© CREATISTA/Shutterstock.com

Irritable or bored customer service workers may enact aggressive nonverbal cues that can negatively influence a business transaction.

chapter eleven

and can escalate an unpleasant encounter with a member of the public. For example, if an angry or frustrated customer slams down a receipt on the counter, yelling, "Just give me my money back!" a customer service rep shouldn't follow suit, or the exchange will escalate, possibly causing other disgruntled customers to get involved.

In sum, communicating effectively with customers and clients is essential in professional contexts (Lin & Lin, 2017). If you work in customer service, we recommend taking responsibility for the excellent service you're expected to provide. Customers and clients want to do business with organizations and professionals who employ effective verbal and nonverbal communication skills—those who are empathetic and responsive to concerns.

LEADERSHIP AND NONVERBAL COMMUNICATION

Scholars have long studied the topic of leadership and communication, providing typologies of leadership styles, strategies, and approaches (Johnson & Hackman, 2018; Men & Stacks, 2013). In this section, we examine nonverbal communication as an essential leadership quality. Here are some questions to get us started: Do you join clubs as a college student and remain just a member, or do you tend to become a leader of those clubs? If you admire leadership as a quality in other people but don't view yourself as a leader, why is that? What are some nonverbal communication skills you might need to develop to become an effective leader?

The Nonverbal Essentials of Leadership

Many people make the mistake of viewing leadership as a title. Once they're promoted or elected into a particular leadership position, they think, "That's it—job over. I've arrived." We emphasize that leadership is a skill, one that needs to be developed and fostered throughout life. One particular skill set that helps leaders emerge is nonverbal communication (Beebe & Mottet, 2016; Remland, 2006). Think about leaders who are successful at what they do. What makes them great? How do they communicate nonverbally?

IMPRESSION MANAGEMENT. An essential leadership ability is impression management, which we defined earlier in this chapter as the formation of an impression, perception, or view of a person. Effective leaders work on creating a desired impression of themselves so that they're perceived as they want to be perceived. They also recognize others' efforts at impression management. Nonverbal communication scholars Crane and Crane (2002) provide the following impression management strategies for leaders:

1. Effective leaders should recognize different factors that lead to the use of impression management strategies by employees. This means that leaders should be able to receive and interpret the cues, both verbal and nonverbal, their employees, coworkers, superiors, and customers/clients extend as they try to affect impressions formed about them.
2. Some degree of impression management will always occur in professional settings. Leaders need to be able to distinguish between honest and manipulative strategies employees use to shape perception.
3. Effective leaders need to be particularly aware of the image they want to project in the workplace and strive to achieve that image, while being receptive to feedback. This audience includes all colleagues in the workplace as well as customers/clients and rivals.
4. It's imperative that leaders know their audience, the situation, and the goal of an encounter before using an impression management strategy.
5. Honest performance should be the hallmark of a leader. Achievement generates a positive impression.
6. The best impression is reality. Leaders always present their real selves and never show a false face to their audiences.

Dress to Impress. Another essential for leaders is to wear clothing and use accessories (artifacts) that signal to others they're leaders. Many of the tips we provided for appropriate interview attire apply to leaders' appearances as well. However, leaders may need to strategically "dress down" when a situation calls for it, such as in situations where they're expected to build rapport with clients or employees, or informally celebrate an organization's accomplishments (Chandor, Hargie, & Crute, 2017; Gurung et al., 2018; Peluchette et al., 2006).

Business and Social Etiquette. Leaders should adhere to the following tips about social etiquette:

1. Know how to make an entrance and work a room; understand appropriate proxemics (the amount of space between people in conversation).
2. Be well versed in first-meeting (initial interaction) strategies, in which such nonverbal cues as the professional handshake are critical.
3. Practice making business and social introductions with confidence and poise, making the best use of vocalics, facial expressions, and other important nonverbal codes.
4. Attend to others' nonverbal cues, as well as the related emotions and attitudes driving those cues. Apply sensitivity and caution when attempting to decipher complex nonverbal cues, rather than relying on stereotypes or past experience.
5. Make use of the skill of perception checking. Check your perceptions of others' nonverbal cues with trusted people so as to formulate appropriate responses and realistic expectations for future behavior.

THE POSTURE OF LEADERSHIP. As we discussed in Chapter 2, Albert Mehrabian is a major contributor to our understanding of many nonverbal behaviors. His work on body movement and posture set an early standard for nonverbal research and applies to our focus on the nonverbal essentials of leadership. Mehrabian (1966, 1968, 1969a, 1969b, 1971, 1972, 1981) contended that three primary dimensions exist, through which we communicate our attitudes, feelings, and status to others.

The first dimension Mehrabian termed **immediacy**, which refers to the degree of perceived physical or psychological closeness between people. The more immediacy behavior someone exhibits, the more we generally like that person or are interested in what she or he says or conveys nonverbally. Kinesic cues related to immediacy include forward lean of the body, symmetric positioning (arms or legs in correspondence with the general body position), and a direct body orientation (body positioned toward someone, rather than in an indirect or sideways configuration). It's easy to see why immediacy cues are important to leaders, who should realize that behaviors that engender liking in coworkers and clients are preferable to behaviors that communicate disinterest or pomposity.

The second component in Mehrabian's framework is **arousal**; as we said in Chapter 2, we don't mean sexual arousal here, but merely activation or interest. Arousal prepares the body for action, so it's important that leaders use their eyes, faces, voices, and body movements to indicate they're fully engaged in what's happening around them. Although this may sound contradictory, it's also important for leaders to show non activation or non arousal at times, meaning they need to know when to nonverbally indicate relaxation or de-escalate emotions. A backward lean or sitting position, asymmetric positioning with others, rocking movements, and general reduced tension in the body, especially in the arms, legs, and feet, are appropriate leader-like nonverbal cues. At times, a leader's sense of calm is what's necessary.

The third dimension of Mehrabian's framework communicates the balance of power in an interaction or relationship. **Dominance** cues communicate status, position, and importance. While the best leaders are confident in their abilities, sometimes leaders are insecure and feel the need to enact dominating, power-based nonverbal cues. Great leaders have no need for obvious power displays, but may indicate their higher status more subtly through dress, posture, and proxemics when interacting with others (Arnette & Pettijohn, 2012; Toscano, Schubert, & Geissner, 2018).

HIRING GOOD PEOPLE. Effective leaders not only pay attention to their own nonverbal communication, but they also attend to the nonverbal cues of people they hire and of those whom others hire to work for them, from the initial interview to performance on the job (Beebe & Mottet, 2016). Leaders set the tone in job interviews: If they look beyond the basic information presented during an employment interview and see through applicant anxiety, which is often communicated nonverbally, they will be more likely to hire and retain good people (McCarthy & Goffin, 2004). On the job, many employers now look beyond technical training and basic competencies in hirees; organizations seek people to join their ranks who are aware of and proactive in their current level of communication skill, open to receiving communication skills training so they can improve, and focused on contributing to a positive organizational culture (Chandor et al., 2017).

OUT OF THE CLASSROOM
onto the page

Most students already have or will soon join the professional workforce. As the job market continues to become more competitive, it's critical that prospective employees learn proper résumé-building and interviewing strategies to gain a leg up on the competition. However, it's important to note that not all employers desire the same traits and communication practices; a correctional officer will need strong, assertive communication practices, while a day-care operator will need sensitive, friendly communication practices.

Classroom discussions often include student input that relates to students' personal lives. Sometimes, contributions include anecdotes from work. Students in our classes often share multiple examples from their work lives that help us understand the role of nonverbal communication in the workplace.

One student named Harrison explained how he always feels nervous before interviews because he doesn't know what to wear. He was afraid of looking like "your average college kid" playing "dress up." His classmate, Madison, agreed with this, stating that she never knew if she was over-dressed or under-dressed for an interview; she wondered how her clothing impacted hiring decisions. Michael, who did the hiring for the hotel where he worked, suggested that his classmates wear something to an interview that was just as formal or slightly more formal than the dress of current employees. If servers at a restaurant wore t-shirts and jeans, an appropriate interview outfit might be a button-down shirt with khaki pants, a casual dress, or a nice slacks outfit. The general consensus among our college students, as they approached employment interviews, was that it was better to err on the side of being too formally dressed than too casually dressed, which could mean you'd blow the interview by looking unprofessional.

We've seen one constant in our teaching of this topic: Students almost always disagree about whether to cover up piercings and tattoos for a job interview. Some believe you have to be your "true self" at an interview, so employers will know the reality of who they're hiring; others believe a few physical appearance adjustments won't take away your authenticity and might help you get the job.

EMOTIONAL INTELLIGENCE. Effective leaders strive for **emotional intelligence**—our ability to monitor our own and others' feelings and emotions, discriminate among them, and use this information to guide our thinking and action (Fiori & Vesely-Maillefer, 2018; Gangai & Agrawal, 2018; Goleman, 1995). While the study of emotional intelligence originated in the discipline of psychology, the concept is particularly applicable in business and leadership contexts (Ashkanasy & Duas, 2017; Santos, Wang, & Lewis, 2018).

© dizain/Shutterstock.com

Obviously, our interest is the connection between emotional intelligence and nonverbal communication. We've included emotional intelligence as a leadership essential since it incorporates nonverbal communication as a skill—specifically, the ability to recognize emotional expressions displayed by oneself and others. Developing our powers of emotional intelligence helps us regulate our own emotions and better understand the emotions of others. In addition, emotional intelligence encourages us to use our emotions for flexible planning, creative thinking, redirecting our attention, and motivating ourselves to accomplish goals and finish tasks (Goleman & Boyatzis, 2013).

REMEMBER

Remember! **11.4**

Customer relations	Also referred to as customer service, the interaction between employees or representatives of an organization or business and the people the organization sells to or serves
Immediacy	Degree of perceived physical or psychological closeness between people
Arousal	Nonverbal cues that show activation, interest, or engagement, such as forward body lean and direct body orientation to others
Dominance	Nonverbal cues that indicate status, position, and importance
Emotional intelligence	Ability to monitor one's own and others' feelings and emotions, discriminate among them, and use this information to guide one's thinking and actions

NONVERBAL COMMUNICATION IN EDUCATIONAL CONTEXTS ■ ■ ■ ▬

In this section of the chapter, we examine critical nonverbal communication codes that inform the teaching–learning process. This information is relevant to students because you spend a good deal of your life in classrooms as you work on your degrees. Attention is given to student nonverbal behavior to help you think about or reflect on your current experience. We also provide information about nonverbal communication in the educational arena, in case you ever decide to take on the role of a teaching professional or currently serve in that capacity.

LEARNING ENVIRONMENTS ■ ■ ■

What types of learning environments do you prefer? Think about colors, lighting, temperature, and seating comfort in a classroom or lab. These are all characteristics of **learning environments**—spaces and locations within which learning occurs. Typical learning environments, like seminar rooms, lecture halls, labs, and classrooms, are communication contexts that affect perceptions of safety, comfort, attitude, and character. Some educational environments actually inhibit learning because of their nonverbal properties (Castilla, Llinares, Bravo, & Blanca, 2017; Neill, 2017).

Classroom size, seating arrangements, and other aspects of the physical structure of an educational space profoundly affect student learning.

From the Sunshine Room to the Lecture Hall

Think back to your first classrooms, perhaps in kindergarten or elementary school. Do you remember the features of those early rooms, like colors, windows, lighting, and furniture arrangement? Now fast-forward to your middle school and high school years. Think about how the learning environments changed. Your textbook authors have had conversations about the bright colors and vivid images of animals, plants, and people present in our lower grades. Dr. Wahl recalled different classroom themes from the first grade, when he was lucky enough to be assigned to the Sunshine Room, while a neighborhood kid was proud to report daily to the Green Room.

What kinds of classrooms do you have now, as college students? It's likely that a lot of your college classroom environments are kind of boring, right? (They're no "sunshine rooms.") We realize that classrooms come in different sizes, configurations, and colors, but here are some features of this particular category of physical environment you should pay attention to:

1. *Colors:* Color matters in an environment (Duan, Rhodes, & Cheung, 2018a, 2018b; Hyodo, 2011; von Castell, Stelzmann, Oberfeld, Welsch, & Hecht, 2018). Elementary-aged students respond better to warm colors (e.g., yellow and pink) in classrooms, while secondary students respond better to cool colors (e.g., blue and green). Research isn't specific when it comes to colors and college students, but as you've no doubt noticed, most college classrooms are painted your basic white, beige, or grey.

2. *Lighting:* Limited light or lighting that is too bright or produces glare can create eye strain and fatigue and contribute to poor concentration, and thus poor learning (Georgieva, Schledermann, Nielsen, & Hansen, 2017).

3. *Temperature:* Students have trouble learning if they're too hot or too cold, but establishing a comfortable temperature is often beyond control within a classroom.

4. *Spatial arrangement:* The amount of space and the way classroom furnishings are arranged determine what communicative relationships are possible and affect the teaching and learning process (Byers, Imms, & Hartnell-Young, 2018; Castilla et al., 2017; Simonds & Cooper, 2011; Tenbrink et al., 2017). Some lecture halls have seats attached to long desks, such that communication beyond a few people around you is pretty near impossible. For communication classes that often involve group work, flexible classrooms with movable chairs and tables tend to work best.

5. *Furnishings:* Due to a lack of funding or attention, some college classrooms look like something right out of the Depression years. The rooms look dingy, as though they haven't been painted in a century, with stained floors or carpeting, broken or missing desks or chairs, antiquated chalkboards (instead of newer whiteboards), peeling walls, and an obvious lack of technology. Research shows that unkempt learning environments—including classrooms that aren't upgraded, don't include modern technology, and don't offer ways to control noise—send negative signals to the teachers and students who attempt to function in such surroundings (Castilla et al., 2017).

Online Learning Environments and Distance Education

When you move beyond face-to-face classroom settings, you see huge growth in online learning environments—computer-mediated, web-based educational forums. Online learning environments are also referred to as **distance education**—courses taught via computer, such that students don't have to be present in traditional classrooms (Keller, Ucar, & Kumtepe, 2018; Seaman, Allen, & Seaman, 2018). Distance education courses use computer-mediated tools to offer students a wider array of courses than their home campuses can offer; they also enable students to take courses from remote locations. For example, many universities offer nursing courses to students working in hospitals at a distance from campus.

Since online learning environments and distance education programs have proliferated with the emergence of new technologies, communication researchers continue to explore how these new learning environments affect the student and teacher experience (Faulconer & Gruss, 2018; Lei & Govra, 2010; Naidu, 2017). Much of this scholarly attention focuses on the role of nonverbal communication in online learning environments and distance education. Because students have particular nonverbal expectations of their teachers in distance learning, teachers must attempt to overcome the distance and replicate the face-to-face arrangement students are more used to (Dixson, Greenwell, Rogers-Stacy, Weister, & Lauer, 2017). Over the years, we've come to understand students' preferences in traditional learning environments, but the growth of distance education and other online learning forums is causing teachers to think about nonverbal communication in a different way.

An alternative to both the traditional classroom and distance learning has recently emerged in many colleges and universities: blended learning. Blended learning involves a hybrid of distance learning and face-to-face interaction (Broadbent, 2017). Researcher Wei-Fan Chen (2012) examined a blended-learning classroom for the potential benefits of this type of instruction. Results indicated that students in blended-learning environments performed significantly better on measures of factual knowledge than did students in a pure online learning environment. Have you taken any blended or hybrid college classes? How would you rate the learning experience? As university learning environments continue to become more diversified, think about what teaching and learning styles you prefer, as well as what nonverbal cues—present or absent in the learning environment—are most critical to how well you learn.

TEACHER NONVERBAL COMMUNICATION ■ ■ ■

A variety of the nonverbal communication codes we've explored earlier in this chapter, as well as in previous chapters in this book, pertain to teaching effectiveness. In fact, many teachers turn to nonverbal communication teacher training forums to become masters in the classroom (Elfenbein, 2006; McCroskey, Richmond, & McCroskey, 2006; Mottet & Beebe, 2006b; Richmond, McCroskey, & Hickson, 2011; Simonds & Cooper, 2011). In this section, we explore instructor nonverbal cues that research suggests positively influence student learning.

Teacher Nonverbal Immediacy

What are some specific nonverbal cues teachers use in the classroom? Teacher nonverbal cues communicate more than their simple like or dislike of students or of teaching, in general; teacher nonverbal cues display attitudes toward subject matter and one's job (Clark-Gordon, Bowman, Watts, Banks, & Knight, 2018; Martin & Mottet, 2011; McCroskey et al., 2006; Neill, 2017).

As we mentioned earlier, Mehrabian (1971) first conceptualized **immediacy**—behavior that enhances psychological and physical closeness between people. Since this conceptualization, teacher immediacy, both verbal and nonverbal, has been studied specifically for its impact on student attitudes, perceptions, and learning (Dannels, 2015; Finn & Schrodt, 2012; Henning, 2012; Kelly, Rice, Wyatt, Ducking, & Denton, 2015; Santilli, Miller, & Katt, 2011). **Teacher nonverbal immediacy** is the use of nonverbal cues (e.g., eye contact, smiling, vocal expressiveness, gestures, relaxed body positions, movement around the classroom, appropriate touch) to signal to students a teacher's approachability, availability, closeness, and warmth. Communication scholars Simonds and Cooper (2011) provide the following list of teacher nonverbal immediacy behaviors, as well as behaviors that show a lack of immediacy.

1. *Accepts student behavior:* Smiles, affirmatively shakes head, pats on the back, winks, places hand on shoulder or head.
2. *Praises student behavior:* Places index finger and thumb together ("okay" sign), claps, raises eyebrows and smiles, nods head affirmatively, and smiles.
3. *Displays student ideas:* Writes comments on board, puts students' work on bulletin board, holds up papers, provides for nonverbal student demonstration.
4. *Shows interest in student behavior:* Establishes and maintains eye contact.
5. *Moves to facilitate student-to-student interaction:* Physically moves into the position of group member, physically moves away from the group.
6. *Gives directions to students:* Points with hands, looks at specified area, employs predetermined signal (such as raising hands for students to stand up), reinforces numerical aspects by showing a number of fingers, extends arms forward and beckons with the hands, points to students for answers.
7. *Shows authority toward students:* Frowns, stares, raises eyebrows, taps foot, rolls book on desk, negatively shakes head, walks or looks away from students, snaps fingers.
8. *Focuses students' attention on important points:* Uses pointer, walks toward students or objects, taps on something, thrusts head forward, thrusts arms forward, employs a nonverbal movement with a verbal statement to add emphasis.
9. *Demonstrates and/or illustrates:* Performs a physical skill, manipulates materials and media, illustrates a verbal statement with a nonverbal action.
10. *Ignores student behavior:* Fails to provide a nonverbal response when one is ordinarily expected.

When teachers exhibit nonverbal immediacy behaviors, a number of positive effects emerge (Dannels, 2015; Malachowski & Martin, 2011; McCroskey et al., 2006; Pogue & AhYun, 2006; Richmond et al., 2011; Schrodt & Witt, 2006; Witt & Kerssen-Griep, 2011): (1) higher student enjoyment of the subject matter and content; (2) increased student–teacher and student–student communication; (3) higher evaluations of instructor effectiveness and credibility; and (4) enhanced learning because students' attention spans are increased and a positive, supportive environment is created.

Teacher Touch: Too Close for Comfort

As we've made clear, effective teachers use nonverbal communication to establish approachability and connection with their students. At the same time, most teachers strive for balance between their personal and private lives, as well as manage the notion of teaching as a mode of friendship (McBride & Wahl, 2005; Rawlins, 2000). It's also important to be aware of **excessive immediacy**, defined as offensive and inappropriate comments, gestures, physical proximity, and touch that can occur in classrooms, hallways, and faculty offices. In some cases, excessive immediacy may be viewed as sexual harassment (Ratliff, Watson, & Hall, 2017; Rester & Edwards, 2007; Weiss & Lolonde, 2001). Research has shown that **teacher misbehaviors**—offensive or disruptive actions by teachers (e.g., yelling, insulting, and harassing students; telling offensive jokes; chronically arriving late to class)—are detrimental to student learning (Claus, Booth-Butterfield, & Chory, 2012; Frymier, Wanzer, & Wojtaszczyk, 2008; Neill, 2017).

Teacher touch must be *appropriate* (Legg & Wilson, 2013; Simonds & Cooper, 2011). If any touch is extended from teacher to student, it should be on a neutral part of the body, which includes the hand, forearm, shoulder, and upper back. Of course, the amount of teacher and student touch will vary with age and grade level, but we urge caution with this particularly powerful form of nonverbal communication. One teacher's sign of affection is one student's idea of sexual harassment.

Professors must respect the personal boundaries of their students.

© ESB Professional/Shutterstock.com

Teacher Appearance and Attire

Physical appearance is another nonverbal communication code that applies to educational contexts, especially in student ratings of teacher attractiveness (Claus et al., 2012; Edwards, Edwards, Qing, & Wahl, 2007; Fromuth, Kelly, Wilson, Finch, & Scruggs, 2013). Websites like ratemyprofessor. com give students the opportunity to evaluate instructors based on their attractiveness, assigning them chili pepper icons indicating "hotness" (Hartman & Hunt, 2013; Liu, Hu, & Furutan, 2013; Miles & Sparks, 2013).

Just as clothing has an impact in professional situations, the same holds true for teacher attire. The way teachers dress does communicate something to students in classrooms, from elementary to college levels (Shoulders & Smith, 2018; Thornbory & White, 2006). What reaction do students have when teachers wear informal or casual attire, compared with when they're dressed formally? Research shows that formally dressed instructors are perceived as organized, competent, and prepared, while informally dressed teachers are viewed as friendly, fun, understanding, and flexible (Simonds & Cooper, 2011). A tension seems to exist between what to wear and what not to wear as a teacher. This can be challenging for less-experienced or beginning teachers whose goal is **homophily**—perceived similarity with others in appearance, background, and attitudes. They may desire to appear hip or "on the students' level" while also establishing their credibility. If beginning instructors or teaching assistants dress in formal attire, they may be viewed as credible but not approachable. On the other hand, if they dress informally, they may be viewed as approachable, but students may lack respect for the teacher and be prone to misbehavior (e.g., talking out of turn, distracting other students, leaving class early, arriving late).

REMEMBER

Remember!
11.5

Learning environments	Spaces and locations where learning occurs
Distance education	Courses for which students don't have to be physically present in traditional classrooms
Immediacy	Behavior that enhances psychological and physical closeness between people
Teacher nonverbal immediacy	Nonverbal cues that reflect a teacher's approachability, availability, closeness, and warmth
Excessive immediacy	Offensive and inappropriate comments, gestures, physical proximity, and touch that can occur in classrooms, hallways, and faculty offices
Teacher misbehaviors	Teachers' offensive or disruptive actions that are detrimental to student learning
Homophily	Perceived similarity in appearance, background, and attitudes

STUDENT NONVERBAL COMMUNICATION

Another factor to consider in the educational context is student nonverbal behavior. Have you ever been distracted by what other students are doing around you in class? Have you thought about how much student nonverbal communication takes place in the classroom? While researchers have given teacher nonverbal communication specific consideration, they've also examined student nonverbal communication (Houser & Waldbuesser, 2017; Mottet, 2004; Mottet & Beebe, 2006a; Neill, 2017).

Student nonverbal communication is important for us to explore so you can be more aware of your own behavior as well as that of other students in your classrooms and other campus settings. Your classmates' behavior affects your own, but you probably knew that. At the same time, this information about student nonverbal cues helps prospective teachers become more aware of what may go on in their classrooms.

Student Adapting Behaviors

Have you ever thought about the nonverbal cues students send in educational settings? There are so many we could cover, but let's focus on the more obvious ones. One category of nonverbal cues, mostly associated with kinesics, is **adaptors**—nonverbal behaviors that help us satisfy a personal need, cope with emotions, or adapt to an immediate situation. As professors, we know that our students prefer to bolt from the classroom as soon as they've finished an exam, but as a nonverbal experiment, the next time you finish a test and some of your classmates are still in the room finishing theirs, stick around and watch the nonverbals. You'll see interesting examples of nervous tension in the bodies of your classmates—frequent shifts of posture in chairs, hair twirling, pencil chewing or tapping on desktops, running of hands through hair repeatedly, and long stares up at the ceiling (hoping for a vision of the right answer)—because most students exhibit some sort of nonverbal signal of test anxiety (Thomas, Cassady, & Heller, 2017). Then there's the thigh shaker. Some students can make one of their legs quiver up and down at a very fast pace, and they don't usually realize they're doing it.

Another common nonverbal category is termed **leave-taking behavior**—nonverbal cues that indicate a departure is imminent, such as sighing or breathing hard, looking at a clock, watch, or cell phone, sitting on the edge of a chair, packing up a backpack or laptop computer, and so on. These cues tell the teacher that students are ready to hit the road! In contrast, some students arrive early to class, wait outside the door for the classroom to become available, or sit in the classroom studying their notes (or catching up on e-mails and text messages) before the professor and other students arrive. What nonverbal signal is sent by students who arrive early to class? Do teachers view them as smarter? More involved and interested in course content? Our point is this: Student nonverbal behavior in educational settings *does* play a role in helping form positive or negative impressions.

Student Misbehaviors

Just as teachers exhibit misbehaviors, students are capable of behaving badly, too. Student behaviors in the classroom that are perceived by teachers and other students to be negative, such as talking out of turn, interrupting the teacher or other students, over-talking (meaning monopolizing class discussion), not offering a contribution during class discussions (silence is a nonverbal cue too), arriving late to class, and leaving class early have been termed in research **student misbehaviors**. Take a moment to think of student misbehaviors that really bother you (but that, of course, you would *never* engage in yourself). How many of these misbehaviors are nonverbal?

Students and teachers alike use more and more technology in the classroom these days. Laptops, tablets, and smartphones are examples of electronic devices that can help us learn. But where do we draw the line when the use of such technology invades the classroom or makes students passive, so that they engage less in class discussion? Consider your teacher's syllabus or class rules for this nonverbal communication course you're taking. Does the syllabus address student use of technology in class? Are more of your professors permitting cell phone use during class than they used to? As communication professors, we've experienced this dilemma firsthand; we've revised our approaches, mainly because so many students now use downloaded textbooks and follow along with course material on their phones and laptops. (Granted, some students are simply addicted to social media.)

Studies have examined student cell phone use in class for its connection to teacher immediacy, student motivation, and achievement. Bottom line? Texting is a recurring behavior in college classrooms; banning phone and laptop use during class sessions has mixed effects on students

Misuse of technology in class can be considered a major misbehavior in higher education.

(Ledbetter & Finn, 2013; Sawang, O'Connor & Ali, 2017; Wei & Wang, 2010). Scholars Kuznekoff and Titsworth (2013) found that students who didn't use their phones in class wrote down 62% more information—*detailed* information—in notes they took during class, had better recall of the class lecture, and scored a full letter grade and a half higher on a multiple choice test on the information than did their counterparts who used their phones during class.

What's the nonverbal message sent when students are preoccupied with texting their friends instead of focusing on the teacher or participating in class discussion? What impressions do teachers have of students who take a cell phone call in the middle of class? What impressions do other students have of this behavior? Have classroom norms evolved along with the growth of technology?

Students with Disabilities

In previous chapters, we've discussed the importance of developing nonverbal competency when communicating with people with disabilities. Nonverbal communication skills of teachers and students are critical to the formation of inclusive, respectful learning environments for students with disabilities. Have you ever had social contact with a student with a disability? Perhaps you, as a student, are living with a disability or have a family member or friend who comes to mind. Our knowledge or first clue that a student is living with a disability is often based on his or her physical appearance. Sadly, the physical appearance of a person with a disability sometimes causes us to make assumptions about her or his communicative capability, and to interact with the person (or not) based on our assumptions (Braithwaite, 1991; Braithwaite & Braithwaite, 2014). If you have a classmate with a physical disability, you may need that person to inform you as to what is needed or expected in educational settings (e.g., holding open the classroom doors; trading seats so someone in a wheelchair or on crutches can more comfortably fit in the room; offering special assistance, such as carrying books and materials; moving out of the way). But it's important for all of us to be careful that we don't assume that a physical disability means a person has diminished mental, intellectual, or communicative capacity. Students with disabilities face and overcome daily obstacles that often don't even register with people who don't have disabilities (Fleming, Plotner, & Oertle, 2017).

Consider how nonverbal communication awareness can help accommodate students with learning disabilities and other challenges, such as test anxiety, dyslexia, attention-deficit disorder (ADD), and attention-deficit hyperactivity disorder (ADHD) (DuPaul, Pinho, Pollack, Gormley, & Laracy, 2015; Enzinna, 2016/2017). For the most part, learning disabilities aren't revealed through nonverbal means (such as physical appearance); students with learning disabilities occasionally reveal their status to their teachers but seldom to classmates. Sometimes you might notice a student's absence on test days, which indicates that she or he takes tests in a more private, often proctored environment so distractions common to classroom settings are reduced. Students with learning disabilities—the hidden or masked kinds of disabilities—remind us all that we need to take care with our nonverbal cues in educational settings, as well as sharpen our powers of nonverbal observation, so we can function and communicate more effectively in instructional contexts (Jeffress, 2018).

Adaptors	Nonverbal behaviors that help a person satisfy a personal need, cope with emotions, or adapt to an immediate situation
Leave-taking behavior	Classroom nonverbal cues that indicate to teachers that students are ready to leave
Student misbehaviors	Negative student behaviors in a classroom that can disrupt learning

SUMMARY

In this chapter, we provided an application of nonverbal communication to two key contexts in daily life: professional and educational settings. We discussed the importance of direct and indirect nonverbal communication in trying to get a job. Recall the impact of direct nonverbal communication cues during job interviews (e.g., physical appearance, clothing, hair length, body smell, professional handshake), and be aware of the more subtle, indirect forms of nonverbal communication before and after an interview (e.g., résumés, handwritten thank-you notes, social media usage). Further, we applied several nonverbal communication codes to on-the-job experiences, such as superior–subordinate relationship development, coworker nonverbal communication, and nonverbal communication with customers and clients.

Next, we discussed the important role of nonverbal communication as a leadership quality in people. Factors such as impression management, hiring good people, and being aware of one's own and others' verbal and nonverbal communication are essential to leadership. Effective leaders not only pay attention to their own nonverbal communication, but they also pay attention to the non-verbals of people they hire. Effective leaders work to develop emotional intelligence—the ability to monitor one's own and others' feelings and emotions, discriminate among them, and use this information to guide one's thinking and actions.

In the next section of this chapter, we examined the significance of nonverbal communication in educational settings, with special attention to learning environments, teacher nonverbal behavior, and student nonverbal behavior. We discussed how distance education and other instructional technologies shape how students and teachers use space on college campuses. We also addressed the effect of teacher nonverbal immediacy on student learning. In addition, we examined teacher misbehaviors—offensive or disruptive actions by teachers that are often detrimental to learning and the creation of a supportive, safe classroom environment.

In the final section of this chapter, we overviewed student nonverbal communication. Specifically, we examined student misbehaviors, such as talking out of turn, interrupting a teacher or other students, monopolizing class discussions, arriving late to class, and leaving class early, for their negative impacts in an instructional setting. We ended the chapter with a discussion of the important role of nonverbal cues when communicating with students with physical and learning disabilities. We trust that your reading of this chapter has provided you with an understanding of some of the more important aspects of nonverbal communication in two critical contexts in which our need to succeed and be perceived as effective communicators is essential.

DISCUSSION STARTERS

1. What forms of direct nonverbal communication do you think are most important when trying to get a job? What indirect nonverbal strategies are most important?
2. In a professional situation, have you ever shaken hands with someone who violated your expectations? Do you think a professional handshake is an important skill for you to work on, or do you have this nonverbal cue down?
3. Think about your use of e-mail in your current job. What nonverbal cues are present in how you send and respond to e-mail messages? Will you have some changes to make once you're in a career-type job after college graduation?
4. If you currently have a job, how do you nonverbally communicate with difficult coworkers? Identify some specific nonverbal communication codes and explain how you use them to help resolve or avoid conflict at work.
5. Review the nonverbal essentials of leadership discussed in this chapter. Do you exhibit these nonverbal qualities? What do you need to work on to develop your leadership abilities and how you're perceived nonverbally?
6. Have you taken an online or blended course in college? If you have, how important was nonverbal communication in that course? How was nonverbal communication different in the online or blended course, compared with a traditionally delivered, face-to-face course?
7. What's your view of student technology use in classroom environments? Do you find cell phone, laptop, and tablet use in the classroom distracting? What do you think of students who text message their friends during class?
8. Make a list of student misbehaviors you find distracting in the classroom. Are most of the behaviors verbal or nonverbal in nature?

chapter eleven

REFERENCES ■ ■ ■

Ames, M. F. (2018). *A good firm handshake (and other essential business tips).* Hilton, NY. Retrieved from michelle@agoodfirmhandshake.com

Arnette, S. L., & Pettijohn, T. F. II. (2012). The effects of posture on self-perceived leadership. *International Journal of Business and Social Science, 3,* 8-12.

Ashkanasy, N. M., & Daus, C. S. (2017). *Emotional intelligence in the workplace.* In P. C. Flood & Y. Freeney (Eds.) *Wiley encyclopaedia of management.* Hoboken, NJ: John Wiley & Sons.

Antonellis, P. J. Jr., Berry, G., & Silsbee, R. (2017). Employment interview screening: Is the ink worth it? *Global Journal of Human Resource Management, 5,* 38-53.

Baert, S. (2018). Hiring a gay man, taking a risk? A lab experiment on employment discrimination and risk aversion. *Journal of Homosexuality, 65,* 1015-1031.

Barth, I., & Wagner, A. L. (2017). Physical appearance as invisible discrimination. In J. Chanlat & M. F. Özbilgin (Eds.), *Management and diversity: Thematic approaches* (pp. 127-146). Bingley, UK: Emerald Publishing Limited.

Beebe, S. A. (1974). Eye contact: A nonverbal determinant of speaker credibility. *Speech Teacher, 23,* 21–25.

Beebe, S. A., Beebe, S. J., & Ivy, D. K. (2019). *Communication: Principles for a lifetime* (7th ed.). Boston: Pearson.

Beebe, S. A., & Mottet, T. P. (2015). *Business and professional communication: Principles and skills for leadership* (3rd ed.). Boston: Pearson.

Bennett, S. (2014). *The elements of résumé style* (2nd ed.). New York: AMACOM.

Bernstein, A. (2018). Preventing sexual harassment in the workplace. *Nursing and Residential Care.* https://doi.org/10.12968/nrec.2018.20.7.344

Boddy, C. R. (2017). Harassment in the workplace. In D. Poff & A. Michalos (Eds.), *Encyclopedia of business and professional ethics.* New York: Springer.

Bonaccio, S., O'Reilly, J., O'Sullivan, S., & Chicchio, F. (2016). Nonverbal behavior and communication in the workplace: A review and an agenda for research. *Journal of Management, 42,* 1044-1074.

Braithwaite, D. O. (1991). "Just how much did that wheelchair cost?": Management of privacy boundaries by persons with disabilities. *Western Journal of Speech Communication, 55,* 254–274.

Braithwaite, D. O., & Braithwaite, C. A. (2014). "Which is my good leg?": Cultural communication of persons with disabilities. In L. A. Samovar, R. E. Porter, E. R. McDaniel, & C. Sexton Roy (Eds.), *Intercultural communication: A reader* (14th ed., pp. 162-173). Boston: Cengage Learning.

Bringhurst, R. (2013). *The elements of typographic style: Version 4.0* (4th ed.). New York: Hartley and Marks.

Broadbent, J. (2017). Comparing online and blended learners' self-regulated learning strategies and academic performance. *The Internet and Higher Education, 33,* 24-32.

Byers, T., Imms, W., & Hartnell-Young, E. (2018). Evaluating teacher and student spatial transition from a traditional classroom to an innovative learning environment. *Studies in Educational Evaluation, 58,* 156-166.

CareerBuilder.com. (2018). Advice for job hunters. Retrieved from https://www.careerbuilder.com/advice/phase/find-the-job

Castilla, N., Llinares, C., Bravo, J. M., & Blanca, V. (2017). Subjective assessment of university classroom environment. *Building and Environment, 122,* 72-81.

Chandor, A., Hargie, O., & Crute, V. (2017). *Professional interviewing*. Abingdon, UK: Routledge.

Chaplin, W. E., Phillips, J. B., Brown, J. D., Clanton, N. R., & Stein, J. L. (2000). Handshaking, gender, personality, and first impressions. *Journal of Personality and Social Psychology, 79*, 110–117.

Chen, W-F. (2012). An investigation of varied types of blended learning environments on student achievement: An experimental study. *International Journal of Instructional Media, 39*, 205–212.

Clark-Gordon, C. V., Bowman, N. D., Watts, E. R., Banks, J., & Knight, J. M. (2018). "As good as your word": Face-threat mitigation and the use of instructor nonverbal cues on students' perceptions of digital feedback. *Communication Education, 67*, 206-225.

Claus, C. J., Booth-Butterfield, M., & Chory, R. M. (2012). The relationship between instructor misbehaviors and student antisocial behavioral alteration techniques: The roles of instructor attractiveness, humor, and relational closeness. *Communication Education, 61*, 161–183.

Crane, E., & Crane, F. G. (2002). Usage and effectiveness of impression management strategies in organizational settings. *International Journal of Action Methods, 55*, 25–34.

Dannels, D. P. (2015). *Eight essential questions teachers ask: A guidebook for communicating with students*. New York: Oxford University Press.

Davies, H. J. (2018, June 4). To beard or not to beard: Is facial hair really a turnoff? Retrieved from https://www.theguardian.com/fashion/shortcuts/2018/jun/04/to-beard-or-not-to-beard-is-facial-hair-really-a-turn-off

Dixson, M. D., Greenwell, M. R., Rogers-Stacy, C., Weister, T., & Lauer, S. (2017). Nonverbal immediacy behaviors and online student engagement: Bringing past instructional research into the present virtual classroom. *Communication Education, 66*, 37-53.

Duan, Y., Rhodes, P. A., & Cheung, V. (2018a). The influence of color on impulsiveness and arousal: Part 1—hue. *Color Research & Application, 43*, 396-404.

Duan, Y., Rhodes, P. A., & Cheung, V. (2018b). The influence of color on impulsiveness and arousal: Part 2—chroma. *Color Research & Application, 43*, 405-414.

Dunbar, N. E., & Abra, G. (2010). Observations of dyadic power in interpersonal interaction. *Communication Monographs, 77*, 657–684.

DuPaul, G. J., Pinho, T. D., Pollack, B. L., Gormley, M. J., & Laracy, S. D. (2015). First-year college students with ADHD and/or LD: Differences in engagement, positive core self-evaluation, school preparation, and college expectations. *Journal of Learning Disabilities, 50*, 238-251.

Eaves, M., & Leathers, D. G. (2016). *Successful nonverbal communication: Principles and applications* (4th ed.). Abingdon, UK: Routledge.

Edwards, C., Edwards, A., Qing, Q., & Wahl, S. T. (2007). The influence of computer-mediated word-of-mouth communication on student perceptions of instructors and attitudes toward learning course content. *Communication Education, 56*, 255–277.

Elfenbein, H. A. (2006). Learning in emotion judgments: Training and the cross-cultural understanding of facial expressions. *Journal of Nonverbal Behavior, 30*, 21–36.

Enzinna, M. N. (2016/2017). Reconsidering nonverbal communication among children with mental and physical disabilities. *Journal of the Communication, Speech, and Theatre Association of North Dakota, 29*, 56-70.

Esfehani, L. (2011). Electronic name address as individual identity. *International Journal of Linguistics, 3*, 1–16.

Farley, S. D. (2008). Attaining status at the expense of likeability: Pilfering power through conversational interruptions. *Journal of Nonverbal Behavior, 32*, 241–260.

chapter eleven

Farr, M. (2011). *The quick résumé and cover letter book.* Indianapolis, IN: JIST Works.

Faulconer, E. K., & Gruss, A. B. (2018). A review to weigh the pros and cons of online, remote, and distance science laboratory experiences. *The International Review of Research in Open and Distributed Learning, 19,* 155-168.

Finn, A. N., & Schrodt, P. (2012). Students' perceived understanding mediates the effects of teacher clarity and nonverbal immediacy on learner empowerment. *Communication Education, 61,* 111–130.

Fiori, M., & Vesely-Maillefer, A. K. (2018). Emotional intelligence as an ability: Theory, challenges, and new directions. In K. V. Keefer, J. D. A. Parker, & D. H. Saklofske (Eds.), *Emotional intelligence in education* (pp. 23-47). New York: Springer.

Fleming, A. R., Plotner, A. J., & Oertle, K. M. (2017). College students with disabilities: The relationship between student characteristics, the academic environment, and performance. *Journal of Postsecondary Education and Disability, 30,* 209-221.

Flynn, N., & Flynn, T. (2003). *Writing effective e-mail: Improving your electronic communication.* Boston: Thomson Course Technology.

Frank, M. G., Maroulis, A., & Griffin, D. J. (2013). The voice. In D. Matusomo, M. G. Frank, & H. S. Hwang (Eds.), *Nonverbal communication: Science and application* (pp. 53–74). Thousand Oaks, CA: Sage.

Fromuth, M. E., Kelly, D. B., Wilson, A. K., Finch, L. V., & Scruggs, L. (2013). An exploratory study of the effects of teacher attractiveness on undergraduates' perceptions of teacher-student sexual involvement. *Journal of Child Sexual Abuse, 22,* 341-357.

Frymier, A. B., Wanzer, M. B., & Wojtaszczyk, A. M. (2008). Assessing students' perceptions of inappropriate and appropriate teacher humor. *Communication Education, 57,* 266–288.

Gang, H., Feng, L., Cheng, S., & Xiaochen, S. (2017). Effect of workplace environment cleanliness on judgement of counterproductive work behavior. *Social Behavior & Personality: An International Journal, 45,* 599-604.

Gangai, K. N., & Agrawal, R. (2018). Relationship among emotional intelligence, employee engagement and workplace stress in hospitality industry: An empirical study. *BULMIM Journal of Management and Research, 3,* 1-10.

Garland-Thomson, R. (2009). *Staring: How we look.* New York: Oxford University Press.

Georgieva, D., Schledermann, K. M., Nielsen, S. M. L., & Hansen, E. K. (2017). Designing user centered intelligent classroom lighting. In A. Brooks, E. Brooks, & N. Vidakis (Eds.), *Interactivity, game creation, design, learning, and innovation* (pp. 314-323). New York: Springer.

Gnisci, A., Sergi, I., DeLuca, E., & Errico, V. (2012). Does frequency of interruptions amplify the effect of various types of interruptions? Experimental evidence. *Journal of Nonverbal Behavior, 36,* 39–57.

Goffman, E. (1971). *Relations in public: Microstudies of the public order.* New York: Harper Colophon.

Goleman, D. (1995). *Emotional intelligence.* New York: Bantam.

Goleman, D., & Boyatzis, R. E. (2013). *Primal leadership: Unleashing the power of emotional intelligence.* Boston: Harvard Business School Publishing.

Guerrero, L. K., & Floyd, K. (2006). *Nonverbal communication in close relationships.* Mahwah, NJ: Erlbaum.

Gurney, D. J., Howlett, N., Pine, K., Tracey, M., & Moggridge, R. (2017). Dressing up posture: The interactive effects of posture and clothing on competency judgments. *British Journal of Psychology, 108,* 436-451.

Gurung, R. A. R., Punke, E., Brickner, M., & Badalamenti, V. (2018). Power and provocativeness: The effects of subtle changes in clothing on perceptions of working women. *The Journal of Social Psychology, 158*, 252-255.

Hall, J. A. (1996). Touch, status and gender at professional meetings. *Journal of Nonverbal Behavior, 20*, 23–44.

Hall, J. A. (2001). Status roles and recall of nonverbal cues. *Journal of Nonverbal Behavior, 25*, 79–100.

Hall, J. A. (2011). Gender and status patterns in social touch. In M. J. Hertenstein & S. J. Weiss (Eds.), *The handbook of touch: Neuroscience, behavioral, and health perspectives* (pp. 329–350). New York: Springer.

Hammermesh, D. (2011). *Beauty pays: Why attractive people are more successful.* Princeton, NJ: Princeton University Press.

Harris, P., & Sachau, D. (2005). Is cleanliness next to godliness? The role of housekeeping in impression formation. *Environment and Behavior, 37*, 81–99.

Hartman, K. B., & Hunt, J. B. (2013). What ratemyprofessor.com reveals about how and why students evaluate their professors: A glimpse into the student mind-set. *Marketing Education Review, 23*, 151-161.

Hastings, S. O., Musambira, G. W., & Ayoub, R. (2011). Revisiting Edward T. Hall's work on Arabs and olfaction: An update with implications for intercultural communication scholarship. *Journal of Intercultural Communication Research, 40*, 3–20.

Haynes, B., Suckley, L., & Nunnington, N. (2017). Workplace productivity and office type: An evaluation of office occupier differences based on age and gender. *Journal of Corporate Real Estate, 19*, 111-138.

Hiemstra, K. M. (1999). Shake my hand: Making the right first impression in business with nonverbal communications. *Business Communication Quarterly, 62*, 71–74.

Hodges-Simeon, C. R., Gaulin, S. J. C., & Puts, D. A. (2010). Different vocal parameters predict perceptions of dominance and attractiveness. *Human Nature, 21*, 406–427.

Houser, M. L., & Waldbuesser, C. (2017). Emotional contagion in the classroom: The impact of teacher satisfaction and confirmation on perceptions of student nonverbal classroom behavior. *College Teaching, 65*, 1-8.

Howlett, N., Pine, K. J., Cahill, N., Orakcioglu, I., & Fletcher, B. C. (2015). Unbuttoned: The interaction between provocativeness of female work attire and occupational status. *Sex Roles, 72*, 105-116.

Hynes, G. E., & Veltsos, J. R. (2018). *Managerial communication: Strategies and applications* (7th ed.). Thousand Oaks, CA: Sage.

Hyodo, J. (2011). Can colors make me happy? The effect of color on mood: A meta-analysis. *Advances in Consumer Research, 39*, 858–867.

Jeffress, M. (2018). *International perspectives on teaching with disability: Overcoming obstacles and enriching lives.* Abingdon, UK: Routledge.

Jia, M., Cheng, J., & Hale, C. L. (2017). Workplace emotion and communication: Supervisor nonverbal immediacy, employees' emotion experience, and their communication motives. *Management Communication Quarterly, 31*, 69-87.

Johnson, C. E., & Hackman, M. Z. (2018). *Leadership: A communication perspective* (7th ed.). Longrove, IL: Waveland.

Kabo, F. W. (2017). A model of potential encounters in the workplace: The relationships of homophily, spatial distance, organizational structure, and perceived networks. *Environment & Behavior, 49*, 638-662.

Keller, J. M., Ucar, H., & Kumtepe, A. T. (2018). *Supporting multiculturalism in open and distance learning.* Hershey, PA: IGI Global.

Kelly, S., Rice, C., Wyatt, B., Ducking, J., & Denton, Z. (2015). Teacher immediacy and decreased student quantitative reasoning anxiety: The mediating effect of perception. *Communication Education, 64*, 171-186.

Khan, S. W., & Omar, N. (2018). Understanding workplace relationships: LMX quality, turnover intention and employee job satisfaction, mediating role of superior subordinate communication. In B. Mohamad, A. I. Omoloso, R. R. Adetunji, S. Memon, & H. Harun (Eds.), *School of multimedia technology & communication postgraduate symposium* (pp. 163-167). Kedah, Malaysia: Universiti Utara Malaysia Press.

Kingsley Westerman, C. Y., & Westerman, D. (2010). Supervisor impression management: Message content and channel effects on impressions. *Communication Studies, 61*, 585–601.

Krapels, R. H. (2000). Communication training in two companies. *Business Communication Quarterly, 63*, 104–110.

Kupritz, V. W., & Hillsman, T. (2011). The impact of the physical environment on supervisory communication skills transfer. *Journal of Business Communication, 48*, 148–185.

Kuzmenko, A. (2017). Proximity as a kind of non-verbal communication. *European Exploratory Scientific Journal, 1*, 1-14.

Kuznekoff, J. H., & Titsworth, S. (2013). The impact of mobile phone usage on student learning. *Communication Education, 62*, 233–252.

Ledbetter, A. M., & Finn, A. N. (2013). Teacher technology policies and online communication apprehension as predictors of learner empowerment. *Communication Education, 62*, 301–317.

Legg, A. M., & Wilson, J. (2013). Instructor touch enhanced college students' evaluations. *Social Psychology of Education, 16*, 317-327.

Lei, S. A., & Govra, R. K. (2010). College distance education courses: Evaluating benefits and costs from institutional, faculty and student perspectives. *Education, 130*, 616–631.

Lin, C. Y., & Lin, J. S. C. (2017). The influence of service employees' nonverbal communication on customer-employee rapport in the service encounter. *Journal of Service Management, 28*, 107-132.

Lin, M-H., Cross, S. N. N., & Childers, T. L. (2018). Understanding olfaction and emotions and the moderating role of individual differences. *European Journal of Marketing, 52*, 811-836.

Liu, J., Hu, J., & Furutan, O. (2013). The influence of student perceived professors' "hotness" on expertise, motivation, learning outcomes, and course satisfaction. *Journal of Education for Business, 88*, 94-100.

Lobmaier, J. S. (2012). Facial expression and eye gaze direction: Are they combined when processing emotionally relevant information? *Journal of Communications Research, 4*, 89–101.

Low, K. E. Y. (2006). Presenting the self, the social body, and the olfactory: Managing smells in everyday life experiences. *Sociological Perspectives, 49*, 607–631.

Lybarger, J. E., Rancer, A. S., & Lin, Y. (2017). Superior-subordinate communication in the workplace: Verbal aggression, nonverbal immediacy, and their joint effects on perceived superior credibility. *Communication Research Reports, 34*, 124-133.

Malachowski, C. C., & Martin, M. M. (2011). Instructors' perceptions of teaching behaviors, communication apprehension, and student nonverbal responsiveness in the classroom. *Communication Research Reports, 28*, 141–150.

Martin, L., & Mottet, T. P. (2011). The effect of instructor nonverbal immediacy behaviors and feedback sensitivity on Hispanic students' affective learning outcomes in ninth-grade writing conferences. *Communication Education, 60,* 1–19.

Masip, J., Garrido, E., & Herrero, C. (2004). Facial appearance and impressions of credibility: The effects of facial babyishness and age on person perception. *International Journal of Psychology, 39,* 276–289.

McBride, M. C., & Wahl, S. T. (2005). To say or not to say: Teacher communication boundary management. *Texas Speech Communication Journal, 30,* 8–22.

McCarthy, J., & Goffin, R. (2004). Measuring job interview anxiety: Beyond weak knees and sweaty palms. *Personnel Psychology, 57,* 607–637.

McCroskey, J. C., Richmond, V. P., & McCroskey, L. L. (2006). Nonverbal communication in instructional contexts. In V. Manusov & M. L. Patterson (Eds.), *The SAGE handbook of nonverbal communication* (pp. 421–436). Thousand Oaks, CA: Sage.

Mehrabian, A. (1966). Immediacy: An indicator of attitudes in linguistic communication. *Journal of Personality, 34,* 26–34.

Mehrabian, A. (1968). Inference of attitudes from the posture, orientation, and distance of a communicator. *Journal of Consulting and Clinical Psychology, 32,* 296–308.

Mehrabian, A. (1969a). Measures of achieving tendency. *Educational and Psychological Measurement, 29,* 445–451.

Mehrabian, A. (1969b). Significance of posture and position in the communication of attitude and status relationships. *Psychological Bulletin, 71,* 359–372.

Mehrabian, A. (1971). *Silent messages.* Belmont, CA: Wadsworth.

Mehrabian, A. (1972). *Nonverbal communication.* Chicago: Atherton.

Mehrabian, A. (1981). *Silent messages: Implicit communication of emotions and attitudes* (2nd ed.). Belmont, CA: Wadsworth.

Men, L., & Stacks, D. W. (2013). The impact of leadership style and employee empowerment on perceived organizational reputation. *Journal of Communication Management, 17,* 171–192.

Merkin, R. S. (2018). *Saving face in business.* Basingstoke, UK: Palgrave Macmillan.

Miles, A. D., & Sparks, W. (2013). Examining social media and higher education: An empirical study on ratemyprofessor.com and its impact on college students. *International Journal of Economy, Management, & Social Sciences, 2,* 513-524.

Milkman, R. (2018). The senior precariat. *New Labor Forum, 27,* 44-52.

Mottet, T. P. (2004). The effects of student verbal and nonverbal responsiveness on teacher self-efficacy and job satisfaction. *Communication Education, 53,* 150–163.

Mottet, T. P., & Beebe, S. A. (2006a). Foundations of instructional communication. In T. P. Mottet, V. P. Richmond, & J. C. McCroskey (Eds.), *The handbook of instructional communication: Rhetorical and relational perspectives* (pp. 3–32). Boston: Allyn & Bacon.

Mottet, T. P., & Beebe, S. A. (2006b). The relationship between student responsive behaviors, student socio-communicative style, and instructors' subjective and objective assessments of student work. *Communication Education, 55,* 295–312.

Naidu, S. (2017). Openness and flexibility are the norm, but what are the challenges? *Distance Education, 38,* 1-4.

Neill, S. (2017). *Classroom nonverbal communication.* Abingdon, UK: Routledge.

chapter eleven

O'Brien, K., Latner, J., Ebneter, D., & Hunter, J. (2013). Obesity discrimination: The role of physical appearance, personal ideology, and anti-fat prejudice. *International Journal of Obesity, 37*, 455–460.

Olszewski, A., Panorska, A., & Gillam, S. L. (2017). Training verbal and nonverbal communication interview skills to adolescents. *Communication Disorders Quarterly, 38*, 206-218.

Osensky, T. S. (2017). *Shortchanged: Height discrimination and strategies for social change.* Lebanon, NH: University Press of New England.

Paludi, M. A. (2015). Introduction. In M. A. Paludi, J. L. Martin, J. E. Gruber, & S. Fineran (Eds.), *Sexual harassment in education and work settings: Current research and best practices for prevention* (pp. xix-lii). Santa Barbara, CA: Praeger.

Paramasivam, S., & Subramaniam, S. K. (2018). Superior-subordinate request email in workplace communication of a Malaysian organisation. *Journal of Intercultural Communication Research, 47*, 161-187.

Peck, J. A., & Levashina, J. (2017). Impression management and interview and job performance ratings: A meta-analysis of research design with tactics in mind. *Frontiers in Psychology, 8*. https://doi: 10.3389/fpsyg.2017.00201

Peluchette, J. V., Karl, K., & Rust, K. (2006). Dressing to impress: Beliefs and attitudes regarding workplace attire. *Journal of Business and Psychology, 21*, 45–63.

Petrician, R., Todorov, A., & Grady, C. (2014). Personality at face value: Facial appearance predicts self and other personality judgments among strangers and spouses. *Journal of Nonverbal Behavior, 38*, 259-277.

Pogue, L. L., & AhYun, K. (2006). The effect of teacher nonverbal immediacy and credibility on student motivation and affective learning. *Communication Education, 55*, 331–344.

Powell, G. N. (2018). *Women and men in management* (5th ed.). Thousand Oaks, CA: Sage.

Quintanilla, K. M., & Wahl, S. T. (2016). *Business and professional communication: Keys for workplace excellence* (3rd ed.). Thousand Oaks, CA: Sage.

Ratliff, L., Watson, J., & Hall, K. R. (2017). Preventing sexual misconduct: A guide for teachers, counselors, and administrators. In C. Schwilk, R. Stevenson, & D. Bateman (Eds.), *Sexual misconduct in the education and human services sector* (pp. 172-183). Hershey, PA: IGI Global.

Rawlins, W. K. (2000). Teaching as a mode of friendship. *Communication Theory, 10*, 5–26.

Re, D., & Rule, N. O. (2016). Making a (false) impression: The role of business experience in first impressions of CEO leadership ability. *Journal of Nonverbal Behavior, 40*, 235-245.

Remland, M. (2006). Uses and consequences of nonverbal communication in the context of organizational life. In V. Manusov & M. L. Patterson (Eds.), *The SAGE handbook of nonverbal communication* (pp. 501–519). Thousand Oaks, CA: Sage.

Rester, C. H., & Edwards, R. (2007). Effects of sex and setting on students' interpretation of teachers' excessive use of immediacy. *Communication Education, 56*, 34–53.

Richmond, V. P., McCroskey, J. C., & Hickson, M. L. III. (2011). *Nonverbal behavior in interpersonal relations* (7th ed.). Boston: Pearson.

Roehling, M. V., & Huang, J. (2018). Sexual harassment training effectiveness: An interdisciplinary review and call for research. *Journal of Organizational Behavior, 39*, 134-150.

Ryan, R. (2016). *60 seconds and you're hired* (Rev. ed.). New York: Penguin.

Saiki, D. (2013). Identification of workplace dress by low-income job seekers. *Journal of Employment Counseling, 50*, 50–58.

Santilli, V., Miller, A. N., & Katt, J. (2011). A comparison of the relationship between instructor nonverbal immediacy and teacher credibility in Brazilian and U.S. classrooms. *Communication Research Reports, 28,* 266–274.

Santos, A., Wang, W., & Lewis, J. (2018). Emotional intelligence and career decision-making difficulties: The mediating role of career decision self-efficacy. *Journal of Vocational Behavior, 107,* 295-309.

Sawang, S., O'Connor, P. J., & Ali, M. (2017). IEngage: Using technology to enhance students' engagement in a large classroom. *Journal of Learning Design, 10,* 11-19.

Scarduzio, J. A., Wehlage, S. J., & Lueken, S. (2018). "It's like taking your man card away": Male victims' narratives of male-to-male sexual harassment. *Communication Quarterly.* https://doi:10.1080/0146337 3.2018.1447978

Schrodt, P., & Witt, P. L. (2006). Students' attributions of instructor credibility as a function of students' expectations of instructional technology use and nonverbal immediacy. *Communication Education, 55,* 1–20.

Seaman, J. E., Allen, I. E., & Seaman, J. (2018). *Grade increase: Tracking distance education in the United States.* Wellesley, MA: Babson Survey Research Group.

Sekerdej, M., Simao, C., Waldzus, S., & Brito, R. (2018). Keeping in touch with context: Non-verbal behavior as a manifestation of communality and dominance. *Journal of Nonverbal Behavior.* https:// doi-org/10.1007/s10919-018-0279-2

Shoulders, C. W., & Smith, L. (2018). Impact of teacher attire on students' views of teacher credibility, attitude homophily, and background homophily within school-based agricultural education programs. *Journal of Agricultural Education, 59,* 275-288.

Simonds, C. J., & Cooper, P. (2011). *Communication for the classroom teacher* (9th ed.). Boston: Pearson.

Sims, C. H. (2017). Genderized workplace lookism in the U.S. and abroad: Implications for organization and career development professionals. In M. Khosrow-Pour (Ed.) *Discrimination and diversity: Concepts, methodologies, tools, and applications* (pp. 61-85). Hershey, PA: IGI Global.

Sohn, E. M., & Lee, K. W. (2018). The effect of chefs' nonverbal communication in open kitchens on service quality. *Journal of Foodservice Business Research.* https://doi:10.1080/15378020.2018.1459125

Sorokowska, A. (2013). Assessing personality using body odor: Differences between children and adults. *Journal of Nonverbal Behavior, 37,* 153–163.

Sorokowska, A., Sorokowski, P., & Szmajke, A. (2012). Does personality smell? Accuracy of personality assessments based on body odor. *European Journal of Personality, 26,* 496–503.

Tenbrink, T., Andonova, E., Schole, G., & Coventry, K. R. (2017). Communicative success in spatial dialogue: The impact of functional features and dialogue strategies. *Language & Speech, 60,* 318-329.

Thomas, C. L., Cassady, J. C., & Heller, M. L. (2017). The influence of emotional intelligence, cognitive test anxiety, and coping strategies on undergraduate academic performance. *Learning and Individual Differences, 55,* 40-48.

Thornbory, G., & White, C. (2006). How to project a professional image. *Occupational Health, 58,* 24.

Timming, A. R. (2014). Visible tattoos in the service sector: A new challenge to recruitment and selection. *Work, Employment and Society, 29,* 60-78.

Toscano, H., Schubert, T. W., & Giessner, S. R. (2018). Eye gaze and head posture jointly influence judgments of dominance, physical strength, and anger. *Journal of Nonverbal Behavior.* https://doi.org/10.1007/s10919-018-0276-5

Tsai, W., Huang, T., & Yu, H. (2012). Investigating the unique predictability and boundary conditions of applicant physical attractiveness and nonverbal behaviors on interviewer evaluations in job interviews. *Journal of Occupational & Organizational Psychology, 85*, 60–79.

Veitch, J. A., Stokkermans, M. G. M., & Newsham, G. R. (2011). Linking lighting appraisals to work behaviors. *Environment & Behavior, 45*, 198–214.

von Castell, C., Stelzmann, D., Oberfeld, D., Welsch, R., & Hecht, H. (2018). Cognitive performance and emotion are indifferent to ambient color. *Color Research & Application, 43*, 65-74.

Wei, F.-Y. F., & Wang, Y. K. (2010). Students' silent messages: Can teacher verbal and nonverbal immediacy moderate student use of text messaging in class? *Communication Education, 59*, 475–496.

Weick, M., McCall, C., & Blascovich, J. (2017). Power moves beyond complementarity: A staring look elicits avoidance in low power perceivers and approach in high power perceivers. *Personality and Social Psychology Bulletin, 43*, 1188-1201.

Weiss, D. S., & Lolonde, R. N. (2001). Responses of female undergraduates to scenarios of sexual harassment by male professors and teaching assistants. *Canadian Journal of Behavioral Science, 33*, 148–163.

Weiss, M., & Morrison, E. W. (2018). Speaking up and moving up: How voice can enhance employees' social status. *Journal of Organizational Behavior, 39*. http://doi.org/10.1002/job/2262

Witt, P. L., & Kerssen-Griep, J. (2011). Instructional feedback I: The interaction of facework and immediacy on students' perceptions of instructor credibility. *Communication Education, 60*, 75–94.

Yoo, S. H., & Noyes, S. E. (2016). Recognition of facial expressions of negative emotions in romantic relationships. *Journal of Nonverbal Behavior, 40*, 1-12.

Youngquist, J. (2009). The effect of interruptions and dyad gender combination on perceptions of interpersonal dominance. *Communication Studies, 60*, 147–163.

Yuksel, A. (2008). Nonverbal service behavior and customers' affective assessment. *Journal of Quality Assurance in Hospitality & Tourism, 9*, 57–77.

chapter twelve

NONVERBAL COMMUNICATION: GENDER, INTIMATE RELATIONSHIPS, AND SEXUALITY

chapter outline

chapter objectives

After studying this chapter, you should be able to
1. distinguish between the terms sex and gender;
2. define the terms androgyny, sexual orientation, and gender identity as subsets of the larger concept of gender;
3. identify key sex differences in nonverbal sending and receiving abilities;
4. discuss major research findings regarding men's and women's behavior within the nonverbal codes of proxemics, physical appearance, kinesics, facial expressions and eye behavior, touch, and vocalics;
5. identify Scheflen's four stages of quasi-courtship behavior and the relevant nonverbal cues present in each stage;
6. identify and provide examples of nonverbal cues within Jones and Yarbrough's three categories of intimate touch;
7. review major research findings on nonverbal cues and relationship maintenance, conflict, and dissolution;
8. define sexuality, sexual orientation, and gaydar, and identify the primary nonverbal codes associated with each; and
9. discuss the impact of nonverbal cues before, during, and after sexual activity.

case study

AN AGE OLD DILEMMA

We all know the world changes FAST. Technology you used in high school is now likely obsolete or, at best, "quaint." Once you upgrade your technology and learn how to use it, it's time to evolve again because something newer, shinier, and faster has likely been introduced on the market. Likewise, what you were taught about people, sexuality, gender, identity, and relationships has likely fluxed and then fluxed again as you've become a college student. Change can be exciting, but also stressful.

You may long for a simpler world, because stability is comforting and change is often work. But that wistful feeling is more often experienced by people whose sexuality, gender, and identity haven't been in question for many decades. These people have been written about, depicted in media, and held up as a standard of what's "normal" in society. But if you're someone who rarely saw herself or himself in mainstream media, who felt like your true identity had to be hidden or at least only revealed in strict circumstances and to only a rare, trusted few people, then societal change is what you long for.

Your textbook authors are in the education business, not the indoctrination business; we won't dictate to you what to think, feel, or do in this chapter on gender, sexuality, and nonverbal communication. All we ask is that you approach the material with an open mind and heart, with a sincere motivation of becoming more educated on these topics so that your views will be more informed and perhaps your relationships will be enriched. Recognize too that what we discuss here will likely be in flux while you're reading it, meaning some information will go out of date quickly and other research findings will replace it. That's the world we live in now.

> "That girl over there is really hot, and she knows she's hot, too. She's not looking at anybody, but everybody's sure looking at her."
>
> "Check out that cute guy—gay or straight? Got any gaydar on him?"
>
> "We've been out a couple of times, and I keep thinking he's going to make a move, and then he doesn't. I think he's attracted to me, but I can't figure out if he's just being polite, if he's shy, or if he's 'just not that into me.'"

Sex, gender, relationships, sexuality. If those words aren't enough to pique your interest in this chapter, check your pulse.

When deciding what application chapters to write for this book, your coauthors felt that this chapter was a "no-brainer"; this topic *had* to be covered. Everyone has a sex and a gender (and we'll discuss later why those are different things), as well as relationships, ranging at different times in our lives from very casual and non-intimate to very close and intimate. But perhaps you've not stopped to think about how nonverbal communication facilitated your establishment of those relationships. Have you considered the role nonverbal communication plays in developing or deepening your relationships, keeping them going, and maybe even ending them?

For you to get the most out of this reading, we challenge you to insert people (including yourself) into the descriptions of the various relationships and experiences we explore here. Try not to read this *objectively* or at an emotional distance, as you might if you were merely preparing to be tested over the material. Read this chapter *subjectively*, putting yourself, your relationships, and your experiences into every page so you can take full advantage of this information.

We broach the important but challenging subject of sexuality in this chapter. Nonverbal cues are a critical part of how we view ourselves as sexual beings, how we communicate our sexuality to other people, and how we express how we feel about certain people in our lives. One disclaimer: Don't

4

think that by tackling the topic of sexuality and relationships we're assuming that (1) all readers are sexually active, (2) all readers are equally interested in sexuality and relationships, and (3) all readers are involved in relationships in which sexual activity may or may not be an integral part. Not everyone is part of an intimate relationship at present; some people are single and celibate. We do believe that all human beings are sexual creatures, but how you choose to express your sexuality (or not) is not subject to our judgment.

From the nonverbal cues, what's going on with this couple? Do they look like their relationship is in trouble?

EFFECTS OF SEX AND GENDER ON NONVERBAL COMMUNICATION ■ ■ ■ ■

Are the sexes more alike when it comes to nonverbal communication, or are the differences more pronounced? How can we possibly address such huge generalizations inherent in this topic? Let's first begin by getting on the same page regarding terminology; then we'll explore the sexes and nonverbal cues.

Sex Versus Gender

In the world outside the walls of your classroom, the terms *sex* and *gender* are used interchangeably. For the sake of clarity, we use them in this chapter with exclusive meanings; however, even *sex* as a form of identity has changed. The term **sex** has traditionally referred to the biological/physiological characteristics that make us female or male (Muehlenhard & Peterson, 2011). In many cases, sex is binary, meaning two choices. However, you may have heard or read about people who are born with both or mixed sets of genitalia and hormonal systems, causing complexity in determining their biological sex. The term used in the past for this occurrence was *hermaphroditism*, but the contemporary term is *intersex*. In fact, the Intersex Society of North America (ISNA) has as its primary goal to bring intersex identity out of the shadows and into the light. Through greater awareness, parents, physicians, and intersex individuals will have more choices, rather than having sex assigned to them at birth and being forced into surgeries to align them with traditional categories of male and female. Some parents are endeavoring to raise "gender neutral" or "gender creative" children whose sex isn't assigned at birth according to their physical characteristics, but their sex and gender is allowed to emerge as the child develops (Morris, 2018). We know that for some of you, this is new information—information that may make you uncomfortable. But to live in our

chapter twelve

current, complicated world, ignorance really isn't bliss. Remember in the opening case study where we encouraged you to keep an open mind?

Another complication with the term *sex* is that, at some points in this chapter, we use the term to refer to sexual activity between people. We'll try to be as clear as possible with our usage of the term.

The term **gender** refers primarily to psychological and emotional characteristics of individuals. Commonly, these characteristics pertain to masculinity, femininity, or **androgyny**—a combination of both feminine and masculine traits (Bem, 1974). But gender encompasses more than this. Like sex, gender isn't binary either; it's complicated. Gender includes the following: biological sex; personality traits and psychological makeup; attitudes, beliefs, and values; **sexual orientation** (related to the sex of a person with whom we wish to engage in sexual activity); and **gender identity** (our view of self relative to feminine, masculine, and androgynous traits, as well as our view of appropriate roles for people in society) (Ivy, 2017; Lippa, 2006).

Gender is socially and culturally constructed, meaning that it's much more extensive than the fact of being born anatomically and hormonally female, male, or intersex (Andersen & Hysock, 2010; Bosson, Vandello, & Buckner, 2019; Sloop, 2012). What's attached to or interpreted from

our biological sex is taught to us through our culture, virtually from the time we're conceived. Culture, with its evolving customs, rules, and expectations for behavior, has the power to affect our perceptions of gender. When we encounter members of other cultures (or our own culture, for that matter) who view sex and gender differently or who operate from rules that contrast with our own, the notable difference may reinforce our original conception of gender or cause it to change (Ivy, 2017).

Thinking of gender as culturally constructed allows us to change or reconstruct

Our ideas about sex and gender are taught to us early on in life, through the values of our culture.

gender, meaning that the way we view masculinity, femininity, and androgyny is not the way we *have* to view them. We can learn to understand gender differently and more broadly if we break through the boundaries of binary sex. Viewing gender through a broader lens helps us understand how nonverbal cues can be construed and realize how culture overlays such interpretations. Then we can choose to accept or reject the interpretations for ourselves. So when studying nonverbal communication, it's important to remember the biological constraints of sex and the cultural constructions of gender that have a profound effect on how we learn to express ourselves and interpret others' nonverbal cues.

REMEMBER	
Sex	Biological/physiological characteristics that make us female, male, or intersex; sexual activity between people
Gender	Our psychological and emotional characteristics
Androgyny	Combination of feminine and masculine traits
Sexual orientation	Related to the sex of persons with whom we wish to engage in sexual activity
Gender identity	View of self relative to feminine, masculine, and androgynous traits; view of appropriate roles for people in society

Sex, Gender, and Nonverbal Codes

Now that we've discussed how gender is a broader construct than sex, which makes it the more interesting concept to explore, we must now admit that this section of information will seem illogical to you. Here's why: Most of the research and literature on the topics of this chapter focus on binary biological sex, not including intersex nor psychological/cultural gender. One reason for this trend is that binary sex research is more readily accomplished than studies that include intersex individuals. People with an intersex identity are still quite closeted in most societies around the world, so they're challenging to recruit as research participants. Another reason relates to the complicated nature of gender; its interesting complications makes it harder to study than binary sex. Imagine you're a researcher: Is it easier to categorize a group of people by sex—female or male—or by gender, which involves many variables? While we would learn more from studying gender and all its complexities, studies of gender are harder to accomplish; therefore, they are less prevalent than studies of binary sex. In this section, we progress through various codes of nonverbal behavior to explore sex effects, as research has investigated them.

NONVERBAL SENDING AND RECEIVING ABILITY. Research on this topic has shown consistently that men and women have varying abilities when it comes to sending (encoding) and receiving (decoding) nonverbal cues, with women having the edge, in general. At least three explanations can be offered for the variation: (1) genetics, (2) brain functioning, and (3) modeling (i.e., socialization). In terms of genetics, biological factors affect our development, which affects our nonverbal behavior (Richmond, McCroskey, & Hickson, 2011). For example, our physicality in terms of body shape, type, and structure is genetically determined, and these characteristics affect how our physical appearance communicates to others, as well as our kinesics, such as walk, stance, gesturing behavior,

chapter twelve

and facial expression. A second explanation comes from studies that suggest that our brains function differently, in terms of how men and women process and interpret stimuli, as well as how we respond verbally and nonverbally to others, although this area of research is controversial (Baron-Cohen, 2004; Hines, 2010; Lenroot & Giedd, 2010). Some experts conclude that brain studies actually show minimal differences (indicating that the sexes' brains are more similar than different) and that these research results are used primarily to engender divisiveness and create unnecessary drama (Halpern, 2012).

In terms of the third explanation, researchers contend that children model the thoughts, emotions, and actions of others, and that this role-modeling has a powerful effect on how children see themselves in terms of sex and gender (Endendijk, Groeneveld, & Mesman, 2018; Lippa, 2006; Schofield, Parke, Castaneda, & Coltrane, 2008). These modeling experiences are most potent in childhood and adolescence, but they continue to affect us as adults, as we continue to redefine ourselves.

In American culture, women and femininity are more associated with affiliation, meaning that women are socialized to emphasize connectedness and culturally shaped to behave in ways that enhance social interaction (Mehrabian, 1981). Women and girls are generally more expressive of emotion than men and boys are, which relates to approachability and the skills of listening, responding, and connecting with others (Chaplin & Aldao, 2013; Fischer & LaFrance, 2015; Minotte, 2017; Smith, LaFrance, Knol, Tellinghuisen, & Moes, 2015). In general, women's nonverbal behaviors—from body positioning to eye and facial expressions to tone of voice—are enacted out of a motivation to be congruent with other people. Thus, women and girls have been found in studies to be better encoders of emotional information, meaning that they more readily display nonverbal cues of emotion than do men and boys (Grossard et al., 2018; Hall, 2006; Yoo & Noyes, 2016).

In contrast, men are socialized toward independence (versus interdependence), and masculinity is associated with status, power, and dominance (Abrams, Maxwell, & Belgrave, 2018; Bailey & Kelly, 2015). Men's nonverbal behaviors primarily serve the purpose of commanding attention and asserting their ideas and identities (Guerrero, Jones, & Boburka, 2006; Hess, Adams, Grammer, & Kleck, 2009; Toscano, Schubert, & Giessner, 2018). These socialization trends affect a great deal of what we are taught, from very young ages, regarding appropriate behavior.

In addition to being more nonverbally expressive than men, women tend to be more sensitive receivers and decoders of others' nonverbal cues, especially those associated with emotions (Fischer & LaFrance, 2015; Hall, 2006). On various tests of nonverbal receiving ability measured over decades of studies, girls and women typically outscore boys and men—a differential that begins in grade school and continues into adulthood. What this means is that a female advantage exists not only when it comes to expressing one's own emotions but also when interpreting others' nonverbal cues, such as processing minute facial expressions and eye behavior, attending to subtle changes in vocal cues, remembering people's appearance, and so forth (Bosson et al., 2019; Hall, Andrzejewski, & Yopchick, 2009; Rosip & Hall, 2004; Schmid Mast & Hall, 2006). This sex difference is consistent across U.S.

and non-U.S. subjects and across age groups (Dickey & Knower, 1941; Hall, 1978; Horgan, Schmid Mast, Hall, & Carter, 2004; Izard, 1971; Rosenthal, Hall, DiMatteo, Rogers, & Archer, 1979). However, two exceptions have been documented in research: Women tend to be less adept than men when it comes to decoding nonverbal expressions of anger (Rotter & Rotter, 1988; Wagner, MacDonald, & Manstead, 1986) and nonverbal cues of deception (Hall & Schmid Mast, 2008; Horgan & Smith, 2006; Lloyd, Summers, Hugenberg, & McConnell, 2018).

PROXEMICS. In Chapter 4, we defined **proxemics** as the way distance and space play a communicative role in everyday life. While proxemic behavior reflects our culture more than it does our sex, some interesting differences exist in how women and men tend to use and relate to space. Research for more than four decades has consistently shown that, in general, women's personal space bubble seems to be smaller than men's (Anand, Du Bois, Sher, & Grotkowski, 2017; Basu, 2011; Hall, 2006; Jenkins & Finneman, 2018; Li & Li, 2007; Maguire & Kinney, 2010; Morman & Whitely, 2012). Research conducted in public settings shows that female dyads stand and sit closer together than male dyads, with the male–female dyad standing and sitting the closest (Santilli & Miller, 2011). Women and girls interact with others more closely than do men and boys, and are less likely to view intrusions into their personal space as violations.

Various explanations for proxemic differences have emerged over the years. One is that males tend to be physically larger than most females and thus require more space. Another explanation relates to how children play and what they play with (Blakemore & Centers, 2005). Typically, girls play with dolls and small objects, which don't take up much room; conversely, boys play with trucks, balls, and larger objects, which encourage play away from the home and often occupy more space. As we mentioned earlier, the female orientation toward affiliation and connection also offers insight into sex differences in proxemics, in that girls and women may feel that getting physically closer to people facilitates psychological closeness. Yet another explanation relates to traditional roles for men and women in U.S. culture—meaning that, even in this day and age, women are more often the primary homemakers, men the primary breadwinners. These roles translate into women more often being in the home with children who invade their space at will, while men are more often in the public sphere, which affords more space and fewer invasions (Riesman, 1990; Wood, 1994). A final explanation is this: Since expansive, highly protected and defended spaces are correlated with higher power and status, particularly in U.S. culture, the tendency is for men to be afforded more personal space, since they hold more economic, political, and social power than do women (Henley, 2001; Ivy, 2017).

PHYSICAL APPEARANCE, ATTRACTIVENESS, CLOTHING, AND ARTIFACTS. In Chapter 5, we explored physical appearance as a significant code of nonverbal behavior, and some obvious differences exist in terms of cultural displays of biological sex. For example, in most cultures, men do not wear dresses or skirts, but there are always exceptions (such as Scottish kilts or tribal sarongs). What's more interesting for our discussion are men's and women's attitudes toward attractiveness and how their choices regarding physical appearance, clothing, and **artifacts** (temporary aspects of physical adornment other than clothing—e.g., jewelry, eyeglasses, cologne, makeup) serve as nonverbal communication.

What's the first question most people in the United States ask when they learn a baby has been born—10 fingers and 10 toes? No, usually they ask, "Boy or girl?" After the sex of the baby is determined, pink and blue clothing and accessories are often lavished on the infant (as well as a whole array of sex-typed behavior; Fagot, Rodgers, & Leinbach, 2000; Ivy, 2017; Tskhay & Rule, 2016). Girls dressed in blue don't face as much ridicule as boys in pink, but for infants, the colored clothing serves as a nonverbal cue to people who wouldn't otherwise be able to detect the sex of the infant (Koller, 2008).

In U.S. culture, as well as many cultures around the world, more emphasis is placed on the physical attractiveness of females than that of males. Girls are given toys related to appearance more often than boys are. Grooming sets (toy brushes, combs, and mirrors), makeup and manicure kits, tutus and other dress-up items, and dolls with endless outfits and accessories can communicate an "appearance is everything" message to young girls (Dittmar, 2010; Forman-Brunell & Whitney, 2015; Weisgram & Dinella, 2018). Is the most important thing about G.I. Joe the outfits he wears?

We know that culture influences clothing choices and trends, but another function of clothing can be to reveal the sex of the wearer.

While clothing has become more generic, fashions for men and women still differ significantly in most cultures around the world. Clothing for men primarily serves as body protection, cultural display, and, for many, an extension of their personalities. Men's clothing and artifacts are less often chosen for their conveyance of masculinity and ability to attract others, but for women, clothing can be an extension of their sexuality and a device for attracting attention. This emphasis has an obvious downside: compromised safety. As Fixmer-Oraiz and Wood (2018) explain, "Most women's shoes are designed to flatter legs at the cost of health, comfort, and safety—how fast can you run in stilettos?" (p. 120).

Volumes have been written on the subject of the sexes and the pressure to be physically attractive; it's beyond the parameters of this chapter to explore it in greater depth. But think about the heat men and women take in American culture when it comes to their appearance: For example, are we as critical of overweight men as we are of overweight women? Granted, anyone can be made to feel bad about her or his weight, fitness, health, and attractiveness nowadays, but research suggests (and we agree) that women feel more intense pressure to be physically attractive than do men (Agthe,

Sporrle, & Maner, 2010; Amon, 2015; Arroyo & Harwood, 2012; Calogero, Pina, & Sutton, 2013; Darlow & Lobel, 2010; Quick, McWilliams, & Byrd-Bredbenner, 2013).

KINESICS. In Chapter 6 we explored **kinesics**, or the study of human movement, gestures, and posture. With regard to movement in general, researchers have obtained mixed results when observing members of both sexes. Some studies have found that men tend to be more active (or restless), in that they move and gesture more than women, which runs opposite to the stereotype that most women couldn't talk if you tied their hands together. Yet other studies have found that women tend to use more gestures than men do (Hall, 2006). What may distinguish the sexes is not the amount of gesturing but the type of gesture or the intention behind its use. Men often use commanding gestures

In American culture, do you think women are judged more harshly for being overweight than men?

for the purpose of indicating dominance, while women more often use gestures in acquiescence or affiliation with other people (Richmond et al., 2011). For example, you're more likely to see a man use a pointing gesture to emphasize a statement, while a woman is more likely to use a palms-up or other less confrontational gesture to say the same thing.

In terms of walking behavior, some sex differences have been detected (Halovic & Kroos, 2018; Moore, Hickson, & Stacks, 2013). For example, nonverbal communication scholar Peter Andersen (2004) explains that men's bodies are somewhat motionless while walking, in that their hips and torso tend to stay facing frontward, their feet move about one foot apart in stride, and their arms swing significantly. In contrast, women have more sway or side-to-side motion in their walks. Women's hips tend to move more than men's, mostly due to the fact that women often put one foot in front of the other when walking, which engages the hips more.

As we discussed in the kinesics chapter, sex differences in sitting behavior have also been observed with regularity in American culture. Typically, men assume open sitting positions, meaning that their legs are often extended and spread apart rather than close together. You may remember in Chapter 6 our description of "manspreading," which occurs when men sit with their legs so far apart that they take up two seats (Petter, 2017; Schuler, 2017). A man is more likely to cross his leg over his other knee in a 90-degree angle to the floor, while a woman is more likely to cross her legs

chapter twelve

at the knee, with the crossed leg hanging down, or to cross her legs at the ankles (Andersen, 2004; Hall, 2006). While some women like the comfort of the 90-degree, crossed-leg position, sitting this way tends to give off a masculine vibe.

FACIAL AND EYE EXPRESSIONS. A subset of kinesics, the facial and eye expressions of the sexes have long been a fascination of nonverbal research. A key difference between women and men has been detected in how often and why they smile. A comprehensive review of more than 400 studies revealed that women smile more than men (LaFrance, Hecht, & Levy Paluck, 2003). Women tend to use more facial animation than men do; they smile as a common facial expression in social interaction, whereas men's smiles are more purposeful and used to reveal their emotions (Ellis, 2006; Fischer & LaFrance, 2015; Guéguen, 2008; Hess et al., 2009; Vatsa & Lata, 2012; Wang, Mao, Li, & Liu, 2017).

In terms of eye contact, research with American subjects shows some sex differences in that women tend to maintain more eye contact in conversation than men do; men tend to hold eye gaze while they are speaking but not while listening (Hall, 2006; Tang & Schmeichel, 2015; Weick, McCall, & Blascovich, 2017). As we explained in Chapter 7, in research terms this is called the **visual dominance ratio**, which is the amount of time spent looking while speaking versus looking while listening (Hall, 2006; Koch, Baehne, Kruse, Zimmermann, & Zumbach, 2010). Individuals, particularly men, who wish to assert dominance will make eye contact when they have something to say but break eye contact when spoken to. However, the athletics context may be an exception to this trend, in that athletes often make direct, continuous eye contact with opponents as a way of "psyching them out" and asserting their dominance (Pearson, 1985). Ever seen two prize fighters face off before a fight and stare each other down?

© Makistock/Shutterstock.com

These people display typical eye behavior for the sexes; the woman's gaze is geared toward the man while the man's gaze is more generalized.

TOUCH (HAPTICS). The study of touch behavior in humans and animals is often referred to as **haptics**, as we explored in depth in Chapter 8. Studies document some sex differences in terms of how women and men give and receive touch. Research has produced mixed results regarding affection between parents and male versus female children (Aznar & Tenenbaum, 2016). While some research has found that, in general, parents extend more affection to daughters than to sons and that touches they extend to daughters are more gentle (Condry, Condry, & Pogatshnik, 1983; Lindsey & Mize, 2001), other research has not detected this differential, nor has it seen any differences in benefits for male or female children who receive affection from either a same-sex or opposite-sex parent (Schrodt, Ledbetter, & Ohrt, 2007).

Many nonverbal researchers have deemed touch more of a "female-appropriate" behavior, primarily because studies from the 1970s to the present have concluded the following: (1) Women express more nonverbal affection than men do; (2) women receive more touch, from both men and other women, than men do; (3) women engage in more frequent and more intimate same-sex touch than men do; (4) women are more comfortable with touch in general and same-sex touch in specific than men are; (5) women in heterosexual stable or married relationships are more likely to initiate touch than their male partners are; and (6) women perceive themselves as being more affectionate than men (Andersen & Leibowitz, 1978; Bombar & Littig, 1996; Bowman & Compton, 2014; Burgoon & Bacue, 2003; Burgoon & Walther, 1990; Derlega, Lewis, Harrison, Winstead, & Costanza, 1989; Emmers & Dindia, 1995; Floyd, 1997, 2000; Floyd & Morman, 1997; Greenbaum & Rosenfeld, 1980; Guerrero & Floyd, 2006; Hall & Veccia, 1990; Harjunen, Spape, Ahmed, Jacucci, & Ravaja, 2017; Harrison & Shortall, 2011; Jones, 1986; Major, Schmidlin, & Williams, 1990; Roese, Olson, Borenstein, Martin, & Shores, 1992; Wallace, 1981; Willis & Rawdon, 1994).

VOCALICS (PARALANGUAGE). The study of how people express themselves through their voices is termed **vocalics**, sometimes referred to as **paralanguage**. Some sex differences in vocal production can be attributed to physiology, meaning how male and female vocal anatomy is structured and the influence of hormones on its functioning. But physiology doesn't tell the whole story. Granted, men's typically thicker vocal folds produce lower pitches, and changes in hormones (specifically, a depletion of estrogen as women age) deepen the average pitch of female voices (Banai, 2017; Eichorn, Kent, Austin, & Vorperian, 2017; Feinberg et al., 2006; Frank, Maroulis, & Griffin, 2013; Stathopoulos, Huber, & Sussman, 2011). But cultural/societal factors (and resulting stereotypes) affect voice production as well; men have been socialized not to use higher pitches, lest they be ridiculed for sounding feminine (Albert et al., 2018; Cartei & Reby, 2012). Masculinity is associated with greater volume, while femininity is associated with a softer-sounding voice, but men and women are equally capable of generating volume when they want to or the situation demands. See how the stereotypes come into play?

One ill effect that stems from the pitch tendency is a monotone problem. Men often go monotone when giving presentations, which can be deadly for an audience. Perhaps men should experiment with more vocal variety for the sake of their listeners, in everyday conversation as well as presentations to audiences, because a modicum of variety is pleasant to the ear (Montano, Tigue, Isenstein, Barclay, & Feinberg, 2017; O'Connor & Barclay, 2017, 2018). Women might do well to monitor their vocal variety, listening for an appropriate use of variation, because too much variation can sound "sing-songy" and diminish credibility.

Proxemics	The way distance and space play a communicative role in everyday life
Artifacts	Temporary aspects of physical adornment other than clothing (e.g., jewelry, eyeglasses, cologne, makeup)
Kinesics	Study of human movement, gestures, and posture
Visual dominance ratio	Amount of time spent looking while speaking versus looking while listening
Haptics	Study of touch behavior in humans and animals
Vocalics (paralanguage)	Study of how people express themselves through their voices

NONVERBAL CUES IN INTIMATE RELATIONSHIPS

Relationships: fascinating, compelling, satisfying, mystifying, thrilling, terrifying, puzzling. For most of us, relationships are what give us life's greatest joy. Sure, we may like our work, enjoy sports, and have hobbies, but if asked what makes life most worth living, the majority of us would answer "other people." So let's start this section on the premise that relationships of all types—family members, friends, coworkers, intimate loved ones—create both satisfaction and frustration in our lives. Given the importance of relationships, it's only natural that we should study the role of nonverbal communication in the initiation, maintenance, and sometimes even termination of relationships.

Many relationships can be intimate, such as those with close friends, family members, and possibly even coworkers, ministers, therapists, attorneys, doctors, or bosses, because the quality of the relationship and the communication within it is of an intimate nature. Because this topic is huge, we've chosen to focus only on the romantic or loving intimate relationship, which may or may not be sexual. What exactly do we mean by intimacy? Couples therapist Jeffrey Fine (2001) defines it this way: "To be intimate is to be totally transparent, emotionally naked in front of another who is equally transparent. You want to see into the other's heart. What people should mean when they say *intimacy* is in-to-me-see" (p. 225). Whether or not you currently have an intimate relationship in your life, these relationships are what most of us seek and hope to experience in our lifetimes; so it's important to consider the role of nonverbal cues in this context.

Relationship Initiation

It may sound old-fashioned, but the activity of getting a relationship going is termed **courtship** in research; a more common term is *dating* (Moore, 2010; Stafford, 2010). However, we realize that few of our college students today actually call their social or relational activity *dating*, preferring such language as *hanging out*, *talking*, *seeing each other* (which is a bit passé), *gayting* (for gay couples), or, if sex is involved, *hooking up* (which typically doesn't lead to a long-term, intimate relationship). To understand this subject better, we rely on the longstanding work of Albert Scheflen (1965), who studied interpersonal encounters and noted patterns of nonverbal behavior over time—patterns that formed into a courtship ritual. (Scheflen's observations were about Western cultures in particular, so understand that courtship in African or Middle-Eastern cultures, for example, is enacted differently.)

Scheflen distinguished between **courtship,** which he defined as romantic attraction and an interest in some form of sexual intimacy, and **quasi-courtship behavior**, which he was much keener on and known for among nonverbal scholars. To make it confusing, the same set of behaviors can indicate courtship—a more serious level of interest—as well as quasi-courtship, in which behavior is flirtatious and not to be taken seriously. Scheflen believed that quasi-courtship behavior is useful, in that it can breathe life into dull interactions or settings, or reinvigorate someone's waning attention. But problems can arise if someone interprets nonverbal cues as courtship while someone else views the behavior as harmless flirtation or seduction—with no intention of forming a deeper connection (Yeomans, 2009). The onus is on the receiver of such nonverbal cues to judge the motivation or intent of the behavior, as to whether it indicates serious interest or "just kidding around" or "having fun." Guerrero and Floyd (2006) contend that "there is often little distinction in the flirtation behaviors used by courters and quasi-courters; where the groups differ is often only in the eventual outcomes they seek" (p. 81).

Scheflen's quasi-courtship ritual includes four categories or stages, summarized in Table 12.1. First are *courtship readiness* cues, or the ways we nonverbally communicate to others that we're open to being approached. Women and men alike engage in these behaviors, which include erect posture (no slouching), having alert eyes and a lifted chin, higher general muscle tone, and a tucked-in stomach. In this phase, we accentuate our best physical features instead of camouflaging or downplaying them, so as to attract people to us. In the second category, *preening behavior* occurs, which involves self-adaptors such as stroking, twirling, or moving our hair; fixing

Multiple nonverbal cues emerge when people are physically and/or sexually attracted to each other.

chapter twelve

TABLE 12.1 Scheflen's Quasi-Courtship Behavior

STAGE	DESCRIPTION	NONVERBAL CUES
Stage 1: Courtship readiness	Cues of approachability; behavior that shows readiness for an interpersonal encounter	Erect posture, alert eyes, high muscle tone, tight stomach, emphasized physical features
Stage 2: Preening	Use of self-adaptors	Touching hair, fixing makeup, touching clothing
Stage 3: Positional cues	Partitioning oneself toward someone and away from others	Blocking proxemics, kinesics that hold someone's focus and that keep him or her away from others
Stage 4: Actions of appeal or invitation	Cues that suggest progress toward a more intimate, private encounter	Extended eye gaze; exposing the skin; rolling the pelvis; muscle flexing; revealing wrists, palms, and neck

makeup (especially when women reapply lipstick; Netchaeva & Ress, 2016); smoothing or rearranging clothing (e.g., tugging on a bra strap, adjusting a tie); checking ourselves in a mirror; and unbuttoning or leaving unbuttoned parts of shirts or blouses.

In the third phase, *positional cues* partition us toward someone and away from others. We can see this happen at social gatherings where people use proxemics as well as their arms, legs, and sitting/standing positions to section themselves off from a group, thereby signaling interest in each other and creating a barrier to ward off in-

© Burlingham/ Shutterstock.com

Positional cues of quasi-courtship can be subtle or obvious, as we nonverbally signal interest in a person and close others off from interaction.

truders. Scheflen termed his fourth phase *actions of appeal or invitation*. These actions typically occur later in the ritual and involve more engaged behaviors, such as holding eye gaze longer than in previous phases; looking at a partner flirtatiously (e.g., looking down, then back up quickly and repeatedly; looking at facial and body parts other than the eyes; "batting" the eyelashes); exposing more of the skin (e.g., rolling up sleeves, removing jackets, shifting or crossing the legs to expose a thigh); rolling the pelvis forward (which sounds odd but is a subtle, subconscious move that reveals attraction); flexing muscles or moving in a way that emphasizes those body parts we're most proud of or that will arouse our partner; and revealing the wrists, palms, or neck (which are considered fairly intimate body parts at this stage in a relationship).

Other systems for understanding courtship behavior have been developed. Birdwhistell (1970) described 24 steps in the male-female "courtship dance"; Morris (1971) developed a 12-step typology for courtship that, like Birdwhistell's steps, begins with initial contact and proceeds through sexual intimacy. One of our favorite approaches to understanding heterosexual courtship comes from British psychologist Peter Collett, who provided commentary for years on the BBC's equivalent of the *Big Brother* TV show. As he explains in his work, *The Book of Tells*, Collett (2004) views nonverbal cues as **tells**—highly informative attributes or actions that reveal a great deal about a person. (If you're a poker player, you'll recognize the language of "tells" immediately.) Of the heterosexual courting context, Collett explains:

> When it comes to romance, men like to think that they're the ones who make the first move and who decide how fast the relationship should progress. All the research on human courtship shows that this is simply not the case. . . . In nightclubs, bars and at parties, it's the woman who invariably makes the first move. She does this by producing an approach tell—a signal which is not too explicit, but which is sufficiently clear to show a man that he may approach her. It's her way of giving him "clearance." (p. 253)

Another approach to this topic of relationship initiation is to examine nonverbal behaviors relevant to **flirting,** or the act of attracting romantic attention, whether conveyed online, in face-to-face contexts, or through text messaging (Punyanunt-Carter & Wagner, 2018; Toma & D'Angelo, 2017). Studies on flirtation have found upwards of 50 gestures and related nonverbal cues that people use to signal their interest (Hall, 2016; Hall, Carter, Cody, & Albright, 2010; Hall & Xing, 2015; Hall, Xing, & Brooks, 2015; Kaspar & Krull, 2013; Meenagh, 2015; Speer, 2017). Among the top flirting cues these studies identified are smiling; surveying a crowded room with the eyes; increased proxemics; prolonged and mutual eye gaze; brief, darting glances; looking at specific body features of another person; animated facial expressions; touching behavior (both purposeful and accidental touches); head tosses (sometimes including the infamous "hair flip"); caressing objects such as a glass or keys; movement to music (not dancing but keeping time to some rhythm one hears); animated vocal inflection, increased rate of speaking, and changes in volume (louder voices to command attention, whispered voices to convey intimacy); and the adjustment of clothing.

Research has found that men tend to view flirting as more sexual than women do; heterosexual men often misinterpret women's friendly behaviors as signs of sexual attraction and interest (Haselton, 2003; Henningsen, 2004; Henningsen, Henningsen, & Valde, 2006; Henningsen, Kartch, Orr, & Brown, 2009; Koeppel, Montagne, O'Hair, & Cody, 1999; Koukounas & Letch, 2001; LaFrance, Henningsen, Oates, & Shaw, 2009; Mongeau, Serewicz, & Thierren, 2004; Moore, 2002). The likelihood of this kind of misinterpretation greatly increases as alcohol consumption increases (Abbey, Zawacki, & Buck, 2005; Delaney & Gluade, 1990).

Intimacy	An experience involving emotions and perceptions of understanding within a relationship characterized by affection and trust
Courtship (dating)	Process of trying to get a relationship going; romantic attraction and an interest in some form of sexual intimacy
Quasi-courtship behavior	Patterns of nonverbal communication that form a ritual of flirtatious behavior
Tells	Highly informative attributes or actions that reveal a great deal about a person
Flirting	Act of attracting romantic attention

Relationship Maintenance

Once a romantic or intimate relationship has been launched, it's equally (if not more) challenging to maintain it. What codes of nonverbal communication strengthen an intimate relationship? Perhaps the nonverbal code most relevant to such a relationship is touch. Physical affection is critical to the success of romantic relationships, the development of intimacy, and satisfaction with one's partner (Hall, 2011; Hesse & Mikkelson, 2017; Horan & Booth-Butterfield, 2010, 2013; Kim, Feeney, & Jakubiak, 2018; Luerssen, Jhita, & Ayduk, 2017; Miller, Denes, Diaz, & Buck, 2014; Rancourt, MacKinnon, Snowball, & Rosen, 2017).

Jones and Yarbrough's (1985) three categories of touch integral to intimacy are helpful here. The first category is *inclusion touch,* which refers to sustained touches that draw attention to the fact that two people are together and in a relationship. These touches mostly involve the lower body parts, such as sitting hip to hip with someone or entwining the legs. The second category, *sexual touch,* includes touches that convey attraction and sexual interest, such as caresses or prolonged holds that involve multiple body parts and typically move from one part of the body to another. The third category is termed *affection touch,* because such actions as placing a hand on a shoulder or squeezing someone's arm in a positive way communicate affection between the parties. Affection touches are just that—pure affection—they don't convey inclusion or sexual interest. Touches in each of the three categories foster an intimate relationship.

Research suggests that touch and several other nonverbal cues tend to be more prevalent in the beginning stages of a relationship (relationship escalation), as opposed to the middle or latter stages (Jakubiak & Feeney, 2017; Punyanunt-Carter, 2004). People in long-term relationships, including marriages, tend to touch each other less frequently and less intimately than people who are working to establish a romantic relationship or to repair one that's in trouble (Debrot, Meuwly, Muise, Impett, & Schoebi, 2017; Patterson, Gardner, Burr, Hubler, & Roberts, 2012; Spott, Pyle, & Punyanunt-Carter, 2010).

Other nonverbal codes besides touch are critical to the successful maintenance of an intimate relationship. Four important cues are interpersonal distance, body lean, body orientation, and the physical plane (meaning the vertical and horizontal distance between people; Andersen, Guerrero,

Your Cheatin' Voice

Have you ever heard that old Hank Williams' song, Your Cheatin' Heart? The refrain in the song goes "Your cheatin' heart will tell on you." The point is that people who cheat on their intimate relational partners usually "fess up" or get exposed for their infidelity. A team of researchers, Susan Hughes and Marissa Harrison, examined whether people could identify cheaters just by the sound of their voices.

Hughes and Harrison (2017) asked study participants to rate voice samples (controlled by attractiveness of sound, age, pitch, and other acoustic qualities) by likelihood to cheat on an intimate partner. In some instances, participants knew that the person behind the voice had cheated on a past partner, meaning subjects were "set up" to perceive the person behind the voice as a cheater. In other instances, no such knowledge of the people behind the voices was given. Hughes and Harrison also manipulated the pitch of the voice samples, moving the voices to lower registers; they then examined the results according to male versus female voices.

As expected, participants rated the voices of those people identified as past cheaters as being highly likely to cheat again on a partner. Female participants in the study were more likely to attach cheating to voices than male participants. Male voices received higher ratings as cheaters, compared to female voices, except when the pitch was manipulated. People in the voice samples with lower than average pitches for both male and female voices were perceived as cheaters, compared with pitches perceived as "typical" or "normal" for each sex.

What can be learned from this study? As we said in Chapter 9, vocalic nonverbal cues are the hardest to control because they are so connected to our physiology, meaning they're affected by hormones, breath control, muscle tension, heart beat, etc. Thus, it's highly likely that listeners pick up on unintended vocal cues and link them to negative perceptions, like a sense that someone is being deceptive or unfaithful. Perhaps because lower pitches in both men and women are associated with sexiness, people connect sexuality—even infidelity—with low tones.

Want to know more about this study? If so, check out Hughes, S. M., & Harrison, M. A. (2017). Your cheatin' voice will tell on you: Detection of past infidelity from voice. *Evolutionary Psychology, 15*, 1-12.

& Jones, 2006). Interpersonal distance means the physical space between partners; research shows that people tend to sit closer to their romantic partners than to their friends (Sluzki, 2016; Szpak, Nicholls, Thomas, Laham, & Loetsher, 2016). Forward lean, a face-to-face body orientation, and interacting on the same physical plane (as opposed to above or below someone) are all associated with enhanced intimacy (Andersen et al., 2006). Kinesic behaviors such as smiling, facial animation, general facial pleasantness, increased eye contact, and synchronized gestures of immediacy, affection, closeness, and warmth are all important in an intimate relationship (Petrician, Todorov, Burris, Rosenbaum, & Grady, 2015; Tickle-Degnen, 2006). As people remain intimate over time, they tend to mimic or acquire each other's nonverbal behaviors, such that they come to look, sound, and behave alike.

WHAT WOULD *YOU* DO?

Desiree is heterosexual; her live-in boyfriend of almost 3 years, Justin, is bisexual. Desiree has always been accepting of Justin's sexual orientation, provided their romantic relationship stays monogamous. Thus far, their relationship is progressing. Desiree has always understood that Justin is one of those people who is attracted to members of both sexes; his attraction to men has never made Desiree feel insecure—it just *is*.

But lately—over the past six months or so—Justin has become distant. Desiree and Justin rarely have sex anymore, much less touch, other than the perfunctory kiss as they head out the door for the day or say goodnight before bed. Desiree comes from a "touchy" family and considers herself an affectionate person—one who gives touch freely and who needs affection from her significant other—so she's feeling a bit lonely and confused. She wonders if the change in Justin is simply related to external factors (e.g., stress at work, demands of a busy life) and not their relationship. In the back of her mind, a little voice makes her wonder if Justin has lost interest in her and, worse, if he's gained interest in someone else. Much as she's tried to fight it, some insecurity related to Justin's bisexuality has cropped up in her mind, as Desiree has begun to worry that Justin's sexual needs might be getting met by a man in his life. She's beginning to wonder about just how open she really is to Justin's sexuality. If Justin is involved with someone else, where does that leave their relationship?

If you were Desiree's friend and counseling her in this situation, *what would you do*? Are her feelings of loneliness over the loss of closeness justified, such that she has a right to confront Justin about what's going on, if anything? Is it understandable that Desiree's insecurity is heightened because of Justin's sexual orientation, or is this a form of discrimination? Would you advise Desiree to try some nonverbal means of fixing the situation, such as increasing her affection to Justin in hopes that he will get the hint and reciprocate? Or might you tell her just to wait out the situation, hoping that as stress reduces, Justin will become affectionate again?

Certain vocal behaviors are associated with intimacy and demonstrations of affection between partners (Farley, Hughes, & LaFayette, 2013). In terms of pitch, research shows that high-pitched female voices and low-pitched male voices communicate affection, rather than the reverse; for both sexes, varying the pitch (i.e., avoiding a monotone delivery) conveys affection as well (Collins & Missing, 2003; Floyd & Ray, 2003). Vocal pleasantness and warmth, as well as laughter, communicate affection between intimates (Montano et al., 2017).

Relational Conflict and Relationship Dissolution

Some people believe that if we've ever had a connection to someone, that relationship supersedes time—meaning that there's no such thing as an ending to a relationship, because these connections and their impact on us are too profound to be considered "terminated." Others believe that many, if not most, relationships end at some point or another but that the truly intimate ones transcend everything, even death. No matter our view of relationship dissolution—lofty, existential, pragmatic, spiritual—nonverbal communication plays a role in the final cycle of relationship development as well as in the initiation and maintenance phases. We approach this topic in two sections: First, let's examine nonverbal cues and conflict, with the understanding that conflict is inevitable and can be constructive in a relationship; it doesn't necessarily signal a relationship's demise (Beebe, Beebe, & Ivy, 2019). But conflict is usually present in a relationship that's on its last legs. Second, let's focus on nonverbal communication and the "parting of ways."

RELATIONAL CONFLICT. Not surprisingly, nonverbal cues are ever-present in conflict situations, often appearing prior to verbal cues (Guerrero, 2013; Patterson et al., 2012). Conflict is wide-ranging, in that it can take the form of a simple disagreement without much emotional toll, an

ongoing feud with patterns of emergent nonverbal cues, or all the way up to a full-blown, knock-down, drag-out fight, with all the heightened nonverbal cues to boot. Many conflicts take place over the phone, through text messaging, via e-mail, and through social media use, but for simplicity's sake, we frame this discussion around face-to-face conflict.

If we were to ask you what romantic relational partners look and sound like when they fight, you might begin with the nonverbal category of proxemics, because couples in conflict use distance in interesting ways.

Nonverbal cues associated with conflict in an intimate relationship are pretty easy to spot; note the rigid body positions, lack of eye contact, and distance between these two guys.

chapter twelve

The most obvious use of proxemic cues is to put physical distance (that parallels the psychological or emotional distance partners feel) between us and our partner (Guerrero & Floyd, 2006). The reverse behavior—getting in someone's face when arguing—is also prevalent, as we decrease distance to appear menacing or gain some sort of advantage. Sometimes we leave the scene of the conflict altogether, preferring time and distance before we can approach our partners again. However, a withdrawal or avoidant response to conflict is seldom effective (Burrell, Allen, Gayle, & Preiss, 2014; Samp, 2016).

Another relevant nonverbal cue related to proxemics is touch—its decrease or absence, or touch that is increasingly controlling, overbearing, or even abusive. When we're in conflict with an intimate partner, most of us decrease our affectionate touch with that person as we increase our distance from him or her (Guerrero, 2013). Even once a conflict has been resolved, it may be hard for partners to express affection toward each other, because the sting of the conflict still hangs in the air.

In terms of touch turned abusive in a conflict, it's beyond our scope here to provide a full discussion of dating or intimate partner violence. But we know that in the heat of an argument, men and women alike may let touch escalate into physical violence when their emotions get out of control. Touches that are extended with more force than usual in a relationship can definitely be characterized as abusive (Ivy, 2017).

What other nonverbal cues are typically present in conflict situations? For some of us, our energy builds to such a degree in an argument that our gestures fly about uncontrollably; others of us pace and gesture in a repetitive fashion, often pointing accusingly at our partner while placing a hand on our chest to signify that we're blameless. A common gesture, besides pointing, is raising the arms up, bent at the elbows, with palms facing out, as if to say, "Stop, I can't take any more" or "Back off." Some of us can't sit and argue—we have to stand, as though towering over our partners will give us an edge.

Facial expressions are usually animated in conflict, although some of us put on a stony face and stay that way until the conflict is over. Some of us use continuous eye contact—staring as though we want to burn a hole into our partner—while others break eye contact in an argument, preferring to look down or stare off into space (Tang & Schmeichel, 2015; Weick et al., 2017). These behaviors are highly individualistic; they depend on the person, the situation, the relationship, and the level of intensity of the conflict.

Vocalic behaviors in conflict are very revealing but, again, quite individualistic. Some of us are vocally aggressive; the more intense the conflict, the faster our rate of speaking, the greater the volume, the more varied the pitch, and the longer our turns at talk. Heightened vocalic cues rarely diffuse a conflict; they tend to escalate it. Others of us have learned the value of the pause and use a dramatic volume, pitch, and rate decrease to reveal the intensity of our emotions. Still others "suffer in silence," preferring not to engage vocally at all in an argument (Cheng & Tardy, 2010; Hocker & Wilmot, 2017). But sometimes an even, calm way of speaking can enrage a partner because it seems manipulative and controlling.

So if we want to improve our conflict-management skills, what does research suggest we do nonverbally? The research offers eight helpful suggestions:

1. Realize that alcohol and conflict don't mix. Research indicates that people who drink when attempting to discuss a relational problem and mediate conflict experience heightened agitation and less positivity toward their partner and the relationship, plus increased erratic behavior (Samp, 2016).

2. Understand that emotion is almost always a factor in conflict; our nonverbal communication will be affected by the emotion we feel during a disagreement or argument (Qin & Andreychik, 2013). It's wise to inventory ourselves in terms of how anger affects our nonverbal cues and then work to mediate those displays so we don't lose it in conflict situations and we can make constructive conflict out of what potentially could be destructive.

3. It's important to monitor our nonverbal behaviors, as well as those of the person (or people) involved in the conflict, rather than getting completely caught up in what's being said.

4. Demonstrating our involvement in conflict resolution means that we show nonverbally that we're in the situation, not checked out of it (Aldeis & Afifi, 2015). Silence rarely resolves anything, and so it's a good idea to speak calmly and normally, modulating the rate, volume, and pitch of our voice; avoid interrupting our partner; and consider the timing of an apology offered to our partner (Cheng & Tardy, 2010; Ebesu Hubbard, Hendrickson, Fehrenbach, & Sur, 2013).

5. Condescending or irritating cues such as eye rolling, accompanied by a "hmmph" or "tsk" vocalization, are clear signals of disdain that won't help mediate or resolve a conflict.

6. We should use direct eye contact but at normal levels—not staring or avoiding gaze, which send negative signals.

7. Maintaining a calm facial expression and body position, and placing ourselves physically on the same plane as the other person so we don't give off power cues are also effective behaviors.

8. Maintaining a respectful, non-antagonistic distance from our partner in conflict is advisable, recognizing that movements toward or away send definite signals and will likely not help diffuse the conflict (Beebe et al., 2019).

RELATIONSHIP DISSOLUTION. So what happens, nonverbally speaking, when a relationship tanks? Communication scholars Knapp, Vangelisti, and Caughlin (2013) provide a five-stage framework for relationship disengagement (de-escalation), summarized in Table 12.2. A couple may enter one or more stages of the de-escalation process, only to revive their relationship and save it from termination. In general, the stages are characterized by avoidance and increased distance, so nonverbal cues related to general avoidance pertain to the phases.

Knapp, Vangelisti, and Caughlin's (2013) first stage, *differentiating*, occurs when the differences between relational partners begin to outweigh the similarities. At this point, partners' identities as individuals become more important than their identity as a couple. Nonverbally, partners begin to increase physical distance, use fewer affirming cues (e.g., smiling, head nodding, forward body lean, direct body orientation), and decrease both public and private touch. In the second stage, *circumscribing*, partners become superficial in their communication with each other and generally are more restrictive in their nonverbal expressions of emotion and affection. If we were at a party and saw a couple in this phase of their relationship, we could hardly tell from their verbal and nonverbal communication that they were a couple.

Stagnating is the third stage, in which communication virtually stops and nonverbal behaviors of closeness and affiliation (e.g., eye contact, physical proximity, touch, facial expressiveness, vocal engagement) shut down. Couples are rarely seen in public together, and when they are, distance and lack of nonverbal engagement are obvious.

The fourth stage of relationship de-escalation is *avoiding*, in which couples physically separate and aren't seen in public together anymore. They tend to avoid going places where they might run into each other; almost all communication ceases. In the final phase, *terminating*, couples end their relationship. While we don't encourage you to stage a breakup just to study the relevant nonverbal cues, it's fascinating to explore how nonverbal cues change as an intimate relationship comes apart.

What does the different spacing between the Obamas and the Trumps communicate about these relationships?

TABLE 12.2 Knapp, Vangelisti, and Caughlin's Stages of Relationship Disengagement

STAGE	DESCRIPTION	NONVERBAL CUES
Stage 1: Differentiating	Differences between partners begin to outweigh similarities.	Increased distance, fewer affirming cues, decreased touch
Stage 2: Circumscribing	Superficial communication and restricted expressions of emotion and affection occur.	Significantly increased distance, few affiliative cues (e.g., facial and vocal expressiveness)
Stage 3: Stagnating	Verbal communication and nonverbal cues of closeness cease.	Little to no touch, almost nonexistent facial and vocal expressiveness
Stage 4: Avoiding	Couples experience physical separation.	Little to no contact, pains taken to avoid partner
Stage 5: Terminating	Couples end their relationship.	No contact, pains taken to avoid partner

NONVERBAL CUES AND SEXUALITY ▪ ▪ ▪

Did the word *sexuality* in the heading of this section catch your eye when you were paging through the chapter, trying to decide what to read and what to skip (er, we mean *postpone* reading for another time)? What exactly do we mean by "sexuality"—how you view yourself as a sexual being? Your sexual orientation? How you express yourself sexually? Your attitudes about sexual activity? Here's our answer: all of the above. There's no way to do a full treatment of this topic here; volumes of books are written on it, and entire TV and radio shows are dedicated to it—not to mention the pornography industry—because sexuality has fascinated human beings since the beginning of time. So what might we possibly add to the discussion?

Our purpose in this final section of the chapter is to overview or hit the high points regarding nonverbal cues and the communication of sexuality. Some of the language you'll read in this section may not be what you're used to seeing in your college textbooks, but we ask you to forge ahead with us for the greater purpose of learning something, rather than feeling embarrassed, shocked, or offended by language you may be unaccustomed to reading. Let's begin by defining a few key terms that will be critical to our discussion.

Sexuality and Sexual Orientation

The online Encarta World English Dictionary offers three definitions for **sexuality**: (1) the state of being sexual, (2) involvement or interest in sexual activity, and (3) sexual appeal or potency. In their

chapter twelve

book on human sexuality, authors Shibley Hyde and DeLamater (2010) explain the complexity of conceptualizing sexuality, given that research on this topic is hampered by a narrow view that tends to focus on how sex is accomplished, how often, and, to a lesser degree, with what effect. They call for a broader conceptualization of sexuality, with an emphasis on **outercourse** instead of intercourse—one that includes the role of thought, emotions, psychological factors (such as aversion or inhibition), identity, and sociocultural factors (such as social norms, family influences, and access to information). For the purposes of clarity in our discussion here, let's view **sexuality** as including sexual behavior, as well as cognitive, emotional, and psychosociocultural factors.

We can operate from the assumption that all human beings are sexual creatures, but the choice of how to communicate our sexuality, if we choose to do so at all, is very individualistic. How do we convey the sexual part of our being? Granted, some of us believe in abstinence, meaning we hold the belief that sexual activity should occur only within the confines of a monogamous, committed partnering, such as marriage. Just because we're not *having* sex doesn't necessarily mean we don't express our sexuality. But how does a person nonverbally convey who she or he is sexually?

This won't surprise you one bit: Physical appearance (which includes attractiveness as well as choices about clothing and artifacts) is the most central nonverbal code related to sexuality. Physical features that we're born with, that we influence by eating right (or not) and working out (or not), that may be altered by illness or accident, and that we accentuate are key conveyors of sexual information. Secondarily, all the things we do to enhance our physical appearance and attractiveness—from clothing choices to alterations of our hair, skin, and bodies, and adornments such as tattoos, piercings, and jewelry—send sexual messages to other people, whether we intend to do so or not.

All the other nonverbal codes can relate to sexuality as well. For example, aspects of kinesics such as our walk, stance, and posture (i.e., how we "carry" ourselves) may attract others to us because we look confident. Or these cues may repel others because we look as though we're carrying the weight of the whole world on our shoulders. Some nonverbal cues are flirtatious, such as the way we use eye contact to show interest in another person, how closely we sit or stand by someone in conversation, how we animate our facial expressions, what kind of touch occurs between us and other people, and how our vocal inflection reveals our interest. All these elements reveal our sexuality, even if acting sexy or seeking sexual activity is not our intent.

A key element within the larger construct of sexuality is **sexual orientation**, defined in the first section of this chapter as being related to the sex of people with whom we wish to engage in sexual activity. Since this isn't a human sexuality textbook, we won't go into detail about theories of the origins of sexual orientation, social and political views, and so forth but will instead focus on the role of nonverbal behavior in the communication of a person's orientation.

Since people who aren't heterosexual are still discriminated against and negatively viewed within U.S. culture and other cultures around the world, many gay, lesbian, bisexual, transgender, and queer people still feel that they must be closeted (or, at least, very private) to function safely in society (Adams, 2016; Baughman & Meyer, 2016; Ding & Rule, 2012; Lick, Johnson, & Rule, 2015; Manning, 2016; Puckett et al., 2017). Briefly, **bisexuality** refers to people who are sexually and emotionally attracted to members of all sexes—those who emphasize the whole individual over the biological sex of the individual. **Transgender** individuals cross over or transcend the traditional boundaries of sex and gender to develop their own unique expression of their sexuality (Capuzza & Spencer, 2015; Criniti & Green, 1016). **Queer** has been reclaimed by some people as an umbrella term for any non-straight identity (Baughman & Meyer, 2016; Ivy, 2017; Killerman, 2013). Granted, things have changed dramatically in the United States, where we've witnessed a Supreme Court ruling legalizing same-sex marriage. And yet complete acceptance and equality have not been achieved. No matter your view on homosexuality, bisexuality, transgender identity, and queer identity, it's hard to deny that things are changing in America and many parts of the world.

Gaydar: Fact or Fiction?

As we've said, discrimination and danger—perceived and real—still exist for people identifying with a non-straight sexual orientation. Given what homosexual, bisexual, transgender, and queer people have always faced and still face, some argue that a way of perceiving someone's sexual orientation continues to operate. You've probably heard the term **gaydar**, referring to an ability to detect the sexual orientation of another person using indirect cues, sometimes referred to as the gay sixth sense (Colzato, van Hooidonk, van den Wildenberg, Harinck, & Hommel, 2010; Rieger, Linsenmeier, Gygax, Garcia, & Bailey, 2010; Woolery, 2008). Gaydar is based primarily on nonverbal cues; it developed within the homosexual community first and was then co-opted by heterosexuals and others as a way of detecting whether someone was gay (Reuter, 2002).

Scholar Cheryl Nicholas (2004) defines gaydar as "a folk concept used within the gay community to name the recognition of verbal and non-verbal behavior associated with gay identity" (p. 60). She elaborates:

> Gaydar suggests that members of the gay and lesbian culture along with straight people familiar with gay/lesbian culture have an innate remote detector that picks up the behavior of individuals within a specified range. The receiver of the stimuli is then of the opinion that the person whose behavior caused the "blip" in gaydar is gay. (pp. 60–61)

Nicholas contends that gaydar is necessary for homosexual people's survival in a world where heterosexuality is the norm or dominant paradigm for relationships. Gaydar protects the invisibility many homosexuals feel is necessary to survive in a discriminatory world. She adds, "Gaydar is possible because gay people believe that it is possible" (p. 66).

However, controversy has emerged among researchers about whether gaydar is real or merely a way of reinforcing stereotypes about people who aren't straight (Brewer & Lyons, 2017; Cox, Devine, Bischmann, & Shibley Hyde, 2016, 2017; Fasoli, Hegarty, Maass, & Antonio, 2018). Many stereotypes stem from nonverbal behavior, so let's expose some stereotypes related to gays and lesbians and call them into question.

Stereotypes about gay men's nonverbal behavior include the following: (1) Gay men have high-pitched voices, use a lot of vocal variety for emphasis and to draw attention to themselves, and talk with a lisp; (2) they have limp wrists, and so their hands flap around a lot while they're talking; (3) they're oversexed, and so they touch people a lot more than straight people do, meaning they're overly and inappropriately affectionate; (4) they're oversexed, and so they're promiscuous; (5) they dress flamboyantly or in the most expensive designer clothing, so as to call attention to themselves and how "different" or "special" they are; (6) they make sexually suggestive eye contact, especially with the sexual body parts of any man they meet; (7) they secretly despise themselves and wish they were women, and so many of them dress in drag and become drag queens; (8) they secretly despise themselves and wish they were women, and so they adopt feminine looks and behaviors; (9) they want to turn straight men gay, and so they come on to straight men by using increased proximity, inappropriate touch, and direct and steady eye contact (which would be considered staring in any other context) so that the straight man succumbs to their charms; (10) they're artistic, with a great sense of style, and so they dress extremely well and are terrific decorators; (11) they use exaggerated facial expressions in interaction, which is related to the need for attention and to appear different; (12) they're obsessed with looking good and attracting men, because sex is very important, and so they work out constantly and have beautiful, virtually flawless bodies; (13) they sit or stand in ways that highlight their crotch or buttocks so other men will notice and be attracted; (14) when they walk, they sashay, using lots of hip movement (as women do); and (15) they like to have women around as camouflage (aka "beards").

Here's the list of stereotypes for lesbians: (1) They're unattractive, both facially and bodily; (2) they wear drab, masculine clothing (such as flannel shirts, trucker caps, boots, and pants—never dresses or skirts) to appear more "butch" and dominant; (3) they use few accessories and prefer to keep a wallet in their pocket rather than carry a purse, or simply carry a nondescript book bag or briefcase; (4) they secretly despise themselves and want to be men, and so they have short haircuts, don't wear makeup, and don't shave their armpits or legs; (5) they're drawn to sports so they can keep in physical contact with other women; (6) they're oversexed, and so they're overly and inappropriately affectionate; (7) they're oversexed, and so they're promiscuous; (8) they make sexually suggestive eye contact, especially with the sexual body parts of any woman they meet; (9) they want to turn straight women into lesbians, and so they come on to straight women by using increased proximity, inappropriate touch, and direct and steady eye contact; (10) they like performing sex acts for the pleasure of straight men; (11) they can't possibly fully enjoy sex since they don't have penises, because everyone knows that the only "true" sex involves penile–vaginal intercourse (and "toys" are no substitute); (12) they have a lousy sense of style, both in dress and home decoration; (13) they appear stone-faced (inexpressive), because too much facial expression looks feminine; (14) they talk in a monotonic fashion, using little vocal variety so as not to seem feminine; and (15) they're overly aggressive and are quick to resort to physical violence to protect their "woman" or lesbian friends.

While *some* of the behaviors listed here might be descriptive of *some* gays and *some* lesbians *some* of the time, since stereotypes typically arise from some observation or experience, you can no doubt see the problem. We run into trouble when we superimpose a stereotype onto new people we meet, expecting them to behave according to type, not as the individuals they are. But if these descriptions are stereotypes, not the "truth," then just how do gays and lesbians act, nonverbally speaking? Do patterns of nonverbal behavior actually emerge among gays and lesbians, and are they detectable with regularity, thus proving the existence and reliability of gaydar? As we said, scholars are divided on these questions (Cox et al., 2016, 2017; Johnson, Gill, Reichman, & Tassinary, 2007; Mack & Munson, 2012; Van Newkirk, 2006).

REMEMBER

Remember!
12.4

Sexuality	Sexual behavior, as well as cognitive, emotional, and psychosociocultural factors that affect one's sexual being
Outercourse	A perspective about sexuality that includes the role of thought, emotions, psychological factors, identity, and sociocultural factors
Sexual orientation	Related to the sex of persons with whom one wishes to engage in sexual activity
Bisexuality	Refers to people who are attracted to members of all sexes and who emphasize the whole individual over the biological sex of the individual
Transgender	Refers to individuals who cross over or transcend the traditional boundaries of sex and gender to develop their own unique expression of their sexuality
Queer	Umbrella term for any non-straight identity
Gaydar	Ability to detect the sexual orientation of a person

chapter twelve

OUT OF THE CLASSROOM
onto the page

One assignment we often "bless" students with is to select a current published journal article on some aspect of nonverbal communication, study that research, and then present it to the rest of the class so that students are exposed to multiple pieces of cutting-edge scholarship on nonverbal communication. One recent class presentation ended up being controversial, leaving students confused.

Manuel was a great student who was always interested in learning as much as he could, participating in discussions whenever possible (but not overly so); he was a joy to have in the classroom. During one class session the discussion centered on nonverbal cues and stereotypes; as part of that discussion, Manuel revealed to the class that he was gay and that he both understood and resented stereotypes about gays. He understood the stereotypes because he had witnessed some of the nonverbal behaviors commonly associated with gay men in his gay friends and acquaintances, but he also resented it when people treated gays like a stereotype, assuming that all gays are the same and no one is an individual.

When it came time to give his presentation on the journal article he'd chosen, Manuel surprised the class by presenting research on whether or not people could accurately identify someone's sexual orientation by looking at photos of their faces. The researchers were specifically interested in identifying characteristics of gay versus straight versus bisexual faces, with special emphasis on bisexuality and physical appearance. In the study, participants were highly accurate when judging straight and gay orientations from faces but highly inaccurate when judging who was bisexual.

Surprisingly, Manuel wasn't critical of the researchers' question or premise, or of their results; Manuel thought that the findings had "real-world applicability," in that the experiences he'd had plus those of friends led them to wonder if someone's face actually could reveal if the person was gay, straight, bi, trans, or queer.

In a classroom setting (or *any* setting, for that matter), when prior information about someone makes you think that he or she rejects stereotypes, and then the person later seems to accept and even make use of those stereotypes, how should you react? Is this confusing or just evidence of a disconnect between research results and everyday living?

Sexual Activity

As we mentioned at the beginning of this chapter, we know that not all of us are currently sexually active. Some are celibate by choice, believing that sexual activity is appropriate only in a committed, monogamous partnering. Others are celibate for certain periods of time, such as those times when they're not in a relationship, their relational partner is at a distance, or they're simply concentrating on other aspects of life. Sexual expression ebbs and flows for most people (even married people and committed partners); this discussion of nonverbal behavior and sexual activity can be applicable to whatever period of life we experience.

What we present in this section sounds contradictory to other information in this book, but in the realm of sex, it's wise to rely more on *verbal* information than on *nonverbal* cues. That's not a typo. We explore some nonverbal cues related to sexual interest and activity, but in this context, *verbal communication is key*, and here's why: While nonverbal cues are important in a sexual context, too much sexual behavior involves reading signals, looking for "body language," "getting vibes," sensing what our partner wants, giving our partner exactly what we perceive is needed, and so forth. The mythology suggests that people are supposed to be so in tune with their own and their partners' bodies that they can somehow read nonverbal cues accurately (while in the midst of their own arousal) and interpret the cues appropriately so that they respond perfectly. Sorry, but what world are these folks living in?

Sexual experience and education can help us develop enhanced nonverbal sending and receiving abilities so we can send clear signals of interest, attraction, and arousal to a potential sexual partner, as well as receive and interpret such cues more accurately (Ivy, 2016; LaFrance, 2010; McGovern, 2017; Orchowski, Gidycz, & Kraft, 2018). But the opportunity for misunderstanding is so great and the consequences so dire that we encourage a little more talking, a little less guessing. (And more verbal communication means more than such statements as, "Ouch! You're on my hair.") Even if it's awkward or embarrassing, talking about such things as sexual needs and wants, what sexual activity means in the greater context of a relationship, and suggestions about sexual behaviors or positions can open the door to deeper intimacy (Brown & Weigel, 2016; Faulkner & Lannutti, 2010).

Clear and effective communication about such subjects as birth control methods, including condom use (i.e., who's responsible for supplying condoms, demanding their use, and actually putting them on before sexual contact), HIV/STI prevention methods, and number of sexual partners (past and present) can greatly enhance the sexual activity and the relationship (Bowleg, Valera, Teti, & Tschann, 2010; Boyle & O'Sullivan, 2010; Hendry, Brown, Dowsett, & Carman, 2017; Rubinsky & Cooke-Jackson, 2017). If more talk about, during, and after sexual activity sounds unromantic to you, we encourage you to think again, because we still advocate for clear communication over media-concocted romance any day. *Real* romance can be highly communicative. Spontaneity and "picking up a vibe" have their definite downsides.

NONVERBAL CUES: BEFORE SEXUAL ACTIVITY. Which nonverbal codes are most related to sexual arousal, meaning the stage before sexual activity might take place or as it is beginning to occur? Certainly physical appearance, sometimes referred to as sex appeal, is a primary factor (Brierley, Brooks, Mond, Stevenson, & Stephen, 2016; Poulsen, Holman, Busby, & Carroll, 2013; Trekels & Eggermont, 2017). In the United States, as well as other cultures around the world, many people go to great lengths to enhance their physical attractiveness, including undergoing cosmetic surgery or procedures. In Chapter 5 on physical appearance and attractiveness, we explored alterations such as breast augmentation, face lifts, butt lifts, and tummy tucks for the nonverbal messages such procedures convey, but one question related to appearance and sexuality should be addressed here: "Does size really matter?" (If you're saying to yourself, "I can't believe they're going there," our view is that *someone* needs to address this issue—someone besides the popular media and pornographers.)

You may not be satisfied with our answer, but the best answer to the size question really is, "It depends." When we refer to size, we're equal opportunists, in that many women struggle with breast and vagina size just as men struggle with penis size. For some people, the size of sexual parts does matter, but others find that their bodies and attitudes about sexuality accommodate any partner, and that focusing on anatomical size misses the point and ruins the enjoyment. Yet another approach is to focus on compatibility of sexual partners, meaning whether people's body parts fit well together sexually. This topic makes some people squeamish, but it's important to focus on how compatible sexual partners are or can become, rather than on some societally concocted notion of what is "enough" or desirable.

In addition to physicality, the way people adorn their bodies can provide clues of sexuality. But here's a caution we've all probably heard before, about assumptions regarding appearance and sexual interest: *Just because someone is dressed in what we deem to be a sexy manner, that doesn't mean the person is looking for sexual activity.* We emphasize this point because the justification, "She was asking for it," is common in relation to sexual assault and rape trials, when perpetrators of these crimes often claim that a victim was dressed or acting provocatively, thereby somehow asking for sex. We can dress in a sexy manner because we want to feel sexy, because we want to express that part of our personality; that doesn't mean we give our consent or want to engage in sexual activity. *Dressing and behaving in a sexy way doesn't equate to an invitation.*

Other nonverbal cues, including kinesic behaviors such as walk, posture, and sitting position, may reveal sexual arousal as well, such as when heterosexual women sometimes exaggerate their hip sway when they walk past men so as to indicate sexual interest, get men's attention, and possibly arouse the men sexually. Likewise, men may accentuate their body parts and move in ways that emphasize their masculinity, hoping to attract attention and sexual interest from onlookers. You may not have thought of dancing as a form of nonverbal communication, but people often reveal their sexuality and attraction to others through the way they move to music.

As we mentioned in the kinesics chapter, an interesting phenomenon to observe when two people are attracted to each other is **interactive synchrony**, defined as a coordination of speech and body movement or a social rhythm between people (Knapp, Hall, & Horgan, 2013). It's fun to watch a couple who appear interested in each other; as their interest and attraction develop over time, their body positions, gestures, touch, facial expressions, and eye behavior will mirror each other, such that they develop a rhythm of behaving (Baimel, Birch, & Norenzayan, 2018; Lozza et al., 2018; Schmidt, Morr, Fitzpatrick, & Richardson, 2012). If we happen to find ourselves in such a situation, it can be exciting and confirming—to be in synch with another person. But again, apply a bit of caution and use all your powers of communication (verbal and nonverbal) to determine if sexual activity should be the outcome of such synchrony.

Proxemics reveal attraction, too, in that decreased distance between people can be a signal of sexual interest, but it's just as likely that the music is too loud to converse at a greater distance. We have to be careful about leaping to an interpretation of sexual interest just because someone gets close to us.

Eye behavior is a fascinating thing to watch among persons of all sexual orientations, because it's a key indicator of interest and attraction. We've already talked about eye contact and its role in gaydar, but in U.S. culture, we rarely give our attention to people without looking at them. When people "undress someone with their eyes," it certainly communicates a pointed message, but this can really backfire, making the receiver of this action feel objectified and degraded. (Women get tired of people who make eye contact with only their breasts.) Eye contact—both continuous and the kind that stops and starts (the double take)—often reveals interest and sexual attraction.

Attraction may be revealed by synchrony, or a mirroring of nonverbal cues between people.

Increased frequency and intimacy of touch may indicate arousal as well, but again we emphasize the word *may*. As we've mentioned elsewhere, research over several decades shows that heterosexual men tend to misinterpret women's touches as being more intimate than women intend (Abbey, 1982, 1987, 1991; Henningsen, 2004; Koukounas & Letch, 2001; LaFrance et al., 2009; Moore, 2002; Orchowski et al., 2018). While women may intend their touches to be an indication of friendship or warmth, men may interpret those touches as indications of love and intimacy (or romantic interest and attraction), leading to sexual arousal. Part of the problem is that some heterosexual men believe that women send mixed signals regarding intimacy, and we grant that this does happen. Women may believe they're just flirting harmlessly and "having a good time," but when their actions are viewed differently than they intend, the results can be devastating.

chapter twelve

A final, important topic warrants discussion in this section—the issue of sexual consent. People usually indicate their consent to sexual activity nonverbally, rather than verbally (Brian, 2016). But how are people likely to indicate that they *don't* consent? We've probably all heard the admonition, "No means no," but sometimes the sexual waters get murky and it isn't all that simple (Ivy, 2016, 2017; Lockwood Harris, 2018; Orchowski et al., 2018). We're going to repeat what many sources say on this point: When anyone says no to sex, that means no—no matter what the body is saying or if that person expresses it without conviction in his or her voice. When anyone says no at any point in sexual activity, activity *must stop*. Throughout this book, we've advised you, when the verbal and the nonverbal contradict, to believe the nonverbal because it usually carries the truer weight of the message; however, in this context, the verbal should override the nonverbal. Translation: If someone's words say no but her or his body says yes, the no should take precedence, sexual activity should stop, and partners should seek clarification before any further action is taken. Beware of sending mixed signals, because it's hard to stop sexual activity when one's partner seems as though he or she is still into it. But if one's partner verbally or nonverbally requests either a breather or for the activity to stop, that request simply *must* be heeded, no matter if any sort of physical affection continues (Ortiz & Shafer, 2017).

Some heterosexual men report being conditioned to view a woman's "no" as **token resistance**, a casual or faked attempt to resist a sexual advance that someone may believe is expected before agreeing to sexual activity (Muehlenhard, 2011; Shafer, Ortiz, Thompson, & Huemmer, 2018). In such a situation, men may believe that "no" actually means "try harder," "try something else," or "try again later." Some women have been conditioned to say no as a tactic of playing hard to get or a way of heightening their partner's arousal, as though sexual activity should be some kind of chase or game. A few of our female students have been honest enough to reveal that they sometimes say no before they agree to or initiate sexual activity, just so the men they're with won't think them easy or slutty. If their bodies and nonverbal actions contradict their lack of verbal consent, the message is that they actually want the activity to continue (Muehlenhard & Rodgers, 2005).

Sexual game playing is inadvisable, because it creates confusion at best and conflict, hurt feelings, and possibly even abuse at worst. The bottom line is this: If we say no to sexual activity, we must say no with our voice *and* our body. We shouldn't say no just to fake people out, mess with their minds, or manipulate their emotions. If we do so, we make the word *no* meaningless *for all of us*. If we hear no from a partner, we have to take it at face value, stop what we're doing, and seek clarification.

NONVERBAL CUES: DURING SEXUAL ACTIVITY. Sexual intimacy is a significant development within a relationship (Mongeau, Serewicz, Henningsen, & Davis, 2006). But saying that this topic is "ticklish" isn't just a pun; it's the reality of delving into such personal waters. It's important to discuss this subject for many reasons, most of which we've already articulated (e.g., misunderstanding, embarrassment, hurt feelings, abusive behavior). Here's another reason: quality.

We wholeheartedly believe, as research, therapists, and self-help books suggest, that sexual activities will be of better quality for both partners if the communication between them is enhanced (Bowleg et al., 2010; Hendry et al., 2017). The media has done us all a disservice here, with films, TV shows, song lyrics, and romance novels depicting sexual encounters primarily in two ways: either as (1) blissful, smooth, perfectly coordinated events, wherein partners don't talk much but seem to know exactly what to do, what feels best, how to gauge how their partner feels, and how to react appropriately, or (2) the complete opposite—awkward, embarrassing, hilarious, uncoordinated, horrible, unsatisfying, and sometimes even abusive encounters.

Decades of research reveals the following nonverbal cues to be related to seduction and sexual encounters: flashing an eyebrow, licking the lips, touching a thigh, tossing the head, presenting one's neck, coming close, making continuous eye contact, flipping one's hair, kissing, and petting (Abbey & Melby, 1986; Anolli & Ciceri, 2002; Grammer, 1990; Kendrick & Trost, 1987; Peck et al., 2016). One of the more obvious codes is haptics (touch behavior). Probably touch is the most integral nonverbal behavior between sexual partners, but some of us assume things about touch, and you know the problem with assumptions. Three common assumptions are: (1) that our current partner will behave and react as our previous partner did, (2) that what we've read or heard about sex works the same way for every partner, and (3) that our partner wants what we want. Granted, we can learn some things from books, Internet sites, and other people's experiences, but we also have to learn to treat our partner as a unique human being who will likely desire and react to us differently than other people do, than what the books say, or than we would. That lack of predictability can be viewed as a positive, not a negative.

For some people, eye contact and facial expressions during sexual activity are very important. Most of us would agree that making love to someone who won't look at us would be a major turnoff (or a dead giveaway that the person would rather be somewhere else or with someone else). What if someone cries during sex? In nonsexual situations, people may cry because they're sad or afraid, but some people cry when they're happy. How do we know what's going on with a sexual partner who's crying if we don't ask? Should we ignore the crying or assume we did something wrong? Some people—men and women alike—cry when they climax, but if we don't understand this reaction, it can be confusing and disconcerting (to say the least).

In terms of kinesics, body positioning and movement are other central aspects of the sexual encounter. Those of us who are comfortable enough to talk about our preferred sexual positions or what feels best to us are more likely to have positive sexual encounters than those of us who just hope for the best or are too afraid or intimidated to discuss our preferences (Sprecher & Cate, 2004). Again, nonverbal cues are important, but they don't replace the power of the good old-fashioned conversation. Studies show that, in general, the more partners talk about sex (and we mean a *quality* conversation), the greater their satisfaction with both sexual and nonsexual aspects of their relationship (Boyle & O'Sullivan, 2010; Brown & Weigel, 2016; Faulkner & Lannutti, 2010).

chapter twelve

One other nonverbal code warrants brief note—vocalics. As we mentioned earlier when discussing nonverbal cues essential in the maintenance of intimate relationships, such aspects of vocal production as volume, pausing, rate, breathiness, and pitch can enhance a sexual situation (Banziger, Patel, & Scherer, 2014; Eddins, Anand, Camacho, & Shrivastav, 2016; Farley et al., 2013). In Chapter 9, we explored a subcategory of vocalics termed **vocalizations,** defined as nonwords or sounds not tied to speech, including those that can substitute for speech (Kurtz & Algoe, 2017). Some sexual messages can be conveyed through vocalizations and the inflection and volume that accompany them. Vocalizations are quite individualistic; over time a sexual partner can come to understand what certain sounds mean from his or her partner. As for other cues, it's unwise to assume that a sound one partner makes means the same thing when a different partner produces it.

One final word on this topic: If certain nonverbal cues heighten our sexual arousal and pleasure, it's important to learn to ask for them rather than expecting or hoping that a partner will read our mind. If we like to be touched in a certain way, how will our partner know? Touching a partner the way we like to be touched may have an impact, but this form of hinting or indirect method often doesn't work. It's better to be explicit and verbalize our desires, but not like a drill sergeant barking out orders, either. Too much instruction can kill the mood, but too little can kill the enjoyment. Nonverbal cues are important, but we shouldn't rely on them to carry sexual messages for us; clear verbal communication is critical.

NONVERBAL CUES: AFTER SEXUAL ACTIVITY. People are as varied in their preferences and approaches for after-sex activity as they are in other phases, so it isn't wise to assume or buy into such stereotypical notions as "All women like to be held" and "If you don't sleep over after sex, it's rude." The intent here is not to take all the spontaneity out of sexual activity—before, during, or after—but, again, we shouldn't try to read our partner's mind if we're unsure of what to do after sexual activity has subsided. It's okay to ask a few simple questions, keeping in mind our own desires and preferences, because then we'll know better how to behave. Some people like a little physical distance after sex, which shouldn't always be interpreted negatively. Not wanting to be touched or finding our own side of the bed when sex has wound down isn't necessarily a judgment about the quality of the sex or a clue as to feelings between partners. Some people like to cuddle and maintain psychological as well as physical closeness, but these kinds of preferences are very individualistic. If we have certain needs or preferences for nonverbal behavior (and verbal behavior, for that matter) after engaging in sexual activity, the best tactic is to make our desires known explicitly but sensitively.

One of the things you may not have thought of regarding the after-effects of sex is this: Being in the throes of passion takes many of us to a different plane, where logic and the best advice pounding in our head have to fight to be heard. But once that passion and lust subsides, reality sets back in and things can get *really* awkward. (Talk about nonverbal cues becoming strange.) So, while we don't want to provide a laundry list of dos and don'ts regarding sexual activity and its aftermath, it's important to take some time to think about these issues, whether or not you're currently sexually active or imagine yourself someday becoming sexually active. Ask yourself, What kind of sexual encounter do I want? How do I want to nonverbally communicate my sexuality, before, during, and after sexual activity? How do I want to verbally communicate? What kind of nonverbal and verbal communication do I want, need, and expect from my partner?

REMEMBER

Remember! **12.5**

Interactive synchrony	Coordination of speech and body movement or a nonverbal rhythm between people
Token resistance	A casual or faked attempt to resist a sexual advance, which someone may believe is expected before agreeing to sexual activity
Vocalizations	Nonwords or sounds not tied to speech, including those that can substitute for speech

SUMMARY

In this chapter, we explored three important aspects of nonverbal communication within our social world. First, nonverbal communication as affected by sex and gender was examined. We began by distinguishing between the terms *sex* and *gender*, and discussed how each forms a part of our identity. We then overviewed key research findings regarding how the sexes are both similar and different in their displays of nonverbal codes of behavior.

Since relationships are what gives most of us life's greatest joy, we turned our attention in this chapter to the role of nonverbal cues in the initiation, maintenance, and sometimes termination of intimate relationships. We first explored various meanings for the term *intimacy*, then highlighted nonverbal cues associated with the development of intimacy in a romantic relationship. Most of us would agree that conflict is inevitable in intimate relationships, but it can also be healthy or constructive if partners are attuned to their own and each other's nonverbal communication. Not all relationships are successful, so we concluded this section of the chapter by looking at predominant nonverbal cues associated with relationship dissolution.

Finally—and, arguably, saving the best for last—we explored the important subject of nonverbal cues and the expression of sexuality. We first defined some key terms, including *sexuality* and *sexual orientation*, as related to LGBTQ identities. We then explored the controversial phenomenon of *gaydar*, since these perceptions rely predominantly on nonverbal cues. We exposed some common stereotypes about gays and lesbians and the pitfalls of relating to someone through a stereotype rather than as a unique human being. We closed the chapter with a discussion of the most critical nonverbal codes of behavior that typically occur before, during, and after sexual activity. We emphasized the utility of relying on *verbal* communication rather than *nonverbal* cues when attempting to determine if sexual consent has been given and received by sexual partners.

DISCUSSION STARTERS ■ ■ ■

1. How do sex and gender differ? If you consider yourself to be androgynous, is that part of your sex, your gender, or both?

2. In your experience, are men and women more alike than different, nonverbally? If you believe the sexes are different, what nonverbal behaviors differ the most, from your perspective and observation?

3. Define quasi-courtship behavior in terms of its four stages; provide some examples of nonverbal communication that might occur in each stage.

4. What nonverbal cues do you use to flirt with someone you find attractive? What nonverbal cues of flirtation have you seen friends or acquaintances enact that you'd like to try or wish you could pull off in social situations?

5. If you have had an intimate relationship in the past, think about the nonverbal cues present when that relationship first began. Then think about how those nonverbal cues changed, if they diminished or disappeared over time. What do you believe caused the change in behavior? Did your behavior change more than your partner's? Why or why not? What do you want to try to do differently the next time?

6. In your experience, does gaydar exist or does it simply reinforce unfortunate stereotypes? What nonverbal cues are most integral to gaydar?

7. In this chapter, we discussed the role of nonverbal communication in sexual activity. What things might you have discovered about yourself in reading this part of the chapter, in terms of how you nonverbally express your sexual self (or not) to other people? What changes do you think you need to make in this regard?

REFERENCES ■ ■ ■

Abbey, A. (1982). Sex differences in attributions for friendly behavior: Do males misperceive females' friendliness? *Journal of Personality and Social Psychology, 42*, 830–838.

Abbey, A. (1987). Misperception of friendly behavior as sexual interest: A survey of naturally occurring incidents. *Psychology of Women Quarterly, 11*, 173–194.

Abbey, A. (1991). Misperception as an antecedent of acquaintance rape: A consequence of ambiguity in communication between men and women. In A. Parrot & L. Bechhofer (Eds.), *Acquaintance rape: The hidden crime* (pp. 96–111). New York: Wiley.

Abbey, A., & Melby, C. (1986). The effects of nonverbal cues on gender differences in perceptions of sexual interest. *Sex Roles, 15*, 283–298.

Abbey, A., Zawacki, T., & Buck, P. O. (2005). The effects of past sexual assault perpetration and alcohol consumption on reactions to women's mixed signals. *Journal of Social and Clinical Psychology, 25*, 129–157.

Abrams, J. A., Maxwell, M. L., & Belgrave, F. Z. (2018). Circumstances beyond their control: Black women's perceptions of black manhood. *Sex Roles, 79*, 151–162.

Adams, T. E. (2016). Sexuality and self-forgiveness. *Women & Language, 39*, 121–125.

Agthe, M., Sporrle, M., & Maner, J. K. (2010). Don't hate me because I'm beautiful: Anti-attractiveness bias in organizational evaluation and decision making. *Journal of Experimental Social Psychology, 46*, 1151–1154.

Albert, G., Pearson, M., Arnocky, S., Wachowiak, M., Nicol, J., & Murphy, D. R. (2018). Effects of masculinized and feminized male voices on men and women's distractibility and implicit memory. *Journal of Individual Differences 39*, 151–165.

Aldeis, D., & Afifi, T. D. (2015). Putative secrets and conflict in romantic relationships over time. *Communication Monographs, 82*, 224–251.

Amon, M. J. (2015). Visual attention in mixed-gender groups. *Frontiers in Psychology, 5*, 1–10.

Anand, L., Du Bois, S. N., Sher, T. G., & Grotkowski, K. (2017). Defying tradition: Gender roles in long-distance relationships. *The Family Journal, 26*, 22–30.

Andersen, M. L., & Hysock, D. (2010). The social construction of gender. In B. Hutchinson (Ed.), *Annual editions: Gender 10/11* (pp. 2–5). New York: McGraw-Hill.

Andersen, P. A. (2004). *The complete idiot's guide to body language.* New York: Alpha.

Andersen, P. A., Guerrero, L. K., & Jones, S. M. (2006). Nonverbal behavior in intimate interactions and intimate relationships. In V. Manusov & M. L. Patterson (Eds.), *The SAGE handbook of nonverbal communication* (pp. 259–277). Thousand Oaks, CA: Sage.

Andersen, P. A., & Leibowitz, K. (1978). The development and nature of the construct touch avoidance. *Environmental Psychology and Nonverbal Behavior, 3*, 89–106.

Anolli, L., & Ciceri, R. (2002). Analysis of the vocal profiles of male seduction: From exhibition to self-disclosure. *Journal of General Psychology, 129*, 149–169.

Arroyo, A., & Harwood, J. (2012). Exploring the causes and consequences of engaging in fat talk. *Journal of Applied Communication Research, 40*, 167–187.

Aznar, A., & Tenenbaum, H. R. (2016). Parent-child positive touch: Gender, age, and task differences. *Journal of Nonverbal Behavior, 40*, 317–333.

Bailey, A. H., & Kelly, S. D. (2015). Picture power: Gender versus body language in perceived status. *Journal of Nonverbal Behavior, 29*, 317–337.

Baimel, A., Birch, S. A. J., & Norenzayan, A. (2018). Coordinating bodies and minds: Behavioral synchrony fosters mentalizing. *Journal of Experimental Social Psychology, 74*, 281–290.

Banai, I. P. (2017). Voice in different phases of menstrual cycle among naturally cycling women and users of hormonal contraceptives. *PLoS ONE, 12*. e0183462.

Banziger, T., Patel, S., & Scherer, K. R. (2014). The role of perceived voice and speech characteristics in vocal emotion communication. *Journal of Nonverbal Behavior, 38*, 31–52.

Baron-Cohen, S. (2004). *The essential difference: Male and female brains and the truth about autism.* New York: Basic Books.

Basu, A. (2011). HIV/AIDS and subaltern autonomous rationality: A call to recenter health communication in marginalized sex worker spaces. *Communication Monographs, 78,* 391–408.

Baughman, L., & Meyer, M. D. E. (2016). Challenging the closet: Living the politics of identity as bisexual/queer identified women. In J. Manning & C. M. Noland (Eds.), *Contemporary studies of sexuality and communication: Theoretical and applied perspectives* (pp. 109–123). Dubuque, IA: Kendall Hunt.

Beebe, S. A., Beebe, S. J., & Ivy, D. K. (2019). *Communication: Principles for a lifetime* (7th ed.). Boston: Pearson.

Bem, S. L. (1974). The measurement of psychological androgyny. *Journal of Consulting and Clinical Psychology, 42,* 155–162.

Birdwhistell, R. L. (1970). *Kinesics and context: Essays on body motion communication.* Philadelphia: University of Pennsylvania Press.

Blakemore, J. E. O., & Centers, R. E. (2005). Characteristics of boys' and girls' toys. *Sex Roles, 53,* 619–634.

Bosson, J. K., Vandello, J. A., & Buckner, C. E. (2019). *The psychology of sex and gender.* Thousand Oaks, CA: Sage.

Bowleg, L., Valera, P., Teti, M., & Tschann, J. M. (2010). Silences, gestures, and words: Nonverbal and verbal communication about HIV/AIDS and condom use in black heterosexual relationships. *Health Communication, 25,* 80–90.

Bowman, J. M., & Compton, B. L. (2014). Self-presentation, individual differences, and gendered evaluations of nonverbal greeting behaviors among close male friends. *The Journal of Men's Studies, 22,* 207–221.

Boyle, A. M., & O'Sullivan, L. F. (2010). General and sexual communication in established relationships: An exploration of possible links to condom use among young adults. *Canadian Journal of Human Sexuality, 19,* 53–64.

Brewer, G., & Lyons, J. (2017). Is gaydar affected by attitudes toward homosexuality? Confidence, labeling bias, and accuracy. *Journal of Homosexuality, 64,* 1241–1252.

Brian, L. A. (2016). A genealogy of sexual consent from the social contract to sex-positive feminism. In J. Manning & C. M. Noland (Eds.), *Contemporary studies of sexuality and communication: Theoretical and applied perspectives* (pp. 35–46). Dubuque, IA: Kendall Hunt.

Brierley, M-E., Brooks, K. R., Mond, J., Stevenson, R. J., & Stephen, I. D. (2016). The body and the beautiful: Health, attractiveness and body composition in men's and women's bodies. *PLoS ONE, 11.* e0156722.

Brown, R. D., & Weigel, D. J. (2016). Beneath the tangled sheets: Examining sexual communication through ecological systems. In J. Manning & C. M. Noland (Eds.), *Contemporary studies of sexuality and communication: Theoretical and applied perspectives* (pp. 47–60). Dubuque, IA: Kendall Hunt.

Burgoon, J. K., & Bacue, A. E. (2003). Nonverbal communication skills. In J. O. Greene & B. R. Burleson (Eds.), *Handbook of communication and social interaction skills* (pp. 179–219). Mahwah, NJ: Erlbaum.

Burgoon, J. K., & Walther, J. B. (1990). Nonverbal expectancies and the evaluative consequences of violations. *Human Communication Research, 17,* 232–265.

Burrell, N. A., Allen, M., Gayle, B. M., & Preiss, R. W. (Eds.) (2014). *Managing interpersonal conflict: Advances through meta-analysis.* New York: Routledge.

Calogero, R., Pina, A., & Sutton, R. (2013). Cutting words: Priming self-objectification increases women's intention to pursue cosmetic surgery. *Psychology of Women Quarterly, 38,* 197–207.

Capuzza, J. C., & Spencer, L. G. (Eds.) (2015). *Transgender communication studies: Histories, trends, and trajectories.* New York: Lexington.

Cartei, V., & Reby, D. (2012). Acting gay: Male actors shift the frequency components of their voices towards female values when playing homosexual characters. *Journal of Nonverbal Behavior, 36*, 79–93.

Chaplin, T. M., & Aldao, A. (2013). Gender differences in emotion expression in children: A meta-analytic review. *Psychological Bulletin, 139*, 735–765.

Cheng, C.-C., & Tardy, C. (2010). A cross-cultural study of silence in marital conflict. *China Media Report Overseas, 6*, 95–105.

Collett, P. (2004). *The book of tells.* London: Bantam.

Collins, S. A., & Missing, C. (2003). Vocal and visual attractiveness are related in women. *Animal Behaviour, 65*, 997–1004.

Colzato, L. S., van Hooidonk, L., van den Wildenberg, W. P. M., Harinck, F., & Hommel, B. (2010). Sexual orientation biases attentional control: A possible gaydar mechanism. *Frontiers in Psychology, 1*(13).

Condry, S. M., Condry, J. C., & Pogatshnik, L. W. (1983). Sex differences: A study of the ear of the beholder. *Sex Roles, 9*, 697–704.

Cox, W. T. L., Devine, P. G., Bischmann, A. A., & Shibley Hyde, J. (2016). Inferences about sexual orientation: The roles of stereotypes, faces, and the gaydar myth. *The Journal of Sex Research, 53*, 157–171.

Cox, W. T. L., Devine, P. G., Bischmann, A. A., & Shibley Hyde, J. (2017). Ecological invalidity of existing gaydar research: In-lab accuracy translates to real-world inaccuracy: Response to Rule, Johnson, & Freeman (2016). *The Journal of Sex Research, 54*, 820–824.

Criniti, S., & Green, E. R. (2016). Understanding transgender identities and experiences. In J. Manning & C. M. Noland (Eds.), *Contemporary studies of sexuality and communication: Theoretical and applied perspectives* (pp. 125–142). Dubuque, IA: Kendall Hunt.

Darlow, S., & Lobel, M. (2010). Who is beholding my beauty? Thinness ideals, weight, and women's responses to appearance evaluation. *Sex Roles, 63*, 833–843.

Debrot, A., Meuwly, N., Muise, A., Impett, E. A., & Schoebi, D. (2017). More than just sex: Affection mediates the association between sexual activity and well-being. *Personality and Social Psychology Bulletin, 43*, 287–299.

Delaney, H. J., & Gluade, B. A. (1990). Gender differences in perception of attractiveness of men and women in bars. *Journal of Personality and Social Psychology, 16*, 378–391.

Derlega, V. J., Lewis, R. J., Harrison, S., Winstead, B. A., & Costanza, R. (1989). Gender differences in the initiation and attribution of tactile intimacy. *Journal of Nonverbal Behavior, 13*, 83–96.

Dickey, E. C., & Knower, F. H. (1941). A note on some ethnological differences in recognition of simulated expressions of emotions. *American Journal of Sociology, 47*, 190–193.

Ding, J., & Rule, N. O. (2012). Gay, straight, or somewhere in between: Accuracy and bias in the perception of bisexual faces. *Journal of Nonverbal Behavior, 36*, 165–176.

Dittmar, H. (2010). *Consumer culture, identity and well-being: The search for the "good life" and the "body perfect."* London: Psychology Press.

Ebesu Hubbard, A. S., Hendrickson, B., Fehrenbach, K. S., & Sur, J. (2013). Effects of timing and sincerity of apology on satisfaction and changes in negative feelings during conflicts. *Western Journal of Communication, 77*, 305–322.

Eddins, D. A., Anand, S., Camacho, A., & Shrivastav, R. (2016). Modeling of breathy voice quality using pitch-strength estimates. *Journal of Voice, 30*, 774.e1-774.e7.

Eichorn, J. T., Kent, R. D., Austin, D., & Vorperian, H. K. (2017). Effects of aging on vocal fundamental frequency and vowel formants in men and women. *Journal of Voice, 31.* http://doi.org/10.1016/j.jvoice.2017.08.003

Ellis, L. (2006). Gender differences in smiling: An evolutionary neuroandrogenic theory. *Physiology and Behavior, 88*, 303–308.

Emmers, T. M., & Dindia, K. (1995). The effect of relational stage and intimacy on touch: An extension of Guerrero and Andersen. *Personal Relationships, 2*, 225–236.

Endendijk, J. J., Groeneveld, M. G., & Mesman, J. (2018). The gendered family process model: An integrative framework of gender in the family. *Archives of Sexual Behavior, 47*, 877–904.

Fagot, B. L., Rodgers, C. S., & Leinbach, M. D. (2000). Theories of gender socialization. In T. Eckes & H. Trautner (Eds.), *The developmental social psychology of gender* (pp. 65–89). Mahwah, NJ: Erlbaum.

Farley, S. D., Hughes, S. M., & LaFayette, J. N. (2013). People will know we are in love: Evidence of differences between vocal samples directed toward lovers and friends. *Journal of Nonverbal Behavior, 37*, 123–138.

Fasoli, F., Hegarty, P., Maass, A., & Antonio, R. (2018). Who wants to sound straight? Sexual majority and minority stereotypes, beliefs and desires about auditory gaydar. *Personality and Individual Differences, 120*, 59–64.

Faulkner, S. L., & Lannutti, P. J. (2010). Examining the content and outcomes of young adults' satisfying and unsatisfying conversations about sex. *Qualitative Health Research, 20*, 275–285.

Feinberg, D. R., Jones, B. C., Law Smith, M. J., Moore, F. R., DeBruine, L. M., Cornwall, R. E., et al. (2006). Menstrual cycle, trait estrogen level, and masculinity preferences in the human voice. *Hormones and Behavior, 46*, 215–222.

Fine, J. (2001, October). Intimacy. *O: The Oprah Winfrey Magazine, 225*.

Fischer, A., & LaFrance, M. (2015). What drives the smile and the tear? Why women are more emotionally expressive than men. *Emotion Review, 7*, 22–29.

Fixmer-Oraiz, N., & Wood, J. T. (2018). *Gendered lives: Communication, gender, and culture* (13th ed.). Boston: Cengage Learning.

Floyd, K. (1997). Communicating affection in dyadic relationships: An assessment of behavior and expectancies. *Communication Quarterly, 45*, 68–80.

Floyd, K. (2000). Affectionate same-sex touch: The influence of homophobia on observers' perceptions. *Journal of Social Psychology, 140*, 774–788.

Floyd, K., & Morman, M. T. (1997). Affectionate communication in nonromantic relationships: Influences of communicator, relational, and contextual factors. *Western Journal of Communication, 61*, 279–298.

Floyd, K., & Ray, G. B. (2003). Human affection exchange: VI. Vocalic predictors of perceived affection in initial interactions. *Western Journal of Communication, 67*, 56–73.

Forman-Brunell, M., & Whitney, J. D. (Eds.) (2015). *Dolls studies: The many meanings of girls' toys and play.* London: Peter Lang.

Frank, M. G., Maroulis, A., & Griffin, D. J. (2013). The voice. In D. Matusomo, M. G. Frank, & H. S. Hwang (Eds.), *Nonverbal communication: Science and application* (pp. 53–74). Thousand Oaks, CA: Sage.

Grammer, K. (1990). Strangers meet: Laughter and nonverbal signs of interest in opposite-sex encounters. *Journal of Nonverbal Behavior, 14*, 209–236.

Greenbaum, P. E., & Rosenfeld, H. M. (1980). Varieties of touching in greetings: Sequential structure and sex-related differences. *Journal of Nonverbal Behavior, 5*, 13–25.

Grossard, C., Chaby, L., Hun, S., Pellerin, H., Bourgeois, J., Dapogny, A., Ding, H., Serret, S., Foulon, P., Chetouani, M., Chen, L., Bailly, K., Grunszpan, O., & Cohen, D. (2018). Children's facial expression production: Influence of age, gender, emotion subtype, elicitation condition and culture. *Frontiers in Psychology, 9*, 446.

Guéguen, N. (2008). The effect of a woman's smile on men's courtship behavior. *Social Behavior and Personality, 36*, 1233–1236.

Guerrero, L. K. (2013). Emotion and communication in conflict interaction. In J. G. Oetzel & S. Ting-Toomey (Eds.), *The SAGE handbook of conflict communication: Integrating theory, research, and practice* (pp. 105–131). Thousand Oaks, CA: Sage.

Guerrero, L. K., & Andersen, P. A. (1991). The waxing and waning of relational intimacy: Touch as a function of relational stage, gender, and touch avoidance. *Journal of Social and Personal Relationships, 8*, 147–165.

Guerrero, L. K., & Andersen, P. A. (1994). Patterns of matching and initiation: Touch behavior and touch avoidance across romantic relationship stages. *Journal of Nonverbal Behavior, 18*, 137–153.

Guerrero, L. K., & Floyd, K. (2006). *Nonverbal communication in close relationships.* Mahwah, NJ: Erlbaum.

Guerrero, L. K., Jones, S. M., & Boburka, R. R. (2006). Sex differences in emotional communication. In D. J. Canary & K. Dindia (Eds.), *Sex differences and similarities in communication* (2nd ed., pp. 241–261). Mahwah, NJ: Erlbaum.

Hall, J. A. (1978). Gender effects in decoding nonverbal cues. *Psychological Bulletin, 85*, 845–857.

Hall, J. A. (2006). Women's and men's nonverbal communication: Similarities, differences, stereotypes, and origins. In V. Manusov & M. L. Patterson (Eds.), *The SAGE handbook of nonverbal communication* (pp. 201–218). Thousand Oaks, CA: Sage.

Hall, J. A. (2011). Gender and status patterns in social touch. In M. J. Hertenstein & S. J. Weiss (Eds.), *The handbook of touch: Neuroscience, behavioral, and health perspectives* (pp. 329–350). New York: Springer.

Hall, J. A. (2016). Interpreting social-sexual communication: Relational framing theory and social-sexual communication, attraction, and intent. *Human Communication Research, 42*, 138–164.

Hall, J. A., Andrzejewski, S. A., & Yopchick, J. E. (2009). Psychosocial correlates of interpersonal sensitivity: A meta-analysis. *Journal of Nonverbal Behavior, 33*, 149–180.

Hall, J. A., Carter, S., Cody, M. J., & Albright, J. M. (2010). Individual differences in the communication of romantic interest: Development of the Flirting Styles Inventory. *Communication Quarterly, 58*, 365–393.

Hall, J. A., & Halberstadt, A. G. (1986). Smiling and gazing. In J. S. Hyde & M. Linn (Eds.), *The psychology of gender: Advances through meta-analysis* (pp. 136–158). Baltimore, MD: Johns Hopkins University Press.

Hall, J. A., & Schmid Mast, M. (2008). Are women always more interpersonally sensitive than men? Impact of goals and content domain. *Personality and Social Psychology Bulletin, 34*, 144–155.

Hall, J. A., & Veccia, E. M. (1990). More "touching" observations: New insights on men, women, and interpersonal touch. *Journal of Personality and Social Psychology, 59*, 1155–1162.

Hall, J. A., & Xing, C. (2015). The verbal and nonverbal correlates of the five flirting styles. *Journal of Nonverbal Behavior, 39*, 41–68.

Hall, J. A., Xing, C., & Brooks, S. (2015). Accurately detecting flirting: Error management theory, the traditional sexual script, and flirting base rate. *Communication Research, 42*, 939–958.

Halovic, S., & Kroos, C. (2018). Not all is noticed: Kinematic cues of emotion-specific gait. *Human Movement Science, 57*, 478–488.

Halpern, D. F. (2012). *Sex differences in cognitive abilities* (4th ed.). New York: Psychology Press.

Harjunen V. J., Spape, M., Ahmed, I., Jacucci, G., & Ravaja, N. (2017). Individual differences in affective touch: Behavioral inhibition and gender define how an interpersonal touch is perceived. *Personality and Individual Differences, 107*, 88–95.

Harrison, M., & Shortall, J. (2011). Women and men in love: Who really feels it and says it first? *Journal of Social Psychology, 151*, 727–736.

Haselton, M. G. (2003). The sexual overperception bias: Evidence of a systematic bias in men from a survey of naturally occurring events. *Journal of Research in Personality, 37,* 34–47.

Hendry, N. A., Brown, G., Dowsett, G. W., & Carman, M. (2017). Association between sexually transmissible testing, numbers of partners and talking to partners and friends about sexual health: Survey of young adults. *Sexual Health, 14,* 378–382.

Henley, N. M. (2001). Body politics. In A. Branaman (Ed.), *Self and society: Blackwell readers in sociology* (pp. 288–297). Malden, MA: Blackwell.

Henningsen, D. D. (2004). Flirting with meaning: An examination of miscommunication in flirting interactions. *Sex Roles, 50,* 481–489.

Henningsen, D. D., Henningsen, M. L. M., & Valde, K. S. (2006). Gender differences in perceptions of women's sexual interest during cross-sex interactions: An application and extension of cognitive valence theory. *Sex Roles, 54,* 821–829.

Henningsen, D. D., Kartch, F., Orr, N., & Brown, A. (2009). The perceptions of verbal and nonverbal flirting cues in cross-sex interactions. *Human Communication, 12,* 371–381.

Hess, U., Adams, R. B., Jr., Grammer, K., & Kleck, R. E. (2009). Face gender and emotion expression: Are angry women more like men? *Journal of Vision, 9,* 1–8.

Hesse, C., & Mikkelson, A. C. (2017). Affection deprivation in romantic relationships. *Communication Quarterly, 65,* 20–38.

Hines, M. (2010). Sex-related variation in human behavior and the brain. *Trends in Cognitive Sciences, 14,* 448–456.

Hocker, J. L., & Wilmot, W. W. (2017). *Interpersonal conflict* (10th ed.). New York: McGraw-Hill.

Horan, S., & Booth-Butterfield, M. (2010). Investigating affection: An investigation of affection exchanges theory and relational qualities. *Communication Quarterly, 58,* 394–413.

Horan, S., & Booth-Butterfield, M. (2013). Understanding the routine expression of deceptive affection in romantic relationships. *Communication Quarterly, 61,* 195–216.

Horgan, T. G., Schmid Mast, M., Hall, J. A., & Carter, J. D. (2004). Gender differences in memory for the appearance of others. *Personality and Social Psychology Bulletin, 30,* 185–196.

Horgan, T. G., & Smith, J. L. (2006). Interpersonal reasons for interpersonal perceptions: Gender-incongruent purpose goals and nonverbal judgment accuracy. *Journal of Nonverbal Behavior, 30,* 127-140.

Hughes, S. M., & Harrison, M. A. (2017). Your cheatin' voice will tell on you: Detection of past infidelity from voice. *Evolutionary Psychology, 15,* 1–12.

Ivy, D. K. (2016). College students' sexual safety: The verbal and nonverbal communication of consent. In J. Manning & C. M. Noland (Eds.), *Contemporary studies of sexuality and communication: Theoretical and applied perspectives* (pp. 405–418). Dubuque, IA: Kendall Hunt.

Ivy, D. K. (2017). *GenderSpeak: Communicating in a gendered world* (6th ed.). Dubuque, IA: Kendall Hunt.

Izard, C. E. (1971). *The face of emotion.* New York: Appleton-Century-Crofts.

Jakubiak, B. K., & Feeney, B. C. (2017). Affectionate touch to promote relational, psychological, and physical well-being in adulthood: A theoretical model and review of the research. *Personality and Social Psychology Review, 21,* 228–252.

Jenkins, J., & Finneman, T. (2018). Gender trouble in the workplace: Applying Judith Butler's theory of performativity to news organizations. *Feminist Media Studies, 18,* 157–172.

Johnson, K. L., Gill, S., Reichman, V., & Tassinary, L. G. (2007). Swagger, sway, and sexuality: Judging sexual orientation from body motion and morphology. *Journal of Personality and Social Psychology, 93,* 321–334.

Jones, S. E. (1986). Sex differences in touch communication. *Western Journal of Speech Communication, 50,* 227–241.

Jones, S. E., & Yarbrough, A. E. (1985). A naturalistic study of the meanings of touch. *Communication Monographs, 52,* 19–56.

Kaspar, K., & Krull, J. (2013). Incidental haptic stimulation in the context of flirt behavior. *Journal of Nonverbal Behavior, 37,* 165–173.

Kendrick, D. T., & Trost, M. R. (1987). A biosocial theory of heterosexual relationships. In K. Kelley (Ed.), *Females, males, and sexuality: Theories and research* (pp. 59–100). Albany: State University of New York Press.

Killerman, S. (2013). *The social justice advocate's handbook: A guide to gender.* Austin, TX: Impetus Books.

Kim, K. J., Feeney, B. C., & Jakubiak, B. K. (2018). Touch reduces romantic jealousy in the anxiously attached. *Journal of Social & Personal Relationships, 35,* 1019–1041.

Knapp, M. L., Hall, J. A., & Horgan, T. G. (2013). *Nonverbal communication in human interaction* (8th ed.). Belmont, CA: Cengage/Wadsworth.

Knapp, M. L., Vangelisti, A. L., & Caughlin, J. (2013). *Interpersonal communication and human relationships* (7th ed.). Boston: Pearson.

Koch, S. C., Baehne, C. G., Kruse, L., Zimmermann, F., & Zumbach, J. (2010). Visual dominance and visual egalitarianism: Individual and group-level influences of sex and status in group interactions. *Journal of Nonverbal Behavior, 34,* 137–153.

Koeppel, L. B., Montagne, Y., O'Hair, D., & Cody, M. J. (1999). Friendly? Flirting? Wrong? In L. K. Guerrero, J. A. DeVito, & M. L. Hecht (Eds.), *The nonverbal communication reader* (2nd ed., pp. 290–297). Prospect Heights, IL: Waveland.

Koller, V. (2008). "Not just a colour": Pink as a gender and sexuality marker in visual communication. *Visual Communication, 7,* 395–423.

Koukounas, E., & Letch, N. M. (2001). Psychological correlates of perception of sexual intent in women. *Journal of Social Psychology, 141,* 443–456.

Krolokke, C., & Sorensen, A. S. (2006). *Gender communication theories and analyses: From silence to performance.* Thousand Oaks, CA: Sage.

Kurtz, L. E., & Algoe, S. B. (2017). When sharing a laugh means sharing more: Testing the role of shared laughter on short-term interpersonal consequences. *Journal of Nonverbal Behavior, 41,* 45–65.

LaFrance, B. H. (2010). What verbal and nonverbal communication cues lead to sex? An analysis of the traditional sexual script. *Communication Quarterly, 58,* 297–318.

LaFrance, B. H., Henningsen, D. D., Oates, A., & Shaw, C. M. (2009). Social–sexual interactions? Meta-analyses of sex differences in perceptions of flirtatiousness, seductiveness, and promiscuousness. *Communication Monographs, 76,* 263–285.

LaFrance, M., Hecht, M. A., & Levy Paluck, E. (2003). The contingent smile: A meta-analysis of sex differences in smiling. *Psychological Bulletin, 129,* 305–334.

Lenroot, R. K., & Giedd, J. N. (2010). Sex differences in the adolescent brain. *Brain and Cognition, 72,* 46–55.

Li, S., & Li, Y. (2007). How far is far enough? A measure of information privacy in terms of interpersonal distance. *Environment & Behavior, 39,* 317–331.

Lick, D. J., Johnson, K. L., & Rule, N. O. (2015). Disfluent processing of nonverbal cues helps to explain anti-bisexual prejudice. *Journal of Nonverbal Behavior, 39,* 275–288.

Lindsey, E. W., & Mize, J. (2001). Contextual differences in parent-child play: Implications for children's gender role development. *Sex Roles, 44,* 155–176.

Lippa, R. A. (2006). *Gender, nature, and nurture* (2nd ed.). Mahwah, NJ: Erlbaum.

Lloyd, E. P., Summers, K. M., Hugenberg, K., & McConnell, A. R. (2018). Revising perceiver and target gender effects in deception detection. *Journal of Nonverbal Behavior.* http://doi.org/10.1007/s10919-018-0283-6

Lockwood Harris, K. (2018). Yes means yes and no means no, but both these mantras need to go: Communication myths in consent education and anti-rape activism. *Journal of Applied Communication Research, 46,* 155–178.

Lozza, N., Spoerri, C., Ehlert, U., Kesselring, M., Hubmann, P., Tschacher, W., & La Marca, R. (2018). Nonverbal synchrony and complementarity in unacquainted same-sex dyads: A comparison in a competitive context. *Journal of Nonverbal Behavior, 42,* 179–197.

Luerssen, A., Jhita, G. J., & Ayduk, O. (2017). Putting yourself on the line: Self-esteem and expressing affection in romantic relationships. *Personality and Social Psychology Bulletin, 43,* 940–956.

Mack, S., & Munson, B. (2012). The influence of /s/ quality on ratings of men's sexual orientation: Explicit and implicit measures of the "gay lisp" stereotype. *Journal of Phonetics, 40,* 198–212.

Maguire, K. C., & Kinney, T. A. (2010). When distance is problematic: Communication, coping, and relational satisfaction in female college students' long-distance dating relationships. *Journal of Applied Communication Research, 38,* 27–46.

Major, B., Schmidlin, A., & Williams, L. (1990). Gender patterns in social touch: The impact of setting and age. *Journal of Personality and Social Psychology, 58,* 634–643.

Manning, J. (2016). Identity, relationships, and culture: A constitutive model of coming out. In J. Manning & C. M. Noland (Eds.), *Contemporary studies of sexuality and communication: Theoretical and applied perspectives* (pp. 93–108). Dubuque, IA: Kendall Hunt.

McDaniel, E. R., & Andersen, P. A. (1998). International patterns of tactile communication: A field study. *Journal of Nonverbal Behavior, 21,* 59–75.

McGovern, J. (2017). Strong women never mumble: Female athlete attitudes about sexual consent. *Journal of Interpersonal Violence.* http://10.1177/0886260517730022

Meenagh, J. (2015). Flirting, dating, and breaking up within new media environments. *Sex Education, 15,* 458–471.

Mehrabian, A. (1981). *Silent messages: Implicit communication of emotions and attitudes* (2nd ed.). Belmont, CA: Wadsworth.

Miller, M. J., Denes, A., Diaz, B., & Buck, R. (2014). Attachment style predicts jealous reactions to viewing touch between a romantic partner and close friend: Implications for Internet social communication. *Journal of Nonverbal Behavior, 38,* 451–476.

Minotte, K. L. (2017). Integrative and masking emotion work: Marital outcomes among dual-earner couples. *Marriage & Family Review, 53,* 88–104.

Mongeau, P. A., Serewicz, M. C. M., Henningsen, M. L. M., & Davis, K. L. (2006). Sex differences in the transition to heterosexual romantic relationship. In K. Dindia & D. J. Canary (Eds.), *Sex differences and similarities in communication* (2nd ed., pp. 337–358). Mahwah, NJ: Erlbaum.

Mongeau, P. A., Serewicz, M. C. M., & Thierren, L. F. (2004). Goals for cross-sex first dates: Identification, measurement, and the influence of contextual factors. *Communication Monographs, 71,* 121–147.

Montano, K. J., Tigue, C. C., Isenstein, S. G. E., Barclay, P., & Feinberg, D. R. (2017). Men's voice pitch influences women's trusting behavior. *Evolution and Human Behavior, 38,* 293–297.

Moore, M. M. (2002). Courtship communication and perception. *Perceptual and Motor Skills, 94,* 97–105.

Moore, M. M. (2010). Human nonverbal courtship behavior—a brief historical review. *Journal of Sex Research, 47,* 171–180.

Moore, N-J., Hickson, M. III, & Stacks, D. W. (2013). *Nonverbal communication: Studies and applications* (6th ed.). Oxford, UK: Oxford University Press.

Morman, M. T., & Whitely, M. (2012). An exploratory analysis of critical incidents of closeness in the mother/son relationship. *Journal of Family Communication, 12*, 22–39.

Morris, A. (2018, April 2-15). It's a theyby! *New York,* 40–43, 91.

Morris, D. (1971). *Intimate behavior.* New York: Random House.

Muehlenhard, C. L. (2011). Examining stereotypes about token resistance to sex. *Psychology of Women Quarterly, 35*, 676–683.

Muehlenhard, C. L., & Peterson, Z. (2011). Distinguishing between sex and gender: History, current conceptualizations, and implications. *Sex Roles, 64*, 791–803.

Muehlenhard, C. L., & Rodgers, C. S. (2005). Token resistance to sex: New perspectives on an old stereotype. In J. K. Davidson & N. B. Moore (Eds.), *Speaking of sexuality* (2nd ed., pp. 280–289). Los Angeles: Roxbury.

Netchaeva, E., & Ress, M. (2016). Strategically stunning: The motivations behind the lipstick effect. *Psychological Science, 27*, 1157–1168.

Nicholas, C. L. (2004). Gaydar: Eye-gaze as identity recognition among gay men and lesbians. *Sexuality and Culture: An Interdisciplinary Quarterly, 8*, 60–86.

Noller, P. (2006). Nonverbal communication in close relationships. In V. Manusov & M. L. Patterson (Eds.), *The SAGE handbook of nonverbal communication* (pp. 403–420). Thousand Oaks, CA: Sage.

O'Connor, J. J. M., & Barclay, P. (2017). The influence of voice pitch on perceptions of trustworthiness across social contexts. *Evolution and Human Behavior, 38*, 506–512.

O'Connor, J. J. M., & Barclay, P. (2018). High voice pitch mitigates the aversiveness of antisocial cues in men's speech. *British Journal of Psychology.* http://doi.org:10.1111/bjop.12310

Orchowski, L. M., Gidycz, C. A., & Kraft, K. (2018). Resisting unwanted sexual and social advances: Perspectives of college women and men. *Journal of Interpersonal Violence.* http://doi.org:10/1177/0886260518781805

Ortiz, R. R., & Shafer, A. (2017). Define your line: Evaluating a peer-to-peer sexual consent education campaign to improve sexual consent understanding among undergraduate students. *Journal of Adolescent Health, 60*, S105–S106.

Patterson, J., Gardner, B. C., Burr, B. K., Hubler, D. S., & Roberts, M. K. (2012). Nonverbal behavioral indicators of negative affect in couple interaction. *Contemporary Family Therapy, 34*, 11–28.

Pearson, J. C. (1985). *Gender and communication.* Dubuque, IA: William C. Brown.

Peck, B., Manning, J., Tri, A., Skrzypczynski, D., Summers, M., & Grubb, K. (2016). What do people mean when they say they "had sex"? Connecting communication and behavior. In J. Manning & C. M. Noland (Eds.), *Contemporary studies of sexuality and communication: Theoretical and applied perspectives* (pp. 3–13). Dubuque, IA: Kendall Hunt.

Petrician, R., Todorov, A., Burris, C. T., Rosenbaum, R. S., & Grady, C. (2015). The look that binds: Partner-directed altruistic motivation and biased perception in married couples. *Journal of Nonverbal Behavior, 39*, 165–179.

Petter, O. (2017, July 27). There's a reason why men take up extra room when they sit down. Retrieved from https://www.independent.co.uk/life-style/manspreading-scientific-explanation-revealed-men-behaviour-public-transport-etiquette-a7862771.html

Poulsen, F. O., Holman, T. B., Busby, D. M., & Carroll, J. S. (2013). Physical attraction, attachment style, and dating development. *Journal of Social & Personal Relationships, 30*, 301–319.

Puckett, J. A., Newcomb, M. E., Ryan, D. T., Swann, G., Garofalo, R., & Mustanski, B. (2017). Internalized homophobia and perceived stigma: A validation study of stigma measures in a sample of young men who have sex with men. *Sexuality Research and Social Policy, 14*, 1–16.

Punyanunt-Carter, N. M. (2004). Reported affectionate communication and satisfaction in marital and dating relationships. *Psychological Reports, 95*, 1154–1160.

Punyanunt-Carter, N. M., & Wagner, T. R. (2018). Interpersonal communication motives for flirting face to face and through texting. *CyberPsychology, Behavior & Social Networking, 21*, 229–233.

Qin, Z., & Andreychik, M. (2013). Relational closeness in conflict: Effects on interaction goals, emotion, and conflict styles. *Journal of International Communication, 19*, 107–116.

Quick, V., McWilliams, R., & Byrd-Bredbenner, C. (2013). Fatty, fatty, two-by-four: Weight-teasing history and disturbed eating in young adult women. *American Journal of Public Health, 103*, 508–515.

Rancourt, K. M., MacKinnon, S., Snowball, N., & Rosen, N. O. (2017). Beyond the bedroom: Cognitive, affective, and behavioral responses to partner touch in women with and without sexual problems. *Journal of Sex Research, 54*, 862–876.

Reuter, D. F. (2002). *Gaydar: The ultimate insider guide to the gay sixth sense.* New York: Crown.

Richmond, V. P., McCroskey, J. C., & Hickson, M. L., III. (2011). *Nonverbal behavior in interpersonal relations* (7th ed.). Boston: Pearson.

Rieger, G., Linsenmeier, J. A. W., Gygax, L., Garcia, S., & Bailey, J. M. (2010). Dissecting "gaydar": Accuracy and the role of masculinity-femininity. *Archives of Sexual Behavior, 39*, 124–140.

Riesman, C. (1990). *Divorce talk: Women and men make sense of personal relationships.* New Brunswick, NJ: Princeton University Press.

Roese, N. J., Olson, H. M., Borenstein, M. N., Martin, A., & Shores, A. L. (1992). Same-sex touching behavior: The moderating role of homophobic attitudes. *Journal of Nonverbal Behavior, 16*, 249–259.

Rosenthal, R., Hall, J. A., DiMatteo, M. R., Rogers, P. L., & Archer, D. (1979). *Sensitivity to nonverbal communication: The PONS test.* Baltimore, MD: Johns Hopkins University Press.

Rosip, J. C., & Hall, J. A. (2004). Knowledge of nonverbal cues, gender, and nonverbal decoding accuracy. *Journal of Nonverbal Behavior, 28*, 267–286.

Rotter, N. G., & Rotter, G. S. (1988). Sex differences in the encoding and decoding of negative facial emotions. *Journal of Nonverbal Behavior, 12*, 139–148.

Rubinsky, V., & Cooke-Jackson, A. (2017). "Tell me something other than to use a condom and sex is scary": Memorable messages women and gender minorities wish for and recall about sexual health. *Women's Studies in Communication, 40*, 379–400.

Samp, J. A. (Ed.) (2016). *Communicating interpersonal conflict in close relationships.* New York: Routledge.

Santilli, V., & Miller, A. N. (2011). The effects of gender and power distance on nonverbal immediacy in symmetrical and asymmetrical power conditions: A cross-cultural study of classrooms and friendships. *Journal of International and Intercultural Communication, 4*, 3–22.

Scheflen, A. E. (1965). Quasi-courtship behavior in psychotherapy. *Psychiatry, 28*, 245–257.

Schmid Mast, M., & Hall, J. A. (2006). Women's advantage at remembering others' appearance: A systematic look at the why and when of a gender difference. *Personality and Social Psychology Bulletin, 32*, 353–364.

Schmidt, R. C., Morr, S., Fitzpatrick, P., & Richardson, M. J. (2012). Measuring the dynamics of interactional synchrony. *Journal of Nonverbal Behavior, 36*, 263–279.

Schofield, T. J., Parke, R. D., Castaneda, E. K., & Coltrane, S. (2008). Patterns of gaze between parents and children in European American and Mexican American families. *Journal of Nonverbal Behavior, 32*, 171–186.

Schrodt, P., Ledbetter, A. M., & Ohrt, J. K. (2007). Parental confirmation and affection as mediators of family communication patterns and children's mental well-being. *Journal of Family Communication, 7,* 23–46.

Schuler, L. (2017, July 18). There's a reason why men take up so much room when they sit. Retrieved from https://tonic.vice.com/en_us/article/evdkwm/manspreading-is-an-anatomical-necessity

Shafer, A., Ortiz, R. R., Thompson, B., & Huemmer, J. (2018). The role of hypermasculinity, token resistance, rape myth, and assertive sexual consent communication among college men. *Journal of Adolescent Health, 62,* S44–S50.

Shibley Hyde, J., & DeLamater, J. D. (2010). *Understanding human sexuality* (11th ed.). New York: McGraw-Hill.

Sloop, J. M. (2012). "This is not natural": Caster Semenya's gender threats. *Critical Studies in Media Communication, 29,* 81–96.

Sluzki, C. E. (2016). Proxemics in couple interactions: Rekindling an old optic. *Family Process, 55,* 7–15.

Smith, J. S., LaFrance, M., Knol, K. H., Tellinghuisen, D. J., & Moes, P. (2015). Surprising smiles and unanticipated frowns: How emotion and status influence gender categorization. *Journal of Nonverbal Behavior, 39,* 115–130.

Speer, S. A. (2017). Flirting: A designedly ambiguous action? *Research on Language & Social Interaction, 50,* 128–150.

Spott, J., Pyle, C., & Punyanunt-Carter, N. M. (2010). Positive and negative nonverbal behaviors in relationships: A study of relationship satisfaction and longevity. *Human Communication, 13,* 29–41.

Sprecher, S., & Cate, R. M. (2004). Sexual satisfaction and sexual expression as predictors of relationship satisfaction and stability. In J. H. Harvey, A. Wenzel, & S. Sprecher (Eds.), *The handbook of sexuality in close relationships* (pp. 235–256). Mahwah, NJ: Erlbaum.

Stafford, L. (2010). Geographic distance and communication during courtship. *Communication Research, 37,* 275–297.

Stathopoulos, E. T., Huber, J. E., & Sussman, J. E. (2011). Changes in acoustic characteristics of the voice across the life span: Measures from individuals 4–93 years of age. *Journal of Speech, Language, and Hearing Research, 54,* 1011–1021.

Szpak, A., Nicholls, M. E. R., Thomas, N. A., Laham, S. M., & Loetsher, T. (2016). "No man is an island": Effects of interpersonal proximity on spatial attention. *Cognitive Neuroscience, 7,* 45–54.

Tang, D., & Schmeichel, B. J. (2015). Look me in the eye: Manipulated eye gaze affects dominance mindsets. *Journal of Nonverbal Behavior, 39,* 181–194.

Tickle-Degnen, L. (2006). Nonverbal behavior and its functions in the ecosystem of rapport. In V. Manusov & M. L. Patterson (Eds.), *The SAGE handbook of nonverbal communication* (pp. 381–399). Thousand Oaks, CA: Sage.

Toma, C. L., & D'Angelo, J. D. (2017). Connecting profile-to-profile: How people self-present and form impressions of others through online dating profiles. In N. M. Punyanunt-Carter & J. S. Wrench (Eds.), *The impact of social media in modern romantic relationships* (pp. 147–162). Lanham, MD: Lexington.

Toscano, H., Schubert, T. W., & Giessner, S. R. (2018). Eye gaze and head posture jointly influence judgments of dominance, physical strength, and anger. *Journal of Nonverbal Behavior.* http://doi.org/10.1007/s10919-018-0276-5

Trekels, J., & Eggermont, S. (2017). Beauty is good: The appearance culture, the internalization of appearance ideals, and dysfunctional appearance beliefs among tweens. *Human Communication Research, 43,* 173–192.

Tskhay, K. O., & Rule, N. O. (2016). People automatically extract infants' sex from faces. *Journal of Nonverbal Behavior, 40,* 247–254.

Van Newkirk, R. (2006). "Gee, I didn't get that vibe from you": Articulating my own version of a femme lesbian existence. *Journal of Lesbian Studies, 10*, 73–85.

Vatsa, S., & Lata, P. (2012). The role of gender in interpreting subtleties of facial expressions. *Journal of Arts and Culture, 3*, 87–91.

Wagner, H. L., MacDonald, C. J., & Manstead, A. S. R. (1986). Communication of individual emotions by spontaneous facial expressions. *Journal of Personality and Social Psychology, 50*, 737–743.

Wallace, D. H. (1981). Affectional climate in the family of origin and the experience of subsequent sexual-affectional behaviors. *Journal of Sex and Marital Therapy, 7*, 296–396.

Wang, Z., Mao, H., Li, Y. J., & Liu, F. (2017). Smile big or not? Effects of smile intensity on perceptions of warmth and competence. *Journal of Consumer Research, 43*, 787–805.

Weick, M., McCall, C., & Blascovich, J. (2017). Power moves beyond complementarity: A staring look elicits avoidance in low power perceivers and approach in high power perceivers. *Personality and Social Psychology Bulletin, 43*, 1188–1201.

Weisgram, E. S., & Dinella, L. M. (Eds.) (2018). *Gender typing of children's toys: How early play experiences impact development.* Washington, D.C.: American Psychological Association.

Willis, F. N., & Rawdon, V. A. (1994). Gender and national differences in attitudes toward same-gender touch. *Perceptual and Motor Skills, 78*, 1027–1034.

Wood, J. T. (1994). Engendered identities: Shaping voice and mind through gender. In D. R. Vocate (Ed.), *Intrapersonal communication: Different voices, different minds* (pp. 145–168). Hillsdale, NJ: Erlbaum.

Woolery, L. M. (2008). Gaydar: A social-cognitive analysis. *Journal of Homosexuality, 53*, 9–17.

Yeomans, T. (2009, November). *Communicating initial interest and attraction: Quasi-courtship versus courtship behaviors.* Paper presented at the meeting of the National Communication Association, Chicago, IL.

Yoo, S., & Noyes, S. (2016). Recognition of facial expressions of negative emotions in romantic relationships. *Journal of Nonverbal Behavior, 40*, 1–12.

glossary

Accenting The use of nonverbal cues to emphasize or draw special attention to a verbal message

Accidental touches Unintentional and meaningless touches

Achieved privacy Actual degree of contact that results from interaction with others

Acronyms Abbreviations for longer terms or phrases, typically formed using the first letter of each word

Adaptors Behaviors that help you adjust to your environment; nonverbal behaviors that help a person satisfy a personal need, cope with emotions, or adapt to an immediate situation

Affect blends Expressing several emotions simultaneously on the face

Affect displays Expressions of emotion

Aggressive communication Self-serving communication that doesn't take into account a listener's feelings and rights

Androgyny Combination of feminine and masculine traits

Anonymity Ability to communicate, participate, and maintain a presence online without revealing one's true identity

Appeals to invitation Fourth stage within Scheflen's quasi-courtship model in which we use more obvious and direct nonverbal cues to signal availability and interest

Arms akimbo A spread-legged stance with the hands on the hips, often indicating dominance or frustration

Aromatherapy Benefits of smell from scented candles or incense used in accord with massage therapy, body wraps, and facials

Arousal A positive or negative reaction to another person; nonverbal cues that show activation, interest, or engagement, such as forward body lean and direct body orientation to others; how stimulated or energized an environment makes us feel; a positive or negative reaction to another person

Articulation (enunciation) How distinctly a person speaks

Artifacts   Temporary aspects of physical adornment other than clothing (e.g., jewelry, eyeglasses, cologne, makeup) that provide clues about our personalities, attitudes, and behaviors and that nonverbally communicate something about us to other people

Attraction   How we are drawn toward other people interpersonally, emotionally, physically, sexually, and/or spiritually for possible friendship, dating, love, partnership, and marriage

Audible pause   A pause in which air is taken in and speech is disrupted

Avatars   Ways people express themselves online and convey emotions through embodiments and manifestations that resemble human characteristics

Back-channel cues   Vocal nonverbal cues that can encourage others to continue speaking and signal our interest in a conversation while also indicating that we'd like a turn at talk

Biological sex   One's sex typically assigned at birth

Bisexuality   Refers to people who are attracted to members of all sexes and who emphasize the whole individual over the biological sex of the individual

Body image   View of ourselves and the amount of mental energy we invest in our physical appearance

Body modification   More permanent methods of changing the way the body looks (e.g., piercings, tattoos, cosmetic procedures)

Body movement, gestures, and posture (kinesics)   People's use of movements of the body to convey information, emotions, and attitudes

Breathiness   Overabundance of air rushing through the vocal folds

Brightness   Intensity of color in an environment

Catfishing   Posing online as someone you're not

Channel   Medium through which a message is sent

Chronemic expectancy violations   Instances when one person's use of time violates what another person deems polite or appropriate

Chronemics   Study of the communicative aspects of time

Civil inattention   When people share the same space or cross paths but acknowledge each other with only a quick look or glance, without starting a conversation

Cocked eyebrow   One brow raised

Cognitive activity   Use of the brain for memory recall and information processing

Communication   Process of acting on information

Communication privacy management (CPM)   Theory that explains how we manage privacy using spatial metaphors

Computer-mediated communication (CMC)   Human communication facilitated by technologies such as chat rooms, e-mail systems, social networking sites, and online gaming

Concealment   How clothing helps us conceal features of our body we don't want others to see

Congruence/incongruence One of Scheflen's postural dimensions; degree of mirroring or imitation of the behavior between two or more people

Conjugate lateral eye movements Involuntary eye movements to the left or right that reveal brain activity or thought processes

Conscious competence Realizing we know something or can do something, but it hasn't yet become an integrated skill or habit

Conscious incompetence Becoming aware or conscious of our own incompetence

Constraint Psychological perception related to getting out of or away from an environment

Contamination The tarnishing of someone's territory with noise or impurity

Control touches Touches used to gain compliance, get someone's attention, or generate a response

Courtship behavior Nonverbal actions we consciously and unconsciously exhibit when we are attracted to someone, someone with whom we possibly want to establish a relationship, typically for the purposes of sexual activity

Courtship (dating) Process of trying to get a relationship going; romantic attraction and an interest in some form of sexual intimacy

Courtship readiness First stage within Scheflen's quasi-courtship model in which we begin to alter our normal nonverbal patterns

Covert observation Appropriately observing nonverbal behaviors of other people without drawing much or any attention to ourselves

Crowding A psychological reaction to a perception of spatial restrictions

Customer relations Also referred to as customer service, the interaction between employees or representatives of an organization or business and the people the organization sells to or serves

Cyber-flirting Representing the body online to attract others

Cyber-infidelity Having an online sexual relationship with someone other than one's face-to-face sexual, monogamous partner

Cybersex Sexual experiences, fantasies, interactions, and descriptions that are exchanged in real time through the Internet

Deception cues Nonverbal indications of dishonesty

Decode Process of receiving and interpreting verbal and nonverbal messages to understand what people mean

Decoration How we decorate our bodies for celebrations and special occasions

Deintensification Reduction of intensity of a facial expression related to a particular emotion due to social or cultural expectations

Density The number of people or objects in a space that have the potential to restrict or interfere with people's activities and the achievement of their goals

Desired privacy Amount of contact desired from others at a given point in time

Dialectic process Instances when we restrict and seek interaction; an interplay between opposing forces; different balances of opening and closing the self to others

Direct nonverbal communication   Nonverbal cues related to face-to-face, telephone, or online communication, as in a live interview with a hiring committee, manager, or business owner

Distance   Perception of physical arrangements—the measurement or dimensions of a space

Distance education   Courses for which students don't have to be physically present in traditional classrooms

Dominance   Nonverbal cues that communicate status, position, and importance; how powerful or in control an environment makes us feel

Duchenne (felt) smile   A form of genuine smile involving the muscles around the eyes, generally communicating a positive message

Duration   How long a touch lasts

Dynamic time   Form of time that usually involves no interruptions between message formation, sending, receiving, and feedback; typical of face-to-face interaction

Ectomorph   One of Sheldon's three body types; a person who is thin, bony, tall, and fragile-looking, with a flat chest and limited muscular development

Emblems   Gestures that have specific, generally understood meanings

Emojis   Images, symbols, or icons used in text fields in electronic communication to express the emotional attitude of the writer, convey information succinctly, and communicate a message playfully without using words

Emoticons   Combination of electronic symbols typed out for the recipient of an electronic message

Emotional intelligence   Ability to monitor one's own and others' feelings and emotions, discriminate among them, and use this information to guide one's thinking and actions

Encode   The ability to send verbal and nonverbal cues to help people understand what we mean

Endomorph   One of Sheldon's three body types; a person with a rounded, oval, or pear-shaped body; usually heavy-set or stocky but not necessarily obese

Environment   Built or natural surroundings that serve as the context in which people interact

Ethnic cosmetic surgery   Medical procedures that make members of other cultures or ethnic minority groups look more Western or Caucasian

Ethnic enclave   City areas that are dominated by a certain demographic of people

Evolution   How species change and adapt over time

Excessive immediacy   Offensive and inappropriate comments, gestures, physical proximity, and touch that can occur in classrooms, hallways, and faculty offices

Exclusion   The use of eye behavior to close others out of a conversation

Expectancy violations model   Suggests that we develop expectations for appropriate nonverbal behaviors in ourselves and others

External factors   Influences on facial expressions such as environment, social norms, and culture

Eye contact   Nonverbal cue that conveys trustworthiness, sincerity, honesty, interest, and respect

Eye gaze (eye contact)   Looking at the general eye area of another person

Eye modification   Permanent or temporary methods of changing the eyes

Face-to-face/parallel   One of Scheflen's postural dimensions; degree to which two people face each other directly versus orienting themselves side by side, with their shoulders in a line (a parallel position)

Facework   A set of coordinated practices in which communicators build, maintain, protect, or threaten personal dignity, honor, and respect

Facial Action Coding System (FACS)   A research coding system that examines the face in three regions: eyebrows and forehead, eyes and eyelids, and lower face (including cheeks, nose, and mouth)

Facial expression   Nonverbal facial cues that reveal thoughts and emotions

Facial modification   More permanent methods of changing the face

Facial symmetry   A face that's equally proportioned in size and shape

Fake smile   A forced and conscious smile that can damage how others view us in social situations

Familiarity   Perception of having been in an environment enough that we know what to expect

Filled pause   A vocalization such as "um" or "er" that fills a pause, typically as a way of covering silence and giving the communicator time to think of what to say, or to encourage others to speak

Flaming   Aggressive online communication that intentionally disrupts, heckles, and harasses others

Flashing eyebrows   Both brows raised and lowered quickly

Flirting   Act of attracting romantic attention

Fluency   How continuously we produce sound

Formality   Perception of a place as "serious," "stuffy," "relaxed," or "casual"; normative rules and expected etiquette associated with a specific computer-mediated channel of communication

Friendship/warmth   Touches that show nonromantic emotion and affection

Functional/professional   Non-intimate touches that serve a specific function, usually within the context of a professional relationship

Fundamental frequency   Most comfortable or often-used pitch of the voice

Gaydar   Ability to detect the homosexual orientation of a person

Gaze   Looking at someone or something in any given context

Gaze aversion   Occurs when someone intentionally doesn't return another person's gaze

Gaze omission   Unintentional avoidance of eye contact

Gender   Psychological and emotional characteristics typically associated with femininity, masculinity, and androgyny

Gender identity   View of self relative to feminine, masculine, and androgynous traits; view of appropriate roles for people in society

Gender swapping   Use of screen names, aliases, and avatars that allow participants to experiment with gender identity

Genuine smile   An unconscious and uncontrolled smile that promotes social relationships and conveys honest emotions

Ghosting   Ending a relationship by disappearing and refusing to respond to phone calls, texts, or e-mail messages

Group identification   How clothing allows us to communicate or celebrate a group we identify with or connect to

Halo effect   Tendency to attribute positive personality qualities to physically attractive people

Haptics   Study of touch behavior in humans and animals

High-contact cultures   Cultures exhibiting frequent touch

Homophily   Perceived similarity in people's appearance, background, and attitudes that benefits relationships

Homophobia   A fear of being labeled homosexual or a general dislike of homosexual people

Hue   Modification of a basic color (e.g., bluish green, red orange) in an environment

Human communication   Process of making sense out of the world and sharing that sense with others by creating meaning

Identity fluidity   How online identities can change at any moment with a simple change of screen name, online format, or avatar

Illustrators   Cues that accompany verbal messages and provide meaning

Image fixation   High degree of concern about physical appearance

Immediacy   Behavior that enhances psychological and physical closeness between people; nonverbal cues that communicate liking and engender feelings of pleasure; how happy or satisfied an environment makes us feel

Impression management   Efforts to affect someone's formation of an impression, perception, or view of oneself

Inclusiveness/noninclusiveness   One of Scheflen's postural dimensions; degree to which a person's body posture includes or excludes people, relative to others

Indirect nonverbal communication   Forms of communication typically expressed before or after a job interview, such as a résumé, cover letter, or thank you note.

Innate behavior   Biological activity or traits that humans have from birth

Information privacy   People's ability to prevent the collection and distribution of information about themselves or their social networks without their knowledge or permission

Intensification   Use of a facial expression that reveals an exaggeration of how we feel about something

Intensity   Power, force, or concentration of bodily contact

Interaction management   How people use verbal and nonverbal communication to conduct or manage their conversations with others

Interactive synchrony   Coordination of speech and body movement or a nonverbal rhythm between at least two speakers

Interpersonal deception theory   Theory that helps explain verbal and nonverbal behavior of deceivers

Interruptions   Obvious and abrupt vocal intrusions into someone's speech that disrupt the flow

Intimacy   An experience involving emotions and perceptions of understanding within a relationship characterized by affection and trust

Intimate space   A distance of 0 to 1 1/2 feet between communicators; considered the most personal range for communication

Intonation   Patterns of pitch

Invasion   An intense and typically permanent encroachment of territory that is driven by an intention to take over the territory

Involvement   The need to interact with other people, even if just with a simple acknowledgement of eye contact or a head nod

Kinesics   Human movement, gestures, and posture

Knitted eyebrows   Both brows lowered toward the nose and eyes

Leakage   Nonverbal cues outside of a deceiver's control that signal dishonesty; ways people nonverbally reveal deception

Learned behavior   Nonverbal expressions acquired through cultural, social, and family experiences over time

Learning environments   Spaces and locations where learning occurs

Leave-taking behavior   Classroom nonverbal cues that indicate to teachers that students are ready to leave

Location   Area of the body where physical contact is made; setting or context within which a touch occurs

Love/intimacy   Highly personal and intimate touches that communicate feelings of romantic affection

Low-contact cultures   Cultures exhibiting little to no touch

Masking   Concealing the facial expressions connected to a felt emotion and replacing them with expressions more appropriate to the situation

Matching hypothesis   Tendency to seek out dating and marital partners we perceive as equal to us in physical attractiveness

Mesomorph   One of Sheldon's three body types; a person with a triangular body shape who is broad-shouldered, tapered at the hip, muscular and proportioned by height and weight, and usually described as athletic

Message duration   A deception cue; the length of someone's message or response to another person's communication

Micromomentary facial expressions (microexpressions)   Dramatic, rapid changes of facial expressions

Mimicry   Intentional mirroring of another person's nonverbal cues

Misspellings   Mistakes in spelling

Monochronic time   View of time as a tangible commodity

Mutual gaze   Occurs when two people look at each other, either in the eyes or within the region of the face

Nasality   Whiny sound produced when air is trapped or too heavily contained in the nasal cavities, instead of resonating through all the vocal structures

Natural selection   Darwin's theory that the organisms best suited to survival in an environment will thrive and pass on their genetic advantages to future generations

Neutralization   Using facial expressions that erase or numb how we really feel

Nonverbal communication   Communication other than written or spoken language that creates meaning for someone

Nonverbal immediacy cues   Nonverbal cues of approachability, availability, closeness, and warmth that decrease psychological and physical distance between people

Normalization   Process of making a viewpoint or action such a normal and everyday part of reality that it can't be questioned

Obesity   Medical term for being significantly overweight

Oculesics   Study of eye behavior, including eye contact, eye movement, and other functions of the eyes

Olfaction   Role of smell in human interaction

One-sided look   A gaze or look toward another person that's not reciprocated

Outercourse   A perspective about sexuality that includes the role of thought, emotions, psychological factors, identity, and sociocultural factors

Overlaps   Vocalizations that tend to occur just as one speaker finishes a turn at talk and another begins a turn

Overt observation   Asking people directly about their own nonverbal behavior or the nonverbal behavior of others

Partial   An emotion that registers in a single area of the face while other facial areas are controlled

Pause (vocal hesitation)   A break or change in the production of sound

Perception checking   Asking direct or third-person parties for their perceptions, which we can compare with our own

Personal space   A distance of 1 1/2 to 4 feet between communicators; conversations with family members and friends usually take place within this zone

Persuasion   Ways clothing influences others' behavior

Physical appearance   How our bodies and appearance communicate to others and impact our view of ourselves; physical attributes of the face and body; typically the first nonverbal cue people perceive in face-to-face situations

Physical attractiveness   Culturally derived perception of beauty formed by features such as height, weight, size, and shape

Physical body   The body that is not mediated but real and existing in face-to-face communication

Physical privacy   Degree to which someone is physically inaccessible to others

Physical space   Where we communicate and how we interact within a given space, as well as how much space is available

Piercings   Form of body modification created by putting holes into the skin for the purpose of wearing jewelry

Pitch   Falling or rising tone heard in the voice

Playful touches   Touches that convey teasing, joking, or mild aggression between people

Polychronic time   View of time that places more value on people than schedules

Popular culture   Products of a culture that are owned and made by businesses for the purpose of generating profit

Positional cues   Third stage within Scheflen's quasi-courtship model in which we use posture and body orientation to draw the attention of another person

Positive affect (affectionate) touches   Touches that indicate a degree of liking or positivity toward another person

Power display   A nonverbal means of indicating dominance over another person

Power stare   A narrowing of the eyelids (almost into a squint) and the maintenance of eye contact without blinking, as a means of establishing dominance

Preening   Second stage within Scheflen's quasi-courtship model in which we attend to our appearance and make adjustments

Primary territories   Territories that have a clear owner and rules or barriers that serve to mark or protect them from invasion

Privacy   Perception of an environment that is protected from others who may overhear what is said

Professional handshake   Full, firm, and equal handshake that makes a good first impression as a professional

Pronunciation   How correctly a person speaks, according to a dictionary's indication of proper pronunciation

Protection   How we use clothing to protect our bodies from intrusion or harm

Proxemics   The way distance and space play a communicative role in everyday life

Psychological privacy   People's ability to exercise control over the expression of their thoughts and feelings

Psychological space   Effect of space on attitude, mood, and emotionality

Public space   A distance of 12 feet and beyond; usually not personal in nature

Public territories   Spaces that are open to anyone for temporary ownership

Pupil dilation   An increase in size or widening of the pupils in the eyes

Quasi-courtship behavior   Scheflen's model of nonverbal actions we consciously and unconsciously exhibit when we are attracted to someone but the motive is not to establish a relationship or make sexual contact; patterns of nonverbal communication that form a ritual of flirtatious behavior

Queer   Umbrella term for any non-straight identity

Raspiness   Hoarseness or a gravelly sound in the voice

Rate (tempo)   Pace at which sounds are uttered

Reflexivity   Actions accomplished automatically rather than purposefully; referring back to the self

Regulating   Eye behavior that lets another person know whether a conversation will begin, continue, or come to an end

Regulators   Cues that control and manage the flow of communication

Résumé   Document indicating educational and professional experience that serves as a reflection of who people are and what they can offer a potential employer

Response latency   How long it takes someone to respond to another person's communication

Rhetoric of architecture   Architectural items (e.g., churches, shopping malls, doors, stairs) that have meaning and influence our behavior

Ritualistic touches   Touches typically associated with rituals, such as greetings and departures

Salience   The fact that what we do with our eyes is more noticeable than other actions of the face and body

Saturation   Amount of color present in an environment

Secondary territories   Territories that are not as important to the owner or as exclusive as primary territories; spaces that one does not own but over which one develops a sense of ownership

Self-disclosure   The sharing of information that people cannot learn about us unless we reveal it to them

Self-silencing   The inhibition of self-expression

Self-synchrony   Coordination of speech and body movement enacted by one person

Sex   Biological/physiological characteristics that make us female, male, or intersex; sexual activity between people

Sexual arousal   Extremely intimate touches that typically target the sexual zones or organs of the body for the purpose of sexual arousal

Sexual attraction   Ways clothing helps draw sexual attention from others

Sexual orientation   Related to the sex of persons with whom one wishes to engage in sexual activity

Sexuality   Sexual behavior, as well as cognitive, emotional, and psychosociocultural factors that affect one's sexual being

Shouting   Typing words in all caps in e-mails, text messages, and online postings

Silence   The absence of sound

Silent pause   Breaks in speech that carry no sound

Social/polite   Touches associated with cultural norms that indicate fairly low intimacy within a relationship

Social privacy   When an individual or group opts to withdraw from social interaction

Social space   A distance of 4 to 12 feet between communicators; used in professional life and many social contexts

Somatyping   Sheldon's system that classifies people according to their body type

Space (proxemics)   How people create and use proximity and distance; includes behavior to protect and defend space

Speech errors   A deception cue; incorrect uses of grammar, mispronounced words, and so forth

State touch avoidance   Tendency to avoid physical contact only with certain people or in certain circumstances

Static time   Form of time that may involve interruptions between message formation, sending, receiving, and feedback; typical of mediated or online interaction

Status   A person's rank or position in an organization; how nonverbal cues communicate social and professional class

Stretching   Practice of expanding a healed piercing by wearing larger and larger gauges to widen the hole in the ear lobe

Student misbehaviors   Negative student behaviors in the classroom that can disrupt learning

Stutter start   Repetition of the first word or first letter or sound of the first word of a statement we want to make

Subordinate   Employees in professional situations who typically rank lower than others in terms of hierarchy

Superior   Supervisors or employers in professional situations who typically rank higher than others in terms of hierarchy

Synchrony   When people's nonverbal cues mirror each other

Task-related touches   Touches that serve an instrumental function, meaning those that help accomplish a task

Tattoos   Form of body modification involving temporary or permanent ink messages and images placed on the body

Teacher misbehaviors   Teachers' offensive or disruptive nonverbal actions that are detrimental to student learning

Teacher nonverbal immediacy   Nonverbal cues that reflect a teacher's approachability, availability, closeness, and warmth

Teacher privacy management   Teachers' decisions about what private information they want to reveal or conceal

Tells   Highly informative attributes or actions that reveal a great deal about a person

Territoriality   Our sense of ownership of an object, a particular space, a person, or even our time

Territorial markers   Cues that indicate ownership and occupancy of space; nonverbal signals to others that a space is taken or reserved

Textese   Writing in textisms

Textisms   Abbreviated, nonstandard forms of language that create a shorthand for communicators

Tie sign   Nonverbal behaviors that express affection between people and also signal the status of the relationship to others

Token resistance   A casual or faked attempt to resist a sexual advance, which someone may believe is expected before agreeing to sexual activity

Tone of voice (prosody)   Elements of sound that the human voice can produce and manipulate

Touch avoidance   Reduction or lack of physical contact with people

Touch deprivation   When individuals or segments of society are deprived of touch from others

Touch ethic   Beliefs about and preferences for touch

Touch (haptics)   Study of human bodily contact; communicates the nature of the relationship between people

Trait touch avoidance   Tendency to avoid physical contact with most people across most circumstances

Transaction   Shared creation of meaning that occurs in a simultaneous, ongoing manner

Transgender   Refers to individuals who cross over or transcend the traditional boundaries of sex and gender to develop their own unique expression of their sexuality

Turn-denying cues   Vocal nonverbal cues that indicate that we want other people to continue talking or don't want to converse at all

Turn-maintaining cues   Vocal nonverbal cues that indicate that we want to maintain the floor or our turn at talk

Turn-requesting cues   Vocal nonverbal cues that signal that we would like to engage in conversation

Turn-taking   A structure for conversation and a means of studying or tracking conversations for the purpose of analysis; when one person speaks or takes a turn in conversation, then another person responds (takes a turn), and so forth

Turn-yielding cues   Vocal nonverbal cues that indicate that we want to relinquish the floor

Typos   Mistakes in typing

Unconscious competence Knowing we can do something but not having to concentrate to be able to act on the knowledge or draw on the skill

Unconscious incompetence Being unaware of our own incompetence

Upper blepharoplasty A surgical procedure that modifies the eyelids

Upspeak/uptalk Ending every statement with an upward pitch shift, as though all sentences are turned into questions

Verbal communication Words you choose to use

Video chat Visual conversations accomplished using technology, such as computers and smartphones, by participants in different geographical locations

Violation Use of someone's primary territory without permission

Virtual body The body that is mediated, represented, or constructed through e-mail messages, pictures, descriptions, avatars, emoticons, and emojis

Visual dominance ratio Amount of eye contact made when talking to someone versus when listening to that person

Vocal expression (vocalics, paralanguage) Communicates emotion and clarifies the meaning of messages through such elements as pitch, rate, and volume

Vocal properties Aspects of the voice that can be purposefully altered to create meaning

Vocal qualities Characteristics of the voice that develop subtly, more as habits than as conscious choices

Vocal variety (inflection) Varying the pitches used in speaking

Vocalics (paralanguage) Study of how people express themselves through their voices

Vocalizations Nonwords or sounds not tied to speech, including those that can substitute for speech

Voice-recognition software/talk to text Technology that allows computers/smartphones/tablets to recognize voices, respond to commands, and post one's words on a screen or in a text message

Volume (intensity) Softness or loudness of the voice

Waist-to-hip ratio Body measurement of the waist in proportion to the hips

Warmth Perception of and desire for a comfortable, welcoming context that is part of our current or past experience

Wink Quickly closing and opening one eye, usually directed toward another person

author index

subject index

subject index

matching hypothesis, 147, *147*
mediated chronemics, 360–361
mediated communication, 349–353
    acronyms, 350, *354*
    emojis, 349
    emoticons, 349
    grammar, 350
    photos, 351
    punctuation, 350
    spelling, 350
    textisms, 350, *354*
    video chats, 351
    videos, 351
Mehrabian's framework, 56–57
    arousal, 56, *57*
    dominance, 57, *57*
    immediacy, 56, *57*
mesomorph, 148, *149*
message duration, 327
micromomentary facial expressions, 227, *230*
mimicry, 189, *191*
monochronic time, 84, *85*
monotone voice, 306
mouth, 230
multichanneled communication, 20–21, *21*

N

nasality, 313
natural selection, 221, *224*
nature of nonverbal communication, 16–21
    ambiguous, 18–20, *21*
    culture-bound, 16–17, *21*
    expectancy violations model, 18
    multichanneled, 20–21, *21*
    perception checking, 20, *42*
      direct, 20
      indirect, 20
    rule governed, 17–18, *21*
neutralization, 224, *226*
nonverbal codes in face-to-face (FtF), 362, *362*
    CMC versus, 362, *362*
nonverbal immediacy cues, 237
normalization, 165
nose, 230

O

obesity, 150, *155*
oculesics, 234, *236*
olfaction, *94*, 153, *155*
online dating, 345
online deception, 366–367
online learning environments, 405–406
online persona, 355–360
outercourse, 449, *452*
overlaps, 322–*324*
overt observation, 36, *42*

P

paralanguage, 48
pausing, 316–320
people with disabilities, 128–130, *130*
perception checking, 20, *42*
    direct, 20
    indirect, 20
perceptions
    of color, 86–87
      brightness, 86
      hue, 86
      saturation, 86
    of environment, 71–97
      constraint, 80, *81*
      distance, 80–81, *81*
      familiarity, 79, *81*
      formality, 76–77, *81*
      privacy, 78–79, *81*
      warmth, 77–78, *81*
    of lighting, 87
    of smell, 89
    of sound, 88
    of temperature, 89–91
    of time, 83–85
personal space, 109, *109*, 119
personality, 160
personalization, 364
persuasion, 158, *161*
pet therapy, 271
photos, 351
physical appearance, 141–173, *147*. *See also* body
    artifacts, 161–163
    eyeglasses, 162–163
    jewelry, 162
    makeup, 163

W

waist-to-hip ratio, 149, *155*
walking, 192–195
warmth, 77–78, *81*
weight, body, 150–151
wink, 229, *230*
withholder, 227

Z

zero proxemics, 265